CLASSICS IN PSYCHOLOGY

CLASSICS IN PSYCHOLOGY

A NOTE ABOUT THE AUTHOR

ROBERT M. YERKES was born in Bucks County, Pennsylvania, in 1876. He received bachelor degrees from Ursinus College and Harvard. After studying zoology and psychology at Harvard as a graduate student, he received a doctorate in psychology and was appointed head of comparative psychology at Harvard in 1902; he remained in this capacity until 1917. While chiefly a comparative psychologist, Yerkes was also instrumental in developing the system for measuring human intelligence used in the "Army Alpha" tests. After leaving Harvard, he taught at Minnesota, then set up Primate Laboratories first at Yale and later at Orange Park, Florida. After his retirement in 1941, the Orange Park Laboratories were renamed the Yerkes Laboratories of Primate Biology. Yerkes died in 1956.

Yerkes studied many different species, chiefly from the viewpoint of their intellectual capacities, but also with attention to other facets of their behavior and bearing. He climbed the evolutionary ladder in his researches, beginning with studies of the lower forms, then moving up through the crab, turtle, frog, dancing mouse, rat, crow, dove, and pig, spending his latter years primarily on higher primates and on man. Two of his charming and representative studies are reprinted here.

THE DANCING MOUSE
AND
THE MIND OF A GORILLA

Robert M. Yerkes

ARNO PRESS
A New York Times Company
New York ★ 1973

156
Y47d

Reprint Edition 1973 by Arno Press Inc.

The Dancing Mouse was reprinted from a copy
in The Newark Public Library

Classics in Psychology
ISBN for complete set: 0-405-05130-1
See last pages of this volume for titles.

Publisher's Note: The Mind of a Gorilla was
reprinted from the best available copy.

Manufactured in the United States of America

———◆———

Library of Congress Cataloging in Publication Data

Yerkes, Robert Mearns, 1876-1956.
    The dancing mouse.

    (Classics in psychology)
    Includes bibliographies.
    1. Dancing mice—Psychology. 2. Gorillas—
Psychology. I. Yerkes, Robert Mearns, 1876-1956.
The mind of a gorilla. 1973. II. Title.
III. Title: The mind of a gorilla. IV. Series.
[DNLM: QL Y47d 1907F]
QL737.R666Y47   156   73-3000
ISBN 0-405-05174-3

THE DANCING MOUSE

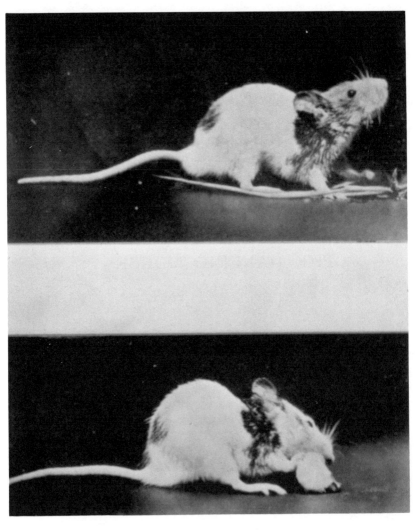

DANCING MICE — SNIFFING AND EATING.

THE ANIMAL BEHAVIOR SERIES. VOLUME I

THE DANCING MOUSE

A Study in Animal Behavior

BY

ROBERT M. YERKES, Ph.D.

INSTRUCTOR IN COMPARATIVE PSYCHOLOGY IN HARVARD
UNIVERSITY

The Cartwright Prize of the Alumni Association of the College of Physicians
and Surgeons, Columbia University, was awarded, in 1907, for an Essay
which comprised the first twelve chapters of this volume.

New York

THE MACMILLAN COMPANY

1907

4/6/76

Norwood Press
J. S. Cushing Co. — Berwick & Smith Co.
Norwood, Mass., U.S.A.

IN LOVE AND GRATITUDE
THIS BOOK IS DEDICATED TO
MY MOTHER

PREFACE

THIS book is the direct result of what, at the time of its occurrence, seemed to be an unimportant incident in the course of my scientific work — the presentation of a pair of dancing mice to the Harvard Psychological Laboratory. My interest in the peculiarities of behavior which the creatures exhibited, as I watched them casually from day to day, soon became experiment-impelling, and almost before I realized it, I was in the midst of an investigation of their senses and intelligence.

The longer I observed and experimented with them, the more numerous became the problems which the dancers presented to me for solution. From a study of the senses of hearing and sight I was led to investigate, in turn, the various forms of activity of which the mice are capable; the ways in which they learn to react adaptively to new or novel situations; the facility with which they acquire habits; the duration of habits; the roles of the various senses in the acquisition and performance of certain habitual acts; the efficiency of different methods of training; and the inheritance of racial and individually acquired forms of behavior.

In the course of my experimental work I discovered, much to my surprise, that no accurate and detailed account of this curiously interesting animal existed in the English language, and that in no other language were all the facts concerning it available in a single book. This fact, in connection with my appreciation of the exceptional value of the dancer as a pet and as material for the scientific study of animal behavior, has led me to supplement the results of my own observation by presenting in this little book a brief and not too highly technical description of the general characteristics and history of the dancer.

The purposes which I have had in mind as I planned and wrote the book are three: first, to present directly, clearly, and briefly the results of my investigation; second, to give as complete an account of the dancing mouse as a thorough study of the literature on the animal and long-continued observation on my own part should make possible; third, to provide a supplementary text-book on mammalian behavior and on methods of studying animal behavior for use in connection with courses in Comparative Psychology, Comparative Physiology, and Animal Behavior.

It is my conviction that the scientific study of animal behavior and of animal mind can be furthered more just at present by intensive special investigations than by extensive general books. Methods of research in this field are few and surprisingly crude, for the majority of investigators have been more deeply interested in getting results than in perfecting methods. In writing this account of the dancing mouse I have attempted to lay as much stress upon the development of my methods of work as upon the results which the methods yielded. In fact, I have used the dancer as a means of exhibiting a variety of methods by which the behavior and intelligence of animals may be studied. As it happens the dancer is an ideal subject for the experimental study of many of the problems of animal behavior. It is small, easily cared for, readily tamed, harmless, incessantly active, and it lends itself satisfactorily to a large number of experimental situations. For laboratory courses in Comparative Psychology or Comparative Physiology it well might hold the place which the frog now holds in courses in Comparative Anatomy.

Gratefully, and with this expression of my thanks, I acknowledge my indebtedness to Professor Hugo Münsterberg for placing at my command the resources of the Harvard Psychological Laboratory and for advice and encouragement throughout my investigation; to Professor Edwin B. Holt for valuable assistance in more ways than I can mention; to Professor Wallace C. Sabine for generous aid in connection with the experiments on hearing; to Professor Theobald Smith for the examination of pathological dancers; to Miss Mary C. Dickerson for the photographs of dancing mice which are reproduced in the frontispiece; to Mr. Frank Ashmore for additional photographs which I have been unable to use in this volume; to Mr. C. H. Toll for the drawings for Figures 14 and 20; to Doctors H. W. Rand and C. S. Berry for valuable suggestions on the basis of a critical reading of the proof sheets; and to my wife, Ada Watterson Yerkes, for constant aid throughout the experimental work and in the preparation of this volume.

R. M. Y.

CAMBRIDGE, MASSACHUSETTS,
August, 1907.

CONTENTS

CHAPTER I

Peculiarities of the dancing mouse — Markings and method
of keeping record of individuals — The dancer in China and
Japan (Kishi, Mitsukuri, Hatai) — Theories concerning the
origin of the race: selectional breeding; the inheritance of
an acquired character; mutation, inheritance, and selectional
breeding; pathological changes; natural selection — Instances of the occurrence of dancers among other kinds of
mice — Results of crossing dancer with other kinds of mice.

CHAPTER II

Methods of keeping and caring for dancers — Cages, nest-
boxes, and materials for nest — Cleansing cages — Food
supply and feeding — Importance of cleanliness, warmth, and
pure food — Relations of males and females, fighting — The
young, number in a litter — Care of young — Course of development — Comparison of young of dancer with young of
common mouse — Diary account of the course of development of a typical litter of dancers.

CHAPTER III

Dancing — Restlessness and excitability — Significance of
restlessness — Forms of dance: whirling, circling, and figure-
eights — Direction of whirling and circling: right whirlers,
left whirlers, and mixed whirlers — Sex differences in dancing — Time and periodicity of dancing — Influence of light
on activity — Necessity for prolonged observation of behavior.

Contents

CHAPTER XI

CHAPTER XII

CHAPTER XIII

CHAPTER XIV

ILLUSTRATIONS

LITERATURE ON THE DANCING MOUSE

1. ALEXANDER, G. UND KREIDL, A. "Zur Physiologie des Labyrinths der Tanzmaus." *Archiv für die gesammte Physiologie,* Bd. 82 : 541–552. 1900.

2. ALEXANDER, G. UND KREIDL, A. "Anatomisch-physiologische Studien über das Ohrlabyrinth der Tanzmaus." II Mittheilung. *Archiv für die gesammte Physiologie,* Bd. 88 : 509–563. 1902.

3. ALEXANDER, G. UND KREIDL, A. "Anatomisch-physiologische Studien über das Ohrlabyrinth der Tanzmaus." III Mittheilung. *Archiv für die gesammte Physiologie,* Bd. 88 : 564–574. 1902.

4. BAGINSKY, B. "Zur Frage über die Zahl der Bogengänge bei japanischen Tanzmäusen. *Centralblatt für Physiologie,* Bd. 16 : 2–4. 1902.

5. BATESON, W. "The present state of knowledge of colour-heredity in mice and rats." *Proceedings of the Zoölogical Society of London,* Vol. 2 : 71–99. 1903.

6. BREHM, A. E. "Tierleben." Dritte Auflage. Saugetiere, Bd. 2 : 513–514. 1890.

7. BREHM, A. E. "Life of Animals." Translated from the third German edition of the "Tierleben" by G. R. Schmidtlein. Mammalia. p. 338. Marquis, Chicago. 1895.

8. CYON, E. DE. "Le sens de l'espace chez les souris dansantes japonaises." *Cinquantenaire de la Société de Biologie* (Volume jubilaire). p. 544–546. Paris. 1899.

9. CYON, E. VON. "Ohrlabyrinth, Raumsinn und Orientirung." *Archiv für die gesammte Physiologie,* Bd. 79 : 211–302. 1900.

10. CYON, E. DE. "Présentation de souris dansantes japonaises." *Comptes rendus du XIII Congrès International de Paris, Section de physiologie,* p. 160–161. 1900.

11. CYON, E. VON. "Beiträge zur Physiologie des Raumsinns." I Theil. "Neue Beobachtungen an den japanischen Tanzmäusen." *Archiv für die gesammte Physiologie*, Bd. 89 : 427–453. 1902.

12. CYON, E. DE. "Le sens de l'espace." Richet's "Dictionnaire de physiologie," T. 5 : 570–571. 1901.

13. DARBISHIRE, A. D. Note on the results of crossing Japanese waltzing mice with European albino races. *Biometrica*, Vol. 2 : 101–104. 1902.

14. DARBISHIRE, A. D. Second report on the result of crossing Japanese waltzing mice with European albino races. *Biometrica*, Vol. 2 : 165–173. 1903.

15. DARBISHIRE, A. D. Third report on hybrids between waltzing mice and albino races. *Biometrica*, Vol. 2 : 282–285. 1903.

16. DARBISHIRE, A. D. ˙On the result of crossing Japanese waltzing with albino mice. *Biometrica*, Vol. 3 : 1–51. 1904.

17. GUAITA, G. v. "Versuche mit Kreuzungen von verschiedenen Rassen der Hausmaus." *Berichte der naturforschenden Gesellschaft zu Freiburg i. B.*, Bd. 10 : 317–332. 1898.

18. GUAITA, G. v. "Zweite Mitteilung über Versuche mit Kreuzungen von verschiedenen Hausmausrassen." *Berichte der naturforschenden Gesellschaft zu Freiburg i. B.*, Bd. 11 : 131–138. 1900.

19. HAACKE, W. "Ueber Wesen, Ursachen und Vererbung von Albinismus und Scheckung und über deren Bedeutung für vererbungstheoretische und entwicklungsmechanische Fragen." *Biologisches Centralblatt*, Bd. 15 : 44–78. 1895.

19a. HUNTER, M. S. "A Pair of Waltzing Mice." *The Century Magazine*, Vol. 73 : 889–893. April, 1907.

20. KAMMERER, P. "Tanzende Waldmaus und radschlagende Hausmaus." *Zoologische Garten*, Bd. 41 : 389–390. 1900.

21. KISHI, K. "Das Gehörorgan der sogenannten Tanzmaus." *Zeitschrift für wissenschaftliche Zoölogie*, Bd. 71 : 457–485. 1902.

22. LANDOIS, H. "Chinesische Tanzmäuse." *Jahresbericht des Westfälischen Provinzial-Vereins*, Münster, 1893–1894 : 62–64.

22a. LOSE, J. "Waltzing Mice." *Country Life in America*, September, 1904. p. 447.

23. PANSE, R. Zu Herrn Bernhard Rawitz' Arbeit: "Das Gehörorgan der japanischen Tanzmäuse." *Archiv für Anatomie und Physiologie*, Physiologische Abtheilung, 1901 : 139–140.

24. PANSE, R. "Das Gleichgewichts- und Gehörorgan der japanischen Tanzmäuse." *Münchener medicinische Wochenschrift*, Jahrgang 48, Bd. 1 : 498–499. 1901.

25. RAWITZ, B. "Das Gehörorgan der japanischen Tanzmäuse." *Archiv für Anatomie und Physiologie*, Physiologische Abtheilung, 1899 : 236–243.

26. RAWITZ, B. "Neue Beobachtungen über das Gehörorgan japanischer Tanzmäuse." *Archiv für Anatomie und Physiologie*, Physiologische Abtheilung, 1901, Supplement : 171–176.

27. RAWITZ, B. "Zur Frage über die Zahl der Bogengänge bei japanischen Tanzmäusen." *Centralblatt für Physiologie*, Bd. 15 : 649–651. 1902.

28. SAINT-LOUP, R. "Sur le movement de manège chez les souris." *Bulletin de la Société Zoölogique de France*, T. 18 : 85–88. 1893.

29. SCHLUMBERGER, C. "A propos d'un netzuké japonais." *Memoires de la Société Zoölogique de France*, T. 7 : 63–64. 1894.

30. WELDON, W. F. R. Mr. Bateson's revisions of Mendel's theory of heredity. *Biometrica*, Vol. 2 : 286–298. 1903.

31. ZOTH, O. "Ein Beitrag zu den Beobachtungen und Versuchen an japanischen Tanzmäusen." *Archiv für die gesammte Physiologie*, Bd. 86 : 147–176. 1901.

32. ANONYMOUS. "Fancy Mice: Their Varieties, Management, and Breeding." Fourth edition. London : L. Upcott Gill. No date.

THE DANCING MOUSE

CHAPTER I

Characteristics, Origin, and History

THE variety of mouse which is known as the Japanese dancing or waltzing mouse has been of special interest to biologists and to lovers of pets because of its curious movements. Haacke in Brehm's "Life of Animals" (7 p. 337) [1] writes as follows concerning certain mice which were brought to Europe from China and Japan: "From time to time a Hamburg dealer in animals sends me two breeds of common mice, which he calls Chinese climbing mice (Chinesische Klettermäuse) and Japanese dancing mice (Japanische Tanzmäuse). It is true that the first are distinguished only by their different colors, for their climbing accomplishments are not greater than those of other mice. The color, however, is subject to many variations. Besides individuals of uniform gray, light yellow, and white color, I have had specimens mottled with gray and white, and blue and white. Tricolored mice seem to be very rare. It is a known fact that we also have white, black, and yellow mice and occasionally pied ones, and the Chinese have profited by these variations of the common mouse also, to satisfy their fancy in breeding animals. The Japanese, however, who are no less enthusiastic on this point, know how to transform the common

---

[1] The reference numbers, of which 7 is an example, refer to the numbers in the bibliographic list which precedes this chapter.

mouse into a really admirable animal. The Japanese dancing mice, which perfectly justify their appellation, also occur in all the described colors. But what distinguishes them most is their innate habit of running around, describing greater or smaller circles or more frequently whirling around on the same spot with incredible rapidity. Sometimes two or, more rarely, three mice join in such a dance, which usually begins at dusk and is at intervals resumed during the night, but it is usually executed by a single individual."

As a rule the dancing mouse is considerably smaller than the common mouse, and observers agree that there are also certain characteristic peculiarities in the shape of the head. One of the earliest accounts of the animal which I have found, that of Landois (22 p. 62), states, however, that the peculiarities of external form are not remarkable. Landois further remarks, with reason, that the name dancing mouse is ill chosen, since the human dance movement is rather a rhythmic hopping motion than regular movement in a circle. As he suggests, they might more appropriately be called "circus course mice" (22 p. 63).

Since 1903 I have had under observation constantly from two to one hundred dancing mice. The original pair was presented to the Harvard Psychological Laboratory by Doctor A. G. Cleghorn of Cambridge. I have obtained specimens, all strikingly alike in markings, size, and general behavior, from animal dealers in Washington, Philadelphia, and Boston. Almost all of the dancers which I have had, and they now number about four hundred, were white with patches, streaks, or spots of black. The black markings occurred most frequently on the neck, ears, face, thighs, hind legs, about the root of the tail, and occasionally on the tail itself. In only one instance were the ears white, and that in the case of one of the offspring of a male which was distinguished from most of his fellows by the possession of one white ear. I have had a few individuals whose markings were white and gray instead of white and black.

The method by which I was able to keep an accurate record of each of my dancers for purposes of identification and reference is illustrated in Figure 1. As this method has proved very convenient and satisfactory, I may briefly describe it. With a rubber stamp [1] a rough outline of a mouse, like that of Figure 1 *A*, was made in my record book. On this outline I then indicated the black markings of the individual to be described. Beside this drawing of the animal I recorded its number, sex,[2] date of birth, parentage, and history. *B*, *C*, and *D* of Figure 1 represent typical color patterns. *D* indicates the markings of an individual whose ears were almost entirely white. The pattern varies so much from individual to individual that I have had no trouble whatever in identifying my mice by means of such records as these.

All of my dancers had black eyes and were smaller as well as weaker than the albino mouse and the gray house mouse. The weakness indicated by their inability to hold up their own weight or to cling to an object curiously enough does not manifest itself in their dancing; in this they are indefatigable. Frequently they run in circles or whirl about with astonishing rapidity for several minutes at a time. Zoth (31 p. 173), who measured the strength of the dancer

---

[1] For the use of the plate from which this stamp was made, I am indebted to Professor W. E. Castle, who in turn makes acknowledgment to Doctor G. M. Allen for the original drawing.

[2] I have found it convenient to use the even numbers for the males and the odd numbers for the females. Throughout this book this usage is followed. Wherever the sex of an individual is not specially given, the reader therefore may infer that it is a male if the number is even; a female if the number is odd.

in comparison with that of the common mouse, found that it can hold up only about 2.8 times its own weight, whereas the common white mouse can hold up 4.4 times its weight.

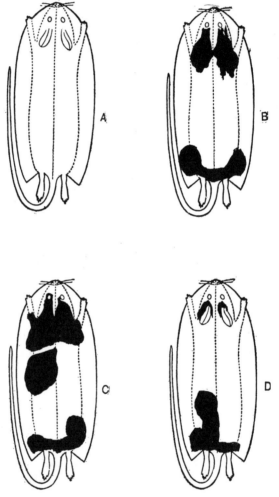

FIGURE 1.—Typical markings of dancers. *A*, blank outline of mouse for record. *B*, markings of No. 2 ♂, born September 7, 1905, of unknown parents, died March 30, 1907. *C*, markings of No. 43 ♀, born November 10, 1906, of 212 and 211. *D*, markings of No. 151 ♀, born February 28, 1906, of 1000 and 5, died February 26, 1907.

No other accurate measurements of the strength, endurance, or hardiness of the dancer are available. They are usually supposed to be weak and delicate, but my own observations cause me to regard them as exceptionally strong in certain respects and weak in others.

What the Japanese have to say about the dancing mouse is of special importance because Japan is rather commonly supposed to be its home. For this reason, as well as because of the peculiar interest of the facts mentioned, I quote at length from Doctor Kishi (21 p. 457). " The dancing mouse has received in Europe this name which it does not bear in its own home, because of the fact that the circular movements which it makes are similar to the European (human) dance. Sometimes it is also called the Japanese or Chinese mouse; originally, however, China must have been its home, since in Japan it is mostly called '*Nankin nesumi*,' the mouse from Nankin. When this animal came from China to Japan I shall inquire at a later opportunity. There were originally in Japan two different species of mouse, the gray and the white; therefore in order to distinguish our dancing mouse from these it was necessary to use the name of its native city.

"In Japan, as in Europe, the animal lives as a house animal in small cages, but the interest which is taken in it there is shown in quite another way than in Europe, where the whirling movements, to which the name dancing mouse is due, are of chief interest. For this reason in Europe it is given as much room as possible in its cage that it may dance conveniently. In Japan also the circular movements have been known for a long time, but this has had no influence upon our interest in the animal, for the human fashion of dancing with us is quite different from that in Europe. What has lent interest to the creature for us are its prettiness, its

cleverness in tricks, and its activity. It is liked, therefore,
as an amusement for children. For this purpose it is kept
in a small cage, usually fifteen centimeters square, sometimes
in a somewhat broader wooden box one of whose walls is of
wire netting. In this box are built usually a tower, a tunnel,
a bridge, and a wheel. The wheel is rather broad, being
made in the form of a drum and pierced with holes on one
side through which the animal can slip in and out. Running around on the inside, the mouse moves the wheel often
for hours at a time, especially in the evening. Moreover,
there are found in the box other arrangements of different
kinds which may be set in motion by the turning of the
wheel. No space remains in the box in which the animal
may move about freely, and therefore one does not easily or
often have an opportunity to observe that the animal makes
circular movements, whether voluntarily or involuntarily.
This is the reason that in its home this interesting little
animal has never been studied by any one in this respect."

It is odd indeed that the remarkable capacity of the dancer
for the execution of quick, graceful, dextrous, bizarre, and
oft-repeated movements has not been utilized in America as
it has in Japan. The mice are inexhaustible sources of
amusement as well as invaluable material for studies in
animal behavior and intelligence.

Concerning the origin and history of this curious variety
of mouse little is definitely known. I have found no mention of the animal in scientific literature previous to 1890.
The fact that it is called the Chinese dancing mouse, the
Japanese dancing mouse, and the Japanese waltzing mouse
is indicative of the existing uncertainty concerning the origin
of the race.

Thinking that Japanese literature might furnish more information bearing on the question of racial history than was

available from European sources, I wrote to Professor Mitsukuri of the University of Tokyo, asking him whether any reliable records of the dancer existed in Japan. He replied as follows: "I have tried to find what is known in Japan about the history of the Japanese waltzing mice, but I am sorry to say that the results are wholly negative. I cannot find any account of the origin of this freak, either authentic or fictitious, and, strange as it may seem to you, no study of the mice in a modern sense has been made, so you may consider the literature on the mouse in the Japanese language as absolutely *nil*." In explanation of this somewhat surprising ignorance of the origin of the race in what is commonly supposed to be its native land, Professor Mitsukuri adds: "The breeders of the mice have mostly been ignorant men to whom writing is anything but easy."

In response to similar inquiries, I received the following letter, confirmatory of Professor Mitsukuri's statements, from Doctor S. Hatai of Wistar Institute, Philadelphia: "If I remember rightly the so-called Japanese dancing mouse is usually called by us *Nankin-nedzumi* (*Nankin* means anything which has been imported from China, and *nedzumi* means rat-like animal, or in this case mouse) or Chinese mouse. I referred to one of the standard Japanese dictionaries and found the following statement: 'The *Nankin-nedzumi* is one of the varieties of *Mus spiciosus* (*Hatszuka-nedzumi*), and is variously colored. It was imported from China. These mice are kept in cages for the amusement of children, who watch their play.' *Mus spiciosus*, if I remember correctly, is very much like *Mus musculus* in color, size, and several other characteristics, if not the same altogether."

In Swinhoe's list of the mammals of China, which appeared in the *Proceedings of the Zoölogical Society of London* for 1870, *Mus musculus* L. is mentioned as occurring in houses in South China and in Formosa. It is further stated that black and white varieties which are brought from the Straits are often kept by the Chinese (p. 637).

The statements of Kishi, Mitsukuri, and Hatai which have been quoted, taken in connection with the opinions expressed by various European scientists who have studied the dancer, make it seem highly probable that the race appeared first in China, and was thence introduced into Japan, from which country it has been brought to Europe and America. Accepting for the present this conclusion with reference to the place of origin of the dancer, we may now inquire, how and when did this curious freak, as Professor Mitsukuri has called it, come into existence? Concerning these matters there is wide divergence of opinion.

Haacke (6 p. 514), as quoted in Brehm's "Tierleben," says that an animal dealer with whom he discussed the question of the possible origin of the dancer maintained that it came from Peru, where it nests in the full cotton capsules, arranging the cotton fibers in the form of a nest by running about among them in small circles. Hence the name cotton mouse is sometimes applied to it. Haacke himself believes, however, that the race originated either in China or Japan as the result of systematic selectional breeding. Of this he has no certainty, for he states that he failed to find any literature on the "beautiful mice of China and Japan." Whether Haacke's description of the dancing mouse was published elsewhere previous to its appearance in Brehm's "Tierleben" I am unable to state; I have found nothing written on the subject by him before 1890. Zoth (31 p. 176) also thinks that the race was developed by systematic breeding, or in other words, that it is a product of the skill of the Asiatic animal breeders.

Another account of the origin of the race is that accepted

by Kishi (21 p. 481) and some other Japanese biologists. It is their belief that the forms of movement acquired by the individual as the result of confinement in narrow cages are inherited. Thus centuries of subjection to the conditions which Kishi has described (p. 6) finally resulted in a race of mice which breed true to the dance movement. It is only fair to add, although Kishi does not emphasize the fact, that in all probability those individuals in which the dancing tendency was most pronounced would naturally be selected by the breeders who kept these animals as pets, and thus it would come about that selectional breeding would supplement the inheritance of an acquired character. Few indeed will be willing to accept this explanation of the origin of the dancer so long as the inheritance of acquired characters remains, as at present, unproved.

Still another mode of origin of the mice is suggested by the following facts. In 1893 Saint Loup (28 p. 85) advanced the opinion that dancing individuals appear from time to time among races of common mice. The peculiarity of movement may be due, he thinks, to an accidental nervous defect which possibly might be transmissible to the offspring of the exceptional individual. Saint Loup for several months had under observation a litter of common mice whose quick, jerky, nervous movements of the head, continuous activity, and rapid whirling closely resembled the characteristic movements of the true dancers of China. He states that these mice ran around in circles of from 1 to 20 cm. in diameter. They turned in either direction, but more frequently to the left, that is, anticlockwise. At intervals they ran in figure-eights (∞) as do the true dancers. According to Saint Loup these exceptional individuals were healthy, active, tame, and not markedly different in general intelligence from the ordinary mouse. One of these mice produced a litter of seven

young, in which, however, none of the peculiarities of
behavior of the parents appeared.

In view of this proof of the occurrence of dancing individuals among common mice, Saint Loup believes that the
race of dancers has resulted from the inheritance and ac-
centuation of an "accidental" deviation from the usual mode
of behavior.   It is scarcely necessary to say that this opinion
would be of far greater weight had he observed, instead of
postulating, the inheritance of the peculiarities of movement
which he has described.   It might be objected, to the first of
his so-called facts, that the litter resulted from the mating
of mice which possessed dancer blood.   Until the occurrence
of dancers among varieties of mice which are known to be
unmixed with true dancers is established, and further, until
the inheritance of this peculiar deviation from the normal
is proved, Saint Loup's account of the origin of the dancing
mouse race must be regarded as an hypothesis.

The occurrence of dancing individuals among common mice
has been recorded by several other observers.   Kammerer
(20 p. 389) reports that he found a litter of young wood
mice (*Mus sylvaticus L.*) which behaved much as do the
spotted dancers of China.   He also observed, among a lot
of true dancers, a gray individual which, instead of spinning
around after the manner of the race, turned somersaults at
frequent intervals.   It is Kammerer's opinion, as a result
of these observations, that the black and white dancers of
China and Japan have been produced by selectional breeding on the basis of this occasional tendency to move in circles.
Among albino mice Rawitz (25 p. 238) has found individuals
which whirled about rapidly in small circles.   He states,
however, that they lacked the restlessness of the Chinese
dancers.   Some shrews (*Sorex vulgaris L.*) which exhibited
whirling movements and in certain other respects resembled

the dancing mouse were studied for a time by Professor Häcker of Freiburg in Baden, according to a report by von Guaita (17 p. 317, footnote). Doctor G. M. Allen of Cambridge has reported to me that he noticed among a large number of mice kept by him for the investigation of problems of heredity [1] individuals which ran in circles; and Miss Abbie Lathrop of Granby, Massachusetts, who has raised thousands of mice for the market, has written me of the appearance of an individual, in a race which she feels confident possessed no dancer blood, which whirled and ran about in small circles much as do the true dancers.

Although it is possible that some of these cases of the unexpected appearance of individuals with certain of the dancer's peculiarities of behavior may have been due to the presence of dancer blood in the parents, it is not at all probable that this is true of all of them. We may, therefore, accept the statement that dancing individuals now and then appear in various races of mice. They are usually spoken of as freaks, and, because of their inability to thrive under the conditions of life of the race in which they happen to appear, they soon perish.

Another and a strikingly different notion of the origin of the race of dancers from those already mentioned is that of Cyon (11 p. 443) who argues that it is not a natural variety of mouse, as one might at first suppose it to be, but instead a pathological variation. The pathological nature of the animals is indicated, he points out, by the exceptionally high degree of variability of certain portions of the body. According to this view the dancing is due to certain pathological structural conditions which are inherited. Cyon's belief raises the interesting question, are the mice normal or ab-

[1] Allen, G. M. "The Heredity of Coat Color in Mice." Proc. Amer. Academy, Vol. 40, 59–163, 1904.

normal, healthy or pathological? That the question cannot
be answered with certainty off-hand will be apparent after
we have considered the facts of structure and function which
this volume presents.

Everything organic sooner or later is accounted for, in
some one's mind, by the action of natural selection. The
dancing mouse is no exception, for Landois (22 p. 62) thinks
that it is the product of natural selection and heredity,
favored, possibly, by selectional breeding in China. He
further maintains that the Chinese dancer is a variety of
Mus musculus L. in which certain peculiarities of behavior
appear because of bilateral defects in the brain. This author
is not alone in his belief that the brain of the dancer is defective, but so far as I have been able to discover he is the
only scientist who has had the temerity to appeal to natural
selection as an explanation of the origin of the race.

Milne-Edwards, as quoted by Schlumberger (29 p. 63), is
of the opinion that the Chinese dancer is not a natural wild
mouse race, but instead the product of rigid artificial selection. And in connection with this statement Schlumberger
describes a discovery of his own which seems to have some
bearing upon the problem of origin. In an old Japanese
wood carving which came into his possession he found a
group of dancing mice. The artist had represented in minute
detail the characteristics of the members of the group, which
consisted of the parents and eight young. The father and
mother as well as four of the little mice are represented as
white spotted with black. Of the four remaining young mice,
two are entirely black and two entirely white. The two pure
white individuals have pink eyes, as has also the mother.
The eyes of all the others are black. From these facts
Schlumberger infers that the dancer has resulted from the
crossing of a race of black mice with a race of albinos; the

two original types appear among the offspring in the carving.

Experimental studies of the inheritance of the tendency to dance are of interest in their bearing upon the question of origin. Such studies have been made by Haacke (19), von Guaita (17, 18), and Darbishire (13, 14, 15, 16), and the important results of their investigations have been well summarized by Bateson (5).

By crossing dancing mice with common white mice both Haacke and von Guaita obtained gray or black mice which are very similar to the wild house mouse in general appearance and behavior. The characteristic movements of the dancers do not appear. As the result of a long series of breeding experiments, Darbishire (16 pp. 26, 27) says: "When the race of waltzing mice is crossed with albino mice which do not waltz, the waltzing habit disappears in the resulting young, so that waltzing is completely recessive in Mendel's sense; the eye-color of the hybrids is always dark; the coat-color is variable, generally a mixture of wild-gray and white, the character of the coat being distinctly correlated with characters transmitted both by the albino and by the colored parent." When hybrids produced by the cross described by Darbishire are paired, they produce dancers in the proportion of about one to five.

Bateson (5 p. 93, footnote), in discussing the results obtained by Haacke, von Guaita, and Darbishire, writes: "As regards the waltzing character, von Guaita's experiments agree with Darbishire's in showing that it was always recessive to the normal. No individual in F_1 [thus the first hybrid generation is designated] or in families produced by crossing F_1 with the pure normal, waltzed. In Darbishire's experiments $F_1 \times F_1$ [first hybrids mated] gave 8 waltzers in 37 offspring, indicating 1 in 4 as the probable average. From von

Guaita's matings in the form DR × DR the totals of families were 117 normal and 21 waltzers. . . .   There is therefore a large excess of normals over the expected 3 to 1.   This is possibly due to the delicacy of the waltzers, which are certainly much more difficult to rear than normals are.   The small number in von Guaita's litters makes it very likely that many were lost before such a character as this could be determined."

Bateson does not hazard a guess at the origin of the dancer, but merely remarks (5 p. 86) that the exact physiological basis of the dancing character is uncertain and the origin of this curious variation in behavior still more obscure.   "Mouse fanciers have assured me," he continues, "that something like it may appear in strains inbred from the normal type, though I cannot find an indubitable case.   Such an occurrence may be nothing but the appearance of a rare recessive form Certainly it is not a necessary consequence of inbreeding, witness von Guaita's long series of inbred albinos."   (von Guaita (17 p. 319) inbred for twenty-eight generations.)

From the foregoing survey of the available sources of information concerning the origin and history of the race of dancing mice the following important facts appear.   There are four theories of the origin of the race: (1) origin by selectional breeding (Haacke, Zoth, Milne-Edwards); (2) origin through the inheritance of an acquired character (Kishi); (3) origin by mutation, inheritance, and selectional breeding (Saint Loup, Kammerer, Cyon); (4) origin by natural selection, and inheritance, favored by selectional breeding (Landois). Everything indicates that the race originated in China.   It is fairly certain that individuals with a tendency to move in circles appear at rare intervals in races of common mice.

It seems highly probable, in view of these facts, that the Chinese took advantage of a deviation from the usual form of behavior to develop by means of careful and patient selectional breeding a race of mice which is remarkable for its dancing. Even if it should be proved that the mutation as it appears among common mice is not inherited, the view that slight deviations were taken advantage of by the breeders would still be tenable. The dancing tendency is such in nature as to unfit an individual for the usual conditions of mouse existence, hence, in all probability human care alone could have produced and preserved the race of dancers.

In answer to the question, how and when did the race of dancers originate, it may be said that historical research indicates that a structural variation or mutation which occasionally appears in *Mus musculus,* and causes those peculiarities of movement which are known as dancing, has been preserved and accentuated through selectional breeding by the Chinese and Japanese, until finally a distinct race of mice which breeds true to the dance character has been established. The age of the race is not definitely known, but it is supposed to have existed for several centuries.

CHAPTER II

Feeding, Breeding, and Development of the Young

In this chapter I shall report, for the benefit of those who may wish to know how to take care of dancing mice, my experience in keeping and breeding the animals, and my observations concerning the development of the young. It is commonly stated that the dancer is extremely delicate, subject to diseases to an unusual degree and difficult to breed. I have not found this to be true. At first I failed to get them to breed, but this was due, as I discovered later, to the lack of proper food. For three years my mice have bred frequently and reared almost all of their young. During one year, after I had learned how to care for the animals, when the maximum number under observation at any time was fifty and the total number for the year about one hundred, I lost two by disease and one by an accident. I very much doubt whether I could have done better with any species of mouse. There can be no doubt, however, that the dancer is delicate and demands more careful attention than do most mice. In March, 1907, I lost almost all of my dancers from what appeared to be an intestinal trouble, but with this exception I have had remarkably good luck in breeding and rearing them.

My dancers usually were kept in the type of cage of which Figure 2 is a photograph.[1] Four of these double cages,

[1] This cage was devised by Professors W. E. Castle and E. L. Mark, and has been used in the Zoölogical Laboratories of Harvard University for several years.

70 cm. long, 45 cm. wide, and 10 cm. deep in front, were supported by a frame as is shown in Figure 3. The fact that the covers of these cages cannot be left open is of practical importance. A similar type of cage, which I have used to some extent, consists of a wooden box 30 by 30 cm. by 15 cm. deep, without any bottom, and with a hinged cover made

FIGURE 2. — Double cage, with nest boxes and water dishes.

in part of 1 cm. mesh wire netting. Such a cage may be placed upon a piece of tin or board, or simply on a newspaper spread out on a table. The advantage of the loose bottom is that the box may be lifted off at any time, and the bottom thoroughly cleansed. I have had this type of cage constructed in blocks of four so that a single bottom and cover sufficed for the block. If the mice are being kept for show or for the observation of their movements, at least one side of the cages should be of wire netting, and, as Kishi suggests, such objects as a wheel, a tower, a tunnel, a bridge, and a turntable, if placed in the cage, will give the animals excellent opportunity to exhibit their capacity for varied forms of activity.

c

The floors of the cages were covered with a thin layer of sawdust for the sake of cleanliness, and in one corner of each cage a nest box of some sort was placed. During the warm months I found it convenient and satisfactory to use berry boxes, such as appear in Figure 2, with a small entrance hole cut in one side; and during the cold months cigar boxes, with an entrance hole not more than 5 cm. in diameter at one end. In the nest box a quantity of tissue paper, torn into fragments, furnished material for a nest in which the adults could make themselves comfortable or the female care for her young. Cotton should never be used in the nest boxes, for the mice are likely to get it wound about their legs

FIGURE 3.—Double cages in frame.

with serious results. Apparently they are quite unable to free themselves from such an incumbrance, and their spinning motion soon winds the threads so tightly that the circulation of the blood is stopped.

The cages and nest boxes were emptied and thoroughly cleaned once a week with an emulsion made by heating together one part of kerosene and one part of water containing a little soap. This served to destroy whatever odor the cages had acquired and to prevent vermin from infesting the nests. In hot weather far greater cleanliness is necessary for the welfare of the mice than in cold weather. The animals attend faithfully to their own toilets, and usually keep themselves scrupulously clean.

For water and food dishes I have used heavy watch glasses[1] 5 cm. in diameter and $\frac{1}{2}$ cm. deep. They are convenient because they are durable, easily cleaned, and not large enough for the young mice to drown in when they happen to spin into one which contains water. It is said that mice do not need water, but as the dancers seem very fond of a little, I have made it a rule to wash the watch glasses thoroughly and fill them with pure fresh water daily. The food, when moist, may be placed in the cages in the same kind of watch glass.

There is no need of feeding the animals oftener than once a day, and as they eat mostly in the evening and during the night, it is desirable that the food should be placed in the cage late in the afternoon. For almost a year I kept a pair of dancers on "force"[2] and water. They seemed perfectly healthy and were active during the whole time, but they produced no young. If the animals are kept as pets, and breeding is not desired, a diet of "force," "egg-o-see,"[2] and crackers, with some bird-seed every few days, is likely to prove satisfactory. As with other animals, a variety of food is beneficial, but it appears to be quite unnecessary. Too much rich food should not be given, and the mice should be permitted to dictate their own diet by revealing their preferences. They eat surprisingly little for the amount of their activity. I have had excellent success in breeding the mice by feeding them a mixture of dry bread-crumbs, "force," and sweet, clean oats slightly moistened with milk. The food should never be made soppy. A little milk added thus to the food every other day greatly increases fertility. About once a week a small

[1] Minot watch glasses.   [2] A cereal food.

quantity of some green food, lettuce for example, should be given. It is well, I have found, to vary the diet by replacing the bread and "force" at intervals with crackers and seeds. Usually I give the food dry every other day, except in the case of mice which are nursing litters. One person to whom I suggested that lettuce was good for the dancers lost four, apparently because of too much of what the mice seemed to consider a good thing. This suggests that it should be used sparingly.

Success in keeping and breeding dancing mice depends upon three things: cleanliness, warmth, and food supply. The temperature should be fairly constant, between 60° and 70° Fahr. They cannot stand exposure to cold or lack of food. If one obtains good healthy, fertile individuals, keeps them in perfectly clean cages with soft nesting materials, maintains a temperature of not far above or below 65°, and regularly supplies them with pure water and food which they like, there is not likely to be trouble either in keeping or breeding these delicate little creatures. Several persons who have reported to me difficulty in rearing the young or in keeping the adults for long periods have been unable to maintain a sufficiently high or constant temperature, or have given them food which caused intestinal trouble.

The males are likely to fight if kept together, and they may even kill one another. A male may be kept with one or more females, or several females may be kept together, for the females rarely, in my experience, fight, and the males seldom harm the females. Unless the male is removed from the cage in which the female is kept before the young are born, he is likely to kill the newborn animals. When a female is seen to be building a nest in preparation for a litter, it is best to place her in a cage by herself so that she may not be disturbed.

The sex of individuals may be determined easily in most cases, at the age of 10 to 12 days, by the appearance of teats in the case of females.

The period of gestation is from 18 to 21 days. The maximum number born by my dancers in any single litter was 9, the minimum number 3. In 25 litters of which I have accurate records, 135 individuals were born, an average of 5.4. The average number of males per litter was precisely the same, 2.7, as the number of females.

On the birth of a litter it is well to see that the female has made a nest from which the young are not likely to escape, for at times, if the nest is carelessly made, they get out of it or under some of the pieces of paper which are used in its construction, and perish. Several times I have observed nests so poorly built that almost all of the young perished because they got too far away to find their way back to the mother. It is surprising that the female should not take more pains to keep her young safe by picking them up in her mouth, as does the common mouse, and carrying them to a place where they can obtain warmth and nourishment. This I have never seen a dancing mouse do. For the first day or two after the birth of a litter the female usually remains in the nest box almost constantly and eats little. About the second day she begins to eat ravenously, and for the next three or four weeks she consumes at least twice as much food as ordinarily. Alexander and Kreidl (3 p. 567) state that the female does not dance during the first two weeks after the birth of a litter, but my experience contradicts their statement. There is a decreased amount of activity during this period, and usually the whirling movement appears but rarely; but in some cases I have seen vigorous and long-continued dancing within a few hours after the birth of a litter. There is a wide range of variability in this matter, and the only safe statement, in the light of my observations, is that the mother dances less than usual for a few days after a litter is born to her.

The development of the young, as I have observed it in the cases of twenty litters, for ten of which (Table 1) systematic daily records were kept, may be sketched as follows. At birth the mice have a rosy pink skin which is devoid of hair and perfectly smooth; they are blind, deaf, and irresponsive to stimulation of the vibrissæ on the nose. During the first week of post-natal life the members of a litter remain closely huddled together in the nest, and no dance movements are exhibited. The mother stays with them most of the time. On the fourth or fifth day colorless hairs are visible, and by the end of the week the body is covered with a coat which rapidly assumes the characteristic black and white markings of the race. For the first few days the hind legs are too weak to support the body weight, and whatever movements appear are the result of the use of the fore legs. As soon as the young mice are able to stand, circling movements are exhibited, and by the end of the second week they are pronounced. Somewhere about the tenth day the appearance of the teats in the case of the females serves to distinguish the sexes plainly. Between the tenth and fifteenth days excitability, as indicated by restless jerky movements in the presence of a disturbing condition, increases markedly; the auditory meatus opens, and, in the case of some individuals, there are signs of hearing. On or after the fifteenth day the eyes open and the efforts to escape from the nest box rapidly become more vigorous. About this time the mother resumes her dancing with customary vigor, and the young, when they have opportunity, begin to eat of the food which is given to her. They now dance essentially as do the adults. From the end of the third week growth continues without noteworthy external changes until sexual maturity is attained, between the fourth and the sixth week. For several weeks after they are sexually mature the mice continue to increase in size.

TABLE 1

DEVELOPMENT OF THE YOUNG

PARENTS	NUMBER IN LITTER		HAIR VISIBLE	TEATS VISIBLE	JERKY MOVEMENTS APPEAR	EARS OPEN	REACT TO SOUND	EYES OPEN
	♂	♀						
152 + 151	5	0	4th day	—	13th day	14th day	14th day	16th day
152 + 151	1	3	4th day	9th day	10th day	12th day	13th day	15th day
410 + 415	4	1	5th day	11th day	14th day	15th day	15th day	17th day
410 + 415	2	4	5th day	10th day	13th day	14th day	14th day	16th day
420 + 425	0	2	4th day	10th day	12th day	14th day	14th day	16th day
210 + 215	4	1		—	17th day	13th day	17th day	15th day
210 + 215	3	3	5th day	11th day	11th day	14th day	No	16th day
212 + 211	1	3	4th day	10th day	15th day	14th day	No	15th day
220 + 225	2	4	4th day	10th day	16th day	14th day	No	15th day
220 + 225	3	3	4th day	10th day	17th day	13th day	No	15th day

A course of development very similar to that just described was observed by Alexander and Kreidl (3 p. 565) in three litters of dancing mice which contained 3, 5, and 7 individuals respectively. These authors, in comparing the development of the dancer with that of the common mouse, say that at birth the young in both cases are about 24 mm. in length. The young common mouse grows much more rapidly than the dancer, and by the ninth day its length is about 43 mm. as compared with 31 mm. in the case of the dancer. According to Zoth (31 p. 148) the adult dancer has a body length of from 7 to 7.5 cm., a length from tip of nose to tip of tail of from 12 to 13 cm., and a weight of about 18 grams. The movement of the dancer from the first tends to take the form of circles toward the middle of the nest; that of the common mouse has no definite tendency as to direction. When the

common mouse does move in circles, it goes first in one direction, then in the other, and not for any considerable period
in one direction as does the true dancer.   Neither the young
dancer nor the common mouse is able to equilibrate itself
well for the first few days after birth, but the latter can follow
a narrow path with far greater accuracy and steadiness than
the former.   The uncertain and irregular movements of
the common mouse are due to muscular weakness and
to blindness, but the bizarre movements of the young
dancer seem to demand some additional facts as an
explanation.

A brief account of the development of the dancer given by
Zoth (31 p. 149) adds nothing of importance to the description given by Alexander and Kreidl.   As my own observations disagree with their accounts in certain respects, I shall
now give, in the form of a diary, a description of the important
changes observed from day to day in a normal litter.   The
litter which I have selected as typical of the course of development in the dancer grew rapidly under favorable conditions.
I have observed many litters which passed through the various
stages of development mentioned in this description anywhere
from a day to a week later.   This was usually due to some
such obviously unfavorable condition as too little food or
slight digestive or bowel troubles.   According to the nature
of the conditions of growth the eyes of the dancer open anywhere from the fourteenth to the twentieth day.   This statement may serve to indicate the degree of variability as to
the time at which a given stage of development is reached
by different litters.

On July 14, 1906, No. 151 (female) and No. 152 (male)
were mated, and on August 3 a litter of six was born to them.
The course of the development of this litter during the first
three weeks was as follows: —

First day. The skin is pink and hairless, several vibrissæ are visible on the nose and lips, but there is no definite response when they are touched. The mice are both blind and deaf, but they are able to squeak vigorously. The mother was not seen to dance or eat during the day.

Second day. There is a very noticeable increase in size. The vibrissæ are longer, but touching them still fails to cause a reaction. No hairs are visible on the body. The mother danced rapidly for periods of a minute several times while the record was being made. She ate very little to-day.

Third day. Scales began to appear on the skin to-day. The animals are rapidly increasing in strength; they can now crawl about the nest easily, but they are too weak to stand, and constantly roll over upon their sides or backs when they are placed on a smooth surface. Because of their inability to progress it is impossible to determine with certainty whether they have a tendency to move in circles. The mother was seen out of the nest dancing once to-day. She now eats ravenously.

Fourth day. One of the six young mice was found under a corner of the nest this morning dead, and the others were scattered about the nest box. I gathered them together into a nest which I made out of bits of tissue paper, and the mother immediately began to suckle them. They are very sensitive to currents of air, but they do not respond to light or sound and seldom to contact with the vibrissæ.

Fifth day. When placed on a smooth surface, they tend to move in circles, frequently rolling over. When placed on their sides or backs, they immediately try to right themselves. They do not walk, for their legs are still too weak to support the weight of the body; instead they drag themselves about by the use of the fore legs. Fine colorless hairs are visible over the entire body surface. When the vibrissæ are touched, the head is moved noticeably. The mother dances a great deal and eats about twice as much as she did before the birth of the litter.

Sixth day.   Certain regions of the skin, which were slightly darker than the remainder on the fourth and fifth days, are now almost black. It is evident that they are the regions in which the black hair is to appear. The movement in circles is much more definite to-day, although most of the individuals are still too weak to stand on their feet steadily for more than a few seconds at a time. Most of their time, when they are first taken from the nest, is spent in trying to maintain or regain an upright position. The hair is now easily visible, and the skin begins to have a white appearance as a result.

Seventh day.   Although they are strong enough to move about the nest readily, none of the young has attempted to leave the nest. They huddle together in the middle of it for warmth. The epidermal scales, which have increased in number since the third day, are dropping off rapidly. Contact with the vibrissæ or with the surface of the body frequently calls forth a motor reaction, but neither light nor sound produces any visible change in behavior. The black and white regions of the skin are sufficiently definite now to enable one to distinguish the various individuals by their markings. The mother was seen to dance repeatedly to-day, and she ate all the food that was given to her.

Eighth day.   A fold is plainly visible where later the eyelids will separate. The black pigment in the skin has increased markedly.

Ninth day.   The eyelids are taking form rapidly, but they have not separated. The body is covered with a thick coat of hair which is either pure white or black. Standing on the four legs is still a difficult task.

Tenth day. To-day teats are plainly visible in the case of four of the five individuals of the litter. Up to this time I had thought, from structural indications, that there were three males and two females; it is now evident that there are four females and one male. The external ear, the pinna, is well formed, and has begun to stand out from the head, but no opening to the inner portion of the ear is present. The eyelids appear to be almost fully formed.

Eleventh day. There are no very noticeable changes in appearance except in size, which continues to increase rapidly. They are able to regain their normal upright position almost immediately when they happen to roll over. The mother dances as usual.

Twelfth day. It appears to-day as if the eyes were about to open. The ears are still closed, and there is no evidence of a sense of hearing. They squeaked considerably when in the nest, but not at all when I took them out to note their development. The mother stays outside of the nest box much of the time now, probably to prevent the young ones from sucking continuously.

Thirteenth day. One of the little mice came out of the nest box while I was watching the litter this morning, and was able to find his way back directly despite the lack of sight. The mice are still dependent upon the mother for nourishment. I have not seen any of them attempt to eat the food which is given to the mother. They are extremely neat and clean. I watched one of them wash himself this morning. Each foot was carefully licked with the tongue. There seems to be special care taken to keep the toes perfectly clean.

Fourteenth day. An opening into the ear is visible to-day. When tested with the Galton whistle, all five responded with quick, jerky movements of the head and legs. They evidently hear certain tones. During the past two days the ears have changed rapidly. In one of the females, which seems to be a little in advance of the others in development, certain peculiarities of behavior appeared to-day. She jumped and squeaked sharply when touched and sprang out of my hand when I attempted to take her up. This is in marked contrast with her behavior previously.

Fifteenth day. The eyes are partly opened. All of the members of the litter came out of the nest box this morning and ran around the cage, dancing frequently and trying to eat with the mother. Three out of the five gave auditory reactions on first being stimulated; none of them responded to repetitions of the stimulus. All appeared to be less sensitive to sounds than yesterday. The quick, nervous, jerky movements are very noticeable.

Sixteenth day. The eyes of all five are fully opened. They dance vigorously and are outside the nest much of the time.

Seventeenth day. No reactions to sound could be detected to-day. The sense of sight gives evidence of being well developed. The nervous jumping movements persist.

Eighteenth day. The young mice continue to suck, although they eat of the food which is given to the mother. They are now able to take care of themselves.

Nineteenth day. There are no noteworthy changes except increase in size and strength.

Twentieth day. No auditory reactions were obtained to-day, but other forms of stimulation brought about unmistakable responses.

Twenty-first day. They are now about half grown and there is no other change of special interest to be recorded. Growth continues for several weeks. The statement made by Alexander and Kreidl to the effect that the dancer is almost full grown by the thirty-first day of life is false. At that age they may be sexually mature, but usually they are far from full grown.

CHAPTER III

BEHAVIOR: DANCE MOVEMENTS

THE peculiarities of behavior of the dancing mouse are responsible alike for the widespread interest which it has aroused, and for its name. In a little book on fancy varieties of mice, in which there is much valuable information concerning the care of the animals, one who styles himself "An old fancier" writes thus of the behavior of the dancer: "I believe most people have an idea that the waltzing is a stately dance executed on the hind feet; this is not so. The performer simply goes round and round on all fours, as fast as possible, the head pointing inwards. The giddy whirl, after continuing for about a dozen turns, is then reversed in direction, and each performance usually occupies from one to two minutes. Whether it is voluntary or not, is difficult to determine, but I am inclined to think the mouse can refrain if it wishes to do so, because I never see them drop any food they may be eating, and begin to waltz in the midst of their meal. The dance, if such it can be called, generally seizes the mouse when it first emerges from its darkened sleeping place, and this would lead one to suppose that the light conveys an impression of shock to the brain, through the eyes, which disturbs the diseased centers and starts the giddy gyrations. The mice can walk or run in a fairly straight line when they wish to do so." Some of the old fancier's statements are true, others are mere guesses. Those who have studied the mice carefully will doubtless agree that he has not adequately described the various forms of behavior of

29

which they are capable. I have quoted his description as an
illustration of the weakness which is characteristic of most
popular accounts of animal behavior. It proves that it is not
sufficient to watch and then describe. The fact is that he
who adequately describes the behavior of any animal watches
again and again under natural and experimental conditions,
and by prolonged and patient observation makes himself so
familiar with his subject that it comes to possess an individuality as distinctive as that of his human companions. To the
casual observer the individuals of a strange race are almost indistinguishable. Similarly, the behavior of all the animals of a
particular species seems the same to all except the observer who
has devoted himself whole-heartedly to the study of the subject
and who has thus become as familiar with their life of action
as most of us are with that of our fellow-men; for him each
individual has its own unmistakable characteristics.

I shall now describe the behavior of the dancing mouse in
the light of the results of the observation of scores of individuals for months at a time, and of a large number of experiments. From time to time I shall refer to points in the
accounts of the subject previously given by Rawitz (25 p.
236), Cyon (9 p. 214), Alexander and Kreidl (1 p. 542),
Zoth (31 p. 147), and Kishi (21 p. 479).

The most striking features of the ordinary behavior of the
dancer are restlessness and movements in circles. The
true dancer seldom runs in a straight line for more than a
few centimeters, although, contrary to the statements of
Rawitz and Cyon, it is able to do so on occasion for longer
distances. Even before it is old enough to escape from the
nest it begins to move in circles and to exhibit the quick,
jerky head movements which are characteristic of the race.
At the age of three weeks it is able to dance vigorously, and
is incessantly active when not washing itself, eating, or sleeping.

According to Zoth (31 p. 149) the sense of sight and especially the sense of smell of the dancer "seem to be keenly
developed; one can seldom remain for some time near the
cage without one or another of the animals growing lively,
looking out of the nest, and beginning to sniff around in the
air (*windet*). They also seem to have strongly developed
cutaneous sensitiveness, and a considerable amount of
curiosity, if one may call it such, in common with their
cousin, the white mouse." I shall reserve what I have
to say concerning the sense of sight for later chapters.
As for the sense of smell and the cutaneous sensitiveness, Zoth is undoubtedly right in inferring from the
behavior of the animal that it is sensitive to certain odors
and to changes in temperature. One of the most noticeable and characteristic activities of the dancer is its
sniffing. Frequently in the midst of its dancing it stops
suddenly, raises its head so that the nose is pointed
upward, as in the case of one of the mice of the frontispiece, and remains in that position for a second or two, as
if sniffing the air.

The restlessness, the varied and almost incessant movements, and the peculiar excitability of the dancer have repeatedly suggested to casual observers the question, why
does it move about in that aimless, useless fashion? To
this query Rawitz has replied that the lack of certain senses
compels the animal to strive through varied movements to
use to the greatest advantage those senses which it does possess. In Rawitz's opinion the lack of hearing and orientation is compensated for by the continuous use of sight and
smell. The mouse runs about rapidly, moves its head from
side to side, and sniffs the air, in order that it may see and
smell as much as possible. In support of this interpretation
of the restlessness of the dancer, Rawitz states that he once

observed similar behavior in an albino dog which was deaf. This suggestion is not absurd, for it seems quite probable that the dancer has to depend for the guidance of its movements upon sense data which are relatively unimportant in the common mouse, and that by its varied and restless movements it does in part make up for its deficiency in sense equipment.

The dancing, waltzing, or circus course movement, as it is variously known, varies in form from moment to moment. Now an individual moves its head rapidly from side to side, perhaps backing a little at the same time, now it spins around like a top with such speed that head and tail are almost indistinguishable, now it runs in circles of from 5 cm. to 30 cm. in diameter. If there are any objects in the cage about or through which it may run, they are sure to direct the expression of activity. A tunnel or a hole in a box calls forth endless repetitions of the act of passing through. When two individuals are in the same cage, they frequently dance together, sometimes moving in the same direction, sometimes in opposite directions. Often, as one spins rapidly about a vertical axis, the other runs around the first in small circles; or again, both may run in a small circle in the same direction, so that their bodies form a living ring, which, because of the rapidity of their movements, appears perfectly continuous. The three most clearly distinguishable forms of dance are (1) movement in circles with all the feet close together under the body, (2) movement in circles, which vary in diameter from 5 cm. to 30 cm., with the feet spread widely, and (3) movement now to the right, now to the left, in figure-eights (∞). For convenience of reference these types of dance may be called *whirling*, *circling*, and the *figure eight dance*. Zoth, in an excellent account of the behavior of the dancer (31 p. 156), describes "manège movements," "solo dances," and "contre dances." Of these the first is whirling, the second one form of circling, and the third the dancing of two individuals together in the manner described above.

Both the whirling and the circling occur to the right (clockwise) and to the left (anticlockwise). As certain observers have stated that it is chiefly to the left and others that it is as frequently to the right, I have attempted to get definite information concerning the matter by observing a number of individuals systematically and at stated intervals. My study of this subject soon convinced me that a true conception of the facts cannot be got simply by noting the direction of turning from time to time. I therefore planned and carried out a series of experimental observations with twenty dancers, ten of each sex. One at a time these individuals were placed in a glass jar, 26 cm. in diameter, and the number of circle movements executed to the right and to the left during a period of five minutes was determined as accurately as possible. This was repeated at six hours of the day: 9 and 11 o'clock A.M., and 2, 4, 6, and 8 o'clock P.M. In order that habituation to the conditions under which the counts of turning were made might not influence the results for the group, with ten individuals the morning counts were made first, and with the others the afternoon counts. No attempt was made in the counting to keep a separate record of the whirling and circling, although had it been practicable this would have been desirable, for, as soon became evident to the observer, some individuals which whirl in only one direction, circle in both.

In Table 2 the results of the counts for the males are recorded; in Table 3 those for the females. Each number in the column headed "right" and "left" indicates the total number of circles executed by a certain dancer in a period of five minutes at the hour of the day named at the head of the column. I may point out briefly the curiously interesting

D

and entirely unexpected new facts which this method of observation revealed to me.

First, there are three kinds of dancers: those which whirl almost uniformly toward the right, those which whirl just as uniformly toward the left, and those which whirl about as frequently in one direction as in the other. To illustrate, No. 2 of Table 2 may be characterized as a "right whirler," for he turned to the right almost uniformly. In the case of the 6 P.M. count, for example, he turned 285 times to the right, not once to the left. No. 152, on the contrary, should be characterized as a "left whirler," since he almost always turned to the left. From both of these individuals No. 210 is distinguished by the fact that he turned now to the left, now to the right. For him the name "mixed whirler" seems appropriate.

Second, the amount of activity, as indicated by the number of times an individual turns in a circle within five minutes, increases regularly and rapidly from 9 A.M. to 8 P.M. According to the general averages which appear at the bottom of Table 2, the average number of circles executed by the males at 9 A.M. was 89.8 as compared with 207.1 at 8 P.M. In other words, the mice dance more in the evening than during the day.

Third, as it appears in a comparison of the general averages of Tables 2 and 3, the females dance more than the males, under the conditions of observation. At 9 A.M. the males circled 89.8 times, the females 151.0 times; at 8 P.M. the males circled 207.1 times, the females, 279.0 times.

Fourth, according to the averages for the six counts made with each individual, as they appear in Table 4, the males turn somewhat more frequently to the left than to the right (the difference, however, is not sufficient to be considered significant); whereas, the females turn much more frequently

TABLE 2

NUMBER OF WHIRLS TO THE RIGHT AND TO THE LEFT DURING
FIVE-MINUTE INTERVALS AS DETERMINED BY COUNTS MADE AT
SIX DIFFERENT HOURS, FOR EACH OF TEN MALE DANCERS

NUMBER OF ANIMAL	9 A.M.		11 A.M.		2 P.M.	
	RIGHT	LEFT	RIGHT	LEFT	RIGHT	LEFT
2	11	2	23	4	194	1
30	20	1	134	1	109	2
34	2	16	2	48	4	92
36	194	21	180	11	143	65
152	7	48	3	171	6	79
156	63	8	53	9	27	6
210	3	9	7	41	225	21
220	168	105	39	43	47	5
410	2	61	10	27	8	103
420	15	142	5	214	16	238
Averages	48.5	41.3	45.6	56.9	77.9	61.2
Gen. Av.	89.8		102.5		139.1	

NUMBER OF ANIMAL	4 P.M.		6 P.M.		8 P.M.	
	RIGHT	LEFT	RIGHT	LEFT	RIGHT	LEFT
2	70	3	285	0	237	10
30	154	0	107	6	134	5
34	7	158	5	118	6	147
36	173	14	170	11	325	19
152	0	91	16	210	9	223
156	85	2	72	26	139	26
210	159	18	31	82	47	201
220	45	38	78	17	69	33
410	9	155	9	394	24	94
420	18	243	16	291	3	320
Averages	72.0	72.2	78.9	115.5	99.3	107.8
Gen. Av.	144.2		194.4		207.1	

TABLE 3

NUMBER OF WHIRLS TO THE RIGHT AND TO THE LEFT DURING
FIVE-MINUTE INTERVALS AS DETERMINED BY COUNTS MADE AT
SIX DIFFERENT HOURS, FOR EACH OF TEN FEMALE DANCERS

NUMBER OF ANIMAL	9 A.M.		11 A.M.		2 P.M.	
	RIGHT	LEFT	RIGHT	LEFT	RIGHT	LEFT
29	9	18	17	30	7	22
33	287	0	329	1	352	3
35	48	15	198	46	208	14
151	13	88	7	75	3	167
157	57	6	50	45	53	12
211	218	21	31	55	66	5
215	67	216	33	105	37	226
225	46	39	72	49	143	44
415	23	0	156	0	34	3
425	43	296	12	201	12	210
Averages	81.1	69.9	90.5	60.7	91.5	70.6
Gen. Av.	151.0		151.2		162.1	

NUMBER OF ANIMAL	4 P.M.		6 P.M.		8 P.M.	
	RIGHT	LEFT	RIGHT	LEFT	RIGHT	LEFT
29	33	114	31	36	45	99
33	436	7	408	3	364	2
35	279	6	165	24	353	10
151	3	8	2	285	2	217
157	52	15	19	125	51	104
211	190	7	86	31	67	250
215	15	292	45	336	150	232
225	133	86	48	39	177	81
415	268	3	437	7	382	8
425	12	242	19	210	4	192
Averages	142.1	78.0	126.0	109.6	159.5	119.5
Gen. Av.	220.1		235.6		279.0	

to the right than to the left. I do not wish to emphasize the importance of this difference, for it is not improbable that counts made with a larger number of animals, or even with another group of twenty, would yield different results.

The most important results of this statistical study of turning are the demonstration of the existence of individual tendencies to turn in a particular direction, and of the fact that the whirling increases in amount from morning to evening.

In order to discover whether the distribution of the dancers among the three groups which have been designated as right, left, and mixed whirlers agrees in general with that indicated by Table 4 (approximately the same number in each group) I have observed the direction of turning in the case of one hundred dancers, including those of the foregoing tables, and have classified them in accordance with their behavior as is indicated below.

	RIGHT WHIRLERS	LEFT WHIRLERS	MIXED WHIRLERS
Males	19	19	12
Females	12	23	15
Totals	31	42	27

The left whirlers occur in excess of both the right and the mixed whirlers. This fact, together with the results which have already been considered in connection with the counts of turning, suggests that a tendency to whirl in a certain way may be inherited. I have examined my data and conducted breeding experiments for the purpose of ascertaining whether this is true. But as the results of this part of the investigation more properly belong in a special chapter on the inheritance of behavior (XVIII), the discussion of the subject may be closed for the present with the statement that the prepon-

TABLE 4

AVERAGE NUMBER OF WHIRLS TO THE RIGHT AND TO THE LEFT FOR
THE SIX INTERVALS OF TABLES 2 AND 3, WITH A CHARACTERIZA-
TION OF THE ANIMALS AS RIGHT WHIRLERS, LEFT WHIRLERS, OR
MIXED WHIRLERS.

MALES	AGE	AVERAGE NO. OF WHIRLS TO RIGHT	AVERAGE NO. OF WHIRLS TO LEFT	CHARACTERIZATION
2	12 mo.	136.7	3.3	Right whirler
30	2 mo.	109.7	2.5	Right whirler
34	2 mo.	4.3	96.5	Left whirler
36	2 mo.	197.5	23.5	Right whirler
152	6 mo.	6.8	137.0	Left whirler
156	1 mo.	73.2	12.8	Right whirler
210	3 mo.	78.7	62.0	Mixed whirler
220	4 mo.	74.3	40.2	Mixed whirler
410	3 mo.	10.3	139.0	Left whirler
420	3 mo.	12.2	241.3	Left whirler
Average		70.4	75.8	4 Right whirlers 4 Left whirlers 2 Mixed whirlers
FEMALES				
29	2 mo.	23.7	53.2	Left whirler
33	2 mo.	362.7	2.7	Right whirler
35	2 mo.	208.5	19.2	Right whirler
151	6 mo.	5.0	140.0	Left whirler
157	1 mo.	47.0	51.2	Mixed whirler
211	3 mo.	109.7	61.5	Mixed whirler
215	3 mo.	57.8	234.5	Left whirler
225	4 mo.	103.2	56.3	Mixed whirler
415	3 mo.	216.7	3.5	Right whirler
425	3 mo.	17.0	225.2	Left whirler
Average		115.1	84.7	3 Right whirlers 4 Left whirlers 3 Mixed whirlers

derance of left whirlers indicated above is due to a strong tendency to turn to the left which was exhibited by the individuals of one line of descent.

The tendency of the dancer's activity to increase in amount toward evening, which the results of Tables 2, 3, and 4 exhibit, demands further consideration. Haacke (7 p. 337) and Kishi (21 p. 458) agree that the dancing is most vigorous in the evening; but Alexander and Kreidl (1 p. 544) assert, on the contrary, that the whirling of the individuals which they observed bore no definite relation to the time of day and apparently was not influenced in intensity thereby. Since the results of my own observations contradict many of the statements made by the latter authors, I suspect that they may not have watched their animals long enough to discover the truth. The systematic records which I have kept indicate that the mice remain quietly in their nests during the greater part of the day, unless they are disturbed or come out to obtain food. Toward dusk they emerge and dance with varying intensity for several hours. I have seldom discovered one of them outside the nest between midnight and daylight. The period of greatest activity is between 5 and 10 o'clock P.M.

Zoth states that he has observed the adult dancer whirl 79 times without an instant's interruption, and I have counted as many as 110 whirls. It seems rather absurd to say that an animal which can do this is weak. Evidently the dancer is exceptionally strong in certain respects, although it may be weak in others. Such general statements as are usually made fail to do justice to the facts.

The supposition that light determines the periodicity of dancing is not borne out by my observations, for I have found that the animals continue to dance most vigorously toward evening, even when they are kept in a room which is constantly illuminated. In all probability the periodicity of activity is an expression of the habits of the mouse race rather than of the immediate influence of any environmental condition. At some time in the history of the dancer light probably did have an influence upon the period of activity; but at present, as a result of the persistence of a well-established racial tendency, the periodicity of dancing depends to a greater extent upon internal than upon external conditions. During its hours of quiescence it is possible to arouse the dancer and cause it to whirl more or less vigorously by stimulating it strongly with intense light, a weak electric current, or by placing two individuals which are strangers to one another in the same cage; but the dancing thus induced is seldom as rapid, varied, or as long-continued as that which is characteristic of the evening hours.

One of the most interesting results of this study of the direction of turning, from the observer's point of view, is the demonstration of the fact that the truth concerning even so simple a matter as this can be discovered only by long and careful observation. The casual observer of the dancer gets an impression that it turns to the left more often than to the right; he verifies his observation a few times and then asserts with confidence that such is the truth about turning. That such a method of getting knowledge of the behavior of the animal is worse than valueless is clear in the light of the results of the systematic observations which have just been reported. But, however important the progress which we may have made by means of systematic observation of the phenomenon of turning, it must not for one moment be supposed that the whole truth has been discovered. Continued observation will undoubtedly reveal other important facts concerning circling, whirling, and the periodicity of dancing, not to mention the inheritance of peculiarities of dancing and the significance of the various forms of activity.

CHAPTER IV

Behavior: Equilibration and Dizziness

Quite as interesting and important as the general facts of behavior which we have been considering are the results of experimental tests of the dancer's ability to maintain its position under unusual spatial conditions—to climb, cross narrow bridges, balance itself on high places. Because of its tendency to circle and whirl, to dart hither and thither rapidly and apparently without control of its movements, the study of the mouse's ability to perform movements which demand accurate and delicate muscular coördination, and to control its expressions of activity, are of peculiar scientific interest.

That observers do not entirely agree as to the facts in this field is apparent from the following comparison of the statements made by Cyon and Zoth (31 p. 174).

Cyon states that the dancer

Cannot run in a straight line,
Cannot turn in a narrow space,
Cannot run backward,
Cannot run up an incline,
Cannot move about safely when above the ground, because of fear and visual dizziness,
Can hear certain tones.

Zoth, on the contrary, maintains that the animal

Can run in a straight line for at least 20 cm.,
Can and repeatedly does turn in a narrow space,
Can run backward, for he has observed it do so,

Can run up an incline unless the surface is too smooth for it to gain a foothold,

Can move about safely when above the ground, and gives no signs of fear or dizziness,

Cannot hear, or at least gives no signs of sensitiveness to sounds.

Such contradictory statements (and unfortunately they are exceedingly common) stimulated me to the repetition of many of the experiments which have been made by other investigators to test the dancer's behavior in unusual spatial relations. I shall state very briefly the general conclusions to which these experiments have led me, with only sufficient reference to methods and details of results to enable any one who wishes to repeat the tests for himself to do so. For the sake of convenience of presentation and clearness, the facts have been arranged under three rubrics: equilibrational ability, dizziness, and behavior when blinded. To our knowledge of each of these three groups of facts important contributions have come from the experiments of Cyon (9 p. 220), Alexander and Kreidl (1 p. 545), Zoth (31 p. 157), and Kishi (21 p. 482), although, as has been stated, in many instances their results are so contradictory as to demand reëxamination. All in all, Zoth has given the most satisfactory account of the behavior and motor capacity of the dancer.

If the surface upon which it is moving be sufficiently soft or rough to furnish it a foothold, the dancer is able to run up or down inclines, even though they be very steep, to cross narrow bridges, to balance itself at heights of at least 30 cm. above the ground, and even to climb up and down on rods, as is shown by certain of Zoth's photographs which are reproduced in Figure 4. Zoth himself says, and in this I am able fully to agree with him on the basis of my own observations, "that the power of equilibration in the dancing

mouse, is, in general, very complete.   The seeming reduction which appears under certain conditions should be attributed, not to visual dizziness, but in part to excitability and restlessness, and in part to a reduced muscular power" (31 p. 161).

FIGURE 5.—Tracks of common mouse. Reproduced from Alexander and Kreidl's figure in *Pflüger's Archiv*, Bd. 82.

The dancer certainly has far less grasping power than the common mouse, and is therefore at a disadvantage in moving about on sloping surfaces.   One evidence of this fact is the character of the tracks made by the animal.   Instead of raising its feet from the substratum and placing them neatly, as does the common mouse (Figure 5), it tends to shuffle along,

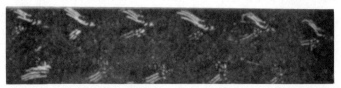

FIGURE 6. — Tracks of dancing mouse. Reproduced from Alexander and Kreidl's figure in *Pflüger's Archiv*, Bd. 82.

dragging its toes and thus producing on smoked paper such tracks as are seen in Figure 6.   From my own observations I am confident that these figures exaggerate the differences. My dancers, unless they were greatly excited or moving under conditions of stress, never dragged their toes as much as is indicated in Figure 6.   However, there can be no doubt that they possess less power of grasping with their toes than do common mice.   The animal is still further incapacitated for movement on inclined surfaces or narrow places by its tendency to move in circles and zigzags. The results of my own experiments indicate that the timidity of the adult is greater than that of the immature animal when it is placed on a bridge 1 or 2 cm. wide at a distance of 20 cm. from the ground. Individuals three weeks old showed less hesitation about trying to creep along such a narrow pathway than did full-grown dancers three or four months old; and these, in turn, were not so timid apparently as an individual one year old. But the younger animals fell off more frequently than did the older ones.

Additional support for these statements concerning equilibrational ability is furnished by the observations of Kishi (21 p. 482). He built a wooden bridge 60 cm. long, 1 cm. wide at one end, and $\frac{1}{2}$ cm. at the other, and supported it at a height of 30 cm. above the ground by posts at the ends. On this bridge ten dancers were tested. Some attempted to move sidewise, others began to whirl and fell to the ground; only one of the ten succeeded in getting all the way across the bridge on the first trial. The second time he was tested this individual crossed the bridge and found the post; and the third time he crossed the bridge and climbed down the post directly. The others did not succeed in descending the post even after having crossed the bridge safely, but, instead, finally fell to the floor from awkwardness or exhaustion. On the basis of these and other similar observations, Kishi says that the dancer possesses a fair degree of ability to orient and balance itself.

Inasmuch as equilibration occurs similarly in darkness and in daylight, Zoth thinks that there is neither visual dizziness nor fear of heights. But it is doubtful whether he is right concerning fear. There is no doubt in my mind, in view of the way the mice behave when placed on an elevated surface, that they are timid; but this is due probably to the uncomfortable and unusual position rather than to perception of their distance from the ground. That they lack visual dizziness seems fairly well established.

When rotated in a cyclostat [1] the dancer, unlike the common mouse, does not exhibit symptoms of dizziness. The following vivid description of the behavior of both kinds of mice when rotated is given by Alexander and Kreidl (1 p. 548). I have not verified their observations.

The common mouse at first runs with increasing rapidity, as the speed of rotation of the cyclostat cylinder is increased, in the direction opposite to that of the cylinder itself. This continues until the speed of rotation has increased to about 60 revolutions per minute. As the rotation becomes still more rapid the mouse begins to crawl along the floor, its body stretched out and clinging to the floor. At a speed of 250 revolutions per minute it lies flat on the floor with its limbs extended obliquely to the movement of rotation, and at times with its back bent against the axis of the cylinder; in this position it makes but few and feeble efforts to crawl forward. When the rotation is suddenly stopped, the animal pulls itself together, remains for some seconds with extended limbs lying on the floor, and then suddenly falls into convulsions and trembles violently. After several attacks of this kind, cramps appear and, despite its resistance, the animal is thrown about, even into the air at times, as if by an external force. This picture of the position assumed during rapid rotation, and of cramps after the cessation of rotation (the typical picture of rotation dizziness), is repeated with great uniformity in the case of the common mouse. Within fifteen minutes after being returned to its cage the animal re-

---

[1] An apparatus consisting of a glass cylinder with a mechanism for turning it steadily and at different speeds about its vertical axis.

covers from the effects of its experience. This description of the symptoms of rotation dizziness in the common mouse applies equally well to the blinded and the seeing animal.

In sharp contrast with the behavior of the common mouse in the cyclostat is that of the dancer. As the cylinder begins to rotate the dancer runs about as usual in circles, zigzags, and figure-eights. As the speed becomes greater it naturally becomes increasingly difficult for the mouse to do this, but it shows neither discomfort nor fear, as does the common mouse. Finally the centrifugal force becomes so great that the animal is thrown against the wall of the cylinder, where it remains quietly without taking the oblique position. When the cyclostat is stopped suddenly, it resumes its dance movements as if nothing unusual had occurred. It exhibits no signs of dizziness, and apparently lacks the exhaustion which is manifest in the case of other kinds of mice after several repetitions of the experiment. The behavior of the blinded dancer is very similar.

If these statements are true, there is no reason to believe that the dancer is capable of turning or rotation dizziness. If it were, its daily life would be rendered very uncomfortable thereby, for its whirling would constantly bring about the condition of dizziness. Apparently, then, the dancer differs radically from most mammals in that it lacks visual and rotational dizziness. In the next chapter we shall have to seek for the structural causes for these facts.

The behavior of the blinded animal is so important in its bearings upon the facts of orientation and equilibration that it must be considered in connection with them. Cyon insists that the sense of vision is of great importance to the dancer in orienting and equilibrating itself. When the eyes are covered with cotton wads fastened by collodion, this writer states (9 p. 223) that the mice behave as do pigeons and frogs whose semicircular canals have been destroyed. They perform violent forced movements, turn somersaults forward and backward, run up inclines and fall over the edges, and roll over and over. In a word, they show precisely the kind of disturbances of behavior which are characteristic of animals whose semicircular canals are not functioning normally. Cyon, however, observed that in certain dancers these peculiarities of behavior did not appear when they were blinded, but that, instead, the animals gave no other indication of being inconvenienced by the lack of sight than do common white mice. This matter of individual differences we shall have to consider more fully later.

No other observer agrees with Cyon in his conclusions concerning vision, or, for that matter, in his statements concerning the behavior of the blind dancer. Alexander and Kreidl (1 p. 550) contrast in the following respects the behavior of the white mouse and that of the dancer when they are blinded. The white mouse runs less securely and avoids obstacles less certainly when deprived of vision. The dancer is much disturbed at first by the shock caused by the removal of its eyes, or in case they are covered, by the presence of the unusual obstruction. It soon recovers sufficiently to become active, but it staggers, swerves often from side to side, and frequently falls over. It moves clumsily and more slowly than usual. Later these early indications of blindness may wholly disappear, and only a slightly impaired ability to avoid obstacles remains.

It was noted by Kishi (21 p. 484) that the dancer when first blinded trembles violently, jumps about wildly, and rolls over repeatedly, as Cyon has stated; but Kishi believes that these disturbances of behavior are temporary effects of the strong stimulation of certain reflex centers in the nervous system. After having been blinded for only a few minutes the dancers observed by him became fairly normal in their behavior. They moved about somewhat more slowly than usually, especially when in a position which required accurately coördinated movements. He therefore fully agrees with Alexander and Kreidl in their conclusion that vision is not so important for the guidance of the movements of the dancer as Cyon believes.

In summing up the results of his investigation of this subject Zoth well says (31 p. 168), "the orientation of the positions of the body with respect to the horizontal and vertical planes seems to take place without the assistance of the sense of sight." And, as I have already stated, this excellent observer insists that the ability of the dancer to place its body in a particular position (orientation), and its ability to maintain its normal relations to its surroundings (equilibration) are excellent in darkness and in daylight, provided only the substratum be not too smooth for it to gain a foothold.

It must be admitted that the contradictions which exist in the several accounts of the behavior of the dancer are too numerous and too serious to be explained on the basis of careless observation. Only the assumption of striking individual differences among dancers or of the existence of two or more varieties of the animal suffices to account for the discrepancies. That there are individual or variety differences is rendered practically certain by the fact that Cyon himself worked with two groups of dancers whose peculiarities he has described in detail, both as to structure and behavior.

In the case of the first group, which consisted of three individuals, the snout was more rounded than in the four individuals of the second group, and there were present on the head three large tufts of bristly black hair which gave the

E

mice a very comical appearance. The animals of the second group resembled more closely in appearance the common albino mouse. They possessed the same pointed snout and long body, and only the presence of black spots on the head and hips rendered them visibly different from the albino mouse.

In behavior the individuals of these two groups differed strikingly. Those of the first group danced frequently, violently, and in a variety of ways; they seldom climbed on a vertical surface and when forced to move on an incline they usually descended by sliding down backwards or sidewise instead of turning around and coming down head first; they gave no signs whatever of hearing sounds. Those of the second group, on the contrary, danced very moderately and in few ways; they climbed the vertical walls of their cage readily and willingly, and when descending from a height they usually turned around and came down head first; two of the four evidently heard certain sounds very well. No wonder that Cyon suggests the possibility of a different origin! It seems not improbable that the individuals of the second group were of mixed blood, possibly the result of crosses with common mice.

As I shall hope to make clear in a subsequent discussion of the dancer's peculiarities of behavior, in a chapter on individual differences, there is no sufficient reason for doubting the general truth of Cyon's description, although there is abundant evidence of his inaccuracy in details. If, for the present, we accept without further evidence the statement that there is more than one variety of dancer, we shall be able to account for many of the apparent inaccuracies of description which are to be found in the literature on the animal.

As a result of the examination of the facts which this chapter presents we have discovered at least six important peculiarities of behavior of the dancer which demand an explanation in terms of structure. These are: (1) the dance movements—whirling, circling, figure-eights, zigzags; (2) restlessness and the quick, jerky movements of the head; (3) lack of responsiveness to sounds; (4) more or less pronounced deficiency in orientational and equilibrational power; (5) lack of visual dizziness; (6) lack of rotational dizziness.

Naturally enough, biologists from the first appearance of the dancing mouse in Europe have been deeply interested in what we usually speak of as the causes of these peculiarities of behavior. As a result, the structure of those portions of the body which are supposed to have to do with the control of movement, with the phenomena of dizziness, and with the ability to respond to sounds, have been studied thoroughly. In the next chapter we shall examine such facts of structure as have been discovered and attempt to correlate them with the facts of behavior.

CHAPTER V

STRUCTURAL PECULIARITIES AND BEHAVIOR

THE activities of an animal are expressions of changes which occur in its structure, and they can be explained satisfactorily only when the facts of structure are known. Such peculiarities of activity as are exhibited by the dancing mouse, as contrasted with the common mouse, suggest at once that this creature has a body which differs in important respects from that of the ordinary mouse. In this chapter I shall present what is known concerning the structural bases for the whirling, the lack of equilibrational ability and of dizziness, the quick jerky head movements, the restlessness, and the partial or total deafness of the dancing mouse.

Comparative physiologists have discovered that the ability of animals to regulate the position of the body with respect to external objects and to respond to sounds is dependent in large measure upon the groups of sense organs which collectively are called the ear. Hence, with reason, investigators who sought structural facts with which to explain the forms of behavior characteristic of the dancer turned their attention first of all to the study of the ear. But the ear of the animal is not, as might be supposed on superficial examination, a perfectly satisfactory natural experiment on the functions of this group of sensory structures, for it is extremely uncertain whether any one of the usual functions of the organ is totally lacking. Dizziness may be lacking, and in the adult hearing also, but in general the functional facts lead the investigator to expect modifications of the sense organs rather than their absence.

I shall now give an account of the results of studies concerning the structure of the ear and brain of the dancer. Since the descriptions given by different anatomists contradict one another in many important points, the several investigations which have been made may best be considered chronologically.

Bernhard Rawitz (25 p. 239) was the first investigator to describe the structure of the ear of the Japanese or Chinese dancers, as he calls them. The definite problem which he proposed to himself at the beginning of his study was, what is the structural basis of the whirling movement and of the deafness of the mice?

In his first paper Rawitz described the form of the ears of five dancers. His method of work was to make microscopic preparations of the ears, and from the sections, by the use of the Born method, to reconstruct the ear in wax. These wax models were then drawn for the illustration of the author's papers (Figures 8, 9, 10).

The principal results of the early work of Rawitz are summed up in the following quotation from his paper: "The Japanese dancing mice have only one normal canal and that is the anterior vertical. The horizontal and posterior vertical canals are crippled, and frequently they are grown together. The utriculus is a warped, irregular bag, whose sections have become unrecognizable. The utriculus and sacculus are in wide-open communication with each other and have almost become one. The utriculus opens broadly into the scala tympani, and the nervous elements of the cochlea are degenerate.

"The last-mentioned degeneration explains the deafness of the dancing mice; but in my opinion it is a change of

secondary nature. The primary change is the broad opening between the utriculus and the scala tympani from which
results the streaming of the endolymph from the semicircular
canals into the cochlea. When, as a consequence of the
rapid whirling movements, a great part of the endolymph is
hurled into the scala tympani, the organ of Corti in the scala
vestibuli is fixed and its parts are rendered incapable of
vibration. The condition of atrophy which is observable
in the sense cells and in the nerve elements is probably due

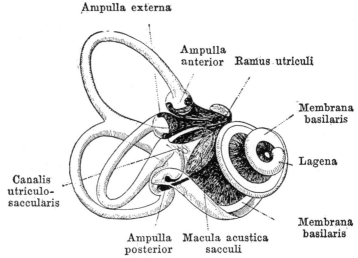

FIGURE 7.—The inner ear of the rabbit. Reproduced from Selenka after
Retzius.

to the impossibility of functional activity; it is an atrophy
caused by disuse " (25 p. 242).

To render the terms which occur in this and subsequent
descriptions of the ear of the dancer somewhat more intelligible to those who are not familiar with the general anatomy
of the vertebrate ear, a side view of the inner ear of the rabbit
is reproduced from a drawing by Retzius (Figure 7). I have
chosen the ear of the rabbit for this purpose, not in preference

to that of the common mouse, but simply because I failed to find any reliable description of the latter with drawings which could be reproduced. The rabbit's ear, however, is sufficiently like that of the mouse to make it perfectly satisfactory for our present purpose.

This drawing of the rabbit's ear represents the three semicircular canals, which occur in the ear of all mammals, and which are called, by reason of their positions, the anterior vertical, the posterior vertical, and the horizontal. Each of these membranous canals possesses at one end, in an enlargement called the ampulla, a group of sense cells. In Figure 7 the ampullæ of the three canals are marked respectively, ampulla anterior, ampulla posterior, and ampulla externa. This figure shows also the cochlea, marked lagena, in which the organ of hearing of mammals (the organ of Corti) is located. The ear sac, of which the chief divisions are the utriculus and the sacculus, with which the canals communicate, is not shown well in this drawing.

Within a few months after the publication of Rawitz's first paper on the structure of the dancer's ear, another European investigator, Panse (23 and 24) published a short paper in which he claimed that previous to the appearance of Rawitz's paper he had sectioned and mounted ears of the common white mouse and the dancing mouse side by side, and, as the result of careful comparison, found such slight differences in structure that he considered them unworthy of mention. Panse, therefore, directly contradicts the statements made by Rawitz. In fact, he goes so far as to say that he found even greater differences between the ears of different white mice than between them and the ears of the dancer (23 p. 140).

In a somewhat later paper Panse (24 p. 498) expresses his belief that, since there are no peculiarities in the general form, sensory structures, or nerve supply of the ear of the dancer, which serve to explain the behavior of the animal, it is probable that there are unusual structural conditions in the brain, perhaps in the cerebellum, to which are due the dance movements and the deafness.   The work of Panse is not very convincing, however, for his figures are poor and his descriptions meager; nevertheless, it casts a certain amount of doubt upon the reliability of the descriptions given by Rawitz.

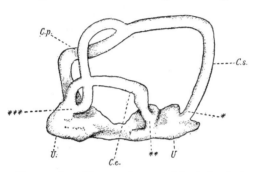

FIGURE 8. — The membranous labyrinth of the dancer's ear.   Type I.   This figure, as well as 9 and 10, are reproduced from Rawitz's figures in the *Archiv für Anatomie und Physiologie, Physiologische Abtheilung,* 1899. *C.s.,* anterior vertical canal; *C.p.,* posterior vertical canal; *C.e.,* horizontal canal; *U.,* utriculus.

The unfavorable light in which his report was placed by Panse's statements led Rawitz to examine additional preparations of the ear of the dancer.   Again he used the reconstruction method.   The mice whose ears he studied were sent to him by the physiologist Cyon.

As has been noted in Chapter IV, Cyon discovered certain differences in the structure and in the behavior of these dancers (11 p. 431), which led him to classify them in two groups.   The individuals of one group climbed readily on the vertical walls of their cages and responded vigorously to sounds; those of the other group could not climb at all and gave no evidences of hearing.   After he had completed his study of their behavior, Cyon killed the mice and sent their heads to Rawitz; but unfortunately those of the two groups became mixed, and Rawitz was unable to distinguish them.   When he examined the structure of the ears of these mice, Rawitz did find, according to his accounts, two structural types between which very marked differences existed. Were it not for the carelessness which is indicated by the confusion of the materials, and the influence of Cyon's suggestion that there should be different structures to account for the differences in behavior, Rawitz's statements might be accepted. As matters stand there can be no doubt of individual differences in behavior, external appearance, and the structure of the ear; but until these have been correlated on the

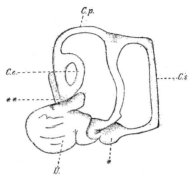

FIGURE 9. — The membranous labyrinth of the dancer's ear. Type II.

basis of thorough-going, careful observation, it is scarcely worth while to discuss their relations.

To his previous description of the conditions of the ear sacs, sense organs,

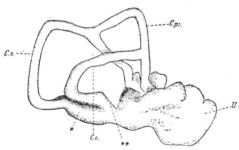

FIGURE 10. — The membranous labyrinth of the dancer's ear. Type III.

and nerve elements of the dancer's ear, Rawitz adds nothing of importance in his second paper (26 p. 171). He merely reiterates his previous statements concerning the form of the canals, on the basis of his findings in the case of six additional dancers. Figures 8, 9, and 10 are reproduced from Rawitz to show the anatomical conditions which he claims that he found. As these figures indicate, the canals were found to be extremely variable, as well as unusual in form, and the sacs distorted. In the ears of some specimens there were only two canals, and in all cases they were more or less reduced in size, distorted, or grown together.

The work of Rawitz was unfavorably criticised by Alexander and Kreidl (2), Kishi (21), and Baginsky (4), as well

FIGURE 11. — Photograph of a wax model of the membranous labyrinth of the ear of the dancer. Reproduced from Baginsky's figure in the *Centralblatt für Physiologie*, Bd. 16.

as by Panse (23 and 24). To their criticisms Rawitz replied by insisting that the other investigators could not with right attack his statements because they had not used the reconstruction method. In order to test the value of this contention, and if possible settle the question of fact, Baginsky had a model of the ear of the dancer constructed by a skilled preparator (Herr Spitz) from sections which had been prepared by the best neurological methods. This model was made eighty times the size of the ear. It was then reduced in the process of photographic reproduction to sixteen times the natural size of the ear in the mouse. Figure 11 is a photograph of Baginsky's model. It shows beyond question the presence of three canals of the same general form and relations as those of the common mouse and of other mammals. Baginsky's paper is brief and to the point. His criticisms of the work of both Cyon and Rawitz are severe, but they are justified in all probability by the carelessness of these investigators in the fixation of their materials. Of the five skilled histologists who have examined the ear of the dancer, Rawitz alone found markedly abnormal canals. It is highly probable, therefore, that the canals in his preparations in some way became distorted before the ears were sectioned. He doubtless described accurately the conditions which he found, but the chances are that those conditions never existed in the living animals.

The conflicting statements of Rawitz and Panse stimulated interest, and as a result two other investigators, without knowledge of one another's work, began careful researches on the dancer's ear. One, Alexander (2 and 3), worked in coöperation with the physiologist Kreidl; the other, Kishi (21), worked independently. The anatomical papers of Alexander and Kishi appeared at about the same time, and since neither contains a reference to the other, it is evident that the investigations were carried on almost simultaneously. Alexander's descriptions are more detailed than those of Rawitz and Panse, and in certain respects Kishi's are even more thoroughgoing. The first paper published by Alexander and Kreidl (1) contains the results of observations on the habits and behavior of the dancers. Having examined the chief facts of function, these investigators attempted to discover the structural conditions for the peculiarities of behavior which they had observed.

As material for their anatomical work they made use of four dancers, one albino mouse, and four common gray mice. The ears of these individuals were fixed, sectioned, and examined microscopically in connection with parts of the brain. In all, eight dancer ears and six common mouse ears were studied.

Very extensive descriptions of these preparations, together with measurements of many important portions of the ear, are presented in their paper, the chief conclusions of which are the following: —

1. The semicircular canals, the ampullæ, the utriculus, and the cristæ acusticæ of the canals are normal in their general form and relations to one another as well as in their histological conditions (2 p. 529). This is contradictory of the statements made by Rawitz.

2. There is destruction of the macula sacculi (2 p. 534).

3. There is destruction also of the papilla basilaris cochleæ, with encroachment of the surrounding tissues in varying degrees.

4. There is diminution in the number of fibers of the branches and roots of the ramus superior and ramus medius of the eighth nerve, and the fiber bundles are very loosely bound together.

5. Similarly the number of fibers in the inferior branch (the cochlear nerve) of the eighth nerve is very much reduced.

6. There is moderate reduction in the size of the two vestibular ganglia as a result of the unusually small number of nerve cells.

7. The ganglion spirale is extremely degenerate.

There is therefore atrophy of the branches, ganglia, and roots of the entire eighth nerve, together with atrophy and degeneration of the pars inferior labyrinthii. The nerve endings are especially degenerate (2 p. 534).

The above structural deviations of the ear of the dancer from that of the common mouse may be considered as primary or secondary according as they are inherited or acquired. Since, according to Alexander and Kreidl, the dancers' peculiarities of behavior and deafness are directly and uniformly inherited, it is obvious that certain primary structural deviations must serve as a basis for these functional facts. But it is equally clear, in the opinion of Alexander and Kreidl (2 p. 536), that other structural peculiarities of the dancer are the result of the primary changes, and in no way the conditions for either the dancing or the deafness. These authors feel confident that the facts of behavior which are to be accounted for are almost certainly due to the pathological changes which they have discovered in the nerves, ganglia, and especially in the peripheral nerve endings of the ear of the mouse (2 p. 537).

It is further claimed by Alexander and Kreidl that there are very marked individual differences among the dancers in the structure of the ear. In some cases the otoliths and the sensory hairs are lacking; in others, they are present in the state of development in which they are found in other varieties of mouse. Sometimes the cochlea is much reduced in size; at other times it is found to be of normal size (2 p. 538). These variations in structure, if they really exist, go far toward justifying the tendency of Cyon and Alexander and Kreidl, as well as many other investigators, to regard the dancer as abnormal or even pathological.

The functions of the ear as at present known to the comparative physiologist are grouped as the acoustic and the non-acoustic. The cochlea is supposed on very good grounds to have to do with the acoustic functions, and the organs of the semicircular canals on equally good evidence are thought to have to do with such of the non-acoustic functions as equilibration and orientation. Just what the functions of the organs of the ear sacs are is not certainly known. These facts are of importance when we consider the attempts made by Alexander and Kreidl to correlate the various peculiarities of behavior shown by the dancer with the structural facts which their work has revealed. This correlation is indicated schematically below. The physiological facts to be accounted for in terms of structure are presented in the first column, and the anatomical facts which are thought to be explanatory, in the second (2 p. 539).

FUNCTION	STRUCTURE
1 Lack of sensitiveness to auditory stimuli.	1 Destruction of the papilla basilaris cochleæ, etc.
	2 Diminution of the inferior branch of the eighth nerve.
	3 Marked degeneration of the ganglion spirale.
2 Defective equilibrational ability.	4 Destruction of the macula sacculi.
3 Lack of turning dizziness.	5 Diminution of the branches and roots of the superior and middle branches of the eighth nerve.
	6 Diminution of both ganglia vestibulii and of the nerve cells.

4 Normal reactions to galvanic stimulation.

Alexander and Kreidl themselves believe that the partial deafness of the dancers (for they admit that the total lack of hearing has not been satisfactorily proved) is due to the defective condition of the cochlea. They account for the imperfect equilibrational ability of the animals by pointing out the structural peculiarities of the sacculus, the vestibular ganglia, and the peripheral nerves. Similarly, the lack of dizziness they suppose to be due to the diminution of the fibers of the nerves which supply the canal organs, the atrophied condition of the vestibular ganglia, and a disturbance of the peripheral sense organs. Furthermore, there are no anatomical facts which would indicate a lack of galvanic dizziness (2 p. 552).

Despite the fact that they seem to explain all the functional peculiarities of the dancer, the statements made by Alexander and Kreidl are neither satisfying nor convincing. Their statements concerning the structure of the ear have not been verified by other investigators, and their correlation of structural with functional facts lacks an experimental basis.

In this connection it may be worth while to mention that a beautiful theory of space perception which Cyon (9) had constructed, largely on the basis of the demonstration by Rawitz that the dancers have only one normal canal, is totally destroyed by Panse, Baginsky, Alexander and Kreidl, and Kishi, for all of these observers found in the dancer three canals of normal shape. Cyon had noted that the most abnormal of the voluntary as well as of the forced movements of the dancer occur in the plane of the canal which Rawitz found to be most strikingly defective. This fact he connected with his observation that the fish Petromyzon, which possesses only two canals, moves in only two spatial dimensions. The dancer with only one functional canal in each ear moves in only one plane, and neither it nor Petromyzon is able to move far in a straight line (11 p. 444). From these and similar surmises, which his eagerness to construct an ingenious theory led him to accept as facts quite uncritically, Cyon concluded that the perception of space depends upon the number and arrangement of the semicircular canals, and that the dancer behaves as it does because it possesses canals of unusual shape and relations to one another. The absurdity of Cyon's position becomes obvious when it is shown that the structural conditions of which he was making use do not exist in the dancer.

The results obtained by Kishi in his study of the ear of the dancer differ in many important respects from those of all other investigators, but especially from those of Rawitz and Alexander and Kreidl.

Kishi's work was evidently done with admirable carefulness. His methods in the preparation of his materials, so far as can be judged from his report, were safe and satisfactory, and his descriptions of results are minute and give evidence of accuracy and conscientious thoughtfulness. The material for his histological work he obtained from three different animal dealers. It consisted of fifteen adult and nineteen young dancers, and, as material for comparison, ten common gray mice. The animals were studied first biologically, that their habits and behavior might be described accurately and so far as possible accounted for in the light of whatever histological results might be obtained subsequently; then they were studied physiologically, that the functional importance of various organs which would naturally be supposed to have to do with the peculiarities of the mouse might be understood; and, finally, they were killed and their ears and portions of their brains were studied microscopically, that structural conditions for the biological and physiological facts might be discovered.

The ear, which was studied by the use of several series of sections, as well as in gross dissections, is described by Kishi under three headings: —

(1) The sound-receiving apparatus (auditory organs).

(2) The static apparatus (equilibrational organs).

(3) The sound-transmitting apparatus (ear drum, ear bones, etc.).

The chief results of his structural investigation may be stated briefly under these three headings. In the sound-receiving or auditory apparatus, Kishi failed to find the important

deviations from the usual structure of the mammalian ear
which had been described by Rawitz. The latter distinctly
says that although the organ of Corti is present in all of the
whirls of the cochlea, the auditory cells in it are noticeably
degenerate. Kishi does not agree with Panse's statement
(21 p. 476) that the auditory organ of the dancer differs in
no important respects from that of the common mouse, for
he found that in certain regions the hair cells of the organ
of Corti were fewer and smaller in the dancer. He therefore
concludes that the auditory organ is not entirely normal,
but at the same time he emphasizes the serious discrepancy
between his results and those of Rawitz. In not one of the
ears of the twelve dancers which he studied did Kishi find
the direct communication between the utriculus and the scala
tympani which Rawitz described, and such differences as
appeared in the organ of Corti were in the nature of slight
deviations rather than marked degenerations.

In the outer wall of the ductus cochlearis of the dancer
the stria vasculosa is almost or totally lacking, while in the
gray mouse it is prominent. This condition of the stria
vasculosa Kishi was the first to notice in the dancer; Alexander and Kreidl had previously described a similar condition in an albino cat. If, as has been supposed by some
physiologists, the stria vasculosa is really the source of the
endolymph, this state of affairs must have a marked influence
on the functions of the auditory apparatus and the static apparatus, for pressure differences between the endolymph
and the perilymph spaces must be present. And, as Kishi
points out, should such pressure differences be proved to
exist, the functional disturbance in the organ of hearing
which the lack of responses to sounds seems to indicate might
better be ascribed to them than to the streaming of the endolymph from the canals into the cochlea as assumed by Rawitz

F

(21 p. 477). Kishi merely suggests that the condition of the stria may account for the deafness of the mouse; he does

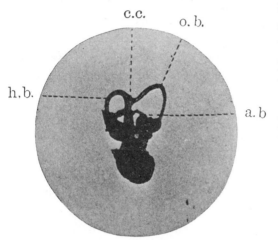

not feel at all confident of the truth of his explanation, and he therefore promises in his first paper a continuation of his work in an investigation of the functions of the stria. This, however, he seems not to have accomplished thus far.

FIGURE 12.—The inner ear of the dancer. Reproduced from Kishi's figure in the *Zeitschrift für wissenschaftliche Zoölogie*, Bd. 71. *c.c.* crus simplex; *o.b.* anterior vertical canal; *h.b.* posterior vertical canal; *a.b.* horizontal canal.

The static apparatus Kishi describes as closely similar in form to that of the gray mouse. In none of his twelve preparations of the ear of the dancer did he find such abnormalities of form and connections in the semicircular canals as Rawitz's figures and descriptions represent. Rawitz states that the anterior canal is normal except in its lack of connection with the posterior and that the posterior and horizontal are much reduced in size. Kishi, on the contrary, insists that all of the three canals are normal in shape and that the usual connection between the anterior and the posterior canals, the crus simplex, exists. He justifies these statements by presenting photographs of two dancer ears which he carefully removed from the head. Comparison of these photographs (Figures 12 and 13) with Rawitz's drawings of the conditions of the canals and sacs as he found them (Figures 8, 9, and 10), and of both with the condition in the typical mammalian ear as shown by Figure 7, will at once make clear the meaning of Kishi's statements. That Rawitz's descriptions of the canals are not correct is rendered almost certain by the fact that Panse, Baginsky, Alexander and Kreidl, and Kishi all agree in describing them as normal in form.

The only important respects in which Kishi found the membranous labyrinth, that is, the canals and the ear sacs, of the dancer to differ from that of the gray mouse are the following. In the dancer the cupola of the crista

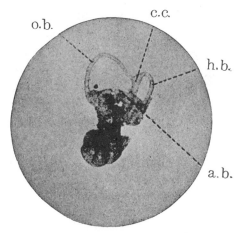

FIGURE 13.—The inner ear of the dancer, showing the spiral form of the cochlea. After Kishi.

acustica is not so plainly marked and not so highly developed, and the raphæ of the ampullæ and canals, which frequently are clearly visible in the gray mouse, are lacking (21 p. 478).

The sound-transmitting apparatus of the dancer, according to Kishi, differs only very slightly from that of the gray mouse, and there is no reason to consider the differences which appear as important (21 p. 478).

Almost as amusing as the way in which Cyon's theory of space perception disappears in the light of critical research is Panse's explanation of the deafness of the dancer. Failing to find any defects in the auditory apparatus of the inner ear which seemed adequate to account for the obvious lack of responsiveness to sounds, this investigator concluded that plugs of wax which he had noticed in the auditory meatus of the dancer excluded sounds or in some way interfered with the functioning of the tympanic membrane. Kishi reports that he found such plugs of wax in the ears of one gray mouse, but in none of the dancers which he examined did he discover them (21 p. 479). Panse's explanation of the defective hearing of the dancer neither needs nor deserves further comment.

As one result of his investigation, Kishi is convinced that the dance movements are not due to peculiarities in the semicircular canals and their sense organs, as Rawitz claimed, for the general form and finer structure of these organs in the dancer is practically the same as in the common mouse. Kishi is just as certain that the whirling is not due to defects in the canal organs, as Rawitz is that it is due to such structural conditions! It is rather surprising that any one should feel confident of the power of the microscope to reveal all those structural conditions which are important as conditions of function. Probably there are histological differences between the ear of the dancer and that of the gray mouse, which, although undetectable by scientific means at present, furnish the structural basis for the marked differences in behavior. As has been set forth already (p. 9), Kishi accounts for the dance movements by assuming the inheritance of an acquired character of behavior. This inherited tendency to dance, he thinks, has been accentuated by the confinement of the mice in narrow cages and their long-continued movement in the wheels which are placed in the cages (21 p. 481).

Rawitz, Cyon, and Alexander and Kreidl felt themselves under the necessity of finding peculiarities of behavior in the dancer which could be referred to the various abnormalities of structure which they had either seen or accepted on faith; Kishi found himself in a very different predicament, for he had on his hands the commonly accepted statement that the animals are deaf, without being able to find any structural basis for this defect. To avoid the difficulty he questions the existence of deafness! If perchance they are deaf, he thinks that it is possibly because of the defect in the stria vasculosa. This suggestion Kishi makes despite the fact that our ignorance of the function of the stria renders it impossible for us to do otherwise than guess at its relation to hearing.

We have now briefly reviewed the results of the various important investigations of the behavior and structure of the dancer.

The observations of Cyon, Zoth, and the writer establish beyond doubt the existence of important individual differences in behavior if not of distinct divisions within the species of mouse, and the general results of the several anatomical investigations make it seem highly probable that the structure of the ear, as well as the externally visible structural features of the animals, vary widely. Unfortunately, the lack of agreement in the descriptions of the ear given by the different students of the subject renders impossible any certain correlation of structural and functional facts. That the whirling and the lack of dizziness and of hearing have their structural bases no one doubts, but whether it is in the brain itself, in the sense organs, or in the labyrinth, our knowledge does not permit us to say. With this statement Rawitz, Cyon, and Alexander and Kreidl would not agree, for they believe that they have discovered structural peculiarities which fully explain the behavior of the dancer. Panse and Kishi, on the other hand, contend that the ear gives no structural signs of such peculiarities as the dancing and deafness suggest; they therefore look to the cerebellum for the seat of the disturbance. With the same possibility in mind the author of "Fancy Varieties of Mice" writes: "These quaint little creatures make amusing pets for any one who is not scientific, or very fond of knowing 'the reason why.' In their case, the reason of the peculiarity which gives them their name is rather a sad one. It is now pretty conclusively established that they are no more Japanese than they are of any other country in particular, but that the originators of the breed were common fancy mice which were suffering from a disease of the brain analogous to the 'gid' in sheep. In the latter, the complaint is caused by a parasite in the brain; in the case of the Waltzing Mouse, it is probably due to an hereditary malformation therein. Be this as it may, the breed is now a firmly established one, and the children of waltzing mice waltz like their parents" (32 p. 45). Although it is quite possible that peculiarities in the central nervous system, rather than in the peripheral nervous system, may be responsible for the forms of behavior exhibited by the dancer, it must be remembered that no such peculiarities have been revealed by the examination of the central nervous system. The old fancier has neither better nor worse grounds for his belief than have Panse and Kishi.

So far as the reliability of the anatomical work which has been discussed is in question, it would seem that Rawitz's results are rendered somewhat unsatisfactory by the carelessness of Cyon in fixing the materials; that Panse's descriptions and comparisons are neither careful nor detailed enough to be convincing; that the work of Alexander and Kreidl, as well as that of Kishi, gives evidence of accuracy and trustworthiness. The fact that the statements of Alexander and Kreidl frequently do not agree with those of Kishi proves that there are serious errors in the work of one or another of these investigators. Cyon's discussion of the anatomy of the dancer is not to be taken too seriously, for by his theory of space perception and of a sixth sense he was unduly biased in favor of the structural peculiarities described by Rawitz. Nevertheless, his discussion is not without interest, for the way in which he succeeded in making every structural fact which Rawitz suggested fit into his theories and help to account for the functional peculiarities which he had himself observed, is extremely clever and indicates a splendid scientific imagination.

To sum up: All the facts of behavior and physiology which have been established lead us to expect certain marked structural differences between the dancer and the common mouse. The bizarre movements, lack of equilibrational ability, and the nervous shaking of the head suggest the presence of peculiar conditions in the semicircular canals or their sense organs; and the lack of sensitiveness to sounds indicates defects in the cochlea. Yet, strange as it may seem to those who are not familiar with the difficulties of the study of the minute structure of these organs, no structural conditions have been discovered which account satisfactorily for the dancer's peculiarities of behavior. That the ear is unusual in form is highly probable, since three of the four investigators who have studied it carefully agree that it differs more or less markedly from that of the common mouse. But, on the other hand, the serious lack of agreement in their several descriptions of the conditions which they observed renders their results utterly inconclusive and extremely unsatisfactory. The status of our knowledge of the structure of the central nervous system is even less satisfactory, if possible, than that of our knowledge of those portions of the peripheral nervous system which would naturally be supposed to have to do with such functional peculiarities as the dancer exhibits. So far as I have been able to learn, no investigator has carefully examined the brain and spinal cord in comparison with those of the common mouse, and only those who have failed to find any structural basis for the facts of behavior in the organs of the ear have attempted to account for the dancer's whirling and deafness by assuming that the cerebellum is unusual in structure. We are, therefore, forced to conclude that our knowledge of the nervous system of the dancing mouse does not at present enable us to explain the behavior of the animal.

It seems highly probable to me, in the light of my observation of the dancer and my study of the entire literature concerning the animal, that no adequate explanation of its activities can be given in terms of the structure of the peripheral or the central nervous system, or of both, but that the structure of the entire organism will have to be taken into account. The dancer's physiological characteristics, in fact, suggest multitudinous structural peculiarities. I have confined my study to its behavior, not because the problems of structure seemed less interesting or less important, but simply because I found it necessary thus to limit the field of research in order to accomplish what I wished within a limited period.

That there are structural bases for the forms of behavior which this book describes is as certain as it could be were they definitely known; that they, or at least some of them, are discoverable by means of our present-day histological methods is almost as certain. It is, therefore, obvious that this is an excellent field for further research. It is not an agreeable task to report inconclusive and contradictory results, and I have devoted this chapter to a brief account of the work that has been done by others on the structure of the ear of the dancer rather for the sake of presenting a complete account of the animal as it is known to-day than because of the value of the facts which could be stated.

CHAPTER VI

The Sense of Hearing

REPEATEDLY in the foregoing chapters mention has been made of the dancer's irresponsiveness to sounds, but it has not been definitely stated whether this peculiarity of behavior is due to deafness or to the inhibition of reaction. This chapter is concerned with the evidence which bears upon the problem of the existence of a sense of hearing. Again I may be permitted to call attention to the observations of other investigators before presenting the results of my own experiments and stating the conclusions which I have reached through the consideration of all available facts.

By the results of various simple tests which he made, Rawitz (25 p. 238) was convinced that the adult dancer is totally deaf. He did not experiment with the young, but he says he thinks they may be able to hear, since the necessary structural conditions are present. This guess which Rawitz made on the basis of very indefinite and uncertain knowledge of the histology of the ear of the young dancer is of special interest in the light of facts revealed by my own experiments. Unfortunately the study of hearing made by Rawitz is casual rather than thorough, and although it may turn out that all of his statements are justified by his observations, the reader is not likely to get much satisfaction from his discussion of the subject.

Inasmuch as he could discover no structural basis for deafness, Panse (23 p. 140) expressed himself as unwilling to believe that the mice are deaf, and this despite the fact that he observed no responses to the sounds made by a series of tuning forks ranging from C_5 to C_8. He believes rather that they are strangely irresponsive to sounds and that their sensitiveness is dulled, possibly, by the presence of plugs of wax in the ears. Since another investigator, Kishi, has observed the presence of similar plugs of wax in the ears of common mice which could hear, there is but slight probability that Panse is right in considering the plugs of wax as the cause of the dancer's irresponsiveness to sounds.

Far more thoroughgoing tests than those of Rawitz or Panse were made by Cyon (9 p. 218), who holds the unique position of being the only person on record who has observed the adult dancer give definite reactions to sounds. To a König Galton whistle so adjusted that it gave a tone of about 7000 complete vibrations per second, which is said to be about the pitch of the voice of the dancer, some of the animals tested by Cyon responded unmistakably, others not at all. In one group of four mice, two not only reacted markedly to the sound of the whistle but apparently listened intently, for as soon as the whistle was blown they ran to the side of the cage and pressed their noses against the walls as if attempting to approach the source of the stimulus. The remaining two mice gave not the slightest indication that the sound acted as a stimulus. By the repetition of this sound from eight to twelve times Cyon states that he was able to arouse the mice from sleep. When thus disturbed, the female came out of the nest box before the male. Similarly when the mice were disturbed by the whistle in the midst of their dancing, the female was first to retreat into the nest box. There is thus, according to Cyon, some indication of sex, as well as individual, differences in sensitiveness to the sound of the whistle. Cyon's statement that in order to evoke a response the whistle must be held above the head of the dancer suggests at once the possibility that currents of air or odors instead of sounds may have been responsible for the reactions which he observed. The work of this investigator justifies caution in the acceptance of his statements. Neither the conditions under which the auditory tests were made nor the condition of the animals is described with sufficient accuracy to make possible the comparison of Cyon's work with that of other investigators. As will appear later, it is of the utmost importance that the influence of other stimuli than sound be avoided during the tests and that the age of the mouse be known. The conclusion reached by Cyon is that some dancers are able to hear sounds of about the pitch of their own cries.

The fact, emphasized by Cyon, that the mice respond to tones of about the pitch of their own voice is of peculiar interest in its relation to the additional statements made by the same author to the effect that the female dancer is more sensitive to sounds than the male, and that the males either do not possess a voice or are much less sensitive to disagreeable stimuli than the females. In the case of the dancers which he first studied (9 p. 218), Cyon observed that certain strong stimuli evoked pain cries; but later in his investigation he noticed that four individuals, all of which were males, never responded thus to disagreeable stimulation (11 p. 431). He asks, therefore, does this mean that the males lack a voice or that they are less sensitive than the females? The fact that he did not succeed in getting a definite answer to this simple question is indicative of the character of Cyon's work. My dancers have provided me with ample evidence concerning the matter. Both the males and the females, among the dancers which I have studied, possess a voice.

The females, especially during periods of sexual excitement, are much more likely to squeak than the males. At such times they give their shrill cry whenever they are touched by another mouse or by the human hand. A slight pinching of the tail will frequently cause the female to squeak, but the male seldom responds to the same stimulus by crying out. The most satisfactory way to demonstrate the existence of a voice in the male is to subject him to the stimulating effect of an induced current, so weak that it is barely appreciable to the human hand. To this unexpected stimulus even the male usually responds by a sudden squeak. There can be no doubt, then, of the possession of a voice by both males and females. The males may be either less sensitive or less given to vocal expression, but they are quite able to squeak when favorable conditions are presented. The possession of a voice by an animal is presumptive evidence in favor of a sense of hearing, but it would scarcely be safe to say that the mice must be able to hear their own voices. Cyon, however, thinks that some dancers can. What further evidence is to be had?

Although they obtained no visible motor reactions to such noises as the clapping of the hands, the snapping of the fingers, or to the tones of tuning forks of different pitches and the shrill tones of the Galton whistle, Alexander and Kreidl (1 p. 547) are not convinced of the total deafness of the dancer, for, as they remark, common mice which undoubtedly hear do not invariably respond visibly to sounds. Furthermore, the anatomical conditions revealed by their investigation of the ear of the dancer are not such as to render sensitiveness to sounds impossible. They recognize also that the existence of the ability to produce sounds is an indication of hearing. They have no confidence in the results reported by Cyon, for they feel that he did not take adequate precautions to guard against the action of other than auditory stimuli.

Zoth (31 p. 170) has pointed out with reason and force that testing the sensitiveness of the mice is especially difficult because of their restlessness. They are almost constantly executing quick, jerky movements, starting, stopping, or changing the direction of movement, and it is therefore extremely difficult to tell with even a fair degree of certainty whether a given movement which occurs simultaneously with a sound is a response to the sound or merely coincident with it. With great care in the exclusion of the influence of extraneous stimuli, Zoth tried a large number of experiments to test the hearing of both young and adult dancers. Not once did he observe an indubitable auditory reaction. As he says, "I have performed numerous experiments with the Galton whistle, with a squeaking glass stopper, with caps and cartridges, without being able to come to any certain conclusion. With reference to the Galton whistle and particularly to the tone which was said to have been heard extremely well by Cyon's mice, I believe I am rather safe in asserting that my mice, young (12-13 days) as well as old, do not react to the König Galton whistle (7210 Vs.). They could not be awakened out of sleep by repetitions of the sound, nor enticed out of their nests, and their dancing could not be interrupted" (31 p. 170). Zoth's experiments appear to be the most careful and critical of those thus far considered.

Last to be mentioned, but in many respects of greatest interest and value, is the work of Kishi (21 p. 482) on the problem of hearing. To this acute observer belongs the credit of calling attention emphatically to the ear movements which are exhibited by the dancer. Frequently, as he remarks, the ears move as if the animal were listening or trying to determine the direction whence comes a sound, yet usually the mouse gives no other sign of hearing. That the absence of ordinary reactions to sounds is due to deafness, Kishi, like Panse, is led to doubt because his anatomical studies have not revealed any defects in the organs of hearing which would seem to indicate the lack of this sense.

This historical survey of the problem of hearing has brought out a few important facts. No one of the several investigators of the subject, with the exception of Cyon, is certain that the dancer can hear, and no one of them, with the exception of Rawitz, is certain that it cannot hear! Cyon almost certainly observed two kinds of dancing mice. Those of his dancers which exhibited exceptional ability to climb in the vertical direction and which also gave good evidence of hearing certain sounds may have been hybrids resulting from the crossing of the dancer with a common mouse, or they may have been exceptional specimens of the true dancer variety. A third possibility is suggested by Rawitz's belief in the ability of the young dancer to hear. Cyon's positive results may have been obtained with immature individuals. I am strongly inclined to believe that Cyon did observe two types of dancer, and to accept his statement that some of the mice could hear, whereas others could not. It is evident, in the light of our examination of the experimental results thus far obtained by other investigators, that neither the total lack of sensitiveness to sounds in the adult nor the presence of such sensitiveness in the young dancer has been satisfactorily proved.

I shall now report in detail the results of my own study of the sense of hearing in the dancer   As the behavior of the young differs greatly from that of the adult, by which is meant the sexually mature animal, I shall present first the results of my experiments with adults and later, in contrast, the results obtained with mice from one to twenty-eight days old.

My preliminary tests were made with noises. While carefully guarding against the interference of visual, tactual, temperature, and olfactory stimuli, I produced noises of varying degrees of loudness by clapping the hands together suddenly, by shouting, whistling, exploding pistol caps, striking steel bars, ringing an electric bell, and causing another mouse to squeak. To these sounds a common mouse usually responds either by starting violently, or by trembling and remaining perfectly quiet for a few seconds, as if frightened. The adult dancers which I have tested, and I have repeated the experiment scores of times during the last three years with more than a hundred different individuals, have never given unmistakable evidence of hearing. Either they are totally deaf or there is a most surprising lack of motor reactions.

Precisely the same results were obtained in tests made with the Galton whistle throughout its range of pitches, and with Appuun whistles which, according to their markings, ranged from 2000 Vs. (C_4) to 48,000 (G_9), but which undoubtedly did not correspond at all exactly to this range, and with a series of König tuning forks which gave tones varying in pitch from 1024 to 16,382 complete vibrations.

I am willing to trust these experimental results the more fully because during all the time I have had adult dancers under observation I have never once seen a reaction which could with any fair degree of certainty be referred to an auditory stimulus. Never once, although I have tried repeatedly, have I succeeded in arousing a dancer from sleep by producing noises or tones, nor have I ever been able to observe any influence of sounds on the dance movements. All of Cyon's signs have failed with my mice. Occasionally what looked like a response to some sound appeared, but critical observation invariably. proved it to be due to some other cause than the auditory stimulus.   A sound produced above the animal is very likely to bring about a motor reaction, as Cyon claims; but I have always found it to be the result of the currents of air or odors, which usually influence the animal when the experimenter is holding any object above it.   I do not wish to maintain that Cyon's conclusions are false; I .merely emphasize the necessity for care in the exclusion of other stimuli.   The mice are extremely sensitive to changes in temperature, such, for example, as are produced by the breath of the experimenter, and one must constantly guard against the misinterpretation of behavior.

In a single experiment with mice over a month old, I observed what might possibly indicate sensitiveness to sound. While holding a mouse, thirty-five days old, in my hand I pursed my lips and made a very shrill sound by drawing in air; the mouse seemed to start perceptibly according to the indications given by my sense of touch.   I repeated the stimulus several times and each time I could see and feel the animal start slightly.   With two other individuals which I tested the reaction was less certain, and with several others I failed to get any indication of response.   This would seem to prove that the three individuals which responded happened to be sensitive to that particular tone at the age of five weeks. The test is unsatisfactory because the vibrations from my own body may have brought about the reaction instead of the air vibrations produced by my lips, and I therefore merely mention it in the enumeration of the various experimental tests which I have made.

If we should conclude from all the negative evidence that is available, or that could be obtained, that the dancer is totally deaf, it might fairly be objected that the conclusion is unsafe, since an animal does not necessarily respond to stimuli by a visible change in the position or relations of its body. Death feigning may fairly be considered a response to a stimulus or stimulus complex, yet there may be no sign of movement. The green frog when observed in the laboratory usually gives no indication whatever, by movements that are readily observable, that it hears sounds which occur about it, but I have been able to show by means of indirect methods of study that it is stimulated by these same sounds.[1] Its rate of respiration is changed by the sounds, and although a sound does not bring about a bodily movement, it does very noticeably influence movements in response to other stimuli which occur simultaneously with the sound. I discovered that under certain rather simple experimental conditions the green frog would regularly respond to a touch on the back by drawing its hind leg up toward the body. Under the same conditions the sound of an electric bell caused no visible movement of the leg, but if at the instant the back was touched the bell was rung, the leg movement was much greater than that brought about by the touch alone. This suggests at once the desirability of studying the sense of hearing in the dancer by some indirect method. The animal may be stimulated, and yet it may not give any visible sign of the influence of the auditory stimulus.

Were not the dancing so extremely variable in rapidity and duration, it might be used as an index of the influence of auditory stimuli. Cyon's statements would indicate that sounds interfere with the dancing, but as I obtained no evidence of this, I worked instead with the following indirect method, which may be called the method of auditory choice. The apparatus which was used is described in detail in

[1] "The Sense of Hearing in Frogs." *Journal of Comparative Neurology and Psychology*, Vol. XV, p. 288, 1905.

Chapter VII, p. 92. Figures 14 and 15 will greatly aid the reader in understanding its essential features. Two small wooden boxes, identical in form and as closely similar as possible in general appearance, were placed in a larger box in such positions that a mouse was forced to enter and pass through one of them in order to get to the nest-box. On the bottom of each of these small boxes was a series of wires through which an electric current could be made to pass at the will of the experimenter. The boxes could readily be interchanged in position. At one side of the large wooden box and beyond the range of vision of the mouse was an electric bell which could be caused to ring whenever the mouse approached the entrance to one of the small boxes. The point of the experiment was to determine whether the dancer could learn to avoid the box-which-rang when it was approached. The method of conducting the tests was as follows. Each day at a certain hour the mouse was placed in that part of the large box whence it could escape to the nest-box only by passing through one of the small boxes. If it approached the wrong box (whether it happened to be the one on the right or the one on the left depended upon the experimenter's decision), the bell began to ring as a warning against entering; if it approached the other box, all was silent. As motives for the choice of the box-which-did-not-ring both reward and punishment were employed. The reward consisted of freedom to return to the nest-box *via* the passage which led from the box-which-did-not-ring; the punishment, which consisted of a disagreeable electric shock, was given whenever the mouse entered the wrong box, that is, the one which had the sound as a warning. Entering the wrong box resulted in a disagreeable stimulus and in the necessity of returning to the large box, for the exit to the nest-box by way of the passage from this box was closed.

My assumption, on the basis of extended study of the ability of the dancer to profit by experience, was that if.it could hear the sound of the bell it would soon learn to avoid the box-that-rang and enter instead the one which had no sound associated with it.

Systematic tests were made with No. 4 from the 3d to the 12th of February, inclusive, 1906. Each day the mouse was permitted to find his way to the nest-box through one of the small boxes ten times in succession. Usually the experimenter rang the bell alternately for the box on the left and the box on the right. The time required for such a series of experiments varied, according to the rapidity with which the mouse made his choice, from ten to thirty minutes. If in these experiments the animal approached and entered the right, or soundless box, directly, the choice indicated nothing so far as ability to hear is concerned; if it entered the wrong, or sounding box, despite the ringing of the bell, it indicated either the lack of the influence of experience or inability to hear the sound; but if it regularly avoided the box-which-sounded it thus gave evidence of ability to hear the sound of the bell. The purpose of the test was to determine, not whether the mouse could learn, but whether it could hear.

For ten successive days this experiment was carried on with No. 4 without the least indication of increasing ability to avoid the wrong box by the association of the sound of the bell with the disagreeable electric shock and failure to escape to the nest-box. In fact, the experiment was discontinued because it became evident that an impossible task had been set for the mouse. Day by day as the tests were in progress I noticed that the animal became increasingly afraid of the entrances to the small boxes; it seemed absolutely helpless in the face of the situation. Partly because of the definiteness of the negative results obtained with No. 4 and partly because of the cruelty of subjecting an animal to disagreeable conditions which it is unable to avoid, the experiment was not repeated with other individuals.   I have never conducted an experiment which gave me as much discomfort as this; it was like being set to whip a deaf child because it did not learn to respond to stimuli which it could not feel.

By a very similar method No. 18 was tested for his sensitiveness to the noise and jar from the induction apparatus which was used in connection with many of my experiments on vision and the modifiability of behavior.   In this experiment the wrong box was indicated by the buzzing sound of the apparatus and the slight vibrations which resulted from it.   Although No. 18 was tested, as was No. 4, for ten successive days, ten trials each day, it gave no evidence of ability to avoid the box-which-buzzed.

Since both direct and indirect methods of testing the hearing of the dancer have uniformly given negative results, in the case of mice more than five weeks old, I feel justified in concluding that they are totally deaf and not merely irresponsive to sounds.

Rawitz's statements, and the fact that what may have been auditory reactions were obtained with a few individuals of five weeks of age, suggest that the mice may be able to hear at certain periods of life.   To discover whether this is true I have tested the young of twenty different litters from the first day to the twenty-eighth, either daily or at intervals of two or three days.   In these tests König forks, steel bars, and a Galton whistle were used.   The results obtained are curiously interesting.

During the first two weeks of life none of the mice which I tested gave any visible motor response to the various sounds used.   During the third week certain of the individuals responded vigorously to sudden high tones and loud noises. After the third week I have seen only doubtful signs of hearing. I shall now describe in detail the method of experimentation, the condition of the animals, and the nature of the auditory reactions.

Between the twelfth and the eighteenth day the auditory canal becomes open to the exterior. The time is very variable in different litters, for their rate of growth depends upon the amount of nourishment which the mother is able to supply. Without exception, in my experience, the opening to the ear appears before the eyes are open. Consequently visual stimuli usually are not disturbing factors in the auditory tests with mice less than sixteen days old. There is also a sudden and marked change in the behavior of the mice during the third week. Whereas, for the first fourteen or eighteen days they are rather quiet and deliberate in their movements when removed from the nest, some time in the third week their behavior suddenly changes and they act as if frightened when taken up by the experimenter. They jump out of his hand, squeak, and sometimes show fight. This is so pronounced that it has attracted my attention many times and I have studied it carefully to determine, if possible, whether it is due to some profound change in the nervous system which thus suddenly increases the sensitiveness of the animal or to the development of the sexual organs. I am inclined to think that it is a nervous phenomenon which is intimately connected with the sexual condition. Within a day or two after it appears the mice usually begin to show auditory reactions and continue to do so for three to five days.

I shall now describe the results obtained with a few typical litters. A litter born of Nos. 151 and 152 gave uniformly negative results in all auditory tests up to the fourteenth day. On that day the ears were open, and the following observations were recorded. The five individuals of the litter, four females and one male, were taken from the nest one at a time at 7 A.M. and placed on a piece of paper in the bright 'sunlight. The warmth of the sun soon quieted them so that auditory tests could be made to advantage. As soon as an individual had become perfectly still, the Galton whistle was held at a distance of about four inches from its head in such a position that it could not be seen nor the currents of air caused by it felt, and suddenly blown. Each of the five mice responded to the first few repetitions of this stimulus by movements of the ears, twitchings of the body, and jerky movements of the legs. The most violent reactions resulted when the individual was lying on its back with its legs extended free in the air. Under such circumstances the four legs were often drawn together suddenly when the whistle was sounded. Similar responses were obtained with the lip sound already mentioned. Two other observers saw these experiments, and they agreed that there can be no doubt that the mice responded to the sound. The sounds which were effective lay between 5000 and 10,000 complete vibrations.

On the fifteenth day the eyes were just beginning to open. Three of the mice responded definitely to the sounds, but the other two slightly, if at all. On the sixteenth day they were all too persistently active for satisfactory auditory tests, and on the seventeenth, although they were tested repeatedly under what appeared to be favorable conditions, no signs of sensitiveness were noted. Although I continued to test this litter, at intervals of three or four days, for two weeks longer, I did not once observe a response to sound.

This was the first litter with which I obtained perfectly definite, clear-cut responses to sounds. That the reactive ability had not been present earlier than the fourteenth day I am confident, for I had conducted the tests in precisely the same manner daily up to the time of the appearance of the reactions. To argue that the mice heard before the fourteenth day, but were unable to react because the proper motor mechanism had not developed sufficiently would be short-sighted, for if the response depended upon the development of such a mechanism, it is not likely that it would disappear so quickly. I am therefore satisfied that these reactions indicate hearing.

With another litter the following results were obtained. On the thirteenth day each of the eight members of the litter responded definitely and uniformly to the Galton whistle, set at 5 (probably about 8000 complete vibrations), and to a König steel bar of a vibration rate of 4096 Vs. The largest individuals, for almost always there are noticeable differences in size among the members of a litter, appeared to be most sensitive to sounds.

On the fifteenth day and again on the seventeenth unmistakable responses to sound were observed; on the eighteenth the responses were indefinite, and on the nineteenth none were obtained. I continued the tests up to the twenty-eighth day without further indications of hearing.

Certain individuals in this litter reacted so vigorously to the loud sound produced by striking the steel bar a sharp blow and also to the Galton whistle, during a period of five days, that I have no hesitation in saying that they evidently heard during that period of their lives. Other members of the litter seemed to be less sensitive; their reactions were sometimes so indefinite as to leave the experimenter in doubt about the presence of hearing.

A third litter, which developed very slowly because of lack of sufficient food, first showed unmistakable reactions to sound on the twenty-first day. On this day only two of the five individuals reacted. The reactions were much more obvious on the twenty-second day, but thereafter they became indefinite.

Still another litter, which consisted of one female and four males, began to exhibit the quick, jerky movements, already mentioned, on the fourteenth day. On the morning of the fifteenth day three members of the litter definitely reacted to the tone of the steel bar, and also to the hammer blow when the bar was held tightly in the hand of the experimenter. My observations were verified by another experimenter. Two individuals which appeared to be very sensitive were selected for special tests. Their reactions were obvious on the sixteenth, seventeenth, and eighteenth days; on the nineteenth day they were indefinite, and on the twentieth none could be detected. Some individuals of this litter certainly had the ability to hear for at least five days.

A sixth litter of four females and two males first gave indications of the change in behavior which by this time I had come to interpret as a sign of the approach of the period of auditory sensitiveness, on the seventeenth day. I had tested them almost every day previous to this time without obtaining evidence of hearing. The tests with the steel bar and the Galton whistle were continued each day until the end of the fourth week without positive results. To all appearances the individuals of this litter were unable to hear at any time during the first month of life.

Practically the same results were obtained with another litter of four females. The change in their behavior was obvious on the eighteenth day, but at no time during the first month did they give any satisfactory indications of hearing.

In the accompanying table, I have presented in condensed form the results of my auditory tests in the case of twelve litters of young dancers.

TABLE 5

Period of Auditory Reaction in Young Dancers

Parents	No. in Litter	Change in Behavior	Ears Open	Auditory Reactions	
				Appear	Disappear
152 + 151	5	13th day	14th day	14th day	16th day
152 + 151	8	(?)	13th day	13th day	17th day
152 + 151	5	13th day	13th day	13th day	17th day
152 + 151	4	10th day	12th day	13th day	15th day
410 + 415	5	14th day	15th day	15th day	19th day
410 + 415	6	13th day	14th day	14th day	18th day
420 + 425	2	12th day	14th day	14th day	17th day
210 + 215	5	17th day	13th day	17th day	19th day
210 + 215	6	11th day	14th day	No reactions	
220 + 225	6	16th day	14th day	No reactions	
220 + 225	6	17th day	13th day	No reactions	
212 + 211	4	15th day	14th day	No reactions	

Certain of the litters tested responded definitely to sounds, others gave no sign of hearing at any time during the first four weeks of life. Of the twelve litters for which the results of auditory tests are presented in Table 5, eight evidently passed through an auditory period. It is important to note that all except one of these were the offspring of Nos. 151 and 152, or of their descendants Nos. 410 and 415 and Nos. 420 and 425. In fact every one of the litters in this line of descent which I have tested, and they now number fifteen, has given indications of auditory sensitiveness. And, on the other hand, only in a single instance have the litters born of Nos. 210 and 215, or of their descendants, given evidence of ability to hear.

These two distinct lines of descent may be referred to hereafter as the 400 and the 200 lines. I have observed several important differences between the individuals of these groups in addition to the one already mentioned. The 200 mice were sometimes gray and white instead of black and white; they climbed much more readily and danced less vigorously than those of the 400 group. These facts are particularly interesting in connection with Cyon's descriptions of the two types of dancer which he observed.

In criticism of my conclusion that the young dancers are able to hear certain sounds for a few days early in life, and then become deaf, it has been suggested that they cease to react because they rapidly become accustomed to the sounds. That this is not the case, is evident from the fact that the reactions often increase in definiteness during the first two or three days and then suddenly disappear entirely. But even if this were not true, it would seem extremely improbable that the mouse should become accustomed to a sudden and startlingly loud sound with so few repetitions as occurred in these tests. On any one day the sounds were not made more than five to ten times. Moreover, under the same external condition, the common mouse reacts unmistakably to these sounds day after day when they are first produced, although with repetition of the stimulus at short intervals, the reactions soon become indefinite or disappear.

The chief results of my study of hearing in the dancer may be summed up in a very few words. The young dancer, in some instances, hears sounds for a few days during the third week of life. The adult is totally deaf. Shortly before the period of auditory sensitiveness, the young dancer becomes extremely excitable and pugnacious.

CHAPTER VII

THE SENSE OF SIGHT: BRIGHTNESS VISION

THE sense of sight in the dancer has received little attention hitherto. In the literature there are a few casual statements to the effect that it is of importance. Zoth, for example (31 p. 149), remarks that it seems to be keenly developed; and other writers, on the basis of their observation of the animal's behavior, hazard similar statements. The descriptions of the behavior of blinded mice, as given by Cyon, Alexander and Kreidl, and Kishi (p. 47), apparently indicate that the sense is of some value; they do not, however, furnish definite information concerning its nature and its role in the daily life of the animal.

The experimental study of this subject which is now to be described was undertaken, after careful and long-continued observation of the general behavior of the dancer, in order that our knowledge of the nature and value of the sense of sight in this representative of the Mammalia might be increased in scope and definiteness. The results of this study naturally fall into three groups: (1) those which concern brightness vision, (2) those which concern color vision, and (3) those which indicate the role of sight in the life of the dancer.

Too frequently investigators, in their work on vision in animals, have assumed that brightness vision and color vision are inseparable; or, if not making this assumption, they have failed to realize that the same wave-length probably has markedly different effects upon the retinal elements of the eyes of unlike organisms. In a study of the sense of sight it is extremely important to discover whether difference in the quality, as well as in the intensity, of a visual stimulus influences the organism; in other words, whether color sensitiveness, as well as brightness sensitiveness, is present. If the dancer perceives only brightness or luminosity, and not color, it is evident that its visual world is strikingly different from that of the normal human being.

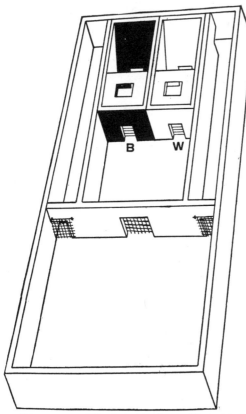

FIGURE 14. — Discrimination box. *W*, electric-box with white cardboards; *B*, electric-box with black cardboards. Drawn by Mr. C. H. Toll.

The experiments now to be described were planned to show what the facts really are.

As a means of testing the ability of the dancer to distinguish differences in brightness, the experiment box represented by Figures 14 and 15 was devised. Figure 14 is the box as seen from the position of the experimenter during the tests. Figure 15 is its ground plan. This box, which was made of wood, was 98 cm. long, 38 cm. wide, and 17 cm. deep, as measured on the outside. The plan of construction and its significance in connection with these experiments on vision will be clear from the following account of the experimental procedure. A mouse whose brightness vision was to be tested was placed in the nest-box, *A* (Figure 15). Thence by pushing open the swinging door at *I*, it could pass into the entrance chamber, *B*. Having entered *B* it could return to *A* only by passing through one of the electric-boxes, marked *W*, and following the alley to *O*, where by pushing open the swing door it could enter the nest-box. The door at *I* swung inward, toward *B*, only; those at *O*, right and left, swung

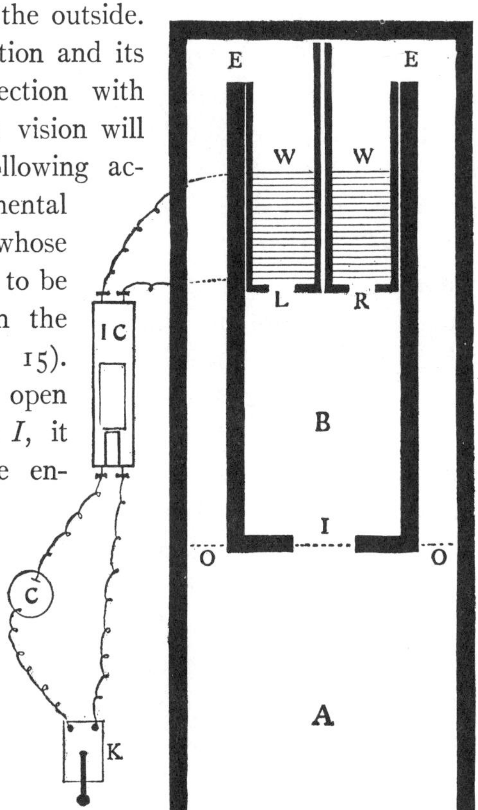

FIGURE 15.—Ground plan of discrimination box. *A*, nest-box; *B*, entrance chamber; *W*, *W*, electric-boxes; *L*, doorway of left electric-box; *R*, doorway of right electric-box; *E*, exit from electric-box to alley; *I*, swinging door between *A* and *B*; *O*, swinging door between alley and *A*; *IC*, induction apparatus; *C*, electric cell; *K*, key in circuit.

outward, toward *A*, only. It was therefore impossible for the mouse to follow any other course than *A-I-B-L-W-E-O* or *A-I-B-R-W-E-O*. The doors at *I* and *O* were pieces of wire netting of $\frac{1}{2}$ cm. mesh, hinged at the top so that a mouse could readily open them, in one direction, by pushing with its nose at any point along the bottom. On the floor of each of the electric-boxes, *W*, was an oak board 1 cm. in thickness, which carried electric wires by means of which the mouse could be shocked in *W* when the tests demanded it. The interrupted circuit constituted by the wires in the two electric-boxes, in connection with the induction apparatus, *IC*, the dry battery, *C*, and the hand key, *K*, was made by taking two pieces of No. 20 American standard gauge copper wire and winding them around the oak board which was to be placed on the floor of each electric-box. The wires, which ran parallel with one another, $\frac{1}{2}$ cm. apart, fitted into shallow grooves in the edges of the board, and thus, as well as by being drawn taut, they were held firmly in position. The coils of the two pieces of wire alternated, forming an interrupted circuit which, when the key *K* was closed, was completed if the feet of a mouse rested on points of both pieces of wire. Since copper wire stretches easily and becomes loose on the wooden base, it is better to use phosphor bronze wire of about the same size, if the surface covered by the interrupted circuit is more than three or four inches in width. The phosphor bronze wire is more difficult to wind satisfactorily, for it is harder to bend than the copper wire, and it has the further disadvantage of being more brittle. But when once placed properly, it forms a far more lasting and satisfactory interrupted circuit for such experiments as those to be described than does copper wire. In the case of the electric-boxes under consideration, the oak boards which carried the interrupted circuits were separate, and the two circuits were joined by the union of the wires between the boxes. The free ends of the two pieces of wire which constituted the interrupted circuit were connected with the secondary coil of a Porter inductorium whose primary coil was in circuit with a No. 6 Columbia dry battery. In the light of preliminary experiments, made in preparation for the tests of vision, the strength of the induced current received by the mouse was so regulated, by changing the position of the secondary coil with reference to the primary, that it was disagreeable but not injurious to the animal. What part the disagreeable shock played in the test of brightness vision will now be explained.

An opportunity for visual discrimination by brightness difference was provided by placing dead black cardboard at the entrance and on the inside of one of the electric-boxes, as shown in Figure 14, *B*, and white cardboard similarly in the other box. These cardboards were movable and could be changed from one box to the other at the will of the experimenter. The test consisted in requiring the mouse to choose a certain brightness, for example, the white cardboard side, in order to return to the nest-box without receiving an electric shock. The question which the experimenter asked in connection with this test really is, Can a dancer learn to go to the white box and thus avoid discomfort? If we assume its ability to profit by experience within the limits of the number of experiences which it was given, such a modification of behavior would indicate discrimination of brightness. Can the dancer distinguish white from black; light gray from dark gray; two grays which are almost of the same brightness? The results which make up the remainder of this and the following chapter furnish a definite answer to these questions.

To return to the experimental procedure, the mouse which is being tested is placed by the experimenter in the nest-box, where frequently in the early tests food and a comfortable nest were attractions. If it does not of its own accord, as a result of its abundant random activity, pass through *I* into *B* within a few seconds, it is directed to the doorway and urged through. A choice is now demanded of the animal; to return to the nest-box it must enter either the white electric-box or the black one. Should it choose the white box, it is permitted to return directly to *A* by way of the doorway *E*, the alley, and the swinging door at *O*, and it thus gets the satisfaction of unobstructed activity, freedom to whirl, to feed, and to retreat for a time to the nest. Should it choose to attempt to enter the black box, as it touches the wires of the interrupted circuit it receives a shock as a result of the closing of the key in the circuit by the experimenter, and further, if it continues its forward course instead of retreating from the "stinging" black box, its passage through *E* is blocked by a barrier of glass temporarily placed there by the experimenter, and the only way of escape to the nest-box is an indirect route by way of *B* and the white box. Ordinarily the shock was given only when the mouse entered the wrong box, not when it retreated from it; it was never given when the right box was chosen. The box to be chosen, whether it was white, gray, or black, will be called the right box. The electric shock served as a means of forcing the animal to use its discriminating ability. But the question of motives in the tests is not so simple as might appear from this statement.

The reader will wonder why the mouse should have any tendency to enter *B*, and why after so doing, it should trouble to go further, knowing, as it does from previous experiences, that entering one of the electric-boxes may result in discomfort. The fact is, a dancer has no very constant tendency to go from *A* to *B* at the beginning of the tests, but after it has become accustomed to the box and has learned what the situation demands, it shows eagerness to make the trip from *A* to *B*, and thence by way of either the right or the left route to *A*. That the mouse should be willing to enter either of the electric-boxes, after it has experienced the shock, is even more surprising than its eagerness to run from *A* to *B*. When first tested for brightness discrimination in this apparatus, a dancer usually hesitated at the entrance to the electric-boxes, and this hesitation increased rapidly unless it were able to discriminate the boxes by their difference in brightness and thus to choose the right one. During the period of increasing hesitancy in making the choice, the experimenter, by carefully moving from *I* toward the entrances to the electric-boxes a piece of cardboard which extended all the way across *B*, greatly increased the mouse's desire to enter one of the boxes by depriving it of dancing space in *B*. If an individual which did not know which entrance to choose were permitted to run about in *B*, it would often do so for minutes at a time without approaching the entrance to the boxes; but the same individual, when confined to a dancing space 4 or 5 cm. wide in front of the entrances, would enter one of the electric-boxes almost immediately. This facilitation of choice by decrease in the amount of space for whirling was not to any considerable extent the result of fear, for all the dancers experimented with were tame, and instead of forcing them to rush into one of the boxes blindly and without attempt at discrimination, the narrowing of the space simply increased their efforts to discriminate. The common mouse when subjected to similar experimental conditions is likely to be frightened by being forced to approach the entrances to the boxes, and fails to choose; it rushes into one box directly, and in consequence it is as often wrong as right. The dancer always chooses, but its eagerness to choose is markedly increased by the restriction of its movements to a narrow space in front of

H

the entrances between which it is required to discriminate. It is evident that the animal is uncomfortable in a space which is too narrow for it to whirl in freely. It must have room to dance. This furnished a sufficiently strong motive for the entering of the electric-boxes. It must avoid disagreeable and unfavorable stimuli. This is a basis for attempts to choose, by visual discrimination, the electric-box in which the shock is not given. It may safely be said that the success of the majority of the experiments of this book depended upon three facts: (1) the dancer's tendency to avoid disagreeable external conditions, (2) its escape-from-confinement-impelling need of space in which to dance freely, and (3) its abundant and incessant activity.

Of these three conditions of success in the experiments, the second and third made possible the advantageous use of the first. For the avoidance of a disagreeable stimulus could be made use of effectively in the tests just because the mice are so restless and so active. In fact their eagerness to do things is so great that the experimenter, instead of having to wait for them to perform the desired act, often is forced to make them wait while he completes his observation and record. In this respect they are unlike most other animals.

My experiments with the dancer differ from those which have been made by most students of mammalian behavior in one important respect. I have used punishment instead of reward as the chief motive for the proper performance of the required act. Usually in experiments with mammals hunger has been the motive depended upon. The animals have been required to follow a certain devious path, to escape from a box by working a button, a bolt, a lever, or to gain entrance to a box by the use of teeth, claws, hands, or body weight and thus obtain food as a reward. There are two very serious objections to the use of the desire for food as a motive in animal behavior experiments — objections which in my opinion render it almost worthless in the case of many mammals. These are the discomfort of the animal and the impossibility of keeping the motive even fairly constant. However prevalent the experience of starvation may be in the life of an animal, it is not pleasant to think of subjecting it to extreme hunger in the laboratory for the sake of finding out what it can do to obtain food. Satisfactory results can be obtained in an experiment whose success depends chiefly upon hunger only when the animal is so hungry that it constantly does its best to obtain food, and when the desire for food is equally strong and equally effective as a spur to action in the repetitions of the experiment day after day. It is easy enough to get almost any mammal into a condition of utter hunger, but it is practically impossible to have the desire for food of the same strength day after day. In short, the desire for food is unsatisfactory as a motive in animal behavior work, first, because a condition of utter hunger, as has been demonstrated with certain mammals, is unfavorable for the performance of complex acts, second, because it is impossible to control the strength of the motive, and finally, because it is an inhumane method of experimentation.

In general, the method of punishment is more satisfactory than the method of reward, because it can be controlled to a greater extent. The experimenter cannot force his subject to desire food; he can, however, force it to discriminate between conditions to the best of its knowledge and ability by giving it a disagreeable stimulus every time it makes a mistake. In other words, the conditions upon which the avoidance of a disagreeable factor in the environment depends are far simpler and much more constant than those upon which the seeking of an agreeable factor depends.

Situations which are potentially beneficial to the animal attract it in varying degrees according to its internal condition; situations which are potentially disagreeable or injurious repel it with a constancy which is remarkable. The favorable stimulus solicits a positive response; the unfavorable stimulus demands a negative response.

Finally, in connection with the discussion of motives, it is an important fact that forms of reward are far harder to find than forms of punishment. Many animals feed only at long intervals, are inactive, do not try to escape from confinement, cannot be induced to seek a particular spot, in a word, do not react positively to any of the situations or conditions which are employed usually in behavior experiments. It is, however, almost always possible to find some disagreeable stimulus which such an animal will attempt to avoid.

As it happens, the dancer is an animal which does not stand the lack of food well enough to make hunger a possible motive. I was driven to make use of the avoiding reaction, and it has proved so satisfactory that I am now using it widely in connection with experiments on other animals. The use of the induction shock, upon which I depended almost wholly in the discrimination experiments with the dancer, requires care; but I am confident that no reasonable objection to the conduct of the experiments could be made on the ground of cruelty, for the strength of the current was carefully regulated and the shocks were given only for an instant at intervals. The best proof of the humaneness of the method is the fact that the animals continued in perfect health during months of experimentation.

The brightness discrimination tests demanded, in addition to motives for choice, adequate precautions against discrimination by other than visual factors, and, for that matter, by other visual factors than that of brightness. The mouse might choose, for example, not the white or the black box, but the box which was to the right or to the left, in accordance with its experience in the previous test. This would be discrimination by position. As a matter of fact, the animals have a strong tendency at first to go uniformly either to the right or to the left entrance. This tendency will be exhibited in the results of the tests. Again, discrimination might depend upon the odors of the cardboards or upon slight differences in their shape, texture, or position. Before conclusive evidence of brightness discrimination could be obtained, all of these and other possibilities of discrimination had to be eliminated by check tests. I shall describe the various precautions taken in the experiments to guard against errors in interpretation, in order to show the lengths to which an experimenter may be driven in his search for safely interpretable results.

To exclude choice by position, the cardboards were moved from one electric-box to the other. When the change was made regularly, so that white was alternately on the right and the left, the mouse soon learned to go alternately to the right box and the left without stopping to notice the visual factor. This was prevented by changing the position of the cardboards irregularly.

Discrimination by the odor, texture, shape, and position of the cardboards was excluded by the use of different kinds of cardboards, by changing the form and position of them in check tests, and by coating them with shellac.

The brightness vision tests described in this chapter were made in a room which is lighted from the south only, with the experiment box directed away from the windows. The light from the windows shone upon the cardboards at the entrances to the electric-boxes, not into the eyes of the mouse as it approached them. Each mouse used in the experiments was given a series of ten tests in succession daily. The experiment was conducted as follows. A dancer was placed in *A*, where it usually ran about restlessly until it happened to find its way into *B*. Having discovered that the swing door at *I* could be pushed open, the animal seemed to take satisfaction in passing through into *B* as soon as it had been placed in or had returned to *A*. In *B*, choice of two entrances, one of which was brighter than the other, was forced by the animal's need of space for free movement. If the right box happened to be chosen, the mouse returned to ·*A* and was ready for another test; if it entered the wrong box, the electric shock was given, and it was compelled to retreat from the box and enter the other one instead. In the early tests with an individual, a series sometimes covered from twenty to thirty minutes; in later tests, provided the condition of discrimination was favorable, it did not occupy more than ten minutes.

To exhibit the methods of keeping the records of these experiments and certain features of the results, two sample record sheets are reproduced below. The first of these sheets, Table 6, represents the results given by No. 5, a female,[1] in her first series of white-black tests. Table 7 presents the results of the eleventh series of tests given to the same individual.

In the descriptions of the various visual experiments of this and the following chapters, the first word of the couplet which describes the condition of the experiment, for example, white-black, always designates the visual condition which the animal was to choose, the second that which it was to avoid on penalty of an electric shock. In the case of Tables 6 and 7, for example, white cardboard was placed in one box,

[1] It is to be remembered that the even numbers always designate males; the odd numbers, females.

TABLE 6

BRIGHTNESS DISCRIMINATION

White-Black, Series 1

Experimented on No. 5   January 15, 1906

TEST	POSITION OF CARDBOARDS	RIGHT	WRONG
1	White left	—	Wrong
2	White right	—	Wrong
3	White left	—	Wrong
4	White right	—	Wrong
5	White left	Right	—
6	White right	Right	—
7	White left	—	Wrong
8	White right	Right	—
9	White left	—	Wrong
10	White right	Right	—
Totals		4	6

black in the other, and the animal was required to enter the white box. In the tables the first column at the left gives the number of the test, the second the positions of the cardboards, and the third and fourth the result of the choice. The first test of Table 6 was made with the white cardboard on the box which stood at the left of the mouse as it approached from *A*, and, consequently, with the black cardboard on the right. As is indicated by the record in the "wrong" column, the mouse chose the black instead of the white. The result of this first series was choice of the white box four times as compared with choice of the black box six times. On the eleventh day, that is, after No. 5 had been given 100 tests in this brightness vision experiment, she made no mistakes in a series of ten trials (Table 7).

Before tests, such as have been described, can be presented as conclusive proof of discrimination, it must be shown that the mouse has no preference for the particular brightness which the arrangement of the test requires it to select. That any preference which the mouse to be tested might have for white, rather than black, or for a light gray rather than a dark gray, might be discovered, what may be called preference test series were given before the discrimination tests were begun. These series, two of which were given usually, consisted of ten tests each, with the white alternately on the left and on the right. The mouse was permitted to enter either the white or the black box, as it chose, and to pass through to the nest-box without receiving a shock and without having its way blocked by the glass plate. The conditions of these preference tests may be referred to hereafter briefly as "No shock, open passages."

TABLE 7

BRIGHTNESS DISCRIMINATION

White-Black, Series 11

Experimented on No. 5 February 2, 1906

TEST	POSITION OF CARDBOARDS	RIGHT	WRONG
1	White left	Right	—
2	White left	Right	—
3	White right	Right	—
4	White right	Right	—
5	White right	Right	—
6	White left	Right	—
7	White left	Right	—
8	White left	Right	—
9	White right	Right	—
10	White right	Right	—
Totals		10	0

The preference tests, which of course would be valueless as such unless they preceded the training tests, were given as preliminary experiments, in order that the experimenter might know how to plan his discrimination tests, and how to interpret his results.

The results given in the white-black preference tests by ten males and ten females are presented in Table 8. Three facts which bear upon the brightness discrimination tests appear from this table: (1) black is preferred by both males and females, (2) this preference is more marked in the first series of tests than in the second, and (3) it is slightly stronger for the first series in the case of females than in the case of males.

That the dancers should prefer to enter the dark rather than the light box is not surprising in view of the fact that the nests in which they were kept were ordinarily rather

TABLE 8

WHITE-BLACK PREFERENCE TESTS

MALES	FIRST SERIES		SECOND SERIES	
	WHITE	BLACK	WHITE	BLACK
No. 10	3	7	3	7
18	5	5	5	5
20	2	8	4	6
152	4	6	6	4
210	4	6	4	6
214	6	4	3	7
220	5	5	3	7
230	4	6	2	8
410	4	6	5	5
420	4	6	9	1
Averages	4.1	5.9	4.4	5.6

TABLE 8 — CONTINUED

FEMALES	FIRST SERIES		SECOND SERIES	
	WHITE	BLACK	WHITE	BLACK
No. 11	5	5	4	6
151	6	4	5	5
215	2	8	2	8
213	2	8	5	5
225	4	6	2	8
227	4	6	6	4
235	6	4	4	6
415	2	8	4	6
425	5	5	8	2
229	2	8	5	5
Averages	3.8	6.2	4.5	5.5

dark. But whatever the basis of the preference, it is clear that it must be taken account of in the visual discrimination experiments, for an individual which strongly preferred black might choose correctly, to all appearances, in its first black-white series. Such a result would demonstrate preference, and therefore one kind of discrimination, but not the formation of a habit of choice by discrimination. The preference for black is less marked in the second series of tests because the mouse as it becomes more accustomed to the experiment box tends more and more to be influenced by other conditions than those of brightness. The record sheets for both series almost invariably indicate a strong tendency to continue to go to the left or the right entrance according to the way by which the animal escaped the first time. This cannot properly be described as visual choice, for the mouse apparently followed the previous course without regard to the conditions of illumination. We have here an expression of the tendency to the repetition of an act. It is only after

an animal acquires considerable familiarity with a situation
that it begins to vary its behavior in accordance with relatively unimportant factors in the situation. It is this fact,
illustrations of which may be seen in human life, as well as
throughout the realm of animal behavior, that renders it im-
perative that an animal be thoroughly acquainted with the
apparatus for experimentation and with the experimenter
before regular experiments are begun. Any animal will do
things under most experimental conditions, but to discover
the nature and scope of its ability it is necessary to make
it thoroughly at home in the experimental situation. As
the dancer began to feel at home in the visual discrimination
apparatus it began to exercise its discriminating ability, the
first form of which was choice according to position.

Since there appears to be a slight preference on the part
of most dancers for the black box in comparison with the
white box, white-black training tests were given to fifty mice,
and black-white to only four. The tests with each individual were continued until it had chosen correctly in all of
the tests of three successive series (thirty tests). As the reproduction of all the record sheets of these experiments
would fill hundreds of pages and would provide most readers
with little more information than is obtainable from a simple
statement of the number of right and wrong choices, only
the brightness discrimination records of Tables 6 and 7 are
given in full.

As a basis for the comparison of the results of the white-
black tests with those of the black-white tests, two representative sets of data for each of these conditions of brightness
discrimination are presented (Tables 9 and 10). In these
tables only the number of right and wrong choices for each
series of ten tests appears.

Tables 9 and 10 indicate—if we grant that the precautionary

TABLE 9

WHITE-BLACK TESTS

SERIES	DATE	No. 210 Age, 28 Days		No. 215 Age, 28 Days	
		RIGHT (WHITE)	WRONG (BLACK)	RIGHT (WHITE)	WRONG (BLACK)
A	June 22	4	6	2	8
B	23	4	6	2	8
1	24	4	6	3	7
2	25	6	4	5	5
3	26	7	3	7	3
4	27	5	5	8	2
5	28	7	3	9	1
6	29	8	2	8	2
7	30	9	1	9	1
8	July 1	10	0	10	0
9	2	10	0	9	1
10	3	10	0	10	0
11	4	—	—	10	0
12	5	—	—	10	0

tests to be described later exclude the possibility of other forms of discrimination — that the dancer is able to tell white from black; that it is somewhat easier, as the preference tests might lead us to expect, for it to learn to go to the black than to the white, and that the male forms the habit of choosing on the basis of brightness discrimination more quickly than the female.

It is now necessary to justify the interpretation of these results as evidence of brightness discrimination by proving that all other conditions for choice except brightness difference may be excluded without interfering with the animal's ability to select the right box. We shall consider in

TABLE 10

BLACK-WHITE TESTS

SERIES	DATE	No. 14 AGE, 32 DAYS		No. 13 AGE, 32 DAYS	
		RIGHT (BLACK)	WRONG (WHITE)	RIGHT (BLACK)	WRONG (WHITE)
1	May 13[1]	5	5	7	3
2	14	8	2	6	4
3	15	7	3	9	1
4	16	9	1	9	1
5	17	10	0	10	0
6	18	10	0	9	1
7	19	10	0	10	0
8	20	—	—	10	0
9	21	—	—	10	0

order the possibility of discrimination by position, by odor, and by texture and form of the cardboards.

The tendency which the dancer has in common with many, if not all, animals to perform the same movement or follow the same path under uniform conditions is an important source of error in many habit-formation experiments. This tendency is evident even from casual observation of the behavior of the dancer. The ease with which the habit of choosing the box on the left or the box on the right is formed in comparison with that of choosing the white box or the black box is strikingly shown by the following experiment. Five mice were given one series of ten trials each in the discrimination box of Figure 14 without the presence of cardboards or of other means of visual discrimination. The electric shock was given whenever the box on the left was entered. Thus without other guidance than that of direc-

[1] No preference tests were given.

tion, for the boxes themselves were interchanged in position, and, as was proved by additional tests, the animals were utterly unable to tell one from the other, the mouse was required to choose the box on its right. Only one of the five animals went to the box on the left after once experiencing the electric shock. The results of the series are given in Table 11.

TABLE 11

CHOICE BY POSITION

	CHOICES OF BOX ON RIGHT	CHOICES OF BOX ON LEFT
First mouse	9	1
Second mouse	8	2
Third mouse	9	1
Fourth mouse	9	1
Fifth mouse	9	1

This conclusively proves that the habit of turning in a certain direction or of choosing by position can be formed more readily than a habit which depends upon visual discrimination. A rough comparison justifies the statement that it takes from six to ten times as long for the dancer to learn to choose the white box as it does to learn to choose the box on the right. Since this is true, it is exceedingly important that the possibility of choice by position or direction of movement be excluded in the case of tests of brightness discrimination. To indicate how this was effectively accomplished in the experiments, the changes in the position of the cardboards made in the case of a standard set of white-black series are shown in Table 12. The number of the series, beginning at the top of the table with the two lettered preference series, is given in the first column at the left, the number of the tests at the top of the table, and the position of the white cardboard, left or right, is indicated below by the letters *l* (left) and *r* (right).

TABLE 12

POSITION OF WHITE CARDBOARDS FOR A SET OF 150 TESTS

SERIES	1	2	3	4	5	6	7	8	9	10
Preference										
A	l	r	l	r	l	r	l	r	l	r
B	r	l	r	l	r	l	r	l	r	l
1	r	l	r	l	r	l	r	l	r	l
2	l	l	r	r	l	r	l	l	r	r
3	r	r	l	r	l	l	r	l	r	l
4	l	l	l	r	r	r	l	r	r	l
5	r	l	r	l	r	l	r	l	r	l
6	l	l	r	l	r	r	l	r	l	r
7	r	l	l	l	r	r	r	l	r	l
8	r	r	l	l	r	l	r	l	r	l
9	r	r	r	l	l	l	r	l	r	l
10	l	l	l	l	r	r	r	r	l	r
11	r	l	r	r	r	l	l	l	r	l
12	r	l	r	l	r	r	l	l	r	l
13	r	l	r	l	l	l	r	r .	r	l
14	l	l	l	l	r	r	r	r	l	r
15	r	l	r	r	r	l	l	l	r	l

It is to be noted that in the case of each series of ten tests the white cardboard was on the left five times and on the right five times. Thus the establishment of a tendency in favor of one side was avoided. The irregularity of the changes in position rendered it impossible for the mouse to depend upon position in its choice. It is an interesting fact that the dancer quickly learns to choose correctly by position if the cardboards are alternately on the left box and on the right.

The prevalent, although ill-founded, impression that mice have an exceedingly keen sense of smell might lead a critic of these experiments to claim that discrimination in all probability was olfactory rather than visual. As precautions against this possibility the cardboards were renewed frequently, so that no odor from the body of the mouse itself should serve as a guiding condition, different kinds of cardboard were used from time to time, and, as a final test, the cardboards were coated with shellac so that whatever characteristic odor they may have had for the dancer was disguised if not totally·destroyed. Despite all these precautions the discrimination of the boxes continued. A still more conclusive proof that we have to do with brightness discrimination, and that alone, in these experiments is furnished by the results of white-black tests made with an apparatus which was so arranged that light was transmitted into the two electric-boxes through a ground glass plate in the end of each box. No cardboards were used. The illumination of each box was controlled by changes in the position of the sources of light. Under these conditions, so far as could be ascertained by critical examination of the results, in addition to careful observation of the behavior of the animals as they made their choices, there was no other guiding factor than brightness difference. Nevertheless the mice discriminated the white from the black perfectly. This renders unnecessary any discussion of the possibility of discrimination by the texture or form of the cardboards.

Since a variety of precautionary tests failed to reveal the presence, in these experiments, of any condition other than brightness difference by which the mice were enabled to choose correctly, and since evidence of ability to discriminate brightness differences was obtained by the use of both reflected light (cardboards) and transmitted light (lamps behind ground glass), it is necessary to conclude that the dancer possesses brightness vision.

CHAPTER VIII

THE SENSE OF SIGHT: BRIGHTNESS VISION (*Continued*)

SINCE the ability of the dancer to perceive brightness has been demonstrated by the experiments of the previous chapter, the next step in this investigation of the nature of vision is a study of the delicacy of brightness discrimination, and of the relation of the just perceivable difference to brightness value. Expressed in another way, the problems of this portion of the investigation are to determine how slight a difference in brightness enables the dancer to discriminate one light from another, and what is the relation between the absolute brightnesses of two lights and that amount of difference which is just sufficient to render the lights distinguishable. It has been discovered in the case of the human being that a stimulus must be increased by a certain definite fraction of its own value if it is to seem different. For brightness, within certain intensity limits, this increase must be about one one-hundredth; a brightness of 100 units, for example, is just perceivably different from one of 101 units. The formulation of this relation between the amount of a stimulus and the amount of change which is necessary that a difference be noted is known as Weber's law. Does this law, in any form, hold for the brightness vision of the dancing mouse?

Two methods were used in the study of these problems. For the first problem, that of the delicacy of brightness discrimination, I first used light which was reflected from gray papers, according to the method of Chapter VII. For the second, the Weber's law test, transmitted light was used, in an apparatus which will be described later. Either of these methods might have been used for the solution of both problems. Which of them is the more satisfactory is definitely decided by the results which make up the material of this chapter. Under natural conditions the dancer probably sees objects which reflect light more frequently than it does those which transmit it; it would seem fairer, therefore, to require it to discriminate surfaces which differ in brightness. This the use of gray papers does. But, on the other hand, gray papers are open to the objections that they may not be entirely colorless (neutral), and that their brightness values cannot be changed readily by the experimenter. As will be made clear in the subsequent description of the experiments with transmitted light, neither of these objections can be raised in connection with the second method of experimentation.

To determine the delicacy of discrimination with reflected light it is necessary to have a series of neutral grays (colorless) whose adjacent members differ from one another in brightness by less than the threshold of discrimination of the animal to be tested. A series which promised to fulfill these conditions was that of Richard Nendel of Berlin. It consists of fifty papers, beginning with pure white, numbered 1, and passing by almost imperceptible steps of decrease in brightness through the grays to black, which is numbered 50. For the present we may assume that these papers are so nearly neutral that whatever discrimination occurs is due to brightness. The differences between successive papers of the series are perceptible to man. The question is, can they, under favorable conditions of illumination, be perceived by the dancer?

On the basis of the fact that the dancer can discriminate between white and black, two grays which differed from one another in brightness by a considerable amount were chosen from the Nendel series; these were numbers 10 and 20. It seemed certain, from the results of previous experiments, that the discrimination of these papers by brightness difference would be possible, and that therefore the use of papers between these two extremes would suffice to demonstrate the

FIGURE 16. Three of Nendel's gray papers: Nos. 10, 15, and 20. To exhibit differences in brightness.

delicacy of discrimination. In Figure 16 we have a fairly accurate representation of the relative brightness of the Nendel papers Nos. 10, 15, and 20.

Pieces of the gray papers were pasted upon cardboard carriers so that they might be placed in the discrimination box as were the white and black cardboards in the tests of brightness vision previously described. Mice which had been trained to choose the white box by series of white-black tests were now tested with light gray (No. 10) and dark gray (No. 20), my assumption being that they would immediately choose the brighter of the two if they were able to detect the difference. As a matter of fact this did not always occur; some individuals had to be trained to discriminate gray No. 10 from gray No. 20. As soon as an individual had been so trained that the ability to choose the lighter of these grays was perfect, it was tested with No. 10 in combination with No. 15. If these in turn proved to be discriminable, No. 10 could be used with No. 14, with No. 13, and so on until either the limit of discrimination or that of the series had been reached.

That it was not necessary to use other combinations than 10 with 20, and 10 with 15 is demonstrated by the results of Table 13. Mouse No. 420, whose behavior was not essentially different from that of three other individuals which were tested for gray discrimination, learned with difficulty to choose gray No. 10 even when it was used with No. 20. Two series of ten tests each were given to this mouse daily, and not until the twentieth of these series (200 tests) did he succeed in making ten correct choices in succession. Immediately after this series of correct choices, tests with grays No. 10 and No. 15 were begun. In the case of this amount of brightness difference twenty series failed to reveal discrimination. The average number of right choices in the series is slightly in excess of the mistakes, 5.8 as compared with 4.2.

From the experiments with gray papers we may conclude that under the conditions of the tests the amount by which Nendel's gray No. 10 differs in brightness from No. 20 is near the threshold of discrimination, or, in other words, that the difference in the brightness of the adjacent grays of Figure 16 is scarcely sufficient to enable the dancer to distinguish them.

This result of the tests with gray papers surprised me very much at the time of the experiments, for all my previous observation of the dancer had led me to believe that it is very sensitive to light. It was only after a long series of tests with

TABLE 13

GRAY DISCRIMINATION

The Delicacy of Brightness Discrimination

No. 420

SERIES	DATE	GRAYS NOS. 10 AND 20		DATE	GRAYS NOS. 10 AND 15	
		No. 10 (RIGHT)	No. 20 (WRONG)		No. 10 (RIGHT)	No. 15 (WRONG)
1	Jan. 26	5	5	Feb. 6	8	2
2	27	8	2	6	5	5
3	28	6	4	7	9	1
4	28	2	8	7	7	3
5	29	1	9	8	5	5
6	29	6	4	8	6	4
7	30	9	1	9	5	5
8	30	7	3	9	6	4
9	31	6	4	10	8	2
10	31	4	6	10	3	7
11	Feb. 1	7	3	11	4	6
12	1	8	2	11	4	6
13	2	7	3	12	7	3
14	2	8	2	12	7	3
15	3	9	1	13	6	4
16	3	9	1	13	4	6
17	4	6	4	14	4	6
18	4	9	1	14	5	5
19	5	6	4	15	5	5
20	5	10	0	15	8	2
Averages		6.6	3.4		5.8	4.2

transmitted light, in what is now to be described as the Weber's law apparatus, that I was able to account for the meager power of discrimination which the mice exhibited in the gray tests. As it happened, the Weber's law experiment contributed quite as importantly to the solution of our first problem as to that of the second, for which it was especially planned.

For the Weber's law experiment a box similar to that used in the previous brightness discrimination experiments (Figure 14) was so arranged that its two electric-boxes could be illuminated independently by the light from incandescent lamps directly above them. The arrangements of the light-box and the lamps, as well as their relations to the other important parts of the apparatus, are shown in Figure 17. The light-box consisted of two compartments, of which one may be considered as the upward extension of the left electric-box and the other of the right electric-box. The light-box was pivoted at A and could be turned through an angle of 180° by the experimenter. Thus, by the turning of the light-box, the lamp which in the case of one test illuminated the left electric-box could be brought into such a position that in the case of the next test it illuminated the right electric-box. The practical convenience of this will be appreciated when the number of times that the brightnesses of the two boxes had to be reversed is considered. The light-box was left open at the top for ventilation and the prevention of any considerable increase in the temperature of the experiment box. In one side of each of the compartments of the light-box a slit (B, B of the figure) was cut out for an incandescent lamp holder. A strip of leatherette, fitted closely into inch grooves at the edges of the slit, prevented light from escaping through these openings in the sides of the light-box. By moving the strips of leatherette, one of which appears in the figure, C, the lamps could be changed in position with reference to the bottom of the electric-box. A scale, S, at the edge of each slit enabled the experimenter to determine the distance of the lamp from the floor of the electric-box. The front of the light-box was closed, instead of being open as it appears in the figure.

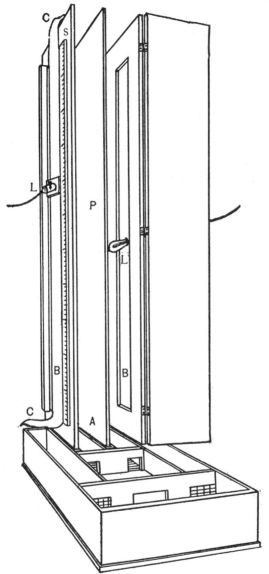

FIGURE 17.—Weber's law apparatus for testing brightness discrimination. Lower part, discrimination box similar to that of Figure 14. Upper part, rotatory light-box, pivoted at *A*, and divided into two compartments by a partition *P* in the middle. *L, L*, incandescent lamps movable in slits, *B, B*, in which a narrow strip of leatherette, *C*, serves to prevent the escape of light. *S*, scale.

This apparatus has the following advantages. First, the electric-boxes, between which the mouse is expected to discriminate by means of their difference in brightness, are illuminated from above and the light therefore does not shine directly from the lamps into the eyes of the animal, as it approaches the entrances to the boxes. Choice is required, therefore, between illuminated spaces instead of between two directly illuminated surfaces. Second, the amount of illumination of each electric-box can be accurately measured by the use of a photometer. Third, since the same kind of lamp is used in each box, and further, since the lamps may be interchanged at any time, discrimination by qualitative instead of quantitative difference in illumination is excluded. And finally, fourth, the tests can be made expeditiously, conveniently, and under such simple conditions that there should be no considerable error of measurement or of observation within the range of brightness which must be used.

It was my purpose in the experiment with this apparatus to ascertain how great the difference in the illumination of the two electric-boxes must be in order that the mouse should be able to choose the brighter of them. This I attempted to do by fixing an incandescent lamp of a certain known illuminating power at such a position in one compartment of the light-box that the electric-box below it was illuminated by what I call a standard value, and by moving the incandescent lamp in the other compartment of the light-box until the illumination of the electric-box below it was just sufficiently less than that of the standard to enable the dancer to distinguish them, and thereby to choose the brighter one. The light which was changed from series to series I shall call the *variable*, in contrast with the *standard*, which was unchanged.

The tests, which were made in a dark-room under uniform conditions, were given in series of fifty each; usually only one such series was given per day, but sometimes one was given in the morning and another in the afternoon of the same day. To prevent choice by position the lights were reversed in position irregularly, first one, then the other, illuminating the right electric-box. For the fifty tests of each initial series the order of the changes in position was as follows: standard (brighter light) on the *l* (left), *l*, *r* (right), *r*, *l*, *l*, *r*, *r*, *l*, *r*, *l*, *r*, *l*, *l*, *r*, *r*, *l*, *l*, *r*, *r*, *l*, *l*, *l*, *r*, *r*, *r*, *l*, *r*, *l*, *r*, *r*, *r*, *l*, *l*, *l*, *r*, *r*, *r*, *l*, *l*, *r*, *l*, *r*, *l*, *r*, *l*, *r*, *l*, *r*, *l*. Twenty-five times in fifty the standard light illuminated the right electric-box, and the same number of times it illuminated the left electric-box. When a second series was given under the same conditions of illumination, a different order of change was followed.

In order to discover whether Weber's law holds in the case of the brightness vision of the dancer it was necessary for me to determine the just perceivable difference between the standard and the variable lights for two or more standard values. I chose to work with three values, 5, 20, and 80 hefners, and I was able to discover with a fair degree of accuracy how much less than 5, 20, or 80 hefners, as the case might be, the variable light had to be in order that it should be discriminable from the other. For the work with the 5 hefner standard I used 2-candle-power lamps,[1] for the 20, 4-candle-power, and for the 80, 16-candle-power.

---

[1] I give merely the commercial markings of the lamps. They had been photometered carefully by two observers by means of a Lummer-Brodhun photometer and a Hefner amyl-acetate lamp previous to their use in the experiment. For the photometric measurements in connection with the Weber's law tests I made use of the Hefner lamp with the hope of attaining greater accuracy than had been possible with a standard paraffine candle, in the case of measurements which I had made in connection with the experiments on color vision that are reported in Chapters IX and X. The Hefner unit is the amount of light produced by an amyl acetate lamp at a flame height of 40 mm. (See Stine's "Photometrical Measurements.") A paraffine candle at a flame height of 50 mm. is equal to 1.2 Hefner units.

For reasons which will soon appear, Weber's law tests were made with only one dancer. This individual, No. 51, had been thoroughly trained in white-black discrimination previous to the experiments in the apparatus which is represented in Figure 17. Having given No. 51 more than two hundred preliminary tests in the Weber's law apparatus with the electric-boxes sufficiently different in brightness to enable her to discriminate readily, I began my experiments by trying to ascertain how much less the value of the illumination ot one electric-box must be in order that it should be discriminable from a value of 20 hefners in the other electric-box. In recording the several series of tests and their results hereafter, I shall state in Hefner units the value of the fixed or standard light and the value of the variable light, the difference between the two in terms of the former, and the average number of wrong choices in per cent.

With the lamps so placed that the difference in the illumination of the two electric-boxes was .53 of the value of the standard, that is about one half, No. 51 made twenty wrong choices in one hundred, or 20 per cent. When the difference was reduced to .36 (one third) the number of errors increased to 36 per cent, and with an intermediate difference of .48 there were 26 per cent of errors (see Table 14).

Are these results indicative of discrimination, or are the errors in choice too numerous to justify the statement that the dancer was able to distinguish the boxes by their difference in brightness? Evidently this question cannot be answered satisfactorily until we have decided what the percentage of correct choices should be in order that it be accepted as evidence of ability to discriminate, or, to put it in terms of errors, what percentage of wrong choices is indicative of the point of just perceivable difference in brightness. Theoretically, there should be as many mistakes as right choices, 50 per cent of each, when the two electric-boxes are equally illuminated (indiscriminable), but in practice this does not prove to be the case because the dancer tends to return to that electric-box through which in the previous test it passed safely, whereas it does not tend in similar fashion to reënter the box in which it has just received an electric shock. The result is that the percentage of right choices, especially in the case of series which have the right box in the same position two, three, or four times in succession, rises as high as 60 or 70, even when the visual conditions are indiscriminable. Abundant evidence in support of this statement is presented in Chapters VII and IX, but at this point I may further call attention to the results of an experiment in the Weber's law apparatus which was made especially to test the matter. The results appear under the date of May 27 in Table 14. In this experiment, despite the fact that both boxes were illuminated by 80 hefners, the mouse chose the standard (the illumination in which it was not shocked) 59 times in 100. In other words the percentage of error was 41 instead of 50. It is evident, therefore, that as low a percentage of errors as 40 is not necessarily indicative of discrimination. Anything below 40 per cent is likely, however, to be the result of ability to distinguish the brighter from the darker box. To be on the safe side we may agree to consider 25 wrong choices per 100 as indicative of a just perceivable difference in illumination. Fewer mistakes we shall consider indicative of a difference in illumination which is readily perceivable, and more as indicative of a difference which the mouse cannot detect. The reader will bear in mind as he examines Table 14 that 25 per cent of wrong choices indicates the point of just perceivable difference in brightness.

If we apply this rule to the results of the first tests, reported above, it appears that a standard of 20 hefners was distin-

TABLE 14

RESULTS OF WEBER'S LAW EXPERIMENTS

Brightness vision

DATE	NUMBER OF TESTS	STANDARD LIGHT	VARIABLE LIGHT	DIFFERENCE	% OF ERRORS
May 13	100	20	9.4	.53	20
15	100	20	12.8	.36	36
16	100	20	10.8	.46	26
20	50	80	37.6	.53	6
21	50	80	51.3	.36	10
22	100	80	71.1	.11	35
24	100	80	60.0	.25	21
25	100	80	65.0	.19	25
27	100	80	80	0	41
28	50	5	2.5	.50	18
29	50	5	4.0	.20	14
29	100	5	4.5	.10	25
31	50	5	4.25	.15	20
June 1	50	5	4.85	.03	48
2	50	20	15.0	.25	16
3	50	20	17.4	.13	22
3	100	20	18.0	.10	22
4	100	80	72.0	.10	18
5	100	5	4.5	.10	12
7	100	5	4.67	.067	46
8	50	80	74.67	.067	56
9	50	20	18.67	.067	44

guished from a variable of 9.4 hefners (.53 difference), for the percentage of errors was only 20. But in the case of a difference of .36 in the illuminations lack of discrimination is indicated by 36 per cent of errors. A difference of .46 gave a frequency of error so close to the required 25 (26 per cent) that I accepted the result as a satisfactory determination of the just perceivable difference for the 20 hefner standard and proceeded to experiment with another standard value.

The results which were obtained in the case of this second standard, the value of which was 80 hefners, are strikingly different from those for the 20 hefner standard. Naturally I began the tests with this new standard by making the differences the same as those for which determinations had been made in the case of the 20 standard. Much to my surprise only 6 per cent of errors resulted when the difference in illumination was .53. I finally discovered that about .19 difference (about one fifth) could be discriminated with that degree of accuracy which is indicated by 25 per cent of mistakes.

So far as I could judge from the results of determinations for the 20 and the 80 hefner standards, Weber's law does not hold for the dancer. With the former a difference of almost one half was necessary for discrimination; with the latter a difference of about one fifth could be perceived. But before presenting additional results I should explain the construction of Table 14, and comment upon the number of experiments which constitutes a set.

The table contains the condensed results of several weeks of difficult experimentation. From left to right the columns give the date of the initial series of a given set of experiments, the number of experiments in the set, the value of the standard light in hefners, the value of the variable light, the difference between the lights in terms of the standard (the variable was always less than the standard), and the percentage of errors or wrong choices. Very early in the investigation I discovered that one hundred tests with any given values of the lights sufficed to reveal whatever discriminating ability the mouse possessed at the time. In some instances either the presence or the lack of discrimination was so clear, as the result of 50 tests (first series), that the second series of 50 was not given. Consequently in the table the number of tests for the various values of the lights is sometimes 100, sometimes 50.

After finishing the experiments with the 80 standard on May 27 (see table) I decided, in spite of the evidence against Weber's law, to make tests with 5 as the standard, for it seemed not impossible that the lights were too bright for the dancer to discriminate readily. I even suspected that I might have been working outside of the brightness limits in which Weber's law holds, if it holds at all. The tests soon showed that a difference of one tenth made discrimination possible in the case of this standard. If the reader will examine the data of the table, he will note that a difference of .20 gave 14 per cent of mistakes; a difference of .03, 48 per cent. Evidently the former difference is above the threshold, the latter below it. But what of the interpretation of the results in terms of Weber's law? The difference instead of being one half or one fifth, as it was in the cases of the 20 and 80 standards respectively, has now become one tenth. Another surprise and another contradiction!

Had these three differences either increased or decreased regularly with the value of the standard I should have suspected that they indicated a principle or relationship which is different from but no less interesting than that which Weber's law expresses. But instead of reading 5 standard, difference one tenth; 20 standard, difference one fifth; 80 standard, difference one half: or 5 standard, difference one half; 20 standard, difference one fifth; 80 standard, difference one tenth: they read 5 standard, difference one tenth; 20 standard, difference one half; 80 standard, difference one fifth. What does this mean? I could think of no other explanation than that of the influence of training. It seemed not impossible, although not probable, that the mouse had been improving in ability to discriminate day by day. It is true that this in itself would be quite as interesting a fact as any which the experiment might reveal.

To test the value of my supposition, I made additional experiments with the 20 standard, the results of which appear under the dates June 2 and 3 of the table. These results indicate quite definitely that the animal had been, and still was, improving in her ability to discriminate. For instead of requiring a difference of about one half in order that she might distinguish the 20 standard from the variable light she was now able to discriminate with only 22 per cent of errors when the difference was one tenth.

As it seemed most improbable that improvement by training should continue much longer, I next gave additional tests with the 80 standard. Again a difference of one tenth was sufficient for accurate discrimination (18 per cent of errors). These series were followed immediately by further tests with the 5 standard. As the results indicated greater ease of discrimination with a difference of one tenth in the case of this standard than in the case of either of the others I was at first uncertain whether the results which I have tabulated under the dates June 3, 4, and 5 of the table should be interpreted in terms of Weber's law.

Up to this point the experiments had definitely established two facts: that the dancer's ability to discriminate by means of brightness differences improves with training for a much longer period and to a far greater extent than I had supposed it would; and that a difference of one tenth is sufficient to enable the animal to distinguish two lights in the case of the three standard values, 5, 20, and 80 hefners. The question remains, is this satisfactory evidence that Weber's law holds with respect to the brightness vision of the dancer, or do the results indicate rather, that this difference is more readily detected in the case of 5 as a standard (12 per cent error) than in the case of 20 as a standard (22 per cent error)?

For the purpose of settling this point I made tests for each of the three standards with a difference of only one fifteenth. In no instance did I obtain the least evidence of ability to discriminate. These final tests, in addition to establishing the fact that the limit of discrimination for No. 51, after she had been subjected to about two thousand tests, lay between one tenth and one fifteenth, proved to my satisfaction, when taken in connection with the results already discussed, that Weber's law does hold for the brightness vision of the dancer.

In concluding this discussion of the Weber's law experiment I wish to call attention to the chief facts which have been revealed, and to make a critical comment. In my opinion it is extremely important that the student of animal behavior should note the fact that the dancer with which I worked week after week in the Weber's law investigation gradually improved in her ability to discriminate on the basis of brightness differences until she was able to distinguish from one another two boxes whose difference in illumination was less than one tenth [1] that of the brighter box. At the beginning of the experiments a difference of one half did not enable her to choose as certainly as did a difference of one tenth after she had chosen several hundred times· Evidently we are prone to underestimate the educability of our animal subjects.

The reason that the experiments were carried out with only one mouse must now be apparent. It was a matter of time. The reader must not suppose that my study of this subject is completed. It is merely well begun, and I report it here in its unfinished state for the sake of the value of the method which I have worked out, rather than for the purpose of presenting the definite results which I obtained with No. 51.

---

[1] Under the conditions of the experiment I was unable to distinguish the electric-boxes when they differed by less than one twentieth.

The critical comment which I wish to make for the benefit of those who are working on similar problems is this. The phosphor bronze wires, on the bottom of the electric-boxes, by means of which an electric shock could be given to the mouse when it chose the wrong box, are needless sources of variability in the illumination of the boxes. They reflect the light into the eyes of the mouse too strongly, and unless they are kept perfectly clean and bright, serious inequalities of illumination appear. To avoid these undesirable conditions I propose hereafter to use a box within a box, so that the wires shall be hidden from the view of the animal as it attempts to discriminate.

A brief description of the behavior of the dancer in the brightness discrimination experiments which have been described may very appropriately form the closing section of this chapter. For the experimenter, the incessant activity and inexhaustible energy of the animal are a never-failing source of interest and surprise. When a dancer is inactive in the experiment box, it is a good indication either of indisposition or of too low a temperature in the room. In no animal with which I am familiar is activity so much an end in itself as in this odd species of mouse. With striking facility most of the mice learn to open the wire swing doors from either side. They push them open with their noses in the direction in which they were intended by the experimenter to work, and with almost equal ease they pull them open with their teeth in the direction in which they were not intended to work. In the rapidity with which this trick is learned, there are very noticeable individual differences. The pulling of these doors furnished an excellent opportunity for the study of the imitative tendency.

When confronted with the two entrances of the electric-boxes, the dancer manifested at first only the hesitation caused

K

by being in a strange place. It did not seem much afraid, and usually did not hesitate long before entering one of the boxes. The first choice often determined the majority of the choices of the preference series. If the mouse happened to enter the left box, it kept on doing so until, having become so accustomed to its surroundings that it could take time from its strenuous running from *A* by way of the left box to the alley and thence to *A*, to examine things in *B* a little, it observed the other entrance and in a seemingly half-curious, half-venturesome way entered it. In the case of other individuals, he cardboards themselves seemed to determine the choices from the first.

The electric shock, as punishment for entering the wrong box, came as a surprise. At times an individual would persistently attempt to enter, or even enter and retreat from the wrong box repeatedly, in spite of the shock. This may have been due in some instances to the effects of fright, but in others it certainly was due to the strength of the tendency to follow the course which had been taken most often previously. The next effect of the shock was to cause the animal to hesitate before the entrances to the boxes, to run from one to the other, poking its head into each · and peering about cautiously, touching the cardboards at the entrances, apparently smelling of them, and in every way attempting to determine which box could be entered safely. I have at times seen a mouse run from one entrance to the other twenty times before making its choice; now and then it would start to enter one and, when halfway in, draw back as if it had been shocked. Possibly merely touching the wires with its fore paws was responsible for this simulation of a reaction to the shock. The gradual waning of this inhibition of the forward movement was one of the most interesting features of the experiment. Could we but discover what the psychical states and the physiological conditions of the animal were during this period of choosing, comparative psychology and physiology would advance by a bound.

If the conditions at the entrances of the two boxes were discriminable, the mouse usually learned within one hundred experiences to choose the right box without much hesitation. Three distinct methods of choice were exhibited by different individuals, and to a certain extent by the same individual from time to time. These methods, which I have designated *choice by affirmation, choice by negation,* and *choice by comparison,* are of peculiar interest to the psychologist and logician.

When an individual runs directly to the entrance of the right box, and, after stopping for an instant to examine it, enters, the choice may be described as recognition of the right box. I call it choice by affirmation because the act of the animal is equivalent to the judgment — " this is it." If instead it runs directly to the wrong box, and, after examining it, turns to the other box and enters without pause for examination, its behavior may be described as recognition of the wrong box. This I call choice by negation because the act seems equivalent to the judgment — " this ·is not it." Further, it seems to imply the judgment — "therefore the other is it." In the light of this fact, this type of choice might appropriately be called choice by exclusion. Finally, when the mouse runs first to one box and then to the other, and repeats this anywhere from one to fifty times, the choice may be described as comparison of the boxes; therefore, I call it choice by comparison. Certain individuals choose first by comparison, and later almost uniformly by affirmation and negation. Whenever the conditions are difficult to discriminate, choice by comparison occurs most frequently and persistently. If, however, the conditions happen to be absolutely indiscrim-

inable, as was true, for example, in the case of the sound
tests, in certain of the Weber's law tests, and in the plain
electric-box tests, the period of hesitation rapidly increases
during the first three or four series of tests, then the mouse
seems to lessen its efforts to discriminate and more and more
tends to rush into one of the boxes without hesitation or
examination, and apparently with the expectation of a shock,
but with the intention of getting it over as soon as possible.
Now and then under such conditions there is a marked tendency to enter the same box each time. Indiscriminable
conditions are likely to render the animals fearful of the experiment; instead of going from *A* to *A* willingly, they fight
against making the trip. They refuse to pass from *A* to *B*;
and when in *B*, they fight against being driven toward the
entrances to the electric-boxes.

In marked contrast with this behavior on the part of the
mouse under conditions which do not permit it to choose
correctly is that of the animal which has learned what is expected of it. The latter, far from holding back or fighting
against the conditions which urge it forward, is so eager to
make the trip that it sometimes has to be forced to wait while
the experimenter records the results of the tests. There is
evidence of delight in the freedom of movement and in the
variety of activity which the experiment furnishes. The
thoroughly trained dancer runs into *B* almost as soon as it
has been placed in *A* by the experimenter; it chooses the
right entrance by one of the three methods described above,
immediately, or after whirling about a few times in *B;* it
runs through *E* and back to *A* as quickly as it can, and almost before the experimenter has had time to record the
result of the choice it is again in *B* ready for another choice.

CHAPTER IX

The Sense of Sight: Color Vision

Is the dancing mouse able to discriminate colors as we do? Does it possess anything which may properly be called color vision? If so, what is the nature of its ability in this sense field? Early in my study of the mice I attempted to answer these and similar questions, for the fact that they are completely deaf during the whole or the greater part of their lives suggested to me the query, are they otherwise defective in sense equipment? In the following account of my study of color vision, I shall describe the evolution of my methods in addition to stating the results which were obtained and the conclusions to which they led me. For in this case the development of a method of research is quite as interesting as the facts which the method in its various stages of evolution revealed.

Observation of the behavior of the dancer under natural conditions caused me to suspect that it is either defective in color vision or possesses a sense which is very different from human vision. I therefore devised the following extremely simple method of testing the animal's ability to distinguish one color from another. In opposite corners of a wooden box 26 cm. long, 23 cm. wide, and 11 cm. deep, two tin boxes 5 cm. in diameter and 1.5 cm. deep were placed, as is shown in part I of Figure 18. One of these boxes was covered on the outside with blue paper (*B* of Figure 18), and the other with orange [1] (*O* of Figure 18). A small quantity of "force"

---

[1] These were the Milton Bradley blue and orange papers.

was placed in the orange box. As the purpose of the test was
to discover whether the animals could learn to go directly

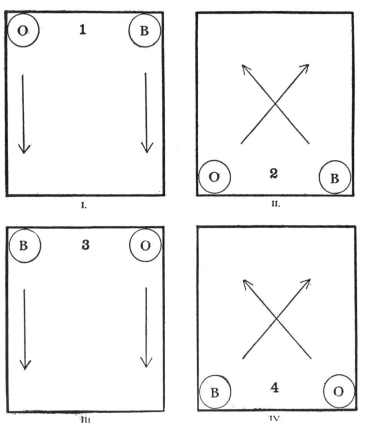

FIGURE 18.—Food-box apparatus for color discrimination experiments. *O*,
orange food-box; *B*, blue food-box; 1, 2, 3, 4, different positions of the food-
boxes, *O* and *B;* I, II, III, IV, figures in which the arrows indicate the direction
in which the food-boxes were moved.

to the box which contained the food, the experiments were
made each morning before the mice had been fed. The
experimental procedure consisted in placing the individual
to be tested in the end of the large wooden box opposite the
color boxes, and then permitting it to run about exploring

the box until it found the food in the orange box. While it was busily engaged in eating a piece of "force" which it had taken from the box and was holding in its fore paws, squirrel fashion, the color boxes were quickly and without disturbance shifted in the directions indicated by the arrows of Figure 18, I. Consequently, when the animal was ready for another piece of "force," the food-box was in the corresponding corner of the opposite end of the experiment box (position 2, 18, II). After the mouse had again succeeded in finding it, the orange box was shifted in position as is indicated by the arrows in Figure 18, II. Thus the

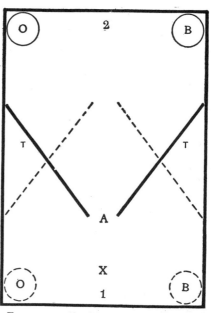

FIGURE 19.—Food-box apparatus with movable partitions. *O*, orange food-box; *B*, blue food-box; *X*, starting point for mouse; *A*, point at which both food-boxes become visible to the mouse as it approaches them; 1, 2, two different positions of the food-boxes; *T, T*, movable partitions. (After Doctor Waugh.)

tests were continued, the boxes being shifted after each success on the part of the animal in such a way that for no two successive tests was the position of the food-box the same; it occupied successively the positions 1, 2, 3, and 4 of the figure, and then returned to 1. Each series consisted of 20 tests.

An improvement on this method, which was suggested by Doctor Karl Waugh, has been used by him in a study of the sense of vision in the common mouse. It consisted in the introduction, at the middle of the experiment box, of two wooden partitions which were pivoted on their mid-vertical axes so that they could be placed in either of the positions indicated in Figure 19. Let us suppose that a mouse to be tested for color vision in this apparatus has been placed at *X*. In order to obtain food it must pass through *A* and choose either the orange or the blue box. If it chooses the former, the test is recorded as correct; if it goes to the blue box first, and then to the orange, it is counted an error. While the animal is eating, the experimenter shifts the boxes to position 1 of Figure 19, and at the same time moves the partitions so that they occupy the position indicated by the dotted lines. The chief advantage of this improvement in method is that the animal is forced to approach the color boxes from a point midway between them, instead of following the sides of the experiment box, as it is inclined to do, until it happens to come to the food-box. This renders the test fairer, for presumably the animal has an opportunity to see both boxes from *A* and can make its choice at that point of vantage.

Two males, A and B, of whose age I am ignorant, were each given seventeen series of tests in the apparatus of Figure 18. A single series, consisting of twenty choices, was given daily. Whether the animal chose correctly or not, it was allowed to get food; that is, if it went first to the blue box, thus furnishing the condition for a record of error, it was permitted to pass on to the orange box and take a piece of "force." No attempt was made to increase the animal's desire for food by starving it. Usually it sought the food-box eagerly; when it would not do so, the series was abandoned and work postponed. "Force" proved a very convenient form of food in these tests. The mice are fond of it, and they quickly learned to take a flake out of the box instead of trying to get into the box and sit there eating, for when they attempted the latter they were promptly pushed to one side by the experimenter and the box, as well as the food, was removed to a new position.

The results of the tests appear in Table 15. No record of the choices in the first two of the 17 series was kept. The totals therefore include 15 series, or 300 tests, with each individual. Neither the daily records nor the totals of this table demonstrate choice on the basis of color discrimination. Either the dancers were not able to tell one box from the other, or they did not learn to go directly to the orange box. It might be urged with reason that there is no sufficiently strong motive for the avoidance of an incorrect choice. A mistake simply means a moment's delay in finding food, and this is not so serious a matter as stopping to discriminate. I am inclined, in the light of result of other experiments, to believe that there is a great deal in this objection to the method. Reward for a correct choice should be supplemented by some form of punishment for a mistake. This conclusion was forced upon me by the results of these preliminary experiments on color vision and by my observation of the behavior of the animals in the apparatus. At the time the above tests were made I believed that I had demonstrated the inability of the dancer to distinguish orange from blue, but now, after two years' additional work on the subject, I believe instead that the method was defective.

The next step in the evolution of a method of testing the dancer's color vision was the construction of the apparatus (Figures 14 and 15) which was described in Chapter VII. p. 92. In connection with this experiment box the basis for a new motive was introduced, namely, the punishment of mistakes by an electric shock. Colored cardboards, instead of the white, black, or grays of the brightness tests, were placed in the electric-boxes.

The Dancing Mouse

TABLE 15

ORANGE-BLUE TESTS, WITH FOOD-BOX

SERIES	DATE 1904	MOUSE A		MOUSE B	
		RIGHT (ORANGE)	WRONG (BLUE)	RIGHT (ORANGE)	WRONG (BLUE)
1	Dec. 6	—	—	—	—
2	7	—	—	—	—
3	8	12	8	12	8
4	9	10	10	9	11
5	10	15	5	10	10
6	11	10	10	12	8
7	12	9	11	9	11
8	13	10	10	9	11
9	14	12	8	12	8
10	15	13	7	12	8
11	16	13	7	10	10
12	17	12	8	10	10
13	18	11	9	10	10
14	19	13	7	8	12
15	20	13	7	.9	11
16	22	14	6	12	8
17	23	10	10	9	11
Totals		177	123	153	147

In preliminary tests, at the rate of four per day, the colored cardboards were placed only at the entrances to the boxes, not inside, and as was true also in the case of brightness tests under like conditions, no evidence of discrimination was obtained from ten days' training. This seemed to indicate that a considerable area of the colored surface should be exposed to the mouse's view, if discrimination were, to be made reasonably easy.

This conclusion was supported by the results of other preliminary experiments in which rectangular pieces of colored papers,[1] 6 by 3 cm., were placed on the floor at the entrances to the electric-boxes, instead of on the walls of the boxes. Mouse No. 2 was given five series of ten tests each with a yellow card to indicate the right box and a red card at the entrance to the wrong box. At first he chose the red almost uniformly, and at no time during these fifty tests did he exhibit ability to choose the right box by color discrimination. I present the results of these series in Table 16, because they indicate a fact to which I shall have to refer repeatedly later, namely, that the brightness values of different portions of the spectrum are not the same for the dancer as for us. Previous to this yellow-red training, No. 2, as a result of ten days of white-black training (two tests per day), had partially learned to go to the brighter of the two electric-boxes. It is possible therefore that the choice of the box in the case of these color experiments was in reality the choice of what appeared to the mouse to be the brighter box. If this were not true, how are the results of Table 16 to be accounted for?

TABLE 16

YELLOW-RED TESTS

In Color Discrimination Box with 6 by 3 cm. Pieces of Hering Papers at Entrances to Boxes

No. 2

SERIES	DATE 1906	RIGHT (YELLOW)	WRONG (RED)
1	Jan. 16	1	9
2	17	3	7
3	18	4	6
4	19	5	5
5	20	5	5

[1] These were the only Hering papers used in my experiments.

Without further mention of the many experiments which were necessary for the perfecting of this method of testing color vision, I may at once present the final results of the tests which were made with reflected light. These tests were made with the discrimination apparatus in essentially the same way as were the brightness discrimination tests of Chapter VII.

In all of the color experiments, unless otherwise stated, a series of ten tests each day was given, until satisfactory evidence of discrimination or proof of the lack of the ability to discriminate had been obtained. The difficulties of getting conclusive evidence in either direction will be considered in connection with the results themselves. For all of these tests with reflected light the Milton Bradley colored papers were used. These colored papers were pasted on white cardboard carriers. I shall designate, in the Bradley nomenclature, the papers used in each experiment.

With colored cardboards inside the electric-boxes as well as at their entrances (see Figure 14 for position of cardboards) blue-orange tests were given to Nos. 2 and 3 until they discriminated perfectly. The papers were Bradley's blue tint No. 1 and orange. Number 2 was perfect in the twelfth series (Table 17), No 3 in the fourteenth and again in the sixteenth. They were then tested with a special brightness check series which was intended by the experimenter to reveal any dependence upon a possible brightness difference rather than upon the color difference of the boxes.

The nature of this brightness check series, as well as the results which No. 2 gave when tested by it, may be appreciated readily by reference to Table 18. Tint No. 1 of the blue, which is considerably brighter, in my judgment, than the Bradley blue, was replaced at intervals in this series by the latter. For it was thought that in case the mouse were

TABLE 17

LIGHT BLUE-ORANGE TESTS IN COLOR DISCRIMINATION BOX

SERIES	DATE 1906	No. 2		No. 3	
		RIGHT (LIGHT BLUE)	WRONG (ORANGE)	RIGHT (LIGHT BLUE)	WRONG (ORANGE)
1	Jan. 26	7	3	1	9
2	27	7	3	5	5
3	28	7	3	6	4
4	29	7	3	7	3
5	30	7	3	4	6
6	31	10	0	7	3
7	Feb. 1	9	1	7	3
8	2	8	2	6	4
9	3	9	1	9	1
10	5	7	3	5	5
11	6	8	2	5	5
12	7	10	0	5	5
Special brightness check series (see Table 18)					
13	8	10	0	7	3
Special light blue-dark blue series					
14	9	8	2	10	0
15	10	9	1	9	1
Special light blue-dark blue series					
16	11	9	1	10	0
				Special brightness check series	
17	12	10	0	9	1

choosing the blue of the series because it seemed brighter than the orange, this substitution might mislead it into choosing the orange. These blues are referred to in the table as light blue (tint No. 1) and dark blue (standard blue). Again a change in the opposite direction was made by substituting Bradley red for orange. As this was for the human eye the substitution of a color whose brightness was considerably less than that of the orange, it seemed possible that the mouse, if it had formed the habit of choosing the box which seemed the darker, might by this change be misled into choosing the red instead of the light blue. In a word, changes in the conditions of the experiments were made in such a way

TABLE 18

LIGHT BLUE-ORANGE

Brightness check series   Mouse No. 2, Series 13

Feb. 8, 1906

TEST	CONDITION	RIGHT	WRONG
1	Light blue on right Orange on left	Right	—
2	Light blue on left Orange on right	Right	—
3	Light blue on right Red substituted for orange	Right	—
4	Light blue on left Red substituted for orange	Right	—
5	Dark blue on right Orange on left	Right	—
6	Dark blue on right Orange on left	Right	—
7	Dark blue on left Orange on right	Right	—
8	Dark blue on right Red substituted for orange	Right	—
9	Dark blue on left Red substituted for orange	Right	—
10	Dark blue on left Red substituted for orange	Right	—
	Totals	10	0

that now one color, now the other, appeared to be the brighter. But I did not attempt to exclude brightness discrimination on the part of the mouse by dependence upon the human judgment of brightness equality, for it is manifestly unsafe to assume that two colors which are of the same brightness for the human eye have a like relation for the eye of the dancer or of any other animal. My tests of color vision have been conducted without other reference to human standards of judgment or comparisons than was necessary for the description of the experimental conditions. In planning the experiments I assumed neither likeness nor difference between the human retinal processes and those of the dancer. It was my purpose to discover the nature of the mouse's visual discriminative ability.

As is indicated in the tables, neither the substitution of dark blue for light blue, nor the replacement of the orange by red or dark blue rendered correct choice impossible, although certain of the combinations did render choice extremely difficult. In other words, despite all of the changes which were made in the brightness of the cardboards in connection with the light blue-orange tests, the mice continued to make almost perfect records. What are we to conclude from this? Either that the ability to discriminate certain colors is possessed by the dancer, or that for some reason the tests are unsatisfactory. If it be granted that the possibility of brightness discrimination was excluded in the check series, the first of these alternatives apparently is forced upon us. That such a possibility was not excluded, later experiments make perfectly clear. The fact was that not even in the check series was the brightness value of the orange as great as that of the blue. Consequently the mice may have chosen the brighter box each time while apparently choosing the blue.

Although conclusive proof of the truth of this statement is furnished only by later experiments, the results of the light blue-orange series, as given in Table 17, strongly suggest such a possibility. Mouse No. 3 had not been experimented with previous to these color discrimination tests. Her preference for the orange, which in the case of the first series was 9 to 1, consequently demands an explanation. If she had been trained previously to choose the white instead of the black, as was true of No. 2, it might be inferred that she went to the orange box because it appeared brighter than the blue. As this explanation is not available, we are driven back upon the results of the white-black preference tests in Chapter VII, which proved that many dancers prefer the black to the white. This may mean that they prefer the lower degree of brightness or illumination, and if so it might be argued, in turn, that the orange was chosen by No. 3 because it appeared darker than the blue. Since, as has already been stated, the orange was far brighter for me than the blue, this would also mean that the brightness values of different colors are not the same for man and mouse.

Practically the same kind of color tests as those described for Nos. 2 and 3 were given to Nos. 1000 and 5. The results appear in Table 19. These tests followed upon the formation of a habit to choose white instead of black (that is, the greater brightness). From the first both No. 1000 and No. 5 chose the light blue in preference to the orange or the red. It therefore seems probable that the former was considerably brighter than the latter. Number 1000, to be sure, was led into three erroneous choices by the brightness check series (series 7), but, on the other hand, No. 5 was not at all disturbed in her choices by similar check tests. It seems natural to conclude from these facts that both of these mice chose the blue at first because of its relatively greater brightness, and that they continued to do so for the same reason. In other words, their behavior indicates that the brightness check tests were valueless because not enough allowance had been made for the possible differences between the vision of mouse and man.

TABLE 19

Light Blue-Orange and Dark Blue-Red Tests

Series	Date	Condition	No. 1000		No. 5	
			Right (Light Blue or Dark Blue)	Wrong (Orange or Red)	Right (Light Blue or Dark Blue)	Wrong (Orange or Red)
1	Jan. 25	Blue-red	8	2	10	.0
2	26	Blue-red or				
		Light blue-orange	10	0	10	0
3	27	Light blue-orange	10	0	5	5
4	29	Light blue-orange	9	1	8	2
5	30	Light blue-orange	10	0	8	2
6	31	Light blue-orange	10	0	10	0
7	Feb. 1	Light blue-orange or				
		Dark blue-red	7	3	10	0

If only the final results of my experiments with the dancer and the conclusions to which they lead were of interest, all of this description of experiments which served merely to clear the ground and thus make possible crucial tests might be omitted. It has seemed to me, however, that the history of the investigation is valuable, and I am therefore presenting the evolution of my methods step by step. To be sure, not every detail of this process can be mentioned, and only a few of the individual results can be stated, but my purpose will have been fulfilled if I succeed in showing how one method of experimentation pointed the way to another, and

L

how one set of results made possible the interpretation of others.

As the results of my color vision experiments seemed to indicate that the red end of the spectrum appears much darker to the dancer than to us, tests were now arranged with colors from adjacent regions of the spectrum, green and blue. The papers used were the Bradley green and tint No. 1 of the blue. They were not noticeably different in brightness for the human eye. Green marked the box to be chosen. Three of the individuals which had previously been used in the light blue-orange series, and which therefore had perfect habits of going to the light blue, were used for the green-light blue tests. Of these individuals, No. 1000 became inactive on the fifth day of the experiment, and the tests with him were discontinued. Twenty series were given to each of the other mice, with the results which appear in Table 20. To begin with, both No. 4 and No. 5 exhibited a preference for the light blue, as a result of the previous light blue-orange training. As this preference was gradually destroyed by the electric shock which was received each time the light blue box was entered, they seemed utterly at a loss to know which box to enter. Occasionally a record of six, seven, or even eight right choices would be made in a series, but in no case was this unquestionably due to color discrimination; usually it could be explained in the light of the order of the changes in the positions of the cardboards. For example, series 9, in which No. 5 made a record of 8 right and 2 wrong, had green on the right for the first three tests. The animal happened to choose correctly in the first test, and continued to do so three times in succession simply because there was no change in the position of the cardboards. I have occasionally observed a record of seven right choices result when it was perfectly evident to the observer that the mouse could not discriminate visually. It was to avoid unsafe conclusions and unfair comparisons, as the result of such misleading series, that three perfect series in succession were required as evidence of a perfectly formed habit of discrimination.

TABLE 20

GREEN-LIGHT BLUE TESTS

SERIES	DATE 1906	No. 1000		No. 4		No. 5	
		RIGHT (GREEN)	WRONG (BLUE)	RIGHT (GREEN)	WRONG (BLUE)	RIGHT (GREEN)	WRONG (BLUE)
1	Feb. 3	2	8	3	7	3	7
2	5	7	3	5	5	5	5
3	6	5	5	6	4	5	5
4	7	5	5	5	5	5	5
5	8	2	8	5	5	4	6
6	9			7	3	7	3
7	10			4	6	3	7
8	10			6	4	4	6
9	12			6	4	8	2
10	13			6	4	6	4
11	14			5	5	3	7
12	15			6	4	7	3
13	16			5	5	7	3
14	17			3	7	6	4
15	19			6	4	6	4
16	20			7	3	5	5
17	21			4	6	8	2
18	22			3	7	4	6
19	23			6	4	4	6
20	24			6	4	5	5

Twenty series, 200 tests for each of the individuals in the experiment, yielded no evidence whatever of the dancer's ability to tell green from blue. As it has already been proved that they readily learn to choose the right box under discriminable conditions, it seems reasonable to conclude either

that they lack green-blue vision, or that they have it in a
relatively undeveloped state.

If it be objected that the number of training tests given was
too small, and that the dancer probably would exhibit discrimination if it were given 1000 instead of 200 tests in such
an experiment, I must reply that the behavior of the animal
in the tests is even more satisfactory evidence of its inability
to choose than are the results of Table 20. Had there been
the least indication of improvement as the result of 200 tests,
I should have continued the experiment; as a matter of fact,
the mice each day hesitated more and more before choosing,
and fought against being driven toward the entrance to the experiment box. That they were helpless was so evident that it
would have been manifestly cruel to continue the experiment.

TABLE 21

VIOLET-RED TESTS

With Odor of All Cardboards the Same

SERIES	DATE	No. 7		No. 998	
		RIGHT (VIOLET)	WRONG (RED)	RIGHT (VIOLET)	WRONG (RED)
A	Mar. 7	8	2	5	5
B	7	3	7	2	8
1	14	3	7	6	4
2	15	4	6	4	6
3	16	5	5	5	5
4	19	4	6	4	6
5	20	5	5	6	4
6	21	4	6	8	2
7	22	8	2	4	6
8	23	4	6	6	4
9	24	6	4	4	6
10	25	4	6	6	4

Further color tests with reflected light were made with violet and red. Two dancers, Nos. 998 and 7, neither of which had been in any experiment previously, were subjected to the ten series of tests whose results are to be found in Table 21. In this experiment the cardboards used had been coated with shellac to obviate discrimination by means of odor. It is therefore impossible to give a precise description of the color or brightness by referring to the Bradley papers.[1] Both the violet and the red were rendered darker, and apparently less saturated, by the coating.

These violet-red tests were preceded by two series of preference tests (*A* and *B*), in which no shock was given and escape was possible through either electric-box. Although the results of these preference tests as they appear in Table 21 seem to indicate a preference for the red on the part of No. 998, examination of the record sheets reveals the fact that neither animal exhibited color preference, but that instead both chose by position. Number 998 chose the box on the right 15 times in 20, and No. 7 chose the box on the left 15 times in 20.

Ten series of tests with the violet-red cardboards failed to furnish the least indication of discrimination. The experiment was discontinued because the mice had ceased to try to discriminate and dashed into one or the other of the boxes on the chance of guessing correctly. When wrong they whirled about, rushed out of the red box and into the violet immediately. They had learned perfectly as much as they were able to learn of what the experiment required of them. Although we are not justified in concluding from this experiment that dancers cannot be taught to distinguish violet from red, there certainly is good ground for the statement

---

[1] The violet was darker than Bradley's shade No. 2, and the red was lighter than Bradley's red.

that they do not readily discriminate between these colors.

The experiments on color vision which have been described and the records which have been presented will suffice to give the reader an accurate knowledge of the nature of the results, only a few of which could be printed, and of the methods by which they were obtained.

In brief, these results show that the dancer, under the conditions of the experiments, is not able to tell green from blue, or violet from red. The evidence of discrimination furnished by the light blue-orange tests is not satisfactory because the conditions of the experiment did not permit the use of a sufficiently wide range of brightnesses. It is obvious, therefore, that a method of experimentation should be devised in which the experimenter can more fully control the brightness of the colors which he is using. I shall now describe a method in which this was possible.

CHAPTER X

The Sense of Sight: Color Vision (*Continued*)

There are three well-known ways in which colors may be used as stimuli in experiments on animals: by the use of colored papers (reflected light); by the use of a prism (the spectrum which is obtained may be used as directly transmitted or as reflected light); and by the use of light filters (transmitted light). In the experiments on the color vision of the dancer which have thus far been described only the first of these three methods has been employed. Its advantages are that it enables the experimenter to work in a sunlit room, with relatively simple, cheap, and easily manipulated apparatus. Its chief disadvantages are that the brightness of the light can neither be regulated nor measured with ease and accuracy. The use of the second method, which in many respects is the most desirable of the three, is impracticable for experiments which require as large an illuminated region as do those with the mouse; I was therefore limited to the employment of light filters in my further tests of color discrimination.

The form of filter which is most conveniently handled is the colored glass, but unfortunately few glasses which are monochromatic are manufactured. Almost all of our so-called colored glasses transmit the light of two or more regions of the spectrum. After making spectroscopic examinations of all the colored glasses which were available, I decided that only the ruby glass could be satisfactorily used in my experiments. With this it was possible to get a pure red. Each of the other colors was obtained by means of a filter, which consisted of a glass box filled with a chemical solution which transmitted light of a certain wave length.

For the tests with transmitted light the apparatus of Figures 20 and 21 was constructed. It consisted of a re-action-box essentially the same as that used in the brightness vision tests, except that holes were cut in the ends of the electric-boxes, at the positions *G* and *R* of Figure 20, to per-mit the light to enter the boxes. Beyond the reaction-box was a long light-box which was divided lengthwise into two compartments by a partition in the middle. A slit in the cover of each of these compartments carried an incandescent lamp *L* (Figure 20). Between the two lamps, *L, L,* and directly over the partition in the light-box was fastened a millimeter scale, *S,* by means of which the experimenter could determine the position of the lights with reference to the reaction-box. The light-box was separated from the reaction-box by a space 6 cm. wide in which moved a narrow wooden carrier for the filter boxes. This carrier, as shown in Figure 20, could be moved readily from side to side through a distance of 20 cm. The filter boxes, which are represented in place in Figures 20 and 21, consisted of three parallel-sided glass boxes 15 cm. long, 5 cm. wide, and 15 cm. deep. Each box contained a substance which acted as a ray filter. Tightly fitted glass covers prevented the entrance of dust and the evaporation of the solutions in the boxes. Figures 20 and 21 represent the two end boxes, *R, R,* as red light filters and the middle one, *G,* as a green light filter. Three filters were used thus side by side in order that the position of a given color with reference to the electric-boxes might be changed readily. As the apparatus was arranged, all the experimenter had to do when he wished to change from

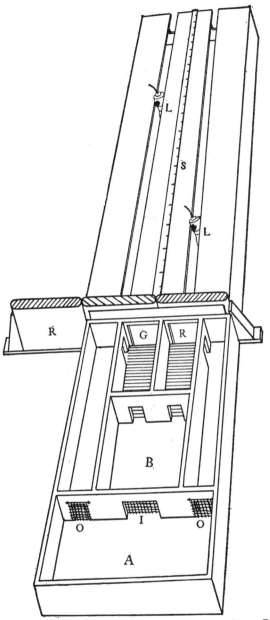

FIGURE 20. — Color discrimination apparatus. *A,* nest-box; *B,* entrance chamber; *R, R,* red filters; *G,* green filter; *L, L,* incandescent lamps in light-box; *S,* millimeter scale on light-box; *I,* door between *A* and *B; O, O,* doors between alleys and *A.*

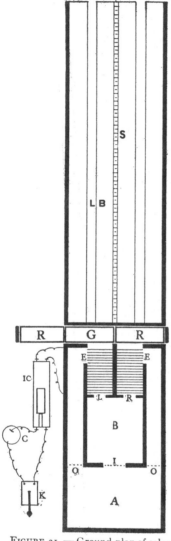

FIGURE 21. — Ground plan of color discrimination apparatus. *E, E,* exits from electric-boxes. *LB,* light-box; *R, G, R,* filter boxes on carrier; *L,* left electric-box; *R,* right electric-box; *IC,* induction apparatus; *C,* electric cell; *K,* key; *S,* millimeter scale.

green-left, red-right to green-right, red-left was to push the carrier towards the right until the green filter covered the hole on the right at the end of the electric-box. When this had been accomplished the red filter at the left end of the carrier covered the hole on the left at the end of the electric-box. Thus quickly, noiselessly, easily, and without introducing any other change in conditions than that of the interchange of lights, the experimenter was able to shift the positions of his colored lights at will.

In the tests which are now to be reported, three portions of the spectrum were used: the red end, the blue-violet end, and a middle region, chiefly green. The red light was obtained by the use of a filter which was made by placing two plates of ruby glass in one of the glass boxes, filling the box with filtered water and then sealing it to prevent evaporation. The blue-violet was obtained by the use of a filter box which contained a 5 per cent solution of copper ammonium sulphate. The green, which, however, was not monochromatic, was obtained by the use of a filter box which contained a saturated solution of nickel nitrate. These three sets of filters were examined spectroscopically both before the experiments had been made and after their completion.[1] The red filters, of which I had two for shifting the lights, transmitted only red light. The blue-violet filters, two also, at first appeared to transmit only portions of the blue and violet of the spectrum, but my later examination revealed a trace of green. It is important to note, however, that the red and the blue-violet filters were mutually exclusive in the portions of the spectrum which they transmitted. Of all the filters used the green finally proved the least satisfactory. I detected some yellow and blue in addition to green in my first examination, and later I discovered a trace of red. Apparently the transmitting power of the solutions changed slightly during the course of the experiments. On this account certain solutions are undesirable for experiments on color vision, for one must be certain of the constancy of the condition of stimulation. It is to be understood, of course, that each of the three filters transmitted, so far as the eye is concerned, only the color named. I consider the red filter perfectly satisfactory, the blue-violet very good, and the green poor Henceforth, in testing color vision in animals, I shall make use of colored glasses as filters, if it is in any way possible to obtain or have manufactured blue, green, and yellow glasses which are as satisfactory as the ruby.

The apparatus needs no further description, as its other important features were identical with those of the reflected light experiment box. The use of artificial light for the illumination of the electric-boxes made it necessary to conduct all of the following tests in a dark-room. The method

[1] A Janssen-Hoffman spectroscope was used.

of experimentation was practically the same as that already described. A mouse which had been placed in *A* by the experimenter was permitted to enter *B* and thence to return to *A* by entering one of the electric-boxes, the red or blue or green one, as the case might be. Mistakes in choice were punished by an electric shock. One further point in the method demands description and discussion before the results of the tests are considered, namely, the manner of regulating and measuring the brightness of the lights.

Regulating brightness with this apparatus was easy enough; measuring it accurately was extremely difficult. The experimenter was able to control the brightness of each of the two colored lights which he was using by changing the position or the power of the incandescent lamps in the light-box. The position of a lamp could be changed easily between tests simply by moving it along toward or away from the electric-box in the slit which served as a lamp carrier. As the distance from the entrances of the electric-boxes to the further end of the light-box was 120 cm., a considerable range or variation in brightness was possible without change of lamps. Ordinarily it was not necessary to change the power of the lamps, by replacing one of a given candle power by a higher or lower, during a series of tests. Both the candle power of the lamps and their distance from the filters were recorded in the case of each test, but for the convenience of the reader I have reduced these measurements to candle meters [1] and report them thus in the descriptions of the experiments.

But measuring the actual brightness of the red light or the green light which was used for a particular series of tests, and the variations in their brightnesses, was not so simple a matter as might appear from the statements which have just been made. The influence of the light filters themselves

---

[1] The illuminating power of a standard candle at a distance of one meter.

upon the brightness must be taken into account. The two red filters were alike in their influence upon the light which entered them, for they were precisely alike in construction, and the same was true of the two blue-violet filters. The same kind of ruby glass was placed in each of the former, and a portion of the same solution of copper ammonium sulphate was put into each of the filter boxes for the latter. But it is difficult to say what relation the diminution in brightness caused by a red filter bore to that caused by a blue-violet or a green filter. My only means of comparison was my eye, and as subjective measurement was unsatisfactory for the purposes of the experiment, no attempt was made to equalize the amounts of brightness reduction caused by the several filters. So far as the value of the tests themselves, as indications of the condition of color vision in the dancer is concerned, I have no apology for this lack of measurement, but I do regret my inability to give that accurate objective statement of brightness values which would enable another experimenter with ease and certainty to repeat my tests. The nearest approach that it is possible for me to make to such an objective measurement is a statement of the composition and thickness of the filters and of the candle-meter value of the light when it entered the filter. The distance from this point to the entrance to the electric-box was 20 cm.

To sum up and state clearly the method of defining the brightness of the light in the following experiments: the candle-meter value of each light by which an electric-box was illuminated, as determined by the use of a Lummer-Brodhun photometer and measurements of the distance of the source of light from the filter, is given in connection with each of the experiments. This brightness value less the diminution caused by the passage of the light through a filter, which has been defined as to composition and thickness of the layer of solution, gives that degree of brightness by which the electric-box was illuminated.

Tests of the dancer's ability to discriminate green and blue [1] in the transmitted light apparatus were made with four animals. An incandescent lamp marked 16-candle-power was set in each of the light-boxes. These lamps were then so placed that the green and the blue seemed to be of equal brightness to three persons who were asked to compare them carefully. Their candle-meter values in the positions selected were respectively 18 and 64, as appears from the statement of conditions at the top of Table 22.

TABLE 22

GREEN-BLUE TESTS

Brightnesses Equal for Human Eye

Green 18 candle meters   Blue 64 candle meters

SERIES	DATE 1906	No. 10		No. 11	
		RIGHT (GREEN)	WRONG (BLUE)	RIGHT (GREEN)	WRONG (BLUE)
A and B [2]	April 2	10	10	12	8
1	3	6	4	5	5
2	4	5	5	6	4
3	5	5	5	5	5
4	6	5	5	5	5
5	7	7	3	5	5
6	8	7	3	3	7
7	9	7	3	5	5
8	10	3	7	7	3
9	11	5	5	4	6
10	12	5	5	6	4

[1] Hereafter the light transmitted by the blue-violet filter will be referred to for convenience as blue.

[2] A single preference series of twenty tests.

Numbers 10 and 11 exhibited no preference for either of these colors in the series of 20 tests which preceded the training tests, and neither of them gave evidence of ability to discriminate as the result of ten series of training tests. In this case, again, the behavior of the animals was as strongly against the inference that they can tell green from blue as are the records of choices which appear in the table. Granted, that they are unable to discriminate green from ·blue when these colors are of about the same brightness for the human eye, what results when they differ markedly in brightness? Table 23 furnishes a definite answer to this question. Numbers 5 and 12 were given eight series of green-blue tests with each light at 18 candle meters. Little, if any, evidence of discrimination appeared. Then, on the supposition that the difference was not great enough for easy discrimination, the blue light was reduced almost to 0, the green being left at 18. The tests (series 9) immediately indicated discrimination. For series 10 the green was made 64 candle meters, the blue 18, and again there was discrimination. These results were so conclusively indicative of the lack of color vision and the presence of brightness vision, that there appeared to be no need of continuing the experiment further.

Accepting provisionally the conclusion that the dancers cannot tell green from blue except by brightness differences, we may proceed to inquire whether they can discriminate other colors. Are green and red distinguishable?

Green-red discrimination now was tested by a method which it was hoped might from the first prevent dependence upon brightness. The light in the light-box on the left was so placed that it had a value of 18 candle meters, that in the light-box on the right so that it had a value of 1800 candle meters. Neither light was moved during the first four series of the green-red tests which were given to Nos. 151 and 152.

TABLE 23

GREEN-BLUE TESTS

Brightnesses Different for Human Eye

Green 18 candle meters   Blue 18 candle meters

SERIES	DATE 1906	No. 5		No. 12	
		RIGHT (GREEN)	WRONG (BLUE)	RIGHT (GREEN)	WRONG (BLUE)
1	April 10	6	4	5	5
2	11	5	5	7	3
3	12	6	4	7	3
4	13	4	6	7	3
5	14	7	3	5	5
6	15	4	6	6	4
7	16	6	4	8	2
8	17	5	5	4	6

As it was now evident that the intensity difference was not sufficient to render discrimination easy, the blue was reduced to 0, and the green left at 18.

9	17	7	3	8	2

Now the brightnesses were made, green 64, blue 18, just the reverse of those of series of Table 22.

10	17	8	2	8	2

Each of these series consisted of 20 tests instead of 10. As a result of the arrangement of the lights just mentioned, the green appeared to me very much brighter than the red when it was on the right and very much darker when it was on the left. If this were true for the mouse also, it is difficult to see how it could successfully depend upon brightness for guidance in its choices. Such dependence would cause it to choose now the green, now the red.

The first four series of green-red tests so clearly demonstrated discrimination, of some sort, that it was at once necessary to alter the conditions of the experiment. The only criticism of the above method of excluding brightness discrimination, of which I could think, was that the red at no time had been brighter than the green. In other words, that despite a value of 1800 candle meters for the red and only 18 candle meters for the green, the latter still appeared the brighter to the mouse. To meet this objection, I made the extreme brightness values 1 and 1800 candle meters in some of the later series, of which the results appear in Table 24. From day to day different degrees of brightness were used, as is indicated in the second column of the table. Instead of having first one color and then the other the brighter, after the fourth series I changed the position of the lights each time the position of the filters was changed; hence, the table states a certain brightness value for each color instead of for each electric-box.

Series 5 to 14 so clearly indicated discrimination, that it seemed necessary to devise some other means than that of changing the brightnesses of the colored lights themselves to test the assumption that the animals were choosing the brighter light. I therefore removed the light filters so that the colors which had been present as conditions of discrimination were lacking, and arranged the apparatus so that first one box, then the other, was illuminated the more brightly. The purpose of this was to discover whether as the result of their green-red training the mice had acquired the habit of choosing uniformly either the lighter or the darker box. One series was given under the conditions of illumination specified in Table 24 with the result that the brighter box was chosen eight times in ten by No. 151 and every time by No. 152. Since neither of these individuals had previously been trained by white-black tests to go to the white, and since, furthermore, the dancers usually manifest a slight preference for the lower

M

instead of the higher illumination, this result may be interpreted as indicative of dependence upon brightness in the
previous color tests. It looks very much indeed as if the
green had been chosen, not because of its greenness, but on
account of its relatively greater brightness.

This test of brightness preference was followed by two
series, 16 and 17, under conditions similar to those of the
first four series of the table. For series 16 the value of the
light in the left box was 1 candle meter, that of the light in
the right box 1800 candle meters. Discrimination was perfect. For series 17 the value for the left remained at 1 candle
meter, but that of the right box was decreased to 0. In this
series No. 152 was entirely at a loss to know which box to
choose. Of course this was an entirely new set of conditions
for choice, namely, a colored box, the green or the red as the
case might be, beside a dark box, the one which was not
illuminated. If the mice really had been choosing correctly
because of a habit of avoiding the red or of seeking the green,
this method should bring out the fact, for the red box, since
with it the disagreeable electric shock had always been associated, should be a box to be avoided. For No. 151 this
seemed to be the case.

Series 23 to 27 of Table 24 were given as final and crucial
tests of the relation of brightness discrimination to color discrimination. As it is not possible to express in a simple
formula the conditions of the tests, a sample series which
indicates the brightness of the colors in each of the twenty
tests of a series, and in addition the results given by No. 151
in the first of these final series, is reproduced in Table 25.
For an animal which had presumably learned perfectly to
choose green in preference to red, the record of 8 mistakes
in 20 choices as a result of changes in relative brightness is
rather bad, and it renders doubtful the existence of color
discrimination in any of these experiments. No. 152 showed

TABLE 24

GREEN-RED TESTS

Brightnesses Extremely Different for Human Eye

Intensities are given in candle meters (c.m.)

SERIES	DATE	CONDITIONS	No. 151		No. 152	
			RIGHT (GREEN)	WRONG (RED)	RIGHT (GREEN)	WRONG (RED)
1	April 26	18 c.m. on left 1800 c.m. on right	11	9	7	13
2	27	Same	16	4	16	4
3	28	Same	20	0	17	3
4	29	Same	19	1	19	1
5	30	Green 18 c.m. Red 18 c.m.	9	1	10	0
6	30	Green 64 c.m. Red 18 c.m.	9	1	8	2
7	May 1	Green 6 c.m. Red 1500 c.m.	7	3	9	1
8	1	Green 4 c.m. Red 1500 c.m.	8	2	7	3
9	2	Both varied from 4 to 1500 c.m.	18	2	18	2
10	3	Green 2 c.m. Red 1800 c.m.	6	4	7	3
11	3	Same	10	0	10	0
12	4	Same	7	3	8	2
13	4	Same	8	2	6	4
14	5	Green 1 c.m. Red 1800 c.m.	19	1	19	1

Filters were now removed. An illumination of 15 c.m. was established on one side and an illumination of 0 on the other side, in order to ascertain whether the mice would choose the brighter box. This was done to test the assumption that the green in the previous tests had always appeared brighter to the mice than did the red, and that in consequence they had chosen the brighter box instead of the green box.

TABLE 24 — CONTINUED

SERIES	DATE	CONDITIONS	No. 151		No. 152	
			RIGHT (GREEN)	WRONG (RED)	RIGHT (GREEN)	WRONG (RED)
15	May 5	Brighter 15 c.m. Darker 0 c.m.	8[1]	2[2]	10[1]	0[2]
16	5	1 c.m. on left 1800 c.m. on right	10	0	10	0
17	5	1 c.m. on left 0 c.m. on right	9	1	4	6
18	8	˙Green 18 c.m. Red 18 c.m.	19	1	17	3
19	9	Same	9	1	9	1
20	9	Same	10	0	10	0
21	10	Same	10	0	10	0
22	11	Same	10	0	10	0
23	June 1	Both varied from 1 to 1800 c.m.	12	8	10	10
24	2	Same	18	2	14	6
25	3	Both varied from 2 to 1800 c.m.	19	1	17	3
26	4	Same	17	3	17	3
27	5	Same	18	2	18	2

no ability whatever to choose the green in the first of the series (series 23 of Table 24) of which that of Table 25 is a sample. His record, 10 mistakes in 20 choices, was even poorer than that of No. 151. That both of these mice learned to choose fairly accurately in these final tests is shown by the results of series 24, 25, 26, and 27. I must admit, however, that these records indicate little ability on the part of the animals to discriminate colors.

These long-continued and varied tests with Nos. 151 and

[1] Brighter.   [2] Darker.

152 revealed three facts: that the mice depend chiefly upon brightness differences in visual discrimination; that they probably have something which corresponds to our red-green vision, although their color experience may be totally unlike ours; and that the red end of the spectrum seems much darker to them than to us, or, in other words, that the least refrangible rays are of lower stimulating value for them than for us.

So many of the results of my color experiments have

TABLE 25

GREEN-RED TESTS

June 1, 1906 No. 151

Test	Position	Brightness Values in Candle Meters		Right (Green)	Wrong (Red)
1	Green on left	Green 4,	Red 448	Right	—
2	Green on right	Green 448,	Red 4	Right	—
3	Green on right	Green 4,	Red 448	Right	—
4	Green on left	Green 448,	Red 4	Right	—
5	Green on left	Green 3,	Red 1800	—	Wrong
6	Green on right	Green 1800,	Red 3	—	Wrong
7	Green on right	Green 3,	Red 1800	—	Wrong
8	Green on left	Green 1800,	Red 3	Right	—
9	Green on right	Green 5,	Red 34	Right	—
10	Green on left	Green 34,	Red 5	Right	—
11	Green on right	Green 6,	Red 74	Right	—
12	Green on left	Green 74,	Red 6	Right	—
13	Green on left	Green 4,	Red 448	—	Wrong
14	Green on right	Green 448,	Red 4	Right	—
15	Green on right	Green 4,	Red 448	—	Wrong
16	Green on left	Green 448,	Red 4	Right	—
17	Green on right	Green 3,	Red 1800	—	Wrong
18	Green on left	Green 1800,	Red 3	—	Wrong
19	Green on right	Green 1800,	Red 3	—	Wrong
20	Green on left	Green 3,	Red 1800	Right	—
	Totals			12	8

indicated the all-important role of brightness vision that I have hesitated to interpret any of them as indicative of true color discrimination. But after I had made all the variations in brightness by which it seemed reasonable to suppose that the mouse would be influenced under ordinary conditions, and after I had introduced all the check tests which seemed worth while, there still remained so large a proportion of correct choices that I was forced to admit the influence of the quality as well as of the intensity of the visual stimulus.

The first of the facts mentioned above, that brightness discrimination is more important in the life of the mouse than color discrimination, is attested by almost all of the experiments whose results have been reported. The second fact, namely, that the dancer possesses something which for the present we may call red-green vision, also has been proved in a fairly satisfactory manner by both the reflected and the transmitted light experiments. I wish now to present, in Table 26, results which strikingly prove the truth of the statement that red appears darker to the dancer than to us.

The brightness conditions which appeared to make the discrimination between green and red most difficult were, so far as my experiments permit the measurement thereof, green from 1 to 4 candle meters with red from 1200 to 1600. Under these conditions the red appeared extremely bright, the green very dark, to the human subject.

According to the description of conditions in Table 26, Nos. 2 and 5 were required to distinguish green from red with the former about 3 candle meters in brightness and the latter about 1800 candle meters. In the eighth series of 20 tests, each of these animals made a perfect record. As it seemed possible that they had learned to go to the darker of the two boxes instead of to the green box, I arranged the following check test. The filters were removed, the illumination of one electric-box was made 74 candle meters, that of the other 3, and the changes of the lighter box from left to right were made at irregular intervals. In February, No. 2 had been trained to go to the black in black-white tests, and at the same time No. 5 had been trained to go to the white in white-black tests. The results of these brightness check tests, as they appear in the table, series 8 *a*, are indeed striking. Number 2 chose the darker box each time; No. 5 chose it eight times out of ten. Were it not for the fact that memory tests four weeks after his black-white training had proved that No. 2 had entirely lost the influence of his previous experience (he chose white nine times out of ten in the memory series), it might reasonably be urged that this individual chose the darker box because of his experience in the black-white experiment. And what can be said

TABLE 26

GREEN-RED TESTS

Brightnesses Different for Human Eye

SERIES	DATE	BRIGHTNESS VALUES	No. 2		No. 5	
			RIGHT (GREEN)	WRONG (RED)	RIGHT (GREEN)	WRONG (RED)
I	May 7	Green 3 c.m. Red 1800 c.m.	10	10	12	8
2	8	Same	12	8	11	9
3	9	Same	15	5	14	6
4	10	Same	18	2	12	8
5	11	Same	18	2	14	6
6	12	Same	19	1	16	4
7	13	Same	19	1	18	2
8	14	Same	20	0	20	0

Brightness tests without colors were now given to determine whether the mice had been choosing the brighter or the darker instead of the green.

TABLE 26 — CONTINUED

SERIES	DATE	BRIGHTNESS VALUES	No. 2		No. 5	
			RIGHT (GREEN)	WRONG (RED)	RIGHT (GREEN)	WRONG (RED)
8a	14	Brighter 74 c.m. Darker 3 c.m.	0[1]	10[2]	2[1]	8[2]
9	15	3 c.m. on left 1800 c.m. on right	8	12	16	4
10	16	4 c.m. on left 36 c.m. on right	5	5	7	3
11	16	Green 4 c.m. Red 36 c.m.	9	1	8	2
12	17	11 c.m. on left 1800 c.m. on right	7	3	6	4
13	17	Green 11 c.m. Red 1800 c.m.	9	1	8	2
14	18	Mixed values 3 to 1800 c.m.	7	3	8	2
15	19	Same	7	3	7	3
16	20	Same	7	3	7	3
17	21	Same	7	3	9	1
18	22	Same	9	1	8	2
19	23	Same	7	3	9	1
20	24	Same	10	0	8	2
21	25	Same	10	0	9	1
22	26	Same	9	1	10	0

in explanation of the choices of No. 5? I can think of no more reasonable way of accounting for this most unexpected result of the brightness tests than the assumption that both of these animals had learned to discriminate by brightness difference instead of by color.

Immediately after the brightness series, the influence of making first one color, then the other, the brighter was studied.

[1] Brighter.   [2] Darker.

Throughout series 9 the brightness value of the left box remained 3 candle meters, that of the right side 1800 candle meters. Number 2 was so badly confused by this change that his mistakes in this series numbered 12; No. 5 made only 4 incorrect choices. Then series after series was given under widely differing conditions of illumination. The expression "mixed values," which occurs in Table 26 in connection with series 14 to 22 inclusive, means that the brightnesses of the green and the red boxes were changed from test to test in much the way indicated by the sample series of Table 25. In view of the results of these 22 series, 320 tests for each of two mice, it is evident that the dancer is able to discriminate visually by some other factor than brightness. What this factor is I am not prepared to say. It may be something akin to our color experience, it may be distance effect. No other possibilities occur to me.

Table 26 shows that discrimination was relatively easy for Nos. 2 and 5 with green at 3 candle meters and red at 1800. That their discrimination was made on the basis of the greater brightness of the red, instead of on the basis of color, is indicated by the results of the brightness check series 8a. Increase in the brightness of the green rendered discrimination difficult for a time, but it soon improved, and by no changes in the relative brightness of the two colors was it possible to prevent correct choice.

In addition to giving point to the statement that red appears darker to the dancer than to us, the above experiment shows that the animals depend upon brightness when they can, and that their ability to discriminate color differences is extremely poor, so poor indeed that it is doubtful whether their records are better than those of a totally color blind person would be under similar conditions. Surely in view of such results it is unsafe to claim that the dancer possesses color vision similar to ours.

Perfectly trained as they were, by their prolonged green-red tests, to choose the green, or what in mouse experience corresponds to our green, Nos. 2 and 5 offered an excellent opportunity for further tests of blue-green discrimination. For in view of their previous training there should be no question of preference for the blue or of a tendency to depend upon brightness in the series whose results constitute Table 27.

To begin with, the blue and the green were made quite

TABLE 27

BLUE-GREEN TESTS

SERIES	DATE	BRIGHTNESS VALUES	No. 2		No. 5	
			RIGHT (BLUE)	WRONG (GREEN)	RIGHT (BLUE)	WRONG (GREEN)
1	June 1	Blue 74 c.m.				
		Green 36 c.m.	3	7	3	7
2	2	Same	5	5	4	6
3	3	Same	5	5	6	4
4	4	Same	6	4	3	7
5	5	Same	6	4	5	5
6	6	Blue 21 c.m.				
		Green 21 c.m.	6	4	7	3
7	7	Same	2	8	3	7
8	8	Same	5	5	4	6
9	9	Same	3	7	6	4
10	10	Same	2	8	4	6
11	12	Same	6	4	3	7
12	13	Blue 36 c.m.				
		Green 21 c.m.	3	7	4	6
13	14	Same	5	5		
14	15	Blue 62 c.m.				
		Green 21 c.m.	4	6		
15	16	Same	5	5		
16	17	Same	5	5		
17	18	Same	6	4		

TABLE 27 — CONTINUED

Now, as a final test, blue and green glasses were placed over the electric-boxes, the brightness of the two was equalized for the human eye, and the tests of series 18 and 19 were given to No. 2: —

| | | | No. 2 | |
SERIES	DATE	BRIGHTNESS VALUES	RIGHT (BLUE)	WRONG (GREEN)
18	18	Blue 62 c.m.		
		Green 21 c.m.	4	6
19	19	Same	6	4
20	20	Blue 21 c.m.		
		Green 88 c.m.	2	8

The green was now made much the brighter.

21	21	Blue 21 c.m.		
		Green 1800 c.m.	7	3
22	23	Same	8	2

bright for the human subject, blue 74 candle meters, green 36. Later the brightness of both was first decreased, then increased, in order to ascertain whether discrimination was conditioned by the absolute strength of illumination. No evidence of discrimination was obtained with any of the several conditions of illumination in seventeen series of ten tests each.

On the supposition that the animals were blinded by the brightness of the light which had been used in some of the tests, similar tests were made with weaker light. The results were· the same. I am therefore convinced that the animals did justice to their visual ability in these experiments.

Finally, it seemed possible that looking directly at the source of light might be an unfavorable condition for color discrimination, and that a chamber flooded with colored light from above and from one end would prove more satisfactory.

To test this conjecture two thicknesses of blue glass were placed over one electric-box, two plates of green glass over the other; the incandescent lamps were then fixed in such positions that the blue and the green within the two boxes appeared to the experimenter, as he viewed them from the position at which the mouse made its choice, of the same brightness.

Mouse No. 2 was given two series of tests, series 18 and 19, under these conditions, with the result that he showed absolutely no ability to tell the blue box from the green box. The opportunity was now taken to determine how quickly No. 2 would avail himself of any possibility of discriminating by means of brightness. With the blue at 21 candle meters, the green was increased to about 1800. Immediately discrimination appeared, and in the second series (22 of Table 27) there were only two mistakes.

The results of the blue-green experiments with light transmitted from in front of the animal and from above it are in entire agreement with those of the experiments in which reflected light was used. Since the range of intensities of illumination was sufficiently great to exclude the possibility of blinding and of under illumination, it is necessary to conclude that the dancer does not possess blue-green vision.

Again I must call attention to the fact that the behavior of the mice in these experiments is even more significant of their lack of discriminating ability than are the numerical results of the tables. After almost every series of tests, whether or not it came out numerically in favor of discrimination, I was forced to add the comment, "No satisfactory evidence of discrimination."

We have now examined the results of green-red, green-blue, and blue-green tests. One other important combination of the colors which were used in these experiments is possible, namely, blue-red. This is the most important of all the combinations in view of the results already described, for these colors represent the extremes of the visible spectrum, and might therefore be discriminable, even though those which are nearer together in the spectral series were not.

As is shown by the results in Table 28, no combination of brightnesses rendered correct choice impossible in the case

TABLE 28
BLUE-RED TESTS

SERIES	DATE	BRIGHTNESS VALUES	No. 2		No. 205	
			RIGHT (BLUE)	WRONG (RED)	RIGHT (BLUE)	WRONG (RED)
I	July 31	1800 c.m. on left			6	4
		24 c.m. on right	5	5		
2	Aug. 1	21 c.m. on left			6	4
		1800 c.m. on right	6	4		
3	2	1800 c.m. on left			6	4
		21 c.m. on right	8	2		
4	3	19 c.m. on left			6	4
		1800 c.m. on right	9	1		
5	4	1800 c.m. on left			5	5
		7 c.m. on right	7	3		
6	5	6 c.m. on left			7	3
		1800 c.m. on right	10	0		
7	6	18 c.m. on left			9	1
		74 c.m. on right	10	0		
8	7	1800 c.m. on left			8	2
		7 c.m. on right	8	2		
9	8	7 c.m. on left			8	2
		1800 c.m. on right	7	3		
10	9	Mixed values			9	1
		6 to 1800 c.m.	8	2		
11	10	Blue 3 c.m.			6	4
		Red 1800 c.m.	7	3		

Brightness tests were now made, without the use of colors.

| 11a | 10 | | 4 | 6 | 5 | 5 |

TABLE 28 — CONTINUED

SERIES	DATE	BRIGHTNESS VALUES	No. 2		No. 205	
			RIGHT (BLUE)	WRONG (RED)	RIGHT (BLUE)	WRONG (RED)
12	10	Blue 3 c.m.				
		Red 8 c.m.	4	6	6	4
13	11	Blue 3 c.m.				
		Red 7200 c.m.	8	2	5	5
14	13	Mixed values				
		3 to 7200 c.m.	7	3	7	3
15	13	Same	7	3	9	1
16	14	Blue 3 to 6 c.m.				
		Red 112 to 3650 c.m.	10	0	10	0

Series were now given to test the assumption that red appears dark to the dancer.

SERIES	DATE	BRIGHTNESS VALUES	No. 2		No. 205	
17	14	Darkness on one side				
		Red 3 c.m.	5	5	7	3
18	14	Blue 3 to 3650 c.m.				
		Red 3 to 3650 c.m.	10	0	10	0
19	15	Darkness on one side				
		Red 3 c.m.	5	5	4	6
20	15	Blue 3 to 3650 c.m.				
		Red 3 to 3650 c.m.	10	0	9	1
21	16	Darkness on one side				
		Red 72 c.m.	5	5	7	3
22	16	Darkness on one side				
		Red 1800 c.m.	6	4	10	0

of the blue-red tests which are now to be described. Choice was extremely difficult at times, even more so perhaps than the table would lead one to suppose, and it is quite possible that color played no part in the discrimination. But that brightness difference in the colors was not responsible for whatever success these mice attained in selecting the right box is proved by the brightness-without-color series which follows series 11 of the table. Neither No. 2 nor No. 205 showed preference for the lighter or the darker box. At the end of the sixteenth blue-red series, I was convinced that one of two conclusions must be drawn from the experiment: either the dancers possess a kind of blue-red vision, or red is of such a value for them that no brightness of visible green or blue precisely matches it.

The latter possibility was further tested by an experiment whose results appear in series 17 to 22 inclusive, of Table 28. The conditions of series 17 were a brightness value of 0 in one box (darkness) and in the other red of a brightness of 3 candle meters. Despite the fact that they had been perfectly trained in *blue-red tests* to avoid the red, neither of the mice seemed able to discriminate the red from the darkness and to avoid it. This was followed by a series in which the brightness of both the blue and the red was varied between 3 and 3650 candle meters, with the striking result that neither mouse made any mistakes. In series 19 red was used with darkness as in series 17, and again there was a total lack of discrimination. Series 20 was a repetition of series 18, with practically the same result. I then attempted to find out, by increasing the brightness of the red, how great must be its value in order that the dancers should distinguish it readily from darkness. For the tests of series 21 it was made 72 candle meters, but discrimination did not clearly appear. At 1800 candle meters, as is shown in series 22, the red was sufficiently different in appearance from total darkness to enable No. 205 to discriminate perfectly between the two electric-boxes. For No. 2 discrimination was more difficult, but there was no doubt about his ability. It would appear from these tests that the dancers had not learned to avoid red. Therefore we are still confronted with the question, can they see colors?

The account of my color vision experiments is finished. If it be objected that other than visual conditions may account for whatever measure of discriminating ability, apart from brightness discrimination, appears in some of the series,

TABLE 29

VISUAL CHECK TESTS

With the Electric-boxes Precisely Alike Visually

SERIES	DATE	No. 151		No. 152	
		RIGHT	WRONG	RIGHT	WRONG
1	Sept. 29	6	4	4	6
2	30	5	5	6	4
3	Oct. 1	3	7	4	6
4	2	5	5	3	7
5	3	3	7	5	5
6	4	6	4	5	5
7	5	5	5	5	5
8	6	—	—	3	7
9	7	—	—	6	4
10	8	—	—	4	6
Averages		4.7	5.3	4.5	5.5

the results of the series of Table 29, in which all conceivable visual means of discrimination were purposely excluded, and those of the several check tests which have been described from time to time in the foregoing account, should furnish a satisfactory and definite answer. I am satisfied that whatever discrimination occurred was due to vision; whether we are justified in calling it color vision is quite another question.

I conclude from my experimental study of vision that although the dancer does not possess a color sense like ours, it probably discriminates the colors of the red end of the spectrum from those of other regions by difference in the stimulating value of light of different wave lengths, that such specific stimulating value is radically different in nature from the value of different wave lengths for the human eye, and that the red of the spectrum has a very low stimulating value for the dancer. In the light of these experiments we may safely conclude that many, if not most, of the tests of color vision in animals which have been made heretofore by other investigators have failed to touch the real problem because the possibility of brightness discrimination was not excluded.

Under the direction of Professor G. H. Parker, Doctor Karl Waugh has examined the structure of the retina of the dancing mouse for me, with the result that only a single type of retinal element was discovered. Apparently the animals possess rod-like cells, but nothing closely similar to the cones of the typical mammalian retina. This is of peculiar interest and importance in connection with the results which I have reported in the foregoing pages, because the rods are supposed to have to do with brightness or luminosity vision and the cones with color vision. In fact, it is usually supposed that the absence of cones in the mammalian retina indicates the lack of color vision. That this inference of functional facts from structural conditions is correct I am by no means certain, but at any rate all of the experiments which I have made to determine the visual ability of the dancer go to show that color vision, if it exists at all, is extremely poor. It is gratifying indeed to learn, after such a study of behavior as has just been described, that the structural conditions, so far as we are able to judge at present, justify the conclusions which have been drawn.

CHAPTER XI

The Role of Sight in the Daily Life of the Dancer

Darting hither and thither in its cage, whirling rapidly, now to the left, now to the right, running in circles, passing through holes in the nest box quickly and neatly, the dancer, it would seem, must have excellent sight. But careful observation of its behavior modifies this inference. For it appears that a pair of mice dancing together, or near one another, sometimes collide, and that it is only those holes with which the animal is familiar that are entered skillfully. In fact, the longer one observes the behavior of the dancer under natural conditions, the more he comes to believe in the importance of touch, and motor tendencies. Sight, which at first appears to be the chief guiding sense, comes to take a secondary place. In this chapter it is my purpose to show by means of simple experiments what part sight plays in the dancer's life of habit formation.

The evidence on this subject has been obtained from four sources: (1) observation of the behavior of dancers in their cages; (2) observation of their behavior when blinded; (3) observation of their behavior in a great variety of discrimination experiments, many of which have already been described; and (4) observation of their behavior in labyrinth experiments which were especially planned to exhibit the importance of the several kinds of vision which the dancer might be supposed to possess. The evidence from the first three of these sources may be presented summarily, for much of it has already appeared in earlier chapters. That from the fourth source will constitute the bulk of the material of this chapter.

My observation of the behavior of the mice has furnished conclusive evidence of their ability to see moving objects. But that they do not see very distinctly, and that they do not have accurate perception of the form of objects, are conclusions which are supported by observations that I have made under both natural and experimental conditions. In Chapters VII, VIII, IX, and X, I have presented an abundance of evidence of brightness vision and, in addition, indications of a specific sensitiveness to wave length which may be said to correspond to our color vision. It is noteworthy, however, that all of the experimental proofs of visual ability were obtained as the result of long periods of training. Seldom, indeed, in my experience with them, have the dancers under natural conditions exhibited forms of activity which were unquestionably guided by vision.

It is claimed by those who have experimented with blinded dancers that the loss of sight decreases the amount and rapidity of movement, and the ability of the animals to avoid obstacles.

By means of the discrimination method previously used in the preliminary experiments on color vision, a full description of which may be found in Chapter IX, p. 133, the dancers' ability to perceive form was tested. Immediately after the two males *A* and *B* had been given the "food-box" tests, whose results appear in Table 15, they were tested in the same apparatus and by the same method for their ability to discriminate a rectangular food-box from a round one. In the case of the color discrimination tests, it will be remembered that the circular tin boxes 5 cm. in diameter by 1.5 cm. in depth, one of which was covered with blue paper, the other with orange, were used. For the form discrimination tests I used instead one of the circular boxes of the dimensions given above and a rectangular box 8.5 cm. long, 5.5 cm. wide and 2.5 cm. deep. "Force" was placed in the circular box. The tests were given, in series of 20, daily.

The results of 15 series of these tests, as may be seen by the examination of Table 30, are about as definitely negative, so far as form discrimination is in question, as they possibly could be. From the first series to the last there is not one which justifies the inference that either of the dancers

TABLE 30

VISUAL FORM TESTS

		MOUSE A		MOUSE B	
SERIES	DATE	RIGHT (CIRCULAR BOX)	WRONG (RECTANGULAR BOX)	RIGHT (CIRCULAR BOX)	WRONG (RECTANGULAR BOX)
1	Jan. 5	10	10	9	11
2	7	12	8	13	7
3	10	6	14	10	10
4	11	7	13	10	10
5	12	9	11	10	10
6	13	11	9	11	9
7	14	13	7	9	11
8	15	10	10	11	9
9	16	10	10	11	9
10	17	11	9	9	11
11	18	11	9	12	8
12	19	12	8	10	10
13	20	10	10	12	8
14	21	10	10	8	12
15	22	10	10	10	10
Totals		152	148	155	145

depended upon the form of the boxes in making its choice. In view of the general criticisms I have made concerning the use of hunger as a motive in experiments on animal behavior, and in view of the particular criticisms of this very method of testing the discriminating powers of the mouse, it may seem strange that space should be given to a report of these tests. I sympathize with the feeling, if any one has it, but, at the same time, I wish to call attention to the fact that almost any mammal which is capable of profiting by experience, and which, under the same conditions, could distinguish the rectangular box from the circular one, would have chosen the right box with increasing accuracy as the result of such experience. The results are important in my opinion, not because they either prove or disprove the ability of the dancer to discriminate these particular forms, the discrimination of which might fairly be expected of any animal with an image-forming eye, but because they demonstrate an important characteristic of the dancing mouse, namely, its indifference to the straightforward or direct way of doing things.

Most mammals which have been experimentally studied have proved their eagerness and ability to learn the shortest, quickest, and simplest route to food without the additional spur of punishment for wandering. With the dancer it is different. It is content to be moving; whether the movement carries it directly towards the food is of secondary importance. On its way to the food-box, no matter whether the box be slightly or strikingly different from its companion box, the dancer may go by way of the wrong box, may take a few turns, cut some figure-eights, or even spin like a top for seconds almost within vibrissa-reach of the food-box, and all this even though it be very hungry. Activity is preeminently important in the dancer's life.

In passing I may emphasize the importance of the fact that at no time did the brightness or color discrimination tests furnish evidence of attempts on the part of the dancers to choose by means of slight differences in the form of the cardboards or the cardboard carriers. Several times form differences, which were easily perceivable by the human subject, were introduced in order to discover whether the mice would detect them and learn to discriminate thereby instead

FIGURE 22. — Cards used for tests of form discrimination.

of by the visual conditions of brightness or color. As these experiments failed to furnish evidences of form discrimination, the following special test in the discrimination box was devised.

The color discrimination box of Chapter X was arranged so that the light at the entrance to each electric-box had a value of 20 candle meters, less the diminution caused by a piece of ground glass which was placed over the end of the electric-boxes to diffuse the light. The windows through which the light entered the electric-boxes were covered with pieces of black cardboard; in one of these cardboards I had cut a circular opening 4 cm. in diameter, and in the other an opening of the same area but markedly different shape.

These openings are shown in Figure 22. As the mouse approached the entrance to the electric-boxes, it was confronted by these two equally illuminated areas, whose chief difference was one of form. Difference in the amount of light within the boxes was excluded so far as possible. The question which I asked was, can the dancer discriminate by means of this difference in visual form?

For the purpose of settling this point and of gaining additional knowledge of the role of vision, two individuals were tested in the discrimination box under the conditions which have just been described. During the first ten days of the experiment each of these mice, Nos. 420 and 425, was given a series of ten tests daily. At the end of this period experimentation with No. 425 had to be discontinued, and the number of daily tests given to No. 420 was increased to twenty.

Instead of taking space for the presentation of the daily records, I may state the general results of the tests. Neither of the mice learned to choose the right box by means of form discrimination. In fact, there was absolutely no sign of discrimination at any time during the tests. This result is as surprising as it is interesting. I could not at first believe that the mice were unable to perceive the difference in the lighted areas, but assumed that they were prevented from getting the outlines of the areas by the blinding effect of the light. However, decreasing the intensity of the illumination did not alter the result. According to the indications of this experiment, the dancer's ability to perceive visual form is extremely poor.

Thus far the purpose of our experiments has been to ascertain what the dancer is enabled to do by sight. Suppose we now approach the problem of the role of this sense by trying to find out what it can do without sight.

For the investigation of this matter the labyrinth method seemed eminently suitable. The first form of labyrinth which was used in these visual tests appears in ground plan in Figure 23. It was made of 1½ cm. boards. The length was 52 cm., the width 17 cm., the depth 10 cm. Each of the doorways, *I* (the entrance), 1, 2, 3, and *O* (the exit), was 5 by 5 cm. The alleys were 2½ cm. wide. For this

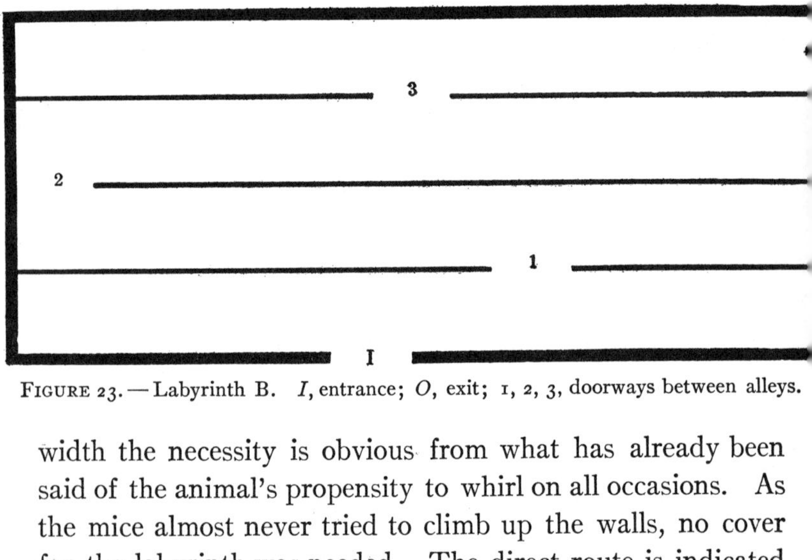

FIGURE 23.—Labyrinth B. *I*, entrance; *O*, exit; 1, 2, 3, doorways between alleys.

width the necessity is obvious from what has already been said of the animal's propensity to whirl on all occasions. As the mice almost never tried to climb up the walls, no cover for the labyrinth was needed. The direct route is indicated by the symbols *I*-1-2-3-*O*. If an error be defined as a choice of the wrong path as the animal progressed toward the exit, five mistakes were possible in the forward course: the first by turning to the left at the entrance; the second by failing to pass through doorway 1; the third by turning to the right after passing through doorway 1; the fourth by failing to pass through doorway 3, and the fifth by turning to the left after passing through 3. In case the mouse retraced its course, any mistakes made as it again progressed towards *O* were counted, as at first, no matter how many times it went over the same ground. Thus an individual might make the same mistake several times in the course of a single test in the labyrinth.

With this labyrinth Nos. 7, 998, 15, 16, 151, and 152 were tested. At first a record was kept of the time which elapsed from the instant the animal entered *I* to the instant it emerged at *O*, of the path which it followed, and of the number of errors which it made; but later only the number of errors was recorded.

TABLE 31

THE ROLE OF SIGHT

Labyrinth-B Experiments

TEST	DATE	No. 7		No. 998	
		TIME	ERRORS	TIME	ERRORS
1	June 16	66″	8	127″	19
2	16	11	0	94	12
3	16	15	2	18	3
4	16	7	0	13	2
5	16	5	0	10	1
6	18	61	15	12	3
7	18	13	3	14	4
8	18	14	5	8	1
9	18	24	9	16	2
10	18	10	1	9	1
11	19	36	13	80	17
12	19	8	3	10	1
13	19	6	1	7	1
14	19	9	1	8	0
15	19	12	2	7	0
16	20	14	1	25	0
17	20	28	3		
18	20	No efforts to escape		No efforts to escape	

TABLE 32

LABYRINTH-B EXPERIMENTS

with

Electric Shock given as Punishment for Mistakes

TEST	DATE	No. 7		No. 998	
		CONDITION	ERRORS	CONDITION	ERRORS
1	June 29	Light	4	Light	9
2	29	Light	1	Light	3
3	29	Light	1	Light	2
4	29	Light	0	Light	0
5	29	Light	0	Light	0
6	29	Light	0	Light	0
7	29	Light	1	Light	0
8	29	Light	0	Light	0
9	29	Light	1	Darkness	0
10	29	Light	1	Light	0
11	29	Light	1	Darkness	0
12	29	Light	0	Light	0
13	29	Light	0	Light	0
14	29	Light	0	Light	0
15	29	Light	0	Light	0
16	29	Light	0	Light	0
17	29	Darkness	2	Darkness	0
18	29	Light	2	Light with paper	0
19	29	Light·	0	Light	0
20	29	Darkness	0	Light with paper	0
21	29	Light	0	Light	0
22	29	Light	0	Darkness	0
23	29	Light	0	Odorless	0

TABLE 32 — CONTINUED

		No. 7		No. 998	
TEST	DATE	CONDITION	ERRORS	CONDITION	ERRORS
24	June 29	Light	0	Darkness	0
25	29	Light	0		
26	29	Darkness	4		
27	29	Light with paper	1		
28	29	Light	0		
29	29	Light with paper	1		
30	29	Darkness	0		
31	29	Odorless	2		
32	29	Darkness	4		

As the results in Table 31 show, the time and number of errors rapidly diminished. Number 7, for example, made no errors in the second test. The chiefly significant fact which appeared in these preliminary experiments, however, was that the mice soon ceased to care whether they got out of the labyrinth or not. After they knew the path perfectly, they would enter the wrong passages repeatedly and wander about indefinitely. It was obvious, therefore, that the labyrinth could not be used to reveal the role of sight unless some sufficiently strong motive for continuous effort to escape from it could be discovered. Naturally I looked to the electric shock for aid.

The labyrinth of Figure 23, which for convenience in distinguishing it from several other forms to be described later I have designated as labyrinth B, was placed upon a board 90 cm. long and 30 cm. wide about which had been wound two pieces of phosphor bronze wire after the manner de-

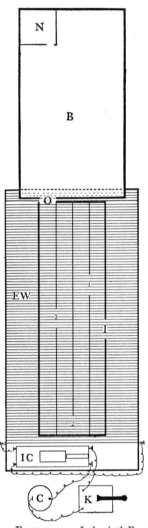

FIGURE 24. — Labyrinth B on an interrupted circuit board. *I-*1-2-3-*O*, labyrinth path; *B*, nest-box; *N*, nest; *EW*, board wound with phosphor bronze wire; *IC*, induction apparatus; *C*, electric cell; *K*, key.

scribed on p. 94. At *O*, Figure 24, there was an opening closed by a swinging door which led into a box 40 by 24 cm. In one corner of this box was a small nest-box. The significance of this rearrangement of the labyrinth is apparent. As in the preliminary tests, the dancer was started at I, but instead of being allowed to wander about without any other result than delay in escape, it was given a shock each time it made an error. The satisfaction of escaping from the narrow bounds of the labyrinth's passages, which alone was not strong enough to impel a dancer constantly to do its best to escape, was thus supplemented by the powerful and all-controlling tendency to avoid the disagreeable stimulus which resulted from entering certain of the passages. The result of this modification of method is strikingly exhibited by the data of Table 32.

This table was constructed for the purpose of exhibiting the principal features of the results obtained with labyrinth *B* in certain preliminary experiments in which the conditions were changed in various ways. Chief among the important facts which appear in the illustrative data (for Nos. 7 and 998) which are presented, are the following. The dancers readily learn the path of labyrinth B so that they can follow it quickly and with perfect accuracy. After familiarity with the direct path from entrance to exit has been gained, they become indifferent about escaping and tend to wander aimlessly. The introduction of the electric shock as punishment for the choice of the wrong passage impels them to do their best to avoid errors. The path once learned can be followed in total darkness with few or no errors. Table 32 indicates marked differences in the behavior of No. 7 and No. 998. The latter learned the path readily and was little disturbed by any of the changes in conditions. In total darkness he followed the path rapidly and accurately, as was indicated by the time of the trip and the path that he left on a sheet of smoked paper that had been placed on the floor of the labyrinth as a means of obtaining a record of the errors made. The presence of the smoked paper did not seem to interfere at all with his behavior, nor did the thorough washing of the labyrinth and the resultant removal of its odors. In the case of No. 7 the opposite was true. She did not learn the path readily, was confused by any change in conditions, had great difficulty in finding her way in darkness, made errors when the smoked paper was placed on the floor and after the odors of the labyrinth had been removed by washing. Of the six dancers which were observed in these preliminary tests, No. 7 alone gave convincing evidence of the importance of sight.

I think we may say in the light of the results of the table that such errors as appear in the darkness tests are due rather to the disturbing influence of a change in the conditions of the experiment than to the exclusion of visual data, for as many or more errors were sometimes caused simply by changing the position of the labyrinth, placing smoked paper on the floor, or by introducing a new odor at some point. The exclusion of the possibility of guidance by smell and touch did not seriously interfere with the animal's ability to follow the path.

The results which have just been considered seemed to be of sufficient interest and importance to justify the further use of the labyrinth method in the investigation of the role of vision. A series of experiments with labyrinth B was therefore planned so that the importance of sight, touch, and smell in connection with this form of habit should be more satisfactorily exhibited. Does the dancer follow the path by sight, touch, smell, by all, or by no one of them?

This series of tests with labyrinth B, whose several purposes may best be explained in connection with the various kinds of tests enumerated below, consisted of:

I. A preliminary test in which the dancer was permitted to wander about in the labyrinth, without being shocked, until it finally escaped to the nest-box by way of the exit. Thus the animal was given an opportunity to discover that escape from the maze was possible.

II. This was immediately followed by a series of tests at the rate of about one per minute, with an electric shock as punishment for every mistake. This was continued without interruption until the path had been followed without error five times in succession.

III. The labyrinth was now moved about 3 cm. to one side so that it covered a new floor area, and a test was given for the purpose of ascertaining whether the mouse had been following a trail on the floor.

IV. Tests with smoked paper on the floor were now alternated with tests in which the floor was plain. The alternation was rendered necessary by the fact that the paper was laid over the electric wires and therefore prevented the punishment of mistakes. The purpose of these tests was to discover whether the smoked paper, which was an essential condition for the next test, was itself a disturbing condition. These tests were continued until the animal had followed the path correctly, despite the smoked paper, twice in succession.

V. The electric lights were now turned out and tests were given in total darkness, with smoked paper on the floor as a means of obtaining a record of the number of errors. These tests were continued until the path had been followed once correctly.

VI. The labyrinth was now thoroughly washed with warm water, to which a little kerosene had been added, and quickly dried over a steam radiator. This usually necessitated a delay of about five minutes. As soon as the labyrinth was dry, tests were given to discover whether the odors of the various passages had been serving as important guiding conditions. These tests were continued until the path had been followed once without error.

VII. A final test in darkness completed the series.

As it was not possible for the observer to watch the animal and thus to count the number of mistakes which it made in total darkness, the simple method of placing a piece of smoked paper on the floor of the labyrinth was used. The mouse left a graphic record of its path on the paper and from this the number of errors could be ascertained. In the tests now to be described the smoked paper was placed upon the electric wires, but later a form of electric labyrinth was devised in which it was underneath and therefore did not interfere with the electric shock.

The above series of tests was given under the same external conditions in a dark-room to six pairs of dancers. In all cases, two individuals, a male and a female, which had been kept in the same cage, were experimented with at the same time, *i.e.* one was permitted to rest in the nest-box while the other was being put through a test. This was done in order that the comparison of the results for males and females should be perfectly fair.

The detailed results of this long series of tests may be presented for only two individuals, Nos. 210 and 215, Table 33. In this table lines separate the results of the seven different kinds of tests.

TABLE 33

THE ROLE OF SIGHT, TOUCH, AND SMELL IN LABYRINTH EXPERIMENTS

	No. 210			No. 215	
TEST	CONDITION	ERRORS		CONDITION	ERRORS
I. 1	No shock	9		I. No shock	2
II. 2	Shock	5		II. Shock	3
3	Shock	4		Shock	1
4	Shock	2		Shock	0
5	Shock	3		Shock	0
6	Shock	0		Shock	0
7	Shock	0		Shock	0
8	Shock	0		Shock	0
9	Shock	0		III. Labyrinth moved	0
10	Shock	0		IV. Paper on floor	4
III. 11	Labyrinth moved	0		No paper (shock)	0
IV. 12	Paper on floor	2		Paper	0
13	No paper (shock)	0		No paper	0
14	Paper	1		Paper	1
15	No paper	0		No paper	0
16	Paper	7		Paper	4
17	No paper	0		No paper	0
18	Paper	0		Paper	0

TABLE 33 — CONTINUED

	No. 210			No. 215	
TEST	CONDITION	ERRORS		CONDITION	ERRORS
19	No paper	0		No paper	0
20	Paper	4		Paper	0
21	No paper	0		No paper	0
22	Paper	2		V. Darkness	0
23	No paper	2		VI. Labyrinth washed	2
24	Paper	1			0
25	No paper	0		VII. Darkness	2
26	Paper	0			
27	No paper	0			
28	Paper	0			
29	No paper	0			
V. 30	Darkness	0			
VI. 31	Labyrinth washed	2			
32		0			
VII. 33	Darkness	0			

The average results for the twelve individuals (six of each sex) which were subjected to the tests, I have arranged in Table 34. The Roman numerals at the top of the table designate the seven groups of tests, and the figures under each, the numerical results of the tests. I may explain and comment upon the averages of the several columns of this table in turn.

Column I gives the number of errors made in the preliminary test. Curiously enough, the males made many more errors than the females.

For the second group of tests (II) two results have been tabulated: the number of the first correct test, and the total number of tests before the path was followed correctly five

o

times in succession.   The first correct trip came usually
after not more than five or six tests, but five successive
correct trips demanded on the average at least fourteen
training tests.

Destruction of the floor path by movement of the labyrinth to one side, without changing its relations to the points
of the compass, disturbed the mice very little.   Only four of
the twelve individuals made any mistakes as a result of the
change in the tactual conditions, and the average error as it
appears in Column III is only .3.

TABLE 34

Role of Sight, Touch, and Smell in Labyrinth Experiments

MALES	I. Preliminary Test. Errors	II. Training Tests. No. of Tests Before Correct		III. Labyrinth Moved. Errors	IV. Smoked Paper on Floor. No. of Times Before Correct Twice
		First Time	Five Times		
210	9	5	9	0	9
212	2	3	8	1	3
214	6	10	28	0	22
220	25	4	8	0	14
410	11	6	20	0	10
420	14	6	14	1	7
Averages	11.2	5.7	14.5	.3	10.8
FEMALES					
211	16	6	10	1	5
213	7	5	14	1	21
215	2	3	7	0	6
225	14	6	18	0	14
415	6	6	13	0	3
425	10	7	13	0	8
Averages	9.2	5.5	12.5	.3	9.5

TABLE 34 — CONTINUED

MALES	V. DARKNESS		VI. LABYRINTH WASHED. ERRORS	VII. DARKNESS. ERRORS
	ERRORS IN FIRST TEST	NO. OF TESTS BEFORE COR'CT		
210	O	I	2	O
212	2	2	O	O
214	O	I	—	O
220	2	4	2	O
410	I	3	2	I
420	2	4	I	4
Averages	1.2	2.5	1.2	0.8
FEMALES				
211	2	2	O	O
213	2	2	—	3
215	O	I	2	2
225	3	2	O	O
415	I	3	2	I
425	I	7	O	O
Averages	1.5	2.8	0.7	1.0

That covering the floor with smoked paper forced the mice to relearn the path, in large measure, is evident from the results of Column IV. An average of ten tests was necessary to enable the mice to follow the path correctly. It is almost certain, however, that the interference with the perfectly formed labyrinth habit which this change in the condition of the floor caused was not due to the removal of important tactual sense data.

As Column V shows, the number of errors in total darkness is very small. Some individuals gave no sign of being disturbed by the absence of visual guidance, others at first seemed confused. I have given in the table the number of errors in the first darkness test and the number of the first test in which no mistakes occurred.

No more disturbance of the dancer's ability to follow the path which it had learned resulted from washing the labyrinth thoroughly than from darkening the room. Indeed it is clear from Column VI that the path was not followed by the use of smell. However, the test in darkness, after the odor of the box had been removed, proved conclusively that in most cases the mice could follow the path correctly without visual or olfactory guidance.

The behavior of 18 individuals as it was observed in labyrinth B makes perfectly evident three important facts. (1) In following the path which it has learned, the dancer in most instances is not guided to any considerable extent by a trail (odor or touch) which has been formed by its previous journeys over the route; (2) sight is quite unnecessary for the easy and perfect execution of the labyrinth habit, for even those individuals which are at first confused by the darkening of the experiment room are able after a few tests to follow the path correctly; (3) and, finally, smell, which according to current opinion is the chiefly important sense of mice and rats, is not needful for the performance of this habitual act.

At this point we may very fittingly ask, what sense data are necessary for the guidance of the series of acts which constitutes the labyrinth habit? I answer, probably none. A habit once formed, the senses have done their part; henceforth it is a motor process, whose initiation is conditioned by the activity of a receptive organ (at times a sense receptor), but whose form is not necessarily dependent upon immediate impressions from eye, nose, vibrissæ, or even from internal receptors. These are statements of my opinion; whether they express the truth, either wholly or in part, only further experimentation can decide.

In considering the results of these labyrinth tests it is important that we distinguish clearly those which have to do with the conditions of habit formation from those which instead have to do with the conditions of habit performance. Sense data which are absolutely necessary for the learning of a labyrinth path may be of little or no importance for the execution of the act of following the path after the learning process has been completed. Thus far in connection with the labyrinth tests we have discussed only the relations of sight, touch, and smell to what I have called habit performance. We may now ask what part these senses play in the formation of a labyrinth habit.

A very definite answer to this question is furnished by observation of the behavior of the dancers in the tests. Most of them continuously made use of their eyes, their noses, and their vibrissæ. Some individuals used one form of receptive organ almost exclusively. I frequently noticed that those individuals which touched and smelled of the labyrinth passages most carefully gave least evidence of the use of sight. It is safe to say, then, that under ordinary conditions habit formation in the dancer is conditioned by the use of sight, touch, and smell, but that these senses are of extremely different degrees of importance in different individuals. And further, that, although in the case of some individuals the loss of sight would not noticeably delay habit formation, in the case of others it would seriously interfere with the process. When deprived of one sense, the dancer depends upon its remaining channels of communication with environment. Indeed there are many reasons for inferring that if deprived of sight, touch, and smell it would still be able to learn a labyrinth path; and there are reasonable grounds for the belief that a habit once formed can be executed in the absence of all special sense data. Apparently the various receptive organs of the body furnish the dancer with impressions which serve as guides to action and facilitate habit formation, although they are not necessary for habit performance.

The reader may wonder why I have not carried out systematic experiments to determine accurately and quantitatively the part which each sense plays in the formation of a labyrinth habit instead of basing my inferences upon incidental observation of the behavior of the dancers. The reason is simply this: the number and variety of experiments which were suggested by the several directions in which this investigation developed rendered the performance of all of them impossible. I have chosen to devote my time to other lines of experimentation because a very thorough study of the conditions of habit formation has recently been made by Doctor Watson.[1]

What is the role of sight in the dancing mouse? How shall we answer the question? The evidence which has been obtained in the course of my study of the animal indicates that brightness vision is fairly acute, that color vision is poor, that although form is not clearly perceived, movement is readily perceived. My observations under natural conditions justify the conclusion that sight is not of very great importance in the daily life of the dancer, and my observations under experimental conditions strongly suggest the further conclusion that movement and changes in brightness are the only visual conditions which to any considerable extent control the activity of the animal.

[1] Watson, J. B., *Psychological Review*, Monograph Supplement, Vol. 8, No. 2, 1907.

CHAPTER XII

EDUCABILITY: METHODS OF LEARNING

NEARLY all of the experiments described in earlier chapters have revealed facts concerning the educability of the dancer. In order to supplement the knowledge of this subject thus incidentally gained and to discover the principles of educability, the specially devised experiments whose results appear in this and succeeding chapters were arranged and carried out with a large number of mice. In the work on the modifiability of behavior I have attempted to determine (1) by what methods the dancer is capable of profiting by experience, (2) the degree of rapidity of learning, (3) the permanency of changes wrought in behavior, (4) the effect of one kind of training upon others, (5) the relation of re-training to training, and (6) the relation of all these matters to age, sex, and individuality.

As it is obvious that knowledge of these subjects is a necessary condition for the intelligent appreciation of the capacities of an animal, as well as of the choice of methods by which it may be trained advantageously, perhaps it is not too much to expect that this investigation of the nature and conditions of educability in the dancing mouse may give us some new insight into the significance of certain aspects of human education and may serve to suggest ways in which we may measure and increase the efficiency of our educational methods.

Merely for the sake of convenience of description I shall classify the methods which have been employed as problem methods, labyrinth methods, and discrimination methods. That these names are not wholly appropriate is suggested by the fact that discrimination necessarily occurs in connection with each of them. As problem methods we may designate those tests of initiative and modifiability which involve the opening of doors by pushing or pulling them, and the climbing of an inclined ladder. An example of the labyrinth method has been presented in Chapter XI. The name discrimination method I have applied to those tests which involve the choice of one of two visual, tactual, or olfactory conditions. The white-black discrimination tests, for example, served to reveal the rapidity and permanency of learning as well as the presence of brightness vision.

In the case of most mammals whose educability has been studied experimentally, problem methods have proved to be excellent tests of docility and initiative. The cat, the raccoon, the monkey, in their attempts to obtain food, learn to pull strings, turn buttons, press latches, slide bolts, pull plugs, step on levers. The dancer does none of these things readily. Are we therefore to infer that it is less intelligent, that it is less docile, than the cat, the raccoon, or the monkey? Not necessarily, for it is possible that these methods do not suit the capacity of the animal. As a matter of fact, all of the tests which are now to be described in their relation to the educability of the dancer bear witness to the importance of the selection of methods in the light of the motor equipment and the habits of the animal which is to be tested. Judged by ordinary standards, on the basis of results which it yields in problem and labyrinth tests, the dancer is extremely stupid. But that this conclusion is not justified is apparent when it is judged in the light of tests which are especially adapted to its peculiarities.

Problems which are easy for other mammals because of their energetic and persistent efforts to secure food in any way which their motor capacity makes possible are useless as tests of the dancer's abilities, because it is not accustomed to obtain its food as the result of strenuous and varied activities. There are problems and problems; a condition or situation which presents a problem to one organism may utterly lack interest for an organism of different structure and behavior. What is a problem test in the case of the cat or even of the common mouse, is not necessarily a problem for the dancer. Similarly, in connection with the labyrinth method, it is clear that the value of the test depends upon the desire of the organism to escape from the maze. The cat, the rat, the tortoise do their best to escape; the dancer is indifferent. Clearly, then, methods of training should be chosen on the basis of a knowledge of the characteristics of the animal whose educability is to be investigated.

The simplest possible test of the intelligence of the dancer which I could devise was the following. Beside the cage in which the mice were kept I placed a wooden box 26 cm. long, 23 cm. wide, and 12 cm. deep. Neither this box nor the cage was covered, for the animals did not attempt to climb out. As a way of passing from one of these boxes to the other I arranged a ladder made of wire fly-screen netting. This ladder was about 8 cm. broad and it extended from the middle of one side of the wooden box upward at an angle of about 30° to the edge of the box and then descended at the same angle into the cage.

A dancer when taken from the nest-box and placed in the wooden box could return to its cage and thus find warmth, food, and company by climbing the ladder. It was my aim to determine, by means of this apparatus, whether the dancers can learn such a simple way of escape and whether they learn by watching one another. As it turned out, a third value belonged to the tests, in that they were used also to test the influence of putting the mice through the act.

In the first experiment three dancers, Nos. 1000, 2, and 6, were together placed in the wooden box. At the end of 15 minutes not one of them had succeeded in returning to the cage. They were then driven to the bottom of the ladder and started upward by the experimenter; with this assistance all escaped to the nest-box. At the expiration of 5 minutes they were again placed in the wooden box, whence the chilly temperature (about 60° F.) and the lack of food made them eager to return to their cage. No attempt to climb up the ladder was made by any of them within 15 minutes, so the experimenter directed them to the ladder and started them upward as in the first test. This completed the experiment for the day. The following day two tests were given in the same way. In the second of these tests, that is, on its fourth trial, No. 1000 climbed over of his own initiative in 5 minutes. The others had to be assisted as formerly. On the third day No. 1000 found his way back to the nest-box quickly and fairly directly, but neither No. 2 or No. 6 climbed of its own initiative in the first test. When their movements were restricted to the region of the box about the base of the ladder, both of them returned to the cage quickly. And on the second test of the third day all the mice climbed the ladder directly.

In Table 35 I have given the time required for escape in the case of 40 tests which were given to these 3 individuals at the rate of 2 tests per day.

When the time exceeded 15 minutes the mice were helped out by the experimenter; a record of 15 minutes, therefore, indicates failure. Naturally enough the motives for escape were not sufficiently strong or constant to bring about the most rapid learning of which the dancer is capable. Sometimes they would remain in the wooden box washing themselves for several minutes before attempting to find a

TABLE 35

LADDER CLIMBING TEST

Time in Minutes and Seconds

No. of Exp.	Date 1905	No. 1000	No. 2	No. 6	Average for All	Daily Av. for All
1	Nov. 14	15′	15′	15′	—	—
2		15′	15′	15′	—	—
3	15	15′	15′	15′	—	—
4		300″	15′	15′	—	—
5	16	480″	15′	15′	—	—
6		180″	300″	420″	300″	300″
7	17	450″	240″	540″	410″	
8		20″	15″	18″	18″	214″
9	18	90″	180″	135″	135″	
10		135″	105″	165″	135″	135″
11	19	480″	240″	330″	350″	
12		30″	120″	90″	80″	143″
13	20	360″	75″	120″	185″	
14		5″	6″	8″	6″	95″
15	21	105″	450″	120″	192″	
16		8″	80″	20″	54″	123″
17	22	255″	300″	180″	245″	
18		10″	30″	270″	103″	174″
19	23	300″	660″	450″	470″	
20		90″	120″	150″	120″	295″
21	24	240″	125″	225″	197″	
22		4″	6″	168″	59″	128″

TABLE 35 — CONTINUED

No. of Exp.	Date	No. 1000	No. 2	No. 6	Average for All	Daily Av. for All
23	Nov. 25	305″	85″	130″	173″	
24		5″	6″	118″	43″	108″
25	26	3″	8″	44″	18″	
26		19″	1″	176″	98″	58″
27	27	150″	79″	269″	166″	
28		26″	3″	31″	20″	93″
29	28	214″	18″	267″	166″	
30		40″	3″	4″	16″	91″
31	29	130″	45″	250″	142″	
32		12″	3″	25″	13″	77″
33	Dec. 2	61″	35″	44″	47″	
34		50″	5″	24″	26″	36″
35	3	66″	18″	2″	29″	
36		8″	5″	10″	8″	19″
37	4	9″	4″	3″	5″	
38		10″	5″	6″	7″	6″
39	5	5″	3″	5″	4″	
40		10″	4″	3″	6″	5″

way of escape. On this account I made it a rule to begin the time record with the appearance of active running about. The daily average time of escape as indicated in the table does not decrease regularly and rapidly. On the fourth day, which was the first on which all three of the dancers returned to the cage by way of the ladder of their own initiative in both tests, the average is 214 seconds. In contrast with this, on the twentieth day the time was only 5 seconds. It is quite evident that the dancers had learned to climb the ladder.

At the end of the twentieth day the experiment was discontinued with Nos. 2 and 6, and after two weeks they were given memory tests, which showed that they remembered perfectly the ladder-climbing act, for when placed in the wooden box, with Nos. 4 and 5 as controls, they returned to the cage by way of the ladder immediately and directly.

One of the most interesting and important features of the behavior of the dancer in the ladder experiment was a halt at a certain point on the ladder. It occurred just at the edge of the wooden box at the point where the ladder took a horizontal position, and led over into the cage. Every individual from the first test to the last made this halt. Although from the point of view of the experimenter the act was valueless, it may have originated as an attempt to find a way to escape from the uncomfortable position in which the animal found itself on reaching the top of the ladder. Its persistence after a way of escape had been found is an indication of the nature of habit. Day after day the halt became shorter until finally it was little more than a pause and a turn of the head toward one side of the ladder. I think we may say that in this act we have evidence of the persistence of a particular resolution of physiological states which is neither advantageous nor disadvantageous to the organism. Had the act resulted in any gain, it would have become more marked and elaborate; had it resulted in injury or discomfort, it would have disappeared entirely. I have observed the same kind of behavior in the frog and in other animals. What the animal begins to do it persists in unless the act is positively harmful or conflicts with some beneficial activity. The only explanation of certain features of behavior is to be found in the conditions of their original occurrence. They persist by sheer force of conservatism. They have value only in the light of the circumstances under which they first appeared. Although this is merely a fact of habit formation, it suggests that many of the problems which have puzzled students of behavior for ages may be solved by a study of the history of activity.

That there are marked individual differences in intelligence in the dancing mice is apparent from the results of the ladder-climbing experiment. No. 1000 learned to climb quickly, and largely by his own initiative; Nos. 2 and 6, on the contrary, learned only by reason of tuition (being put through the required act by the experimenter). It occurred to me that this experiment, since it was difficult for some individuals and easy for others, might be used to advantage as a test of imitation. If a dancer which knows how to escape to the cage by way of the ladder be placed in the wooden box with one which, despite abundant opportunity, has proved unable to form the habit on his own initiative, will the latter profit by the activity of the former and thus learn the method of escape?

On November 20, Nos. 4 and 5 were placed in the wooden box and left there for half an hour. As they had failed to escape at the end of this interval, they were taken out of the box by the experimenter and returned to the nest-box. November 21 and 22 this test of their ability to learn to climb the ladder was repeated with the same result. On November 23 they were placed in the box with the three mice which had previously been trained to climb the ladder. The latter escaped at once. Apparently the attention of Nos. 4 and 5 was drawn to the ladder by the disappearance of their companions, for they approached its foot and No. 5 climbed up a short distance. Neither succeeded in escaping, however, and they made no further efforts that day. On the 24th, and daily thereafter until the 29th, these two dancers were placed in the box for half an hour, with negative results. At the end of the half hour on the 29th, Nos. 2 and 6 were placed in the box and permitted to go back and forth from one box to the other repeatedly within sight of Nos. 4 and 5. The latter made no attempts to follow them, although at times they seemed to be watching their movements as they ascended the ladder.

To render the results of this test of imitation still more conclusive No. 5 was given further opportunity to learn from No. 1000. Beginning December 2, the following method of experimentation was employed with these two individuals. They were placed in the wooden box together. No. 1000 usually climbed out almost immediately. Sometimes No. 5 apparently saw him disappear up the ladder; sometimes she paid no attention whatever either to the presence or absence of her companion. After he had been in the nest-box for a few seconds, No. 1000 was returned to the wooden box by the experimenter and again permitted to climb out for the benefit of No. 5. This mode of procedure was kept up until No. 1000 had made from three to ten trips. No. 5 was left in the box for half an hour each day. This test was repeated on 18 days within a period of 3 weeks. No. 5 showed no signs of an imitative tendency, and she did not learn to climb the ladder.

To this evidence of a lack of an imitative tendency in the dancer I may here add the results of my observations in other experiments. In the discrimination tests and in the laby-rinth tests I purposely so arranged conditions, in certain instances, that one individual should have an opportunity to imitate another. In no case did this occur. Seldom indeed did the animals so much as follow one another with any considerable degree of persistence.   They did not profit by one another's acts.

Excellent evidence in support of this conclusion was furnished by the behavior of the mice in the discrimination experiments.   Some individuals learned to pull as well as to push the swinging wire doors of the apparatus and were thus enabled to pass through the doorways in either direction; other individuals learned only to pass through in the direction in which the doors could be pushed open.   Naturally I was interested to discover whether those which knew only the trick of opening the doors by pushing would learn to pull the doors or would be stimulated to try by seeing other individuals do so.   At first I arranged special tests of imitation in the discrimination box; later I observed the influence of the behavior of one mouse upon that of its companion in connection with visual discrimination experiments. This was made possible by the fact that usually a pair of individuals was placed in the discrimination box and the tests given alternately to the male and to the female.   Both individuals had the freedom of the nest-box and each frequently saw the other pass through the doorway between the nest-box, A, and the entrance chamber, B (Figure 14), either from A to B by pushing the swing door or from B to A by pulling the door.

Although abundant opportunity for imitation in connection with the opening of the doors in the discrimination box was given to twenty-five individuals, I obtained no evidence of ability to learn by imitation.   The dancers did not watch the acts which were performed by their companions, and in most instances they did not attempt to follow a mate from nest-box to entrance chamber.

These problem tests, simple as they are, have revealed two important facts concerning the educability of the dancer.

First, that it does not learn by imitation to any considerable extent, and, second, that it is aided by being put through an act. Our general conclusion from the results of the experiments which have been described in this chapter, if any general conclusion is to be drawn thus prematurely, must be that the dancing mouse in its methods of learning differs markedly from other mice and from rats.

CHAPTER XIII

Habit Formation: The Labyrinth Habit

THE problem method, of which the ladder and door-opening tests of the preceding chapter are examples, has yielded interesting results concerning the individual initiative, ingenuity, motor ability, and ways of learning of the dancer; but it has not furnished us with accurate measurements of the rapidity of learning or of the permanency of the effects of training. In this chapter I shall therefore present the results of labyrinth experiments which were planned as means of measuring the intelligence of the dancer.

The four labyrinths which have been used in the investigation may be designated as A, B, C, and D. They differ from one another in the character of their errors, as well as in the number of wrong choices of a path which the animal might make on its way from entrance to exit. In the use of the labyrinth method, as in the case of the discrimination method of earlier chapters, the steps by which a satisfactory form of labyrinth for testing the dancer was discovered are quite as interesting and important for those who have an intelligent appreciation of the problems and methods of animal psychology as are the particular results which were obtained. For this reason, I shall describe the various forms of labyrinth in the order in which they were used, whether they proved satisfactory or not. At the outset of this part of my investigation, it was my purpose to compare directly the capacity for habit formation in the dancer with that of the common mouse. This proved impracticable because the same labyrinth is not suited to the motor tendencies of both kinds of mice.

The first of the four labyrinths, A, appears in ground plan in Figure 25. It was constructed of wood, as were the other labyrinths also, and measured 60 cm. in length and width, and 10 cm. in depth. The outside alleys were 5 cm. wide. In the figure, *I* marks the starting point or entrance to the maze, and *O* the exit through which the mouse was permitted to pass into its nest-box.

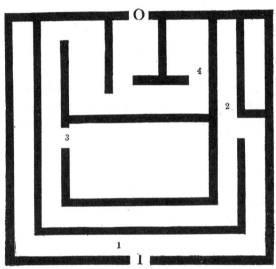

FIGURE 25. — Labyrinth A. *I*, entrance; *O*, exit; 1, 2, 3, 4, blind alleys.

Any turn in the wrong direction which the animal made in its progress from entrance to exit was recorded as an error. The four errors, exclusive of the mistake of turning back, which were possible in this labyrinth, are indicated in the figure by the numerals 1, 2, 3, and 4. By retracing its steps a mouse might repeat any one or all of these errors, and add to them the error of turning back.

In the experiments a mouse was permitted to enter the maze from a small box which had been placed by the experimenter at *I*, and an accurate record was kept of the number of errors which it made in finding its way from entrance to exit, and of the time occupied. Each of five dancers was given

31 tests in this labyrinth. The number of tests per day varied, as is indicated in Table 36, from 1 to 4. The results of the tests, so far as errors and times are in question, appear in the table. *T* at the head of a column is an abbreviation for time, *E* for errors.

The dancers did not learn to escape from this labyrinth easily and quickly. In fact, the average time of the thirty-first test (198″) is considerably longer than that of the first (130″). The number of errors decreased, it is true, but even for the last test it was 6.6 as compared with only a little more than twice that number for the first test. The last column of the table furnishes convincing proof of the truth of the statement that the animals did not acquire a perfect labyrinth-A habit. Was this due to inability to learn so complex a path, or to the fact that the method is not adapted to their nature? Observation of the behavior of the mice in the experiments enables me to say with certainty that there was no motive for escape sufficiently strong to establish a habit of following the direct path. Often, especially after a few experiences in the maze, a dancer would wander back and forth in the alleys and central courts, dancing much of the time and apparently exploring its surroundings instead of persistently trying to escape. This behavior, and the time and error results of the accompanying table, lead me to conclude that the labyrinth method, as it has been employed in the study of the intelligence of several other mammals, is not a satisfactory test of the ability of the dancer to profit by experience. That the fault is not in the labyrinth itself is proved by the results which I obtained with common mice.

On the basis of two tests per day, two common mice, a white one and a gray one, quickly learned to escape from labyrinth *A* by the shortest path. The time of escape for the gray individual (Table 37) decreased from 180″ in the

TABLE 36

RESULTS OF LABYRINTH-A TESTS WITH DANCERS

TEST	DATE 1905	No. 1000 T	E	No. 2 T	E	No. 6 T	E	No. 4 T	E	No. 5 T	E	AVERAGE FOR ALL T	E
1	Nov. 23	130″	14	100″	8	170″	13	60″	6	190″	26	130″	13.4
2	24	140	19	78	7	60	8	149	6	211	25	128	13.0
3	25	392	31	87	1	98	5	185	13	120	9	176	11.8
4	26	448	38	38	3	47	2	50	3	121	12	141	11.3
5	27	142	8	21	2	27	3	27	2	17	1	47	3.2
6	28	45	2	61	7	63	5	102	8	33	4	61	5.2
7	29	303	17	64	7	36	3	42	2	57	4	100	6.6
8	30	222	15	26	2	37	5	42	3	7	0	67	5.0
9	Dec. 1	185	9	36	5	48	3	63	3	94	8	85	5.6
10	2	52	2	71	4	19	0	196	5	95	11	87	4.4
11	3	180	8	32	2	107	4	52	3	38	4	82	4.2
12	4	310	10	133	11	65	3	242	6	125	6	175	7.2
13	4	153	9	335	55	130	10	195	15	154	18	193	21.4
14	5	330	7	69	2	42	2	201	6	130	10	154	5.4
15	5	287	7	34	4	61	4	136	7	25	2	109	4.8
16	5	455	15	65	4	25	0	110	8	160	15	183	8.4
17	6	120	15	280	9	33	0	168	4	39	2	128	6.0
18	6	120	4	164	10	81	4	101	5	85	4	110	5.4
19	6	132	12	78	7	110	6	40	2	151	12	102	7.8
20	7	258	10	223	16	33	1	92	5	37	1	129	6.6
21	7	110	7	23	3	44	4	20	4	305	23	100	8.2
22	7	100	4	60	8	167	15	44	7	58	4	86	7.6
23	8	43	1	179	7	356	6	34	3	65	3	135	4.0
24	8	92	5	56	5	42	3	17	1	23	1	46	3.0
25	9	85	5	114	3	62	3	129	8	31	0	84	3.8
26	9	30	2	36	4	109	15	12	1	34	2	44	4.8
27	9	69	5	40	4	85	6	36	3	16	1	49	3.8
28	10	160	7	80	3	28	0	142	5	35	2	89	3.4
29	10	155	5	266	8	91	5	27	0	37	2	115	4.0
30	10	29	1	25	2	124	14	83	6	111	12	74	7.0
31	10	465	6	208	8	95	3	65	3	159	13	198	6.6

first test to 21″ in the tenth, and the number of errors from 6 to 1. Similarly in the case of the white individual, the time decreased from 122″ to 8″, and the errors from 5 to 1. A fraction of the number of tests to which the dancer had been subjected sufficed to establish a habit of escape in the common mouse. It is evident, therefore, that the dancer differs radically from the common mouse in its behavior in a maze, and it is also clear that the labyrinth method, if it is to be used to advantage, must be adapted to the motor tendencies of the animal which is to be tested.

TABLE 37

RESULTS OF LABYRINTH-A TESTS WITH COMMON MICE

TEST	GREY MOUSE		WHITE MOUSE	
	T	E	T	E
1	180″	6	122″	5
2	26	2	80	6
3	37	1	56	4
4	18	0	27	1
5	68	2	33	2
6	10	1	19	1
7	11	1	17	1
8	13	1	17	1
9	10	0	8	1
10	21	1	8	1

The behavior of the dancer made obvious two defects in labyrinth A. Its passages are so large that the mouse is constantly tempted to dance, and it lacks the basis for a strong and constant motive of escape by the direct path. To obviate these shortcomings labyrinth B was constructed, as is shown in Figures 23 and 24, with very narrow passages, and a floor which was covered with the wires of an interrupted electric circuit so that errors might be punished. The length of this labyrinth was 52 cm. and the passages were 2.5 cm. wide and 10 cm. deep. Dancing in these narrow alleys was practically impossible, for the mice could barely turn around in them. In the case of all except the common mice and two dancers, a depth of 10 cm. was sufficient to keep the animals in the maze without the use of a cover.

As an account of the behavior of the dancer in labyrinth B has already been given in Chapter XI, I may now state the general results of the experiments. In all, thirty individuals were trained in this labyrinth. Each individual was given tests at the rate of one per minute until it had succeeded in following the correct path five times in succession. The weak electric shock, which was given as a punishment for mistakes, provided an activity-impelling motive for escape to the nest-box.

An idea of the extreme individual difference in the rapidity with which the labyrinth-B path was learned by these dancers may be obtained by an examination of Table 38, from which it appears that the smallest number of training tests necessary for a successful or errorless trip through the maze was one and the largest number fourteen. It is to be remembered that each mouse was given an opportunity to pass through the labyrinth once without punishment for errors, and thus to discover, before the training tests were begun, that a way of escape existed. This first test we may designate as the preliminary trial. Table 38 further indicates that the females acquired the labyrinth habit more quickly than did the males.

A graphic representation of certain of the important features of the process of formation of the labyrinth-B habit is furnished by Figure 26 in which the solid line is the curve of learning for the ten males of Table 38, and the broken line for the ten females. These two curves were plotted from the number of errors made in the preliminary trial (*P* in the figure)

TABLE 38

RESULTS OF LABYRINTH-B EXPERIMENTS, WITH TWENTY DANCERS

MALES			FEMALES		
No. OF MOUSE	No. OF FIRST CORRECT TEST	No. OF LAST OF FIVE CORRECT TESTS	No. OF MOUSE	No. OF FIRST CORRECT TEST	No. OF LAST OF FIVE CORRECT TESTS
76	8	14	75	4	15
78	5	20	77	7	11
86	13	22	87	12	22
58	2	14	49	1	5
50	6	23	57	3	20
60	13	37	59	14	28
410	6	20	415	4	13
220	4	8	225	6	18
212	3	7	211	6	10
214	10	28	213	5	14
Av.	7.0	19.3	Av.	6.2	15.6

and in each of the subsequent tests up to the sixteenth.   In the case of both the males and the females, for example, the average number of errors in the preliminary trial was 11.3, as is indicated by the fact that the curves start at a point whose value is given in the left margin as 11.3.   In the second training test the number of errors fell to 3.3 for the males and 2.7 for the females.   The number of the test is to be found on the base line; the number of errors in the left margin.   If these two curves of learning were carried to their completion, that for the males would end with the thirty-seventh test, and that for the females with the twenty-eighth.

Time records are not reported for these and subsequent labyrinth tests because they proved to be almost valueless as measures of the rapidity of habit formation. At any point in its progress through a labyrinth, the dancer may suddenly stop to wash its face, look about or otherwise examine its surroundings; if a shock be given to hurry it along it may

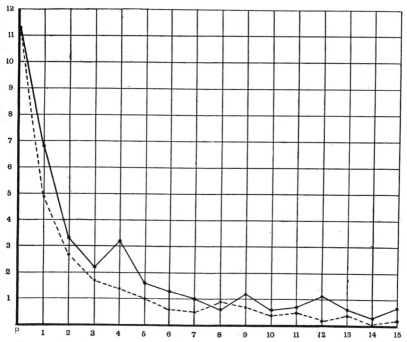

FIGURE 26. — Curves of habit formation, plotted from the data of labyrinth-B tests with ten males and ten females. The figures in the left margin indicate the number of errors; those below the base line the number of the test. *P* designates the preliminary test. Males ———; Females – – – – – .

be surprised into an error. It is my experience, and this is true of other animals as well as of the dancing mouse, that a long trip, as measured in time units, does not necessarily indicate the lack of ability to follow the labyrinth path correctly and rapidly. Hence, whenever it is possible (and the experimenter can always plan his tests so that it shall be possible), the number of errors should be given first importance and the time of the test second place. I have presented in Table 38 the number of the first correct test, and the number of the last of five successive correct tests. Space cannot be spared for records of the errors made in the several tests by each individual.

In general, labyrinth B proved very satisfactory as a means of testing the ability of the dancer to learn a simple path. The narrow passages effectively prevented dancing, and the introduction of the electric shock as a punishment for mistakes developed a motive for escape which was uniform, constant, and so strong that the animals clearly did their best to escape from the labyrinth quickly and without errors. This maze was so simple that it did not tend to discourage them as did the one which is next to be described. It must be admitted, however, that, though labyrinth B is perfectly satisfactory as a test of the dancer's ability to learn to follow a simple path, it is not an ideal means of measuring the rapidity of habit formation. This is due to the fact that the preliminary trial and the first training test play extremely different roles in the case of different individuals. A dancer which happens to follow the correct path from entrance to exit in the preliminary trial may continue to do so, with only an occasional error, during several of the early training tests, and it may therefore fail for a considerable time to discover that there are errors which should be avoided. The learning process is delayed by its accidental success. On the other hand, an individual which happens to make many mistakes to begin with immediately attempts to avoid the points in the maze at which it receives the electric shock. I was led to conclude, as a result of the labyrinth-B experiments, that the path was too easy, and that a more complex labyrinth would, in all probability, furnish a more satisfactory means of measuring the rapidity of habit formation.

On the basis of the supposition that a maze whose path was so complex that the animal would not be likely to follow it correctly in the early trials would be more to the purpose

Title of investigation..................................Labyrinth C..

Experimented on..........................No. 2...

HARVARD PSYCH. LAB.,...............February 26,..................., 1907.

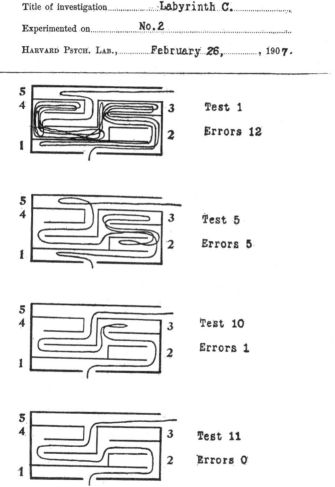

Test 1

Errors 12

Test 5

Errors 5

Test 10

Errors 1

Test 11

Errors 0

FIGURE 27.—A record sheet, showing the plan of labyrinth C (as made on the sheet by means of a rubber stamp) on which the experimenter recorded the path followed by the mouse. This sample sheet presents the path records for the first, fifth, tenth, and eleventh tests of No. 2 in labyrinth C. 1, 2, 3, 4, 5 designate the several errors of the labyrinth.

than either A or B, labyrinth C was devised. As is shown in the plan of this maze, Figure 27, five mistakes in choice of path were possible on the forward trip. These errors, as a rule, were more difficult for the dancers to avoid than those of labyrinths A and B. Those which are designated by the numerals 2, 3, and 4 were especially difficult. Error 4 was much more troublesome for left whirlers than for right whirlers because, after turning around abruptly at the entrance to the blind alley, the former type of dancer almost always followed the side wall of the maze so far that it missed the correct path. Undoubtedly the various errors are not of the same value for different individuals; but it would be extremely difficult, if not impossible, to devise a maze which should be equally difficult for several normal individuals.

In order that records of the path followed by a mouse in test after test might be kept with ease and accuracy by the experimenter, the plan of this labyrinth, and also that of labyrinth D, were cast in rubber. The outlines of labyrinths C and D which appear in Figures 27 and 28 respectively were made with the rubber stamps which were thus obtained. Figure 27 is the reproduction of a record sheet which presents the results of the first, the fifth, the tenth, and the eleventh tests of No. 2 in labyrinth C. The path followed by this individual in the first test was far too complex to be traced accurately on the record sheet. The record therefore represents merely the number of errors which was made in each region of the maze. For the fifth test, and again for the tenth and the eleventh, the path was recorded accurately. This simple device for making record blanks which can readily be filled in at the time of the experiment should recommend itself to all students of animal behavior.

In labyrinth C ten pairs of dancers were given continuous training tests at the rate of one test per minute until they were able to follow the direct path correctly. Because of the difficulty in learning this maze perfectly, it was not demanded of the mice that they should follow the path correctly several times in succession, but instead the training was terminated after the first successful trip.

The results of the experiments with this labyrinth as they are presented in Table 39 indicate that its path is considerably more difficult for the dancer to learn than that of labyrinth B, that the females learn more quickly than the males, and finally, that individual differences are just as marked as they were in the case of the simpler forms of labyrinth. It therefore appears that increasing the complexity of a labyrinth does not, as I had supposed it might, diminish the variability of the results. Certain of the individual differences which

TABLE 39

RESULTS OF LABYRINTH-C EXPERIMENTS, WITH TWENTY DANCERS

MALES		FEMALES	
NO. OF MOUSE	NO. OF FIRST CORRECT TEST	NO. OF MOUSE	NO. OF FIRST CORRECT TEST
2	11	29	15
30	33	49	34
50	49	57	15
52	22	59	15
58	16	215	10
60	17	415	10
76	3	75	8
78	6	77	11
86	5	87	9
88	25	85	11
Av.	18.7	Av.	13.8

appear in Table 39 are due, however, to the fact that in some
cases training in labyrinth B had preceded training in labyrinth C, whereas in the other cases C was the first labyrinth
in which the animals were tested. But even this does not
serve to account for the wide divergence of the results given

by No. 2 and No. 50, for the
latter had been trained in B
previous to his training in C,
and the former had not been so
trained. Yet, despite the advantage which previous labyrinth
experience gave No. 50, he did
not learn the path of C as well
in fifty tests as No. 2 did in
eleven. The facts concern-

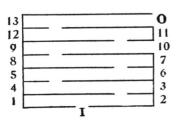

FIGURE 28. — Plan of Labyrinth
D, as reproduced from a print made
with a rubber stamp. *I*, entrance;
O, exit; numerals 1 to 13, errors.

ing the value of training in one form of labyrinth for the learning of another, as they were revealed by these experiments,
may more fittingly be discussed in a later chapter in connection with the facts of memory and re-learning.

Labyrinth C is a type of maze which might properly be
described as irregular, since the several possible errors are
extremely different in nature. In view of the results which
this labyrinth yielded, it seemed important that the dancer
be tested in a perfectly regular maze of the labyrinth-D type.
The plan which I designed as a regular labyrinth has been
reproduced, from a rubber stamp print, in Figure 28. As
is true also of the mazes previously described, it provides
four kinds of possible mistakes: namely, by turning to the
left (errors 1, 5, 9, and 13), by turning to the right (errors
3, 7, and 11), by moving straight ahead (errors 2, 4, 6, 8, 10,
and 12), and by turning back and retracing the path just
followed. The formula for the correct path of *D* is simple
in the extreme, in spite of the large number of mistakes which

are possible, for it is merely "a turn to the right at the entrance, to the left at the first doorway, and thereafter alternately to the right and to the left until the exit is reached." This concise description would enable a man to find his way out of such a maze with ease. Labyrinth D had been constructed with an exit at 10 so that it might be used as a nine-error maze if the experimenter saw fit, or as a thirteen-error maze by the closing of the opening at 10. In the experiments which are now to be described only the latter form was used.

Can the dancer learn a regular labyrinth path more quickly than an irregular one? Again, I may give only a brief statement of results. Each of the twenty dancers, of Table 40, which were trained in labyrinth D had previously been given opportunity to learn the path of C, and most of them had been trained also in labyrinth B. All of them learned this regular path with surprising rapidity. The numerical results of the tests with labyrinths B, C, and D, as well as the behavior of the mice in these several mazes, prove conclusively that the nature of the errors is far more important than their number. Labyrinth D with its thirteen chances of error on the forward trip was not nearly as difficult for the dancer to learn to escape from as labyrinth C with its five errors. That the facility with which the twenty individuals whose records are given in Table 40 learned the path of D was not due to their previous labyrinth experience rather than to the regularity of the maze is proved by the results which I obtained by testing in D individuals which were new to labyrinth experiments. Even in this case, the number of tests necessary for a successful trip was seldom greater than ten. If further evidence of the ease with which a regular labyrinth path may be followed by the dancer were desired, it might be obtained by observation of the

TABLE 40

RESULTS OF LABYRINTH-D EXPERIMENTS, WITH TWENTY DANCERS

MALES			FEMALES		
No. OF MOUSE	No. OF FIRST CORRECT TEST	No. OF LAST OF TWO CORRECT TESTS	No. OF MOUSE	No. OF FIRST CORRECT TEST	No. OF LAST OF TWO CORRECT TESTS
2	3	7	29	10	11
58	7	10	49	7	8
30	9	10	57	3	6
60	10	14	215	6	10
402	10	11	415	7	8
76	4	7	75	4	13
78	4	5	77	11	12
86	3	9	87	4	9
88	4	8	85	3	4
90	7	8	83	4	7
Av.	6.1	8.9	Av.	5.9	8.8

behavior of an individual in labyrinths C and D. In the former, even after it has learned the path perfectly, the mouse hesitates at the doorways from time to time as if uncertain whether to turn to one side or go forward; in the latter there is seldom any hesitation at the turning points. The irregular labyrinth is followed carefully, as by choice of the path from point to point; the regular labyrinth is followed in machine fashion, — once started, the animal dashes through it.

From the results of these labyrinth experiments with dancers I am led to conclude that a standard maze for testing the modifiability of behavior of different kinds of animals should be constructed in conformity with the following suggestions. Errors by turning to the right, to the left, and by moving forward should occur with equal frequency, and in such order that no particular kind of error occurs repeatedly in succession. If we should designate these three types of mistake by the letters *r*, *l*, and *s* respectively, the error series of labyrinth C would read *l-l-r-s-l*. It therefore violates the rule of construction which I have just formulated. In the case of labyrinth D the series would read *l-s-r-s-l-s-r-s-l-s-r-s-l*. This also fails to conform with the requirement, for there are three errors of the first type, four of the second, and six of the third. Again, in a standard maze, the blind alleys should all be of the same length, and care should be taken to provide a sufficiently strong and uniform motive for escape. In the case of one animal the desire to escape from confinement may prove a satisfactory motive; in the case of another, the desire for food may conveniently supplement the dislike of confinement; and in still other cases it may appear that some form of punishment for errors is the only satisfactory basis of a motive for escape. Readers of this account of the behavior of the dancing mouse must not infer from my experimental results that the electric shock as a means of forcing discrimination will prove satisfactory in work with other animals or even with all other mammals. As a matter of fact it has already been proved by Doctor G. van T. Hamilton that the use of an electric shock may so intimidate a dog that experimentation is rendered difficult and of little value. And finally, in connection with this discussion of a standard labyrinth, I wish to emphasize the importance of so recording the results of experiments that they may be interpreted in terms of an animal's tendency to turn to the right or to the left. My work with the dancer has clearly shown that the avoidance of a particular error may be extremely difficult for left whirlers and very easy for right whirlers.

I hope I have succeeded in making clear by the foregoing account of my experiments that the labyrinth method is more

Q

satisfactory in general than the problem method as a means of measuring the rapidity of habit formation in the dancer, and I hope that I have made equally clear the fact that it is very valuable as a means of discovering the roles of the various senses in the acquirement of a habit (Chapter XI). From my own experience in the use of the labyrinth with the dancer and with other animals, I am forced to conclude that its chief value lies in the fact that it enables the experimenter so to control the factors of a complex situation that he may readily determine the importance of a given kind of sense data for the formation or the execution of a particular habit. As a means of measuring the intelligence of an animal, of determining the facility with which it is capable of adjusting itself to new environmental conditions, and of measuring the permanency of modifications which are wrought in its behavior by experimental conditions, I value the labyrinth method much less highly now than I did previou; to my study of the dancer. It is necessarily too complex for the convenient and reasonably certain interpretation of results. Precisely what is meant by this statement will be evident in the light of the results of the application of the discrimination method to the dancer, which are to be presented in the next chapter. The labyrinth method is an admirable means of getting certain kinds of qualitative results; it is almost ideal as a revealer of the role of the senses, and it may be used to advantage in certain instances for the quantitative study of habit formation and memory. Nevertheless, I think it may safely be said that the problem method and the discrimination method are likely to do more to advance our knowledge of animal behavior than the labyrinth method.

CHAPTER XIV

Habit Formation: The Discrimination Method

DISCRIMINATION is demanded of an animal in almost all forms of the problem and labyrinth methods, as well as in what I have chosen to call the discrimination method. In the latter, however, discrimination as the basis of a correct choice of an electric-box is so obviously important that it has seemed appropriate to distinguish this particular method of measuring the intelligence of the dancer from the others which have been used, by naming it the discrimination method.

It has been shown that neither the problem nor the labyrinth method proves wholly satisfactory as a means of measuring the rapidity of learning, or the duration of the effects of training, in the case of the dancer. The former type of test serves to reveal to the experimenter the general nature of the animal's capacity for profiting by experience; the latter serves equally well to indicate the parts which various receptors (some of which are sense organs) play in the formation and execution of habits. But neither of them is sufficiently simple, easy of control, uniform as to conditions which constitute bases for activity, and productive of interpretable quantitative results to render it satisfactory. The problem method is distinctly a qualitative method, and, in the case of the dancing mouse, my experiments have proved that the labyrinth method also yields results which are more valuable qualitatively than quantitatively. I had anticipated that various forms of the labyrinth method would enable me to measure the modifiability of behavior in the dancer with great accuracy, but, as will now be made apparent, the discrimination method proved to be a far more accurate method for this purpose.

Once more I should emphasize the fact that my statements concerning the value of methods apply especially to the dancing mouse. Certain of the tests which have proved to be almost ideal in my study of this peculiar little rodent would be useless in the study of many other mammals. An experimenter must work out his methods step by step in the light of the daily results of patient and intelligent observation of the motor capacity, habits, instincts, temperament, imitative tendency, intelligence, hardihood, and life-span of the animal which he is studying. The fact that punishment has proved to be more satisfactory than reward in experiments with the dancer does not justify the inference that it is more satisfactory in the case of the rat, cat, dog, or monkey. Methods which yielded me only qualitative results, if applied to other mammals might give accurate quantitative results; and, on the other hand, the discrimination method, which has proved invaluable for my quantitative work, might yield only qualitative results when applied to another kind of animal.

The form of the discrimination method whose results are to be presented in this chapter has already been described as white-black discrimination. In the discrimination box (Figures 14 and 15, p. 92) the two electric-boxes which were otherwise exactly alike in appearance were rendered discriminable for the mouse by the presence of white cardboards in one and black cardboards in the other. In order to escape from the narrow space before the entrances to the two electric-boxes, the dancer was required to enter the white box. If it entered the black box a weak electric shock was experienced. After two series of ten tests each, during which the animal was permitted to choose either the white or the black box without shock or hindrance, the training was begun. These two preliminary series serve to indicate the natural preference of the animal for white or black previous to the training. An individual which very strongly preferred the white might enter, from the first, the box thus distinguished, whereas another individual whose preference was for the black might persistently enter the black box in spite of the disagreeable shocks. First of all, therefore, the preliminary tests furnish a basis for the evaluation of the results of the subsequent training tests. On the day succeeding the last series of preliminary tests, and daily thereafter until the animal had acquired a perfect habit of choosing the white box, a series of training tests was given. These experiments were usually made in the morning between nine and twelve o'clock, in a room with south-east windows. The entrances to the electric-boxes faced the windows, consequently the mouse did not have to look toward the light when it was trying to discriminate white from black. All the conditions of the experiment, including the strength of the current for the shock, were kept as constant as possible.

Choice by position was effectively prevented, as a rule, by shifting the cardboards so that now the left now the right box was white. The order of these shifts for the white-black series whose results are quantitatively valuable appear in Table 12 (p. 111). That the order of these changes in position may be criticised in the light of the results which the tests gave, I propose to show hereafter in connection with certain other facts. The significant point is that the defects which are indicated by the averages of thousands of tests could not have been predicted with certainty even by the most experienced investigator in this field.

In Table 41 are to be found the average number of errors in each series of ten white-black discrimination tests for five males and for five females which were trained by being given ten tests per day, and similarly for the same number of individuals of each sex, trained by being given twenty tests per day. Since the results for these two conditions of training are very similar, the averages for the twenty individuals are presented in the last column of the table. For the present we may neglect the interesting individual, sex, and age differ-

TABLE 41

WHITE BLACK DISCRIMINATION TESTS. NUMBER OF ERRORS IN THE VARIOUS SERIES

	MALES			FEMALES			AVERAGES FOR ALL (20) MALES AND FEMALES
SERIES	AVERAGES FOR 5, 10 TESTS PER DAY	AVERAGES FOR 5, 20 TESTS PER DAY	GENERAL AVERAGES FOR 10	AVERAGES FOR 5, 10 TESTS PER DAY	AVERAGES FOR 5, 20 TESTS PER DAY	GENERAL AVERAGES FOR 10	
A	5.8	6.0	5.9	5.8	5.8	5.8	5.85
B	5.6	6.2	5.9	5.8	5.6	5.7	5.8
1	5.0	5.0	5.0	5.6	4.6	5.1	5.05
2	2.6	4.6	3.6	4.4	5.0	4.7	4.15
3	3.0	3.4	3.2	3.4	3.4	3.4	3.3
4	2.6	3.8	3.2	2.4	2.2	2.3	2.75
5	2.4	2.0	2.2	2.6	1.8	2.2	2.2
6	1.6	1.6	1.6	1.0	2.2	1.6	1.6
7	1.0	1.4	1.2	2.0	0.4	1.2	1.2
8	0.2	0.6	.4	1.4	1.6	1.5	.95
9	0.2	1.0	.6	0.6	0.8	.7	.65
10	0	.8	.4	1.0	0.8	.9	.65
11	0	.8	.4	0.8	0	.4	.40
12	0	.6	.3	0.4	0	.2	.25
13	0	0	0	0	0	0	0
14	0	0	0	0		0	0
15	0	0	0	0		0	0

ences which these experiments revealed and examine the significant features of the general averages, and of the white-black discrimination curve (Figure 29).

The preference series, *A* and *B*, reveal a constant tendency to choose the black box, whose strength as compared with

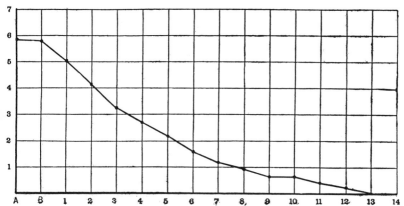

FIGURE 29. — Error curve plotted from the data given by twenty dancers in white-black discrimination tests. The figures in the left margin indicate the number of errors; those below the base line, the number of the series. *A* and *B* designate the preference series.

the tendency to choose the white box is as 5.8 is to 4.2. In other words, the dancer on the average chooses the black box almost six times in ten. The first series of training tests reduced this preference for black to zero, and succeeding series brought about a rapid and fairly regular decrease in the number of errors, until, in the thirteenth series, the white was chosen every time. Since I arbitrarily define a perfect habit of discrimination as the ability to choose the right box in three successive series of ten tests each, the tests ended with the fifteenth series.

The discrimination curve, Figure 29, is a graphic representation of the general averages of Table 41. It is an error curve, therefore. Starting at 5.85 for the first preliminary series, it descends to 5.8 for the second series, and thence abruptly to 5.05 for the first training series. This series of ten tests therefore served to reduce the black preference very considerably. The curve continues to descend constantly until the tenth series, for which the number of errors was the same as for the preceding series, .65. This irregularity in the curve, indicative, as it would appear, of a sudden cessation in the learning process, demands an explanation. My first thought was that an error in computation on my part might account for the shape of the curve. The error did not exist, but in my search for it I discovered what I now believe to be the cause of the interruption in the fall of the error curve. In all of the training series up to the tenth the white cardboard had been on the right and the left alternately or on one side two or three times in succession, whereas in the tenth series, as may be seen by referring to Table 12 (p. 111), it was on the left for the first four tests, then on the right four times, and, finally, on the left for the ninth test and on the right for the tenth. This series was therefore a decidedly more severe test of the animal's ability to discriminate white from black and to choose the white box without error than were any that had preceded it. If my interpretation of the results is correct, it was so much more severe than the ninth series that the process of habit formation was obscured. It would not be fair to say that the mouse temporarily ceased to profit by its experience; instead it profited even more than usually, in all probability, but the unavoidably abrupt increase in the difficultness of the tests was just sufficient to hide the improvement.

As I have suggested, the plan of experimentation may be criticised adversely in the light of this irregularity in the error curve. Had the conditions been perfectly satisfactory the curve would not have taken this form. I admit this, but at the same time I am glad that I chose that series of shifts in the position of the cardboards which, as it happens, served to exhibit an important aspect of quantitative measures of the modifiability of behavior that otherwise would not have been revealed. Our mistakes in method often teach us more than our successes. I have taken pains, therefore, to describe

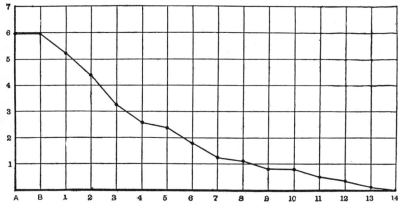

FIGURE 30. — Error curve plotted from the data given by thirty dancers, of different ages and under different conditions of training, in white-black discrimination tests.

the unsatisfactory as well as the satisfactory steps in my study of the dancer.

The form of the white-black discrimination curve of Figure 29 is more surprising than disappointing to me, for I had anticipated many more irregularities than appear. What I had expected, as the result of training five or even ten pairs of mice, was the kind of curve which is presented, for contrast with the one already discussed, in Figure 30. This also is an error curve, but, unlike the previous one, it is based upon results which were got from individuals of different ages which were trained according to the following different methods. Ten of these individuals were given two or five tests daily, ten were given ten tests daily, and ten were given twenty tests daily. The form of the curve serves to call attention to the importance of uniform conditions of training, in case the results are to be used as accurate measures of the rapidity of learning.

Examination of the detailed results of the white-black discrimination tests as they appear in the tables of Chapter VII will reveal the fact that some individuals succeeded in choosing correctly in a series of ten tests after not more than five series, whereas others required at least twice as many tests as the basis of a perfect series. In very few instances, however, was a perfect habit of discrimination established by fewer than one hundred tests. As the averages just presented in Table 41 indicate, fifteen series, or one hundred and fifty tests, were required for the completion of the experiment. One might search a long time, possibly, for another mammal whose curve of error in a simple discrimination test would fall as gradually as that of the dancer. It is fair to say that this animal learns very slowly as compared with most mammals which have been carefully studied. It is to be remembered, however, that quantitative results such as are here presented for the dancer are available for few if any other animals except the white rat. Neither in the form of the curve of learning nor in the behavior of the animal as it makes its choice of an electric-box is there evidence of anything which might be described as a sudden understanding of the situation. The dancer apparently learns by rote. It exhibits neither intelligent insight into an experimental situation nor ability to profit by the experience of its companions. That the selection of the white box occurs in various ways in different individuals, and even in the same individual at different periods in the training process, is the only indication of anything suggestive of implicit reasoning. Naturally enough comparison of the two boxes is the first method of selection. It takes the dancers a surprisingly long time to reach the point of making this comparison as soon as they are confronted by the entrances to the two electric-boxes.

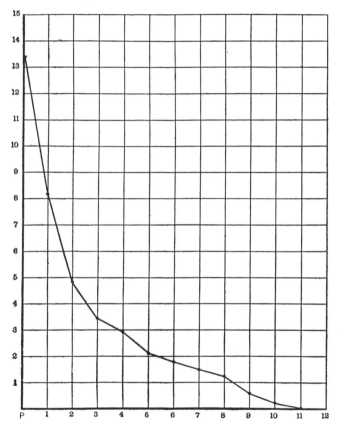

FIGURE 31. — Curve of habit formation, plotted from the data of labyrinth-D tests with ten males and ten females.

The habit of running from entrance to entrance repeatedly before either is entered, once having been acquired, is retained often throughout the training experiments. But in other cases, an individual finally comes to the point of choosing by what appears to be the immediate recognition of the right or the wrong box. In the former case the mouse enters the

white box immediately; in the latter, it rushes from the black
box into the white one without hesitation.   So much evidence the discrimination tests furnish of forms of behavior
which in our fellow-men we should interpret as rational.

Comparison of the error curves for the labyrinth tests
(Figures 26 and 31) with those for the discrimination tests
(Figures 29 and 30) reveals several interesting points of difference.   The former fall very abruptly at first, then with decreasing rapidity, to the base line; the latter, on the contrary,
fall gradually throughout their course.   Evidently the labyrinth habit is more readily acquired by the dancer than is the
visual discrimination habit.   Certain motor tendencies can
be established quickly, it would seem, whereas others, and
especially those which depend for their guidance upon visual
stimuli, are acquired with extreme slowness.   From this it
might be inferred that the labyrinth method is naturally far
better suited to the nature of the dancer than is any form of
the discrimination method.   I believe that this inference is
correct, but at the same time I am of the opinion that the
discrimination method is of even greater value than the
labyrinth method as a means of discovering the capacity of
the animal for modification of behavior.

Inasmuch as my first purpose in the repetition of white-
black discrimination tests with a number of individuals
was to obtain quantitative results which should accurately
indicate individual, age, and sex differences in the rapidity
of learning, it is important to consider the reliability of the
averages with which we have been dealing.   Possibly two
groups of five male dancers each, chosen at random, would
yield very different results in discrimination tests.   This
would almost certainly be true if the animals were selected
from different lots, or were kept before and during the tests
under different environmental conditions.   But from my

experiments it has become apparent that the average of the results given by five individuals of the same sex, age, and condition of health, when kept in the same environment and subjected to the same experimental tests, is sufficiently constant from group to group to warrant its use as an index of modifiability for the race. This expression, index of modifiability, is a convenient mode of designating the average number of tests necessary for the establishment of a perfect habit of white-black discrimination. Hereafter I shall use it instead of a more lengthy descriptive phrase.

As an indication of the degree of accuracy of measurements of the rapidity of learning which are obtained by the use of 5 individuals I may offer the following figures. For one of two directly comparable groups of 5 male dancers which were chosen from 16 individuals which had been trained, the number of tests which resulted in a perfect habit of white-black discrimination was 92; for the other group it was 96. These indices for strictly comparable groups of 5 individuals each differ from one another by less than 5 per cent. Similarly, in the case of two groups of females, the indices of modifiability were 94 and 104. These figures designate the number of tests up to the point at which errors ceased for at least three successive series (30 tests).

The determination of the probable error of the index of modifiability further aids us in judging of the reliability of the measure of the rapidity of learning which is obtained by averaging the results for 5 individuals. For a group of 5 males (Table 43, p. 243) the index was 72 ± 3.5; and for a group of 5 females of the same age as the males and strictly comparable with respect to conditions of white-black training, it was 104 ± 2.9. A probable error of ± 3.5 indicates the reliability of the first of these indices of modifiability; one of ± 2.9, that of the second.

I do not doubt that 10 individuals would furnish a more reliable average than 5, but I do doubt whether the purposes of my experiments would have justified the great increase in work which the use of averages based upon so large a group would have necessitated.

Further discussion of the index of modifiability may be postponed until the several indices which serve as measures of the efficiency of different methods of training have been presented in the next chapter.

From the data which constitute the materials of the present chapter it is apparent that the results of the discrimination method are amenable to much more accurate quantitative treatment than are those of the problem method or the labyrinth method. But I have done little more as yet than describe the method by which it is possible to measure certain dimensions of the intelligence of the dancer, and to state some general results of its application. In the remaining chapters it will be our task to discover the value of this method and of the results which it has yielded.

CHAPTER XV

The Efficiency of Training Methods

The nature of the modifications which are wrought in the behavior of an organism varies with the method of training. This fact is recognized by human educators, as well as by students of animal behavior (makers of the science of comparative pedagogy), but unfortunately accurate measurements of the efficiency of our educational methods are rare.

Whatever the subject of investigation, there are two pre-eminently important aspects of the educative process which may be taken as indications of the value of the method of training by which it was initiated and stimulated. I refer to the rapidity of the learning process and its degree of permanency, or, in terms of habit formation, to the rapidity with which a habit is acquired, and to its duration. Of these two easily measurable aspects of the modifications in which training results, I have chosen the first as a means to the special study of the efficiency of the training to which the dancing mouse has been subjected in my experiments.

The reader who has followed my account of the behavior of the dancer up to this point will recall that in practically all of the discrimination experiments the number of tests in a series was ten. Some readers doubtless have wondered why ten rather than five or twenty tests was selected as the number in each continuous series. I shall now attempt to answer the question. It was simply because the efficiency of that number of tests, given daily, when taken in connection with the amount of time which the conduct of the experiments required, rendered it the most satisfactory number. But this statement demands elaboration and explanation.

Very early in my study of the dancer, I learned that a single experience in a given experiment day after day had so little effect upon the animal that a perfect habit could not be established short of several weeks or months. Similarly, experiments in which two tests per day were given proved that even a simple discrimination habit cannot be acquired by the animal under this condition of training with sufficient rapidity to enable the experimenter to study the formation of the habit advantageously. Next, ten tests in succession each day were given. The results proved satisfactory, consequently I proceeded to carry out my investigation on the basis of a ten-test series. After this method had been thoroughly tried, I decided to investigate the efficiency of other methods for the purpose of instituting comparisons of efficiency and discovering the number of tests per day whose efficiency, as measured by the rapidity of the formation of a white-black discrimination habit, is highest.

For this purpose I carefully selected five pairs of dancers of the same age, descent, and previous experience, and gave them white-black tests in series of two tests per day (after the twentieth day the number was increased to five) until they had acquired a perfect habit of discriminating. Similarly other dancers were trained by means of series of ten tests, twenty tests, or one hundred tests per day. Since it was my aim to make the results of these various tests strictly comparable, I spared no pains in selecting the individuals, and in maintaining constancy of experimental conditions. The order of the changes in the position of the cardboards which was adhered to in these efficiency tests was that given in Table 12.

At the beginning of the two-test training I thought it possible that the animals might acquire a perfect habit with only a few more days' training than is required by the ten-test method. This did not prove to be the case, for at the end of the twentieth day (after forty tests in all) the average number of mistakes, as Table 42 shows, was 3.2 for the males and 3.0 for the females. Up to this time there had been clear evidence of the formation of a habit of discriminating white from black, but, on the other hand, the method had proved very unsatisfactory because the first test each day usually appeared to be of very different value from the second. On account of the imminent danger of the interruption of the experiment by the rapid spread of an epidemic among my mice, I decided to increase the number of tests in each series to five in order to complete the experiment if possible before the disease could destroy the animals. On the twenty-first day and thereafter, five-test series were given instead of two-test. Unfortunately I was able to complete the experiment up to the point of thirty successive correct tests with only six of the ten individuals whose numbers appear at the top of Table 42. That the results of this table are reliable, despite the fact that some of the individuals had to be taken out of the experiment on account of bad condition, is indicated by the fact that all the mice continued to do their best to discriminate so long as they were used. Possibly the habit would have been acquired a little more quickly by some of the individuals had they been stronger and more active.

It should be explained at this point that the results in all the efficiency-of-training tables of this chapter are arranged, as in the previous white-black discrimination tables, in tens, that is, each figure in the tables indicates the number of errors in a series of ten tests. In all cases *A* and *B* mark preliminary series of tests which were given at the rate of ten tests per

R

series. The numbers in the first column of these tables designate groups of ten tests each, and not necessarily daily series. In Table 42, for example, 1 includes the results of the first five days of training, 2, of the next five

TABLE 42

EFFICIENCY OF TRAINING. WHITE-BLACK TESTS AT THE RATE OF 2 OR 5 PER DAY

SETS OF 10	MALES						FEMALES					
	80	82	84	86	88	Av.	73	79	83	85	89	Av.
A	5	5	4	8	5	5.4	5	6	7	7	6	6.2
B	5	3	6	5	6	5.0	7	5	7	6	7	6.4
1	7	7	6	6	6	6.4	7	6	9	4	6	6.4
2	2	1	0	6	6	3.0	6	5	6	5	5	5.4
3	4	5	4	1	2	3.2	6	5	2	4	1	3.6
4	3	4	7	2	0	3.2	4	3	1	4	3	3.0
5	2	3	3	2	4	2.8	—	3	4	3	1	2.7
6	2	2	—	2	2	2.0	—	0	2	2	0	1.0
7	—	1	—	0	1	0.7	—	1	0	2	1	1.0
8	—	—	—	1	1	1.0	—	1	1	0	0	0.5
9	—	—	—	0	1	0.5	—	1	1	0	0	0.5
10	—	—	—	0	0	0	—	0	0	0	0	0
11	—	—	—	0	0	0	—	0	0			0
12	—	—	—		0	0	—	0	0			0

days, and so on. The table shows that No. 80 made seven wrong choices in the first five series of two tests each. This method of grouping results serves to make the data for the different methods directly comparable, and at the same time it saves space at the sacrifice of very little valuable information concerning the nature of the daily results. It is to be noted, with emphasis, that the two-five tests per day training established a perfect habit after four weeks of training. This method is therefore costly of the experimenter's time.

The results of the ten-test training as they appear in Table 43 need no special comment, for quite similar data have already been examined in other connections. In the case of this table it is to be remembered that each figure represents the number of errors for a single day as well as for a series of ten successive tests. The results of Table 44, on the other

TABLE 43

EFFICIENCY OF TRAINING. WHITE-BLACK TESTS AT THE RATE OF
10 PER DAY

SETS OF 10	MALES						FEMALES					
	210	220	230	410	420	Av.	215	225	235	415	425	Av.
A	6	5	6	6	6	5.8	8	4	4	8	5	5.8
B	6	8	8	5	1	5.6	8	7	6	6	2	5.8
1	6	7	6	2	4	5.0	7	6	5	6	4	5.6
2	4	3	1	2	3	2.6	5	6	4	2	5	4.4
3	3	1	4	3	4	3.0	3	3	4	3	4	3.4
4	5	0	3	3	2	2.6	2	1	3	3	3	2.4
5	3	0	4	1	4	2.4	1	3	3	3	3	2.6
6	2	1	4	0	1	1.6	2	1	1	1	0	1.0
7	1	0	3	1	0	1.0	1	1	2	3	3	2.0
8	0	0	1	0	0	0.2	0	0	2	2	3	1.4
9	0	0	0	1	0	0.2	1	0	0	1	1	0.6
10	0		0	0		0	0	2	1	0	2	1.0
11		0	0			0	0	3	0	1	0	0.8
12			0		0	0	0	0	0	2	0	0.4
13								0	0	0	0	0
14								0		0		0
15										0		0

TABLE 44

EFFICIENCY OF TRAINING. WHITE-BLACK TESTS AT THE RATE OF
20 PER DAY

SETS OF 10	MALES						FEMALES					
	72	74	208	240	402	Av.	217	239	245	403	407	Av.
A	4	6	7	7	6	6.0	5	4	7	7	6	5.8
B	6	4	6	8	7	6.2	7	3	5	8	5	5.6
1	3	5	7	5	5	5.0	3	6	4	4	6	4.6
2	4	3	7	5	4	4.6	7	3	5	4	6	5.0
3	3	3	3	5	3	3.4	4	3	3	2	5	3.4
4	6	3	1	4	5	3.8	5	0	1	2	3	2.2
5	4	1	0	2	3	2.0	6	0	0	1	2	1.8
6	3	1	0	2	2	1.6	4	1	1	0	6	2.2
7	3	2	0	1	1	1.4	1	0	0	0	1	0.4
8	2	0		0	1	0.6	0	3	3	0	2	1.6
9	2	1		1	1	1.0	1	0	0		3	0.8
10	1	2		1	0	0.8	0	1	1		2	0.8
11	3	1		0	0	0.8	0	0	0		0	0
12	1	2		0	0	0.6	0	0	0		0	0
13	0	0		0		0		0	0		0	0
14	0	0				0						
15	0	0				0						

hand, appear as subdivided series, since each daily series was constituted by two series of ten tests, or in all twenty tests.

Finally, in Table 45 I have arranged the results of what may fairly be called the continuous training method. In connection with several of the labyrinth experiments of Chapter XIII continuous training proved very satisfactory. It therefore seemed worth while to ascertain whether the same method would not be more efficient than any other for the establishment of a white-black discrimination habit. That this method was not applied to ten individuals as were the two-five-test, the ten-test, and the twenty-test methods is due to the fact that it proved practically inadvisable to continue the tests long enough to complete the experiment. I have usually designated the method as one hundred or more tests daily. I applied this training method first to individuals Nos. 51 and 60. At the end of one hundred and twenty tests with each of these individuals I was forced to discontinue the experiment for the day because of the approach of darkness. In the table the end of a series for the day is indicated by a heavy line. The following day Nos. 51 and 60 succeeded in acquiring a perfect habit after a few more tests.

TABLE 45

EFFICIENCY OF TRAINING. WHITE-BLACK TESTS AT THE RATE OF 100 OR MORE PER DAY

SETS OF 10	51[1]	60	87	Av.	SETS OF 10	51	60	87	Av.
A	5	5	6	5.3	12	2	1	1	1.3
B	5	3	7	5.0	13	4	1	2	2.3
					14	1	2	1	1.3
1	6	6	5	5.7	15	3	1	5	3.0
2	3	2	5	3.3	16	3	3	2	2.7
3	5	4	7	5.3	17	1	0	1	0.7
4	7	4	5	5.3	18	2	0	1	1.0
5	6	2	3	3.7	19	0	0	2	0.7
6	1	1	3	1.7	20	0		0	0
7	4	2	3	3.0	21	0		1	0.3
8	3	3	0	2.0	22			—	
9	2	2	3	2.3	23			—	
10	5	0	2	2.3	24			—	
11	1	2	2	1.7					

[1] Age of No. 51, 22 weeks. Age of No. 60, 17 weeks. Age of No. 87, 8 weeks.

The results of the continuous training method for these two mice were so strikingly different from those yielded by the other methods that I at once suspected the influence of some factor other than that of the number of tests per day. The ages of Nos. 51 and 60 at the time of their tests were twenty-two and seventeen weeks, respectively, whereas all the individuals used in connection with the other efficiency tests were four weeks of age. It seemed possible that the slow habit formation exhibited in the continuous training experiments might be due to the greater age of the mice. I therefore selected a healthy active female which was only eight weeks old, and tried to train her by the continuous training method. With this individual, No. 87, the results were even more discouraging than those previously obtained, for she was still imperfect in her discrimination at the end of two hundred and ten tests. At that point the experiment was interrupted, and it seemed scarcely worth while to continue it further at a later date. The evidence of the extremely low efficiency of the continuous method in comparison with the other methods which we have been considering is so conclusive that further comment seems superfluous.

We are now in a position to compare the results of the several methods of training which have been applied to the dancer, and to attempt to get satisfactory quantitative expressions of the efficiency of each method. I have arranged in Table 46 the general averages yielded by the four methods. Although these general results hide certain important facts which will be exhibited later, they clearly indicate that an increase in the number of tests per day does not necessarily result in an increase in the rapidity of habit formation. Should we attempt, on superficial examination, to interpret the figures of this table, we would doubtless say that in efficiency the two-five-test method stands first, the continuous-

test method last, while the ten-test and twenty-test methods
occupy intermediate positions.

TABLE 46

EFFICIENCY OF TRAINING

Number of Errors in White-Black Series for Different Methods of
Training

SETS OF 10	2 OR 5 TESTS PER DAY	10 TESTS PER DAY	20 TESTS PER DAY	100 OR MORE TESTS PER DAY
A	5.8	5.8	5.9	5.3
B	5.7	5.7	5.9	5.0
1	6.4	5.3	4.8	5.7
2	4.2	3.5	4.8	3.3
3	3.4	3.2	3.4	5.3
4	3.1	2.5	3.0	5.3
5	2.7	2.5	1.9	3.7
6	1.5	1.3	1.9	1.7
7	0.9	1.5	0.9	3.0
8	0.7	0.8	1.1	2.0
9	0.5	0.4	0.9	2.3
10	0	0.5	0.8	2.3
11	0	0.4	0.4	1.7
12	0	0.2	0.3	1.3
13		0	0	2.3
14		0	0	1.3
15		0	0	3.0
16				2.7
17				0.7
18				1.0
19				0.7
20				0

We may now apply to the results of our efficiency-of-training tables the method of measuring efficiency which was
mentioned at the end of the preceding chapter as the *index*

of modifiability (that number of tests after which no errors occur for at least thirty tests). By taking the average number of tests for the several individuals in each of the Tables 42, 43, 44, and 45 we obtain the following expressions of efficiency: —

Method	Index of Modifiability (Efficiency)
Two-five-test	81.7 ± 2.7
Ten-test . , ...	88.0 ± 4.1
Twenty-test	91.0 ± 5.3
Continuous-test	170.0 ± 4.8

Since the difference between the indices for the ten-test and the twenty-test methods lies within the limits of their probable errors (± 4.1 and ± 5.3) it is evident that it is not significant. Except for this, I think these indices may be accepted as indications of real differences in the value of the several methods of training.

A somewhat different interpretation of our results is suggested by the grouping of individuals according to sex. In Table 47 appear the general averages for the males and the females which were tested by the several methods. The most striking fact exhibited by this table is that of the high efficiency of the twenty-test method for the females. Apparently

TABLE 47

EFFICIENCY OF TRAINING

CONDITION	MALES INDEX OF MODIFIABILITY	FEMALES INDEX OF MODIFIABILITY
2 or 5 tests per day	85.0	80.0
10 tests per day	72.0	104.0
20 tests per day	94.0	88.0
100 or more tests per day	160.0	180.0

they profited much more quickly by this method than by the ten-test method, whereas just the reverse is true of the males. I present the data of this table merely to show that general averages may hide important facts.

From all considerations that have been mentioned thus far the reader would be justified in concluding that I made a mistake in selecting the ten-test method for my study of the modifiability of the behavior of the dancer. That this conclusion is not correct is due to the time factor in the experiments. If the dancer could acquire a perfect habit as a result of twelve days' training, no matter whether two, five, ten, or twenty tests were given daily, it would, of course, be economical of time for the experimenter to employ the two-test method. But if, on the contrary, the two-test method required twice as many days' training as the five-test method, it would be economical for him to use the five-test method despite the fact that he would have to give a larger number of tests than the two-test method would have demanded. In a word, the time which the work requires depends upon the number of series which have to be given, as well as upon the number of tests in each series. As it happens, the ten-test method demands less of the experimenter's time than do methods with fewer tests per day. The twenty-test method is even more economical of time, but it has a fatal defect. It is at times too tiresome for both mouse and man. These facts indicate that a balance should be struck between number of tests and number of series. The fewer the tests per day, within the limits of two and one hundred, the higher the efficiency of the method of training, as measured in terms of the total number of tests necessary for the establishment of a perfect habit, and the lower its efficiency as measured in terms of the number of series given. The greater the number of tests per day, on the other hand, the higher the efficiency of the method in terms of the number of series, and the lower its efficiency in terms of the total number of tests.   By taking into account these facts, together with the fact of fatigue, we are led to the conclusion that ten tests per day is the most satisfactory number.

If my time and attention had not been fully occupied with other problems, I should have determined the efficiency of various methods of training in terms of the duration of habit, as well as in terms of the rapidity of its formation.   As these two measures of efficiency might give contradictory results, it is obvious that a training method cannot be fairly evaluated without consideration of both the rapidity of habit formation and the permanency of the habit.   *A priori* it seems not improbable that slowness of learning should be directly correlated with a high degree of permanency.   By the further application of the method which I have used in this study of the efficiency of training we may hope to get a definite answer to this and many other questions concerning the nature of the educative process and the conditions which influence it.

CHAPTER XVI

THE DURATION OF HABITS: MEMORY AND RE-LEARNING

THE effects of training gradually disappear. Habits wane with disuse. In the dancer, it is not possible to establish with certainty the existence of memory in the introspective psychological sense; but it is possible to measure the efficiency of the training to which the animal is subjected, and the degree of permanency of habits. The materials which constitute this chapter concern the persistence of unused habits, and the influence of previous training on the re-acquisition of a habit which has been lost or on the acquisition of a new habit. For convenience of description, I shall refer to certain of the facts which are to be discussed as facts of memory, with the clear understanding that consciousness is not necessarily implied. By memory, wherever it occurs in this book, I mean the ability of the dancer to retain the power of adaptive action which it has acquired through training.

I first discovered memory in the dancer, although there was previously no reason for doubting its existence, in connection with the ladder-climbing tests of Chapter XII. In this experiment two individuals which had perfectly learned to escape from the experiment box to the nest-box by way of the wire ladder, when tested after an interval of two weeks, during which they had remained in the nest-box without opportunity to exercise their newly acquired habit, demonstrated their memory of the method of escape by returning to the nest-box by way of the ladder as soon as they were given opportunity to do so. As it did not lend itself readily to quantitative study, no attempts were made to measure the duration of this particular habit. At best the climbing of a wire ladder is of very uncertain value as an indication of the influence of training.

Similarly, the persistence of habits has been forced upon my attention day after day in my various experiments with the mice. It is obvious, then, that the simple fact of memory is well established, and that we may turn at once to an examination of the facts revealed by special memory and re-learning experiments.

The visual discrimination method, which proved invaluable as a means of measuring the rapidity of habit formation, proved equally serviceable in the measurement of the permanency or duration of habits. Memory tests for discrimination habits were made as follows. After a dancer had been trained in the discrimination box so that it could choose the correct electric-box, white, red, blue, or green as it might be, in three successive daily series of ten tests each, it was permitted to remain for a certain length of time without training and without opportunity to exercise its habit of visual discrimination and choice. At the expiration of the rest interval, as we may designate the period during which the habit was not in use, the mouse was placed in the discrimination box under precisely the same conditions in which it had been trained and was given a series of ten memory tests with the box to be chosen alternately on the right and on the left. In order that the entire series of ten tests, and sometimes two such series given on consecutive days, might be available as indications of the duration of a habit, the mouse was permitted to enter and pass through either of the electric-boxes without receiving a shock. Had the shock been given as punishment for a wrong choice, it is obvious that only the first test of the memory series would be of value as an indication of the existence of a previously acquired habit. Even under the conditions of no shock and no stop or hindrance the first test of each memory series is of pre-eminent importance, for the mouse tends to persist in choosing either the side or the visual condition (sometimes one, sometimes the other) which it chooses in the first test. If the wrong box is chosen to begin with, mistakes are likely to continue because of the lack of punishment; in this case the animal discriminates, but there is no evidence that it remembers the right box. Likewise, if the right electric-box is chosen in the first test, correct choices may continue simply because the animal has discovered that it can safely enter that particular box; again, the animal discriminates without depending necessarily upon its earlier experience. I have occasionally observed a series of ten correct choices, made on the basis of an accidental right start, followed by another series in which almost every choice was wrong, because the animal happened to start wrong.

As the results of my tests of memory are of such a nature that they cannot advantageously be averaged, I have arranged in Table 48 a number of typical measurements of the duration of visual discrimination habits. In this table I have indicated the number and age of the individual tested, the habit of discrimination which had been acquired, the length of the rest interval, the result of the first test (right or wrong), and the number of errors made in each series of ten memory tests.

This quantitative study of the duration of simple habits of choice showed that in the majority of cases a perfectly acquired habit persists for at least two weeks. To be perfectly fair to the animal I must restrict this statement to visual conditions other than colors, for the dancer exhibited little

TABLE 48

MEASUREMENTS OF THE DURATION OF A HABIT

Memory

No.	Age	Name of Test	Rest Interval	First Choice	Errors First Series	Errors Second Series
1000	25 weeks	White-black	4 weeks	Right	o	
5	27	White-black	4	Right	5	7
210	15	White-black	8	Right	5	
220	15	White-black	8	Right	4	
230	15	White-black	8	Wrong	5	
215	15	White-black	8	Right	5	
225	15	White-black	8	Right	2	
235	15	White-black	8	Right	7	
410	15	White-black	8	Wrong	4	
415	15	White-black	8	Wrong	6	
420	15	White-black	8	Wrong	3	
425	15	White-black	8	Right	3	
2	28	Black-white	4	Wrong	9	
7	17	Black-white	2	Wrong	1	
7	21	Black-white	6	Right	1	
7	27	Black-white	10	Right	1	6
998	18	Black-white	2	Wrong	3	
998	22	Black-white	4	Right	o	
998	28	Black-white	10	Right	5	5
13	10	Black-white	4	Right	3	
14	10	Black-white	4	Right	3	
15	10	Black-white	4	Right	2	
16	10	Black-white	4	Right	4	
1000	25	Light blue-orange	4	Right	4	
2	28	Light blue-orange	2	Wrong	5	
5	28	Light blue-orange	6	Wrong	4	6
3	25	Light blue-orange	4	Wrong	8	
10	24	Light blue-orange	2	Right	8	
10	26	Light blue-orange	2	Right	5	
11	25	Light blue-orange	2	Right	6	
11	27	Light blue-orange	2	Wrong	5	
151	13	Green-red	2	Right	1	o
152	13	Green-red	2	Right	5	1

ability either to acquire or to retain a habit of distinguishing spectral colors. Altogether, I made a large number of white-black and black-white memory tests after rest intervals of four, six, eight, or ten weeks. The results for the four-week interval show extreme individual differences in memory. Number 1000, for example, was able to choose correctly every time in a series of white-black tests after a rest interval of four weeks, whereas No. 5 was wrong as often as she was right after the same interval. I have placed the results for these two individuals at the head of the table because they suggest the variations which render averages undesirable. Number 1000 had a perfect habit at the end of four weeks of disuse; No. 5 had no habit whatever. I shall reserve further discussion of age, sex, and individual differences in the permanency of habits for the next chapter.

With Nos. 7 and 998 memory tests were made after three different rest intervals. At the end of two weeks the black-white habit was present in both individuals, although it was not perfect. After six and four weeks, respectively (see Table 48), it still persisted; in fact, it apparently had improved as the result of additional training after the earlier memory tests. At the expiration of ten weeks it had wholly disappeared. In her first series of memory tests after the ten-week interval No. 7 made only one error, but a chance choice of the black (right) in the first test and the subsequent choice of the box in which no shock had been received serve to account for results which at first appear to be indicative of memory. That this explanation is correct is proved by the fact that a second memory series, in which the first choice happened to be wrong, resulted in six mistakes. Evidently she had lost the habit.

In no instance have memory tests definitely indicated the presence of a habit after a rest interval of more than eight weeks. It is safe, therefore, to conclude from the results which have been obtained that a white-black or black-white discrimination habit may persist during an interval of from two to eight weeks of disuse, but that such a habit is seldom perfect after more than four weeks.

The measurements of memory which were made in connection with color discrimination experiments are markedly different from those which were obtained in the brightness tests. As might have been anticipated (?), in view of the extreme difficulty with which the dancer learns to discriminate colors, the habit of discriminating between qualitatively different visual conditions does not persist very long. I have never obtained evidence of a perfect habit after an interval of more than two weeks, and usually, as is apparent from Table 48, the tests indicated very imperfect memory at the end of that interval. It seems probable that even in these so-called color tests discrimination is partly by brightness difference, and that the imperfection of the habit and its short duration are due to the fact that the basis of discrimination is inadequate. This is the only explanation which I have to offer for the difference which has been demonstrated to exist between the duration of brightness discrimination habits and color discrimination habits.

The duration of a discrimination habit having been measured with a fair degree of accuracy, I undertook the task of ascertaining whether training whose results have wholly disappeared, so far as memory tests are in question, influences the re-acquisition of the same habit. Can a habit be re-acquired with greater facility than it was originally acquired? Is re-learning easier than learning? To obtain an answer to the question which may be asked in these different forms, ten individuals were experimented with in accordance with a method whose chief features are now to be stated. In each of these ten individuals a perfect white-black habit was established by the use of the standard series of tests the order of which is given in Table 12. At the expiration of a rest interval of eight weeks precisely the same series of tests were repeated as memory and re-training tests. In this repetition,

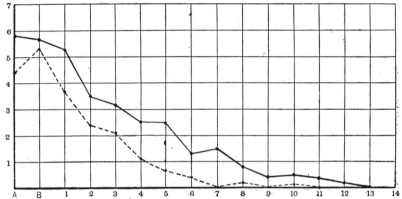

FIGURE 32. — Error curves plotted from the data given by ten dancers in white-black discrimination tests. The solid line (———) is the error curve of the original learning process; the broken line (- - - - - -) is that of the re-learning process, after an interval of eight weeks.

the preliminary series, *A* and *B*, served as memory tests, and the subsequent training series, as re-training series.

The striking results of this investigation of re-learning are exhibited in the curves of learning and re-learning of Figure 32. These curves make it appear that the mice re-acquired the white-black discrimination habit much more readily than they had originally acquired it. But in addition to furnishing the basis for some such statement as the foregoing, the curves suggest a serious criticism of the experiment.

In the original tests, the preliminary series indicated a strong preference for black. In series *A* it was chosen on the average 5.8 times in 10, and in series *B*, 5.7 times. This preference was rapidly overcome by the training series, and

s

at the end of 130 tests discrimination was perfect. All this appears in the curve of learning (solid line of figure). On the other hand, these preliminary series when repeated as memory tests, after a rest-interval of eight weeks, gave markedly different results. Series *A* indicated preference for white (5.6 times in 10) instead of black, and series *B* indicated only a slight preference for black. In brief, series *A* and *B* show that the preference for black was considerably stronger at the beginning of the training than at the beginning of the re-training.

In the light of these facts it is fair to claim that the effects of the white-black training had not wholly disappeared as the result of eight weeks of rest, and that the experiment therefore fails to furnish satisfactory grounds for the statement that re-learning occurs more rapidly than learning. I accept this criticism as pertinent, although not necessarily valid, and at the same time I freely admit that the results have a significance which I had not anticipated. But they are not less interesting or valuable on that account. Granting, then, that at least some of the ten individuals which took part in the experiment had not completely lost the memory of their white-black training at the end of eight weeks, it is still possible that an examination of the individual results may justify some conclusion concerning the question which was proposed at the outset of the investigation. Such an examination is made possible by Tables 49 and 50, in which I have arranged separately the results for the males and the females.

Only three of the ten individuals failed to re-acquire the habit of white-black discrimination more quickly than it had originally been acquired, and, in the case of these exceptions, No. 220 required exactly the same number of tests in each case, and No. 420 was placed at a slight disadvantage

TABLE 49

WHITE-BLACK TRAINING. TEN TESTS PER DAY

Males

	TRAINING						RE-TRAINING					
	210	220	230	410	420	Av.	210	220	230	410	420	Av.
A	6	5	6	6	6	5.8	5	4	5	4	3	4.2
B	6	8	8	5	1	5.6	8	4	5	4	6	5.4
1	6	7	6	2	4	5.0	3	3	4	7	3	4.0
2	4	3	1	2	3	2.6	2	4	2	5	3	3.2
3	3	1	4	3	4	3.0	1	4	1	4	1	2.2
4	5	0	3	3	2	2.6	0	1	0	1	2	0.8
5	3	0	4	1	4	2.4	0	2	0	2	0	0.8
6	2	1	4	0	1	1.6	0	1	0	0	2	0.6
7	1	0	3	1	0	1.0	0			0	0	0
8	0	0	1	0	0	0.2	0			0	1	0.2
9	0	0	0	1	0	0.2	0				0	0
10	0		0	0		0					1	0.2
11			0	0		0					0	0
12			0			0					0	0
13											0	0
14												
15												

in the re-learning series by an interruption of the training between the seventh and the eighth series. Had his training been completed by the sixth series he too would have had the same number of tests in training and re-training. Moreover, and this is of preëminent importance for a fair interpretation of the results, in several instances even those individuals which exhibited as strong a preference for the black in the memory series as in the preliminary series re-learned more quickly than they had learned. Number

TABLE 50

WHITE-BLACK TRAINING. TEN TESTS PER DAY

Females

	TRAINING						RE-TRAINING					
	215	225	235	415	425	Av.	215	225	235	415	425	Av.
A	8	4	4	8	5	5.8	5	2	7	6	3	4.6
B	8	7	6	6	2	5.8	8	5	6	4	3	5.2
1	7	6	5	6	4	5.6	4	1	5	4	3	3.4
2	5	6	4	2	5	4.4	1	1	1	2	3	1.6
3	3	3	4	3	4	3.4	1	0	3	6	0	2.0
4	2	1	3	3	3	2.4	0	0	3	3	1	1.4
5	1	3	3	3	3	2.6	0	0	died	2	0	0.5
6	2	1	1	1	0	1.0	0			1	0	0.2
7	1	1	2	3	3	2.0				0	0	0
8	0	0	2	2	3	1.4				1		0.2
9	1	0	0	1	1	0.6				0		0
10	0	2	1	0	2	1.0				0		0
11	0	3	0	1	0	0.8				0		0
12	0	0	0	2	0	0.4						
13		0	0	0	0	0						
14		0		0		0						
15				0		0						

210, for example, although he gave no evidence of memory, and, in fact, chose the black more frequently in the memory series than he did in the preliminary series, re-acquired the discrimination habit in less than half the number of tests which had been necessary for the establishment of the habit originally.

The facts which have been presented thus far become more significant when the indices of modifiability for the learning and the re-learning processes are compared.

INDICES OF MODIFIABILITY

	LEARNING	RE-LEARNING
Females	104	42.5
Males	72	54

The behavior of the mice in the experiments, the detailed results of Tables 49 and 50, and the indices of modifiability together justify the following conclusions. Most of the ten dancers, at the end of a rest interval of. eight weeks, had so far lost the habit of white-black discrimination that memory tests furnished no conclusive evidence of the influence of previous training; a few individuals seemed to possess traces of the habit after such an interval. In the case of each group of individuals re-training brought about the establishment of a perfect habit far more quickly than did the original training. This suggests the existence of two kinds or aspects of organic modification in connection with training; those which constitute the basis of a definite form of motor activity, and those which constitute the bases or dispositions for the acquirement of certain types of behavior. There are several indications that further study of the modifiability of behavior will furnish the facts which are necessary to render this suggestion meaningful.

Closely related to the facts which have been revealed by the re-training experiments are certain results of the labyrinth experiments. For the student of animal behavior, as for the human educator, it is of importance to learn whether one kind of training increases the efficiency of similar forms of training. Can a dancer learn a given labyrinth path the more readily because it has previously had experience in another form of labyrinth?

The answer to this question, which my experimental results furnish, is given in Table 51. In the upper half of the table have been arranged the results for six individuals which were trained first in labyrinth B, then in labyrinth C, and finally in labyrinth D.   Below, in similar fashion, are given the results for six individuals which were trained in the same three labyrinths in the order C, B, D, instead of B, C, D.   My purpose in giving the training in these two orders was to ascertain whether labyrinth C, which had proved to be rather difficult

TABLE 51

THE INFLUENCE OF ONE LABYRINTH HABIT UPON THE FORMATION OF ANOTHER

No.	LABYRINTH B		LABYRINTH C		LABYRINTH D	
	NO. OF FIRST CORRECT TEST	NO. OF LAST OF FIVE CORRECT TESTS	NO. OF FIRST CORRECT TEST	NO. OF LAST OF FIVE CORRECT TESTS	NO. OF FIRST CORRECT TEST	NO. OF LAST OF TWO CORRECT TESTS
76	8	14	3	19	4	7
78	5	20	6	14	4	5
86	13	22	5	12	3	9
75	4	15	8	19	4	13
77	7	11	11	29	11	12
87	12	22	9	20	4	9
Av.	8.2	17.3	7.0	18.8	5.0	9.2
	LABYRINTH C		LABYRINTH B		LABYRINTH D	
58	16	—	2	14	7	10
60	17	—	13	37	10	14
88	25	35	9	22	4	8
49	34	—	1	5	7	8
57	15	—	3	20	3	6
85	11	18	2	11	3	4
Av.	19.7	26.5	5.0	18.2	5.7	8.3

for most individuals, would be more easily learned if the training in it were preceded by training in labyrinth B.

The results are sufficiently definite to warrant the conclusion that experience in B rendered the learning of C easier than it would have been had there been no previous labyrinth training. Those individuals whose first labyrinth training was in C made their first correct trip as the result of 19.7 trials, whereas those which had previously been trained in labyrinth B were able to make a correct trip as the result of only 7.0 trials. Similarly the table shows that training in C rendered the subsequent learning of B easier. To master B when it was the first labyrinth required 8.2 trials; to master it after C had been learned required only 5 trials. In addition to proving that the acquisition of one form of labyrinth habit may facilitate the acquisition of others, comparison of the averages of Table 51 furnishes evidence of the truth of the statement that no results of training can be properly interpreted in the absence of knowledge of the previous experience of the organism.

CHAPTER XVII

Individual, Age, and Sex Differences in Behavior

ALL dancers are alike in certain important respects, but to the trained observer of animal behavior their individual peculiarities are quite as evident, and even more interesting than their points of resemblance. Omitting consideration of the structural marks of individuality, we shall examine the individual, age, and sex differences in general behavior, rapidity of learning, memory, and discrimination, which have been revealed by my experiments. Observations which bear on the subject of differences are scattered through the preceding chapters, but in no case have they been given sufficient prominence to force them upon the attention of those who are not especially interested in individual peculiarities. It has seemed worth while, therefore, to assemble all the available material in this chapter for systematic examination and interpretation.

In the pages which follow, individual, age, and sex peculiarities are discussed in turn. Within each of these three groups of differences I have arranged in order what Royce has appropriately named the facts of discriminating sensitiveness, docility, and initiative. Individuals of the same age and sex no less than those which differ in sex or age exhibit important differences in ability to discriminate among sense impressions ("discriminative sensitiveness"), in ability to profit by experience ("docility"), and in ability to try new kinds of behavior ("initiative").

Individual differences in sensitiveness to visual, auditory, tactual, and olfactory stimuli have been revealed by many of my experiments. The brightness discrimination tests conclusively proved that a degree of difference in illumination which is easily detectable by one dancer may be beyond the discriminating sensitiveness of another. Both the tests with gray papers and those with the Weber's law apparatus furnished striking evidence of individual differences in the kind of visual sensitiveness which throughout this book has been called brightness vision. I suspect that certain of the differences which were observed should be referred to the experience of the individuals rather than to the capacity of the visual organs, for training improves visual discrimination to a much greater extent than would ordinarily be thought possible. To the truth of this statement the results of the Weber's law experiments with No. 51 bear witness. Likewise in color discrimination there are individual differences, examples of which may be discovered by the examination of the results given in Chapters IX and X.

No differences in auditory sensitiveness appeared in my adult dancers, for in none of them was there definite response to sounds, but among the young individuals differences were prominent. I may call attention to the data on this subject which Table 5, p. 89, contains. The mice in four out of twelve litters gave no indications of hearing any sounds that I was able to produce; the remaining individuals responded with varying degrees of sensitiveness. I made no attempt to measure this sensitiveness, but it obviously differed from mouse to mouse. I feel justified, therefore, in stating that the young dancers exhibit extreme individual difference in sensitiveness to sounds.

My observations of differences in sensitiveness to other forms of stimulation were made in connection with training tests, and although they are not quantitative, I venture to call attention to them. Indeed, I am led by the results of my study of various aspects of the dancer's behavior to conclude that the race exhibits individual differences in discriminating sensitiveness to a far greater extent than do most mammals, not excepting man. The importance of this fact (for I am confident that any one who carefully examines the detailed results of the various experiments which are described in this book will agree that it is an established fact) cannot be overlooked. It alters our interpretation of the results of training, memory, heredity, and discrimination experiments, and it leads us to suspect that the dancing race is exceedingly unstable. I do not venture to make comparison of my own observations of the dancer's sense equipment with those of Cyon, Rawitz, Zoth, and Kishi, for the differences are too great in many instances to be thought of as other than species or variety peculiarities. It has seemed fairer to compare only individuals of the same breed, or, as I have done and shall continue to do throughout this chapter, of two lines of descent.

With respect to docility individual differences are prominent. We need only turn to the various tables of results to discover that in modifiability of behavior, in memory, in re-learning, not to mention other aspects of docility, dancers of the same sex and age differed strikingly. Let me by way of illustration cite a few cases of difference in docility. Number 1000 learned to discriminate white from black more quickly and retained his habit longer than any other dancer with which I have experimented. I should characterize him as an exceptionally docile individual. Table 44 offers several examples. Numbers 403 and 407, though they were born in the same litter and were alike in appearance and in conditions of life, acquired the white-black habit with a difference in rapidity which is expressed by the indices of modifiability 50 and 100. In other words, it took No. 407 twice as long to acquire this habit as it took No. 403. Similarly the ladder-climbing tests revealed important individual differences in ability to profit by experience. In the tables of labyrinth tests (38, 39, 40) individual differences are too numerous to mention. It required forty-nine tests to establish in No. 50 a labyrinth-C habit which was approximately equal in degree of perfection to that which resulted from twenty-two tests in the case of No. 52. The figures in this and other instances do not exaggerate the facts, for repeatedly I have tested individuals of the same litter, the same sex, and, so far as I could judge, of the same stage of development, and obtained results which differ as markedly as do those just cited. If space limits permitted, I could present scores of similar differences in docility which the problem, labyrinth, and discrimination methods have revealed.

In examining the detailed individual results of the various tables for differences of this sort, it is important to bear in mind that sex, age, and descent should be taken into account, for with each of them, as will be shown clearly later in this chapter, sensitiveness, docility, and initiative vary. I have therefore based my statements concerning individual differences in docility upon the results of comparison of mice of the same litter, sex, and age. It is safe to say that human beings similarly selected for comparison do not exhibit greater differences in ability to profit by experience than did these dancing mice.

The facts concerning individual differences in initiative which I have discovered are not less definite than those of the preceding paragraphs. From the beginning of my study of the dancer I observed that what one individual would readily learn of his own initiative another never learned. For example, in the ladder-climbing experiment No. 1000 distinguished himself for his initiative, whereas Nos. 4 and 5 never acquired the habit of escaping from confinement by using the ladder. I noticed, in this test of the animal's ability to learn, that while one individual would be scurrying about trying all ways of escape, investigating its surroundings, looking, sniffing, and dancing by turns, another would devote all its time to whirling, circling, or washing itself. One in the course of its activity would happen upon the way of escape, the other by reason of the limited scope of its activity, not the lack of it, would fail hour after hour to discover even the simplest way of getting back to its nest, to food, and to its companions. Hundreds of times during the past three years I have noticed important individual differences in initiative in connection with the discrimination experiments. The swinging wire doors which one dancer learned to push open before he had been in the box five minutes, another might not become familiar with through his own initiative for hours or days. In fact, it was not seldom that I had to teach an individual to pass from one compartment to the other by gently pushing him against the door until it opened sufficiently to allow him to squeeze through. Occasionally a mouse learned to pull the doors open so that he could pass through the openings in either direction with facility. This was a form of individual initiative which I had not anticipated and did not especially desire, so I did not encourage its development, but, nevertheless, at least one fourth of the mice which I experimented with in the discrimination box learned the trick. The other three fourths, although they were used in the box day after day sometimes for weeks, never discovered that they might return to the nest-box by pulling the swing-door through which they had just passed as well as by entering one of the electric-boxes.

Another indication of individual initiative in action appeared in the tendency of certain mice to climb out of the experiment boxes or labyrinths. It would have been extremely easy for any of the mice to escape from the labyrinths by scaling the walls of the alleys, for they were only 10 cm. in height, and when a dancer stood on its hind legs it could easily reach the top with its nose. But, strange though it will seem to any one who has not worked with the dancer, not more than one in ten of the animals which I observed made any attempt to escape in this manner. They lacked initiative. That it was not due to a lack of the power to climb, I abundantly demonstrated by teaching a few individuals that a scramble in one corner meant easy escape from the maze of paths. I do not think any one of the mice was physically incapable of climbing, but I am confident that they differed markedly, not only in the willingness to try new modes of action, but in the readiness with which they could climb. I have already said that individuals differ noticeably in the scope of their activity. By this statement I mean that they try a varying number of kinds of activity. As in the case of men, so in mice, one individual will do a greater number of things in a few hours than another will in weeks or months. The dancers differ in versatility, in individual initiative, as do we, albeit not so markedly.

Important differences which may with certainty be described as age differences are not so obvious as are such marks of individuality as have been set forth in the preceding pages. I have noted few changes in discriminative sensitiveness, other than those with regard to auditory sensitiveness, which could be correlated with age. In certain instances adults appeared to be able to discriminate more accurately and more easily than young mice, but it is difficult to say whether this change belongs under sensitiveness or docility. I have not made an ontogenetic study of the senses, and I am therefore unable to describe in detail the course of their development and decline. Of one important fact I am certain, that discriminative sensitiveness increases up to a certain point with age and with training.

Differences in docility which are obviously to be correlated with age abound. In the prime of its life (from the second to the tenth month) the dancer is active, full of energy, quick to learn; in its senility (during the second year) it is inactive, but at times even more docile than during the period of greatest physical development. Frequently I have noticed in connection with labyrinth tests that individuals of the age of a year or more learn much more quickly than do individuals of the age of two or three months. But, on the other hand, I have contradictory observations, for now and then I obtained just the opposite result in experiments to test docility. Evidently this is a matter which demands systematic, quantitative investigation. Casual observation may suggest conclusions, but it will not justify them.

Early in my investigation of the behavior of the dancer I conceived the idea of determining the relation of modifiability of behavior (docility) to age. The question which was foremost in my mind and for which I first sought an answer may be stated thus: can the dancer acquire a given habit with the same facility at different ages? Since the visual discrimination experiment seemed to be well suited for the investigation of this problem I planned to train, in the white-black discrimination experiment, five pairs of dancers at the age of one month, and the same number for each of the ages four, seven, ten, thirteen, sixteen, and nineteen months.[1]

---

[1] I have not been able thus far to determine the average length of the dancer's life. The greatest age to which any of my individuals has attained is nineteen months.

To test the same individuals month after month would be the ideal way of obtaining an answer to our question, but I could devise no satisfactory way of doing this. The effects of training last so long, as the results of the previous chapter proved, and the uncertainty of their entire disappearance is so serious, that the same training process cannot be used at successive ages. The use of different methods of training is even more unsatisfactory because it is extremely difficult to make accurate quantitative comparison of their results. It was these considerations that forced me to attempt to discover the relation of docility to age by carrying out the same experiments with groups of individuals of different ages.

As my plan involved the execution of precisely the same set of tests with at least seventy individuals whose age, history, and past experience were accurately known, and of which some had to be kept for nineteen months before they could be trained, the amount of labor and the risk of mishap which it entailed were great. To make possible the completion of the investigation within two years, I accumulated healthy individuals for several months without training any of them. In March, 1907, I had succeeded in completing the tests for the age of one month, and I had on hand for the remaining tests almost a hundred individuals, whose ages ranged from a few days to eighteen months. Had everything gone well, the work would have been finished within six months. Suddenly, and without discoverable external cause, my mice began to die of an intestinal trouble, and despite all my efforts to check the disease by changing food supply and environment, all except a single pair died within a few weeks. Thus ended a number of experiments whose final results I had expected to be able to present in this volume. However, the work which I have done is still of value, for the single pair of survivors have made possible the continuance of my tests with other individuals of the same line of descent as those which perished, and I have to regret only the loss of time and labor.

As I have on hand results for ten individuals of the age of one month, and for four individuals of the age of four months, it has seemed desirable to state the problem, method, and incomplete results of this study of the relation of modifiability to age. The indices of modifiability for these two groups of dancers differ so strikingly that I feel justified in

TABLE 52

PLASTICITY (RELATION OF MODIFIABILITY TO AGE)

Number of Errors in Successive Daily Series of Ten White-Black Tests, with Dancers Four Months Old

SERIES	MALES			FEMALES			
	No. 76	No. 78	Av.	No. 75	No. 77	Av.	GENERAL AV.
A	7	7	7.0	4	8	6.0	6.50
B	8	6	7.0	6	5	5.5	6.25
1	5	5	5.0	5	5	5.0	5.00
2	5	4	4.5	2	2	2.0	3.25
3	4	5	4.5	2	5	3.5	4.00
4	3	4	3.5	1	1	1.0	2.25
5	5	2	3.5	0	1	0.5	2.00
6	3	2	2.5	1	0	0.5	1.50
7	2	1	1.5	1	2	1.5	1.50
8	5	1	3.0	0	0	0	1.50
9	1	3	2.0	0	0	0	1.00
10	1	2	1.5	1	0	0.5	1.00
11	1	1	1.0	0		0	0.50
12	1	1	1.0	0		0	0.50
13	0	0	0	0		0	0
14	0	0	0				0
15	0	0	0				0

persisting in my efforts to obtain comparable data for the seven ages which have been mentioned.

The detailed results for the one-month old individuals appear in Table 43; those for the four-month individuals in Table 52. The general averages for the former are to be found in the third column of Table 46, under the heading

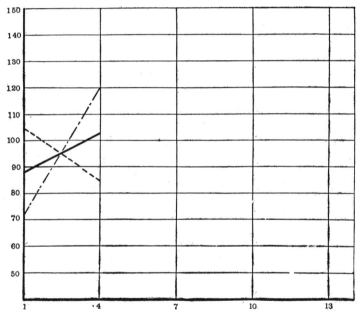

FIGURE 33.—Plasticity curves. In the left margin are given the indices of modifiability (the number of tests necessary for the establishment of a perfect habit). Below the base line the age of the individuals is given in months. Curve for males, — · — · — · —; curve for females, - - - -; curve for both males and females, ——. When these three plasticity curves are completed, they will represent the indices of modifiability as determined for ten individuals at the age of 1 month, and similarly for the same number of individuals at each of the ages, 4, 7, 10, 13, 16, and 19 months.

"10 tests per day"; those for the latter in the last column of Table 52. Mere inspection of these tables reveals the curious sex difference which goes far towards justifying the presentation of this uncompleted work. The index of modifiability

T

for the ten one-month individuals is 88 (that is, 88 tests were necessary for the establishment of a habit); for the four-month individuals it is 102.5. The heavy solid line of Figure 33 joins the points on the ordinates at which these values are located. Apparently, then, the dancer acquires the white-black discrimination habit less readily at the age of four months than at the age of one month.

Further analysis of the results proves that this statement is not true. When the averages for the two sexes are compared, it appears that the males learned much less quickly at four months than at one month, whereas just the reverse is true of the females. The dash and dot line of the figure extends from the index of modifiability of the one-month males (72) to that of the four-month males (120); and the regularly interrupted line similarly joins the indices of the one-month (104) and the four-month (85) females. In seeking to discover age differences in docility or ability to profit by experience we have stumbled upon what appears to be an important sex difference. Perhaps I should add to this presentation of partial results the following statement. Since there are only four individuals in the four-month group, two of each sex, the indices are not very reliable, and consequently too much stress should not be laid upon the age and sex differences which are indicated.

In view of this impressive instance of the way in which averages may conceal facts and lead the observer to false inferences, I wish to remark that my study of the dancer has convinced me of the profound truth of the statement that the biologist, whether he be psychologist, anthropologist, physiologist, or morphologist, should work with the organic individual and should first of all deal with his results as individual results. Averages have their place and value, but to mass data before their individual significance has been carefully sought out is to conceal or distort their meaning. Too many of us, in our eagerness for quantitative results and in our desire to obtain averages which shall justify general statements, get the cart before the horse.

Figure 33 presents the beginning of what I propose to call plasticity curves. When these three curves are completed on the basis of experiments with five dancers of each sex for each of the ages indicated on the base line of the figure, they will indicate what general changes in plasticity, modifiability of behavior, or ability to learn (for all of these expressions have been used to designate much the same capacity of the organism) occur from the first month to the nineteenth in the male and the female dancer, and in the race without respect to sex. So far as I know, data for the construction of plasticity curves such as I hope in the near future to be able to present for the dancing mouse have not been obtained for any mammal.

At present it would be hazardous for me to attempt to state any general conclusion concerning the relation of docility to age.

The initiative of the dancer certainly varies with its age. In scope the action system rapidly increases during the first few months of life, and if the animal be subjected to training tests, this increase may continue well into old age. The appearance of noticeable quiescence does not necessarily indicate diminished initiative. Frequently my oldest mice have shown themselves preëminent in their ability to adjust their behavior to new conditions. However, I have not studied individuals of more than eighteen months in age. One would naturally expect initiative to decrease in senility. All that I can say is that I have seen no indications of it.

We may now briefly consider the principal sex differences which have been revealed by the experiments. In sensitiveness I have discovered no difference, but it should be stated that no special attention has been given to the matter. In docility the males usually appeared to be superior to the females. This was especially noticeable early in my visual discrimination tests. The males almost invariably acquired a perfect habit quicker than the females. I may cite the following typical instances. Number 14 acquired the black-white habit with 40 tests; No. 13, with 60 (Table 10, p. 109). Of the five pairs of individuals whose records in white-black training appear in Table 43, not one contradicts the statement which has just been made. It is to be noted, however, that under certain conditions of training, for example, 20 tests per day, the female is at an advantage. Recently I have with increasing frequency obtained measures of docility which apparently favor the female. That this difference in the results is due to a difference in age is probable.

In labyrinth tests the female is as much superior to the male as the male is to the female in discrimination tests. From the tables of Chapter XIII I may take a few averages to indicate the quantitative nature of this difference. A degree of proficiency in labyrinth B attained by the males after 7.0 trials was equaled by the females after 6.2 trials. In labyrinth C the males acquired a habit as a result of 18.7 trials; the females, as a result of 13.8. And similarly in labyrinth D, 6.1 trials did no more for the males than 5.9 did for the females.

That at the age of about one month the male dancer should be able to acquire a visual discrimination habit more rapidly than the female, whereas the female can acquire a labyrinth habit more readily than the male, suggests an important difference in the nature of their equipment for habit formation. One might hazard the suggestion that the male depends more largely upon discrimination of external conditions, whereas the female depends to a greater extent than does the male upon the internal, organic changes which are wrought by acts. At any rate the female seems to follow a labyrinth path more mechanically, more accurately, more easily, and with less evidence of sense discrimination than does the male.

Finally, in concluding this chapter, I may add that in those aspects of behavior which received attention in the early chapters of this volume the dancers differ very markedly. Some climb readily on vertical or inclined surfaces to which they can cling; others seldom venture from their horizontally placed dance floor. Some balance themselves skillfully on narrow bridges; others fall off almost immediately. My own observations, as well as a comparison of the accounts of the behavior of the dancer which have been given by Cyon, Zoth, and other investigators, lead me to conclude that there are different kinds of dancing mice. This may be the result of crosses with other species of mice, or it may be merely an expression of the variability of an exceptionally unstable race.

I can see no satisfactory grounds for considering the dancer either abnormal or pathological. It is a well-established race, with certain peculiarities to which it breeds true; and no pathological structural conditions, so far as I have been able to learn, have been discovered.

I have presented in this chapter on differences a program rather than a completed study. To carry out fully the lines of work which have been suggested by my observations and by the presentation of results would occupy a skilled observer many months. I have not as yet succeeded in accomplishing this, but my failure is not due to lack of interest or of effort.

CHAPTER XVIII

The Inheritance of Forms of Behavior

In a general way those peculiarities of behavior which suggested the name dancing mouse are inherited. Generation after generation of the mice run in circles, whirl, and move the head restlessly and jerkily from side to side. But these forms of behavior vary greatly. Some individuals whirl infrequently and sporadically; others whirl frequently and persistently, at certain hours of the day. Some are unable to climb a vertical surface; others do so readily. Some respond to sounds; others give no indications of ability to hear. I propose in this chapter to present certain facts concerning the inheritance of individual peculiarities of behavior, and to state the results of a series of experiments by which I had hoped to test the inheritance of individually acquired forms of behavior.

My study of the nature of the whirling tendency of the dancer has revealed the fact that certain individuals whirl to the right almost uniformly, others just as regularly to the left, and still others now in one direction, now in the other. On the basis of this observation, the animals have been classified as right, left, or mixed whirlers. Does the dancer transmit to its offspring the tendency to whirl in a definite manner?

Records of the direction of whirling of one hundred individuals have been obtained. For twenty of these mice the determination was made by counting the number of com-

plete turns in five-minute intervals at six different hours of
the day. For the remaining eighty individuals the direction
was discovered by observation of the activity of the animals
for a brief interval at five different times. Naturally, the
former results are the more exact; in fact, they alone have
any considerable quantitative value. But for the problem
under consideration all of the determinations are sufficiently
accurate to be satisfactory.

The distribution of the individuals which were examined as
to direction of whirling is as follows.

	Right Whirlers	Left Whirlers	Mixed Whirlers	Total
Males	19	19	12	50
Females	12	23	15	50

The frequency of occurrence of left whirlers among the
females is unexpectedly high. Is this to be accounted for
in terms of inheritance? In my search for an answer to this
question I followed the whirling tendency from generation
to generation in two lines of descent. These two groups of
mice have already been referred to as the 200 line and the
400 line. The former were descended from Nos. 200 and
205, and the latter from Nos. 152 and 151. Individuals
which resulted from the crossing of these lines will be referred
to hereafter as of mixed descent. There were some striking
differences in the behavior of the mice of the two lines of
descent. As a rule the individuals of the 200 line climbed
more readily, were more active, danced less vigorously,
whirled less rapidly and less persistently, and were in several
other respects much more like common mice than were the
individuals of the 400 line. It is also to be noted (see Table
5, p. 89) that few of the litters of the 200 line exhibited
auditory reactions, whereas almost all of the litters of the
400 line which were tested gave unmistakable evidence of

sensitiveness to certain sounds. These differences at once suggest the importance of an examination of the whirling tendency of each line of descent.

The results for the several generations of each line which I had opportunity to examine are unexpectedly decisive so far as the question in point is concerned.

INDIVIDUALS OF THE 200 LINE

	MALES	FEMALES
First generation	No. 200, ?	No. 205, ?
Second generation	No. 210, Mixed whirler	No. 215, Left whirler
Third generation	No. 220, Mixed whirler	No. 225, Mixed whirler
Fourth generation	No. 230, Right whirler	No. 235, Mixed whirler
Fifth generation	No. 240, Right whirler	No. 245, Left whirler

INDIVIDUALS OF THE 400 LINE

	MALES	FEMALES
First generation	No. 152, Left whirler	No. 151, Left whirler
Second generation	No. 410, Left whirler	No. 415, Right whirler
Third generation	No. 420, Left whirler	No. 425, Left whirler

One line of descent exhibited no pronounced whirling tendency; the other exhibited a strong tendency to whirl to the left. Are these statements true for the group of one hundred individuals whose distribution among the three classes of whirlers has been given? In order to obtain an answer to this question I have reclassified these individuals according to descent and direction of whirling.

INDIVIDUALS OF THE 200 LINE

	RIGHT WHIRLERS	LEFT WHIRLERS	MIXED WHIRLERS	TOTAL
Males	7	6	8	21
Females	5	8	8	21
	12	14	16	42

Individuals of the 400 Line

	Right Whirlers	Left Whirlers	Mixed Whirlers	Total
Males	4	9	1	14
Females	6	9	4	19
	10	18	5	33

Individuals of Mixed Descent

9	10	6	25

Three interesting facts are indicated by these results: first, the inheritance of a tendency to whirl to the left in the 400 line of descent; second, the lack of any definite whirling tendency in the 200 line; and third, the occurrence of right and left whirlers with equal frequency as a result of the crossing of these two lines of descent.

It is quite possible, and I am inclined to consider it probable, that the pure dancer regularly inherits a tendency to whirl to the left, and that this is obscured in the case of the 200 line by the influences of a cross with another variety of mouse. It is to be noted that the individuals of the 200 line were predominantly mixed whirlers, and I may add that many of them whirled so seldom that they might more appropriately be classed as circlers.

The Inheritance of Individually Acquired Forms of Behavior

The white-black discrimination experiments which were made in connection with the study of vision and the modifiability of behavior were so planned that they should furnish evidence of any possible tendency towards the inheritance of modifications in behavior. The problem may be stated thus. If a dancing mouse be thoroughly trained to avoid black, by being subjected to a disagreeable experience every time it enters a black box, will it transmit to its offspring a tendency to avoid black?

Systematic training experiments were carried on with individuals of both the 200 and 400 lines of descent. For each of these lines a male and a female were trained at the age of four weeks to discriminate between the white and the black electric-boxes and to choose the former. After they had been thoroughly trained these individuals were mated,

TABLE 53

The Inheritance of the Habit of White-Black Discrimination

Number of Errors in Daily Series of Ten Tests

SERIES	MALES				FEMALES			
	First Genera-tion	Second Genera-tion	Third Genera-tion	Fourth Genera-tion	First Genera-tion	Second Genera-tion	Third Genera-tion	Fourth Genera-tion
	No. 210	No. 220	No. 230	No. 240	No. 215	No. 225	No. 235	No. 245
A	6	5	6	7	8	4	4	7
B	6	8	8	8	8	7	6	5
1	6	7	6	5	7	6	5	4
2	4	3	1	5	5	6	4	5
3	3	1	4	5	3	4	4	3
4	5	0	3	4	2	1	3	1
5	3	0	4	2	1	3	3	0
6	2	1	4	2	2	1	1	1
7	1	0	3	1	1	1	2	0
8	0	0	1	0	0	0	2	3
9	0	0	0	1	1	0	0	0
10	0		0	1	0	2	1	1
11			0	0	0	3	0	0
12				0	0	0	0	0
13				0		0	0	0
14						0		

and in course of time a male and female, chosen at random from their first litter, were similarly trained. All the individuals were trained in the same way and under as nearly the same conditions as could be maintained, and accurate records were kept of the behavior of each animal and of the number of errors of choice which it made in series after series of tests. What do these records indicate concerning the influence of individually acquired forms of behavior upon the behavior of the race?

I have records for four generations in the 200 line and for three generations in the 400 line.[1] As the results are practically the same for each, I shall present the detailed records for the former group alone. In Table 53 are to be found the number of errors made in successive series of ten tests each by the various individuals of the 200 line which were trained in this experiment. The most careful examination fails to reveal any indication of the inheritance of a tendency to avoid the black box. No. 240, in fact, chose the black box more frequently in the preference series than did No. 210, and he required thirty more tests for the establishment of a perfect habit than did No. 210. Apparently descent from individuals which had thoroughly learned to avoid the black box gives the dancer no advantage in the formation of a white-black discrimination habit. There is absolutely no evidence of the inheritance of this particular individually acquired form of behavior in the dancer.

---

[1] This experiment was interrupted by the death of the animals of both lines of descent.

INDEX

ABNORMAL dancers, 277.
Acquired forms of behavior, 281.
Act, useless, repeated, 106, 205.
Activity, periods of, 34.
Affirmation, choice by, 131.
Age, peculiarities, 264, 269; maximum age, 270; and intelligence, 272.
Albino cat, 65; dog, 32.
Alexander and Kreidl, young dancer, 21, 23; behavior, 30, 42; tracks of mice, 44; behavior in cyclostat, 46; behavior of white mouse and dancer, 48; structure of ear, 58–65; deafness, 76.
Allen, G. M., drawing of dancer, 3; heredity in mice, 11.
Alleys, width of, in labyrinths, 214.
Amyl acetate for photometry, 121.
Anatomy of dancer, 52.
Animals, education of, 200.
Appuun whistles, 79.
Audition. *See* Hearing.
Averages, dangers in, 274.

BAGINSKY, B., model of ear of dancer, 58, 59, 63, 67.
Bateson, W., breeding experiments, 13, 14.
Behavior, of dancer, 5, 29; inheritance of, 37, 278; when blinded, 42, 47; equilibration, 42; dizziness, 45; structural bases of, 52; of young, 22; changes in, 21, 85; useless acts, 106, 205; under experimental conditions, 120; in indiscriminable conditions, 122; value of sight, 178; in labyrinth experiments, 188; modifiability of, 199; history of, 206; explanations of, 206; individual differences in, 264, 277.

Blinded dancers, behavior of, 42, 47.
Blue-orange tests, 140; blue-red tests, 145, 173; blue-green tests, 170; blue-green blindness, 172.
Bradley papers, 133, 140.
Brain, structure of, 29, 69, 71.
Breeding of dancers, 1, 13, 20.
Brehm, A. E., "Tierleben," 1, 8.
Brightness vision, 91; preference, 105; check experiments, 140; relation to color vision, 177.

CAGES for dancers, 16.
Candle meter, 156.
Candle power, 121.
Cardboards, for tests of vision, 95; positions of, 111.
Care of dancer, 18.
Castle, W. E., drawing of mouse, 3; cages, 16.
Cat, albino, 65; training of, 200, 228.
Cerebellum of dancer, 72.
Characters, acquired, 281.
Check experiments, 140.
China, dancers of, 5, 14.
Choice, exhibition of, 96; by affirmation, 131; by negation, 131; by comparison, 131; methods of, 200, 234.
Circling, a form of dance, 32.
Circus course mice, 2.
Cleghorn, A. G., 2.
Climbing of dancer, 42, 269, 277.
Cochlea, functions of, 61.
Color blindness, 169.
Color discrimination apparatus, 134, 151.
Colored glasses, 151, 155.
Colored papers, 133, 139, 140.
Color patterns of dancers, 1, 4.
Color vision, problem, 91, 177; methods of testing, 133, 137, 151;

285

CHILD BEHAVIOR, DIFFERENTIAL AND GENETIC PSYCHOLOGY

Single Nos. $2.00
$7 per annum
This Issue $3.00

Jan. and March, 1927
Vol. II, Nos. 1 and 2

GENETIC PSYCHOLOGY MONOGRAPHS

JANUARY—MARCH, 1927

THE MIND OF A GORILLA*

BY

ROBERT M. YERKES

Institute of Psychology, Yale University

*Transmitted to the Editors by Carl Murchison

WORCESTER, MASS.

ACKNOWLEDGMENTS

I am filled with gratitude as I record the circumstances which paved the way for my study of Congo. Mr. Carl Akeley acted as a friend, disinterestedly, broad-mindedly, generously. Mr. Richard Sparks, impelled by the conviction that Congo was potentially a scientific prize, made it his business to create opportunity for the study of her mentality and to discover someone who would eagerly utilize it.

In my experience the friendliness and generosity of Mr. Ben Burbridge are unexcelled. Without reserve or hampering limitations he placed Congo at my disposal for study. Sharing my interest in the discovery of facts about her mental constitution he eagerly coöperated in the work and aided me. His Akeley camera and his experience and skill enabled us to secure valuable records of her performance in various psychological experiments. I find it impossible adequately to express my appreciation of his kindness and my admiration of his attitude toward our work.

Congo owes much to Mr. and Mrs. James Burbridge, for they have given her a wonderfully beautiful and comfortable home in Florida, and their intelligent and sympathetic care has kept her healthful and contented. To me, a stranger on a strange mission, they were no less kind. Their genuine interest, ready coöperation, and hospitality made my laborious weeks with Congo seem like a Florida holiday.

To the five friends who thus helped me to make an exploratory journey into the mind of the gorilla I am deeply obligated.

For aid cheerfully rendered I am indebted also to my colleagues Raymond Dodge and Harold C. Bingham, to my research assistant Margaret S. Child, and to my wife. Miss Child, Mrs. Yerkes and my secretary, Mrs. Morford, helped especially with the manuscript and proofs.

CONTENTS

LIST OF ILLUSTRATIONS

I

HISTORY OF "CONGO" AND OF OPPORTUNITY TO STUDY HER

All my life I had longed for opportunity to study the mind of the gorilla. Suddenly and without warning it came. I was at work in the Yale Primate Laboratory, Thanksgiving morning of 1925, when over the telephone my friend Carl Akeley greeted me with the surprising question: "Yerkes, would you like to have a young gorilla for scientific study?" Doubtless my voice trembled with excitement as I replied, "Would I!" "With me," Akeley continued, "is a lifelong friend of Ben Burbridge, the captor and owner of a little mountain gorilla which is now in Jacksonville, Florida. His name is Richard D. Sparks and he thinks Burbridge would be willing to loan you the gorilla, or at least to give you opportunity to study it. Can you come to New York to discuss the matter?" Without stopping to consult my calendar I said, "Yes, tomorrow morning." The next day Dr. Harold C. Bingham, Research Associate in the Institute of Psychology, and I met Mr. Akeley and Mr. Sparks in the former's studio at the American Museum of Natural History, New York. It was an assemblage of enthusiasts, and the outcome of the conference might readily have been predicted. We psychologists made no attempt to conceal our eagerness for intimate acquaintance with the gorilla, one or many, or our willingness to accept responsibility for using any opportunity that Mr. Burbridge might offer us. With Mr. Akeley standing as mutual acquaintance, mediator, and sympathetic adviser, Mr. Sparks promised to present immediately to Mr. Burbridge a plan and proposal for the scientific utilization of his gorilla "Congo" and thus favorably to initiate negotiations.

By letter, telegraph, and telephone, conference with Mr. Burbridge in Florida proceeded, and on December 10 the writer left New Haven for Jacksonville to visit the gorilla and to confer with her owner about possible arrangements for observation. This also proved to be a meeting of enthusiasts and a conference which could not fail of interesting results. Willingly and generously Mr. Burbridge offered the Yale Institute of Psychology the privilege of observing "Congo" in her Florida home, and of making physical and mental measurements. Neither of us considered it practicable to remove her in the midst of winter to New Haven; but as "Shady Nook," the home of Mr. James Burbridge, where Congo resided as a welcome visitor, promised to be a highly favorable place for scientific observation, and as both Mr. and Mrs. James Burbridge made us feel that it would be a kindness to them to accept their generous offer of coöperation, immediate study of Congo on the spot seemed practicable.

Encouraging also was the attitude of Congo herself. From my experience with children and anthropoid apes I realized that I should not force myself on this highly organized, rare, and reputedly conservative creature. Our first meeting occurred with the wire-netting cage wall between us. I approached to let her examine me and we exchanged finger-shakes. As each was adequately protected from the other, neither was a bit nervous or uneasy and curiosity dominated. The following day when Mrs. Burbridge entered the cage to play with Congo I accompanied her, and as she took the gorilla-child on her lap, stroking her heavy coat and talking to her the while gently and assuringly, I stood at one side waiting for Congo to make the first advance. Presently she reached out her left hand to me and when I grasped it she drew me to her. Then followed close visual and olfactory scrutiny of my hands, face, and hair. Satisfied, apparently, that I was worthy of her friendly confidence she put an arm

Plate 1.

Ben Burbridge and the little female mountain gorilla Congo,
October, 1925.
Courtesy of O'Brien and Russell, Jacksonville.

about my neck. From that moment Congo and I were trusting friends. She probably would be as much surprised and disturbed if I deceived or struck her as I if she maliciously attacked me.

On my return a week later to New Haven I reported favorably on the opportunity for the study of gorilla psychology offered by Mr. Burbridge, and recommended to 'its Governing Board that the Institute of Psychology authorize and enable me to arrange as soon as possible for a sojourn of several weeks in Jacksonville to study Congo. The recommendation was promptly and heartily approved, and on January 2, 1926, I found myself in Jacksonville arranging for psychological work. Monday, January 4, I actually began my experimental inquiry.

Instead of proceeding with an account of the experiments and their results I must digress in order to share with the reader the story of Mr. Burbridge's adventures with mountain gorillas in the Belgian Congo.

Born with a love of hunting, Ben Burbridge has had more thrilling experiences, more narrow escapes, more fascinating glimpses of the home and family life of big game animals in North America and in Africa than would seem credible. The secret of his success as hunter with gun and camera and of his survival is found, I surmise, in his extraordinary energy, patience, clear-headedness, insight, and determination. He has the will to succeed and the physical stamina to support it. However little appeal hunting to kill may make to one, he cannot refuse admiration to faith, courage, and persistence in the study of wild animals.

Four times Mr. Burbridge has journeyed to Africa and each time he has safely returned home with treasures of experience, which unhappily he has not put on record, and with rarely valuable pictorial stories. In the last two expeditions it was his purpose to trail, study, and make motion pictures of the mountain gorillas of the Eastern Belgian Congo, and if possible to capture some of the young animals alive.

It is not my task to describe the hardships of those who elect to follow *Gorilla beringei* in its mountain habitat near Lake Kivu. Various collectors and hunters have returned from the region to tell interestingly and more or less convincingly of their adventures with this rare species of huge manlike ape.

Initially it was Mr. Burbridge's intention to familiarize himself with the form, manner of life, and environment of the mountain gorillas by trailing them, observing the behavior of individuals and bands, shooting typical specimens, and making motion picture records. Conditions for photography were extremely unfavorable; but refusing to accept defeat or yield to discouragement, he finally succeeded in making some truly remarkable, as well as scientifically useful, pictures of wild gorillas at close range and often in action. They are pictures which even in these days of incredible discovery and invention, one having seen, will not forget. Success was achieved chiefly through continued and thoughtful observation of the ways of the gorilla. Amidst plentiful difficulties and hazards Mr. Burbridge at last developed a procedure which enabled him to lure them almost to the camera. Mostly he depended on curiosity, parental solicitude, or timidity. It is for him to describe his methods completely; here one must suffice as an illustration.

The following play upon parental solicitude proved effective in many instances. The hunter and his helpers having trailed a band of gorillas to a location reasonably favorable for photographic work, arrangements were speedily and quietly made for attracting the animals toward the camouflaged camera. As soon as the members of the hunting group were properly disposed, one imitated the cry of the leopard and another responded with the scream of a young gorilla. The leopard, it seems, is a deadly enemy of the gorilla and according to Mr. Burbridge's report succeeds in destroying many of the animals while immature. Naturally then, the associated cries of leopard and young gorilla command the attention of the adults of the band and immediately draw parents to the defense of their young. By this ruse Mr. Burbridge states that he has sometimes succeeded in luring several members of a band into clear sight and occasionally to within a few feet of his concealed camera. Before they could retreat the faithful "Akeley" had done its work. Thrilling moments these must have been for photographer as well as for gorillas. Even the pictures are thrilling. It is a temptation to continue this description of Mr. Burbridge's observations, insights, and their practical applications; but it is his right and obligation to tell the story, and I desist.

Some of the same ruses which lured gorillas within camera range served to bring the young within grasp of the hunter. The word thrilling has been used to characterize motion picture experiences. How shall we characterize the act of capturing gorillas alive!

From his first journey into the gorilla mountains Mr. Burbridge returned to the plains with four captive youngsters. Each had been taken barehanded, by main force, and in contempt of risk of damage by gorilla teeth and nails. It was in May, 1922, that these young animals were captured on Mt. Mikeno. They were named Congo (the first), Kivu, Quahalie, and Lulangua. Of these individuals Mr. Burbridge says Congo was a male weighing some twenty-three pounds, savage and unrelenting; Kivu, also a male, weighed sixty pounds and was almost untamable. Quahalie, a female, weighed about thirty-five pounds, and was "the handsomest of all." Full of life and spirit she took readily to captivity and shortly became gentle and tame. Lulangua, also a female, the smallest of all, was gentle, friendly, and of excellent disposition. Of the four, Quahalie, which means in Swahili "good-bye," was the last captured and the only one to survive the journey to Europe. In accordance with agreement she was delivered by Mr. Burbridge to the Zoölogical Garden in Antwerp for the Belgian Government. It is reported that she has since died.

Two incidents in connection with the capture and care of

young gorillas I have asked Mr. Burbridge to permit me to report. They prove that capturing wild gorillas is hardly more exciting, difficult, and dangerous than the task of bringing them home. Kivu and Lulangua died before·they reached the port of Dar-es-Salaam. There Congo succumbed. He was found one morning in Quahalie's arms dead. She, now companionless, screamed piteously when the body was removed.

It was after his return from the gorilla country, and while resting and recuperating self and captive animals, en route to the coast, at the Mission of the White Fathers beside Lake Kivu, that this disagreeable adventure came to Mr. Burbridge. Early one morning he heard a disturbance in the shed in which the four young gorillas were housed. Hastily slipping on shoes and a long coat he made his way in the dim light to the shed. As he opened the door and started to step into the building one of the animals hurled itself upon him from the darkness. The unexpected shock bore him to the ground and the hunter found himself beset by his captives. Ruthlessly they tore at him with tooth and nail. Protecting his head and face with his arms, Mr. Burbridge groped in the darkness for the chain which held Kivu. the largest and the savagest of them all. By the time he had succeeded in getting Kivu throttled, the animals had about stripped him of clothing and inflicted many wounds, of which a severe bite on the knee later caused most trouble. Luckily for the victim, help arrived quickly and he was rescued from his sad predicament.

From this expedition with its multitudinous risks, hardships, and injuries, Mr. Burbridge returned home to the United States without a single live specimen and with photographic records which far from satisfied his ambition to record fully the story of the wild life of the mountain gorilla. Two years passed, and the lure of Africa and his persistent desire to bring a young mountain gorilla alive to America, drew Mr. Burbridge back to the volcanic mountains on which at altitudes of several thousand feet *Gorilla beringei* lives.

In June and July, 1925, four more young animals were captured. One of these, named by the natives Bula Matadi (great master or fine fellow), weighed about one hundred and twenty-six pounds. Mr. Burbridge thinks this is the largest mountain gorilla ever taken alive. Certainly his capture would have made a prize picture! It happened thus. A band of gorillas had been trailed by the hunters, closely approached, and then startled by alarming sounds in order that the adults might be frightened away. In their hasty retreat the aforesaid Bula Matadi scrambled over a rock behind which crouched Mr. Burbridge. On the instant the hunter, set for the capture of a little gorilla, seized the animal. Immediately he realized that he had more of a gorilla than he bargained for or could manage. Nevertheless he kept his grip. The approved procedure was to grasp the young animal by the throat and forcing it to the ground hold it determinedly until a helper arrived to slip a stout burlap bag over its head. In this case the gorilla was so much stronger than the man that it at once drew both of his hands into its mouth. Probably Bula Matadi would have escaped to follow his elders but for Mr. Burbridge's iron will and quickness of wit. Realizing his inability to overpower the gorilla, or even to release his hands, he thrust them with all his might into the throat of the young animal, thus at once frustrating its attempt to crush his hands and choking it. Several natives quickly arrived and by concerted effort they at last overpowered the young giant and securely bound him. The first burlap bag he split asunder, but a multiple application proved effective and he was triumphantly carried to camp. Mr. Burbridge states that this young lord of the forest-clad mountains never accepted captivity. Utterly untamable and bitterly resentful of his humiliation, he finally died in camp from the bites of a swarm of ants, from which, because of his restraint, he was unable adequately to protect himself.

Of the remaining three captives, one died in Africa and two reached Europe in good health. Marzo, a little male, was presented by Mr. Burbridge to the Zoölogical Garden in Antwerp. It was there seen by friends of the writer late in the summer of 1925. A few weeks later the papers reported its death. Congo (the second), a female, arrived in New York with Mr. Burbridge in October, 1925. She was in splendid condition, but unhappily her owner was seriously ill and as soon as he had safely landed her in his home city, Jacksonville, Florida, and arranged for her care, he betook himself to a hospital, whence a few weeks later he emerged cured.

This is all we know of the history of Congo, the subject of this report. Of her antecedents, her age, her experiences prior to capture, we unhappily are entirely ignorant. Mr. Burbridge has done his best, but it is impossible for him to answer our chief questions. This is a serious handicap, albeit a common one, in the study of the mental constitution of an animal, but mountain gorillas are far too rare, precious, and little known to justify over-exactingness on the part of the student of behavior.

Our subject, Congo, is then a female of the species *Gorilla beringei,* estimated from size and condition of teeth to be four to five years of age. Apparently she is in perfect condition and normally developed. Her weight in January, 1926, was approximately sixty-five pounds and she was said to be growing steadily. The only anatomical peculiarity noted was the complete fusion of the second, third, and fourth toes so that they functioned as one. Each toe was perfect even to its independent nail, and the condition of fusion was the same on each foot.

Apparently the mountain gorilla is built for strength rather than speed. Congo, considering her presumable age and her actual size and weight, was amazingly strong. It was possible to make only rough measurements of strength and speed, but the daily impressions of the investigator abundantly confirmed them. Pulling with both arms, her feet braced firmly, Congo several times drew one hundred and sixty pounds on a heavy spring balance (see p. 82). Without a brace for

Plate 2. Portraits and extremities

Fig. 1, upper left. Hands of Congo and the experimenter.
Fig. 2, upper right. Foot of Congo, showing fusion of toes.
Fig. 3, middle left. A characteristic resting attitude. Fig. 4,
middle right. The fused toes again displayed. Fig. 5, lower
left. A half profile for nose, lips, and chin. Fig. 6, lower
right. Profile for ear, facial angle, and nostril.

Courtesy of the *Jacksonville Journal,* January, 1926.

her feet she was able to draw one hundred and twenty pounds.
During the period of my observation she played acceptably
with a young Airedale dog, but it has since been reported
that she is so rough that the dog no longer tolerates her attentions. Although ready and eager to climb, in this she
could scarcely excel a well-conditioned and practiced boy. It
was easy for the investigator to outrun her, whether he was
leading or following.

The animal's eyes are large, dark brown, and expressive,
the surrounding sclera is yellowish. The ears are small and
set close to the head. The nose is flat, very broad, and with
large nostrils. The mouth, although large, seems less so than
that of a chimpanzee of corresponding size, and the lips are
less prominent than those of the chimpanzee and are used
quite differently in feeding, for Congo seldom protrudes her
lips either in connection with taking food or examining it.
The chin is obvious and gives the impression of strength. On
the face, hands, and feet the skin is jet black, while on the
body it is dark brown to black.

Sweat glands apparently are numerous and widely distributed, for drops of perspiration were frequently observed
on the extremities as well as on the head and face. The
secretion has a pronounced odor which by certain observers
is said to be similar to that of the Negro. The writer has
not been able to confirm the latter observation.

Congo's body is covered, with the exception of portions of
the face, head, and feet, with black hair. A small patch of
white hair appears about the anus. On the abdomen the hair
is fine, thick, and kinky, suggesting wool. The remainder of
the body is covered with a coarse black coat from two to four
inches long. Possibly the hair is somewhat less coarse on
the head than on the remainder of the body. There is no
definite crest or ruff on the head, but there is apparently
some tendency for the hair on the back of the head to be
directed upward or straight backward rather than to lie flat.
This, however, may be due in part to a collar which is regu-

larly worn. It is entirely evident that the mountain gorilla is adapted to the low temperature of its high altitude habitat. Presumably it suffers more or less serious inconvenience when brought to sea level. Congo obviously is uncomfortable when active in temperatures of seventy degrees or upward or when in the direct sunlight of a warm winter day in Florida. Apparently temperatures of fifty-five to sixty degrees were most favorable to her comfort and activity.

It was found difficult to make complete observations on the teeth, for Congo persistently refused to open her jaws sufficiently wide to expose her molars. The incisors and canines and the first molars of each jaw were frequently seen and their condition recorded, but I never succeeded, despite repeated efforts, in obtaining a complete record of her dentition. In January, 1926, she had regularly placed and in excellent condition in the upper jaw two pairs of incisors, of which the second was considerably 'smaller than the first; and in the lower jaw, one pair which by position and size were identified as second incisors. They apparently were abnormally near the median line and interfered with the growth of the first pair of which the member on the right side appeared somewhat back of its proper position. The one on the left side was absent. One pair of canines, strong, conicle in shape, appeared in each jaw. Although certain of the molars were obviously present in good condition, my data do not justify attempt at description. It is significant that Congo should have refused to permit examination of her teeth. I have seldom had difficulty in making satisfactory examination of the dentition in the chimpanzee and orang-utan of approximately her age and degree of domestication.

Anthropometric observations on Congo were peculiarly difficult because of her failure to coöperate. Doubtless with sufficient persistence her confidence might have been won and her full coöperation commanded; unfortunately my time did not suffice. Several attempts were made to get important measurements, but the results in most cases were either nega-

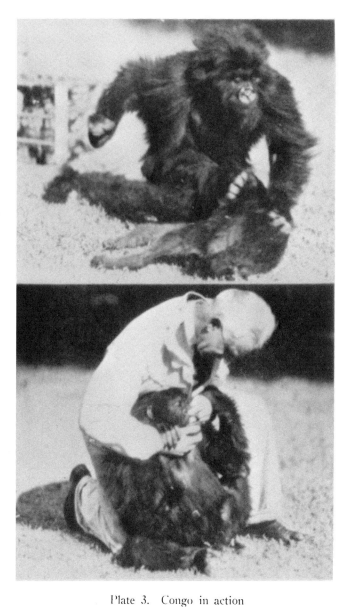

Plate 3. Congo in action

Fig. 1, upper. Playmates, gorilla and dog. Fig. 2, lower. Experimenter examining a new tooth.

Courtesy of *Florida Times-Union*, January, 1926.

tive or of such low degree of reliability that they do not justify publication. As already stated, Congo's weight in January, 1926, was somewhere about sixty-five pounds. At this time her standing height was 38 ± 1 inches; her sitting height approximately 25 inches; her chest girth at level of nipples, 34 ± 1 inches; her maximal arm reach or span 59 to 60 inches. The length of the right ear was approximately 2.1 inches; that of the left, 2 inches. The circumference of the wrists, approximately 7 inches. The maximal foot length, approximately 8 inches. All other measurements, including those of the head, were unsatisfactory. These facts are reported rather because of their psychological than their anthropometric significance.

Healthfully active, of good appetite, and normally ready for work or play, Congo from the first impressed me as a well developed, vigorous, young specimen, typical probably of her species, and neither injured nor otherwise unfavorably affected by her capture and her short period of life in confinement. I had no special difficulties in commanding her confidence and her coöperation, except in the anthropometric work. She was uniformly friendly with me and if not gentle at least not rougher than an animal of her strength and habits of life might be expected to be. There were no signs whatever of maliciousness or viciousness. I noticed that vigorous play quickly left her short of breath and that at such times her heart action was very rapid. Considering, however, the radical change of environment from an altitude of perhaps eight thousand feet to sea level, and from low to high temperatures, perhaps her respiratory and circulatory reactions were entirely normal and adaptive.

As a visitor at Shady Nook, Congo appears to be eminently contented. She has now (July, 1926) been there for slightly more than eight months, and in addition to becoming increasingly at home in her surroundings she has obviously gained interest in people and friendliness with them. Whereas at first she sometimes resented the approach of visitors and acted as though a camera were distasteful to her, she now delights in opportunity to "show off" and has developed several friendships.

II

OUR KNOWLEDGE OF THE MENTAL LIFE OF
THE GORILLA*

In this section attempt is made to present certain general information about gorillas and to provide historical setting for the study of Congo.

Of living great manlike apes there are three types, the gorilla, the orang-utan, and the chimpanzee, which differ among themselves more than do the races of man. Largest, strongest, and seemingly least docile of all is the gorilla. If this remarkable creature was known to the ancients, records should exist. Actually none has been found which unquestionably describes it. The following reference by Hanno, the Carthaginian Admiral (16), is the earliest known, and typically difficult to evaluate.

"On the third day, having sailed from thence, passing the streams of fire, we came to a bay called the Horn of the South. In the recess there was an island like the first, having a lake, and in this there was another island full of wild men. But much the greater part of them were women, with hairy bodies, whom the interpreters called 'Gorillas.' But, pursuing them, we were not able to take the men; they all escaped, being able to climb the precipices, and defended themselves with pieces of rock. But three women (females), who bit and scratched those who led them, were not willing to follow. However, having killed them, we flayed them, and conveyed the skins to Carthage; for we did not sail any further, as provisions began to fail." (Quoted from translation by Bishop Maltby, 27, p. 22).

The use of the word gorillæ by Hanno in the fifth century, B. C., by no means proves that the great ape had been dis-

---

*Because we have in preparation a systematic historical work on anthropoid behavior, this section is restricted to an outline in which only certain major orientational references are cited to acquaint the reader with the discovery and nature of *Gorilla gorilla* and *Gorilla beringei*.

covered. Rather the evidence suggests that either the chimpanzee or a type of native wild man was met by Hanno who, as Ogilby says:

"No ways daunted at such strange Sights, sail'd from *Sierra Liona* Southerly to the *Æquinox* where he discover'd an Island not far from the *African* Coast, inhabited by a rough and hairy People, to take some of whom, he us'd all possible means, yet could not; onely two Women, being incompass'd by Soldiers, were taken, and carried aboard; but being very salvage, and barbarously wild, could not be tamed, or brought to any complacency; so they kill'd them, and carried their stuff'd-up Skins to *Carthage,* where they were a long time gaz'd upon with great admiration." (26, p. 20).

Brief references like that of Hanno, meager descriptions, and confusion of nomenclature leave us uncertain whether the gorilla was known to naturalists prior to the sixteenth century, when Andrew Battell, an English sailor captured by the Portuguese and sent to Angola, Africa, for military service, observed and described a huge powerful ape to which he gave the name Pongo.

"The Woods," writes Battell, "are so couered with Baboones, Monkies, Apes, and Parrots, that it will feare any man to trauaile in them alone. Here are also two kinds of Monsters, which are common in these Woods, and very dangerous.

"The greatest of these two Monsters is called, *Pongo,* in their Language: and the lesser is called, *Engeco.* This *Pongo* is in all proportion like a man, but that he is more like a Giant in stature, than a man: for he is very tall, and hath a mans face, hollow eyed, with long haire upon his browes." (This description finds place in the remarkable book of Samuel Purchas, 28, p. 981).

It is reasonably certain that during the following two centuries the gorilla was referred to under various names by Buffon (7, 8, 9), Monboddo (25), and other naturalists.

Doubt as to the existence of the gorilla and of fairly reliable although limited information concerning it had partially disappeared when in 1819 Bowdich (5, p. 441) described in contrast with "the African ourang-outan," as he called the chimpanzee, the Ingēna, an animal comparable with the ourang-outan "but much exceeding it in size, being generally five feet high and four feet across the shoulders; its paw was said to be even more disproportionate than its breadth, and one blow of it to be fatal."

Whereas during the centuries much information about the structure, manner of life, and environment of the orang-utan and chimpanzee had accumulated, relatively little was known with certainty about the gorilla when in the middle of the last century Savage and Wyman published their description (29). To the former we owe the earliest reliable account of general appearance, habits, and disposition; to the latter, similarly useful anatomical description. Savage, with acuteness, recognized from published descriptions, the identity with the gorilla of Battell's Pongo and Bowdich's Ingēna and stated that the gorilla or Engé-ena of the natives of the Gaboon is distinct from the chimpanzee (called by him *Troglodytes niger*), and from the orang-utan found in Borneo and Sumatra.

From the publication of the observations of Savage and Wyman, the name gorilla came to be used for the giant ape and information about it became more abundant and reliable (see Hartmann, 17). For a long time it was not known whether one species or many existed and whether the characteristics of structure and behavior attributed to the type gorilla were generic or specific. Descriptions of appearance and structure were incomplete and misleading chiefly because of the inadequacy of material and ignorance of the age of specimens. Similarly, descriptions of habits and mental traits were of uncertain value because based partly on the statements of natives and partly on the chance observations of hunters.

Although the report of Savage and Wyman established the gorilla as an animal peculiarly interesting to comparative anatomists, naturalists, and psychologists, it remained for the traveler Du Chaillu (12) to command the interest of the reading public by his almost unbelievable account of the characteristics and life of the creature. In 1861 appeared his "Explorations and adventures in Equatorial Africa." Previously his observations had been presented in lectures, and he had sent gorilla skins and skeletons to interested students of anatomy. His book, with its highly colored descriptions of gorilla hunting, its portrait of the ape as a monstrous and ferocious beast, and its varied evidences of the hostility of the gorilla toward man, immediately aroused unfavorable comment, adverse criticism, and flat contradiction. The author was accused by many authorities of conscious misrepresentation as well as of gross carelessness of statement. Shortly it became unfashionable to accept anything that Du Chaillu said of the gorilla. Opposition and incredulity replaced the usual open-mindedness and charitableness of the scientist. Probably adverse criticism was seriously overdone, for it now appears that despite exaggeration and the mingling of truth, half truth, and misstatement, much of the traveler's description was correct. We are able to-day, as Du Chaillu's contemporaries were not on account of prejudice, to read the book cautiously, critically, fairly, and to conclude that its role in advancing knowledge of the gorilla has been important. But even now no contribution to natural history better proves the necessity for critical caution, combined with open-mindedness, than does Du Chaillu's at once famous and infamous account of the gorilla.

It is almost unbelievable that a century ago the gorilla should have been practically unknown to the scientific world. Words there were which more or less certainly identified it, but useful descriptions were lacking. Even at the close of the nineteenth century only one species was definitely recognized by taxonomists. Forbes, in his handbook of the primates (14, vol. 2, p. 180), states that the genus contains but a single species, *Gorilla gorilla,* which is found in western equatorial Africa between the Cameroons and the Congo. This West African form is undoubtedly the gorilla of Battell and Bowdich, of Savage and Wyman, and of Du Chaillu and

the majority of his critics. Indeed, most descriptions of gorilla structure, natural history, and mentality appear to be
based on observation of West African specimens.

Even as late as 1913, Elliot in his taxonomic work "A review of the primates," wrote, "From the Gaboon two forms
have been described, *Gorilla gorilla,* longest known species of
the genus, and *Gorilla gorilla castaneiceps,* but it is extremely
doubtful if the last one is entitled to any racial distinction"
(13, vol. 3, p. 210).

The discovery in 1903 of a second and markedly differing
species of gorilla in German East Africa surprised the scientific world. This new form was found on the volcano Sabinio
by the German-Colonial official Captain von. Beringe. It was
promptly described by the zoölogist Matschie and given the
name *Gorilla beringei.* Because of its high altitude mountain
habitat, it is commonly known as the mountain gorilla. From
the lowland gorillas of West Africa it differs importantly in
many respects conspicuous among which are shape of cranium
and jaws, stature and build, and texture and color of the
hair. In view of what is now known about the West and
East African types of gorilla, it would be rash indeed to attempt a general description of the genus on the basis of study
of either type, for it seems that these two species are at least
as markedly different as are the Negro and the Malay. Obviously, then, our descriptions of structure and behavior should
have specific reference to *Gorilla gorilla* or *Gorilla beringei.*

Prior to the World War little beyond Matschie's original
description was added to our knowledge of the mountain
gorilla. A few specimens were collected and their anatomical
characteristics studied. It was not until 1920 that opportunity
offered for collectors, hunters, and naturalists to intrude themselves upon the previously unmolested bands of *G. beringei.*
First to arrive with gun and permit was the English collector,
Barns. In addition to securing museum specimens, he
gathered data for interesting chapters on the life of the animals
(2, 3).

Inasmuch as Barns considers the mountain gorilla less intelligent than the chimpanzee and the orang-utan it is appropriate to quote the following paragraph, descriptive chiefly of disposition and attitude toward life.

"The gorilla, shunning observation at all times, is of a silent, morose, and even phlegmatic disposition. He seldom utters a sound unless thoroughly alarmed, and then his screaming roar is quite terrifying. When interested and curious he utters a loud whine like a great dog, following this by a resonant 'clopping' made by beating the closed hand on the bare chest below the nipples. Apart from using this beating of the chest to frighten away an intruder, it seems to be made both as a danger signal and to locate each other's whereabouts, and also, I think, to 'hearten' themselves, for I have heard it when there was no possibility of the animals being alarmed. In the course of many weeks spent in observing these apes in the forest, I have never heard them utter a sound at night, and not often in the daytime, by which I judge they are not quarrelsome—the exact opposite to chimpanzis or the baboons. I found open wounds from fighting on the crest of only one of the old males I shot; they were apparently teeth marks, and this same animal, by the way, had several big boils in different parts of its body, especially on the glands of one armpit" (3, p. 131).

In the tracks of Barns came Prince Wilhelm of Sweden and Count Gyldenstolpe, armed with a permit to kill as many as fourteen gorillas, and especially desirous of obtaining materials to answer certain questions about local subspecies or varieties. They were successful perhaps beyond their hopes, and their publications have added not inconsiderably to our naturalistic information. Unique in the literature of gorilla social relations are the following paragraphs from Prince Wilhelm's "Among pygmies and gorillas."

"We had not gone many steps before we found traces of a great herd of gorillas which had come down into the valley from Karissimbi. The gorillas had not hurried—you could see that by the appearance of the tracks. On the way they had evidently been busy taking their breakfast, this time consisting of the juicy stalks of the chervil. Whilst taking specially great care not to make any noise, we crept cautiously forward. Soon we were near the gorillas. Now and then you could hear faint gruntings and movements and rustlings in the undergrowth, announcing the presence of the animals. Unfortunately they themselves were completely hidden by the high vegetation. On the spot where the tracks had first been seen the greater part of my followers were left with strict orders to keep perfectly quiet and motionless, whatever happened.

"I, my gun-bearer Simba and one of the guides crept forward slowly till we had reached the foot of a tree from which we could' peep out over a small, fairly open place in the forest. In the middle of this opening lay a biggish tree thrown down, whose branches rose above the rich vegetation which everywhere covered the ground. My hiding-place was situated only about twenty yards from the place where the gorillas were. With very natural excitement I expected to catch sight of the animals any moment and perhaps behold a sight that few, if any, Europeans had had the luck to see. I had not long to wait before I caught sight of a baby gorilla slowly and cautiously climbing up the fallen tree trunk. This baby was soon followed by another and the two young ones now began to play a clumsy game of 'tick' with each other. Now and then they let themselves down on the ground. They never jumped straight down, but first hung by their arms, after which they threw themselves down on the ground with a thud and then after a short time got up onto the tree trunk again and continued the game afresh. Their movements were slow and very clumsy. Once when one of the young ones was trying to catch hold of its play-fellow and made a violent movement it simply tumbled over, and in the surprise of seeing its play-fellow disappear so suddenly the other one very nearly followed its example. Before it succeeded in regaining its equilibrium it took a real header.

"On some occasions the young ones clasped each other in their arms and once I noticed how one of them, after an unsuccessful attempt to catch the other, began to beat the tree trunk with both hands, evidently in order to make its play-fellow come nearer out of curiosity. Then suddenly there was a lively movement amongst the feeding animals and slowly and lazily a full-grown female gorilla climbed up the trunk. There she sat looking around. The young gorillas kept perfectly motionless for some moments. They resumed their dizzy game, however, as soon as the mother had convinced herself that no danger threatened. The female soon joined in the game, to the visible and audible delight of the young ones. Once I saw the female gorilla take one of the young ones in her arms. She remained sitting like that a long while, with the other young one jealously looking on. By and by the female climbed down to the ground again and the young ones continued their interrupted game alone.

"A little further away there stood a dry tree, in the lower branches of which another female and a young one sat crouched, evidently no longer hungry, but content with their existence. To the left of me there was a fallen tree on which a big male sat on guard. Now and then he went down from his elevated post and broke off leaves and plants which, after he had carefully examined them, he put into his mouth with one hand and ate with a smacking sound. In the middle of the opening—unfortunately, however, completely hidden from my curious eyes—was the remainder of the herd, which, as appeared afterwards, consisted of about thirty members. Among these was the leader, who now and then made his presence known by a grunting sound. From time to time some short angry growls were heard from some gorilla who disputed with one of the others the possession of some specially delicate and juicy stalk, and sometimes we heard hollow sounds when one of them beat its bare chest. This habit of beating the chest seems to me to be a sort of signal of warning, or else it is to show their power and strength and to warn others to keep at a proper distance.

"For more than half an hour I lay and enjoyed this rare and splendid sight of the gorillas' home-life in the wild forest. Unfortunately there was a drizzle that made photography impossible" (31, p. 190).

Before the bewildered gorillas had time to recover from the disturbing presence of the Barns and Prince Wilhelm hunting parties, Carl Akeley and the Bradleys arrived in search of specimens for the American Museum of Natural History and of pictorial records. Akeley came with the full-grown idea that the gorilla is not a dangerous animal and will not ordinarily and unprovoked attack or injure man. That he was not disappointed is made clear by his book "In brightest Africa" (1) and by Mary Hastings Bradley's "On the gorilla trail" (6). But how much previous successful hunting may be responsible for the mountain gorilla's lack of aggressiveness and seeming timidity is a fair question which these observers leave unanswered.

Many of the observations recorded by Barns and Prince Wilhelm were confirmed and some were supplemented by those of Akeley and the Bradleys. Much disturbed by the small numbers—estimated as fifty to one hundred—of mountain gorillas, Akeley conceived the idea of recommending to the King of the Belgians the establishment of a gorilla sanctuary in which *Gorilla beringei* might live unmolested, multiply, and furnish ideal opportunities for naturalistic and experimental studies of its behavior and mentality. This suggestion, favorably received by the Belgian Government, has gained expression in the establishment of the Albert National Park, of which the triangle of three extinct volcanoes, Mikeno, Karissimbi, and Visoke, is at once the central feature and the inviolable sanctuary of the gorilla.

It was Akeley's distinction to secure also the first motion pictures of the mountain gorilla in its native forest. Thus, by the skillful mounting of specimens for his natural gorilla group in the American Museum of Natural History, and by bringing about the establishment of a preserve for *G. beringei*, he has contributed significantly to scientific progress.

In 1923, and again in 1925, Benjamin Burbridge, an American hunter, betook himself to the gorilla mountains to collect specimens, obtain motion pictures of the wild life of the gorillas, and to capture and carry home with him young individuals. He alone of the notable train of hunter-collectors has failed to make into a book his varied and enlightening experiences with the gorilla. As recounted in previous pages, his first expedition yielded excellent motion pictures and four young captives; his second, additional observational data, pictorial records, and another quartet of captive youngsters.

It is doubtful whether anyone knows the mountain gorilla more intimately or, for the purposes of hunter and photographer, more usefully than does Burbridge. The only approach to an account of his adventures and knowledge is "The gorilla hunt" by him (10), and a popular article by Richard D. Sparks (30) on Congo, the subject of this psychological report.

Probably at least as much is now known of the natural history of *Gorilla beringei* as of *Gorilla gorilla*. It is not my purpose to compare them. Instead I have attempted to present certain general information preparatory to my description of the behavior of Congo. During the hundred years which have elapsed since the publication of Bowdich's paper (5) several accounts of the mind and behavior of gorillas have appeared. When I remark that they are disappointing, I reflect unfavorably on the status of gorilla study but not necessarily on the ability, effort, insight, or honesty of the observers or recorders. As a fact, the only contributions to gorilla psychology are impressionistic, fragmentary, and almost as difficult to evaluate as are Du Chaillu's descriptions.

Of the mental traits of the chimpanzee we know much; of those of the orang-utan somewhat; but of the psychology of gorillas next to nothing with certainty. The present report is unique because it records the first mental measurements of a gorilla. It is a pioneer contribution also in that for the first time a professional student of animal behavior and a specialist in the psychology of the primates offers the results of a systematic, general survey of the mental constitution of *Gorilla beringei*. It is hoped that the reader will constantly bear in mind the purpose and limitations of the investigation and the fact that the author's statements are not made of gorillas in general, or even of the species beringei, but of the individual specimen Congo. If she is not typical of her species, sex, and age it is our misfortune.

III

THE OBSERVATIONAL SITUATION AND ITS VALUES

From New York Ben Burbridge took Congo directly to Jacksonville. There he arranged with his brother, James Burbridge, that the gorilla' should be housed and cared for at Shady Nook, which is a quiet beautiful home-spot on the banks of the St. Johns River some two miles out of South Jacksonville and approached by the San José Boulevard. The buildings are located several hundred yards from the highway and the heavy traffic therefore is not disturbing. There is a cottage, a separate study, a garage, and for Congo a cage especially built. The buildings are set among immense live oak trees which effectively shelter them from sun and rain.

The gorilla cage is located about six feet north of the study. It is some sixty feet from the cottage and approximately the same distance from the garage. To describe the cage in some detail is necessary since many of the experiments to be reported were made in or about it.

It is twenty feet long, ten feet wide, and eight feet high. Plate 4 gives a view of the cage from the east and also a view of the north end of the interior. Wooden posts 3¾ by 3¾ inches and rails 3¾ by 1¾ inches carry Page wire netting, 2 inch mesh and no. 9 gauge. This netting covers the top as well as the sides of the cage. When the cage was originally constructed in November, 1925, it was possible for Congo to get her hands through the wire netting, but her growth has since eliminated this possibility. At the north end of the cage an area four by ten feet has been floored and roofed. One-half of this covered portion of the cage has been finished as a sleeping room for Congo (see plate 4, lower left figure). The room has an entrance door which can be closed on cold nights, and at the level of the floor in the east wall an opening six inches deep by five feet long, to facilitate cleaning the floor. This opening, too narrow for Congo to squeeze through, is closed by a door hinged on the upper edge and locked by a hasp at the bottom. Except when opened to air and dry the nest-room or in connection with cleaning, it was kept closed and locked. It is particularly described because it figures importantly in certain experiments. The north end of the cage is solidly boarded to break the cold winds of winter, and for the same reason the other three sides are partially boarded, the east and west, to a height of thirty-two inches from the ground; the south side, to a height of fifty-four inches.

The long dimension of the cage extends from somewhat west of north to east of south. I shall, however, for simplicity of description, hereafter refer to the several sides as north, south, east, and west. In the wooden portion of the south side of the cage, approximately thirty inches from the southwest corner post and thirty inches from the ground, is a ten by ten inch opening, with hinged door. Through this aperture Congo was given her meals when it did not happen to be convenient for the caretaker to enter the cage. The bottom of the cage, with the exception of the boarded portion at the north end, consists of sandy soil. It has the great advantages of dryness and cleanliness. The cage can be entered by a door located at the south corner of the west side. At the corresponding corner of the east side, indicated by an X in the lower right figure of plate 4, the board siding was removed and replaced by one-half inch iron rods, set vertically and at four inches between centers. This spacing enabled Congo readily to reach through the grill with hand and arm or foot and leg. The grill space is approximately forty-one inches long by twenty-two inches high. This modification of Congo's cage was effected to provide a convenient situation for setting problems outside the cage which Congo from within could work at, or the reverse.

Aside from the shelter room and porch at the north end of the cage, it contains, for Congo's amusement, three heavy iron

Plate 4. Glimpses of Congo's Florida home

Fig. 1, upper left. The Burbridge cottage, Shady Nook, with Betty in the foreground. Fig. 2, upper right. Congo resting in a favorite position in a live oak near her cage. Fig. 3, lower left. Interior of cage, showing Congo's nest-room. Fig. 4, lower right. Cage as seen from the east. X marks the section of side wall which was replaced by grill.

rings suspended from the ceiling by chains, and along the sides the following benches. On the west side is a wooden bench eighteen inches wide, eighteen inches from the ground, extending from the edge of the porch to within two feet of the entrance door of the cage. In the middle of the east side there is a bench twenty-four inches wide, forty inches from the ground, and approximately eight feet long. Similarly, at the southeast corner there is a corner bench approximately fifty inches from the ground and filling the triangular space between the southeast corner post and the adjacent posts on the south and east respectively.

The study is southeast of the cage, the cottage approximately south, and the garage west. Conveniently placed in relation to the cage are several large oaks in or under which arrangements were made for several of the experiments to be described.

Prior to my period of observation Congo had been fed regularly three times daily by either Mrs. or Mr. James Burbridge. The principal articles of food were baked bananas, baked sweet potatoes, apples, and oranges, and skimmed milk mixed with an equal quantity of water. She ate eagerly and evidently was well nourished. No particular pains had been taken to extend her diet by teaching her to eat other things or to train her to the use of knife, fork, and spoon, and to care and cleanliness in the handling of foods. Although eager for the diluted milk given her, she drank little water.

As bedding a plentiful supply of clean, dry straw was kept in the shelter or bedroom. With this Congo made herself comfortable by shaping a crude nest. There is no evidence that she ordinarily covered herself with the straw as protection against the cold, but she evidently did burrow into it, thus making for her body a hole in the center of the heap Every clear day this straw was removed from the room and placed in the sunlight to dry. Once or twice a week it was replaced, and the floor of the nest-room was thoroughly washed. The ground floor of the cage ordinarily required no attention because the sand quickly absorbed moisture, and Congo early formed the habit of using the northwest corner between the porch edge and the adjacent end of the side bench as a toilet.

The young gorilla, it might be expected, would be lonesome in this environment without anthropoid companionship, but she obviously was not. During the period of my work she was on friendly terms with a bulldog named Bobby and an Airedale named Betty, both of whom were young enough to be playful. The gorilla quite evidently enjoyed their companionship, and they in their quite different dog ways sometimes sought and at other times merely tolerated hers. Neither dog had access to the gorilla cage and their only opportunities for play or other intimate association were when Congo happened to be chained to a tree or post outside of her cage. There can be no doubt, I think, that the principal objects in Congo's social environment were the Burbridges, and that her contentment from the first was chiefly conditioned by the friendly, sympathetic attitude of Mrs. Burbridge and the latter's interest and skill in feeding her and in making her feel at once welcome and at home.

My initial decision was to adapt myself and my research interests as far as practicable to the conditions at Shady Nook instead of attempting to convert it into a scientific establishment. At first things looked a little discouraging, but I shortly discovered ways in which it seemed possible to go forward profitably. No laboratory was available and under the circumstances only the simplest equipment could be used. But in spite of the lack of even ordinary facilities for experimental work it seemed that mental measurement in connection with a general survey of the psycho-biological characteristics of Congo should be more profitable than strictly naturalistic observation and might importantly supplement what little is already known about the gorilla.

I therefore accepted out-of-doors at Shady Nook·as my laboratory. The only essential change made in Congo's imme-

diate environment was the construction of the grill already
described (p. 30) in the southeast corner of the cage. There
were distractions, and conditions were far more variable than
one would permit in a laboratory environment. Such success
as was obtained in the work doubtless depended rather on the
practical experience and adaptability of the investigator than
on what are commonly considered essential material requirements of experimental research. Ordinarily working hours
were free from curious visitors, and I am inclined to think
that the relative naturalness of the conditions of work goes a
long way toward compensating for variability and the lack of
conventional and customary controls.

With the idea of a survey of Congo's mental equipment in
mind I planned to observe under simple experimental conditions and to measure with a serviceable degree of accuracy,
both intellectual and affective responses and adaptations.
Realizing that it would be impossible to make even a preliminary study of the animal's sensory and perceptual equipment if I were to do much with intellectual and affective responses, I subordinated the former to the latter psychological
categories and proceeded on what appeared to be a practicable course. Experimental situations from the first were
chosen or devised primarily to display the nature and degree
of Congo's adaptivity, to reveal whatever measures of insight
or understanding she might possess, and to elicit characteristic affective expressions and adjustments.

The abbreviated notes hastily made during each morning's
observational work, were written up in detail each afternoon
and thus made to constitute a record complete, detailed, intelligible, and trustworthy. Many photographic records also were
made, and the four score still pictures and thousand feet of.
motion picture film which were obtained, in important and unexpected ways supplement my verbal descriptions.

Unless otherwise stated, Congo had opportunity to see the
experimental situation arranged. As soon as everything was
ready she was permitted to work for food. Had the condi-

tions favored it, doubtless I should have introduced her to completely prepared situations instead of letting her watch me. There can be no doubt that the conditions under which I worked held the possibility of suggestion and possibly also other influence of the experimenter on the subject. In advance of observation I had considered the necessity of setting certain problems in Congo's presence unfortunate and made up my mind to avoid it as far as possible. But as experimental observation progressed I became less certain of the disadvantages and finally decided that except for standardization of procedure the advantages, temporarily at least, were in favor of the course which circumstances had forced upon me. I now feel reasonably certain that had I worked more conventionally and in accord with laboratory practice I should have acquired less information and insight.

Usually also the observer was where Congo could see him during her periods of effort. Mostly he sat a few feet away taking notes. No reason appeared for believing that this relation was objectionable because of suggestion or inhibitory influence. In a few experiments the observer hid himself from the subject's view or was absent from the vicinity of the cage; when he thus took remote positions or was out of Congo's sight the fact is indicated in the description of experiments.

When working within her cage Congo ordinarily was given full freedom, and although a leather collar was always kept about her neck no chain nor rope was attached to it. But when she was taken out of the cage for experiments, exercise, or to be moored to a nearby tree, her freedom was restricted by a stout chain attached to her collar. This chain could be fastened to stake, tree, or other stable object and thus made to keep her within bounds.

Food was used as reward or lure in all experiments, and Congo's desire for it was so strong, persistent, and dependable that it constituted an adequate incentive to determined effort in the solution of problems. Each morning before my arrival at Shady Nook Congo was given about a pint of diluted milk.

The remainder of her breakfast and her midday meal she obtained by working for rewards in experimental situations. Four foods were used chiefly as lures: baked banana, baked sweet potato, raw apple and orange. They have been named in the order of preference usually exhibited by Congo. At the end of the morning's experimental work Congo was given whatever remained of her usual allowance of food.

As the work progressed, and Congo learned that situations arranged by the experimenter were worth attending to, she came to work more spontaneously, eagerly, persistently, and confidently, if not also increasingly for the pleasure of activity and success, even apart from the reward itself.

Punishment was employed to supplement reward only in the experiments with the multiple-choice apparatus. Unquestionably the hope and expectation of reward proved more serviceable as condition of effort toward adaptation than did the fear of punishment. This generalization applies only to my experiments with Congo. Quite possibly under other circumstances the relative values of these motivating stimuli might be reversed.

The climatic conditions in North Florida during my period of experimentation varied widely and were sometimes decidedly unfavorable. About one-fifth of the days were rainy, and on a few occasions it rained so hard and steadily that out-of-door work was next to impossible. The remaining days were about equally divided between fair and cloudy. But except as rain drove Congo and the observer to shelter the degree of clearness was important chiefly because of its relation to temperature, which indeed proved by far the most important environmental factor.

At eight to nine a. m. the temperatures during my period of work ranged from 38° to 68° Fahrenheit. At twelve noon to one p. m. they ranged from 42° to 70°. The average temperature at the beginning of my day's work was 51° and at the end of the morning's work 57°. On the whole these temperatures were a trifle low for Congo's comfort and activity. She seemed to prefer and to work best at temperatures ranging from 55° to

65°. Below 50° she tended to seek shelter, and shivering indicated her unfavorable condition; and similarly at temperatures above 70°, and especially in the direct sunlight, she tended to become quiescent.

If this section has given the reader the impression that conditions of work were other than highly favorable at Shady Nook I have failed in my attempt at effective description, for the trying circumstances, although important enough for mention, seemed rather to stir the interest and determination of Congo and the experimenter than to discourage them.

IV

MEASURES OF ADAPTIVITY OF BEHAVIOR

The experimental inquiry of which this is an account began January 5, 1926. On the morning of that day the grill described on page 30 had been installed and other preparations made. It was my plan and desire to begin work by presenting to Congo some relatively simple problem. Degree of coöperation, industry, and energy could not be predicted, but I assumed that for the reward of much desired food she might be induced to work for at least a few minutes. The use of a stick as tool or instrument with which to obtain desired food was selected as the initial problem.

Although strictly chronological account of observations is for many reasons desirable, I shall in the following pages depart somewhat from it in order to condense the description. The departures, however, are in the direction merely of the grouping of closely related problems. This compromise between the strictly chronological order and the logical seems to be indicated by the plan of work as well as by the results obtained. The reader, however, must constantly bear in mind that the experimental situation steadily became more complicated as new problems were presented to Congo. At the outset I had slight hope that she would work effectively more than thirty minutes at a stretch, but instead she proved very nearly inexhaustible in her interest in experimental situations and her patience in trying to meet them properly. Whereas I had assumed that most of my time might be devoted to planning and preparing experiments, I shortly discovered that I could present one problem after another for as many as four or five hours with no appreciable lessening in Congo's interest or activity if she was reasonably successful in obtaining the desired reward. Starting with one problem per day the number was gradually increased to eight, and as each problem required the setting of an experimental situation, followed by period of observation and the recording of results, we were kept very busy from nine a. m. to at least one p. m. with eight problems.

In order that the reader may have a general view of the more important experimental situations used to measure Congo's intellectual and affective responses and adaptations, the following list is given with the date, hour, and, whenever significant, the duration of each trial. The problems are arranged in order of presentation and the list of dates indicates not only this order but the number of presentations and the succession of problems for a given day. The experiments were always conducted in the morning beginning at eight forty-five to nine o'clock and continuing in accordance with the number of problems to as late as two p. m.

List of problems with dates of presentation

1. Shelf and stick.
   Jan. 5, 12:15, 60'; 7, 9:00, 60'; 8, 9:15, 60', 12:10, 2'; 9, 8:50, 15'. M. p. r.* Jan. 19 and Feb. 1.
2. Diagonal rope.
   Jan. 7, 10:18, three trials in an hour.
3. Hooked rope.
   Jan. 8, 10:20, 20', 10:55, 60'; 10, 9:21, 17'; 11, 9:32, 4'; 12, 9:50, 4'; 13, 9:13, 1' 15"; 14, 9:20, 1' 30"; 15, 9:35, 30"; 16, 9:15, 30"; 17, 9:40, 30". M. p. r. Jan. 19.
4. Platform and stick.
   Jan. 8, 12:12, 3'; 9, 9:06, 15'; 10, 9:03, 15'; 11, 9:12, 15'; 12, 9:25, 15'; 13, 8:55, 15'; 15, 9:15, 15'; 16, 9:00, 12'; 17, 9:42, 8'; 18, 11:02, 23'; 20, 10:40, 15'; 21, 9:45, 15'; 22, 9:10, 21'; 23, 9:15, 9'; 25, 10:00, 60'; 26, 9:15, 10'; 27, 11:35, 10'; 28, 12:20, 5'; 29, 9:17, 53'; 30, 9:10, 7', 9:47, 8', 12:15, 2'. M. p. r. Jan. 19 and Feb. 1.
5. Pull rope.
   Jan. 8, 12:45, 12', 12:57, 30'; 9, 10:10, 3', 10:15, 3'; 10, 9:45, 1'; 11, 9:38, 1'; 12, 10:12, 1' 30"; 13, 9:15, 30"; 14, 9:50, 5' (estimated); 15, 10:25; 16, 9:42; 17, 10:15. M. p. r. Jan. 19.
6. Milk bottle.
   Jan. 9, 10:00, 2'; 29, jar instead of milk bottle.

---

*M. p. r. stands for motion picture record.

7. Buried food jar.
   Jan. 10, 11 :00, 30'; 11, 10:55, 15'; 12, 11 :03; 13, 10 :26, 20'; 14, 10 :00, 30"; 15, 10:20; 16, 10 :00; 17, 10 :10. M. p. r. Jan. 19.
8. Suspended food and stick.
   Jan. 10, 10 :35, 5'; 11, 10 :20, 30'; 12, 10 :30, 30'; 13, 9 :43, 15'; Feb. 3, 10 :08, 2'; 4, 9 :48, 1' 30".
9. Pipe, wire, and stick.
   Jan. 11, 11 :30, ˙3'; 12, 11 :46, 12'; 13, 10 :08, 15'; 14, 9 :35, 15'; 15, 9 :55, 25'; 16, 9 :26, 14'; 17, 9 :53, 16'; Feb. 3, 10 :27, 13'. M. p. r. Jan. 19.
10. Suspended food and boxes.
    Jan. 14, 11 :19, 30'; 15, 10 :50, 40 ; 16, 10 :07, 30'; 17, 9 :03, 16'; 19, 10 :55, 30'; 20, 10 :08, 30'; 21, 10 :10, 30'; 22, 9 :43, 30'. M. p. r. Jan. 19 and Feb. 1.
11. Hasp and padlock.
    Jan. 15, 12 :48, 45'; 16 to 28 inclusive, daily. M. p. r. Jan. 19.
12. Spring bolt box.
    Jan. 17-18, 20-22, 23, box inverted.
13. Hammer and nail imitation.
    Jan. 18.
14. Delayed response, multiple-choice apparatus.
    Jan. 21, 11 :00; 22, 10 :25; 23, 10 :25, 11 :30; Feb. 2, 10 :45; 3, 10 :45; 4, 10 :20. M. p. r. Feb. 1.
15. Identical object, multiple-choice.
    Jan. 23, 10 :25. M. p. r. Feb. 1.
16. Box imitation.
    Jan. 23, 11 :00, 20'; 26, 9 :20, 22'; 27, 9 :50, 33'; 28, 9 :14, 16 ; 30, 9 :20, 4'.
17. First object to left, multiple-choice.
    Jan. 23, 11 :30.
18. Mirror.
    Jan. 25, 11 :05, 5'-8'; 26, 12 :30, 5'-8'; 27, 12 :02, 5'-8'; 28, 12 :05, 5'-8'; 29, 11 :00, 5'-8'; Feb. 3, 11 :50, 5'-8'. M. p. r. Feb. 1.
19. Arm and leg reach.
    Jan. 26; 28; Feb. 3. M. p. r. Feb. 1.
20. Wound chain.
    Jan. 26, 10 :40, 55'; 27, 10 :30, 60'.
21. Box and weight obstruction.
    Jan. 26, 11 :26, 30'; 27, 9 :10, 30'.
22. Middle object, multiple-choice.
    Jan. 28, 10 :30; 31, 11 :16; Feb. 2, 10 :45.

23. Box stacking.
     Jan. 30, 10:01, 1′, 10:15, 30′; 31, 9:25, 30′, 10:15, 22′;
     Feb. 2, 9:56, 30′; 3, 11:55, 1′; 4, 10:00, 4′. M. p. r.
     Feb. 1.
24. Hidden stick.
     Jan. 31, 10:00, 2′; Feb. 1, 9:05, 10′; 2, 9:27, 2′; 3,
     9:30, 30′; 4, 9:20,. 1′.

The more or less problematic situations arranged to reveal
the nature and extent of Congo's adaptability logically fall into
three groups: (1) the use of objects as appliances or tools, as
for example in the stick and box problems; (2) the manipulation of environment, as in the several rope problems and in
the multiple choice, and (3) the modification of environment,
as in the buried food problem. It was my endeavor to select
from previously used methods, or to devise, simple experimental situations which should differ widely in type of adaptive response required and in complexity or difficulty for the
gorilla. Many of the situations which I employed are described
by Hobhouse (19) to whom I gratefully acknowledge my exceptional indebtedness.

With the thought that the use of objects as tools might be
the simplest and most effective way to exhibit at once the animal's acquisitions and resourcefulness, I planned a series of
problems involving the utilization of sticks or boxes and covering a wide range of requirement. That my plans were completely upset by Congo is made clear in the following description of her behavior.

A. THE STICK AS INSTRUMENT

As soon as general preparations for experimental work had
been completed on the morning of January 5, a wooden shelf
was placed at the south end of Congo's cage, sloping from the
wall of the adjacent study to the cage at an angle of about fifteen degrees. The cage end of this shelf was slightly below
the 10 by 10 inch door described on page 30 as feeding door.
Nailed to the shelf at either side of the feeding door and extending from cage to study were strips of wood which served
as guards to prevent food placed on the shelf from rolling off

or being swept off during experiments. These guard rails were eighteen inches apart at the feeding door end of the shelf and thirty inches apart at the study end. The shelf itself was approximately 60 inches long by 30 inches wide. It was found necessary, in order to discourage Congo's attempt to squeeze through the feeding door, to lessen its width by two inches, making the dimensions 10 inches by 8 inches.

Problem 1. Shelf and stick. When this construction had been completed Congo's reach through the feeding door was determined as about twenty-four inches. Then while the animal's attention was otherwise occupied a stick 1 by 1 by 12 inches was placed on the bench on the west side of the cage, and another approximately ⅓ by 2 by 18 inches on the floor of the cage some six feet from the feeding door. Each was clearly visible to Congo as she wandered about the cage. At approximately 12:15 p. m. a whole baked banana was placed on the shelf thirty-six inches from the feeding door. The door was opened and Congo given opportunity to obtain the food.

Going promptly to the opening she saw the banana and desiring it tried energetically to squeeze through the opening, at the same time reaching to her utmost repeatedly with her right arm. After nearly a minute of work and eight determined reaches she paused and for a few seconds looked at the banana. Then she went to the grill and looked out; then to the house shelf, as we shall hereafter designate the shelf on the west side of the cage and facing the kitchen door of the cottage. The hour for her midday meal was near and Congo quite obviously was eager for food. Further to stimulate effort toward the solution of the problem, I placed a baked sweet potato beside the banana on the shelf at 12:25 p. m. Seeing me by the feeding door she returned to it and reached twice for the food. As she left the door to go to the grill she noticed the stick on the floor of the cage and in passing picked it up, but promptly put it down again almost in the same spot. Evidently the act was a response to an unfamiliar object and had no relation to her food seeking. During the next half-hour she moved about the cage deliberately and several times went to the feeding door and reached for the food or tried to squeeze through the opening. Usually she reached first with her right arm and then sometimes with the left. The right was decidedly preferred.

The test was continued for one hour during which she went to the feeding door and either reached for the food or looked at it intently some twelve different times. Toward the end of the period the impulse to reach decidedly lessened and several times it was inhibited almost at the beginning. Once on seeing Mr. Burbridge approach she patted her chest rapidly in apparent expression of impatience.

During this initial period of experiment to test Congo's ability to use the stick as a tool it became increasingly clear that she had neither natural nor acquired ability to use sticks, straws, or functionally similar objects in her cage to aid her in reaching desired food. She used but two methods: the attempt to squeeze her head and body through the feeding aperture, and reaching with extended arm. To my great surprise there was no overt expression of excitement or anger because of difficulties encountered and failure to achieve the desired reward. She was hungry, evidently wanted the food, and yet acted calmly. Surprising also to the observer were Congo's poise in the experiment, her deliberateness of movement and adaptive effort, and her self-control and emotional stability.

At the conclusion of the observational period Congo was immediately fed by Mrs. Burbridge.

The following day was too rainy for experimental work, so Congo was given her second opportunity at the shelf and stick problem at 9 a. m., January 7. This time a baked banana, a baked sweet potato, and a raw apple were placed on the shelf thirty-six inches from the feeding aperture. On the floor of the cage within six to twelve feet of the aperture were three sticks, 12, 18 and 18 inches long respectively, with any one of which Congo could readily have reached the food on the shelf.

When the feeding door was opened Congo came eagerly, put her head as far as possible through the opening, and reached determinedly with her left arm. After a single effort she gave up and wandered about the cage, stopping from time to time at favorite resting places and looking about with a peculiarly disinterested and unconcerned air. The most frequented resting place at such times was the house bench which gave her clear view of the kitchen door and was her nearest approach to the usual source of food.

About 9:10 a. m. she came to the aperture, put her head through but did not reach. Again fifteen minutes later she came to the opening, put her head through and with her right arm reached once. Several times she made a smacking sound with her lips which suggested expectation of food.

She gave no heed whatever to the sticks and her behavior differed from that on the 5th only in lessened tendency to reach and increased effort to squeeze her body through the aperture. At the end of the first half-hour, as she sat on the house bench, I pushed a 24-inch stick through in front of her and let it rest on the bench with one end in the wire netting of the cage. She saw but did not touch it. I accepted this fact with difficulty because all of my experience in working with primates justified expectation of examination on the basis of curiosity, and play or fooling with the object.

Once in the next fifteen minutes she reached for the food. At 9:45 a. m., with intent to increase incentive, I placed the food six inches nearer the aperture. This immediately commanded her attention and stirred her to effort to get through the opening. She worked quietly and with such strength that for a moment I was fearful she might break her way through the end of the cage. After a few well directed attempts she gave up and patting her chest vigorously walked about the cage.

A few times during the remainder of the hour she came to the aperture and occasionally reached for the food. It now was almost within reach and her behavior clearly enough indicated its increased value as lure.   Effort is related to apparent chance of success.

Thus without sign of ability or tendency to use objects as aids in obtaining desired reward, the second period of experimentation ended.

To alleviate at least partially the discouraging influence of Congo's failure in the shelf and stick experiment she was introduced on January 7 to the diagonal rope test.   In this, fortunately, she was successful, as will appear from subsequent description.   The matter is mentioned at this point because the rope test undoubtedly influenced somewhat Congo's behavior in the stick test.

On January 8 Congo was given another one-hour trial with the shelf and stick problem.   On the shelf were a banana, sweet potato, and apple, and on the cage floor at various points lay four sticks.   Since the beginning of this experiment the sticks had not been removed from the cage: the number had been increased from two to four.   There was no indication that Congo had moved them about in play or otherwise.   Apparently they simply failed to command her interested attention.

Beginning at 9:15 a. m. Congo eagerly sought the food and for two minutes she struggled hard but vainly to force her way through the aperture first with one shoulder and arm, then the other shoulder and arm, and finally feet foremost. After this attempt she settled down on the house bench quietly. Once she whined in high pitched voice.   It was as though she were begging for food and complaining because of my failure to supply it.   This morning for the first time she greeted me with lively and seemingly expectant interest.   Evidently as the setter of more or less promising, although problematic, situations I was acquiring value.

After some five minutes she tried once more to force her way to the food.   Again, about the middle of the hour, she went to the aperture and reached hard with the right arm, then with the left arm.   Returning to the house bench she whined in characteristic tremulous high pitched tone. This plaintive and, as it were, beseeching sound from so sturdy an animal seemed strangely incongruous. Later in the hour, two or three half-hearted efforts were made to reach the food. At no time was attention given to the sticks.

Problem 4. Platform and stick. As Congo had now had three full hours to exhibit any possible appreciation of the stick as a tool and as the results were entirely negative, I decided to change the form of the problem somewhat and to make it easier.

The new stick problem, listed as no. 4 on page 38, is briefly described as "platform and stick." In the transition to this new problem-situation, which was first presented to Congo on January 8, the shelf as well as the platform was used in accordance with the description which follows.

At 12:10 p. m. food was placed on the shelf thirty-six inches from the door and a stick laid on the shelf with one end resting on the edge of the aperture. When Congo came to the aperture she smelled of the stick and promptly pushed it aside and out of the way with one hand. Then without even trying to reach the food she turned away. The performance was so definitely negative that I decided to terminate the observation and to proceed immediately with the similar platform and stick form of experiment.

In front of the grill on the east side of the cage, a platform approximately 40 inches wide by 60 inches long was laid on the ground and staked down. Its surface was some four inches below the level of the lower edge of the grill. On this platform, twenty-eight inches from the grill, I placed a baked sweet potato and between it and the grill a 1 by 2 by 24 inch stick. Congo, having seen the food, came directly to the grill and reached through it. Next she touched the stick with her right hand, but instead of picking it up and using it definitely she pushed it to one side and out of her way as if irritated by its presence. Not satisfied with merely pushing it off the platform, she continued until it was almost beyond her reach.

With the thought that frequent repetitions of opportunity to work at the problem might be more favorable than the previous long periods of work, the trial was discontinued at 12:15 p. m.

The following day, January 9, at 8:50 a. m., food was placed on the shelf, the stick, as previously, with one end resting in the aperture. Congo came eagerly, looked at the food, pushed the stick to one side, and tried to squeeze through the opening head first, then feet first. After this attempt she gave up and went away. At 8:55 a. m. she came back, looked, smacked her lips, but did not reach for the food. When I imitated the lip-smacking she looked eagerly toward the food as though the sound suggested it. After a total of fifteen minutes the trial was discontinued and at 9:06 a. m. the same problem was presented on the grill platform. Here an apple, a banana, and a potato were placed as possible rewards of effort. Congo promptly reached for the food and tried to move the platform itself. The stick between the grill and the food she next grasped and pushed away from her sidewise and toward the food. Leaving the grill she walked about the cage, to return after a few minutes and attempt to squeeze through the grill sidewise. Next she reached hard. Touching the stick with one hand she moved it slightly but indirectly and if not accidentally, at least with no indication of definite intent. Later she again returned to her task and after pushing the stick away from her with her hand, she reached for and pulled it back with her foot. At intervals in the remainder of the fifteen-minute period she returned to the stick, touching it usually with her right hand and moving it about. Obviously her attention was increasingly commanded by it, perhaps because of its proximity to the food, but more likely because she had discovered she could push it toward the latter. Is this, perhaps, a logical approach to the use of the stick as tool?

From this time forth the shelf was abandoned as experimental situation and the grill platform used instead. When food and stick were placed on the platform at 9:03 a. m., January 10, Congo came eagerly, pushed the stick to one side with her left hand, then reached for it with the same hand and drew it back toward her. The morning was cool, temperature 44°, and the gorilla shivered as she worked. At first as she saw and reached for the reward she growled with eagerness. It seemed as though she fully expected to get the food. As usual, after each determined effort she left the grill for some favored position in the cage. During the fifteen-minute interval of observation she made in all not more than four definite attempts to solve her problem. No appreciable increase in her interest in the stick on the platform, or in those previously placed on the floor of the cage for problem no. 1, was noted and it seemed doubtful whether she had made any progress.

As an aside, which however is not irrelevant, it may be stated that on this date, January 10, the suspended food and stick problem, no. 8 in the list, was presented to Congo. She therefore from this time on had opportunity to become familiar with sticks and to use them in at least two differing situations.

With apple, banana, and potato on the platform thirty-six inches from the grill, and the stick placed between them and the grill and pointing to the food, Congo at 9:12 a. m. on January 11 made a few futile, non-adaptive moves. She went to work immediately, trying first to squeeze through the grill; then she turned to the stick, looked it over carefully, held it against the bars of the grill and put it down on the platform. Her actions were characteristically calm and deliberate—more like those of an elderly person than a youngster. After this initial performance she left the grill. When more food was added to the store in view, her hopefulness seemed to increase slightly and she looked through the grill eagerly, but neither reached nor touched the stick. Somewhat later she did reach for the food, and also took up the stick and smelled it. But when, after fifteen minutes, the trial was discontinued I had to record in my notes "no visible progress."

On January 12, when at 9:25 a. m. the platform-stick problem was presented, Congo's performance was not essentially different from previously. Suspecting that her initiative might be inhibited by my presence I went to the other side of the study, where completely out of Congo's sight I waited for five minutes. When I returned there was no indication that she had attempted to use the stick or done anything else unusual. She now had practically abandoned the futile method of reaching for the food, which at first was so much in evidence, and her interest in sticks or other objects which might be used as aids was increasing slowly if at all. As yet they were uninteresting commonplaces.

First thing on the morning of January 13 Congo was given her usual fifteen-minute trial with the platform-stick problem. She came to the grill and watched the food intently as I placed it, but she made no effort to reach it, nor did she touch the stick. After a few minutes she went to her nest-room where several times she whined. Although at the time I feared she might be indisposed, I am now convinced that she was merely complaining because of her inability to get the desired food. After some ten minutes she returned to the grill, scratched in the sand beside the platform and also fingered the stick. There was no further activity directed toward the food.

On six successive days this problem had been presented with gradual diminution of Congo's interest in the situation, of her initiative, and her persistence in the use of her few methods of attack. As continuation of the experiment threatened to develop discouragement and resentment toward me which might be decidedly unfavorable to further work, I decided to convert the problem into an imitation test by undertaking to show Congo how a stick might be used as tool.

Beginning January 15, the first thing in the morning as usual, I arranged the platform-stick situation and then taking my position at the northeast corner of the grill, with Congo watching, I used the 24-inch stick to move about an apple which I had placed on the platform. First I would pull it toward the grill slightly, then push it away. After doing this a number of times I laid the stick down where Congo could reach it. At intervals I repeated this performance up to six times, but with no attempt on the part of Congo to imitate me. Finally, I pulled the apple toward the grill and left the stick lying with one end against it. Immediately Congo grasped the stick and in moving it chanced to move the apple also. It was just enough, however, to enable her to reach the reward. This, a fortunate accident, had marked effect.

After a few minutes I continued the copy-setting, using the stick to move the apple, then putting it down as above described. This was done about a dozen times without imitative response. Then I again laid the stick down in contact with the apple. Congo immediately grasped the stick with her right hand and with it swept the apple to her left toward the corner of the grill and within reach. But even now when I laid the stick down apart from the apple she paid no attention to it. Evidently her natural tendency to imitate my acts was slight indeed. Prior to observation I had supposed that she would use the stick readily, if not by visual imitation, then by way of the tuition which this experiment provides.

The imitation test was varied somewhat on January 16 when I used small pieces of apple, usually quarters, and showed Congo that they might readily be moved about either toward or away from the grill by grasping and manipulating the stick. Whenever the stick happened to come into contact with the apple, or be left by me in that position, she eagerly seized it and swept the apple toward her left. If, however, the stick was placed on the left side of the apple, instead of the right side, she would make precisely the same motion, sweeping it futilely toward her left and there abandoning it. Although opportunity was provided many times in the course of this copy-setting, never once did she appropriately place the stick in relation to the apple and definitely direct its motion. The act of grasping the stick when it lay in contact with the piece of apple and at the right, and of sweeping it definitely to the left, seemed like an automatism.

The tuitional procedure was continued on four successive

days, January 15 to 18, an average of fifteeen minutes a day being devoted to the task. Ordinarily, Congo's attention was excellent throughout the interval and she undoubtedly would have worked much longer, if continuation had seemed advisable.

Struck by the value of Congo's behavior as evidence of the impossibility of properly describing or understanding an action except in the light of its genetic history, I arranged on January 19, with the coöperation of Mr. Ben Burbridge, to make a motion picture record of Congo's use of a stick to secure food. For the purpose of demonstration, a half orange was placed on the platform with the stick just to the left of it, from Congo's point of view. A record then was made of Congo approaching, grasping the stick, and sweeping it vigorously toward her left, and therefore away from the orange. I am not sure that the film shows any look of disappointment, chagrin or foolishness, but it certainly seems as though something of the sort should appear! In the next instance the stick was placed to the right of the orange and a record made of Congo grasping it and definitely sweeping the orange toward the left corner of the grill.

Anyone ignorant of the history of this behavior might naturally interpret the one act as stupidly unadaptive and the other as definitely adaptive. Actually, as viewed in the light of the foregoing description, they differ slightly in value, and the one probably is neither more stupid nor more intelligent than the other. Indeed, Congo's persistence in sweeping the stick toward her left irrespective of its position in relation to the desired food was the most remarkable result of the experiment.

At the conclusion of the motion picture performance Congo did something which unexpectedly and essentially altered the course of experimentation. She took up the stick and used it far more skillfully than ever before. There seemed also to be some promise of escape from her well established automatism. I thereupon decided to continue the imitation form of the test, varying it according to circumstances and giving Congo large

Plate 5. The gorilla using a stick as a tool

opportunity for initiative, imitation, or original solution. So, on January 20 at 10:40 a. m., the platform-stick situation was once more presented. It chanced that in her first attempt orange and stick happened to get into proper relation and by moving the stick toward her left she obtained the food. Thereupon her behavior with reference to the stick changed markedly. She began to handle it with eager interest and a previously unseen measure of freedom. With it she succeeded in raking in a bit of apple without assistance from me. Her work was extraordinarily crude, but by persistence she achieved her purpose. There was very definite initiative and in addition directed effort. Previously neither of these had appeared, except in the action following the motion picture record. Can it be that she was aroused from her automatism and stirred to freedom of action by the novelty of the motion picture experience?

Again I placed a bit of food in position and the stick within reach. She at once set to work, using the stick however, with amazing clumsiness and inefficiency. Often she dropped it or it flew out of her hand and got beyond reach. Never was it well directed. Apparently it was just as likely to go in the opposite direction as in the one intended. She uniformly grasped the stick with her right hand to-day. Once she worked continuously for about two minutes in a fruitless effort to draw in a small piece of apple.

Presently I placed half of a banana on the platform and the stick near the grill. This time she took the stick in her left hand and swept the food toward the right and entirely off the board. Again later she tried to use the stick with her left hand. Apparently she has entirely abandoned her stereotyped action and achieved a useful measure of freedom.

Whether this adaptation is the result of individual initiative, imitation, or tuition, it is impossible to say. Probably all had contributed. The interesting question was whether her technique would improve, and if so how and to what degree. It was important also to note whether the acquired ability to use a stick as tool would spread to other experimental situations.

Congo's change of attitude toward the stick undoubtedly merits detailed and careful description. Yet I have nothing beyond what has already been reported to bridge the gap between her stereotyped and seemingly unintelligent behavior of January 18 and the obviously free efforts at adaptation which appeared on January 19 and still more notably on January 20. The behavior is illuminating and indicative I think of ability crudely to analyze the situation and adapt to it. Of insight or understanding there is no convincing evidence.

The experiment beginning January 21, and continuing daily to the 27th, with the exception of the 24th, was so arranged as to give Congo opportunity to improve her technique and to acquire the visual-motor coördinations necessary for the skillful and efficient use of the stick.

On January 21 an interesting observation was her evident desire to be helped by the experimenter. Handling the stick she found both difficult and laborious. She much preferred to have the experimenter place it in proper relation to the food, so that by one simple movement she could achieve success. Her attitude reminded me of the belief attributed to certain African natives that the chimpanzee refuses to talk because it fears it might be compelled to work.

On January 22 and 23 appeared the tendency to push the stick toward the food as though it were expected thus to change the latter's position. This developed rather pronouncedly in spite of its relative uselessness. Although Congo often worked hard and persistently, her efforts were so ill-directed that they yielded little. Often they suggested the uncoördinated movements of a newborn infant, or the ill-coördinated movements of a child trying for the first time to draw or write.

My notes for January 25, on which Congo was given sixty minutes work on the platform-stick problem, read as follows: Congo was repeatedly given opportunity to get food with the stick. At first she came to the grill readily and worked energetically, even though it was a wet day; but later she came reluctantly and finally she refused to come. Her efforts to use the stick were as crude as ever, consisting chiefly of pushing, throwing, jabbing, instead of well-coördinated, steady, directed movements. Apparently she had her objective definitely in mind and knew what she wanted to do, but lacked the ability to make hand and eye work together. So great is her difficulty in using the stick that I am by no means sanguine that she will ever attempt to use it in other situations. It is hard, discouraging work; probably not less so to-day than when she originally achieved freedom from her initial automatism.

But the very next day she used the stick better than ever before and repeatedly secured bits of food in from thirty seconds to a minute. Her success heartened her greatly and her technique improved steadily and markedly. At times she placed the stick fairly well and made steady as contrasted with jerky movements. Either hand was used and apparently with no great difference in ease or skill.

January 27 records continued progress and Congo's unabated interest in the use of the stick. On the following day I decided to vary the situation by placing the stick at the edge of the grill and with the greater part of its length either (1) on the platform side of the grill or (2) on the cage side of the grill. This, of course, meant that in the former case Congo had no particular difficulty in grasping and thrusting it toward the food, whereas in the latter case it was necessary to push it out between the bars of the grill before it could be used. The behavior was unexpectedly interesting. When Congo first encountered the stick inside the grill she grasped it with her right hand, drew it in to her, and laid it down on the floor of the cage. Then she looked toward the food and made incipient motions to reach for it with her hands and then with her feet. Thereupon she picked up the stick and moved as if to carry it through the grill, but instead put it down beside her. Abandoning her efforts, she turned toward her nest-room, but on the way stopped and looked back as if expecting something to happen which would correct the change in the experimental situation.

When the stick was placed in position (1) with the greater part of its length outside the cage she used it promptly as a tool; but when again it was offered in position (2) inside the cage she acted as before, laying it down on the floor of the cage beside her. There she abandoned it, but returning later to the grill she grasped the stick with her left hand and thus holding it pushed her right arm through the grill as if expecting to reach the food. Indeed, she seemed surprised by the result.

Evidently the stick is intimately a part of the platform-food situation and the interposition of the grill puts it into a new realm of action or gorilla world.

Repetition of ·this experiment on January 29 yielded results very similar to those described above, but in addition exhibited Congo's initial efforts to push the stick through the grill to the platform. In her first effort she placed it lengthwise against the grill and pressed against it. When she put it down it chanced to rest with one end on the lower end of the grill and projecting through some six inches. A moment later she noticed the end of the stick on the outside of the grill and immediately pushed it all the way through and used it as a tool. That she had something corresponding to the idea of getting the stick to the opposite side of the grill is conceivable, but appearances did not convince me that her actual success was other than a happy accident. She seemed surprised when the stick went through and suddenly became available in its customary relation to the food.

In my notes on this day's work I find the following reflections: I suspect that slight changes in the stick itself, its relative position, etc., may suffice to upset Congo's adaptation. The matter certainly should be thoroughly tested. The more I observe her, the more evidence I see that she is perceptually, and presumably ideationally also, in the status of an infant. Sensory interrelations appear to be meager and manual adjustments and coördinations often are lacking where I should have expected them. Yet the animal must be four to five years old, for already she has acquired some of her permanent teeth.

It does not seem probable that the gorilla develops less rapidly than does man. Thus far she has failed entirely to dissociate the stick as a tool from its immediate setting. It possesses its experiential value solely because of and in connection with the whole of which it is an essential part. Is dissociation possible? And will Congo presently come to use sticks as tools irrespective of their surroundings?

When on the morning of January 30 the platform-stick problem was re-presented with the stick inside the cage, Congo almost immediately picked it up and thrusting it through the bars used it effectively. This radically different performance from those previously observed suggests that she may have waked up. Evidently there was no particular point in further repetitions of this form of test for she now definitely and without hesitation transferred the stick from inside the grill to outside.

To pursue further the question of dissociation I now varied the experiment by placing food in the customary position on the platform and, walking to the opposite (west) side of the cage, offering to Congo the stick which, without her knowledge, I had taken up on my way around the cage. As I pushed the stick through the cage wire toward her she noticed but did not touch it. Instead she turned away and busied herself with other matters. Quietly I pushed the stick through the netting and left it with one end resting on the house bench and the other on the floor of the cage. Its position was conspicuous. A few seconds later when Congo returned to that part of the cage she picked up the stick, went directly to the grill, pushed it through and used it to obtain the food. The entire performance required less than thirty seconds.

At last the stick has acquired definite value as a tool and has become at least partially dissociated from the platform-stick situation. My notes state that I was very much surprised by Congo's quick, definite, well-directed action this morning, for it seemed almost as though she had over-night learned how to use the stick when it appeared in the cage, and, I wondered,

"Why do such things so often in the anthropoid apes appear thus suddenly and as critical points in intelligent learning? Or is it unintelligent?"

At 12:15 p. m. on January 30 I placed a sweet potato on the platform, called Congo's attention to it, and walking around to the west side of the cage offered her an old stick, of different length from that she had been using, and badly chewed up by the dogs. She took it unhesitatingly, promptly turned and made for the grill. Without difficulty she thrust the stick through and proceeded to use it.

Problem 24. Hidden stick. The next question was, Will Congo hunt up the stick and bring it to the platform for use if it is anywhere in the cage? And will she also come to use other objects to reach with? As a possible way of obtaining answers to these questions, the stick experiment hereupon was transformed into the "hidden stick" problem, listed as no. 24 on page 40.

At 10 a. m. on January 31 food was placed on the platform, and on the floor of the cage about six feet from the grill a stick was laid. This was done while Congo was out of the cage and also out of sight. When she was brought back to the cage she at once noticed the food on the platform, and as there was no stick at hand she turned and moved toward the nest-room. In so doing she walked over the stick without touching or apparently seeing it. When a few feet beyond it she suddenly stopped, turned back to it and after a few seconds' delay, perhaps for recognition, took it up and carried it directly to the grill. She had some difficulty in getting it through between the bars because of a tendency to place it broadside. There was also a tendency for her right arm to get ahead of the stick, and several times she seemed puzzled and baffled because the stick did not follow the arm. How strange this world of experiments must seem to Congo! Having got the stick through to the platform she obtained her reward immediately.

It was not until February 1 that the stick was so hidden as

to require "searching" as contrasted with "recognition." That morning, at 9:05, having placed food on the platform, I entered the cage with the 24-inch stick in my hand and approached Congo who was on the roof of her nest-room. There I handed the stick to her and moved it about in her hand to attract her attention definitely to it and made perfectly sure that she had clearly noticed its presence. As usual, she at once laid it down beside her.

Leaving the cage, I went around to the grill corner and called Congo. She came promptly, saw and desired the food, but after looking about for the customary tool she turned away baffled and shortly settled on the house bench as though convinced that nothing more could be done about it. Apparently she had no recollection of the presence of the stick in the cage, and "out of sight" was definitely "out of mind." For ten minutes I waited on the chance that she might seek the stick. She did not do so.

Immediately after this test a motion picture record was made of Congo discovering food on the platform and turning to get a stick which had been placed on the floor of her cage. The stick in this case was not out of sight, and she very evidently noticed it as she approached the grill initially, but apparently lacked sufficient forethought to bring it with her.

The hidden stick problem was presented once again on February 2 at 9:27 a. m. This time I went into the cage with two sticks in my hand, the one an old one previously described as much chewed, and the other the regulation stick of the platform experiment. Congo was in her nest-room. I laid the old stick on the floor of the porch without directing her attention to it, and handed the new stick to her in the nest-room. After playing with it a few seconds while I held one end, she put it down on the straw of her nest. I now left the cage, went directly to the grill and called "Come get your apple, Congo!" She came promptly but empty-handed, leaving the sticks where they had been dropped. She looked at the food, scratched the floor of the platform for a few seconds, picked up a bit of sweet potato skin with abstracted air, then quickly turned, went directly to the porch, got the old stick and with it returned to the grill where she shortly succeeded in obtaining her reward. The time of the performance was approximately two minutes. In this case "out of sight" was not "out of mind," for neither stick could be seen from the grill and she surely would not have returned in such a purposeful manner to the porch floor if she had not remembered the presence of the stick.

Although the preceding observation definitely enough indicates adaptation on the basis of a representative process, it seemed distinctly worth while to get additional evidence and if possible to discover whether Congo would recall the presence of the stick on the roof of the nest-room. Therefore on February 3, at 9:30 a. m., I entered the cage with a piece of shingle in one hand and both the new and the old stick in the other hand. Instead of retreating to the nest-room or its roof, as she often did on my approach, Congo waited for me at the door of her room, and as soon as I had cleaned the cage she partly led, partly pushed me toward the exit door, desiring apparently to get me out, presumably in order to have experiments begin. This behavior was new and in view of all the circumstances I feel reasonably certain of the meaning which I have attributed to it.

My next move was to attract Congo to the roof of her nest-room and hand her the new stick. She seized it and, scrambling down, carried it to the grill, but as there was no food in sight she willingly let me retrieve it and I again placed it on the roof of the nest-room. In that position I attracted her attention to it and made sure that she knew it was there; but before leaving the cage I induced her to come down from the roof so that I might be sure she did not bring the stick with her.

On leaving the cage I took with me all sticks except the one on the roof. Passing to the platform side of the cage I placed a piece of apple in position and called Congo to work. She came eagerly and at the grill picked up a piece of straw which she fumbled with for a moment. She then gathered in one hand a piece of chain which was fastened to her collar and pushed it through the bars toward the apple. In this she persisted for some two minutes, but she could not quite succeed in reaching the apple. Had she thrown the chain her efforts might have succeeded. After a time she gave up and occasionally whined as though begging for food or help in getting it. Later she returned to the grill and again tried to use the chain. For a few seconds she worked at her collar as though trying to loosen the chain. This act, if correctly interpreted, is significant indeed.

In the fifteen minutes during which observation was continued, Congo gave no indications whatever of remembering the stick on the roof. Before terminating the test I decided to place a stick where she could see it in order to make certain that if seen it would be recognized as a possible tool and applied. To this end, while Congo was occupied at the opposite end of the cage and looking in the other direction, I quietly placed a stick on the floor of the cage near the entrance door. After some minutes she happened to pass near the stick. No sooner did she see it than she stopped, picked it up and carried it to the grill for use. Apparently her recognition was slow, for she walked about the cage several times before she gave evidence of appreciating the presence of a possible tool. Whether she must closely approach the stick or touch it in order to recognize it I do not know, but at any rate she did not react appropriately until she chanced to pass close by the object.

Out of sight assuredly was out of mind in this particular trial. Is it that Congo's memory is short, or was she not sufficiently attentive to the stick on the roof?

My final observation in this connection was made on February 4 when at approximately 9:20 a. m. I entered the cage carrying a shingle to clean up with and the old and new sticks. Congo came and taking the sticks from me carried them to the nest-room. In a moment she emerged with the old stick and, carrying it to the grill, attempted to use it. As no food was available this proved futile. But it made me wonder whether this was a way of asking for food. As soon as she laid the old stick down I gathered it in and removed it from the cage. The new stick alone remained in the nest-room where Congo had placed it. I now put a piece of apple on the platform and called Congo to work. Coming, she looked about, with her finger nails scratched the floor of the platform, turned, went directly to the nest-room, and with the stick promptly returned to the grill where she quickly succeeded in getting the food. The time required was about one minute, and the performance seemingly involved representational processes.

This concludes the description of observations in connection with problems numbered 1, 4 and 24, shelf and stick, platform and stick, and hidden stick. Further discussion, interpretations, and inferences based on the data supplied by these simple experiments will be reserved for later sections of the report.

Problem 9. Pipe, wire, and stick. In the midst of the series of trials with the shelf and stick and platform and stick problems, Congo was presented with a situation described as the pipe, wire, and stick problem. It is virtually the equivalent of what in previous experiments with the orang-utan and chimpanzee I have described as the box and pole test (32, p. 99; 34, p. 48). To save labor in construction I used with Congo an iron pipe, instead of a rectangular wooden box with hinged lid. The pipe was 48 inches long, 2 inches inside diameter at the one end, and 3 inches at the other end. On January 11 I placed this pipe on the ground outside of Congo's cage, and three feet from it a no. 9 gauge wire, 54 inches long, and bent at right angles at two-inch intervals, and alternately in opposite directions, to form a zigzag. With Congo moored to a stake nearby and watching I slipped into the pipe a piece of banana, pushing it so far from the end that it could not be reached by her fingers. She was then allowed to try to obtain the food. At once she began to pull at the pipe and to roll it about on the ground. Then she peered in through the larger end. As she did so, she raised the pipe to the level of her eyes. After taking a good look she went to the smaller end and, as the banana had moved in that direction, she was able to reach it with her hand. No attention was given to the wire, nor indeed was its use necessary.

Following this preliminary trial, the pipe was firmly fixed to a heavy timber which in turn was securely staked to the ground under an oak tree some forty feet from Congo's cage. At one side of the pipe near the larger end and two feet from it the 54-inch wire lay on the ground. On the opposite side, and the same distance from the pipe, lay a 48-inch broomstick. At 11:46 on the morning of January 12 Congo was brought from her cage to this apparatus and chained to a stake which had been driven into the ground about four feet from the pipe. She was given freedom of movement in a radius of six feet about the stake and could readily reach the stick, wire, and either end of the pipe. My next move was to slip a piece of banana so far into the larger end of the pipe that she could not reach it. Naturally her initial effort was to force her hand into the pipe and thus reach the food. This failing, she looked in first at the one end, then at the other. I observed her behavior at a distance of about ten feet. There was no evidence that she was disturbed by my presence. During her first trial of twelve minutes duration she tried repeatedly to reach the food, and tugged vainly at the pipe to tear it from its moorings. Not once did she attend to either stick or wire.

Practically the same description applies to her behavior in the succeeding five daily trials, the average time for which was about sixteeen minutes, the minimum time being fourteen and the maximum twenty-five.

After the second trial, which was given on January 13, I decided to give her opportunity to imitate me in the use of the stick. During that particular trial she had picked up the stick and carried it toward the larger end of the pipe, there dropping it without attempt to thrust it into the pipe.

Beginning on January 14 I let her watch me put the banana into the pipe and with the stick push it through and out the opposite end. She was always very attentive and soon learned to run to the opposite end of the pipe and await the arrival of the food. After each demonstration I re-set the apparatus and gave her opportunity to imitate or to obtain the food on her own initiative. Usually in the course of fifteen minutes I demonstrated the use of the stick four times, using a quarter banana as reward each time. This performance was repeated in similar fashion on four successive days, January 14 to 17, with negative result in that Congo did not imitate me and gave no convincing evidence of increasing interest in the stick or of ability to use it. Occasionally I left the stick in the pipe with one end projecting. Seeing it thus she would promptly pull it out instead of pushing it through.

In my notes for January 15 I wrote: I discover no influence of copy-setting or other tuitional efforts. It is almost as though she had decided not to do what I do. Although she is eager for the food, her interest in the problem appears to be slight, and her failure is sharply contrasted with the relatively prompt and ready success of both orang-utan and chimpanzee of corresponding age.

On the last day, January 17, of this imitative copy-setting, I thrice demonstrated the customary method of obtaining the food, and when it came to the use of the last piece of banana I placed it in the larger end of the pipe beyond Congo's reach and entered the stick behind it, so that all that was necessary was to push it through. Thereupon I retired from her sight so that she might work without inhibition. Her activities were as usual: looking in and attempting to reach the banana. The stick she merely withdrew and cast to one side.

Following the making of a motion picture record of Congo's behavior in the pipe, wire, and stick experiment on January 19, work with it was discontinued since progress was extremely slight and it appeared desirable to reserve the problem as a test of transfer of ability from one situation to another.

Surprising, indeed, was Congo's utter lack of imitativeness and of versatility in method of attack on this problem.

The one and only transfer test with this problem was made on February 3 when at 10:27 a. m. I placed a piece of banana as usual in the larger end of the pipe, and the stick and wire within reach. Since, in the meantime, Congo had learned to use a stick as tool in the platform-stick situation, it seemed not improbable her newly acquired interest in the stick and her discovery of its usefulness might lead her to apply it in the pipe-stick problem.

At the outset she looked through both ends of the pipe and wandered around it. She then took up the stick and for a few seconds carried it about with her, holding it first with a hand, then with a foot. During the next five minutes she frequently touched and handled the stick, and occasionally beat her chest as though with impatience.

In the middle of the test, and after she had been working for about eight minutes, I allowed her to see me place a second piece of banana in the pipe. She watched me, looked in at the ends, reached as usual, but made no motion toward the use of either stick or wire. At 10:40 a. m. the experiment was discontinued because of lack of initiative on Congo's part and her entirely evident loss of interest in the situation and lack of expectation of success.

Had my time sufficed I should have repeated this transfer test on three or four successive days, in order to give her abundant opportunity to utilize her recently acquired experience or to demonstrate her inability to do so.

Problem 8. Suspended food and stick. In the list of experiments on page 39 is one described as suspended food and stick. Initial steps in the setting of this problem were taken on January 10 when from the limb of a large oak tree midway between the cage and the garage I suspended an apple on a light cord, at a distance of six feet from the ground. As the apple was eighteen feet from the main trunk of the tree, and the limb at the point of string attachment was only three inches in diameter, and, indeed, only about five inches in diameter where it emerged from the trunk, I felt reasonably certain that Congo could not obtain the apple by climbing along the limb. Instead, I supposed that she at first might reach or jump for it from the ground, and, failing to obtain it, look about for something to strike or reach with or perhaps to climb upon. But in this, prophetic insight failed me. The moment she caught sight of the apple, after she had been led from her cage and chained to a stake under the oak tree, she quickly climbed the tree and walked out on the branch until she was able to reach the cord and secure the food. This preliminary observation proved the necessity of chaining her to a stake at such distance from the trunk of the tree that she could not climb it.

The problem was therefore set as follows. A cord fastened to the aforesaid limb of the oak tree suspended food, used as lure, at sixty-six inches from the ground. The point directly under the suspended food will hereafter be referred to as the center. A stake to which Congo could be moored was driven into the ground five feet west of the center. Five feet north of the center a 48-inch broomstick lay on the ground, and five feet south of the center was a rectangular stick approximately 1 by 1 by 60 inches. Congo was given a range of six feet.

On January 11, with the experimental situation as above described, Congo was brought from her cage and chained to the stake. Immediately she looked toward the tree and started for it, evidently with the intention of climbing, but coming to the end of the chain she was halted abruptly. After looking at the apple for a few seconds she attempted to lay hold of her playmate, the Airedale dog Betty, who happened to be near, and to use her as a stepping block. The dog quickly escaped. Then Congo placed herself beneath the apple and reached for it. Failing in this attempt she went to the stake, pulled at it vigorously, and worked with the chain and the snap which fastened it to the stake. From time to time thereafter she played with Betty, ran about, patted her chest or the ground vigorously with both hands, and occasionally reached for the apple. Quite evidently her failure to obtain the food irritated her. Presently she picked up a bit of stick and began to chew it.

Mrs. Burbridge now approached and I asked her to stand so that Congo might, if she wished, lead her to a position in which she might be used as means of approach to the apple. But this the gorilla, despite opportunity, did not do. Her previous attempt to use Betty as a stepping block was due, doubtless, to the fact that the dog happened to be nearly under the · apple and that therefore a familiar visual configuration was presented.

When, after a few minutes, Mrs. Burbridge retired from the scene of the experiment, the dogs Bobby and Betty were locked n the house, since they tended to distract Congo and possibly to lessen her chances of solving the problem.

It was twenty-three minutes after the beginning of the trial before Congo gave attention to either of the sticks. She then picked up the broomstick, put it down, beat her chest vigorously, again took up the stick and looked toward the apple. It seemed as though she were about to use the stick to aid her, but she promptly abandoned it and began to dig in the sand.

Her behavior made me wonder whether the incentive was sufficiently strong to elicit her best effort. Clearly the nature and quantity of food offered as reward bears an important relation to Congo's interest and effort, and presumably also to the measure of success achieved.

In her attempts to secure the apple by reaching from the ground Congo during this interval of trial stood beneath it and reached directly up. Her maximum reach with one hand certainly did not exceed fifty-eight inches. Each time she stood firmly with both feet on the ground. Not once did she attempt to jump or even to increase her reach by standing on one foot and stretching to the utmost with the arm of the opposite side.

On January 12, and again on January 13, Congo was given opportunity to work for suspended food. A half banana was added to the whole apple on the 12th to increase the value of the lure and they were suspended at a distance of sixty instead of sixty-six inches from the ground. Thus by increasing the quantity of food and diminishing the distance I thought to stimulate Congo's interest, effort, and persistence. The sticks previously present were used, and on the chance that a larger, heavier one might prove more readily serviceable, a stout piece of board 1 by 2 by 66 inches was placed within reach. Each stick was at least five feet off center. As Congo watched me place the food in position she gave evidence of eagerness for it, and when brought from her cage and fastened to the stake she worked diligently, but deprived of opportunity to climb, she relied on reaching, which proved futile. My notes describe in detail her efforts to free herself from the stake and to approach the tree. In thirty minutes of almost continuous activity no new method appeared. At one time she played with the broomstick for a few seconds and again with the new, large stick. Later she threw the broomstick out of her way and drawing the large stick to the stake amused herself with it. The trial terminated without yielding evidence of approach to the use of a stick as tool.

On January 13 when the situation was re-presented, despite the fact that a whole banana as well as an apple were offered as reward, Congo was obviously less eager to work for them and decidedly less sanguine of success. As formerly, she reached from beneath the food, tugged at her chain, and cir-cuited about as though endeavoring to achieve freedom or sufficiently increase her range of movement to reach the tree trunk. She merely fingered the sticks. As the time of the trial passed, her attention to the food diminished and before discontinuance of observation she had given up effort and there was complete lack of interest. She seemed to have de-cided that attempt to secure the food was wholly futile. In view of this behavior I decided to discontinue the suspended food and stick problem temporarily in favor of a suspended food and box problem.

It was not until one week later, January 20, that opportunity to use a stick in a suspended food situation was again offered. On that date, and in a situation essentially like that of experiment no. 8, a 60-inch stick was placed within reach in an experimental setting in which boxes were the primary objects offered as aids. The stick was added with the thought that its presence might possibly lead to the use of stick or box, or perhaps their combination, as aid in obtaining the suspended food. This experiment is no. 10 in the list, suspended food and boxes. As usual the food was suspended from the limb of an oak tree, the boxes and stick placed at least five feet off center, and Congo chained to a stake with sufficient range readily to reach and handle any of the objects which constituted essential parts of the experimental situation.

On January 20, 21 and 22 Congo was given a half-hour for work at this problem. At no time did she attempt to use the stick as tool. Once or twice she touched it or pushed it out of her way as though considering it an obstruction.

Following January 22 the use of the stick was again discontinued, and it was not until February 2 that Congo was given opportunity to display, in the suspended food type of experiment, whatever she may in the meantime have learned from other experiments about the usefulness of sticks. In this case the stick was made auxiliary to the box-stacking experiment, no. 23 in the series. As formerly, the food was suspended from the limb of the tree, this time, however, at a height of seventy-eight inches from the ground, two boxes were placed, one on either side of the center and at a distance of five feet, and near the stake to which Congo was chained a stick five feet long. The trial began at 9:56 a. m., and up to 10:15 Congo had worked with the boxes as tools in a manner later to be described, without giving attention to the stick which was within easy reach. Then suddenly she went to the stick, picked it up, carried it directly and with obvious purpose to box 1, climbed upon the box, and holding the stick with one end on the ground, tried to raise it toward the suspended food.

For a first attempt she managed fairly well, although she was extremely awkward. The upper figure of plate 7 (p. 110) is a photographic record of this first attempt to use the stick as aid in securing suspended food.

In the midst of her attempt to raise the stick toward the food Congo paused and holding the stick in position remained quiet for a few seconds. It was as though she were reflecting on, or puzzling over, her problem, for there was no evidence of distraction or attention to irrelevant things. Her next move was to abandon the stick and return to the use of the boxes, which for a short time she continued to manipulate. Failing, however, to get them placed successfully she took up the stick and with it in her hand mounted one of the boxes which happened to be directly under the food. It seemed as though she were just about to strike at the food with the stick when suddenly something happened within and she put down the stick and began efforts to place the one box upon the other. In this she presently succeeded, and obtained her reward.

Although in this experiment we have excellent evidence of Congo's desire to use the stick as aid in obtaining suspended food, little credit for invention, or even initiative, can be given her since in all probability interest in the stick and ability to use it transferred directly from the platform and stick experiment. Nevertheless, the behavior has significance as evidence of representational experience and as indication of a mode of adaptation which appears to differ radically from that of "trial and error."

A definite test of transfer was made on February 3 in an experimental setting practically identical with that of problem 8, suspended food and stick. The food, consisting of a banana, sweet potato, and half apple, was suspended sixty inches from the ground. Congo was chained to a stake at one side of the center, and five feet off center, lying on the ground, was a light stick sixty inches long. Observation began at 10:08 a. m.. Within two minutes Congo had noticed the stick, taken it up, carried it directly toward the food, and there tried to raise it as if to strike with. Her action was somewhat difficult to interpret and suggested as much a sweeping movement as an attempt to hit directly. In this we find additional evidence of transfer, for the sweeping movement was appropriate to the platform and stick situation. She seemed to be groping her way toward effective use of the stick in a new situation. Of a sudden her method changed and she began to lean her weight on the stick and with it to push herself toward the food. A moment later, with the stick very nearly vertical under the reward, she climbed on it to a sufficient height to reach the food and to obtain it. For this particular kind of use the stick was too slender and the task correspondingly more difficult than it would have been with a stick two inches instead of one inch in diameter. Nevertheless Congo's work was promptly successful.

This experiment was repeated on February 4, on which date she immediately gathered in the stick, carried it under the food, looked up, and with one end of the stick nearer, raised it toward the desired reward. In a moment she had it vertical and began awkwardly to climb, grasping the stick as though she would pull herself up by it. Thus in less than ninety seconds from the beginning of observation she succeeded in getting her reward.

We have therefore convincing evidence that Congo's training and success in the platform and stick situation spread to the suspended-food type of problem and enabled her to use the stick as tool.

Evidently it is only a matter of time and practice until she will use the stick readily as tool in varied situations.

B. Preferential use of hands and feet

Problem 19. Arm and leg reach. Related to the stick problems, and therefore appropriate for report at this point, are certain observations on Congo's preferential use of the right hand and arm and the left foot and leg. Right-handedness was early manifested in the various forms of stick problem, and by a systematic test in which the gorilla was made to reach for food I discovered that she used the right hand and arm approximately two-thirds of the time. Her vigor and persistence in reaching for things suggested to me the possibility of using the response for an experimental problem. It is listed as no. 19, page 39, under the title of arm and leg reach. In setting the problem I had three questions in mind: (1) Will Congo reach with her leg and foot if a desired object is beyond the reach of arm and hand? (2) Will she exhibit leg and foot preference as in case of arm and hand? and (3) Will she reach further and as skillfully with foot as compared with hand?

The problem was first presented on January 26, when at 9:45 a. m., with Congo chained to a stake in the open, by offering bits of food I quickly determined her maximum arm reach. Thereupon I placed a baked sweet potato six inches beyond her maximum reach. She seemed to realize at a glance that the food was out of reach and turned to busy herself with other things. At once I moved the food two inches nearer. After playing about the stake for some seconds she came toward the potato and throwing herself on her right side reached for the food with her left leg and foot. She made one quick thrust which failed to reach the food and then desisted. Promptly I moved the potato closer, until it was barely three inches beyond her maximum arm reach. In this position, after a few attempts, she secured it with her left foot.

The test was immediately repeated and she secured her reward promptly by reaching backward with her left leg and grasping the potato with the foot. Measurement now indicated that she could reach from six to eight inches farther with her left leg than with her right arm. The collar to which chain was attached of course restricted her freedom of motion, and in accordance with its position and the exact status of the chain, the maximum reach varied somewhat from trial to trial.

This problem was presented again on January 28 when with bits of apple as prospective reward Congo repeated her previous performance in all essentials. Always she threw herself on her right side and reaching with the left leg grasped the food with the left foot and carried it to within reach of her hand. In order further to test her preference I presented the reward in several different positions with relation to the stake to which she was moored, but in every case Congo's response was the same.

The experiment supplies definite answers to the three questions initially proposed, for Congo promptly adapted to the situation by using her leg and foot where arm and hand were useless, she exhibited preference for the left leg and foot, and she demonstrated ability to reach six to eight inches farther with them than with arm and hand.

At the conclusion of the arm and leg reach observations of January 28, I gave her opportunity in the same setting to use objects as aids. The food was placed twenty-four inches beyond her reach and within easy reach I put a plain stick, a garden hoe, and a rake. Her first act on noticing these objects was to pull them toward her and lay them down. Later she touched them and examined visually and olfactorily especially the iron portions of the hoe and rake. In the fifteen minutes during which I continued to watch her she made no attempt to use any one of the objects to aid her in obtaining the food. It should be recalled that this test was made after the animal had learned to use a stick in obtaining food on the platform outside the grill, but before she had come to dissociate the stick from that particular situation and look for it in the cage as a possible tool. Probably if I had had time to present the situation described above one week later the result would have been positive instead of negative.

On February 1 a motion picture record was made of Congo reaching first with her right arm and then, for a more distant object, with her left leg.

Finally on February 3 I again confirmed the above observations of preferential use of right arm and left leg. This time I set the problem in six different locations and despite the variation of conditions Congo consistently reached with her right arm and hand, if the object was near, and with her left leg and foot, if the object was beyond arm reach. These confirmatory observations are mentioned because of the unexpectedness of the marked preference and its possible significance in connection with further investigation of handedness, footedness, and eyedness in relation to neurological conditions.

C. MANIPULATION OF ROPES AND FOOD CONTAINERS

Logically the following problems belong together and should be described in connection with the stick problems because they supplement them in ways which are important although not at first obvious. Perhaps the most significant relationship is that of counteracting the discouraging effects of failure in the stick problems. In fact the first rope problem to be presented was arranged especially to give Congo opportunity to obtain a reward, and thus in a measure at least to compensate for her failures in the shelf and stick situation.

The more I experiment with animals which are highly organized neurologically, the more certain I am that experimental failures and misleading results are usually due to the investigator's lack of insight, foresight, common sense, or ingenuity. I suspect that Congo might have been ruined, temporarily at least, by persistence on my part in presenting problems in which she could not succeed. The whole matter was one of effective motivation, and by properly relating problems in order of presentation, and controlling the conditions of work on a given problem, it was possible to maintain the gorilla's interest, expectation of success, and willingness to work.

In this section two inextricably associated groups of problems will be described. The first includes three forms of rope problem and the second three forms of food-container problem. Certain violence will have to be done to the temporal relations of my observations in order to adhere to this logical grouping. It is essential in order to minimize words.

On the third day of experimentation, January 7, immediately following Congo's unsuccessful efforts to solve the shelf and stick problem, the following situation was arranged. To Köhler (20) and Bingham (unpublished notes) I acknowledge the suggestions which determined the form of the test.

Problem 2. Diagonal rope. Outside the grill, on the east side of the cage, and approximately thirty inches above the ground so that it was on a level with the upper edge of the grill space, I placed a half-inch manila rope, one end of which was tied securely to one of the supporting posts on the east side of the cage, and the other to a post at the southeast corner of the study. The rope was drawn taut and so adjusted that it passed diagonally in front of the cage at a distance twenty-four inches from the grill at its north end and thirty-six inches from it at the south end. I knew from previous observations that Congo could just reach the rope at twenty-four inches distant.

My next step was to tie an apple securely to the rope at a point precisely thirty-six inches from the grill. With everything in readiness I stepped aside and permitted Congo to see and attempt to obtain the food. Her first impulse was to reach directly, but this she inhibited before its completion and she went to the nearer end of the rope and reaching hard succeeded in grasping it first with the one hand, then with the other. Pulling hard on the rope she stretched it so that had she followed up her advantage she might readily have obtained the apple. Instead, as the rope gave only slightly and the apple did not come appreciably nearer, she quit and climbing to the bench above the grill sat there watching me and occasionally beating her chest.

After a few minutes I attracted her attention by saying, "Congo, come get your apple!" She looked at me and as if in reply beat her chest. Then she came to the ground, looked toward the apple, reached for the rope at the nearer end, pulled hard at it, let go and went to the cage post to which the rope was fastened. Here she pulled at and chewed the rope; then she went to the feeding door which opened on the shelf and

stick situation. This door was closed but she looked through
the crack at food which had been left on the shelf. Turning
away, she came back briskly to the grill and in a manner which
clearly enough betokened determination and expectation of success, began to work systematically for the apple. She grasped
the rope at the nearer end with her left hand and pulling it
toward her grasped it also with her right hand. Then hand
over hand she moved along the grill toward the more distant
end of the rope and her reward. It was a somewhat difficult
performance because of the obstructing grill, but she managed
it well and in a few seconds had reached the southeast corner
of the grill and was awkwardly trying to bring her right hand
and arm into play. The corner post of the cage made this difficult. After three vain attempts she succeeded in thrusting
out her arm, grasped the apple and drew it to her by pulling
on the rope with her left hand. The apple was carried to the
nest-room while I recorded her success in the solution of this
problem.

While the gorilla was in the nest-room I re-set the problem, placing a sweet potato on the rope as bait. When after
a minute she returned to the grill and saw the new reward
she immediately set to work to obtain it, but in her vigorous
hauling at the rope she broke the potato loose and it fell to the
ground beyond her reach. I picked it up and stored it for
future use. This sorely disappointed her and she growled
deep-throatedly. There was no other visible sign of emotion.

I now tied a whole orange to the rope. Congo looked at it,
but made no move to obtain it. Instead she took her place on
the shelf above the grill, beat her chest and growled occasionally, looked toward the house, and watched me as I wrote my
notes a few feet from the grill.

Some ten minutes later, in order to test my suspicion that
Congo was inhibited by my presence and because of my removal of the sweet potato, I stepped around the corner of the
study out of sight and there watched developments. Scarcely
had I left before she climbed down from the shelf and went

to work. Peeping around the corner of the study I saw her grasp the rope with her left hand, reach out and seize it with the right, and then move along hand over hand as previously until she reached the orange. This time there was no delay and no fumbling at the corner of the cage. She worked rapidly and with impressive calm, steadiness, and efficiency.

A few minutes later the test was again repeated with an orange as reward. Congo secured it in a perfectly ordered series of acts. There were no useless movements and I could not discover the possibility of improvement over her performance.

Following these observations I recorded in my notes: The diagonal rope test can be scored and underscored plus. It is now appropriate to devise a more difficult form of rope problem.

Problem 3. Hooked rope. The new situation was set immediately and Congo was given opportunity to work at it that same morning.

The hooked-rope experiment was arranged as follows in front of the grill. At the extreme corner of the south end of the base bar of the grill a hook with one-inch opening was placed, and at the extreme end of the north corner a screw eye one inch in diameter. Each was heavy enough to stand a pull of at least two hundred pounds. Directly in front of the middle of the grill, outside the cage, and seventy-two inches from it, a heavy wooden stake was securely driven into the ground. To this stake, three inches above the ground level, was attached an iron ring three inches in diameter. With the permanent fixtures thus arranged, I prepared for use a piece of one-half inch manila rope. To one end of this rope a three-inch iron ring was fastened. This ring was then slipped over the hook at the south corner of the grill and the other end of the rope was carried through the ring attached to the stake and thence through the screw eye at the north end of the grill, extending freely into the cage to a length of about one foot. The rope was now drawn taut and a brick was tied into it on the screw eye side of the stake, and between this stop and the screw eye a tin can to serve as food-carrier was securely wired to the rope. This can was four inches in diameter by six inches in length, with an aperture of approximately four inches. The apparatus as set was designed to give Congo opportunity to secure the reward of food by removing the ring from the hook at south end of grill and pulling on the free end or free arm of the rope at the north end of the grill. If she hauled on that arm of the rope without unhooking the ring of the other arm it availed her nothing, or if she hauled on the other arm the stop prevented her from wrecking the apparatus. Thus the problem was to discover the relationship of the ring-on-hook to the possibility of drawing the food-container within reach.

The accompanying drawing, fig. 1, p. 77, will serve to supplement this verbal description and to make clearer the relation of the several features of the situation.

At 10:20 a. m., on January 8, with Congo sitting before the grill, I placed a sweet potato in the food-carrier and offered her opportunity to discover how to get it. Sight of the reward stimulated her to vigorous effort. Naturally enough she began by pulling on the carrier arm of the rope. The ring arm she entirely ignored. On the former she hauled and tugged persistently, pressing her feet against the base of the grill and making the rope sing as she stretched it. To my surprise and satisfaction the apparatus held and the food-carrier did not come within reach. After this spell of determined effort Congo retreated to the shelf above the grill where, except for an occasional trial of the rope as above described, she spent her time for several minutes.

One feature of her initial attack on this problem is peculiarly interesting in relation to the previously described diagonal rope problem. When Congo first seized the carrier arm of the rope she began to haul it in hand over hand, reaching between successive bars precisely as she had done to good

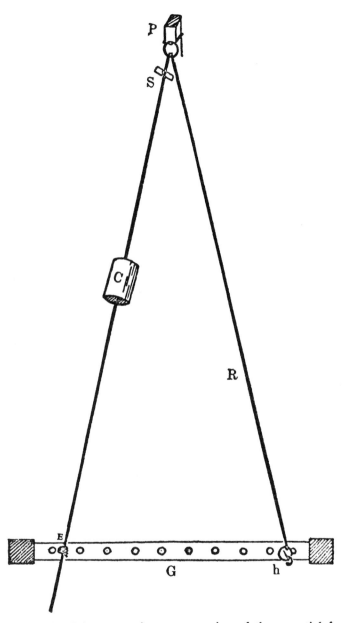

Figure 1. Diagrammatic representation of the essential features and setting of the hooked-rope mechanism. P, stake to which ring for rope was tied; S, stop tied in rope to prevent it passing through ring in direction of hook; C, tin can used as food carrier; E, screw eye through which free end of rope passed into cage; G, base of grill, with circles representing iron rods; R, hook arm of half-inch rope; h, hook in base-bar of grill which held ring end of rope.

purpose in the diagonal rope situation. This procedure proved useless and she promptly abandoned it.

At 10:30 a. m. I stepped forward to readjust the carrier so that the potato should not fall out. This attracted her attention and, coming to the grill, she pulled once on the carrier arm, paused, went to the opposite end of the grill and pulled on the ring arm; another pause, and she returned to the carrier arm and chewed at the end of the rope. This alternation continued, but shortly she approached the hooked end of the rope. Pulling on the ring and the knot which fastened it to the rope she loosened the former from its hook and let it fall to the edge of the grill. Evidently she failed to notice the change in the relationship of the ring to the hook, for she went to the house bench without giving the rope further attention. The unhooking of the ring clearly was accidental and profited her not at all. When several minutes later she returned to the grill and pulled on the carrier arm she naturally secured the food.

For various reasons, but chiefly in order to test my conviction that the removal of the ring from its hook had been wholly accidental, I immediately re-set the problem and gave her opportunity for new solution. The trial began at 10:55 a. m. Congo came eagerly and pulled on the carrier arm with such vigor that the apple which I had placed in the can bounced out. Before I could retrieve it she had seized it and was on her way to the nest-room to eat it. Presumably this retreat to the nest-room with her treasure was an expression of her anxiety lest I try to take the food from her.

There remained in the carrier a second piece of apple. When after a short interval she returned to her task she first paused and looked at the bit of apple as though appraisingly. It was a small piece! Attracted apparently by some sound from the house she left the grill for the house bench. Returning, she pulled on the ring arm of the rope without unhooking it. It was 11:01 when, abandoning her efforts, she mounted to the bench above the grill and there rested.

To increase the incentive, I now placed a whole sweet potato in the carrier together with the segment of apple. Down she came immediately and pulled hard first on the carrier arm, then on the ring arm. This continued at intervals for several minutes. Then she retreated to the grill shelf and watched me quietly without apparent resentment and as if waiting for food. The voice of Mrs. Burbridge was heard in the nearby study and Congo patted her chest vigorously. Was it to attract attention, to beg for food, or as an expression of impatience or discouragement?

Presently she returned to the grill and as usual pulled now on the one arm of the rope, now on the other. There was no attention, however, to the ring or hook and not the slightest indication that Congo appreciated their relationship to the possibility of hauling in the food container.

After a very active period she once more retreated to the grill shelf and there whined tremulously. It seemed like an expression of discouragement and begging to be fed.

At 11:55 a. m. the observation terminated with convincingly negative results. It was entirely clear that the initial success was accidental and that Congo had no insight into the essential relations of the objects which I had arranged to give her opportunity for adaptive behavior.

The hooked-rope problem was not presented the following day, January 9, but work was resumed on January 10, and thereafter a single trial per day was given regularly until January 17. The total number of trials between the beginning of work, January 8, and the completion of the experiment on January 17 was ten. In the first trial on January 8, twenty minutes was required for success; in the second trial, sixty minutes resulted in failure; thereafter the time required for success decreased from seventeen minutes on January 10 to one and one-half minutes, January 14, and one-half minute on January 17.

On the morning of January 10 an important change was made in the apparatus in that the hook which engaged the iron ring at end of rope was straightened and two nails driven in beside it at angle of 50°. In its previous position it was difficult for Congo to remove the ring from the hook, but as altered the ring could readily be lifted off when the appropriate arm of the rope was loosened. This change I assumed would facilitate work while in no degree lessening the chance for display of insight.

At 9:21 a. m. on January 10 Congo began her efforts to secure the banana and piece of apple which had been placed in the food-carrier. By strong sudden pull on the carrier arm of the rope she succeeded, contrary to my expectation and intention, in bringing the food within reach and in obtaining it. From later events I infer that the accident was not unfortunate. While Congo was eating the fruit I re-set the apparatus, moving the carrier back on the arm to a position thirty-six inches from the grill. Congo shortly returned to the task and worked vigorously but intermittently for fourteen minutes, when she obtained her reward in the following manner. She had pulled on the ring arm of the rope and without definitely directed effort had removed the ring from its hook. She then let the ring fall to the platform outside the grill and almost immediately went to the carrier arm of the rope and hauling on it pulled the reward within reach. Although the directness and sequence of events might suggest insight I doubt its existence and am inclined to attribute this success as well as the previous one to random manipulation of the rope and fortunate accident in the freeing of the ring.

The following day success was achieved more quickly but with no clear indication that Congo had associated removal of the ring with the possibility of drawing in the food-carrier. In the next trial there appeared a strong tendency to shift rapidly from one arm of the rope to the other, this doubtless being an effect of her discovery that success ordinarily followed manipulation first of the ring arm of the rope and then of the carrier arm. Teeth as well as hands were used in this trial in removing the ring from its hook.

The performance on January 13 is worthy of somewhat more detailed description to indicate stages in the progress of adaptation. Congo attacked her problem with enthusiasm. She pulled first on the carrier arm twice, then on the ring arm, then back to the carrier arm which she again pulled twice; now to the ring arm, and by attention to and manipulation of the ring she freed it from the hook. This, according to my notes, is the first time she has manipulated the ring with indication of definite purpose and intent to free it from the hook. Having succeeded in unhooking the ring, instead of going directly to the carrier arm of the rope and pulling in her food she pulled once on the ring arm. Her next act was to take up the carrier arm and secure the reward. The total time required in this trial was seventy-five seconds.

The problem thus far had elicited gradual as contrasted with sudden adaptation. There was an elimination of useless movements or errors on the basis rather of repeated trial than of understanding of the essential features of the situation. No evidence of insight or understanding had appeared. Although Congo had definitely solved the problem it seemed desirable to give her a few more trials in order to trace the further improvement of technique and the manner in which errors were eliminated.

In the very next trial, after a few vain pulls on the rope, Congo gave attention to the ring and deliberately and definitely freed it from the hook. This marked the most radical improvement in technique yet noted.

But even in the final and tenth trial, given on January 17, the gorilla instead of going directly to the ring and freeing it, began her work by touching the carrier arm of the rope tentatively but without pulling, then similarly the ring arm, the carrier arm again, the ring arm, the carrier arm, and, finally, returning to the ring arm she directly freed the ring, went at once to the carrier arm and pulled in the food-container. All this was done very quickly, requiring not more than half a minute, and it exhibited in a most instructive way the gradual inhibition of profitless tendencies in favor of essential adaptive acts. Never once did she actually execute the pulling movement until she had freed the ring, but several times she went through all of the preparations for it. One may not fairly score these inhibited acts as errors, yet they count against the subject in the time-record and indicate that the acquisition of the correct mode of response was incomplete.

The hooked-rope problem was committed to motion picture record on January 19, when Congo after a number of false moves solved the problem by fairly expert removal of the ring. Her technique continued far from perfect, and the gradualness with which useless features of her original performance were eliminated was surprising.

On January 19 the hooked-rope situation was utilized to secure measurements of strength. A spring balance measuring to perhaps three hundred pounds was tied into the carrier arm of the rope midway between it and the stake P (see figure 1, page 77, for relations). When food was placed in the carrier, Congo pulled on the free arm of the rope, directly against the spring of balance. Several readings were obtained: (a) when with feet braced against the base of grill she pulled with both arms, and (b) when she pulled with both arms without bracing herself. This simple method of measuring strength of arm proved quite unexpectedly satisfactory. It was economical also, as it involved slight labor for preparation of apparatus and no special training of the subject since the hooked-rope habit was available.

The above direct measurements of strength are supplemented by observation of Congo's ability readily to drag about with her a one hundred and five pound iron weight which earlier in her life at Shady Nook had been a secure anchor. Often she dragged this obstacle by her collar, sometimes walking directly forward and sometimes backing; again, she seized the chain between her collar and the weight with her hands and thus moved the impediment.

Congo's enthusiastic interest in the manipulation of ropes

encouraged me to develop and use the following simple problems. What I call the pull-rope situation always involved the placement at some accessible point within or without the cage of the free end of a rope to the opposite end of which was attached a tin can carrying food. The various forms and settings of this type of problem will not be described in detail. Instead I shall attempt to present the essential structural features of the situations and those features of response which seem to have peculiar interest or value for our understanding of modes of adaptation.

Problem 5. Pull rope. The initial form of the pull-rope problem was presented to Congo on January 8 when at the south end of the cage I placed the food-carrier some ten feet from the grill and then carried the rope over the top of the cage and dropped the free end through the wire of the top so that it reached the floor of the cage about two feet from the southwest corner. Congo from within the cage watched the placing of the rope. I next went to the food-carrier and put into it the reward. Congo, seeing this, came to the east side of the cage and attempted to pull the rope through the two-inch mesh wire. As the rope was one-half inch diameter and quite stiff this was impossible. It was about fifteen minutes later that she happened to go toward the door of the cage and seeing the end of the rope dangling there pulled on it. This drew the carrier toward the grill. Instantly she saw that the food was within reach and going to the grill obtained it.

Following description of this experiment I recorded in my notes: Thus far the tests have indicated heaviness or a certain mental inaptitude, together with the absence of insight, but Congo is rapidly acquiring interest in the experimental situations and is gradually warming to her tasks. It is too early to risk conclusions, but at least the differences of her behavior from those of the orang-utan and chimpanzee are clear and significant.

Repetition of this form of test on January 9, 10, and 11, with the rope shifted to different positions, but always giving

Congo opportunity to draw the food-container within reach, yielded results essentially similar to those described.

The performance on January 12 demands description. In this instance Congo was removed from her cage while the problem was set. With her out of sight, I ran the rope across the top of the cage from the southeast corner to the north-east corner and dropped the free end to a point on the floor of the cage just in front of the nest-room porch. A piece of sweet potato was placed in the carrier, and the latter as well as the rope were held beyond Congo's reach through the grill.

At 10:12 a. m. the animal was brought to the door of the cage and allowed to enter. Immediately she climbed to the shelf above the grill and reached for the rope through the wire. A few seconds of this vain endeavor and her eyes were seen to follow the rope along the top of the cage. Immediately thereafter she ran along the east side bench to the front of the nest-room, descended to the ground, and began to haul at the rope. The instant the metal carrier struck against the bars of the grill she stopped pulling and coming to the grill took the carrier in her hands and reaching in removed the food. The time required for this solution of the problem was approximately one and a half minutes.

The following day the setting was again varied in that the rope ran diagonally across the top of the cage from the south-east to the middle of the west side where it was allowed to fall inside but close to the side wall of the cage so that the end passed through to the ground back of the house bench. This setting also was arranged with Congo out of the way.

Just as soon as Congo entered the cage she ran to the rope and quickly pulled the carrier to the level of the grill. In less than half a minute she had solved the problem of getting her reward.

It was evident that the rope had acquired meaning, and that Congo was inclined to haul at it whenever she had opportunity. Further light on the problem of adaptation will have to be obtained with different types of setting.

Following the idea just expressed, on January 14, with Congo parked outside of the cage and out of sight, I placed the food-container outside the cage at the middle of the west side, carried the rope over the top of the cage and allowed the free end to touch the ground at the middle of the east side but outside of the cage. Always heretofore Congo worked with the rope inside the cage and the food-container outside.

With everything in readiness Congo was led on a chain toward the east side of the cage. As she approached she glanced at the rope, hesitated a moment, and then passed on toward the grill. Probably at this moment she was influenced primarily by the supply of food which was ordinarily stored at the corner of the study nearest the grill. As she proceeded toward the food supply I checked her by fastening the end of her chain about one of the grill rods. Thereupon she promptly went to work on a test later to be described as the buried food problem. When her work on this problem had been rewarded by success, I unfastened the chain and led her back along the east side of the cage so that she might again have opportunity to see and, if she chose, manipulate the rope. This time as soon as she was within reach of the rope she eagerly grasped and began to pull on it. Pulling continued until she had drawn the carrier within reach. There is thus indication of recognition of the rope as a means of securing food even when it appears in a novel situation.

The next day a setting of the pull-rope problem designed as a roundabout route test (Köhler, 20, p. 8) was arranged. The carrier containing food was placed on the west side and outside the cage at a distance of about two feet from the nest-room porch. The free end of the rope was then run through the west side wall at approximately four feet from the ground, across the cage, and out through the east side wall where its free end just touched the ground. The setting was made with care that Congo should not see what was being done.

As previously when everything was in readiness Congo was led on her chain as leash toward the east side of the cage.

She passed the rope without stopping although the indication was fair that she noticed it. Her interest unquestionably was centered in the buried food problem and the supply of food at the corner of the study. As soon as she had completed her work on the buried food task and had eaten her reward, she was led back along the east side of the cage. As she came near the free end of the rope she hesitated, then approached and making as if to pass it, suddenly seized it and began to pull vigorously. Quickly she had hauled the food carrier against the wire wall of the west side of the cage. Even her most vigorous hauls failed to disrupt the apparatus, so she presently desisted. I now permitted her to follow her own will and she turned from the rope and walked toward the study. At the southeast corner of the study she stopped and failing to find food there, turned back and retraced her steps. As she passed beside the rope she stopped and pulled at it again vainly; then she took her course around the north end of the cage. Arriving at the northwest corner, I fully expected her to make directly for the large oak tree between the cage and the garage, for she usually was moored to it during a part of the day and it was her favorite climbing and resting place. But instead she turned abruptly to her left about the corner of the cage, went directly to the food-carrier, and grasping it, hauled it down and extracted a sweet potato. Her behavior had every appearance of being the pursuit of a roundabout course with definite purpose and in anticipation of the reward of food.

The pull-rope problem, set as previously on the outside of the cage, was arranged for use on January 16 with the free end of the rope about thirty inches from the ground and thus less conspicuous and more difficult to get at. As formerly the setting was made with Congo out of sight. She was led along the east side of the cage and in her eagerness to get to the grill apparently did not notice the rope. But when a few moments later she retraced her steps along the east side of the cage she saw the rope promptly, went to it and pulled on it until the food-container was against the opposite side wall. Thereupon she stopped pulling, looked about for a few seconds, and then briskly started north around the cage. At the northwest corner she turned sharply and took the shortest possible course to her reward. This, although entirely confirmatory of yesterday's observation, adds nothing by way of additional evidence of representational process.

Yet another variation of the pull-rope problem is worthy of brief description. It was on January 17 that the rope was arranged with the food-carrier inside the cage and suspended from the iron ring directly in front of the nest-room. Thence the rope ran diagonally across the cage, through the wire of the west side at the south corner, and hung free with the end approximately four feet from the ground. In this position it was considerably above the level of Congo's head as she walked along. Naturally Congo was not permitted to observe the arranging of the apparatus. When everything was ready she was brought to the cage and permitted to walk around it at will. From the grill she went directly to the point on the east side of the cage where the free end of the rope had previously appeared. Failing to find it, she circled about the cage and coming again to the previously significant point of the east side, stopped and looked through, doubtless at the food container which from that point was visible. Thence she continued her way around the north end of the cage. This time as she came abreast of the end of the rope on the west side of the cage she promptly reached for and began to haul on it, thus dragging the can across the floor of the cage until it finally was against the wire wall in front of her. I now opened the door of the cage for her and she ran in and made directly for the door of the nest-room, but suddenly checking her progress she came back to the food-container and took her reward. The impression this behavior gave me was that she recalled the initial position of the food-container beside the iron ring in front of the nest-room and started to look for it there.

With the making of motion picture records of the pull-rope problem, as set on the outside of the cage, on January 19, this type of test was discontinued, but further descriptive reference is essential because of values which appeared in connection with Congo's manipulation of the food container.

Both the hooked-rope and the pull-rope situations involved food carriers or containers. As a matter of fact, the same type of tin can was used in both instances. It was a substantially made container $3\frac{1}{2}$ inches in diameter by $3\frac{3}{4}$ inches deep, with a substantially bound opening $3\frac{3}{4}$ inches in diameter. This was large enough to enable Congo to thrust her hand in and with patience and perseverance to extract from the can whatever food it contained. As in the early trials with the hooked-rope and the pull-rope problems I observed the gorilla's method of extracting her reward from the container, I became convinced that something might be learned from the more explicit use of food containers as problematic situations. Almost invariably Congo reached into the container and picked out the food bit by bit. Occasionally the can was turned over by accident and the food fell out, but in the course of the score or so of experiences which she had with this container in the hooked-rope and pull-rope situations she never once deliberately and skillfully inverted it to obtain the food, and this in spite of the fact that it often was extremely difficult for her to extract large pieces of baked sweet potato. My notes make mention of general improvement in her method of extracting food, but it was in skill in inserting her hand and withdrawing it full of food instead of by the discovery or invention of a better method.

Problem 6. Milk bottle. Naturally enough it occurred to me that the presentation of desired food in a quart milk bottle, the aperture of which was too small for the insertion of Congo's hand, might yield significant results. This was arranged on January 9 when at 10 a. m. I put three sections of apple and a section of banana into a milk bottle. All of the pieces were small enough to fall out readily if the bottle were inverted. I then took the bottle with me into the cage and handed it to Congo, who, seeing the food through the glass, took it with eagerness. Her first procedure was to try to reach the food directly through the glass; her next to bite at the rim of the bottle as if to enlarge the opening. Failing in this she again tried to poke her fingers through the glass. Now in her manipulation of the bottle she tilted it over and rolled it along on the ground, the while intently watching the food as it moved within. Presently in this process, and without any well directed effort on Congo's part, a piece of apple dropped out. Having disposed of it, she carried the bottle with her to the nest-room. There she continued to work with it, tilting and turning it in all directions and reaching into the opening with her fingers. Shortly this steady manipulation emptied out the remaining pieces of apple, but the banana stuck to the side and it was not until Congo held the bottle up and shook it vigorously that it fell out.

Although the solution of this problem was not so prompt and clear-cut as to convince one of ideation, I am by no means sure that the average child of two to three years of age would act more intelligently. At any rate here is one of unnumbered possibilities for comparison of the nature and development of adaptive behavior in child, anthropoid, or other primate on the basis of observation in simple experimental situations.

It was not until January 29 that this particular problem was re-presented to Congo, and then I substituted a quart fruit jar for the milk bottle, chiefly because it had previously been used repeatedly in the test hereafter described under the title "buried food problem."

In preparation for this experiment I put two sweet potatoes into the quart jar and placed it between my feet as I sat on the porch outside of Congo's nest-room. At first she did not notice the food so I attracted her attention to it. Then she immediately took the jar from me and carried it into the nest-room, where holding it with hands or feet, as came convenient, she turned it end over end slowly. One of the potatoes fell out immediately, but it escaped her notice as it rolled into the straw of her nest, and she continued to work steadily for the other, using a combination of jar-tipping and finger-reaching methods.

From my notes it appears that the one thing Congo had definitely learned in her experience with food carriers was that tipping the container is profitable. Usually she merely slid the food toward the opening, where she could reach it with her fingers. She seldom definitely inverted the container and shook out the food. On the whole the performances with milk bottle and jar seem stupid, and unless one were very definitely biased in favor of ideational learning one might naturally attribute success to persistent effort and fortunate accident.

Problem 7. Buried food jar. On the same day, January 9, that Congo was given opportunity to extract food from a milk bottle, a problem was set to test at once her memory for location and her ingenuity in manipulating a food container. On a line perpendicular to the side of the cage, drawn from the northeast end of the grill and at a point sixty inches from it, I dug a hole in the sand approximately six inches deep by eight inches in its other dimensions, and with Congo at the grill watching me I put into a quart glass jar a baked banana, a baked sweet potato, and a piece of apple. I then stuffed the opening of the jar with dry moss, placed it in the hole, covered it with sand, and smoothed over the surroundings so that the place of burial was completely disguised. The jar was buried beneath three inches of sand. It was 11 a. m. when the jar was buried, and on the following day at 11 a. m. I took Congo from her cage, led her to its southeast corner and fastened her chain to a bar of the grill with six feet slack so that she could move about freely and, in case she remembered the buried food, could dig for it within a six foot radius. She looked about, tried to escape by tugging at the chain, and amused herself in a variety of ways for fifteen minutes, giving no sign whatever of memory of the buried treasure. I then called her to me and with my hands began to dig near the jar. She exhibited no interest. Next I partially uncovered the jar and a piece of yellow-red apple appeared through the glass. She saw it immediately and reached for it. Failing to get it she directed her attention elsewhere, apparently not realizing that food was at hand and obtainable. I uncovered the jar completely, exposing the remainder of the food and the moss-plugged aperture. Thereupon she became interested and removed the jar from the hole. Again she tried to get the food through the glass. After a few seconds she pulled out the plug of moss and began her usual procedure to extract the food. As the mouth of the jar was too small to admit her hand she poked her fingers in and thus succeeded in getting bits of the sweet potato. Holding the jar with her feet she rotated it with her hands. This and other manipulations served no useful purpose. Eventually, however, she inverted the jar, the food dropped to the mouth, and with her fingers she pulled most of it out. Although the jar was left with her for several minutes, she failed to obtain the remainder of its contents. After a total of thirty minutes work on this problem she was returned to her cage. The score for memory and method of emptying the jar was very nearly zero.

On January 10 at 12:40 p. m. the jar was loaded with food and, as previously described, buried, with Congo watching through the grill; and on the next day at 10:55 a. m. Congo, moored to the grill, was given the usual opportunity to exhibit memory. She walked and looked about calmly but aimlessly. Sitting on the sand in front of the grill she played with her feet placidly and as though perfectly contented with her lot. For fifteen minutes I waited for some indication of memory of the buried food. Then I assisted her by beginning to dig in the sand near the jar. As the jar appeared she saw it and at once became alert. Although no food had become visible, she began to dig vigorously and in a moment had pulled the jar out. As she drew it from the hole the moss dropped from the mouth and the food slid in that direction, so that she was able to reach it with her fingers. Although she did not definitely invert the jar and shake out the food, she managed to get it quickly and with slight labor.

From this time forth I regularly buried the food-containing jar each morning after the experiment, and the following day gave her opportunity to locate and obtain it. The repetitions of the experiment numbered eight on successive days, January 10 to 17. On January 12, her third experience with the problem, Congo after looking about for a few seconds, went to a nearby stake in the ground and pulled at it, then suddenly began to dig with both hands nearly over the jar. She happened to be a little too far to her right. Three times she dug in different nearby spots, but as nothing appeared she gave up. Whether this digging was purely accidental or conditioned by memory of the buried food it is impossible to tell. To avoid discouraging her I now stepped to the spot and began to scratch the sand over the jar. My first scratch revealed the glass and Congo, at my side, eagerly took over my task. This time she pulled out the moss plug and reached the food with her fingers.

At 12:15 p. m. on this date I varied the conditions for burying the jar by chaining Congo to the grill outside the cage so that she should watch the process of burial from the same point at which she would later have opportunity to locate the hidden treasure. She watched with concentrated attention and it required all of my strength to prevent her from unearthing the jar when I loosed her from the grill to return her to the cage. She used her surprising strength determinedly and also with craft and cunning.

It was 10:26 a. m. when on January 13 she was brought to the front of the grill for the buried food experiment. At once she began to dig near the end of the hooked-rope stake which was opposite the middle of the grill and slightly farther away than the buried jar. During the next ten minutes she scratched and dug at a dozen places near the correct spot and remote from it. She had the impulse to dig, but lacked ability accurately to locate the spot. For a long time she continued to go from place to place, digging a little at each point. Finally she had covered an area of six square feet rather thoroughly. At this time as it began to rain it became necessary either to discontinue observation or assist her. I began to dig at the right spot. She watched me, but did not offer to help until the jar appeared. Then she unearthed it and skillfully removed the food by tipping the jar and then reaching in with her fingers. All of this required twenty minutes.

The following day, in her fifth trial on this problem, she began to dig at the first opportunity. Her location was correct and in less than thirty seconds she had the jar in hand. At first she dug with her left hand, using chiefly the index finger, but toward the end she similarly used her right hand. The food was extracted expeditiously and skillfully, but not by holding the jar upside down and shaking it out. Having eaten what was at hand Congo began digging for more hidden treasure!

The succeeding trial occurred in connection with one of the pull-rope tests and it was apparently memory of the buried food which temporarily diverted her from the rope. At any rate, when she was led from her distant mooring toward the cage and along its east side, she continued to her customary position in front of the grill and there promptly began to dig in the sand. Her first attempt was made about six inches too near the grill. After a moment of work in this spot she shifted to the proper location and promptly disinterred the jar. In this instance her handling of the fruit jar was notable. She withdrew the plug, inverted the jar, and let the pieces fall toward the opening. This process she repeated until she had obtained all of the bits of food. On this occasion also, as soon as she had disposed of the food she began to dig for more.

The next day her response to the buried-food problem was similar, but her initial location inaccurate. First she dug some eighteen inches north of the jar, then nearer the grill. After a wasted minute she returned to a point near the stake and dug vigorously and persistently, going so deep that she finally unearthed the jar from the side instead of the top. The food was extracted this time also by inversion of the jar.

Finally, on January 17, when she was given her eighth and last trial on this problem, she initially missed her location by a few inches, instantly· corrected it, exposed the jar, pulled it out, and in doing so shook out the plug and also the food. At no time did evidences of olfactory location of the jar appear.

On the whole it would seem that the rope problems and the associated food-container problems supply meager evidence for other than trial solutions and slow rather than sudden adaptation. Nevertheless, the behavior is illuminating, and materially increases one's understanding of Congo's mental constitution.

When it came to the making of a motion picture record of the buried-food performance Congo showed off to advantage, for when led from a distant mooring to the front of the grill she located the jar correctly and immediately, as well as expeditiously, unearthed it and obtained her reward.

D. Mechanical Devices

In this section it is proposed to describe problems, tests, or other observations which involve Congo's manipulation of and adaptation to simple mechanisms. Although not numerous they will at least serve to indicate the nature of Congo's mechanical aptitude and its degree of development. Especially to be considered are the hook and ring of the hooked-rope problem, the hasp and padlock problem, the spring-bolt problem, and behavior toward latches, bolts, snaps, and hooks used to fasten doors, chains, or to anchor Congo to trees or other objects.

Inasmuch as the gorilla's performances in the hooked-rope problem have already been described with some detail, it will be necessary here merely to summarize the results. Congo showed surprisingly little interest in the *mechanism* of the hooked rope. Neither hook nor ring especially attracted her attention or was examined thoroughly and manipulatively. It was seemingly because of the chance separation of ring from hook as she hauled on the rope that she gradually came to be interested in the relationship of ring and hook and finally learned how to dissociate them. The impression which this particular experiment gave was that she lacked special mechanical interest and aptitude.

Problem 11. Hasp and padlock. Desiring a more systematic and definite exhibition and measurement of mechanical adaptability than could be provided by such situations as the hooked rope, I arranged what is listed as problem 11, hasp and padlock. The mechanism and setting of this problem are simple and readily describable. Between two of the cage posts and just above the bench on the west side of the cage I nailed a 3¾ by 1¾ inch wooden rail, on the center of which, as appears in the middle right figure of plate 6, was securely fastened a wooden box which carried the hasp and padlock. This box, made of ⅞ inch stock, was 3½ inches deep, 5 inches wide, and 15 inches long, outside measurements. The inside space was sufficient to accommodate oranges or apples cut in half, whole bananas, or whole sweet potatoes. At the left end of the box, as appears in the illustration, a chain attached to the side of the cage carried the key to the padlock. This device was arranged to test Congo's interest and ingenuity in manipulating the key, padlock and hasp.

It was on January 15 at 12:48 p. m. that the hasp-padlock problem was first presented. Congo, having watched me place a whole banana, a half orange, and a sweet potato in the box and close and lock it, apparently observed also my repeated use of the key in unlocking the padlock and in removing it from the hasp staple. Fearing, however, that the padlocked box would be entirely beyond her ability and would prove discouraging, I initially set the box with the lock merely hooked into the hasp. As soon as I stepped aside Congo went to the box and worked with and about it almost continuously for seven minutes. Much of the time she fumbled with the lock or looked and felt under and about the box. In the midst of her work, I was called away for fifteen minutes and when I returned she had ceased to give attention to the box. The lock, however, was in position and she evidently had failed to solve the problem. For this first trial she was given a total of forty-five minutes.

Because of the gorilla's obvious inaptitude I decided to leave the problem set continuously so that, if able and so disposed, she might at any time during the day or night unfasten the box lid and obtain the food. When I arrived at Shady Nook about 9 a. m., January 16, the first thing I noticed was that Congo was working at the hasp and padlock box. Whether my appearance suggested work I cannot be certain, but I strongly suspect that it did and that her attention to what proved an amazingly difficult problem for her was only incidental to my arrival, and momentary.

About 1 p. m. on this date I attracted Congo's attention to the locked box in her cage by replacing the food with fresh and again letting her see me manipulate the fasteners several times. Into the box this time I put a whole banana and a half orange which she very much desired. Indeed she was so eager that she very nearly reached the box before I could close and fasten the lid. As previously I merely hooked the lock into the staple.

It would be tedious indeed to recite the complete history of this experiment, and probably also a mark of poor judgment, for the important things that happened in the course of the two weeks during which the problem was before Congo can be condensed into a very few sentences. Since it early became clear that Congo had almost no interest in the hasp and padlock, and as little knack in handling them, I decided to try to teach her how to remove the lock when it was merely hooked into the hasp and how to unfasten the hasp itself. For several days I went through the necessary motions with her watching me. Then as she gave not the slightest sign of

Plate 6. Some Problems

Fig. 1, upper. The wound-chain problem. Congo registering dissatisfaction because of failure. Fig. 2, middle left. Box and weight obstruction problem as seen from outside the cage and through the grill. Fig. 3, middle right. The hasp and padlock box as set for work in the cage. Fig. 4, lower. Box and weight obstruction problem as seen within the cage. The weight is covered by a sheet of white paper to make it conspicuous.

imitative effort I simplified the problem by placing the lock so that it would fall out of the hasp even if touched. Under this condition she occasionally got it off, although quite as frequently she knocked it back into position. With the lock out of the way, she shortly learned to lift the lever of the hasp and open the box. Day after day I continued to demonstrate the unfastening of this box and the uncovering of food, and each day Congo, stimulated by my success and the apparent availability of the food, would fumble with the mechanisms for a few seconds or even a minute at a time. As there was no visible progress toward solution of the problem or acquisition of skill in handling lock or hasp, the key to the lock remained a needless and unused complication.

On January 28 I recorded in my notes the following reflections. This morning the padlocked box was again found untouched, or at least unopened. Chiefly because of the demand which the multiple-choice experiments now make on my time and their promise of valuable results, I have decided to discontinue the padlocked box experiment. Here endeth the mutually tiresome lesson. I shall, however, leave the box in position and shall replace the food daily in order that Congo may have unlimited opportunity to solve this simple problem. Her hands clearly enough are not clever in manipulating such mechanical devices as locks and hasps, but I suspect that the acts would be performed readily enough if her mental equipment were equal to the demand. This is of a piece with her almost complete lack of attention to the snaps, hasps, hooks, latches, and bolts in her environment which in many instances are essential conditions of her captivity. Never yet have I seen her try to remove from its eye the hook which fastens the cage door on the inside when one enters. Fancy a chimpanzee, or even an orang-utan, letting this simple mechanism alone!

The above affective reflections on Congo's mechanical aptitude are consistent with, and I think wholly justified by, my observations, for they are monotonously similar and almost without exception indicative of meager ability. I have, it is true, seen the little gorilla fumble with the spring snaps which at various times were used to fasten her chain to trees or other objects, but not once did I see her loosen one of these snaps, and only once did she succeed in breaking such a mechanism. That was when she with her teeth bit off the little button which projects from the spring bolt of the snap. The mechanical precautions taken for safe-guarding Congo's captivity would be wholly inadequate for either the chimpanzee or the orang-utan.

Problem 12. Spring bolt box. But there is one problem, in the category which we are considering, with which Congo succeeded fairly well. It is no. 12 in our series, the spring bolt. Although the setting of this problem is extremely simple, it is perhaps justifiable to describe it fully because of the unexpectedly positive nature of Congo's behavior.

On one of the 13 by 20 inch sides of a wooden box 20 inches long by 13 inches high by 11 inches wide, a door 7 inches wide by 20 inches long was attached by two hinges on one 20 inch edge and held closed by a spring bolt placed on the other edge. The mechanism was so arranged that when the button of the spring bolt was pushed downward, that is, toward the ground, the door of the box would fall open, thus exposing to view whatever food had been placed within the box as reward for success.

This apparatus was presented first to Congo at 11:15 a. m. on January 17. I took the box into her cage and placed it on the house bench beside me. Then, calling the animal to me, I opened the door of the box, let her see me put an apple and a sweet potato into it, and quickly closed and locked it. At once she began to pull at the button on the spring bolt, then at the ends of the door, but as this availed her nothing she gave up in a few seconds. Thereupon I quickly opened the door of the box to let her see the food and immediately closed it. Congo was evidently displeased by this act, and after I had repeated it five times she refused to return even when I opened the lid. One may fool a gorilla once, but it can not be done repeatedly! This, by the way, is an adaptation well worth noting. Its nature and the conditions under which it manifests itself in any organism are worthy of careful study. It indicates a kind and degree of mental development which probably are found only in certain mammals. This dogmatic form of statement should be followed by an interrogation point!

The following day the spring-bolt box was once more taken into Congo's cage and with her attentive I demonstrated how to open it and get the food which it contained. She, keen and eager to get the food, attacked almost every part of the box except the critical point, using her teeth, fingers, and toes on the edges and ends, the door battens, and indeed everything accessible except the bolt which held the door shut. From time to time I opened the box to aid her, if possible, by setting copy for successful act. Twenty minutes given to this experiment failed to yield signs of progress toward manipulation of the spring bolt.

To vary the situation, and remove this new mechanical problem from intimate geographical association with the hasp and lock problem, on January 20 I presented the box on the platform before the grill. Congo attacking it as eagerly as ever, directed her attention to the battens on the outside of the door. She worked also at the edges of the door, trying to get a hold which would enable her to tear it open. After a few seconds she began to pull at the button and the door promptly opened. When I again set the apparatus she opened the door promptly in five seconds; on the next setting, in two seconds, and the next at least as quickly. At last she had discovered the trick. Would she carry it until the morrow?

The question was very definitely answered on the morning of January 21 by Congo's successful manipulation of the spring bolt. In her first trial she first pulled at the door battens instead of grasping the button and pulling it downward. This of course is comparable with her persistent indirection in the hooked-rope situation.

With intent to make the spring-bolt problem more difficult, on January 23 I presented the box outside the grill as before, but inverted so that the button must be pushed in the opposite direction in order to release the door. Congo failed on this problem even after I had tried repeatedly to show her what to do. Later the same day, with the box in her cage, she solved it and quickly learned how to open the door when the spring bolt was at the bottom instead of the top of the door.

Other evidences of mechanical inaptitude might be supplied (see problem 13, hammer and nail imitation, p. 140). It seems unnecessary, for there was nothing in which Congo was more consistently unsuccessful than the handling of simple mechanisms. It is impossible for me to say whether this is characteristic of the species, the sex, the individual, or merely of Congo's stage of development.

E. Obstructions

There are only a few situations which belong in the category "obstruction problems." I had planned and hoped to devise many, but the nature of my outdoor laboratory, the resources which were at hand, and the limitations of my time restricted them to the following few. There are first the roundabout route observations in which the cage itself was a barrier; second, a box-weight obstruction problem, and third and last, the wound or shortened chain as an obstruction to free movement or to the obtaining of food.

In the limited opportunity afforded her Congo showed certain ability to orient herself in accordance with a previously perceived but no longer visible objective—as for example when she went around the end of the cage, by a course not customarily followed, apparently to obtain food from the container on end of rope. A single observation is difficult to evaluate, and until this sort of experiment has been repeated many times, and in various forms, one certainly should not infer that the gorilla follows a roundabout course because of a remembered objective.

When on January 19 attempt was made to make a motion picture of her in the roundabout route form of the pull-rope test Congo, instead of running around the cage in order to get at the food container which she had pulled into view, took the short cut over the top of the cage. Undoubtedly this was because she had been released from her chain and felt free to do as she pleased.

Problem 21. Box and weight obstruction. The form of problem described below was suggested to me obviously by certain of Köhler's experiments (21, p. 179). The situation was arranged in the grill corner of the cage. A wooden platform approximately four feet square had been placed on the ground in that corner, and on the platform, as appears in figure 4 of plate 6, (p. 96), had been placed a wooden box twenty-four inches in each dimension. This box was tightly wedged into the southeast corner of the cage so that one side was against the grill and the other against the wooden end of the cage. At the free end of the box, as shown in the illustration, a block of iron was placed. It weighed slightly over one hundred pounds, and attached to the front of it was a staple and chain by which it could readily be pulled forward off the platform. Finally, beyond the weight, a strip of wood was nailed to the platform so that the weight could be moved readily in only one direction. The box could not be moved sidewise without removal of the weight, and a wooden strip nailed diagonally from post to post above it made it impossible to raise it upward from the platform. In the setting of this obstruction problem a plate of food was placed twelve inches from the southeast corner of the cage where it could readily be seen through the grill by Congo, but could not be reached until the box was moved out of the way. Obviously the necessary succession of acts was removal of the block of iron by pulling it forward off the platform and pulling the box cageward away from the grill. This done, Congo could readily squeeze in between the end of the box and the grill and reach the food.

The problem was presented on January 26 with an abundance of food displayed on the plate and Congo apparently in good working condition. Her behavior will be detailed. She first pulled at the grill corner of the box, then mounted the box and pulled at the upper corner next the grill. This temporarily ended her pulling and she retired to the nest-room and tried to squeeze through an opening approximately six inches wide which ordinarily was closed by hinged door but which at the moment was open to permit ventilation of the room. Perhaps this act is as significant of ideation as anything well could be. To be sure, everything depends upon the circumstances and the facts. All that I observed was that she rather early in her endeavor quit work at the box itself and went to the nest-room. If this was because she remembered that the ventilating door was open and with the idea that through this space she might escape to the plate of food, we have an attempted solution of a high order of complexity. If, on the other hand, somewhat discouraged with her attack on the box, she went to the nest-room for rest or diversion and chancing to see the door open tried to squeeze through, her act lacks peculiar psychological significance. I incline to the first interpretation of her behavior because I observed practically the same action in the platform-stick experiment. On that occasion also Congo suddenly quit work when there seemed no adequate reason for discouragement, quickly and directly went to the nest-room, and attempted to get through the ventilation opening. As that opening could not be seen from the grill and as her quickness and directness of movement were such as to command my attention on the instant, I feel reasonably certain that her behavior was controlled by representational processes.

On returning from the nest-room to the box-weight situation Congo fingered the chain on the weight, then looked at the plate of food, and climbed to the shelf above the grill where she watched me. Here she lay for full five minutes. Whenever I moved or anything unusual happened, she became alert and often descended from the shelf as if hoping for some change in the situation, assistance or encouragement. Her actions suggested that she had already accepted the problem as insoluble.

For thirty minutes I awaited her removal of the obstructions, but beyond the acts already described she made no progress. The box-weight construction was left in the cage overnight, but in the morning there was no indication that Congo had disturbed anything. This deserves special emphasis, for one might expect almost any primate to amuse itself by pulling at the several objects and attempting to dismember them.

At 9:10 a. m. on January 27 Congo's entire breakfast was placed on a plate before the grill and she was given thirty minutes in which to obtain it by removing the obstructions. The food was so close to her that she could come within four or five inches of reaching it, but not once did she try. This is characteristic and indicates an accuracy of visual measurement, together with a willingness to act in accordance with observation that are, to say the least, unusual in infrahuman organisms.

In this trial Congo came, saw the food, gave up without so much as a tug at the box or weight, and climbed to the shelf above the grill where she placidly watched me. Why, one inevitably asks, this astounding lack of initiative and this remarkable calm before a good breakfast which is just beyond reach?

At 9:20 she was lying on her back with her hands under her head, a picture of comfort, contentment, and satisfaction with her world. At 9:35 I held the plate of food toward Congo and spoke to her encouragingly. This stirred her interest and hopefulness. She became active, pulled at the grill corner of the box and also at the top of the box; went to the weight and with one pull on the chain dragged it forward nearly six inches. Another six inches and the box would have been free and in all probability Congo within a few seconds would have solved the problem and obtained her reward. So near she came to success without realizing it and perhaps without even deserving to achieve it.

There followed quiescence, and at the end of the thirty minute period Congo had made no progress whatever toward the solution of her problem. Her random activity is so limited that except as she definitely and determinedly attacks the obstruction there is slight chance of success.

Unfortunately the continuation of this experiment was impossible because of its interference with other work, and the two trials which have been described stand alone. At least they serve to indicate that Congo could not quickly see through the situation and by manipulation of a relatively simple environment secure the desired food.

Problem 20. Wound chain. In certain of the experiments it was noted that Congo when her chain was fastened to a stake would give particular attention to the stake, sometimes trying to pull the chain loose from it and again apparently unwinding the chain or straightening it out as if to increase her range. It was these acts that suggested to me the possibility of setting a chain problem which might yield significant results.

On two successive days, January 26 and 27, what I am calling the wound-chain problem was presented. On each of these days Congo was placed in the following situation. Between her cage and the garage was a large oak tree which almost at the ground divided into six portions. To one of these trunks, at about two feet from the ground, Congo's chain was fastened. It was then twice wound around an adjacent large trunk. The remaining free portion of the chain measured approximately six feet. By unwinding the chain Congo could extend her range between four and five feet. At approximately twelve feet from the trunk of the tree, and therefore some three or four feet beyond Congo's reach unless she unwound the chain, was a plate containing a banana, an apple, and a half orange. At 10:40 a. m. on the morning of January 26

Congo was led from her cage to the tree and the free end of the chain was attached to her collar. From her previous behavior I supposed that she might rather promptly and directly unwind the chain and get the food. But apparently she did not see the problem as soluble, for after playing about in the tree for a few seconds she made strenuous efforts to reach the plate. Thereafter she played sometimes on the ground, sometimes in the tree. Once she was noticed to examine the chain carefully where it was fastened to the base of the tree. After fifteen minutes, despite abundant activity, the chain was in its original status. On the chance of stirring her interest and activity, I placed the food two feet nearer the tree. Promptly she came down and without trying to reach with her hands threw herself on her side and reached with one foot. As I had not foreseen this possibility it was necessary for me quickly to draw the plate back a few inches to prevent her from getting the reward. This was resented, with a low growl.

At the expiration of fifty-five minutes the situation was unaltered and there was not the least evidence of approaching solution of the problem.

When the problem was re-presented at 10:30 a. m. on January 27 she made incipient motions toward reaching for the food, but promptly climbed the tree and began to amuse herself by swinging there. For a full hour she was given opportunity to manipulate the chain as she liked, but nothing happened. This experiment also it was necessary to discontinue in favor of other and seemingly more important tasks.

F. THE BOX AS INSTRUMENT

My initial expectation and plan of using the stick as the chief factor in a series of problems of increasing complexity were wholly thwarted by Congo's lack of interest in the stick as tool and slowness in learning to manipulate it and in the acquisition of skill. I had hoped to use the box also as the basis for a series of problems. The results of my attempts are reported in this section.

Problem 10. Suspended food and boxes. On the morning of January 14 I arranged the following experimental situation, and at 11:19 gave Congo opportunity to work at the problem. On a cord tied to the limb of a large oak tree north of the kitchen door of the cottage, and some fifty feet from it, I suspended at sixty inches from the ground a banana and an apple. Five feet off center in one direction was an irregular wooden box approximately 18 inches long, 15 inches wide, and 12 inches deep. One of the 15 by 18 inch sides was open. Five feet off center in the other direction was a stake to which Congo's chain could be attached.

When brought to this problem Congo went to the box, which was the only new object at hand, sniffed it, walked about at the length of her chain, and pulled in the direction of the tree trunk with evident intent to use the tree as an approach to the food. The next ten minutes of her time were spent mostly in playing with her feet or in the sand, beating her chest or the ground as though impatient, and occasionally climbing upon the box. Once she turned the box over and for a time picked at nail heads on the inside. Satisfied apparently by her previous experience (problem 8, p. 65ff.), that the food was beyond her reach she made no attempt to get it directly. During a total of thirty minutes she behaved thus, with a degree of calm placidity which amazed me. Undoubtedly she desired the food and if she had discovered any way to get it would eagerly have used it.

The following day at 10:50 a. m. this experiment was repeated with the addition of another box, numbered 2. Its dimensions were 20 by 13 by 10 inches. The box previously used was now given the number 1. Each box was five feet off center and they were placed on opposite sides of the lure, the mooring stake being midway between them but also five feet off center. As reward an apple and a banana were suspended as previously at a height of sixty inches. Congo was given forty minutes to work at the problem. This time she handled both boxes somewhat, often mounting them and sitting or lying on them for brief intervals. Occasionally she would glance toward the food and sometimes approach and reach for it. She was not very active, and with the hope of increasing her eagerness to get the reward I once directed her attention to the food and set the cord swinging. This dislodged the apple which she promptly appropriated and ate. When she had finished with it she was keen for the banana, reached for it several times, and then rolled box 2 over toward it. Apparently this movement of the box was accidental, as far as possible relation to the food is considered, for she gave no attention to the food or the changed relation of the box to it. Once, reaching for the banana, she touched it with her finger tips. Instead of following her near success with increasingly determined efforts, as I fully expected from my experience with other anthropoid apes, she went away quietly and amused herself with other things as if nothing of consequence had happened. The chimpanzee in this situation would have been stirred to energetic and persistent effort and probably would have obtained the reward before giving up, or have exhausted itself in the attempt.

At the expiration of the period of observation I had to record fair effort and continuity of attention to the task, but lack of definite progress toward the solution of the problem.

On January 16 at 10:07 a. m. the problem was re-presented. It was a warm morning and Congo seemed unusually quiet and contented. She lay on the boxes or on the ground much of the time during the first twenty minutes, unconcerned about the food which was just beyond her reach, and apparently entirely content to ignore man-created problems.

Once I noticed her gaze intently at the food and then follow the cord visually to the limb of the tree. Her look the subjectivist would have to describe as thoughtful or meditative. Then she went back to the manicuring or massaging of her feet.

On the morning of January 17, I decided to present the box problem before Congo had her breakfast. I noticed as I went to set the problem that a small wooden box lay beneath the oak tree near the trunk and beside it an old rocking chair which was one of Congo's playthings. The presence of these objects near where Congo was customarily parked on fair afternoons made me wonder whether something unusual had happened the previous evening.

At 9:03 a. m. work was begun. From·the first Congo's attitude was markedly different from previously. She seemed interested, hopeful, energetic. At once she made for the boxes. First she moved 1 and then 2 toward the food. A quick sharp pull on the side of box 2 pulled off one of the. boards, but I was able to substitute immediately another box and the experiment proceeded. Abandoning the boxes she now, after some four minutes of work, went toward the food and started to reach for it when a distant sound distracted her and she looked toward her cage.

About this time Mr. and Mrs. Burbridge came from the house on their way to the garage and stopping told me that the previous afternoon when a group of visitors was at hand, Congo had been given opportunity to reach for a sweet potato and had used the chair to help her. Perhaps this is the explanation of her increased interest in the boxes and her more hopeful and energetic attitude.

Scarcely had the Burbridges left when Congo took her position directly under the food and reached for it. Then she went to box 2 and moved it slightly toward the food; thence to box 1 on which she stood for a few seconds. Box 2 she now turned over with the open side uppermost. It was not more than two feet off center and quickly noticing its proximity to the food she mounted the corner nearest the food and balancing herself reached as far as possible. As her fingers touched the fruit she lost her balance and fell forward, her weight the same instant tipping the box over toward the food. Picking herself up she noticed the advantage thus accidentally gained and mounting the box easily reached her reward. The time was sixteen minutes.

Can this success be described as the result of spontaneous, purposeful action, or was it perhaps the result of the previous day's experience in using the chair to reach from? Did she in that way get the idea, or its equivalent, of using something to climb upon and reach from? It is impossible to be certain of the correct answer. Although at first suspicious that unwittingly aid had been given her by Mrs. Burbridge in the solution of this problem, I considered significant the fact that Congo had been accustomed to have the rocking chair within reach and to climb upon and from it, also that boxes had frequently been at hand and available for use as she desired. All things considered, I tentatively decided not to give Congo credit for spontaneous and original solution of the box problem. But the following repetitions of the experiment are pertinent and should be described before we accept any conclusion.

In order to minimize chances of interference with the box experiment and distractions in the course of trials, I transferred the observational situation from directly in front of the kitchen door of the cottage to a large oak tree northeast of the cage and about forty feet from it. This location was out of sight of the cottage and was in many other ways more favorable for quiet work. Here on January 19 at 10:55 a. m. Congo was given her fifth trial. Two boxes closed on all sides were used: no. 1 measuring 11 by 13 by 15 inches, and no. 2, 11 by 13 by 20 inches. They were located five feet off center as previously and at equal distances from the stake to which Congo was attached. Apple and banana were used as prospective reward.

As soon as released Congo went to work and, after momentarily examining each box, stood under the food and tentatively reached for it. A motion picture record was made of parts of this performance, but because of Congo's lack of initiative it shows nothing of special interest. Two or three times in the course of the half hour she stood on the one box or the other, as if remembering her experience of yesterday and about to profit by it. At no time did she manipulate the boxes or give other evidence of influence of her previous success. It would seem therefore that my suspicion concerning the accidental character of her previous action is justified.

On January 20 Congo was given a thirty-minute trial in the box problem. In addition to the two boxes, a five-foot stick was placed within reach so that she might use either box or stick as tool. Once more she limited her activities to occasional reaching from the ground without jumping or even lifting one foot, mounting and sitting or lying on the boxes from time to time, digging in the sand, and sunning herself. It is perhaps significant that this morning she came from her cage to the experiment unwillingly. In the cage I had to coax her with food in order to get opportunity to attach the chain to her collar.

Another interesting type of behavior was noted. Once as she was lying on box 1 Congo was made uncomfortable by the pull of her chain which had become wound about the stake so that her range of movement was considerably restricted. Scrambling down she went to the stake and definitely unwound the chain and straightened it out, as though to make sure that she should have the use of its full length. She then returned to the box and lay down comfortably. This was the act which suggested to me the desirability of presenting the wound-chain problem (see p. 104).

A little later, from directly beneath the food she reached upward with both arms and then primarily with her right. Not once during the thirty minutes did she move one of the boxes or the stick except incidentally by contact with them and aimlessly.

The story of the half-hour trial given on January 21 is essentially similar to the foregoing except that attention to the food was decidedly less and there were more evidences of lack of expectation of success. Photographs were made of Congo in the experimental setting and of several of her characteristic attitudes.

Plate 7. Initial success with box and stick

Fig. 1, upper. First attempt to use stick to obtain suspended food. Fig. 2, lower. First success in obtaining suspended food (apple being grasped) by stacking boxes.

What has just been written applies also to the thirty-minute trial on January 22, the eighth in succession. I made a complete notebook inventory of Congo's activities during the half hour, but they were so limited in number and variety that only two pages were required. Mostly she spent her time resting comfortably on the boxes or on the sand. From time to time she reached for the food more or less determinedly. There were occasional intervals of play, but on the whole she was little disposed to strenuous activity. She did not manipulate the boxes, and when her chain once happened to catch in the stick she pushed the latter away, giving it no further notice.

At the end of the period of observation I wrote: Continuation of this experiment under the circumstances seems futile, and especially so since my time is so limited and there are so many other experiments which promise interesting results. Probably I should pass at once to the imitative form of the problem. I am still puzzled over Congo's early success in using a box to reach from, but I am increasingly convinced that her good fortune was due to the influence of the chair situation and to the accidental overturning of the box.

Problem 16. Box imitation. In accordance with the above reflections, I proceeded on January 23 to set for Congo imitative copy in the box problem. This I did systematically and in three stages, using the boxes of problem 10. At the beginning of the experiment for a period of five minutes I gave her opportunity to use the box unaided and on her own initiative. The next five minutes I devoted to demonstrating to her the use of a box as an aid in securing the food. My constant method was to grasp a box with both hands, carry it toward the food, in two or three stages, and when it was nearly under the food step upon it and let Congo watch me touch or pretend to eat the reward. In the early stages of copy-setting she was not allowed to mount the box and obtain the food for herself, but merely to watch my act, chained sufficiently far away to prevent her from molesting me. Finally, came the third five-minute period, in which the ape was given opportunity to imitate me or to use the box on her own initiative as an aid in solving the problem.

On the first day of imitative copy-setting the results throughout were negative. In the initial five-minute period she exhibited no new or unusual behavior and in general acted as though discouraged with the problem and entirely convinced of its insolubility. She watched my copy-setting with fair attention and with evident impatience, especially when I closely approached or touched the food. But when she was given opportunity to imitate, or otherwise achieve her reward, she either stood on the boxes in their original positions or reached for the food from the ground. My behavior evidently stirred her to new endeavor, but gave her no definite aid.

On January 26 Congo and I went through the same performance. She exhibited almost no initiative in the first period of work, in my copy-setting she seemed relatively little interested and much of the time did not watch me, and when given a chance to imitate she merely reached from the ground or mounted the one or the other box without moving it.

The copy-setting was varied on January 27 in that after moving a box toward the food and letting her see me stand upon it and handle the reward, I allowed her to profit by my act by climbing on the appropriately placed box and obtaining the food. I varied the performance considerably in three different repetitions on this date, making it difficult in one instance for her to reach the food from the box, and in another case pushing the box out of her way just as she was about to mount it. Thus I tried to stir her interest and eagerness, while giving definite suggestion as to useful procedure.

That the results of this period of work were not highly encouraging appears from the following sentences in my notebook: I shall discontinue tuitional effort for to-day and await with interest her behavior to-morrow. Seemingly the use of boxes, as in the box-stacking problem, is so far beyond Congo's present capacity that it might take an indefinite time to teach her. I am beginning to understand why there are no stage gorillas! Congo, at least, is incomparably slow in learning anything outside her natural system of adaptations.

At 9:14 a. m. on January 28 Congo without breakfast or other preliminaries was conducted to the box situation and given opportunity to solve the problem. Once in awhile in the five-minute period which she was allowed for initiative she looked toward the food and approached it; occasionally also she went to the boxes. But most of her time was spent in gazing about as though she were entirely unconcerned with the problem and utterly hopeless of obtaining in this situation any part of her delayed breakfast.

The period of copy-setting was filled as previously with my manipulation of the boxes, my several approaches to the food, and finally Congo's utilization of the situation as prepared by me to reach the suspended food. Once I placed a box so nearly under the food that I thought Congo surely would reach it by jumping, but standing on the box she refused to risk the short jump. The net result of the day's work is an underscored "no sign of progress."

On January 29 the box problem was not presented, and on the 30th came a surprise. It was 9:20 a. m. when Congo was taken to the experimental situation. An apple had been suspended sixty inches from the ground and Congo as usual was chained to the stake while with my notebook I sat some thirty feet away watching. From the first she was alert and active, as if something of importance had happened since her last experience with the situation and she now came to it with new hope and expectation of success. She went to box 2, mounted it, then to box 1 and stood on it; then she returned and sat on box 2. Suddenly and without visible warning she scrambled down from the box, seized it with both hands and carried it to a point almost exactly beneath the apple. Promptly she climbed upon it and easily reached her reward. This success required four minutes. There was no fumbling, nothing suggesting accident. Instead it was as though an idea had suddenly come to her and instantly become motor. If I had

chanced to be looking away from the experimental situation
for even as much as two seconds I should have missed the critical moment and have been utterly unable to give the above
descriptive and interpretative statement. Unfortunately there
was no time to make photographic records.

Problem 23. Box stacking. Up to this point problems 10,
suspended food and boxes, and 16, box imitation, have been
described. I now arranged to present the box problem in the
more difficult form listed as problem 23, box stacking. The
essential difference in the setting of the problem was that the
reward was raised to a point which required either the use of
a particular box on its maximum dimension, or two boxes, the
one upon the other.

The first move toward the box-stacking experiment was
made on January 30 shortly after the success just described.
Indeed, it was 10:01 a. m. when, with the situation as previously described, except that the boxes were placed eight feet
off center, Congo was given opportunity to repeat her performance. Scarcely had she been moored to the stake than
she began to move box 2 by rolling it toward the food. She
rolled it over three or four times with unmistakable intent, but
she stopped too soon and when she mounted the box it was
too far off center. Nevertheless, she made an attempt and by
good luck succeeded in grasping the food and carrying it with
her as the box toppled over and she fell to the ground. The
time of this success was about one minute.

While I was writing my notes she finished eating the food
and returning to the box placed it on center, and mounted it
as if expecting to find the food even when she could not see it
in position.

At 10:15 the situation was rearranged and an apple and a
sweet potato were placed at seventy-eight inches from the
ground so that either the boxes would have to be stacked to
reach them or the 20-inch length of box 2 would have to be
used. This will be referred to hereafter as use of the longest
dimension of box 2. In no other position would this box or

box 1 suffice to enable Congo to reach the reward. As previously, the five-foot stick was a part of the situation so that Congo might use it if she so desired.

When given opportunity to go to work Congo rolled and carried box 2 under the bait and climbed upon it, changing its position frequently as she met with failure. After trying all except the longest dimension she gave up, went to box 1 and rolled it to the center and against 2. Now she worked hard first with one box, then the other, mounting them frequently, and quite evidently surprised by her lack of success.

Suddenly after a short pause she grasped box 2, carried it to box 1, and tried to place it on the latter. Three attempts were made with the boxes in such positions that success would have resulted if she had completed the stacking and climbed upon the structure. But each time in these initial efforts the top box slipped off. Presently she gave up and after another pause she drew the two boxes together beneath the bait and sat on them looking somewhat disconsolate. At the end of thirty minutes the test was discontinued.

In my notes I find various questions as to why Congo did not imitate more directly and immediately, and why finally her success should have come with such suddenness and seeming spontaneity. It seems almost as though she had reacted negatively to my suggestions, but nevertheless had been aided by them.

On January 31 Congo was given two trials in the box-stacking experiment. The first was at 9:25 a. m. when with a banana seventy-eight inches from the ground, boxes 1 and 2 and the five-foot stick at hand, she was allowed to display her initiative. Promptly she went to box 1 and from it looked at the reward. There was conspicuous lack of interest and of determination as compared with yesterday. Much of the time she spent looking about and resting or playing. Indeed she acted, as my notes record, as though she had definitely decided that the food could not be obtained. Once she rolled box 2 over several times until it was slightly beyond the center, but except for this act she made slight effort to use it. Later she moved box 1 about, with a peculiarly puzzled air as though surprised, disappointed, baffled. After a half hour the experiment was discontinued with the decision on my part to repeat it after a short interval, with the quantity of reward doubled.

The repetition was duly staged at 10:15 a. m. with an alluring banana and apple so placed as prospective reward that box 2 on its longest dimension would enable Congo readily to reach them. Introduced to the situation she looked at the bait appraisingly, went to box 2 and stood on it, then going beneath the food she looked at it and at me. This performance was repeated several times with variations and each time with lessening of interest and assurance of movement.

Fearing that Congo might become utterly discouraged and abandon the problem, at 10:30 I lowered the food six inches, leaving it at seventy-two inches above the ground. This stirred her visibly. Promptly she rolled box 2 beneath the reward. She reached from its shortest dimension, then turned it over and reached from the middle dimension. Her next move was to place it very nearly on end in a position which would have yielded success, but she started to climb a trifle too soon and the box fell back to an unfavorable position. Thereupon she definitely quit work. It was 10:35. After a short interval of rest she returned to her problem and began again to manipulate box 2. Placing it under the bait on its middle dimension she was just able to reach the food with her finger tips. This greatly stirred her enthusiasm and she began to work with unusual energy as if intending to succeed. For about a minute she steadily manipulated box 2, and then, getting it on its longest dimension, she mounted almost directly beneath the food and easily reached it. Placement was perfect and she made no false moves once she had the box on end. Success was achieved after twenty-two minutes of work.

In this experiment Congo rolled or carried the boxes. Either method was easy for her. She placed them more accurately

Plate 8. Using boxes as tools

Fig. 1, upper left. Reaching vainly for suspended food. Fig. 2, upper right. Discouraged by failure. Fig. 3, middle left. Moving a box. Fig. 4, middle right. Mounting the box. Fig. 5, lower left. Using the longest dimension of box successfully. Fig. 6, lower right. One method of stacking boxes.

and with far better judgment than the chimpanzee and orang-
utan usually do. Possibly this is because of her unwillingness
to reach at the risk of losing her balance, or to jump. Except
in this experiment I have never seen her fall. She takes few
chances with the boxes, and usually places them securely.

The scene of the box-stacking experiment was the next day,
February 1, shifted to an open space so that motion pictures
of Congo's handling of the boxes could be made satisfactorily.
The food was suspended seventy-five inches above the ground
from a convenient telephone wire and the two boxes placed as
previously. It is to be recalled that Congo had not thus far
succeeded in stacking the boxes and thus obtaining the reward.
Once only had she made definite attempts (p. 115). At first
she was reluctant to work in the new setting of the problem.
Apparently she mistrusted the adequacy of her resources. I
encouraged her, however, by word of mouth and by moving
the boxes within her reach whenever they chanced to get into
awkward positions. This was done chiefly to facilitate photography. Mr. Ben Burbridge the while operated his Akeley
camera and with a Graflex camera I took still pictures. It
happened that we were both at our posts and watching our opportunity when quite unexpectedly the box-stacking behavior
appeared. Congo began to work with the boxes and, with
skill and exactitude which very much surprised us, she placed
the one upon the other (I think it was no. 2 on no. 1), mounted the pile, and balancing herself perfectly reached the food
and disengaging it from the string descended quietly and seat-
ing herself on the ground proceeded to devour it. The lower
figure of plate 7 is my Graflex record of the moment of
initial success in box stacking. Unfortunately, it is impossible
to reproduce the motion picture record, which I have no doubt
is the first ever made of the *original solution* of the box-stacking problem by a gorilla, or indeed any other anthropoid ape.

It was on the following day, February 2, that Congo, with
the box-stacking problem again set under the oak tree, the food
at a height of seventy-eight inches and a five-foot stick as well

as boxes 1 and 2 at hand, first attempted to use, as described on page 67, the stick as an aid in obtaining suspended food. In this trial also she finally achieved success by stacking the boxes. The experiment began at 9:56 a. m. and at 10:20 she had failed to arrange the boxes successfully. It was immediately thereafter that she tried to use the stick and then, as if impelled by another idea, dropped it and began efforts to place box 1 on box 2. She worked from the ground and lifted box 1 instead of pulling it. Three attempts were made before she finally got it into a stable position which met her requirements and enabled her to mount the pile and stand securely. All this time, and the total period of effort was not less than three minutes, she worked steadily, concentratedly, and as if thoroughly enjoying her task. The boxes as she finally used them were perfectly placed and she obtained her reward with ease and evident satisfaction.

During the course of this solution of the box-stacking problem I made seven Graflex pictures of different phases of the performance. One of the most valuable is the first use of the stick in this particular situation, presented as the upper figure of plate 7 (p. 110).

I was greatly impressed by Congo's judgment and skill in placing the boxes with relation to one another and to the food. The impulsive carelessness of the chimpanzee was lacking, and so also the peculiar uncertainties and relative clumsiness of the orang-utan. It would seem that Congo's strength and judgment might enable her to build a tower of boxes. If the time could be spared it certainly would be worth while to give her opportunity. Even more important would be experiments with cubes and rectangular boxes of different dimensions, to discover whether she would use the dimensions appropriately, and also place the cubes suitably in accordance with their size.

A further test of box-stacking ability was made on February 3, when in the customary setting Congo, contrary to my expectation and intent, succeeded in reaching the food at a height of seventy-one inches from the longest dimension of box 2. The act was done quickly and cleverly, following perfect placement of the box.

February 4 I placed the food eighty inches from the ground. Immediately Congo rolled box 1 under it, looked up and then proceeded to try the box rapidly in all possible positions without stopping to climb upon it or reach from it. Each time she measured the distance between box and food visually. Then, for the first time, she did something which I have repeatedly observed in the orang-utan and chimpanzee (32, p. 96). She lifted box 1 into the air toward the food. After a few seconds she turned to box 2 and half rolled, half carried it toward 1. Again she turned to box 1 and for a time worked with it. Frequently she tried to climb upon a box when it rested on an edge or corner and, although exhibiting its maximum height, was unstable. This tendency appeared in every one of her tests and apparently it was not inhibited by uniformity of failure. Now she went to box 2, deftly placed it on end nearly under the food, and balancing herself on it reached down and pulled box 1 up in front of her. Quickly she placed 1 stably on 2 and climbed upon them. Until she reached forward for the food her equilibrium was secure. Then she lost her balance and with the boxes toppled over, carrying the food with her. Her success in this trial came after four minutes of work and it was achieved with ease, deliberation, good judgment, and without a false move from the moment she began to stack the boxes.

The box-stacking performance was repeated later on the same day in order that pictures might be obtained. Congo, having demonstrated to her satisfaction that the food at eighty inches from the ground could not be reached from one box, quickly put the one upon the other and obtained her reward. Several excellent photographic records, of which some are presented in plate 8, were obtained during the performance.

V

RELATIONAL PROBLEMS AND DELAYED RESPONSE

It seemed desirable to explore Congo's mental equipment by means of the method of multiple-choices as well as by other and varied types of experimental problem. Therefore it was planned that a simple form of multiple-choice apparatus which could be used out-of-doors and depended on to give indicative if not quantitatively useful results, should be constructed in New Haven and shipped to Jacksonville. The essential portions of this apparatus were: (1) A board 30 inches long by 6 inches wide, on which were mounted, as shown in plate 9, five brass boxes which were placed two inches apart. Each box was 2 inches wide by 3 inches long by approximately 2½ inches high, outside measurements. The corresponding inside measurements were approximately 1¾, 2¾ by 2⅜ inches. (2) An inductorium and the necessary electrical connections to supply induced current through the multiple-choice boxes.

This particular form of multiple-choice apparatus, previously undescribed, and here described only so far as necessary in connection with the particular needs of this work, was designed by Harold C. Bingham especially for use with primates. It has been employed by him in an apparatus consisting of eleven boxes, for a study of multiple-choice reactions in children. The purpose of the manual form of apparatus is to reduce the time required for observations as well as the costs of construction over the original form of box multiple-choice apparatus designed by the writer.

The board which carried the metal reaction mechanisms was set up before the cage grill on a wooden platform so arranged that the ends of the board slid in ways on the platform. This enabled the investigator at will to push the stimulus mechanisms to a fixed position twelve inches from the grill so that the gorilla could reach and manipulate them, or to withdraw them

Plate 9. Multiple-choice and delayed-response apparatus

Fig. 1, upper. The apparatus as seen from the animal's position in the cage. Fig. 2, middle. The apparatus as seen from outside the cage, with two reaction-boxes open and three closed and locked. Fig. 3, lower. Apparatus set for use of electric shock. Congo is cautiously pushing a reaction-box to discover whether it is alive.

to a position thirty-two inches from the grill and therefore beyond the animal's reach.

Each of the brass reaction boxes is hinged to the board on the side away from the grill and can be lifted and thrown back as appears in the illustrations. When a box is thus opened it clearly is out of use and can not be mistaken by the animal as a possible source of reward. In order that the reaction mechanisms might be used with electrical stimulation as punishment for hasty or careless choices, the boxes were so constructed that a metal key could be thrust into the board and through a hole in a flange on the front edge of the reaction box. As long as the box retained its normal position on the board the circuit was not made, but the instant it was lifted it came into contact with the metal key and thus completed a circuit through the primary coil of an inductorium. Thus it was possible to electrify any one or all of the five reaction mechanisms.

Just inside the grill, and on a wooden platform which rested on the ground of the cage, was installed a sheet of brass 18 by 48 inches which, connected by a wire with the inductorium, constituted the second electrode of which the brass reaction mechanism was the first. When Congo, seated on the sheet of brass beyond the grill, attempted to lift a locked reaction mechanism she thereby completed the electrical circuit and received a shock.

Never previously, so far as I know, has electrical stimulation been used as a means of conditioning or controlling behavior in an anthropoid ape. It has been stated by Buytendijk that it cannot be used satisfactorily with the monkey Cercopithecus (11, p. 70).

With this meager description of apparatus, we may proceed with a summary account of the results of multiple-choice experiments. The work was wholly exploratory and intended rather to reveal characteristics of gorilla response, to furnish basis for formulation of problems and adaptation of apparatus than to solve any specific problem. Incidentally the investigator was keenly interested in discovering whether electrical stimulation might be used to advantage in controlling the behavior of the gorilla.

Problem 14.   Delayed response, multiple-choice apparatus. Initially the apparatus was not electrified and the only motive depended upon for appropriate response was the animal's desire to obtain food.   At 11 a. m. on January 21 Congo was confronted at the grill with the multiple-choice apparatus and given opportunity for preliminary practice with it.   This was in the form of settings for delayed response.   With the boxes concealed from Congo by a screen, a piece of banana was placed in each.   Then all except box 1, the first at the left end of the board as viewed by Congo, were locked by the use of the appropriate keys.   Next, with Congo watching, box 1 was lifted, she was shown the banana in it, and it was then closed; and after one minute's delay the board was pushed forward so that she could attempt to open the boxes to locate and obtain the banana.   The point in the experiment, obviously, was to ascertain the maximum duration or persistence of the factors —sensory, perceptual, or imaginal—which condition correct response.

Five trials were given, the boxes 1 to 5 being used in turn as correct or reward boxes.   In the first trial, with box 1 unlocked and containing food, Congo after one minute's delay chose 4 and pulled at it vigorously, next 3, then 2.   As each was locked she could not lift it but simply pulled and pushed at it determinedly.   Next she raised box 1 and got the concealed banana.

Summary statement will suffice for the description of the remaining trials.   In no case, after one minute's delay, did she choose the correct box directly.   Usually she first tried two or more of the locked boxes.

After a few minutes intermission, the series of trials was repeated with the following order of correct boxes: 3, 1, 5, 2, 4.   Again the period of delay was one minute and again Congo failed to choose the correct box first in any of the trials.   Her tendency to pull, instead of pushing or lifting, the boxes continued unabated. Although she watched eagerly while the experimenter placed the food in the correct box and there concealed it, the experience appeared to be valueless to her after the enforced period of delay. For several seconds she would keep her eye on the box and usually she stayed close to the grill, awaiting an opportunity to work, until the reaction mechanisms were pushed forward.

In these preliminary series, to prevent her from playing with the brass boxes, I withdrew the reaction mechanism board as soon as Congo had obtained her reward.

A series of five trials given later the same morning with two minutes delay yielded similar results. There were no correct first choices, but Congo at least learned how to operate the mechanisms, although even at the end of this series she often pulled the box toward her instead of pushing it up and thus opening it.

My general impression from this preliminary work was that. in this experiment, the gorilla might demand a rare combination of rewards and punishments as condition for maximal attention, effort and persistence.

The above initial observations were made on January 21. The following day at 10:25 a. m. the delayed-reaction experiment was continued. As formerly food was placed in each box, and Congo was permitted to observe the process only in the case of the box designated as the correct one. which was left unlocked. Throughout three series of five trials each on this date a delay of two minutes was used. From the beginning Congo was alertly attentive to the multiple-choice apparatus, evidently because of her success yesterday in getting a small reward at regular intervals and with relatively little delay and no serious disappointments or discomforts. The boxes were used in different order in the three series so that she might not acquire position habits. In the first series the order was 3, 1, 5, 2, 4. In the first trial she chose box 3 immediately, pushed it up with her fingers bent in the walking position, and took her reward. In no one of the remaining four trials was the initial choice correct.

At the end of the series I recorded in my notes my conviction that conditions of work are required which will make it worth the animal's while to avoid touching wrong boxes and to select the right box directly and immediately. As this apparently indicated the electrification of the apparatus, I proceeded at once to get the necessary equipment.

My notes record the comment, Congo likes this experiment far beyond my expectation. Presumably it is because she gets her reward regularly and, if not quickly, at least with certainty. She promises to be an excellent subject in this type of experiment.

In the second series of five trials begun at 11 a. m. there were no correct first choices. In the first trial with box 5 as correct, her choices were 4, 3, 2, 1, 2, 3, 4, 1, 5. Each time she pushed the box open with her knuckles.

Most of her time during the series was spent before the grill, but usually during the two minute interval of delay she went to the house bench, the nest-room, or the padlock box for a few seconds. Whereas yesterday she repeatedly grasped the board when I started to withdraw it from the grill and pulled as well as pushed the boxes, these useless activities to-day had almost disappeared.

The third series of trials with the order 1, 2, 3, 4, 5, yielded two correct first choices. The fifth trial was interrupted by a sudden shower; consequently the choices were fifty per cent correct, a very marked improvement.

Description of additional delayed-response observations is given on pages 125 and 134.

Problem 15. Identical object, multiple-choice. On the morning of January 23 the delayed-response problem was modified to that of the selection of the same or identical box in successive trials. My reason for the change was Congo's slow progress in adapting herself to the initial form of delayed-response problem.

In this case the middle box, no. 3, was designated as the correct one and throughout a series of five trials the delay was increased by one minute increments from one minute to five minutes. The following results appeared: In trial 1, with right hand placed on 3 and left hand on 2, Congo pushed 3 open and obtained reward; in the second trial, with two minutes delay, she used the same procedure; in the third trial, with three minutes delay, she pushed open box 3 directly with the knuckles of her right hand; in the fourth trial, with four minutes delay, she placed her right hand on 3 and her left hand on 2, but directly opened the former; finally, in the fifth trial, with five minutes delay, with her left hand she tried first to open 1 and 2, then with her right hand 4 and finally 3. In this the last trial of the series she apparently lost her orientation. Her attention was excellent and although during the delay interval she usually left the grill for a short time, she almost always was back in position and ready for the trial before the reaction mechanisms were pushed forward into position.

In this form of the experiment, as previously, Congo was allowed to see the food placed in the correct box which was thereupon closed but left unlocked as the key which was inserted did not serve as a locking mechanism.

Hereupon a series of five trials was given to see whether on the basis of her previous experience Congo would choose box 3 although she had not seen food placed in it. All of the boxes were supplied with food, closed and locked with the exception of 3 which, as formerly, was unlocked. There was an interval of two minutes between trials, but no other delay. Consistently and throughout the series Congo chose correctly, thus indicating that she had from the previous series acquired the habit of choosing box 3 initially.

Congo was still working splendidly in the multiple-choice experiment. Apparently she would continue much longer than had yet been required. But what, I wondered, would happen when the electrical shock was used to enforce deliberateness and reliance on previous experience in locating the right mechanism?

Problem 17. First object to left, multiple-choice. At 11:30 a. m. on this same day the multiple-choice problem usually described as the first mechanism on the subject's left was presented. Secretly food was placed in each of the boxes. No preliminary practice or form of instruction was given Congo. The time between trials was one minute. It is unnecessary to describe the several settings since only one series of trials was given and the essential results can be presented in a sentence.

In trials 1 to 5 Congo made one correct first choice; in trials 6 to 10, three. The indication was convincing that the experimental situation did not assure deliberateness and maximum care in choice, for whether or not a subject gets the reward on the initial trial it is inevitably obtained within a few seconds. It seemed therefore hardly better than a waste of time to continue this type of experiment. Congo liked it and worked eagerly and with certain indications of improvement, but it appeared to be desirable to introduce as quickly as possible some form of deterrent for careless or random choices to supplement the food reward and thus more stably and constantly to motivate the animal's entire behavior in the experimental situation.

Problem 22. Middle object, multiple-choice. It was not until January 28 that the necessary electrical appliances became available. On the morning of that day the assembling and construction were completed and experimentation resumed. The electrified multiple-choice apparatus does not demand detailed description; it appears in the lower figure of plate 9. Two "Ever Ready" dry cells in series were used to actuate a Porter inductorium. With the coil set at seven on the scale the shock obtained by placing one hand on the sheet of brass inside the cage and grasping one of the locked multiple-choice reaction mechanisms with the other hand, was tested in turn by Mrs. Burbridge, a negro laborer who was at hand, and the experimenter. Each described the stimulus as lively but not especially disagreeable. At 10:30 a. m. the problem of the middle mechanism was presented to Congo in accordance with the following series of settings which indicates not only the keys in use in a given trial but in addition the reactions of Congo.

Problem, Middle mechanism

Trial	Mechanism in use	Reaction
1	1, 2, 3	2 direct
2	3, 4, 5	4 direct
3	1, 2, 3, 4, 5	3 direct
4	2, 3, 4	2, 3, (4 also)
5	1, 2, 5	2 direct
6	2, 4, 5	4 direct
7	1, 3, 4	3 direct
8	1, 2, 4	2 direct
9	1, 3, 5	3 direct
10	1, 4, 5	5, 4

The conditions for a preliminary series of trials were as follows. Congo was permitted to see food placed in the middle mechanism, but all of the others were filled secretly and then locked. The boxes not in use were thrown back on their hinges so that they could not be mistaken for parts of the group of boxes to be chosen among. The mechanisms were not withdrawn until Congo ceased to manipulate them. Because of the introduction of the electrical stimulus as a supplementary factor in motivation, it is necessary to describe with some detail Congo's behavior in this initial series.

In the first trial Congo, having selected the middle box, 2, directly, and obtained the food, tried to open the other boxes. Although she apparently felt the shock, there was no indication of annoyance. Her choice in the second trial also was initially correct, and although she pushed at the other boxes there was no convincing evidence that the electrical stimulus was appreciable. Therefore the coil was set at six. Thereupon, in the third trial, she chose correctly. But in the fourth trial she tried first box 2, from which she evidently received an appreciable shock. The coil was now set at five, and in the next trial, the fifth, after choosing the middle box initially she refrained from touching the other mechanisms. In subsequent trials however she returned occasionally to the testing of locked boxes.

In this preliminary series she was right initially in eight of the trials, wrong in two. Doubtless she was aided by seeing the food placed in the right box. Many times in the course of the series she attempted to open locked boxes. Often she quite evidently received electrical stimulation, but sometimes there was no clear evidence. The apparatus as used in these experiments was crude and although it served well for exploratory work it could not be depended on for constancy and uniformity.

At 11 a. m. the same series of ten settings was presented in the above order, but no indication of the right mechanism was given to Congo. Instead the setting was arranged behind a screen which hid the mechanisms from her view, and at the proper instant the screen was removed and the board pushed into position before the grill. As each trial required between one and two minutes, the total time for the series was approximately fifteen minutes. Initially the coil of the inductorium was set at five on the scale, but in the middle of the series, following trial 5, it was shifted to four.

The number of correct first choices in this series was four. The stimulus strength appeared to be sufficient to assure careful choice and attention to the avoidance of shock. Congo did not seem to be startled or frightened by the electrical stimulation but rather surprised and interested. Sometimes she persistently pushed at the boxes, using her hands in various ways as though experimenting. Noted particularly were the following methods: use of the second joint of the closed fingers, where because of use of the hand in this position in walking the skin is very thick and hard; use of the ends of the fingers involving perhaps the nails as insulators; use of the knuckles, and finally, the back of the hand or wrist which carry heavy coat of hair. A number of times she was observed to pause for a few seconds before a box and then to proceed in some manner or other with her experimentation. It became evident that the resistance of Congo's skin to the current is considerably greater than ours.

In this, the first series of experiments in which Congo repeatedly received a shock of decidedly deterring if not otherwise disturbing strength, one important physiological expression appeared. She urinated three or four times, an entirely exceptional circumstance and probably due to the electrical stimulation. Of vocal, facial, or attitudinal responses to the stimuli there were almost none. One wonders, are they inhibited by the observer's presence, or is the gorilla naturally inexpressive?

Then at 11:30 a. m. followed a third repetition of the series of ten trials—the second series after the preliminary trials. Conditions were maintained as described above except that following the third trial in the series the coil was set at three, whereupon Congo quite obviously tried to minimize the shock by using the back of her hand to push open the boxes. The numerical result of this series was eight right choices and two wrong. Not only numerically but in performance there was obvious improvement over the previous series, for Congo more and more avoided tampering with the locked boxes and contented herself with obtaining the food by manipulation of the right box. My notes record many interesting observations made in the course of the trials. Once after receiving from box 2 a shock which apparently puzzled and interested her, Congo turned to box 1 and tested it tentatively as though trying to find out whether it also would tickle or sting.

Although the strength of stimulus with the coil set at three was decidedly disagreeable to the experimenter, and painful in case of firm continued contact, Congo gave no visible indication of pain or of such degree of disagreeableness as to inhibit search for the right box. The stimulus evidently did encourage extreme caution.

On the whole the results of this first day's use of electrical punishment in the multiple-choice experiment were decidedly encouraging. It appeared that the combination of food as reward and electric shock as punishment may be used to advantage with this anthropoid ape. My notes indicate that the solution of the "middleness" problem may be expected promptly, but that the problem is not very difficult when only five mechanisms are used. Further, that since Congo has given no sign of pain or marked discomfort as result of the electrical stimulation it seems reasonable to continue with what for the experimenter would be a painful stimulus.

Wet weather necessitated delay in the multiple-choice experiment. Attempt was made to use the apparatus on January 30 but the ground was so wet that the stimulating current was short-circuited. The following day, however, January 31, it was possible to resume work, and at 11:16 a. m., with the coil set at four, the problem of middle mechanism was re-presented by means of the series of settings described on page 127 used in reverse order.

In this series Congo made three correct first choices, seven incorrect. Chiefly because of her tendency to use her right hand she selected most frequently boxes 3, 4, and 5. Box 1 was not touched during the series, and box 2 was selected only when it was the right mechanism. In order still further to discourage Congo's tendency to test the boxes, even after she had made her correct choice, the coil was set at three following trial 5.

It is indicated by my notes that Congo's performance to-day was markedly different from previously, for instead of choosing the middle box directly in most of the trials she instead tentatively tested the first box at her right and then usually attacked the middle mechanism. This testing was done with the second joint of the 'fingers of the right hand. She rarely grasped a box to try to raise it. This procedure obviously would give maximum shock and with the setting above designated she has excellent reason to minimize contact with the electrodes. How she arrived at this new procedure is an important question. Apparently it had worked itself out in the interval since the previous period of experimentation. Her behavior very definitely suggests that she is not inactive psychobiologically between experiments or over night.

This series of trials made me wonder whether, after all, by the use of electrical punishment in the present multiple-choice apparatus Congo can be held to maximum effort and care. It begins to look as though she may sufficiently well control the strength of stimulation to frustrate my plans, for when she uses either finger nails or the back of her wrist she evidently gets only a slight shock.

At 11:40 the series of trials was repeated again in reverse order, this time with performance strikingly similar to that above described, but with five correct and five incorrect first choices. Her testing of the boxes showed extreme caution by comparison with her work last week. Quite obviously she did not care for the shock and was seeking in every feasible way to avoid it while at the same time endeavoring to obtain the food.

The series was given in its original order beginning at 12 o'clock, but in this case the coil was set at two. In the first six trials she was not once correct; then followed three successive correct first choices, making her score for the series three right, seven wrong. Use of the back of the fingers, especially at the second joint and knuckles, evidently minimized the electrical stimulus and enabled her to proceed without extraordinary risk of discomfort.

A final series with the trials in the original order was given at 12:43 p. m. with the coil set at zero. The reactions for these trials are reported in detail since they are fairly typical, and at the same time seem to indicate Congo's failure with eighty trials to get the idea of middleness, or any other safe basis of selection.

Trial	Mechanism in use	Reaction
1	1, *2*, 3	2 direct
2	3, *4*, 5	5 tentatively tried, 4
3	1, 2, *3*, 4, 5	4 carefully tested 3 carefully lifted
4	2, *3*, 4	3 direct but touched carefully
5	1, *2*, 5	2 direct but tried carefully
6	2, *4*, 5	2 tentatively touched, 4
7	1, *3*, 4	3 direct
8	1, *2*, 4	2 direct, carefully touched
9	1, *3*, 5	3 direct carefully
10	1, *4*, 5	4 direct; before the board could be withdrawn she tried also 1 and 5.

These observations left me uncertain about the value of the electrical stimulation. Congo, despite the strong stimulus, continued to like the experiment and worked eagerly. Even when she was not particularly hungry she seemed to be fascinated by the novelty of the apparatus and the peculiar experiences which it affords. A serious difficulty arose from the extreme variableness of the stimulus received. She quickly and skillfully achieved adaptations which enabled her to avoid the shock entirely in some incorrect choices and in most instances to minimize it.

In connection with motion picture photography on February 1 record was made of Congo's performance in the multiple-choice experiment. This was done as much to supply a satisfactory representation of the apparatus in use as to record Congo's behavior. The picture, however, does show in a valuable way her approach to the boxes and her method of using the back of her fingers tentatively to try the boxes and to push them sufficiently to discover whether they were locked, while at the same time avoiding disagreeable stimulation.

Continuation of the "middleness" experiment proceeded on February 2 when at 10:45 a. m., with the coil at zero, the series of trials, presented in the original order, yielded nine correct first choices. There was a mistake only in trial 1, when mechanism 3 was first tried. This series made it appear that Congo had solved the problem, but needed an initial trial to provide orientation.

Beginning at 11 a. m., the series was given in reverse order with the coil at zero, and there were as many incorrect as correct first choices. This seemed to be due in part at least to Congo's dissatisfaction with the reward supplied. I was using apple, and she made clear her desire for banana and sweet potato which she very markedly preferred to either orange or apple. Her attitude toward the experiment changed in the course of the series of trials and I am reasonably certain that the increasing number of mistakes was due on the one hand to her dissatisfaction with the reward, and on the other to her dislike of risking electrical stimulation. Although from time to time she received a shock which discomforted her, her only visible expression was quick withdrawal of her hand from the reaction mechanism and attempt to find a more resistant portion of her body to apply to the mechanism.

When at 11:15 I attempted to repeat once more the series of trials, Congo refused to work. For nearly half an hour she stayed away from the apparatus, most of the time resting comfortably in her nest-room. Suspicious that the value of the punishment was relatively greater than that of the reward, I set the coil at four for this series of trials. About 11:50 a. m. she returned to the grill and worked very circumspectly and without eagerness or enthusiasm. For seven trials she proceeded, choosing wrongly in every case except trial 7. Then she again retired from the apparatus and refused to work.

This series of observations is described somewhat fully because the results indicate convincingly the unsatisfactoriness of the experimental situation. Evidently I failed properly to relate and control reward and punishment and thus discouraged the subject.

Thinking now to make further exploratory use of the multiple-choice apparatus which might assist in the formulation of problems and the profitable development and trial of the apparatus and procedure, on February 3 I presented the mechanisms with distinctive black and white markings on the surfaces before Congo. The face of each box was covered by a piece of paper. Box 1 displayed alternate white and black vertical stripes; box 2, a plain white surface; box 3, a white surface with a black circle one inch in diameter in its center; box 4, a white surface with a half-inch black stripe horizontally across its center, and box 5, a uniform black surface.

With these visual differences as basis for choice, it was arranged to give Congo further opportunity in the delayed response type of experiment. A piece of baked banana approximately two inches long was provided as reward. The coil was set at four and the period of delay was uniformly five minutes. It was my procedure to place the food in the correct box, Congo watching, and then to close all of the others and lock them.

A series of five trials under the above conditions revealed no tendency whatever on Congo's part to select the correct box after five minutes delay. I now decreased the delay by one minute intervals until it was reduced to one minute, but still Congo exhibited no ability to choose correctly. In the course of an hour about twenty trials were given her and with few exceptions her initial choice was incorrect. Evidently the experiment had been bungled by one or both of us and she had either become discouraged or definitely settled into an attitude or reaction habit which was unfavorable to the adaptation required. The series of observations indicated that she gave slight attention to the placement of the food, and chose, wheth-

er immediately or after delay, without reference to her prior
visual experience.

Use of the multiple-choice apparatus with combined reward
and punishment has demonstrated its serviceability. Neither
my time nor my experimental resources permitted sustained
and systematic observation. I therefore, by sudden and radical variations of problem and conditions, tried to discover what
might be expected of the little gorilla under relatively unfavorable circumstances. I had hoped for pronounced emotional
expressions and perhaps the appearance of forms of adaptation which would throw additional light on her behavior in
previous experiments. But emotionally she was inexpressive,
and I found it peculiarly difficult to relate the adaptive aspects
of her behavior toward the multiple-choice apparatus to her
modes of solving other types of problem. Probably this section of the report will seem to some readers like an elaborate
description of stupidity in the experimenter. Perhaps it is.
But in any event the exploratory use of the multiple-choice
method with Congo has demonstrated the applicability of electrical stimulation, and has supplied partial basis for the formulation of problems and the adaptive re-designing of the apparatus and procedure.

VI

FOOLING, APING, IMITATING

Definite experimental study of Congo's sensory and perceptual equipment was not attempted, but nevertheless a great many of the observations in connection with experimental situations or incidental to them and to my care and handling of Congo, threw valuable light on receptivity and perceptual status. My descriptive statements must be made with extreme reserve, however, for they are generalizations from a short acquaintance with Congo and are rather in the nature of impressions tentatively advanced than of scientifically accurate assertions.

With this sweeping apology I should say that the visual receptivity of Congo seems to be comparable with our own. Lacking measures of acuity I may not venture on further comparison. Her use of vision seems to be highly effective. I have no indications whatever of the nature and development of color vision, but I gained the very definite impression that vision is the dominant sense in Congo's life.

As my work progressed it became clear that the animal's visual configurations are more or less radically different from our own. This appeared, for example, in her manipulation of such objects as the stick and the box. But always in such instances my knowledge remained inadequate because I failed to analyze the factors of motor adjustment or motor coördination. Perhaps Congo's failure to use the stick definitely and appropriately as a tool was due more largely to lack of the necessary visual-motor coördination than to the nature of visual perception. This idea, however, would not seem to apply to the same extent when the animal placed a rectangular box on the corner of one edge in order to achieve the nearest approach to suspended food; or when instead she lifted the box toward the food and holding it in mid-air tried to climb upon it. Such instances of peculiarity of visual configuration might be multiplied indefinitely.

It is the careful, detailed, analytic study of just such performances on the part of our animal subjects that may be expected to qualify us properly as experimenters and enable us increasingly to devise and create experimental situations suitable to their sensory-perceptual equipment, and calculated to exhibit on the one hand the animal's capacity for adaptation and on the other the modifiability or transformability of sensory configurations. It is increasingly clear to the writer, from his study of Congo, that the results of a considerable proportion of the presumably important studies of methods of learning, adaptive capacity, habit-formation, etc., in animals are determined in the main by the intellectual equipment, experience, pre-suppositions, and prejudices, and above all, the types of perceptual configuration of the experimenter. The experiment may be a human masterpiece, but as likely as not it is so contrived as to give the animal meager opportunity to utilize its peculiar adaptive or expressive capacities. We need, in my opinion, general familiarity with our animal subjects and a sympathetic understanding of them, before we even attempt to design crucial experiments to test their abilities.

Of hearing and auditory perception in Congo I can say little. She seemed to be as keenly aware of the sounds in our common environment as was I; at least as alert in detecting novel or unexpected sounds, and in general interested in the world of sounds and continuously ready to utilize them to her advantage. No experiments on acuity or range of hearing or any aspects of auditory perception were made, but I took considerable pains to record the various forms of vocal expression of the young gorilla, and my natural inference from the nature and variety of these sounds is that Congo has a sense of hearing which is comparable in its development with her sense of sight.

The senses of taste and smell were commonly called into service by new or novel objects whose possible food value was to be tested.   Visual inspection seldom convinced Congo that an unfamiliar object might not be eaten.   If accessible, it was promptly carried to the nose or mouth, usually both.   The few tests of olfactory sensitivity which I carried out had slight value.   I discovered that Congo quickly noticed unusual odors, but that the familiar odors of foods, as for example a banana, would cause her to ignore any strange odor which was not positively disagreeable.   On the other hand she was quick to detect disagreeable, penetrating, or irritating odors and to form associations which enabled her to avoid them.   One demonstration of this was in connection with tear gas which quite evidently irritated her nose even at a distance of several feet.

We are accustomed to think of the primates, especially in early life, as peculiarly and wantonly destructive.   Is this impression in accord with the facts?   In experimental as well as other types of situation I have worked over considerable periods with six widely differing primates: marmoset, cebus monkey, orang-utan, chimpanzee, gorilla, and man, and I have observed that they exhibit extreme differences in degree of natural destructiveness.   Perhaps in proportion to its strength the monkey deserves first place, but certainly the chimpanzee and the human infant and child compete closely, if not for first then certainly for second place.   It has seemed in my experience that destructiveness ordinarily is more or less incidental to the sensory examination and the sensory-perceptual testing or manipulation of objects which in the long run acquaint the organism with the qualities of its environment and give it measured control thereof.

Between a typical chimpanzee of the same age and the gorilla Congo there is an amazing difference in natural destructiveness.   Whereas the chimpanzee pounces eagerly upon new things, examines them with every available sense, tests them, manipulates them, and usually in short order demolishes them if this can be done, Congo mostly confined herself to a rather demure and ladylike examination of unfamiliar objects. The scrutiny is primarily visual, tactual, olfactory, and gustatory. If this examination indicates edibility, the appropriate reaction immediately ensues; otherwise the object, unless capable of some peculiar sort of manipulation, tends to be neglected. Never did I see Congo wantonly destroy an object. Yet in her cage at various times, and partly for the express purpose of testing destructiveness, I placed wooden and paper boxes, carpenter's tools, pieces of experimental apparatus, and even a corncob pipe. So much did her lack of destructiveness impress me that I one day recorded in my notes my willingness to trust my best hat in her cage. I should feel fairly confident· that if it were left there overnight I should be able to reclaim it the next day, somewhat crumpled and soiled but still a hat. With a monkey or chimpanzee at hand I should feel equally certain that the hat would not be identifiable as such a few hours after its commitment to the cage.

I am coming to suspect that destructiveness is importantly related on the one hand to curiosity and perhaps on the other to mode of learning and to the functioning of different learning processes in specific situations. It therefore is particularly in point to consider Congo's display of curiosity.

From my first meeting with Congo I was impressed by the relative infrequency of indications of curiosity about unusual objects or events. I continue uncertain whether the animal represses or inhibits the usual primate expressions of curiosity or instead lacks the experience. In addition to the observations which I made in the course of our daily contacts, I planned many simple experimental situations with intent to elicit gorilla curiosity. The evidences are so abundant that I must limit description to typical examples, whereas I base my impressions and generalizations upon the totality of my observations.

In the several stick problems it will be recalled that Congo initially paid little or no attention to sticks placed on the floor of her cage, put in front of her, or even handed to her. At first she completely ignored these objects; later she sometimes pushed or brushed them aside as if in irritation, and still later she occasionally picked them up, smelled them, and either laid them down or for a few seconds carried them about with her. Even though the stick was of unusual color, texture, or shape, she ordinarily displayed little or no interest in it or concern about it.

It would be difficult for me to forget my genuine surprise in the following experience. One day as I was working on the roof of the cage I accidentally dropped my two-foot rule through the wire netting and it fell to the floor of the cage where Congo could readily see and get it. Assuming, from my previous contacts with monkeys and apes that it would be ruined by Congo before I could get there, I made all haste down the ladder, around the cage, and hastily opened the door and rushed in. The rule lay undisturbed where it had fallen and Congo sat placid and unconcerned on the porch of her nest-room. In the course of weeks of continuous experimental work many similar happenings commanded my attention.

Problem 13. Hammer and nail imitation. An intentional test of curiosity and desire to manipulate things I made one day as I was constructing apparatus. With hammer, wooden block, wire, and boards at hand I was doing certain simple mechanical things which involved frequent use of the hammer. Congo was chained nearby. I called her to me to let her watch or, if she desired, help. She came, but giving almost no attention to what I was doing promptly climbed on my back and wished to remain there. Neither the noise nor my manipulation of the objects seemed to have interest for her. This further stirred my wonder and I became increasingly eager to find something which would really command her attention and examination.

One morning when conditions seemed favorable, I handed her through the netting of her cage a wooden door stop and a two by four inch sheet of red rubber. Each was tested by smell and taste and then, despite their varied qualities and possible uses as amusing objects, she put them to one side and ignored them. The same response was given to a corncob pipe and to various tools and mechanical appliances which I used in working about the cage, in making or setting apparatus, or solely as tests of Congo's natural response.

Her attention, to be sure, could be attracted momentarily by unusual auditory or visual stimuli, and she always was curious about strange people and objects which might possibly prove to have food value. In general, however, I found it true that she was almost unbelievably lacking in active exploratory tendency and destructiveness when faced by novel objects or with familiar objects which might readily be used as playthings or be dismembered.

One sure way to get and hold her attention appeared, and that was to eat something before her or display some object which she suspected of being edible. In this type of situation she made scant effort to control or inhibit expressions of lively interest and eagerness to participate in the activities of the experimenter. An amusing incident illustrates these points. One day as I was busily engaged writing in my notebook while seated on a box on Congo's porch, she came up beside me and before I realized her intent suddenly reached out, seized the page I was writing on, and tearing it from the book hastily made off with it. As soon as she was beyond my reach she started to stuff the page into her mouth, but finding it tasteless and probably otherwise disagreeable, immediately desisted and threw it to one side. Hugely amused by her disappointment and discomfiture, I quietly recovered my notes and proceeded with my work. It would seem that she was interested in the notebook chiefly, if not solely, because of possible edibility.

I have dwelt perhaps tediously on evidences of destructiveness and curiousity because they appear to be keys to the understanding of Congo's mental make-up. Her relatively low degree of active curiosity surely accounts in part for the slightness of her destructive propensity; and these in turn would seem necessarily to condition imitativeness and other modes of adaptation of behavior. It is a pity not to have reasonably accurate descriptive measures of these aspects of response, but in my hasty general survey of Congo's mental characteristics it was impossible sufficiently well to control observational situations and often enough to repeat experiments to provide statistically reliable data, or the basis for reasonably assured generalizations as contrasted with the somewhat impressionistic general statements that I have made.

To pass, then, to the subject of imitativeness, we first of all recognize the fact that there was no opportunity for Congo during my period of observation to imitate other members of her species. The only social factors in her environment were her dog playmates and the persons who visited her, took care of her, or studied her. Almost from the first I gave special attention to imitativeness of persons because I was struck and surprised by Congo's apparently negativistic attitude. In many of the experiments opportunity offered to record imitative responses or the absence of them, and in several it was possible to get something in the nature of measurements of imitative tendency.

Although in the use of the stick Congo eventually learned something by watching me, I am inclined to think it was far less than my notebook descriptions appear to indicate, for what she actually followed observationally was the food and the relation of the stick to it. When the stick happened to come in contact with the food she was alert and eagerly reacted to it as though it were actually a part of the food. Nothing I ever did by way of manipulating objects, whether sticks, boxes, hammer and nails, pencil and paper, pipe, or the parts of my own body, as for example by opening my mouth, grimacing, making gestures, etc., had obvious effect on the form of her response. Sometimes she appeared to be watching intently and with interest; but always her subsequent behavior gave me the feeling that she intended and perhaps preferred to do something different from what I did. This is what I have called negativism. I do not think I am exaggerating Congo's lack of imitativeness of me when I use this term; yet I fully realize that I am going a long way beyond the simple statement that she did not tend to reproduce my acts or to be pronouncedly influenced by them in her solution of problems.

In the several stick, box, and lock problems which I attempted to help Congo with, she gained more I think by watching the result of my series of acts than by following the acts themselves and attempting to reproduce them. In the aggregate I devoted hours to the task of copy-setting, and the acts which I performed with particular intent to assist Congo in learning how to solve various problems ranged all the way from such extremely simple things 'as merely opening my mouth to show my teeth, to the use of a long stick to push food out of a metal pipe. Usually the copy-setting had some practical objective. Thus I did my best to get Congo to open her mouth so that I might obtain her dental formula and observe the condition of her teeth, but neither imitatively nor otherwise, except by force, could she be induced to spread her jaws widely. Or, again, day after day she saw me working in and about her cage with a pipe in my mouth; yet when this object was handed to her or placed where she could examine it at her leisure, instead of imitating my use of the object she bit at the corncob bowl as though it were a nut. Never did she give any indication of being influenced by my use of the pipe. How I literally wore myself out trying to get her to imitate me in removing the padlock from its hasp in experiment no. 11 already has been told.

Recalling the natural love of the captive chimpanzee to use for its own amusement, and apparently imitatively, such things as tooth brushes, hair brushes, scrubbing brushes, brooms, wash cloths, I gave Congo similar opportunity, especially with broom and brush; but her interest and response were limited to fingering the objects for a few seconds, smelling or biting at them and pushing them out of the way as though they were not useful parts of her world.

Were it not for my experience in trying to teach Congo to eat unaccustomed foods I should have to say that she almost entirely lacked tendency to imitate me, and that I saw no convincing evidence of imitation of other persons or other animals. But the story of her response to edible things is as different from the above as well could be. When I arrived on the scene, I learned that Congo's diet was very limited, primarily because of her refusal to eat most of the things that were offered her. She was diligently specializing on baked banana, baked sweet potato, orange and apple, and skimmed milk heavily watered. Lettuce, celery, carrots, eggs, bread, meats and various other things which had been offered she had regularly cast aside either with a casual taste or merely a sniff. Knowing that her health and growth might at any time demand a more varied diet I promptly decided to try to teach her to eat other things. This offered an excellent opportunity for copy-setting and I fully availed myself of it.

Our first experiment looking toward a liberalized diet may be described in detail. With Congo chained to one of the big oaks after her morning's experimental work, I seated myself on a box just beyond her reach and producing two graham crackers proceeded to eat one ostentatiously and with gusto. She watched intently for a few seconds, then turned away to the tree. I continued to munch my cracker. Shortly she approached and watched me eating. I held out a piece of cracker to her and she took it, smelled it, then dropped it to the ground. Now she went again to the tree while I continued to enjoy my cracker. Very soon she came back, picked up the piece of cracker which she had dropped, and carrying it to the foot of the tree broke off a small piece and nibbled at it. Soon she climbed to her favorite resting place in a crotch of the tree and settled there *with her back toward me*. When a little later I walked around to the opposite side of the tree so that I could see her, I noted that she was nibbling at the cracker. My notes at this point record this reflection: Congo's apparent negativeness and obvious reluctance to accept suggestions from or to imitate me may prove to be a valuable clue to her psychology.

Some two minutes later, attracting Congo's attention, I took another cracker from the box and taking a bite of it myself held the remainder toward Congo saying, "Don't you want some cracker, Congo?" She came for it spryly and somewhat to my surprise took it from my hand eagerly and retired with it to her tree crotch where a moment later I discovered her eating it with apparent relish although slowly. I can but wonder whether taking a position in the tree in which she was hidden from me and could not be seen eating the cracker was a part of her negativism.

My note record of this observation concludes: Even if Congo cannot be driven to eat things she may be led by imitation! I fancy one new article of diet a day is enough, so here endeth the first lesson in catholicity of diet.

Subsequently several other articles were added to Congo's meal by similar procedure. She was induced to eat cereal and milk and to use a spoon in feeding herself by observing me. Apparently my act gave her confidence in the edibility of strange substances; and whereas if I merely offered food to her without taking some myself she often would throw it away or push it to one side, she usually could be induced at least to give it a fair trial if I acted as though I liked it. This behavior probably indicates important tuitional relationship between parent and young. Indeed it is more than likely that most of the new foods which in nature are gradually added to the young gorilla's dietary are eaten first in the presence of the parents, and probably in face of their imitative copy, and possibly also their effort to induce the young to imitate.

Entirely consistent with Congo's limited imitativeness of human beings is her social independence. She is interested in persons mainly as sources of food or desired attentions. During my observation of her she paid relatively little attention to strangers, but I am told that her attitude has changed and that she now takes very considerable satisfaction in acting for the entertainment of a "gallery." To those of us who attended to her daily needs or studied her behavior she was consistently friendly, although as a rule not demonstratively so.

Often, but not so frequently as one might expect, she was playful, sometimes making initial advances and at other times responding willingly to approaches. Similarly with her dog friends, Bobby and Betty, her moods and attitudes were variable. Occasionally she would play with them vigorously and until they were tired out or frightened off, but more often she gave them only passing notice or was so rough in her approaches that they quickly retired. Her play so far as observed by me was extremely simple, consisting of chasing or the reverse, climbing, a sort of hide and seek, and fist or foot cuffing. Because of her relatively great strength, romping with her was strenuous exercise and especially so because of her tendency to grasp and throw her whole weight on one, or climb upon and over and about one. Little originality or ingenuity was displayed in play activity, and I saw no indications of the invention of games or of any considerable variations from the simple activities already described.

More perhaps than anything else Congo's apparent contentment with her captive lot surprised me. For hours at a time she would sit in one of the great oaks, gazing about, watching happenings within the range of vision, alert for unusual sounds, but the while placid and seemingly wholly satisfied with herself and her world. Always she watched with interest the comings or goings of those of us upon whom she was dependent for subsistence or companionship. Occasionally when left alone for long intervals she would complain in a whining tone. But her ordinary mood is best described as placid. This remarkable self-dependence, or independence, combined with contentment, even in an unusual environment and in isolation, made me wonder whether the gorilla is unsocial and perhaps also an introvert. A possible way of approaching the problem was to let Congo become familiar with her mirror image. I therefore arranged the following experiment.

Problem 18. Mirror. A mirror twenty-four by fourteen

inches, mounted in a stout wooden frame, was made available
by the kindness of the Burbridges, who told me that at least
twice previously Congo had been given opportunity to examine
herself in it and that she had exhibited marked interest and
eagerness to establish contact with the reflection.

On my first opportunity, and with Congo in placid mood, I
took the mirror into the cage. She was on the roof of her nest-
room and did not come to me when I called her. But when I
held up the mirror so that she could see its reflecting surface
she quickly approached. Either she recognized the mirror as
something of peculiar interest to her or she saw her image at a
distance of six feet and was attracted by it. I held the mirror
firmly upright on the ground before me. Congo approached
and began to touch the glass with her fingers, hands, head, lips,
and face. Then she pressed her lips against the image, apparently kissing it. She also tried to explore it with her tongue. After
somewhat more than a minute, filled with such direct exploratory activities, she looked behind the mirror; then, returning to
the front, she watched the image while reaching around behind
the mirror with one arm and feeling and grasping for what she
evidently assumed to be there. This type of performance was
continued for between one and two minutes. I now placed the
mirror on the floor of the porch of the cage where I could hold
it more firmly and be more comfortable, while closely following Congo's behavior. As I attempted to move it from the
middle of the cage toward the porch she clung to it tenaciously,
evidently intent on keeping it within reach. It was almost
pathetic to see her persistent search for the companion which
she evidently felt must be near at hand. She simply would not
give up the futile search. After some eight minutes of this
behavior on Congo's part, I broke her hold on the mirror and
removed it from the cage.

Peculiarly significant is the gorilla's tactual exploration and
search where visual might have been expected to predominate.
Important also are the degree of her persistence in examining
the mirror image and in trying to locate its original, and her
utter unwillingness to let the mirror go.

So fruitful was this initial presentation of the mirror that I promptly decided to repeat the experiment in order, among other things, to observe changes in Congo's reactions from day to day, and the probable waning of her interest in the image. I was told by Mrs. Burbridge that when previously shown the mirror she had gone behind it and in her eagerness to locate the animal imaged had torn the cardboard from the back of the frame.

The first period of mirror observation was on January 25. There followed similar periods of observation on Jan. 26, 27, 28, 29, and again on February 1 and 3. On each day I held the mirror accessible to Congo for from five to eight minutes. These periods of observation, in addition to those reported by the Burbridges, doubtless would total approximately one hour. Now it happens that giving a mirror to a primate is a not uncommon form of amusement, so there are numerous records available of the behavior of monkeys and apes toward their mirror-images. So far as I am aware, all of these accounts indicate that the animal, even if intensely interested at first, quickly satisfies its curiosity and ceases its examination, exploratory efforts, and vain search for the original of the image. Not so Congo. On the last day of observation, as far as I could see, she was as keenly interested in the companionship of the mirror as originally. This is at once so unexpected and so significant socially that I shall briefly describe her behavior toward the mirror on successive days.

On the second day she exhibited all of the exploratory reactions previously described and also with her hands groped behind the mirror. After about five minutes of almost continuous attention to the image she tried to carry the mirror into her nest-room. I refused to permit this and started toward the door of the cage. She clung persistently to me and to the mirror until I forced her to let go.

Is it that Congo is lonesome for her kind and eager for sympathetic companionship, or if not, how are we to understand or interpret these activities? They are indeed extraordinary in comparison with those of other primates and not less so in comparison with Congo's behavior in other types of experiment and toward persons.

When on the third day I entered the cage with the mirror I carefully held the back toward her so that she should not see her image. Nevertheless she came eagerly, sought out the reflecting surface, and with unabated interest examined the image deliberately from face to hands and feet. Her activity was less energetic than formerly and she did not reach behind the mirror so often as before. Although she kissed the face of the image, she did not lick it with her tongue as previously. Also, instead of crowding against the image and maintaining her contact as though she feared the animal might escape, for a considerable portion of the time to-day she watched it at a distance of from two to three feet. Several times I noticed her look from the mirror to me as though becoming suspicious that in some way I was responsible for the phenomenon. This behavior is new and peculiarly significant. It reminds me vividly of the behavior of one of my monkey subjects in the multiple-choice experiments, when after a long period of work he suddenly came to attribute all of his difficulties to me and behaved accordingly (32, p. 58).

When after the usual period of observation I started to leave the cage, Congo clung to the mirror and did her best to keep it. Although I could not be certain that there was no abatement of her interest, it still was surprisingly strong and varied and she quite evidently found the image more fascinating than anything else at hand and wished to retain it.

The fourth day yielded yet other novel and significant reactions. Congo approached the moment the mirror was introduced and she was much more energetic and rough than in the previous period of observation. Everything by way of exploratory or searching activity previously noted reappeared and in addition she once seized the mirror, turned it suddenly edge toward her and reached out quickly as if to catch the other animal unawares. Once also I saw her strike the image with her fist.

Each day she made it plain to me that she wished to have the mirror to herself. Repeatedly she tried to take it from me, that she might carry it into her nest-room. I resisted because I feared it might accidentally get broken. To-day after one vain effort to drag the mirror, and me with it, into the nest-room she gave up and tried a ruse which certainly should have worked. Taking me by the arm she led me to the exit door and tried to push me out of the cage, while at the same time clinging to the mirror and hoping evidently to retain it. It was clearly enough the equivalent of saying "You may go" or "Get out of here." As I would not be separated from the mirror she carried it back to the door of the nest-room and once more tried to break my hold on it and carry it into the room.

Nothing new happened on the fifth day, but most of the activities previously recorded reappeared. Her searching persisted and several times she quickly turned the mirror and grabbed behind it. Following this day's experiment I mounted the mirror in the open so that a motion picture might be made of Congo's behavior. This was attempted on February 1, but our efforts were frustrated by the conditions. Congo was in the open and the chain had been removed from her collar to give her complete freedom of action. When she was brought into the presence of the mirror it immediately commanded her attention, but she was so far distracted by the unusual appearances and happenings about her, and so promptly became conscious of her freedom, that she only casually looked at the mirror image and thereupon devoted most of her time and attention to trying to escape us. The photographic record is not valueless, but unhappily it does not contain the several characteristic and significant responses which I have taken pains to describe.

With the period of observation on February 3 the mirror experiment had to be abandoned, not because Congo's interest flagged but because I had to return to New Haven. In this, the seventh trial, Congo was keen, active, energetic. She mouthed and kissed the image, felt for it on the glass and behind the frame, turned the frame about and searched behind it, tried to carry it with her into the nest-room, and finally was unwilling to let me take it from the cage with me.

I could not see that there had been any abatement of interest in the mirror-image and I was extremely reluctant to discontinue observation because it would seem worth while to find out how long this peculiar social behavior would continue. Possibly further study might convince one that it is due primarily to lonesomeness for members of her species, or instead to slowness of intelligent adaptation to a novel type of situation. Perhaps after all this apparently innocent and almost absurdly simple type of experiment exhibits something which is extremely important in gorilla psycho-biology. Often we have heard that gorillas die of lonesomeness or as a result of separation from those they are attached to. Do these observations make the statements more easily believable and do they give us some clue to the social psychology of the gorilla, or are we putting together things which are unrelated? Whatever may be the answer, I suspect that we have happened on a line of inquiry which if properly followed up will help us to an understanding of the gorilla mind.

The highly self-dependent attitude of Congo and her aloofness from human beings, except as she feels dependent upon them for her material needs, suggest the term introvert. Are we perhaps dealing in this case with a type of organism which when separated from its kind and compelled to associate with man becomes extremely introverted? And is this condition so far due to the unusual circumstances of life in captivity and of relative isolation from its species that we gain a very misleading notion of the mental traits of the gorilla? Or are shut-in-ness, negativism toward man, and a seeming haughty aloofness characteristic of this king among apes? I have recourse to questions because statements would be even more liable to misconstruction. Congo's behavior has deeply stirred my curiosity, and I have many times asked as I observed her and as I have worked over my notes and manuscript: What are the social and

other biological advantages and disadvantages of extraversion
and introversion, and why has the gorilla, even as compared
with the chimpanzee and orang-utan, lost in the struggle for
existence? It is this question which leads me to consider in
the following paragraphs, modes of adaptation of behavior as
they appear in what I wish to designate as fooling, aping, and
imitating.

Fooling, in the sense of working with objects in a seemingly
purposeless but exploratory fashion, is characteristic of certain types of mammal, and especially of the primates; characteristic also of certain periods of development, as for example
human infancy and the early stages of many of the infrahuman
primates. Presumably the more readily and persistently an animal fools with the objects of its environment, the more rapidly
it learns their qualities and comes to adjust itself profitably to
them. From one point of view what I term fooling or monkey-
ing is the initial or primitive form of research!

In aping, as contrasted with fooling, the influence of social
suggestion or copy becomes dominant and determining. The
act or assemblage of acts may be no more purposeful, or indeed
profitable, than those of fooling, but they at least tend to reproduce more or less precisely the reaction of another organism
or some other type of object, and are direct and immediate responses to those external events. In us yawning, coughing,
sneezing, smiling, frequently occur in response to similar acts
of other organisms and are in the sense of this paragraph instances of aping.

I have reserved the term imitating for acts the stimulus of
which is supplied by the activity of another organism and the
form of which is determined primarily by the objective obviously attained by the other organism. There are, to be sure,
many usages of the term imitation, and it is undeniable that imitative tendency in organisms expresses itself in varied forms of
activity and with varying degrees of consciousness of end and
of means as leading to that end.

I have burdened the reader with these somewhat labored definitions in preparation for the following statements concerning Congo's activities. In the above sense of the term, she fools surprisingly little with the objects in her new world. I have almost no convincing evidence of her tendency to ape. It is difficult to believe that she would not ape others of her kind, but I can truthfully say that I never saw her ape me or any other person. True, this may be a case of contrariness or of complete suppression of an ordinarily natural mode of expression. When it comes to imitating with reference rather to purpose than the precise means, the facts are in no wise different, for Congo simply does not imitate persons with such frequency, freedom, and explicitness that one can feel sure of it. Again I hesitate to believe that she is utterly non-imitative. It seems far more probable that she is non-imitative of us while perhaps somewhat imitative of others of her kind.

What bearing, we may now ask, has Congo's apparent negativism and peculiarity of responsiveness, as compared with the other great apes, on her ability to adapt herself to such problems as I busied myself in presenting to her? Offhand it would seem that she is at a very considerable disadvantage in learning new things because of her lack of abundant and impulsive activity, tendency to test and try everything that comes within reach, and to do what other persons or other animals do, or at least to imitate their actions to the extent of attaining the ends or goals which she sees them attain. If Congo is relatively impulsive, destructive, curious, imitative, she has deceived or misled me amazingly. Her behavior has filled my mind with the impression that she is too much aloof from her environment, too little adventurous, or, in the scientific sense, inquiring, to readily and quickly discover solutions of novel problems and adapt herself to extraordinary environmental demands. If this be true, one can understand why the gorilla should be a disappearing race, and perhaps also why so little relatively is known about its mental traits, and so little sympathy exists between man and gorilla.

Fooling and aping, as do the infrahuman primates and we in

our infancy, are conducive to serviceable adaptation through the popularized process of "trial and error." But it would appear that learning on the basis of insight, understanding, or appreciation of relationships between environmental ends and means, or among means themselves, is relatively at least independent of fooling and aping, while conversely largely dependent on that crude form of the spirit of inquiry which we commonly call curiosity and on the tendency to attend to situations as wholes, to survey them completely and in a seemingly appraising way, and then to try out thoroughly and with patient persistence one after another the methods which are made available by the combined native and acquired reactive capacities of the individual. Just because the chimpanzee is much fuller of curiosity and more imitative than the gorilla, it has I suspect outstripped its gigantic fellow-ape in the race for anthropoid supremacy.

VII

EVIDENCES OF INSIGHT

Insight is used throughout this report to designate varieties of experience which in us are accompaniments of sudden, effective, individually wrought adaptations to more or less distinctly new and problematic situations. For us as students of animal behavior its indications are aspects of the adaptive behavior itself, and in our work the essential thing is to observe and accurately describe the facts, irrespective of any interest or bias we may have respecting methods of learning or types of experience in the organism under observation.

During my study of Congo I acquired new light on at least one important aspect of the methodology of psycho-biology. It was in connection with photographic record versus direct observation. Heretofore I have assumed that the span and distribution of my attention are adequate to enable me to see what my reacting subject does, my memory adequate to hold the facts in mind long enough for abbreviated description, and my training in objectivity adequate to enable me later safely and accurately to transcribe and elaborate my outline notes. It was a considerable shock when from comparison of the results of direct observation with still and motion picture records I discovered that I was overlooking, or otherwise missing or confusing, some of the most important aspects or phases of Congo's behavior. When, for example, she was reaching for something with hand or foot, using a stick or other object as tool, or manipulating the multiple-choice mechanisms, I succeeded as a rule in getting certain important points in the response, perhaps for the actual course and result of the behavior, the essential points. But as often as not I was uncertain which hand or foot had been used, or if both were used, in what order; or realizing that I had actually observed a certain series of acts, I could not be perfectly certain of the exact order or temporal relations. The photographic records in numerous instances, and to a startling degree, corrected and supplemented what I thought I had seen. I am now convinced that especially in the study of those varieties of adaptation which after more or less prolonged attention to a situation and the trial of differing methods of solution are effected directly, expeditiously, and perhaps even suddenly, a complete photographic record is essential to satisfactory description.

In acts which by us are performed with insight or understanding of relations of means to ends, we are familiar with certain characteristics which are important if not also differential. The following is a partial list of features of such behavior. It is presented here with the thought that the comparative study of behavior with insight. in different organisms, may reveal common characteristics.

(1) Survey, inspection, or persistent examination of problematic situation. (2) Hesitation, pause, attitude of concentrated attention. (3) Trial of more or less adequate mode of response. (4) In case initial mode .of response proves inadequate, trial of some other mode of response, ,the transition from the one method'to the other being sharp and often sudden. (5) Persistent or frequently recurrent attention to the objective or goal and motivation thereby. (6) Appearance of critical point at which the organism suddenly, directly, and definitely performs required adaptive act. (7) Ready repetition of adaptive response after once performed. (8) Notable ability to discover and attend to the essential aspect or relation in the problematic situation and to neglect, relatively, variations in non-essentials.

Some such list of characteristics or aspects of behavior with insight may ultimately serve as our criterion of such behavior, in the absence of definite and adequate knowledge of psychoneurological events and their relations. It is unquestionably desirable that we continue to add to our list such observed features as regularly appear in human ideational behavior; and it is even more important that we make it our business to find out whether these characteristics are peculiar to ideational forms of response or appear also in other sorts of behavior. Without worrying unduly about objectivism or subjectivism, introspection, or other modes of observation, we may proceed with an unprejudiced study of the facts of behavior, profiting as much as may be from observation of our own experience and its varieties of expression, and following carefully, critically, persistently, the course of adaptive process in our animal subjects by means and methods which, as above suggested, should be relatively independent of the observer's limitations.

I hold no brief for ideation, insight, understanding, or any other variety or assemblage of experiences in my subject Congo, but I consider it a part of my descriptive task to state in direct, simple, and intelligible manner, what happened in the experiments. The observations have confirmed my suspicion that the conventional formula for habit-formation is incomplete, and the process of "trial and error" wholly inadequate as an account of anthropoid adaptations.

The foregoing descriptions of Congo's behavior must have impressed the reader with the frequency of failure and apparent stupidity where those who are familiar with the chimpanzee and orang-utan would naturally expect success, and perhaps also suggestions of understanding. I admit surprise at almost every turn in my study of the animal. This is one of the chief reasons for the length of this report. It has seemed that I must make clear to the reader the grounds of surprise, and as well as I could, the relations of the successive events which progressively enlightened me.

In the forms of the stick problem with which Congo was from time to time faced, a few responses stand out as possibly involving ideation. All have been mentioned in the previous chapters, but it may be excusable to review them here in what I consider their appropriate category.

Indication that "out of sight" is not necessarily "out of mind" is found in Congo's search for a stick when none was visible, and in her attempt to use as a means of egress the narrow ventilating space on the east side of her nest-room which only occasionally was open. Such behavior might be either idea-tional or non-ideational, but I maintain that its observable characteristics would differ markedly in the two cases. This is not the place to re-examine such characteristics as were ac-tually noted. Among them are several of those mentioned in a previous paragraph.

The use of the stick as a tool presented convincing evidence that visual configurations are important. I was especially im-pressed by the fact that Congo became interested in the particu-lar stick which was provided in the platform-stick problem only when, and seemingly because, it was in contact with, and there-fore a continuation of, the food which she desired to obtain. Slowly and with extreme difficulty she finally acquired the ability so to manipulate the stick as to make it continuous with the food. But even then efficiency was lacking because it was as likely to be moved in the wrong as in the right direction when it came to pushing or drawing the desired object toward her. On the whole I saw numerically and qualitatively more evidences of what superficially seemed like random trial be-havior than of what would naturally impress one as carefully planned and definitely directed effort to achieve a certain end. Yet in us just such behavior may express a motivating idea.

In the various box problems the outstanding evidences of in-sight were the suddenness of success, the relative initial skill in placing a box with its longest dimension in appropriate rela-tion to the food, and finally, the extraordinary indication of "good judgment" in placing one box upon another. Neither one nor all of these acts would be likely to convince objectively minded observers that Congo really understood her problem and had definitely thought out ways of solving it. I do not pretend to know, and I am not arguing the fact. It is solely and simply a matter of appearances, and they, I contend, are strongly suggestive of a measure of insight. If, however, we deny the experience of insight in Congo, we should deny it also in human infants and children, when, as often happens, the appearances are the same.

The orang-utan, from whom I learned most, once tried to use me as an aid in solving a problem. I should be distinctly beyond the observed facts if I inferred that he expected something of my intelligence, but it seems wholly fair to say that he accepted me as a fitting substitute for a pole, ladder, or box. Whereas Congo never happened to exhibit this particular interest in one who was standing by in her suspended-food experiments, she did in other connections, as previously described, show similar behavior, for her attempts to induce the experimenter to leave her cage when she desired to have the mirror to herself, or to have food placed on the platform so that she might reach it, were as intelligible as speech could make them. It was the appearance of this sort of behavior in various connections which first made me suspect a development of craft and cunning in Congo far beyond anything I had previously noted in other anthropoid apes. And although it would be inappropriate on the basis of my present scant knowledge to discuss the matter at length, I have also the suspicion that her degree of penetration and practical understanding of her environment and of the transformations in it for which I was responsible, far exceeded that made apparent by my descriptions of experiments. Much of the time she made me feel that she was concealing rather than revealing her insights.

In the past twenty-five years I have become familiar in one experimental connection or another with the behavior of a considerable variety of highly organized infrahuman creatures. In no one of them have I noted the definite relationship of reward to attitude and effort which appeared in Congo. Three factors obviously affected the value of the reward: the nature and quality of the food offered, its amount, and its difficultness of access. Many times I have seen Congo glance in the direction of much desired food and refrain even from moving toward or reaching for it because it was just beyond reach, or because she was incapable of using satisfactorily the object provided as instrumental aid. Often, too, she would refuse to work because she did not at that moment care for the particular sort of food offered.   When orange did not provoke effort, apple might; or when that failed, either sweet potato or banana almost certainly would.   These observations I can match from my study of the other manlike apes, but the following with much less assurance.

Congo evidently was influenced in marked degree by the quantity of food offered. Whereas half a banana might command scant attention and no effort, a whole banana might stir her to strenuous and prolonged attempts to obtain it.   As from day to day I followed her behavior and its development in the experimental situations I became increasingly certain that in the problem of the relationship of attention, effort, and characteristics of response to the nature of the reward, objective, or incentive, we have an assemblage of problems whose solution is important at once for our general understanding of the behavior of animals in experimental situations and for our analysis of those types of adaptive behavior which involve ideation. Is not something akin to ideation necessary for the sort of regulation of action in relation to quality, quantity, and accessibility of reward displayed by Congo?   It is unnecessary to defend here the presentation of these observations under "evidences of insight."   I am sure of the considerable significance of the facts themselves.   The interpretation is of secondary importance or, if you like, negligible.

Yet another species of "evidence" is difficult alike to describe and evaluate.   I have in mind inter-test activity. Whether it is implicit or explicit behavior I do not know, for I have not observed it.   Something, however, happens between trials or experiences in a given problem which materially affects the nature and rapidity of adaptation.   Presumably it is analogous to what is known to happen in human learning, for it has been demonstrated that the process of habituation occurs between training intervals as well as during those intervals. Scores of times in my experiments with other apes and with Congo I have noted that the solution of a problem or the development of a new method or a new attitude toward the situation progressed between trials, or as I have sometimes described it, over-night. I am by no means sure that this necessarily involves ideational processes. Instead I am inclined to believe that it is dependent on certain fundamental characteristics of neural tissue. But the fact nevertheless remains that the phenomenon has been observed most frequently and definitely in types of organism which possess elaborate and highly organized neural mechanisms, and which also exhibit marked ability to solve novel problems in seemingly ideational manner. Of course no thoughtful observer will miss the point that intertest progress always makes it seem that the animal has continued to attend to the problematic situation, or think about it and its demands, when it was not present to the senses. Sometimes doubtless this is the case. Whether it usually or ever is in Congo I do not know. It seems distinctly worth finding out.

Pauses in the midst of eager effort to solve an experimental problem are commonly observed in various types of organism, but it would appear that in all of the manlike apes these pauses have characteristics which differentiate them from similar interruptions of effort in most other mammals. Attention in Congo, as in the chimpanzee and orang-utan, is very definitely directed, concentrated, or intense, and can be observed to cover rather systematically the total experimental situation. It often makes the observer feel that the animal is calmly and deliberately, as well as thoroughly, taking in or sizing up the situation, and that in accordance with the result of this sensory examination, action will be directed or inhibited. It is this sort of examination or survey which leads sometimes to deliberate abandonment of the problem, and again to persistent effort. In the midst of such effort, and especially if success seems not to be approaching, Congo occasionally would pause and seemingly meditate or reflect. I have noticed pauses in response to visual and auditory stimuli; but quite as often there seemed to be no external cause apart from the immediate experimental situation, and one can but suspect that neural activity of the utmost significance for adaptive behavior is going on. In previous descriptions of the behavior of the manlike apes these pauses, suggestive of our own interruptions in work for reflection, have been described (33, p. 120). They deserve careful attention in our experimental situations, more accurate description than we have at present, and intensive analytical study in order that we may discover the sequence of psycho-biological events.

In many of the tests I was far more impressed by Congo's lack of adaptiveness than by its presence or nature. Thus in the wound-chain experiment, she failed within the time allowed, although from her weeks of experience in being chained to trees and posts about the place, and from her evident interest in and ability to untangle or unwind a chain when it was fastened to a stake in certain experiments, I should have expected her to solve this problem promptly. So also in her habits of eating she was careless and seemingly unintelligent, in obvious contradiction to her occasional performance in other types of situation. Neatness, cleanliness, deftness and skill in obtaining and handling food are, I suspect, in general, indications of a high level or degree of adaptivity. The most intelligent chimpanzee I have ever studied showed these qualities conspicuously. Congo sometimes markedly lacked them. But it would be tedious and unprofitable to review evidences of stupidity. I have tried to do justice to them in the previous chapters and similarly in this to the positive evidences of adaptation with insight. It remains to give a circumstantial account of what I may designate as "warming up or awakening."

On several occasions during continued experimental work with anthropoid apes I have observed the phenomenon which I am about to describe as warming up. The striking thing about it is a sudden radical change in the animal's attitude toward its task and markedly increased effort and success. An illustrative instance was mentioned on page 50 when after the making of a motion picture record of the gorilla's behavior in the platform-stick problem there was an accession of energy and interest in the problem, coupled with initiative and sudden breaking away from the automatism which previously had been characteristic of her attempts to use the stick as tool.

Probably what is meant by warming up or awakening can still better be conveyed to the reader by summary description of typical work-days before and either in the midst of or after warming up. For other reasons also it is worth while to describe the daily program of work. We shall start with Thursday, January 7, which was the third day of experimentation. It was a cloudy day with temperature of 58° about 9 a. m. Between that hour and approximately 11 a. m. Congo was given a chance to work in two experiments, the first being the shelf-stick situation; the second, the diagonal rope problem. To the latter considerable time was devoted since three different trials were made.

At this time I had no idea how long Congo might be willing to work each morning. I naturally expected rapid fatigue and resultant loss of interest and attention. But even at this early date in our acquaintance and our observational association she worked steadily and well for two hours.

January 17, also cloudy but warm, contrasts sharply with January 7 in that eight problems were presented to Congo in succession. Work began at 9:03 a. m. with the suspended food and boxes problem in which Congo worked with interest and energy and by happy accident obtained her reward. At 9:40 this was followed by the hooked-rope problem, in which a trial and error procedure led to success. The imitation phase of the platform-stick problem was presented at 9:42, but without sign of influence on Congo or a vestige of evidence of insight on her part. At 9:53 there followed the pipe and stick experiment with its usual type of negative result. The buried-food problem was presented at 10:10 with speedy solution and complete success both in location of the buried treasure and in its recovery from the jar. This was followed immediately and at approximately 10:15 by a form of the pull-rope test in which she also worked eagerly and with success. Then followed the hasp and padlock experiment. Although in this I set copy for

Congo she exhibited relatively little interest and no progress. Work in this test continued from 10:25 to approximately 11 o'clock. The spring-bolt problem was thereupon presented and Congo worked at it fruitlessly from 11:15 for a few minutes. It was followed by observation of feeding habits and the attempt to induce Congo to take oatmeal imitatively. At 11:45 measurements of weight and strength were made, and before one o'clock the day's work had been completed except for the transcription of notes.

Throughout this varied and undoubtedly fatiguing series of experiences Congo well maintained her customary placidity, eagerness for food, and willingness to do her best to get it. It seemed that eight problems presented in rapid succession the same morning yielded no less satisfactory results than had one or two problems in the early days of observation. On several days six, seven, or eight problems were presented in succession, but my time did not suffice to go beyond that number; whether Congo's patience and energy would, I am not sure, but I had no indication that they were about to give out. Even her appetite was enduring, and by discreet handling of food as reward it was possible to maintain her eagerness for hours and in one experiment after another.

Now, in contrast with the experimental procedure and responsive behavior of January 7 and 17, I shall describe them for January 30. It was cloudy and raining slightly. The temperature at 9 a. m. was 52° and I considered conditions unfavorable for experiments. Nevertheless I proceeded as usual. It should be stated at once that on January 27 Mr. and Mrs. Burbridge found it necessary to leave home, and from the evening of that day Congo was dependent on me, or on the negro helper Bill, for both food and companionship. Sometimes Mrs. Burbridge called during the day and for a few minutes saw Congo, but there was a radical change in her social environment and relations because of the absence of her usual caretakers and her most intimate and devoted friends. Then too on January 28 I had inaugurated electrical punishment in the multiple-choice experiments and probably for the first time in her life Congo had experienced the peculiar qualities of electrical stimulation. There were then these two unusual sets of circumstances which may have served to modify her attitude toward me and the experiments which I was associated with, and also have stimulated or otherwise aroused her to more varied and abundant effort.

I have said that on the morning of the 30th climatic conditions looked bad. Congo was not even in sight when I arrived at Shady Nook about 9 o'clock. The place had been deserted from 5 o'clock the preceding day until Bill arrived in the morning, and even then Congo was not fed. The day's work was inaugurated at 9:10 with the platform-stick problem. Congo came to the task with every show of interest, confidence, and eagerness. The stick which had been placed inside the cage she almost immediately noticed, picked up, and poking it through the bars of the grill used it to obtain her reward. Following description of the performance in my notes I wrote: This is radically different from previous performances when the stick has been placed in the cage. Has she waked up? Continuation of this experiment yielded still further evidences of unusual confidence as well as initiative. It was her quickness, definiteness and directness of action that most surprised me.

Immediately following work with the stick, I set the box-imitation problem. It was 9:20 and the food was sixty inches from the ground. From the start Congo was alert and active. The natural term to use would be full of purpose, for she acted precisely as though she knew perfectly what she wanted and how to get it. In a few seconds she had placed one of the boxes in appropriate position and obtained her coveted reward. There was no fumbling, nothing seemingly accidental about the success. Instead it appeared as though an idea, or its equivalent, had suddenly struck her and as suddenly become motor. It was my good fortune to be watching intently when this behavior occurred and to obtain as accurate and complete a description as my direct observation could afford. It was my misfortune to be unable to supplement direct observation by a motion picture record.

Wholly consistent with the above was Congo's action in a repetition of the platform-stick problem. At 9:47 this was set with a stick on the house bench at the left of the cage door, and food on the platform outside the grill. Congo, coming eagerly to the grill and finding no stick there, made incipient reaching motions with her legs. This was new. Then in the midst of this futile effort, which however was merely tentative, she suddenly turned and with wholly unusual speed and directness ran from the grill to the nest-room. Even as she did so I wondered what had struck her, for it was behavior quite different from the usual. In a moment her head appeared through the open space of the ventilating door in the nest-room and I realized that she must have remembered that that door was open and have gone to the nest-room to try to escape through the opening and thus to approach the food on the platform. This, to be sure, may be incorrect interpretation. The facts of behavior, however, stand as of peculiar interest and value whatever their conscious accompaniment or condition.

The box-stacking problem when presented at 10:01 seemed to stir Congo to exceptional effort. In her first attempt she promptly secured the reward contrary to my plan and expectation by the use of a single box. And when at 10:15 the experiment was re-set with the food suspended at seventy-eight inches from the ground, Congo fairly promptly made her initial effort to place one box upon another and thus to build a tower which would enable her to reach the reward. She did not succeed.

These are the essential and differentiating features of the day's work which on the one hand characterize it as a good or favorable day and on the other as a day of warming up or awakening. I feel reasonably certain that condition or degree of hunger or desire for food was not chiefly responsible for the peculiarities of behavior, and that the change in Congo's attitude toward her work and the uniquely numerous and varied evidences of ideation or insight must be attributed rather to other circumstances than those common to our daily work. The only exceptional conditions of which I have knowledge I mentioned at the beginning: the modified social situation, and the use of electrical stimuli as punishment for incorrect choices in the multiple-choice apparatus. The absence of Mr. and Mrs. Burbridge might naturally enough increase Congo's sense of dependence upon me and correspondingly her interest in the situations for which I was primarily responsible. The electrical stimulation may have so far stirred her bodily functions that her brain on January 30 was capable of far more efficient work than previously. I do not know positively that either of these conditions had anything to do with her surprising exhibition of interest, initiative, and intelligent adaptation on this date, but I am convinced that as opportunity can be made it will be worth our while to find out if warming up or awakening as I have described it for the anthropoid apes is an obserable phenomenon in various mammals, and if so what are its conditions and characteristics. I have satisfied myself as to the fact in the apes, but I admit my ignorance as to its nature and conditions. In my opinion it is one of the most important matters for further investigation revealed by my work with Congo. Pursuit of the clue thus given to an assemblage of psycho-biological problems of adaptivity of behavior is likely to discover the essential, but now lacking, factor in ideational learning, and enable us to understand the "critical point" in adaptation with insight.

Throughout the remaining days of my observation of Congo, the exceptional level of achievement which marked January 30 was pretty well maintained; and when on February 4 it was necessary for me to discontinue my observations I had the conviction that another month of continuous experimentation would have yielded indefinitely more illuminating results than did the initial period. It was Congo's increasingly favorable attitude toward the work itself that chiefly shaped my expectation. She seemed at last to have gained a certain general understanding of what the experimental situations were about, and, as a result of this functional equivalent of understanding or insight, worked with greatly increased willingness, confidence of success, and persistency. Every critical reader will wonder whether she had discovered some cue to guide her to the solution of her problems. Naturally I thought of this and did my best to discover any conditions which might have helped her. I found none.

To sum up this too casual survey of evidences of ideation in Congo, I may say that they are fewer than I should have expected in the light of my experience with chimpanzees and orang-utans of comparable age. Evidences of other modes of adaptation than the ideational are more abundant. Also there are good indications that in Congo ideational adaptations are made with difficulty and extreme fatigue. It was chiefly for this reason that I doubted initially the possibility of working with Congo for as much as a half-day continuously. Probably her ability to work at several different problems in the same morning owes as much to her natural conservation of energy as to her splendid physique and constitution. She wastes very little effort, whether in muscular activity or in ill-directed attention. If a problem looks insoluble or a reward not worth working for, she inhibits effort. But when the account is finally cast, it is only fair that we recall that Congo's age is certainly not more than five years and probably less. In psycho-physiological development she is comparable with a young child. As I review my records of her behavior I am increasingly surprised, considering her age, by the amount and variety of her directed effort in the solution of novel problems, her patience, economy of effort, and steadily increasing ability to meet the general requirements of experimentation. Her relatively high level of intelligence, or adaptivity involving ideation, is evidenced by her general adjustment to the conditions of experimentation and her sudden solution of certain novel problems.

VIII

AFFECTIVE TRAITS AND BEHAVIOR

Congo's temperament and disposition I found peculiarly interesting and puzzling because so utterly different from those of the chimpanzee and orang-utan. It is not easy to describe them adequately, but in this section I shall do my best to present those observations of emotional response which seemed at once most enlightening and most valuable as suggesting problems or furthering their formulation.

Congo's social relations with the Burbridges and me were entirely agreeable. Even apart from our consideration of her needs she seemed to feel friendly toward us, and when not particularly interested in our behavior at least indifferently tolerated our presence or our demands on her. Always she maintained a dignified mien. At first it struck me as distrust, but I later came to interpret it as independence or aloofness. So far as I could make out she was quite as aloof from other objects, including for example her dog playmates, as from us humans. Often it gave one the feeling that she felt superior and I sometimes found myself attributing to her a "superiority complex."

Her interest in things whose value she knew or suspected was ordinarily strong and she was capable of continued and concentrated attention to any situation which particularly interested her. My various experiments demonstrate these facts. But on the other hand she was capable also of ignoring objects and events which I should ordinarily have expected to command or compel her attention. Thus it happened that she would often give up work on problems which I should have expected to be easily soluble, or would abandon trial of a given method because evidently it seemed to her wasteful of effort. Indeed she was quite as ready to quit work on the basis of inadequate prospect of success as to exert her utmost effort persistently when she was satisfied that the environmental situation could be satisfactorily adjusted to or manipulated.

During my few weeks of association with the little gorilla I remarked steady although slow adaptation to the human portion of her social environment. She became distinctly more tolerant of strangers and increasingly willing to try to hold their attention and interest or divert them by her actions. The chimpanzee is notoriously an actor, but Congo when I first met her was mildly resentful of even the gaze of a stranger, and apparently preferred to be let alone or ignored except by those few of us whose acquaintance she had made and whom she moderately trusted.

As I continuously studied her intellectual and affective life I came more and more to feel that hers is a markedly shut-in or introverted personality. Frequently in my notes I used the words reserved, repressed, inhibited. Whether this characteristic attitude is one of shyness, timidity, or superiority I could never be certain, but gradually I eliminated the former and became increasingly confident that self-dependence and a certain superior aloofness best describe her affective attitude. Many times I attempted to call forth emotional expressions, but seldom did I get marked explicit response. To disagreeable or painful stimuli she reacted by withdrawal or attempted avoidance. Every sort of punishment she received stoically. Even the electrical shock called forth no cry of fright or pain; neither would disappointment in obtaining food stir her to cries of anger or resentment. Constantly she reminded me of the descriptions of human stoicism. Finally I came to think of her as relatively inexpressive. This of course rendered it extraordinarily difficult to understand her mood or attitude and to get into such intelligently sympathetic relations with her that work or play could go forward with mutual assurance of perfect adaptation. Accustomed as I was to the varied and often violent emotional outbursts of the young chimpanzee I marveled at Congo's calm when her dinner or some other desired object almost within reach was suddenly removed by the experimenter, for her only sign of disappointment or disapproval would be a frowning countenance and perhaps a growl or grunt.

That emotional reactions occurred one cannot doubt; their unusualness is equally certain. Gradually I came to understand that often when I least suspected it Congo was profoundly stirred, but where I looked for visible response of face, bodily attitude, voice, she responded internally or implicitly. A single illustration of this may well be described in detail, for it is typical and was to me extraordinarily illuminating.

Desiring to obtain measurement of Congo's weight I enlisted the aid of a young man in South Jacksonville who was good enough to loan a platform scale. The morning he came to Shady Nook to help me with the weighing it happened that Mr. and Mrs. James Burbridge and also Mr. Ben Burbridge were with me watching Congo's behavior. Having placed the platform scales in a convenient position outside the cage and arranged that my assistant should make the readings, I led Congo forth and tried to induce her to step on the platform. She refused to do this and I found it necessary to put her into position by force. Once placed on the scale she sat there quietly for a sufficient time to enable us to get the weight, but she evidently did not care for the situation. The second time I placed her on the platform she still more obviously resisted and resented my insistence. When I made a third attempt in order to verify our previous weighings she threatened to bite my hand for the first time in all of my contact with her, and then made vigorous effort to escape by running away from me. All of this naturally should have suggested to me that she was profoundly disturbed and was experiencing either fear, anger, or both. But as a fact I was so fully occupied with the task in hand and with securing her coöperation and through it reliable measurements, that I never for a moment suspected the strength of her emotion. I wondered why she should try to bite me or escape, but because of her lack of vocal or other usual anthropoid signs of strong emotion I completely misunderstood or misinterpreted her attitude. Light came to me only after she had been restored to her cage, for her behavior was then unusual in its indication of relief from strain and reaction. The most marked physiological response, and I think the most significant because seldom observed in Congo although extremely common in the chimpanzee, was temporary diarrhoea. There can be no doubt from this and other unusual signs or symptoms that the weighing procedure had caused Congo extraordinary alarm and had perhaps discomforted her more than anything I had previously done. This was a lesson which I shall never forget. I know now that Congo's emotional life works itself out internally to a far greater extent than externally, and that the term introvert is not inappropriate.

Lest the above illustration should leave the reader with the impression that vocal expressions of affective or other conditions are few or lacking in the gorilla I hasten to describe sound production. There is first the extremely low, seldom loud, and relatively short, grunt of satisfaction. I several times heard Congo give it when she was especially pleased with her food or with some attention shown her by a friendly human. Occurring under similar circumstances, but perhaps expressive of even keener satisfaction, is a still lower sound which I can describe only by the word purr. When I first heard it I could not believe that it came from the gorilla, it was so low and apparently remote; but on repetition I succeeded in localizing it and in identifying it as most like the purring of a great cat. It is short and seldom produced. A high pitched whine, previously referred to in various connections, is common in conditions which induce lonesomeness or mild discomfort and dissatisfaction. It is perhaps midway between the growl of discontent and the scream of anger or terror. The chief peculiarities of this whine are its high pitch and tremulousness. It is extremely tenuous and therefore utterly incongruous with the build and known strength and vigor of Congo. Contrasted with the short grunt of satisfaction is the growl of resentment or anger. I heard it several times, but never observed its repetition or prolongation. Clearly it is indicative of incipient anger. Occasionally when she was working for food or expecting its appearance from the house Congo would smack her lips, and, as already noted, pages 43 and 46, I convinced myself that this sound has very definite meaning for her and suggests either food or eating.

All of the above vocalizations I heard from time to time, although most of them infrequently, during my days of observation. Quantitative statements are impossible, for I have only impressions to guide me, but as I recollect, the purr I heard not more than three or four times, the grunt of satisfaction perhaps a dozen times, the growl of resentment possibly as frequently as the grunt, the whine of lonesomeness or discontent possibly a score of times. It is safe to add that vocalizations under experimental or natural conditions are rare in Congo the captive; what would be true in nature I cannot say.

Another sound which Congo is said to produce I never heard. It is the somewhat prolonged and vigorous scream indicative of anger and perhaps also of extreme fear. The negro helper described it as occurring when Congo apparently enraged by her bondage attempted to break her chain and escape from the tree to which she had been moored.

Mr. Ben Burbridge has spoken to me frequently of the screams of young gorillas and of the deep growls and roars of adults. I have no other basis, aside from my reading, for description of these vocalizations as I have not had opportunity to hear them.

Of other sounds indicative of emotions there are several. Congo in my presence frequently beat on her chest rhythmically with her two fists, and somewhat less frequently on the ground or convenient objects. As a rule not very much noise resulted, but she evidently took considerable satisfaction in the expression itself. I gathered the impression that chest-beating indicates impatience or other mild dissatisfaction, sometimes lonesomeness or slight irritation, and that it may be done to attract attention or to startle or intimidate the observer.

Mr. Ben Burbridge has described to me two other methods

of sound production which he has observed in wild mountain gorillas, namely, cheek and chin-beating. In the former the mouth is opened widely and the stretched cheeks are struck rhythmically and in turn with the palm of the hand. Naturally a peculiar sound is produced. Whether this action is common to old and young, male and female gorillas I do not certainly know, but I infer from Mr. Burbridge's observations that it probably is more common in the female of the species and perhaps in partially grown males than in adult males. Chin-beating also is a novelty. Mr. Burbridge says that the animal relaxes the lower jaw and letting it hang with mouth opened widely, rotates the two hands rapidly under the chin, striking the point of the chin and knocking the jaws together so that the teeth make a rattling sound. I have found no record in the literature of either cheek or chin-beating, but Mr. Burbridge says he has observed the performances repeatedly in wild mountain gorillas and is convinced that they, as well as chest-beating and roaring, are used by the wild animals to intimidate and frighten away any creatures which alarm or threaten them. Especially the chest-beating and roaring of the adult male are calculated to be intimidating, for they inevitably give one the feeling that a creature that can behave in such fashion must be savage and dangerous.

Congo's sound production was extremely limited in quantity and variety. My description is somewhat inadequate but not unfair I think to her behavior. On the whole, sounds gave me little information about her emotional status. Naturally therefore I looked for enlightenment from other modes of response, and from experience with other types of organism attempted to observe facial expression and bodily attitude.

Occasionally in the previous sections I have referred in passing to facial appearance. There is no denying that the eyes, mouth, nose, and lips of the young gorilla are potentially expressive. In spite of evidence to the contrary it still seems to me that they should be as expressive as in us. On the one hand, I am certain that Congo's face is capable of varied expression, and on the other I am equally sure that it seldom clearly reflects her attitudes, or perhaps I might more safely say that it usually reflects a calm, placid, self-dependent state. This emotional equilibrium was so stable, so seldom upset in the course of our day's work, so rarely disturbed to any considerable degree even by the extraordinary things I did and demands I made, that I possibly relaxed my vigil for facial changes and therefore missed certain minor modifications which photographic records would have revealed. I found it extremely difficult to read Congo's eyes; her lips were little used, affectively speaking, by comparison with those of the chimpanzee, and her nose changed its configuration only under very exceptional conditions and stress.

As to bodily attitude I find myself in somewhat the same plight as in the case of facial expression. The most commonly expressed affective state was one of contentment or placidity. In this case Congo would stretch herself on the ground on side or belly and lie completely relaxed, sunning herself and perhaps finding amusement in playing in the sand or pulling at the grass about her, or quite as often in playing with her toes. Even a more extreme attitude of relaxation appeared when throwing herself on her back she would place her arms under her head and thus relaxed, enjoy the warm sunshine. These attitudes clearly enough expressed genuine satisfaction. Resentment and incipient anger I have seen in a tense muscular condition. My observation does not enable me to go farther than to say that her bodily condition gave one the feeling of motor preparedness.

Pleasure, delight, or joy in recreation and play I tried to elicit by various games and forms of romping with the little gorilla. Usually, however, I could not be quite certain whether she entirely approved of my playfulness or not. Often she would retreat from me, but it usually seemed rather a ruse to lead me on than a mark of disapproval. When in active, playful, physical contact with me, other persons, or her dog playmates, her face sometimes lighted up and her rather cumbersome body became extremely pliable. Although she evidently had no desire to hurt us but instead sought enjoyment in lively games of running about or chasing, her strength was such that the dogs found her grip anything but comfortable, and even we adults discovered reason to dread her strength of limb and her weight. Extreme anger or terror I never had opportunity to observe. This was a perpetual surprise to me, for I should have considered it impossible to subject a young gorilla to experimental inquiry for a period of weeks without at some time so far running counter to her natural interest and desires as to make her thoroughly angry. I should have expected also very considerable degrees of fear in some of the unusual experimental situations. But here as elsewhere Congo surprised and disappointed me.

It is often said that only man laughs. I am by no means certain that this is true. Indeed I am sure it is not unless one defines laughter subjectively, for the facial expressions of laughter appearing in the gorilla, chimpanzee, and orang-utan are strikingly like those of man. That a sense of humor is involved except in man is doubtful. It was possible to make Congo chuckle or smile with satisfaction, but she seldom responded to any mode of approach with the hilarious chuckles, facial and bodily contortions, and vocalizations of the tickled or amused young chimpanzee. Evidences of sadness or discontent I noticed in Congo only in her facial expression, which I am utterly incapable of describing. It obviously involved certain changes in the eyes and lips. Tears apparently are never shed, and I saw nothing which might appropriately be described as weeping.

Of gestures there are a few to which emotional significance might be attributed. In general they are suggestive of repulsion or attraction. In this connection I am reminded of Congo's behavior when on her chain as leash I conducted her to and from experiments, or for other reasons shifted her from one part of her limited environment to another. Often, if not usually, when we started out on such a short trip she would desire to go in some other direction than that chosen by me.   It was therefore necessary for me to exercise restraining and directing force.   Mostly in such cases she would for a few seconds drag on the chain with intent to have her own way. Then as though convinced that mine was the stronger and dominant personality she would suddenly give in and go my way. The really striking thing about this behavior was the suddenness and completeness of the change in 'attitude.   Almost in a flash she became transformed from a strongly resistant animal to one entirely docile and willing to do my bidding.

Shut-in though she may be, Congo proved an extraordinarily coöperative and docile subject.   Even when I made her work hard and long for small   rewards, disappointed or apparently deceived her, and otherwise gave reason for keen resentment, she was calm, completely self-controlled and amazingly lenient in her attitude toward me.   As I critically review the hundreds of pages of notes descriptive of her behavior, the scores of still pictures and the thousand feet of motion picture record which with Mr. Burbridge's generous coöperation I was able to get, I am increasingly impressed by her relative superiority to the petty annoyances which constantly disturb the affective life of most infrahuman primates and of not a few in the genus Homo.   Her temperament is almost ideally even, her moods predictable.

IX

COMPARISONS, SUMMARY, CONCLUSIONS

It is proposed in this section to summarize the principal characteristics of behavior observed in Congo and to contrast them with the traits of chimpanzees and orang-utans. I must remind the reader that, with the exception of quotations, the statements of this report refer to anthropoid apes of early age, say approximately five years. Many misunderstandings and misconceptions arise from oversight in the matter of age, sex, or species. I have endeavored to be explicit and I desire here once more to disclaim intention of generalizing from the behavior of Congo to that of her species or of gorillas in general. It does seem to me fair, however, to compare the behavior of this child-gorilla with that of orang-utans and chimpanzees of like age. But here again one must be cautious, for individual differences may be as marked and as significant as are those of age or species.

The following rough comparisons are based on fairly intimate knowledge of a few individuals. They indicate merely characteristics from which we may safely take our departure in studying the different types of anthropoid ape, and they can be of value only as they aid one in the formulation of problems and the control of experimental situations.

In physique the chimpanzee is ordinarily well but lightly built; the orang-utan by contrast somewhat loosely built with arms which strike us as disproportionately long and liable to be in the way, whereas the gorilla is stocky and of impressively strong build. Color and facial characteristics readily enable one to distinguish the three sorts of great ape, for the orang-utan with its reddish hair and skin is thus sharply distinguished from the chimpanzee and gorilla. The latter ordinarily is jet black as to coat, except that the adult male acquires a gray back, and black also in skin. The chimpanzee ranges from gray to black in coat color and from very light to jet black in skin color. There is no single distinctive difference as to face. In general the chimpanzee has large ears and the orang-utan and gorilla relatively small ones set closer to the head; but there are individual chimpanzees or perhaps varieties whose ears are very like those of the gorilla. The same applies to the nose, for although ordinarily the gorilla's nose is flat, broad, and with large nostrils and that of the chimpanzee somewhat smaller, more prominent, and with smaller nostrils, there are in it conditions which closely approach those of the gorilla. To distinguish the types on physical appearance alone is far more difficult than on the basis of physique coupled with behavior.

Certain of the types contrast at least as markedly in temperament as in physical characteristics. It is dangerous to depend on single-word descriptions, yet the following are strongly suggested by my acquaintance with the young of the various types. I have found the chimpanzee to be sanguine, the orang-utan melancholy, the gorilla reserved. There are differences of habit which seem to correlate with these temperamental peculiarities, for the orang-utan is primarily arboreal and seemingly able with the aid of its long arms to manage existence fairly easily in the trees. The chimpanzee, also arboreal but at the same time very much at home on the ground, is almost monkey-like in its nimbleness and its variety of action. The gorilla, only slightly arboreal, is built for defense on the ground, and by its strength of jaw and limb is able to achieve the same ends that the chimpanzee's alertness and agility command.

My first-hand knowledge of the wild life of these apes is entirely inadequate for safe description, so what follows will be based almost wholly on observation of captive specimens. I have no assurance that my statements would similarly apply to the animals in nature and I suspect that many of them would not.

Each of the types exhibits habits of cleanliness of bodily condition and appearance when kept under good conditions.

If closely confined they gradually lose, through the discourage-ment of extremely unfavorable conditions, their habits of self-care. Ordinarily they are careful also with their food and eat with reasonable neatness and cleanliness. There are notable exceptions, but I am attempting to make statements which fairly apply to the types rather than to single individuals. I have seen no evidences of marked differences in the develop-ment or use of the senses or in perceptual characteristics. The same is true of behavior of the imaginative sort. There is, it seems, a fair degree of memory of the visual, auditory, kines-thetic, and chemical varieties in each sort of great ape. For this statement our evidence is meager and I present it merely as a generalization from such experience as I have and that which has been definitely reported in the literature. Possibly I should more nearly do justice to my feeling in the matter if I followed it with an interrogation point in order to suggest that it implies rather an assemblage of problems than a dog-matic assertion.

When it comes to attitude toward work or play, natural tendencies and acquired tendencies in these directions, there are again notable differences, for the extreme activity and buoyancy of the chimpanzee make it preëminently leader of the manlike apes in playfulness and invention of ways of amusing itself. It is quick, impulsive, energetic, but like per-sons of extreme optimism and enthusiasm tends to fatigue rapidly, especially when faced by problems which demand close attention and "intellectual" activity. The orang-utan, working more slowly and cautiously, with less evidence of optimism and impulsiveness, makes one feel that it is some-what more stable and dependable than the chimpanzee, but it too fatigues rapidly and it is more readily depressed or dis-couraged than its livelier cousin. The gorilla, calm, reserved, and apparently cool and calculating in its attack on problems, seems almost the dispositional opposite of the chimpanzee. The terms sullen and morose, often applied to the adult of the species, certainly are not applicable to Congo, for she is habitually placid, self-dependent and reasonably superior to the accidents of her captive environment.

In nothing is the contrast sharper between these three sorts of ape than in exhibition of curiosity and destructivenes. The chimpanzee heads the list; the orang-utan is a close second, but is obviously less enthusiastic and hopeful in its investigation of things than is the chimpanzee, while the gorilla, however much it may be stirred internally by curiosity or impelled to manipulate its environment, usually acts as though it considered itself superior to such childish expressions. This is one of the things that first, chiefly, and all the time impresses one as he observes Congo's behavior.

As to modes of learning, the facts revealed in my fairly intimate acquaintance with each of the manlikes apes suggest that the chimpanzee is naturally the most imitative of all in its association with man, the orang-utan although distinctly less given to imitation is by no means negativistic, but the gorilla, as exemplified by Congo, seems to show positive resistance to imitative tendency and, as in the case of curiosity, to be under compulsion or impulsion to act independently and superiorly. These statements apply only to imitation of human acts. My opportunities to study inter-species imitative tendency have been meager except in the case of the chimpanzee, and it may well be that among themselves gorillas are highly imitative by comparison with other apes

It is in their relative imitativeness of man that we seem to discover the secret of the great apes' peculiar values as performing animals. In this class the chimpanzee easily leads, for it can readily be trained to a considerable variety of skilled acrobatic performances, imitations of human habits or customs and interesting tricks. It loves applause, becomes devoted and strongly attached to its keeper or trainer, and, barring accidents, is loyal and dependable as long as kindly and fairly treated. When one adds to these advantages relative hardiness in captivity, ability to withstand the hard conditions of the life of a traveling troupe and to find grounds for optimism in whatever situation presents itself, it is obvious enough that the chimpanzee is the showman's prize.

By comparison with chimpanzees there are few performing orang-utans on the stage. They lend themselves much less readily to the process of training and they appeal less strongly to the public because of their apparent melancholy. The sanguine temperament of the chimpanzee expresses itself in delightful ways, while the appearance of dejection, depression, or discouragement in the orang-utan has the opposite effect. Then, too, the orang-utan is distinctly less well built for dressing up in imitation of man or for most stage tricks. It gives the impression rather of awkwardness than of grace and may repel even those who have become accustomed to the caricature of man which is seen in the chimpanzee.

The reason why performing gorillas are practically non-existent is, I suspect, difficulty in training. Judging from my experience with Congo, I should say it would be an extremely discouraging task to prepare her adequately for a stage performance and to keep her in the mood for exhibition and properly in mind of it. I think it is not so much inability to learn to do what is required as natural resistance to performance of the expected, or as I have elsewhere put it, negativism to human acts and expectations. Coupled with this extraordinary resistance to training is a heaviness, clumsiness, and near awkwardness of build and behavior which tend to disqualify the gorilla for anything except exhibitions of muscular strength. Although these facts apparently are sufficient to account for the gorilla's absence from the vaudeville stage, there must be added the extraordinary difficulty which has been experienced in keeping the animals in health and contentment. Being rare, and therefore expensive, few persons have been able to afford the risk of trying to train and exhibit them.

In order of ability to acquire new adaptations and habit-systems on the basis of trial and error the three types rank: chimpanzee, orang-utan, gorilla; for this mode of profiting by experience seems to depend chiefly on impulsiveness and versatility in action. That creature which with definitely direct-ed attention most thoroughly investigates its environment and tries the largest number of responses to it, has, other things being equal, the best chance of hitting upon the satisfactory mode of response and possibly also of repeating it and thus marking its peculiar value. The young chimpanzee far out-strips its more deliberate cousins in this respect; and the orang-utan in turn is considerably in advance of Congo.

But when it comes to modes of profiting by experience which turn rather on systematic, deliberate examination of the environment, observation of relations, and whatever processes are implied in insight and understanding, it is by no means so clear that the chimpanzee holds first place. I am not prepared to say that it does not, but I am doubtful. Congo has many advantages for what, lacking an adequate objective term, I must call ideational learning. In this variety of adaptation her concentration of attention, deliberateness, and self-depend-ence are unexcelled assets, whereas the impulsiveness of the chimpanzee may be a serious disadvantage. My guess on the basis of the meager data at hand is that the order of dimin-ishing ability for trial and error learning—chimpanzee, orang-utan, gorilla—is the order of increasing ability for ideational learning. Again, however, I should like to substitute an in-terrogation point for the apparently dogmatic period. I sus-pect rather than know, and I realize that we shall have to study the behavior of several individuals of each type of great ape under experimental as well as natural conditions before any such generalization as I have suggested can be made with assurance.

If, however, the gorilla is intellectually more highly devel-oped than the orang-utan or chimpanzee, how can we account for the fact that it has lost relatively in the struggle for ex-istence? We incline to believe that intelligence is a condition of success and survival. If in this we are correct, gorillas perhaps should be more abundant than chimpanzees or orang-utans; yet the opposite is true. I surmise that many other factors than those of intelligence. have operated to extend or restrict the spread of the great apes and to determine their relative abundance. I am not convinced that superiority of intelligence assures human survival, but on the contrary I am prepared to believe that an intellectually superior type of man may from time to time have been swamped by inferior hordes.

There are numerous other superstitions affecting especially our notions about the manlike apes. Among them are the beliefs that these animals cannot be bred in captivity, that they are delicate by comparison with us, peculiarly subject to various human diseases, and on the whole of low resistance and difficult to maintain in health. All of these I venture to class as superstitions, arising from inadequacy of observation and false interpretation. I do not believe from the evidence available that the chimpanzee, orang-utan, or gorilla is physically more delicate than man, less resistant to unfavorable hygienic, nutritional, or other conditions affecting health, or more likely to succumb to respiratory or digestive disorders than are we. Fairness of comparison of course demands that we take into account acquired resistance and immunities. While animals exposed suddenly to the usually unhealthful conditions of captivity have but slight chance to acquire immunities, it is doubtful whether we humans would respond more successfully than they if similarly treated. On precisely the same ground, and with evidence in support of my position at hand, I contend that if maintained in health and comfort, properly nourished and given adequate social environment, the great apes can be bred and reared in captivity. Likewise they are capable of adaptation to climatic conditions precisely as is man. and instead of being limited to tropical existence may be kept anywhere in the world under properly controlled conditions for man's adaptation to extremes of temperature or to the sun is limited, and he manages to exist through a wide range of environments only by the control of conditions for protective purposes. The adaptation of the manlike ape must be similarly conditioned by the use of shelters and by appropriate feeding

The principal mental traits or characteristics of gorilla behavior which have been presented in this report as result of my observation of Congo are summarized below in association with the tentative conclusions which I feel justified in offering.

Congo, a seemingly normal and presumably typical female specimen of *Gorilla beringei*, estimated to be approximately five years of age, was studied intensively by the writer for nearly six weeks. She proved friendly, coöperative, docile— an excellent subject for studies in behavior.

With out-of-doors as a laboratory, and by observation under natural and experimental conditions, a survey of the gorilla's mental traits was made. Attention was given chiefly to modes of adaptation to environmental demands and to affective expressions. Sensory and perceptual phenomena were observed frequently but incidentally.

Contrary to expectation, the subject initially exhibited neither ability nor tendency to use such objects as sticks, wires, or boxes as appliances or aids in adaptation. Eventually, by a combination of initiative and imitation of the experimenter, she learned to use a few objects as tools in certain situations. Evidence appeared that ability to use an object tends to spread from a specific problem-situation to radically different types of situation.

Notable was the slightness of Congo's destructiveness, random activity, curiosity, and imitativeness of the experimenter. Either she inhibited expressions of curiosity or she is decidedly less curious about strange or novel objects and events than are other apes.

Toward the experimenter she appeared to be negativistic, usually refusing to accept suggestions of means or modes of procedure, but sometimes accepting objectives and striving for them in her own way. Only in the case of food and food-seeking activities did she willingly imitate the experimenter. This of course does not prove the absence of a high degree of inter-species imitativeness. If, however, it should appear that gorillas are as little given to imitate one another's acts as was Congo to imitate mine, the word "ape" is peculiarly inappropriate and inapplicable.

In most of the problem-situations Congo worked energetically, diligently, and often with prolonged concentration. She wasted relatively little energy and exhibited, as has not been observed in any other ape, keen appreciation of, and regulation of behavior in accordance with, the value of the prospective reward and the probability of obtaining it.

Whether lacking in affectivity or merely inexpressive of her emotions, she appeared to be strangely calm, placid, even-tempered. and self-dependent. It seemed at times as though she were repressing or inhibiting acts. Especially when confronted with trying situations, such as insoluble problems, disappointment, or disagreeable stimuli, she exhibited often a degree of self-control which was suggestive of stolidity. Her aloofness and air of independence suggested also superiority. She seldom acted impulsively, and a fit of temper such as young chimpanzees and orang-utans frequently exhibit, was never observed.

There appeared in various types of experimental situation marked preference for the right arm and hand, associated with like preference for the use of the left leg and foot. Although Congo was skillful enough in using her hands and feet and apparently possessed normal motor coördination, she lacked, by comparison with other types of ape, interest in mechanical devices, tendency to fool with them, or even to manipulate them with definite intent when they appeared in problem-situations. Neither spontaneously nor imitatively did she, in this investigation, use or learn to manipulate skillfully such devices as hooks, snaps, hasps, and locks.

By means of sticks, ropes, chains, bottles, boxes, a mirror, and other simple appliances, more than a score of novel problems were set for Congo. Most of them she solved eventually, some by what appeared like random action and the selection of profitable acts, others by observation of essential features or relations in the situation and immediate adaptation. Evidences of psycho-physiological processes in the gorilla are abundant and varied. Clearly "trial and error" as a descripton of adaptive procedure is incomplete and frequently in applicable. Often there appear evidences of "critical points" in adaptive endeavor at which the nature of activity suddenly changes. Many of the objective characteristics in these suddenly achieved adaptations are observed in human ideational behavior. It therefore seems probable that the animal experiences insight. Various experiments prove that "out of sight" is not necessarily "out of mind."

Two important points in experimental technique are suggested by my experience with Congo: the one has to do with the preparedness of the experimenter, the other with the supplementation of his observational ability. One who would satisfactorily devise or design problems or other types of experimental situation for the study of a primate, should know intimately the life history, temperament, interests, and chief perceptual configurations of his subject. Ordinarily we put the cart before the horse, excusing our poor logic by saying that we experiment in order to learn how to do so, but belying our apology by failing to repeat our experiments after we have achieved familiarity with our animal subject. When it comes to direct observation and description of the behavior of a primate, even an experienced observer is inadequate. The activity is too rapid, varied, and unexpected, the transitions from method to method and the final solution too sudden and unpredictable. An objective recorder is essential, and a motion picture camera is clearly indicated as an invaluable resource.

LIST OF PUBLICATIONS REFERRED TO IN TEXT

1. Akeley, Carl E. In brightest Africa. 1923, Garden City.
2. Barns, T. Alexander. The wonderland of the eastern Congo. 1922, London.
3. .... Across the great craterland to the Congo. 1923, London.
4. Battell, Andrew. See Purchas.
5. Bowdich, Thomas Edward. Mission from Cape Coast Castle to Ashantee, etc. Pp. 440-441. 1819, London.
6. Bradley, Mary Hastings. On the gorilla trail. 1922, New York.
7. Buffon, Georges L. L. Comte de. Historie naturelle, générale et particulière. Vol. 14. 1766, Paris.
8. .... Supplèment à l'Historie naturelle, générale et particulière. Vol. 7, 1774, Paris.
9. .... Historie naturelle, générale et particulière. Nouvelle édition. Edited by Latreille. Vol. 35. 1799-1808, Paris.
10. Burbridge, Ben. The gorilla hunt. *Forest and Stream,* 1926 (Nov.) pp. 645 ff.
11. Buytendijk, F. J. J. Considérations de psychologie comparée à propos d'expériences faites avec le singe cercopithecus. *Arch. Néer. de Physiol. de l'Homme et des Animaux,* 1920, *5,* 42-88.
12. Du Chaillu, Paul B. Explorations and adventures in equatorial Africa, etc. 1861, London.
13. Elliot, Daniel Giraud. A review of the primates. 1913, New York.
14. Forbes, Henry O. A hand-book of the primates. 1894, London.
15. Garner, Richard L. Gorillas and chimpanzees. 1896, London.
16. Hanno. Periplus: A voyage of discovery down the west African coast, by a Carthaginian admiral of the fifth century B. C. Translated and edited by Wilfred H. Schoff. 1912, Philadelphia.
17. Hartmann, Robert. Die menschenähnlichen Affen. 1876, Berlin.

18. .... Der Gorilla: zoologisch-zootomische Untersuchungen. 1880, Leipzig.
19. Hobhouse, L. T. Mind in evolution. 2nd ed. 1915, London.
20. Köhler, Wolfgang. Intelligenzprüfungen an Menschenaffen. 1921, Berlin.
21. .... The mentality of apes. Trans. from the German by E. Winter. 1925. New York.
22. Kohts, Nadie. Untersuchungen über die Erkenntnisfähigkeiten des Schimpansen. Aus dem zoopsychologischen Laboratorium des Museum Darwinianum in Moskau. (In Russian). Accompanied by a German translation of the summary. 1923, Moscow.
23. Maltby. See Owen.
24. Matschie, Paul. Einen Gorilla aus Deutsch-Ostafrika. *Sitzb. d. Gesell. Natur. Freunde, Berlin,* 1903, 253-259.
25. Monboddo, James Burnet. Of the origin and progress of language. 2nd ed. Vol. 1. 1774, Edinburgh.
26. Ogilby, John. America: being the latest and most accurate description of the New World. 1671, London.
27. Owen, Richard. On the gorilla (*Troglodytes gorilla.* Sav.) *Proc. Zool. Soc. London,* 1859, 1-23. (Owen in this article quotes Maltby's translation of the Hanno reference to *gorillæ*).
28. Purchas, Samuel. Hakluytus Posthumus or Purchas his pilgrimes. 4th ed. Vol. 2, 981-982. 1625, London.
29. Savage, Thomas S. and Wyman, Jeffries. Notice of the external characters and habits of Troglodytes Gorilla, a new species of orang from the Gaboon River. . . . . Osteology of the same. . . . *Bost. Jour. Nat. Hist.,* 1847, 5, 417-443.
30. Sparks, Richard D. Congo: a personality. *Field and Stream,* 1926 (Jan.) pp. 18-20, 72-73.
31. Wilhelm, Prince of Sweden. Among pygmies and gorillas with the Swedish zoological expedition to Central Africa 1921. 1923, London.
32. Yerkes, Robert M. The mental life of monkeys and apes: a study of ideational behavior. *Behav. Monog.,* 1916, 3, no. 1.
33. .... Almost human. 1925, New York.
34. .... and Learned, Blanche W. Chimpanzee intelligence and its vocal expressions. 1925, Baltimore

INDEX

CHILD BEHAVIOR, DIFFERENTIAL AND GENETIC PSYCHOLOGY

Single Nos. $2.00
$7.00 per annum

November, 1927
Volume II, No. 6

GENETIC PSYCHOLOGY MONOGRAPHS

NOVEMBER, 1927

THE MIND OF A GORILLA:
Part II. Mental Development*

BY

ROBERT M. YERKES

Institute of Psychology, Yale University

*Received for publication by Carl Murchison of the Editorial Board.

ACKNOWLEDGMENTS

Comparable with the satisfaction of contributing to knowledge of the psycho-biology of an uniquely interesting primate is my pleasure in thanking those who have made the investigation possible and have contributed to its progress.

For continuance of his disinterested and wise coöperation I am increasingly indebted to Mr. Ben Burbridge. His generous loan of Congo as subject of observation, no less than his sympathetic interest in my work and tactful encouragement, commands my admiration and gratitude.

Once more, Mr. and Mrs. James Burbridge gave the freedom and facilities of Shady Nook, their Jacksonville home, for the conduct of experiments. From her arrival in Florida in October, 1925 until her transfer to Mr. John Ringling in March, 1927, Shady Nook was Congo's home. The Burbridge's was no ordinary contribution of time, labor, and responsibility to the welfare of the gorilla and the furtherance of my study of her. I cannot thank them adequately.

After acquiring control of Congo in February, 1927, Mr. John Ringling kindly permitted the continuance of my experiments at Shady Nook until the middle of March, when he removed the gorilla to Sarasota, Florida. Thereupon he cordially invited the continuance of my investigation during the following winter.

Mr. Richard D. Sparks, who originally proposed and in coöperation with Mr. Carl Akeley arranged with her owner, Mr. Ben Burbridge, for the study of Congo, continued his lively interest in my work and always stood ready to aid in any practicable manner. His rôle, though a self-effacing one, may not justly be overlooked.

But one of those who prepared the way for my work is beyond the reach of praise or appreciation. Carl Akeley, preserver and historian of the mountain gorilla, in March, 1927 was laid to rest on the slopes of Mount Mikeno in the scenes of gorilla life which he had learned to love. Him we may not thank, but his memory we may honor by recognizing the unselfish devotion, determination and persistence, enthusiasm and faith with which to the end he followed his scientific grail. Enduring memorial to his personal sacrifice and to his originality is the Gorilla Sanctuary which, because of his vision and initiative, stands as the very heart of the great "Parc National Albert." The fruits of his labors continue to multiply, although his spirit has escaped.

The Governing Board of the Institute of Psychology, Yale University, heartily approved my plans for further study of Congo, and with funds supplied by the Laura Spelman Rockefeller Memorial and the Rockefeller Foundation adequately financed them.

Acknowledgment is gratefully made also to the Committee for Research in Problems of Sex, National Research Council, whose coöperation with the Primate Laboratory of Yale University made available the photographic recording equipment used in my experiments with Congo.

For skillful assistance with manuscript and proofs I am deeply indebted to my secretary, Mrs. Helen S. Morford, my research assistant, Mrs. Margaret Child Lewis, and Mrs. Yerkes. Mrs. Morford, in addition, accurately transcribed in New Haven all reports of experiments from Ediphone records made in Jacksonville.

CONTENTS

HISTORICAL SETTING AND RELATIONS OF INVESTIGATION

When in the winter of 1926 opportunity came to me to study intensively for a few weeks the mental life of a young mountain gorilla, I hoped for but dared not expect continuance of the availability of the animal and recurrence of opportunity for observation. Happily, I was able to resume the work under identical external conditions just a year later and to carry it forward with steadily increasing satisfaction and success.

The results of the initial period of observation have been published under the title, "The mind of a gorilla" (Yerkes, 1927). In this report, knowledge of the content of that publication will be assumed and repetition avoided by reference, for the two may be considered chapters of a continuing story which it is hoped may carry description of Congo's behavioral development to maturity.

Whereas in 1926, when approximately six weeks were available for the task, I attempted a general survey of the psychobiological traits of the gorilla, in 1927, from the middle of January to the middle of March, I devoted myself especially to aspects of mental development and mnemonic processes. As a matter of course, the results of the initial survey were confirmed or corrected and supplemented by new data on adaptivity and expressivity.

A kindly critic has inferred from the title "The mind of a gorilla" that the writer is interested either solely or primarily in mental phenomena. As a fact, the term mind (and in the present title mental) is used as a protest against what he deems unwarranted and unprofitable assumptions of the cult of behaviorism and as indication that he considers mental, no less than behavioral phenomena, materials of biological science.

With the exception of an account by Ben Burbridge, captor of Congo, of his experiences in hunting, photographing, and capturing mountain gorillas alive (Burbridge, 1926-27), and reviews, nothing to my knowledge bearing directly on the subject of inquiry has been published since the appearance of my first report.[1]

---

[1]For summary account of knowledge of the mental life of the gorilla and of the discovery of the mountain species, the reader is referred to Yerkes, 1927, pp. 19-28.

STATUS OF CONGO, THE SUBJECT OF OBSERVATION

During Congo's sojourn of approximately eighteen months at Jacksonville, Florida, her health was uniformly excellent and she appeared to develop normally and to thrive exceedingly. In the interval between the discontinuance of my observations in February, 1926 and their resumption in January, 1927, she was used for a short time as subject of motion picture studies, some of which were subsequently incorporated in the widely known Burbridge film, "The gorilla hunt," and a few times she was exhibited in a local theatre. Otherwise, hers was a placid, uneventful life at Shady Nook. Housing, feeding, and general care continued essentially as previously described (Yerkes, 1927, pp. 16-18, 29-32). By the beginning of 1927 the animal's rapidly increasing size and strength rendered it unsafe for Mrs. Burbridge to play with or feed her as formerly. Under the supervision of Mr. and Mrs. Burbridge her care therefore was committed increasingly to Bill, the Negro choreman at Shady Nook.

On my return to Jacksonville, January 14, 1927, I at once went to see Congo. As I approached she came to the side of her cage and gazed at me intently and steadily. Surprised by the directness and duration of her stare I returned it. She seemed not in the least disconcerted by my direct and continued inspection, but for an interval of perhaps one to two minutes looked me over carefully, and for a considerable time looked directly into my eyes. The fact is noteworthy because most animals will not meet the human gaze directly for more than a few seconds. There was no affective demonstration or other unmistakable sign that she remembered me. I take it, however, that her very marked interest in me on first appearance is indicative of memory. My suspicion, in this connection, was confirmed on the following day by the behavior described in subsequent paragraphs.

Inasmuch as a few days before my return the gorilla had bitten Bill rather severely on the forearm, I was warned by Mr. Burbridge to be cautious in approaching and handling her. Partly on this account, I contented myself on my first call with renewal of acquaintance through the cage netting. The following day, after first attaching a chain to Congo's collar, I entered her cage and played with her. She was extremely rough but entirely good-natured and made no attempt to harm me. It was on this date, January 15, that I obtained the following additional evidence of memory.

I started to remove a wooden shutter which during my absence had been nailed over the grill at the easterly corner of the cage. Seeing what I was doing, Congo came and assisted by pushing against the shutter from within the cage. Her action was eagerly aggressive and at once aroused my suspicion of interest which had carried over from experiences in our experiments of the previous winter. No sooner had the shutter been removed and the grill thus cleared, than Congo hunted up a stick and bringing it to the grill tried to use it to obtain things outside the cage. This behavior convinced me of memory of certain experimental situations in which she previously had worked.

Before my return to Florida I had been informed by Mr. Burbridge that Congo in a year had nearly doubled in size and weight. I had taken the information light-heartedly and humorously, assuming that it was intended as exaggeration; but it proved to be fact. Indeed, my first glance at Congo convinced me that the task of working with her would be far different from previously. Therefore, prior to planning experimental procedures and construction of apparatus, I made a few observations on size and strength to compare with those of the previous season.

For the strength measurements the situation previously used was employed, but the spatial relations of the parts of the apparatus were necessarily altered in correspondence with the growth of the animal. I promptly discovered that with moderate effort, using both arms but without bracing her feet against anything, Congo could draw two hundred and forty pounds on a spring balance. Despite a score or more of trials under differing conditions of hunger and with slightly varying settings of the apparatus, I never observed maximal effort. My impression from these observations and from my subsequent experience in trying to control and direct her when on leash was that if she had determinedly tried she could have drawn the balance to its limit of three hundred pounds. A year before, her pulling strength was roughly one hundred and sixty pounds, and although my measurements apparently do not justify it, I feel safe in saying that it had approximately doubled within the year (Yerkes, 1927, pp. 14, 82).

Measurement of weight was made by inducing Congo to enter a traveling crate, and thereupon, by means of the spring balance, determining the weight of crate and animal. The procedure was simple since she coöperated perfectly, but because of the inaccuracy of the weighing mechanism a large margin of error must be allowed. Congo's weight in January, 1926 was approximately sixty-five pounds; in January, 1927 it was approximately one hundred and twenty-eight pounds. Eight weeks later, in March, it was nearly ten pounds more, indicating increase of at least one pound per week during my period of work.

Lacking an assistant, and also suitable anthropometric devices, it was impossible for me to obtain reliable physical measurements, but, with an anthropometric tape and other crude aids, I succeeded in obtaining observations which are comparable in accuracy with those I have previously recorded (Yerkes, 1927, pp. 16-17). They are presented below as indication of the remarkable rapidity of growth during what presumably was the fifth or possibly the sixth year of the gorilla's life. This rate exceeds one pound per week in weight and approaches one inch per month in height.

	January 1926		January 1927		March 7, 1927
Weight	65±5	lbs.	128±5	lbs.	137½±5 lbs.
Height, standing	38±1	in.	47±1	in.	
Maximum standing reach with one arm	58	in.	70	in.	
Circumference of wrist	7	in.	9	in.	
Length of foot	8	in.	9½	in.	
Strength of arms	160	lbs.	240	lbs.	

These physical data are significantly related to nutrition. Assimilation was excellent, and appetite keen and unfailing. Ordinarily the animal received during her life in Jacksonville from one to two quarts of milk per day, usually somewhat diluted, and from one to two pounds of baked sweet potato and approximately the same quantity of baked banana. During the acorn season she ate them at will, as they were available under the oak tree to which she was fastened when taken from her cage. She drank little water. Apparently she obtained sufficient exercise to maintain excellent physical condition, but it presumably was much less than would have been necessary for existence in her native habitat.

Scarcely less remarkable than her physical growth was Congo's psycho-biological development during her first year in Florida. It appeared in almost every comparison of her behavior in the winter of 1926 with that in the winter of 1927. General adaptivity had increased markedly. There was obviously greater interest in problematic situations and in the experimenter as part of the general environment as well as of specific experimental situations. Whereas during the first period of observation there were no unmistakable indications of sex interest, it was noted during the second period in her play with dogs, and in other signs of approaching adolescence. There were also marked changes in sensory-motor ability and in motor coördination: witness, the more persistent and efficient handling of sticks and other objects as implements. Interest in environmental objects and events, curiosity, imitativeness and destructiveness, all had changed notably, and generally by increase. Even apart from her extraordinary changes in physical appearance, Congo gave one the impression of greater maturity and of correspondingly larger store of adaptations. That this impression was not illusory is proved by the results of the experiments which are to be reported.

The reader may find it interesting and helpful to compare the portraits and representations of Congo at work in experiments which are presented in the two reports. In varied ways they supplement the verbal descriptions and comparisons. As it is impracticable to compare in detail the results obtained during the two periods of observation, it is hoped that the reports may be considered as one. Assuredly, the second cannot be understood except by use of the first, and certainly also the first is supplemented in varied and important ways by the second.

ESSENTIAL FEATURES OF THE OBSERVATIONAL
SITUATION

The scene of investigation was the same in 1926 and 1927.
During both winters Shady Nook proved aesthetically and
scientifically an ideal spot for work or play, and equally con-
genial apparently to subject and observer. Except that Congo's
cage had been reënforced to guarantee her security, no changes
affecting the observational situation had been made. Nor had
the personnel changed, for Mr. and Mrs. Burbridge were in
residence, Bill was regularly on duty, and as formerly, Mr.
Ben Burbridge made frequent visits to Shady Nook.

Climatically the two periods of work were extremely different. The winter of 1925-26 was exceptionally wet and
cold; that of 1926-27, unusually dry and warm. The first
was trying to the gorilla because she occasionally suffered
discomfort from the cold, and to the observer because frequent rains interfered with work in his out-of-doors laboratory.
By contrast, the second winter was altogether comfortable and
delightful for subject and observer, and highly favorable for
work. The contrast which has been indicated appears no less
emphatically in the following quantitative data.

	1926	1927
Average temperature, 9 a. m.	51°	59°
Range of temperature	38-68°	31-74°
Average temperature, 12 noon	57°	69°
Range of temperature	42-70°	42-81°

In 1926 about one-fifth of the days were rainy, and of the
remainder approximately one-half were cloudy. By contrast,
in 1927 one-eighth was the proportion of rainy days, and cloudy
days were rare.

Quite as important probably, for the success of observational work, as the favorable meterological conditions was the
following change in the nature of the experimental situation.
During the first winter the majority of experiments were ar-

ranged at the grill so that Congo could work within her cage while the observer controlled the situation and recorded results outside. A few experiments were made under one or other of the oak trees near the cage, with the subject moored to a conveniently placed stake. Chiefly because of my greater familiarity with the characteristics and capacities of the gorilla and confidence in my ability to control to advantage both the observational situation and the animal, I ventured during the second winter to arrange the majority of problematic situations under the trees instead of at the grill (see plates 4 and 5 especially).

Because of Congo's markedly increased strength, aggressiveness, and destructiveness, it was found necessary to use in 1927 much larger and more resistant apparatus than in 1926. Several of the boxes and sticks which had served satisfactorily during the first period of observation were quickly destroyed when presented in 1927. A broomstick, for instance, which came through the original pipe-and-stick experiment none the worse for wear, was promptly and easily broken in half when offered for use a year later. Size, stability, resistance of apparatus, all had to be proportionately increased. This fact was promptly grasped by the experimenter and the necessary adaptations were made.

For experiments which were conducted outside the cage in the open, the procedure in general was as follows. A chain approximately ten feet long was attached by a spring snap to the ring of a stout leather collar which Congo continuously wore. Thereupon the gorilla was conducted either from her cage or from site of previous outdoor experiment to the experimental situation in which it was desired to observe her. She there was moored to a stake which had been driven into the ground in definite spatial relation to the apparatus of the experiment, and arrangements having previously been made for a trial, the observer took his customary position and noted the behavior of the animal. At the beginning of each day's work it usually required patience and caution to attach the leash without mishap, for Congo even after weeks of work refused to come at command to have the chain attached but instead persisted in making a rough game of the performance. This seldom was dangerous to the experimenter, but frequently it was wasteful of time and involved uncomfortable risks. The transfers from one mooring stake to another were effected more easily and expeditiously, for whether she had succeeded or failed in a given experiment she usually was eager for change of scene and therefore welcomed transfer.

Except as otherwise stated in descriptions of experimental procedure, Congo, if she wished, observed preparations for experiments. Ordinarily they involved arrangement of apparatus so that its essential parts were in predetermined positions and relations, and the placement of lure or reward. In all situations uniformity of arrangement was striven for. Undoubtedly her interest in the problematic situations was increased by their visibility during the experimenter's manipulation of apparatus in preparation for trials. One naturally, in a suitable laboratory, would prevent the subject from observing the setting of an experiment, unless it were desired to discover the influence of such observation on behavior. However, there are advantages and disadvantages in either case, and the question of desirability in my work with Congo often was definitely settled by necessity, for in many instances it was either impossible or impracticable to prevent the subject from seeing or hearing what was necessarily done in preparation for an experiment.

In most of the out-of-the-cage experiments the gorilla was given a range of six to ten feet, and as her arm reach enabled her to go considerably beyond the length of the mooring chain she was able to work in a circle of fifteen to twenty-five feet diameter. The observer, with notebook and recording cameras at hand, ordinarily sat about fifteen feet from the mooring stake, which was the center of operations. In this position he usually was able to observe clearly and appropriately to record Congo's behavior in the problematic situation. When she was working in her cage, either through the feeding-door or through the grill, the position of the observer was five to fifteen feet from her. Wherever it seems essential in the following descriptions of experiments, specific information will be given on such points as are mentioned in the above paragraphs.

With a few exceptions, which are specifically noted, experiments were made between eight-thirty in the morning and two in the afternoon. Congo almost always worked willingly and often eagerly in as many as six or eight different problems and over a period of three to five hours each day. There were, of course, intervals between experiments required for the recording of observations, the preparation of apparatus, and the transfer of the subject. In general, her attitude toward an experimental situation varied more markedly with the nature of the problem and its relation to her adaptive ability or expectation of success than with the hour or the length of time she had been working. In a newly presented experiment she usually worked most energetically and determinedly at the beginning of the trial, and if success was not achieved or clearly approached she tended after a few minutes to abandon her attempts, either temporarily and for a rest interval or for the remainder of the fixed period of observation. Not rarely, however, even after some minutes of inattention to her task, she would return to it with energy and evident determination and hopefulness.

With respect to motivation, it should be said that during the second winter, as during the first, reliance was placed almost wholly on hunger and desire to escape from the experiment either to the more familiar cage or to the oak tree to which the animal was moored daily in order that she might climb about for exercise. In both seasons food proved a highly satisfactory incentive. It was not necessary to starve Congo, or even to deprive her of food for unusually long periods, in order to have her work energetically. Instead, as previously stated (Yerkes, 1927, pp. 34-35), during the course of the morning's work the regular ration for both breakfast and the midday meal was used as reward for success. Initially a pint of milk was given early in the morning before my arrival at Shady Nook, but when it became desirable even this was withheld until the beginning of the day's work. Baked banana, baked sweet potato, and occasionally orange, apple, and milk, were used as rewards. The significance of quantity, quality, and location of food appears in connection with descriptions of specific experiments.

Although stronger motivation at various times might have increased her eagerness and effort for the solution of a problem, it is by no means self-evident, nor would it be fair to assume, that it would necessarily favor quicker or more nearly adequate solution. There is abundant indication that in many, if not all, organisms an optimal condition of work in problematic situations exists and that the combination of factors experimentally or otherwise arranged to induce motivation may fall either below or above this optimum. Prior to definite proof of the fact, I should not be willing to admit that in my experiments Congo usually worked with sub-optimal motivation. On the other hand, I feel reasonably certain that she rarely worked under super-optimal conditions, and I am even more certain that occasionally she was inadequately motivated.

Given her evening meal between five and six o'clock and introduced to the first experimental problem of the day about nine o'clock the following morning, she usually, as result of approximately fifteen hours without food, was very eager for it. It then became the task of the experimenter so to apportion the regular ration and manage the other conditions of experimentation that motivation should continue at a satisfactory level throughout several hours of intermittent work in a variety of situations. This was done in ways which varied in accordance with the program of the day and the nature of the several experiments. As a rule, the rewards initially given were relatively small, and if at the end of the day's work Congo had not received her regular quantity of food, it was given to her in her cage. It is important to note that in the majority of experiments on a given day, she failed to solve her problem and consequently received no reward. Ordinarily the daily program was so arranged that failures and successes should approximately equal one another and be distributed throughout the total period of work. In certain experiments, as for example wound chain, box and pole, box stacking, and delayed response, extraordinarily large quantities of food were occasionally presented as prospective rewards. This was in itself an experiment and is so considered in the descriptions which follow.

It may not be assumed that food and escape from the experimental situation were the sole, or indeed necessarily the most important, factors in motivation. Actually, as evidenced by behavior, motivation was suprisingly complex, variable, and in many instances dominated by conditions which the observer would not have expected to prove important. As examples of such factors, mention may be made of the subject's mood and emotional attitude toward the experimenter, her previous experience in the general situation in which the experiment happened to be set, and her previous experience in the particular experiment. Any one of these factors, or assemblages of factors, might in a given trial dominate and completely overshadow the food lure.

Motivating conditions are especially mentioned because in adverse criticism of my previous experiments with Congo it has been suggested that she could not reasonably be expected to exhibit, under the easy and assured conditions of life and experimentation at Shady Nook, the modes and degrees of adaptivity which she might show in the more exacting conditions of her native habitat. This critical surmise may be correct, but on the other hand it may presently be demonstrated that the opposite is true. In any event, it is possible for us psycho-biologists to maintain fairly comparable conditions of work with the several types of anthropoid ape and with man, and it is peculiarly significant in this connection that objective rewards which failed to induce adaptation to certain situations in Congo, commonly do so in the chimpanzee. Obviously it is the task of the psycho-biologist to study not only adaptation, in its varied modes and aspects, but also motivation, for knowledge of its factors, their values and relations is indispensable.

OBJECTIVES, PLAN OF WORK, AND LIST OF EX-PERIMENTS

The primary objective in continuing observation of the gorilla was completion of general account of the psycho-biological traits of the individual, but as secondary aim appeared the desire to observe the changes in reactive tendency and capacity associated with growth and development. It is hoped now that it may be possible to observe Congo periodically until she is physically mature. Assuming that she was approximately five years old when first observed, she was in her sixth year during the last period of observation. There are evidences, later recorded, which suggest approach to adolescence, so it is possible that I have under-estimated her age. Mr. Ben Burbridge, however, disagrees with me in that he believes she is at least a year younger than I have estimated.

In the winter of 1927 I attempted to verify, correct, and supplement previous observations, to follow the development of processes previously observed, and to note the appearance and characteristics of others. Since the general survey of traits originally contemplated was well advanced, it was possible to work somewhat more intensively on certain problems. It was decided to concentrate attention on behavior involving representational processes, and especially on memory reactions.

As a most natural means of obtaining a measure of the behavioral development of Congo during the year I decided to re-present most of the types of problematic situation in which she had been given opportunity to work the previous winter. In many instances this required little time, because of immediate perfect adaptation to the situation, but in other cases solution of problems continued to be difficult or impossible and often observations were continued over several days.

Wherever opportunity offered in connection with repetition of experiments, promising forms of variation were introduced and former experiments were supplemented by new ones. As the work advanced the new experiments came to predominate, and in the final weeks of work, attention was devoted almost wholly to experiments on mnemonic processes.

The methods employed were, as formerly, crude and capable of yielding with few exceptions only qualitative results.[2] Certain progress, however, was made toward the development and application of more exact methods. Especially in the study of memory responses, quantitative data were obtained. Naturally it was impossible to make other than rough measurements of the changes in reactive tendency exhibited by the gorilla. Yet in many instances these changes were so marked as to justify dogmatic statement.

For the convenience of the reader in seeing at a glance the program of experiments and essential facts concerning the presentation of each of the several problematic situations, a *chronological* list, comparable with that of the previous report (Yerkes, 1927, pp. 38-40), is offered herewith. By consultation of this list one may discover in order, on the first line, the number, name or title, relation to the series of 1926, and location of the experiment. Beneath follow in sequence the number (figure in parenthesis), date, hour, and duration of each trial. In a few instances the duration of trial lacks significance and is omitted.

For some experiments a number of variations or forms are indicated. Thus, for example, no. 7, box and pole, is recorded as a new experiment, that is, one not presented to Congo the previous winter, which was used in three forms: first, as offering the animal opportunity for solution by its own initiative, and therefore indicated, following (a), as *initiative;* second, as presented with imitative copy set by the experimenter, and therefore designated, following (b), as *imitation,* and third,

---

[2] Acknowledgment should be made to Hobhouse (1915) for suggestion of several forms of problematic situation.

with tuitional aid supplied by the experimenter, designated as (c), *tuition*. Similarly, in certain other experiments there appear two or three variations. Where in addition to initiative, imitation or tuition appeared, the first form of experiment is regularly designated by the term initiative, the second by imitation, and the third by tuition; but in other cases, for example, no. 14, wound chain, the word variation, with appropriate letter, is employed. Thus, in the instance cited, the initial form of the experiment is recorded as no. 14 (a), and a modification thereof as no. 14 (b), variation A.

Following the title of each experiment is a number or the word new in parenthesis. The number indicates the experiment of the original report which is identical with the present experiment or most closely resembles it. Use of the word new indicates an experiment not previously presented.

Experiments were conducted in so many different locations about Shady Nook, and location is so obviously important by reason of associated successes or failures, that it has seemed desirable to adopt a system of symbols and to indicate, both in the following list of experiments and in text descriptions of problems, the observational location. The following definitions of abbreviated designations are here presented for reference: Tree 1 designates the home tree, that to which Congo was regularly moored when taken from her cage for fresh air and exercise. Tree 2 designates an oak adjacent to Tree 1 and some five yards northerly of it. Tree 3 designates one some ten yards northerly of the cage. It was the site of many of the out-of-doors experiments in 1926 and 1927. Tree 4 designates an oak some twenty-five yards northerly of the cage under which during 1927 the box problems were arranged.

List of problems with dates of presentation

1. Shelf and stick (1). In cage.
   (1) Jan. 17, 12:07, 3'; (2) 18, 9:32, 3'.
2. Hooked rope (3). In cage.
   (1) Jan. 18, 12:15, 30"; (2) 19, 9:16, 1'; (3) 20, 9:39, 1'; (4) 21, 10:04, 10"; (5) 22, 12:05, 5".

3. Platform and stick (4). In cage.
    (1) Jan. 19, 9:30, 1' 30", (2) 12:15, 7'; (3) 20, 9:44, 2';
    (4) 21, 10:07, 20"; (5) 22, 12:06, 20'.
4. Suspended food and stick (8). Under Tree 3.
    (1) Jan. 19, 10:40, 16'; (2) 20, 10:20, 5'; (3) 21, 9:19,
    1'; (4) 22, 11:11, 10', (5) 11:53, 8'.
5. Pipe and stick or rod (9); (a) initiative, (b) imitation.
    Under Tree 3.
    (a) (1) Jan. 21, 9:25, 30'; (2) 22, 11:22, 30'.
    (b) (1) Jan. 23, 10:32, 30'; (2) 24, 10:25, 30'.
6. Suspended food and auxiliary stick (new). Under Tree 3.
    (1) Jan. 23, 9:40, 56'; (2) 24, 9:40, 41'; (3) 25, 9:35,
    41'; (4) 26, 9:38, 41'; (5) 28, 9:25, 24'; (6) 29, 9:27,
    20'; (7) 30, 10:11, 25'; (8) 31, 9:55, 13'; (9) Feb. 1,
    9:41, 40'; (10) 2, 9:21, 17' 30"; (11) 3, 9:42, 4'; (12)
    4, 10:13, 2'; (13) 5, 10:50, 2'; (14) 6, 10:15, 2'; (15) 11,
    10:56, 3'.
7. Box and pole (new); (a) initiative, (b) imitation, (c)
    tuition. Under Tree 3.
    (a) (1) Jan. 25, 10:25, 30'; (2) 26, 10:24, 30'; (3) 28,
    10:00, 30'; (4) 29, 9:53, 30'; (5) 30, 10:43, 30'; (6)
    31, 10:13, 30'.
    (b) (1) Feb. 1, 10:24, 23'; (2) 2, 10:20, 25'; (3) 3,
    9:52, 26'; (4) 4, 10:20, 25'; (5) 5, 10:58, 12'; (6) 6,
    10:25, 13'; (7) 7, 9:43, 22'; (8) 8, 9:56, 22'.
    (c) (1) Feb. 9, 9:20, 16', (2) 9:45, 33"; (3) 10, 9:22,
    11'; (4) 11, 9:48, 13'; (5) 12, 9:52, 18', (6) 10:12, 15',
    (7) 10:34, 12', (8) 10:50, 12'; (9) 13, 9:55, 16', (10)
    10:12, 16', (11) 10:30, 11', (12) 10:43, 11'; (13) 14,
    9:44, 6'; (14) 15, 9:32, 14', (15) 9:48, 11', (16) 10:06,
    1', (17) 10:09, 2', (18) 10:15, 2'; (19) 17, 9:13, 5', (20)
    9:20, 30", (21) 9:24, 2', (22) 9:27, 28".
8. Hasp and padlock (11). In cage.
    (1) Jan. 24, 10:58, 15'; (2) 25, 11:05, 15'; (3) 26, 9:21,
    15'; (4) 28, 10:40, 15'; (5) 29, 10:41, 15'; (6) 30, 11:35,
    38", (7) 11:37, 55"; (8) 31, 11:20, 1'27", (9) 11:25,
    48"; (10) Feb. 1, 11:22, 4', (11) 11:27, 27"; (12) 2,
    11:12, 19", (13) 11:14, 4"; (14) 3, 11:25, 49"; (15) 4,
    11:52, 30"; (16) 5, 12:16, 15"; (17) March 2, 12:35,
    3"; (18) 3, 9:45, m. p. r.[3]
9. Spring snap (new); (a) initiative, (b) imitation. Under
    Tree 3 or in cage.

---

[3]M. p. r. stands for motion picture record.

(a) (1) Jan. 25, 10:25, 30'; (2) 26, 10:24, 30'; (3) 28, 10:00, 30'; (4) 29, 9:53, 30'; (5) 30, 10:43, 30'; (6) 31, 10:13, 30'; (7) Feb. 1, 10:24, 23'; (8) 2, 10:20, 25', (9) 10:55, 3", (10) 10:56, 15'; (11) 3, 11:09, 15'; (12) 4, 11:35, 15'; (13) 5, 12:00, 15'.

(b) (1) Feb. 7, 10:33, 10'; (2) 8, 10:38, 10'; (3) 9, 10:20, 10'; (4) 10, 10:05, 10'; (5) 11, 11:06, 10'; (6) 12, 11:29, 10'; (7) 13, 11:34, 10'; (8) 15, 10:27, 10'; (9) 17, 10:26, 10'; (10) 18, 11:12, 10'; (11) 19, 10:55, 10'; (12) 20, 9:14, 55"; (13) 21, 9:13, 11'; (14) 22, 8:54, 14'; (15) 23, 9:47, 9'; (16) 25, 8:44, 21"; (17) 26, 8:55, 56"; (18) 27, 9:15, 14"; (19) 28, 8:50, 8"; (20) March 2, 12:30, 32". M. p. r. Feb. 21 and March 3.

10. Greatest dimension of box (23). Trials 1 and 2 under Tree 3; trial 3 under Tree 4.
(1) Jan. 26, 11:21, 9'; (2) 28, 10:35, 45"; (3) Feb. 28. 9:52, 1'.

11. Diagonal rope (2). In cage.
(1) Jan. 28, 11:15, 5". M. p. r. March 3.

12. Box stacking with two boxes (23). Trial 1 under Tree 3; trial 2 under Tree 4.
(1) Jan. 29, 10:30, 1'; (2) March 1, 9:27, 4'52".

13. Box stacking with three boxes (new). Under Tree 4, except preliminary trial, which was under Tree 3.
(Preliminary trial) Jan. 30, 11:20, 10'; (1) Jan. 31, 10:46, 30'; (2) Feb. 1, 10:50, 30'; (3) 2, 9:45, 30'; (4) 3, 10:28, 30'; (5) 4, 9:40, 30'; (6) 5, 9:45, 60'; (7) 6, 9:33, 21'; (8) 7, 10:10, 2'10"; (9) 8, 10:20, 15'; (10) 11, 10:20, 30'; (11) 13, 11:05, 8'; (12) March 2, 9:29, 3'12".

14. (a) Wound chain (20), under Tree 2; (b) Variation A, under Tree 1.
(a) (1) Feb. 3, 11:33, 1'; (2) 4, 10:55, 30'; (3) 5, 11:25, 30'; (4) 6, 10:55, 30'; (5) 9, 10:52, 30'; (6) 10, 9:38, 10'; (7) 11, 11:22, 30'; (8) 12, 11:54, 30'; (9) 13, 11:55, 30'; (10) 15, 10:43, 30'; (11) 17, 10:39, 30'; (12) 18, 11:59, 30'; (13) 19, 10:02, 7'; (14) 20, 10:39, 20"; (15) 21, 11:23, 30'; (16) March 5, 12:30, 30'.
(b) (1) Feb. 7, 10:52, 30"; (2) 8, 10:51, 10"; (3) 9, 10:41, 12", (4) 11:25, 9"; (5) 10, 9:49, 1'; (6) 11, 11:53, 1'; (7) 12, 12:28, 1'; (8) 13, 12:43, 14'; (9) 17, 11:10, 1'; (10) 18, 11:50, 6'; (11) 19, 1:01, 20"; (12) March 5, 1:20, 7'.

15. (a) Milk bottle (6); (b) Variation A. Under Tree 1.
(a) (1) Feb. 4, 12:00, 15"; (2) 5, 12:30, 1'5".
(b) (1) Feb. 20, 1:10; (2) 21, 1:20; (3) 22, 1:06; (4) 23, 1:10; (5) 25, 1:25; (6) 26, 1:28; (7) 28, 12:38; (8) March 1, 11:30; (9) 2, 12:40; (10) 3, 12:15; (11) 4, 12:55; (12) 5, 1:01; (13) 6, 12:15; (14) 7, 12:10; (15) 8, 12:30; (16) 9, 12:00.

16. Slot box (new); (a) with hand, (b) with stick. Under Tree 3.
(a) (1) Feb. 8, 9:40, 6' 30"; (2) 9, 10:04, 47"; (3) 11, 10:05, 5"; (4) 13, 10:58, 1'; (5) 23, 9:35, 3' 10"; (6) 26, 10:47, 14'; (7) 27, 11:20, 4' 30".
(b) (1) Feb. 18, 9:42, 30'; (2) 20, 9:40, 30'; (3) 21, 10:31, 30'.

17. Delayed response (new). Under Tree 3.
Table of trials in this experiment, with essential details, is given on page 485.

18. Box and pole to pipe and rod transfer (new). Near Tree 4.
(1) Feb. 18, 9:06, 28'; (2) 20, 11:25, 25'; (3) 21, 10:23, 1' 18"; (4) 22, 10:04, 1' 3"; complication experiment, March 8, 9:15, 15' (see p. 423).

19. Box stacking with four boxes (new). Under Tree 4.
(1) Feb. 21, 12:05, 30'; (2) 22, 10:14, 30'; (3) 23, 9:45, 30'; (4) 25, 9:43, 30'; (5) 26, 11:05, 30'; (6) 27, 10:47, 30'; (7) March 2, 10:23, 30'; (8) 4, 10:00, 30'; (9) 5, 9:51, 60'; (10) 6, 9:27, 15'; (11) 7, 8:37, 15'; (12) 8, 9:33, 3' 21"; (13) 9, 9:30, 28'.

20. Buried food (like 7, but for different purpose). Specified locations.
(1) March 1, 9:45, to March 2, 9:20, 4'; March 2, 9:40, to March 4, 9:55, 5'; March 4, 11:00 to March 5, 1:05, 10'; March 8, 10:00, to March 10, 9:45, 15'.

21. Mirror (18). East of Tree 3.
(1) March 4, 12:00, 10'; (2) 5, 10:55, 10'; (3) 6, 9:47, 10'; (4) 7, 8:55, 10'; (5) 8, 9:45, 10'.

22. Round-about course, with stick (new). In cage.
(1) March 9, 8:32, 30', (2) 11:10, 30'; (3) 10, 8:33, 30'.

The reader who for any reason desires to consider the experimental program of a given day, the work which preceded or followed a given trial, the number of trials in a given situation, the duration of a trial, the total amount of time given to a certain problem, or similar information which may

prove important in evaluating results or in studying the relations of performance in one problematic situation to that in
another, will find the information contained in the "list of
problems" indispensable. The data have been assembled and
presented in tabular form for the sake of condensation, and
in reading the description of an experiment it is desirable
that one may refer to and review the appropriate data given in
the list of problems.

In the account of observations which follows, space is econ-
omized as far as possible by reference to the original report
for descriptions of apparatus and arrangement of experimental
situation. In most instances certain modifications of the original situation were necessitated by the changes in Congo, but
for several of the experiments it was possible to use the appliances which had been prepared the previous winter.

V

USE OF STICK, OR FUNCTIONAL SUBSTITUTE, AS IMPLEMENT

Whereas when I first began to work with Congo in the winter of 1926, she exhibited no aptitude for using sticks or functionally similar objects as implements, at the beginning of the second period of work she used various objects freely, eagerly, and with notably greater facility. At least three assemblages of factors suggest themselves as possible conditions of this behavioral change: (1) previous experience in experiments which demanded the use of sticks; (2) effects of association with man, and (3) psycho-physiological growth and development. Although it is impossible to segregate and evaluate the contributory factors or conditions, it is almost certain that these three are important. It seems logical to place experience in experiments first, but it is possible that development is of even greater importance. My observations indicate the lesser and subordinate significance of association with man and observation of his actions.

Problem 1. Shelf and stick. It was with great difficulty that Congo was at first induced to use a stick in securing food. Indeed, in the initial problematic situation, shelf and stick, which stands as problem 1 in the current list as well as in the previous one, she failed completely in 1926. In the repetition experiments this simple situation was presented first of all with reward thirty-six to thirty-eight inches from the feeding-door in end of cage. When on January 17, five minutes after a hard-wood stick twenty-four inches in length had been placed in her nest-room, the door giving access to the shelf had been opened and one-half of an apple thus exposed to view, Congo came, repeatedly reached for it, tried to squeeze through the doorway; then desisted, went to the grill and there sat for a few seconds. Soon she returned to the shelf with a bit of stick about six inches long which, while sitting at the grill, she had picked up from the floor of the cage. With this she reached vainly for the apple. Finally, she threw it toward the food so that it was beyond her reach. Withdrawing from the doorway, she now walked first toward the grill, then toward the nest-room. Near the porch of the latter lay the 24-inch stick where she had dropped it after playing with it in the room. Picking it up she walked quietly to the feeding-door and pushed it through the opening to use it on the shelf. Her first attempt was unsuccessful, but in her second, holding the stick with her right hand, she touched the apple by sweeping the stick toward her left and gradually pushed it along until it came into contact with the left side-rail of the shelf. Along this she carefully drew it until it was some twenty-eight inches from her, when with her right hand she reached it readily and carried it away to devour.

Although in this experiment she did not seem especially hungry, she nevertheless worked eagerly, and after obtaining the apple ate it. The total time of the trial was three minutes, but of this less than one minute was used in obtaining the reward after the stick had been carried to the shelf. The observation clearly demonstrates that ability to use a stick as implement, in the interim between the shelf and stick experiments of 1926 and the observation herein recorded, transferred from other problematic situations to this particular situation. Never previously had she succeeded in obtaining food from the shelf by use of a stick. She was given no aid whatever in this experiment, and her initiative and success surprised the observer, whose prediction it was that she would not use the stick as implement and under the conditions of experimentation could not succeed, even by brute strength, in obtaining the reward.

The shelf and stick experiment was repeated on January 18 with the difference that a large sweet potato was used as reward instead of piece of apple. Congo's behavior in this trial is, I think, clearly indicative of the developmental status of her ability to act ideationally. When the situation was presented, she went to the feeding-door and reached for the potato with her left hand. Failing, she went to the grill, then to the nest-room, thence back to the shelf and reached with her right hand, then again with her left hand, with which she next pushed toward the potato a bit of straw which she had carried to the shelf. Two minutes after the beginning of the trial she walked from the feeding-door directly to the 24-inch stick, which lay on the floor of the cage, and taking it up returned to the shelf where after a few seconds of awkward effort she succeeded in pushing it through the door and then, grasping it with her right hand, in sweeping the potato within reach. The total time for the second trial in the shelf and stick experiment was three minutes, but of this interval only a few seconds were actually required for success by use of the stick.

Image or other representation of the stick as an essential feature of the situation apparently was not at first in her mind. Indeed, she spent the first two minutes of the trial in the vain use of methods which she had persistently tried during the previous winter. To the observer it seemed as though she had failed in the experiment before she turned to the stick, but on the other hand it may be that she actually turned away from the door in search of the stick instead of merely going in its direction and happening to observe it. From the totality of my observations I am of the opinion that she is somewhere between the concrete stage of adaptive ability which would require presentation of the stick as condition of use and the definite representative stage in which it might be sought in response to mental content. Although her behavior in this experiment is by no means so strongly suggestive of the functioning of images or other representational processes as is that of the chimpanzee in comparable problematic situations, this may be largely because of the more leisurely way in which the gorilla proceeds and her apparent lack of intense interest and eagerness.

As no obvious reason for additional repetitions of this experiment appeared, the shelf was removed after the second trial in order that the feeding-door might be used conveniently when it was necessary to feed Congo in the cage.

Problem 3. Platform and stick. For repetition of this experiment which appears as no. 4 in the original list, a platform was constructed before the grill and on it were securely nailed guard rails to prevent food or other objects from being swept off as Congo attempted to obtain them with sticks or other implements. The space between the side-rails was forty-five inches; the distance from the grill to the rail parallel with it and between the side-rails was fifty-six inches. Originally, in 1926, Congo solved the platform and stick problem with the tuitional aid of the experimenter and after a prolonged series of attempts, which exhibited not only her inability to imagine the stick as an essential feature of the situation, but also her utter incapacity to direct and control it when she attempted to bring it into contact with the desired food and by its manipulation draw the food within her grasp. It is needless to review the story of ontogenetic development in connection with this problematic situation which appears on pages 45-56 of the earlier report. Instead I shall describe the results of repetition of the experiment after an interval of one year. The conditions were essentially as follows.

Previous to placing food on the platform, the narrow door at the east side of the nest-room was opened and propped up by means of a 12-inch stick. Then the 24 by 2 by 1 inch stick which was regularly used in both the shelf and stick and the platform and stick experiments was placed within and close to the south wall of the nest-room. This was done quietly and without effort to attract Congo's attention. Nevertheless she evidently noticed the opening of the door, although she did not come to the nest-room. Approximately one minute after placing the sticks as above described, I put a banana on the platform thirty-two inches from the grill and called Congo from the east side bench to get the food. She came, looked at it, but did not reach for it. Instead, she pushed and threw some bits of paper toward it. After some fifteen seconds she turned and *ran* to the nest-room, removed the prop from the door, and with it and the other stick returned directly and quickly to the grill, where she immediately began her characteristically clumsy efforts to sweep the banana toward her with the stick. First she held both sticks in her right hand and used them as one. Later she pushed the sticks as well as the banana beyond her reach and it was necessary for me to replace them in order that she might continue her work. This I did four times before she finally succeeded in drawing the banana within reach. All the while her intent was clear and definite; her execution crude.

In commenting on the results of this trial I wrote in my notes: The use of a stick for reaching and drawing things toward her is now well established as a visual-motor coördination, and execution has markedly improved since last winter, but ability to direct and control the movement of the stick is still imperfect. As in the previous season's trials, Congo in this repetition held the stick in her right hand and sweeping the food toward her left drew it within reach along the left side-rail.

Since from repetition of this experiment only increase in skill might reasonably be expected, it was decided to vary the problem in order to discover whether Congo would definitely search for sticks to use as aids when none were visible or to be found in usual places. Therefore in the second trial, which as indicated in the list of experiments, p. 398, was presented on the same date as trial 1, namely January 19, beginning at 12:15, the observational situation was thus prepared.

While she was moored to an oak tree some twenty-five feet from the cage, three sticks were placed in unusual positions in the cage: (1) a 36-inch broomstick on a ledge above the house-bench; (2) a 24-inch stick on the roof of the nest-room close to the rear of the cage, and (3) a second 24-inch stick on the floor of the porch close to the west side of the cage. She was then brought to the cage and saw a banana and a small sweet potato placed on the platform thirty-six inches from the grill. She looked at the food for a time without making effort to obtain it, meantime sitting or lying on the floor of her cage before the grill. At 12:21 she walked directly across the cage to the house-bench and taking up the broomstick which had been placed there, returned with it directly to the grill and with evident purpose succeeded in about half a minute in obtaining both the banana and sweet potato. The stick was held in her right hand and the food drawn along the left edge of the platform.

Although it is impossible to say whether the stick was in mind when Congo got up and walked toward the house bench, her alertness and quickness of vision were notable, for the stick was in an unusual and relatively inconspicuous position, and moreover it was of entirely different sort from those which she had previously used on the platform.

For the third trial, similarly, a stick was placed in an unusual position. This time it was the broomstick, outside the open side-door of the nest-room and at one corner of the door some eighteen inches from the opening. It was so placed that Congo could see it as she looked through the doorway, but could reach it only with difficulty. The stick was placed without her knowledge. In further preparation for the trial a whole banana was placed on the platform thirty inches from the grill. So far as observed, she had not noticed the broomstick prior to her approach to the grill and her initial efforts to obtain the banana. These involved reaching and pushing bits of grass and straw toward the food. Once also she pulled at the right side-rail as if to loosen it for use. Suddenly she paused in her half-hearted efforts, hesitated a few seconds, and turning toward the house-bench walked toward it, looking directly at the spot where the broomstick had been placed in trial 2 on the previous day. Thence she went directly to the nest-room, glancing about the cage as she progressed. Entering the room she reached through the doorway, grasped the broomstick, and hastily returned with it to the grill. With her left hand she poked it through the grill, and then seizing it with her right hand swept the banana toward the left, and with a single movement drew it within reach. This was done with exceptional skill and with evident satisfaction. The performance was recorded by the observer as excellent in its adaptive features and affording unusual evidence of the functioning of representative processes. It seemed indeed as though she had the idea, or equivalent, of using the stick and went in search of it.

In preparation for the fourth trial, while Congo was out of the cage and also out of sight, I placed the broomstick on the west side of the cage outside the netting but with one end projecting for about three inches into the cage just above the house-bench. As viewed from within the cage the stick was inconspicuous. It had not previously been placed in this or similar positions.

Congo, after being returned to the cage, entered the nest-room. While she was there a piece of sweet potato was placed on the platform and she was called to the grill. As, in response to the call, she ran out of the nest-room she swerved abruptly toward the house-bench, drew the broomstick through the netting, and without even pausing rushed with it to the grill and with a single stroke of the stick, held in her right hand, swept the potato to her. The total time from call to work to success was approximately twenty seconds, and the performance was in every observed respect perfect. I had no idea that she had even noticed the stick in its seemingly inconspicuous position and was therefore greatly surprised when she went directly to it on her way to the grill. Evidently her vision is keen and her observation excellent for things which have either natural or acquired interest for her.

In the fifth trial, with Congo out of sight, the broomstick was stood at the northwest corner of the porch before the nest-room, between the corner post and the side wall. Again it was not only inconspicuous but in an entirely unusual position; and again when she had been returned to the cage and everything was in readiness, a piece of sweet potato was placed on the platform. Observing it, she ran directly to the nest-room and returned with a handful of straw which she pushed toward the potato and in various ways manipulated in trying to reach it. After a few seconds she walked across the cage to the middle of the house-bench. Her behavior suggested that she might be looking for a stick or other implement. Shortly she returned to the grill and looked toward the potato. Then walking along the east side of the cage she looked about her. Returning to the grill she mounted the shelf above it and there lay down, apparently convinced that she could not obtain the potato. After a few minutes she again went to the nest-room and getting another handful of straw used it as formerly for a few seconds. The trial was continued thus for twenty minutes, and as Congo gave no indication of perceiving the stick I placed another on the roof of the nest-room. This she saw me do. Immediately she ran to the roof, grasped the stick, and scrambling down, almost falling in her haste, she ran to the grill and within fifteen seconds had obtained her reward.

Finally, in commenting on Congo's various performances in these five repetitions of the platform and stick experiment, it may be confidently stated that she is *approaching* a behavioral condition in which if a stick or similar functional object is required, she will definitely search for it. Indications of this adaptive attitude or condition are sufficiently numerous to be impressive, although they are by no means so definite as in the chimpanzee. From her behavior in this experiment it may be asserted that although she is on the alert for anything that can be used to reach with, she does not when faced with a familiar need make continuous systematic search of the cage for sticks or other possible implements. Instead, her observational efforts are rather casual and sporadic, and her successes, even if imaginally conditioned, appear to be in considerable measure happy accidents.

Problem 4. Suspended food and stick. This type of problematic situation was previously employed to discover whether Congo would use a stick to knock down suspended food. Although she did not exhibit such tendency, she solved the problem by using the stick to climb upon and jump or reach from. The experiment was repeated in 1927 in order to discover whether she now would employ the stick to strike with or as formerly as an aid in jumping.

The observational situation for the trials now to be described was set under a large oak tree (Tree 3) some fifteen yards northerly of the cage. To one of the lower limbs of this tree a stout cord was attached, and nearly under the cord a stake, to which Congo's chain could be attached, was driven into the ground. The situation was used not only to test her manner of adaptation, but also to measure her maximal standing reach.

Initially a sweet potato was suspended sixty-six inches from the ground, and four feet from the mooring stake a stick approximately 1 by 1½ by 40 inches lay on the ground. When brought to the stake Congo reached the potato with her hand on her first attempt. It was replaced by another potato at a height of seventy-two inches. This, after glancing toward, she refused to reach for. Instead she gave her undivided attention to efforts to break loose from the mooring stake. During the period of observation no attention was given to the stick, but this is not surprising inasmuch as she succeeded, in the first instance, in reaching the food directly, and in the second instance was on the one hand discouraged by the height of the reward, and on the other encouraged by the inadequate strength of her mooring stake to labor with it for escape.

A second trial in the suspended food and stick experiment reëstablished Congo's ability to reach the food at a height of sixty-six inches above the ground, and demonstrated also her ability to use a stick as formerly to reach from. In this particular trial two sticks, the one three feet long, the other five feet long, were placed about four feet from the mooring stake. She promptly used the longer stick to push herself toward the food and thus obtained it at a height of seventy-two inches.

For the third repetition of the experiment a small sweet potato was placed seventy-two inches from the ground and the three-foot stick was within reach. Congo promptly brought the stick to the mooring stake, placed it vertically before her with one end on the ground, and grasping it near the top with the left hand and near the bottom with the right foot, she readily raised herself toward the food and reaching out with her right hand grasped it. When she was brought from the cage for this particular observation she was unusually rambunctious and tried to escape, but when moored to the stake she wasted no time in solving her problem.

By repetitions four and five, which occurred on January 22, it was demonstrated on the one hand that Congo would not jump for suspended food even if it were very nearly within reach, and on the other, that she would use available sticks or poles readily and efficiently to climb upon and reach from.

In no instance, either in the original experiments or in these repetitional trials, did she use a stick or exhibit any tendency to attempt to use it to reach or strike the food. Her single and sole use was as an aid in climbing, and even in this case she did not jump from the stick as does the chimpanzee, but instead pushed herself upward and clinging to it reached from it. The experiment is not particularly informing or illuminating, except in its negative results and in the contrast which it exhibits between this mountain gorilla and the chimpanzee of corresponding age. The latter, in comparable situations, uses sticks much more freely, skillfully, and in varied ways, as for example, to reach or strike with, to push off from, or to climb and reach or jump from. The only marks of improvement in Congo's use of the stick in the suspended food situation in 1927, as contrasted with 1926, were greater readiness to avail herself of it and increased facility.

Problem 6. Suspended food and auxiliary stick. This problem, taken from Köhler, was intended to discover whether Congo, in the suspended food situation, would use a stick which was too short to use in climbing, to draw within reach a longer stick which would satisfactorily meet her need. The situation was arranged as that for problem 4, except that two sticks were provided in definite relation to the mooring stake, the one 6 feet long by 1¾ inches in its other dimensions, was placed eleven to twelve feet north of the stake, and the other, 3 feet long by 1¾ by 1¾ inches, was placed four feet south of the stake.[4] Almost exactly above the shorter stick, and suspended from the limb of the oak tree at a distance of ninety-two to ninety-six inches from the ground, was a paper bag which contained the food reward. Usually sweet potato was used. Congo had eight feet of free chain.

During her first trial she repeatedly used the shorter stick to climb with, but it was impossible for her thus to obtain the food. In the course of her efforts she succeeded in reaching the six-foot stick with one foot. Drawing it to her she promptly used it successfully as a climbing stick; but instead of placing it under the food she carried it toward the trunk of the tree and there used it to grasp a limb along which she climbed toward the suspended food. Failing in this effort she shortly used it successfully directly beneath the food.

Her performance in this trial is particularly significant as indicating plan and execution of indirect approach. The observer did not at first suspect her intent, but wondered why she was placing the stick so far away from the food. Actually, as it later appeared, she was intending to approach it by way of a limb of the tree, and the stick was to serve as an aid in reaching the limb. In the performance she exhibited patience, craft, persistence, and excellent method.

The second trial yielded quite different, although not less interesting, results. The small stick was repeatedly placed on end under the food, but Congo did not attempt to climb on it. While engaged in placing the shorter stick upright, first on one

[4]It was shortly discovered that the three-foot stick, because of its smoothness, could not be used readily to draw the other stick within reach, so on one end of it a small block was nailed, thus rendering it a hooking device. Also it was discovered that Congo's feet slipped badly when she attempted to climb on the six-foot stick. To facilitate its use, small blocks were nailed on opposite sides at distances of one foot apart.

end then on the other, her attention suddenly turned to the longer stick, and with the shorter in hand she hurried toward it and used the latter as she did the stick on the platform (problem 3, platform and stick) by sweeping it toward the longer stick. Although she was not able to reach it, because her chain happened to be wrapped about the stake, the intent to obtain the longer stick by means of the shorter was apparent.

The answer to my initial question had thus been obtained, and my primary interest in continuing the experiment was to follow the development of skill in obtaining the longer stick by means of the shorter. It required many trials for Congo so to master the situation that she would promptly take up the shorter stick and endeavor to obtain the longer. Instead, she usually carried the shorter stick toward the 'food and went through the motions of preparing it for use as an aid in climbing.

The contrast between her early behavior and that which subsequently appeared is well exhibited by the results of trial 14. The reward had been placed ninety-two inches from the ground and the sticks in their standard positions. Congo, when brought to the stake, immediately took up the shorter stick and moved with it toward the longer. From the moment of beginning to use the shorter stick she persisted in her efforts until in fifty-five seconds she obtained the longer one. Although she was clumsy and crude in her manipulation of the stick, reaching, pushing, sweeping it along the ground, and throwing it toward the other stick without letting go of it, she finally succeeded in hooking it over the six-foot stick and drawing the latter toward her. Persistence was the most significant feature of her behavior. Clearly enough she had the right idea, but lacked adequate motor control and coördination to succeed promptly. Having drawn the longer stick to her she hurried with it toward the food and in a few seconds obtained it.

Among the notable results of this experiment, the detailed records of which I have thus briefly and inadequately summarized, were: (1) the promptness with which she exhibited use of the one stick to obtain the other; (2) her extreme crudity of action in this type of endeavor; (3) the remarkable persistence of her use of the shorter stick, or if not actual use, the handling and repeated placing of the stick before she finally sought and obtained the efficient longer stick, and finally (4) the very gradual and slow appearance of immediate adequate response and of a fair amount of skill in using the one stick to obtain the other. Perhaps it should be added that whereas psychologically the problem proved to be somewhat less difficult for Congo than I had expected, manually it was much more so.

Problem 5. Pipe and stick or rod. The experimental situation does not require description since it appears as problem 9 of the previous report (p. 60 ff.). During the winter of 1926 Congo failed completely in this experiment. Neither of her own initiative nor on the basis of the imitative copy supplied by the experimenter did she succeed in obtaining the desired objective by use of a stick or a wire.

In the first repetitional trial a broomstick four feet long was placed three feet from the larger end of the pipe in which a raw banana appeared as prospective reward. When brought to the experimental situation Congo exhibited eagerness to obtain the banana and tried in various ways to do so. As all of them proved ineffective, she presently went to the stick and taking it up carried it directly to the larger end of the pipe, seemingly with intent to use it. But in that position she appeared uncertain and puzzled, and after a moment's hesitation the stick was laid on the ground between the mooring stake and the pipe. Although the trial was continued over a period of thirty minutes, no progress toward solution of the problem, other than that indicated above in the initial handling of the stick, was made.

The second trial differed from the first in that after thrice handling the stick in a puzzled way, she deliberately broke it in half, thus rendering it useless. Immediately it was replaced by a galvanized iron pipe one inch in diameter and fifty-two inches long (hereafter referred to as a rod). This also she tried to break, but she made no attempt to use it to push the banana through the pipe.

Convinced by these two trials, the results of which were definitely negative, that she had not acquired the ability to solve this particular problem, I proceeded in two trials of thirty minutes each to set imitative copy. This was done as in the previous winter; and also as then, Congo instead of imitating my use of the rod to push the food through the pipe, often grasped it and pushed it to one side out of her way as though it annoyed her. As the two trials furnished no indication of approaching imitative solution of the problem, I decided on a modification of the experimental situation in line with its previous use with the orang-outan and chimpanzee. This involved employment of a wooden box instead of the pipe and of a pole instead of the stick or rod. It seemed not impossible that the problem set with this form of apparatus might for some reason be easier of solution than the pipe-and-stick problem. Without further comment on the results of this experiment as originally presented, and as repeated during the winter of 1927, I shall proceed with description of its modified form.

Problem 7. Box and pole. It is necessary in this case to offer description of apparatus as well as experimental procedure.

Approximately eight feet east of the pipe referred to above, a wooden box 6 feet long by 6 inches by 6 inches, inside measurements, with each end open, was securely fastened to the ground by four stakes, one at each corner, to which it was nailed. In the middle of the upper surface of this box was a door twelve inches long which was strongly hinged on one side and on the other fastened by a hasp in which either spring snap or padlock could be used. Parallel with the box, and from three to four feet east of it, lay a pole 7 feet long by 1¾ by 1¾ inches. In preparation for an experiment Congo was permitted to see food placed in the center of the box. This the experimenter did by opening the door and, having arranged the food, closing and fastening it. The reward could be obtained by using the pole to push it through the box. Congo was moored to a stake about four feet west of the box with approximately ten feet of free chain. For the six trials of (a), the initiative form of this experiment, a spring snap was used to fasten the door. Inasmuch as Congo had had previous experience with spring snaps, although she had never learned to remove them, she was interested in this fastening and gave more or less attention to it. This will be taken account of in subsequent description of the spring snap as a mechanical problem (no. 9).

Results of the box and pole experiment may be presented with extreme brevity because of their wholly negative character. In the six trials above mentioned the period for each of which was thirty minutes, not once was the pole handled in such a way as to indicate definite intent to insert it at one end of the box in order to push it through. Precisely as in the case of the pipe and stick or rod experiment, Congo occasionally took up the pole and carried it toward the box as if intending to use it, but in every instance she abandoned it even when it happened to be in position for easy insertion into the box. Often her behavior suggested perplexity. The natural inference is that interest in the pole as a possible implement carried over from other experiments, but that there lacked definite notion of the effective manner of using it, and perhaps also the necessary motor coördination for such use. Conflict of impulses may also have resulted from her previous experience with sticks.

Assuming that if able to do so of her own initiative she would have solved this problem within six trials, the total time of which was three hours, I planned for its continuation as a test of imitative ability (see (b) imitation, p. 398). The following paragraphs record the procedure and results for eight trials, the times of which ranged from twelve to twenty-six minutes, and in which the following procedure was employed. Regularly in each of the first four trials there were four stages: (1) with Congo watching at a nearby mooring stake

I baited the box; then entering the pole at one end of the box I pushed the food through so that she might see the entire process and also obtain the reward when it appeared at the opposite end; (2) thereupon, with Congo watching, I again baited the box, and transferring her to the mooring stake of the box and pole situation I gave her ten minutes for initiative in securing the reward by using the pole; (3) repetition of (1), except that the pole was entered from the opposite end of the box, and (4) repetition of (2). In this series of trials the door of the box was fastened by a padlock instead of a spring snap.

In stage 4 of the very first trial Congo, when given opportunity for initiative, almost immediately took up the pole and seemingly attempted to enter it at the south end of the box. Her efforts, however, were crude and she did not succeed in approximating the end of the pole to the opening of the box. Instead, she pushed it along outside the box and then temporarily abandoned it. Later she carried it to the opposite end of the box and for a time swung it about in the air as though trying to get it in proper position to push into the box. After a few seconds she laid it down end to end with the box, without further attempt to enter it. This initial performance was remarkably interesting as indicating desire to use an object as implement in the absence of the necessary sensory-motor ability.

In subsequent trials she occasionally endeavored to use the pole, but the usual result was that instead of so orienting it that it could be pushed into the box, she thrust it along outside, sometimes parallel to the box and close to it, and again at an angle. It was thus indicated that she had not only the desire to get the pole into the box but the tendency to push it along as she saw me do.

As the trials progressed, interest in the pole as an implement with possible relation to the food in the box markedly lessened, and she seldom attended to it except to play with it or to use it to climb with. Following the fourth trial, and during the subsequent four trials, the procedure was modified in that imitative copy was set initially, whereupon an unusually large quantity of food, sometimes her entire breakfast, was placed in the box and she was given ten to twenty minutes for initiative. This change, the chief purpose of which was to improve motivation and give more ample opportunity for initiative, did not revive her hopeful attitude toward the situation. Indeed, in the eighth and last trial, she did not touch the pole, and instead of attending to the problem as she had done in early trials, amused herself by playing in the sand or walking about the mooring stake.

As progress toward solution of the problem by imitation of the experimenter failed to appear, it was decided to modify again the form of the experiment, this time by tuitional effort. The following paragraphs briefly describe the form and results of part (c) tuition.

With Congo moored beyond reach of the box, I let her see me bait it as in the imitation form of the experiment. Thereupon I took up the pole and entering it pushed it back and forth in the box, without pushing the food through. She was then permitted to come to the box and sitting beside me to grasp the pole. Her initial tendency was to withdraw it, but after a few attempts she started to push it through. Even after doing so she failed to go to the opposite end to look for the reward. Finally she obtained it, but in such an indirect manner that she could scarcely be expected to profit by her success.

In a second trial on the same day, I similarly baited the box and entered the pole, whereupon Congo was permitted to work. Immediately she grasped the pole and pushed it some four feet into the box, at the same time looking in to see if it had moved the food. She next pulled the pole out all the way, looked into the box, and rising carried the pole to the opposite end, where she dropped it on the ground beside her and reaching in secured the food.

Possibly in this case had I placed the pole near the box instead of actually entering it, she would have solved the problem of her own initiative. Her interest was unusually great and she seemed also optimistic. Subsequently the tuitional procedure was employed, with variations suggested by the immediate circumstances, through twenty-two trials, of which several sometimes were given on a single day. Congo's progress was amazingly slow. Her difficulty, it appeared, lay in so orienting the pole that it could be thrust into the opening of the box. This is illustrated by the behavior in trial (c) 4. She took the pole, looked into the box, and then tried to insert the pole at the north end. The intent was definite, but instead of getting the end of the pole into the box she pushed it along outside, just a few inches east of the box, for its entire length. The act was a most interesting instance of failure properly to relate pole and box.

As the trials progressed, I varied my tuitional efforts. Whereas initially I actually entered the pole at one end of the box, after a few trials I instead placed it directly before the opening and parallel with the box but three or four inches away. Yet later this distance was increased to a foot; and finally, the pole was restored to its original position at the beginning of the box and pole experiment, namely, parallel to the box and approximately three feet east of it.

Even after Congo had thoroughly mastered the handling of the pole when once it was properly entered, she found it extremely difficult so to orient it that she could insert it herself. This required a considerable amount of practice. In connection with her progress toward success, her behavior in trial (c) 14 is significant. The pole in this instance was initially placed three feet east of the box. Congo carried it to the north end of the box and there sat looking about. Presently she looked into the box and then tried hard to insert the pole, but she missed the opening and pushed it for some feet along the east side of the box. A little later she again attempted to insert it at the north end, looked into the box, looked at the end of the box, then at the end of the pole, paused, and then rather abstractedly handled the pole as though puzzled over its relationship to the box. This seemed very much like a reflective pause, and to the observer it naturally suggested approaching mastery of the problem.

Yet another interesting phase of behavior was exhibited in trial (c) 16. In this instance, having taken possession of the pole, she tried to get one end approximated to the open end of the box. Succeeding in this and having inserted the pole, she immediately pulled it out and again tried to enter it. This she repeated several times. To the observer it looked as though she were practicing, but more likely she was trying to get the right sensory "feel" of the pole in the box before proceeding to push it through.

The tuitional phase of the box and pole experiment was completed with the twenty-second trial, on February 17. To test Congo's initiative the pole was placed several feet to the northwest of the box. When brought to the experiment she immediately ran to the pole, carried it quickly to the south end of the box, entered it almost instantly, and shoving it all the way through pushed the food along and immediately obtained it. The time required for success was only twenty-eight seconds. Not only had the box and pole problem been definitely solved, but she had acquired very considerable skill in the manipulation of the pole as implement.

Conditions seemed favorable for test of the possible transfer of acquired interest and ability from the box and pole to the pipe and rod situation. The reader will recall that whereas Congo after many trials and by diligent effort had succeeded in learning how to get food out of the box by using the pole, she had completely failed during a long series of trials in the winter of 1926, and in a number of initiative and imitation trials in 1927, to use stick, or wire, or rod to obtain food placed in the pipe. Since the extent to which sensory-motor adaptations transfer from a specific situation to others differing more or less markedly from it, although possessing certain of its essential characteristics, is of very considerable psychological and pedagogical importance, it was decided to arrange a pipe and rod transfer experiment.

Problem 18. Box and pole to pipe and rod transfer. Both pipe and box were transferred from their original locations to a new position some sixty feet distant. There each was securely staked to the ground, the one parallel to the other, and each approximately three feet distant from the mooring stake which was securely driven into the ground between them. Three feet southwest of the pipe was placed the iron rod which had previously been used in the pipe and rod experiment. The observer seated himself about twenty feet east of the pipe. In preparation for this crucial test Congo was moored to a stake beyond reach of the pipe, where she could easily see it baited with a ripe banana.

With the situation in readiness, she was moored to the pipe and rod stake at 9:06 on February 18 and given opportunity to exhibit initiative. Almost her first move was to take up the rod, walk with it to the north end of the pipe and look in. Thereupon she laid it down without giving certain indication of intent to use it. The next twenty-five minutes she spent in varied activity about mooring post and pipe. The rod occasionally was handled, but without effort to use it as implement in obtaining the food. I had set thirty minutes as limit of the period of observation, and I was writing in my notebook, "No sign whatever of idea of entering the rod in order to obtain banana," when of a sudden Congo jumped up from where she had been playing in the sand, patted her chest rapidly, ran in a circle about the mooring stake, and then sat for a few seconds quietly beside it. Next she was up and away toward the south end of the pipe, where taking up the rod she almost instantly oriented it properly and inserting it pushed its full length into the pipe, thus forcing the banana out of the opposite end. Success occurred at 9:34, just two minutes before the expiration of the thirty-minute period. Immediately after pushing the rod through, she walked quickly to the north end of the pipe and taking up the banana ate it with perfect calm and evident satisfaction.

Her behavior in utilizing the rod was strikingly like that in using the pole. In spite of the small opening of the pipe she had little difficulty in entering the rod. There were only three or four attempts in rapid succession and each time she missed the opening by not more than an inch. Her method was to take the end of the rod in her hands and direct it definitely toward the opening. Since the diameter of the pipe was only slightly greater than that of the banana, there was no chance of missing the latter, and consequently success was assured when the rod was pushed through the pipe.

As soon as Congo had finished eating her reward, she withdrew the rod from the north end of the pipe and looked in. Then dropping the rod to the ground she went away toward the stake, but almost immediately came back and picking up the rod entered it at the north end and pushed it through the pipe, whereupon she walked to the south end and looked in as though expecting food.

Whereas formerly she had failed utterly in this problem, her present solution was adequate. It affords convincing evidence of transfer, for the pipe and rod are of course different in general appearance, dimensions, and sensory-motor requirements, from the box and pole.

To forestall the possible criticism that Congo's performance was accidental, she was given three additional trials in the pipe and rod transfer situation. The second was used primarily to obtain photographic records of her behavior, and she undoubtedly was somewhat disturbed by the activities of the observer. Nevertheless she used the rod successfully to obtain her reward. In the third trial the rod was placed close to the west side of the box, approximately six feet from the pipe, and in an obscure position. As soon as Congo was brought to the situation she ran directly to the rod, took it in her right hand, and hurrying to the south end of the pipe deliberately oriented it and entered it with her left hand. Immediately she pulled it out with the same hand and again entered it, but instead of pushing it through the pipe she now, seemingly dissatisfied with her position, shifted to the opposite side of the rod and grasping it with her right hand pushed it into the pipe and forced the banana out the opposite end, where she promptly obtained it. The time occupied by this performance was approximately seventy-eight seconds.

Mention was previously made, page 403, of the seeming transfer of ability acquired in the platform and stick experiment of 1926, to the shelf and stick situation when it was represented in the winter of 1927. It may be objected that success in the latter experiment was due to maturation, and that transfer is an unnecessary inference. This may be true, but in the case of the pipe and rod experiment the conditions are so different that transfer would appear to be the natural inference, and maturation the improbable explanation.

There is yet another observation in connection with the pipe and rod and box and pole situations which should be mentioned. At the conclusion of the trials whose results have just been described, it occurred to the experimenter that it might be of interest to set the box and pole and pipe and rod experiments simultaneously and contiguously, so that when moored to the stake Congo might obtain food from either pipe or box and might endeavor to use either implement. The rod, as a matter of fact, was a possible means of obtaining the food from either pipe or box, but because the diameter of the pole was greater than that of the pipe it could be used successfully only in the box. To tax Congo's discriminative ability and exhibit effects of her previous experience in the experiments, the pole was placed ten feet west of the stake and therefore closer to the pipe than to the box, while the rod was placed correspondingly ten feet east of the stake and therefore closer to the box. The appropriate implements therefore were interchanged and each approximated to the wrong food container.

This single test in complication of experiments was made on March 8; when after watching from a nearby stake the baiting of pipe and box, Congo was brought to the experimental situation and permitted to work. She immediately took up the pole and carried it toward the box. Apparently she was about to use it when, noticing the rod, she walked on beyond the box and placing the pole on the ground took up the rod and with it returned to the south end of the box. There after a few futile efforts, in which she placed the rod almost at right angles to the end of the box, she succeeded in entering it and pushing the banana through to the opposite end. Promptly she thus obtained her reward. The time required for success was fifty-eight seconds.

Having eaten the food, she went to the pipe and looked in. Then she picked up the pole and carried it to the pipe where she vainly tried to enter it. Repeatedly she placed it at right or acute angles to the end of the pipe. The pole was too large for use in the pipe, but she nevertheless persisted in her efforts to use it, and for about seven minutes she worked diligently, much of the time with the pole so oriented that had it been possible to push it through the pipe she would have obtained her reward. The rod meantime lay completely concealed in the box where she had left it. As I watched her working vainly with the pole for the food in the pipe I naturally wondered whether she would remember the rod and search for it.

At 9:25, just ten minutes after the beginning of the experiment, she left the pipe, and pole in hand went to the box, where she entered it at the south end and proceeded to push it through. She then ran to the north end of the box and began to pull at the pole. This caused the rod to rattle in the box. Hearing the sound she ran back to the south end of the box, looked in, and drew the rod out. Instantly she seemed to recognize its applicability and with it ran to the south end of the pipe. There she tried to enter it, but failed at first to get the appropriate orientation. She worked hard for somewhat more than a minute. Apparently somewhat discouraged by her lack of success, she next went to the box and for a few seconds manipulated the pole. Then returning to the pipe and taking the rod in hand she promptly inserted, pushed it through, and running to the north end, obtained the reward.

The total time of observation was fifteen minutes. Solution of the second problem came slowly and Congo's behavior indicated marked confusion. Nevertheless, I believe that the results of this complication experiment are entirely fair to her mentality and indicative of her present ability in meeting problems. That, she should have confused pole with rod initially and used them in their inappropriate relations and unusual associations surprised the observer. It is natural to suppose that the rod should be preferred to the pole because smaller and more easily handled; so probably it would have been used immediately in the pipe had it not been hidden from view within the box.

Problem 16. Slot box. The suggestion for this experiment was taken from Harold C. Bingham, who in the Yale Primate Laboratory has observed the response of chimpanzees in an apparatus and with an observational procedure similar to that herein described. Description of his method and results has not yet been published.

The apparatus used for Congo consisted of a wooden box 72 inches long, 6 inches deep, and 4½ inches wide, inside measurements. One end of the box was closed, the other was left open. The bottom, that is, the side placed next to the ground, was solid, but in each of the other sides was cut a slot 24 inches long by 1¼ inches wide. Each slot was placed in the middle of the width of the side and was designated by a number. The box was mounted with the closed end resting on the ground and the other end six inches above the ground. This slope was intended to increase the difficulty of obtaining food which had been placed inside the box and at the closed end. The apparatus was securely fastened to the ground under Tree 3 by stakes. Its long axis extended from north to south, the closed end being directed toward the north. The three slots, designated hereafter by the numbers 1, 2, 3, were located as follows: slot 1, on the west side of the box, began at the closed end and extended twenty-four inches toward the open end; slot 2 was located precisely in the middle length and width of the upper surface of the box; slot 3, on the east side of the box as placed for use, began at the open end and extended for twenty-four inches toward the closed end. Both the placement of the box and the location of slots may be observed in plate 6, figure 1 of which shows slot 3 and also a milk bottle containing pieces of banana ready to be used in the box as food container. Figure 2 of this plate represents Congo at work at slot 1. Slots 2 and 3 are visible.

In the initial trials with this apparatus, pieces of banana used as bait were placed in a quart glass milk bottle, and the latter was pushed into the box bottom foremost until it rested against the closed end. The bottle fitted easily, with about three-fourths inch leeway in the width of the box. This strong container was used to prevent the gorilla from drawing the food directly through a slot or crushing it in her attempts to do so.

The experiment was used in two forms: (a) for use of animal's hand as means of obtaining the bottle from the box, and (b) for use of stick instead of hand to obtain bottle. These procedures will be described in turn.

For this experiment Congo was moored to a stake driven into the ground at the closed end of the box. She was allowed the freedom of eight feet of chain. The observer sat about sixteen feet west of the box.

Because of Congo's unexpectedly prompt adaptation to this type of situation she was given only seven trials with direct use of hand and three trials with use of stick as implement.

When, on February 8, this situation was first presented I did not take the trouble to prepare my cameras for action, for I did not expect substantial progress toward the solution of the problem. Congo watched me place several pieces of banana in the milk bottle and push it into the box. She was then moored to the slot box stake with the following result. Directly she went to the open end of box and looked in. Then she ran to the closed end and through slot 1 observed the bottle. Immediately she began to work for it, using both hands to try to pull it through the slot, the latter being just wide enough to enable her to get her fingers and part of the palm of the hand through. After a few seconds of vain effort thus to obtain the food, she desisted and going to the open end again looked in. She then went to slot 2 and looked through it. Then away from the box for a few seconds. Returning she stood at the open end and pounded the box hard with both hands. Next she ran to slot 1 and sitting down before it worked at the bottle with both hands, but especially with the right hand, evidently trying to get it through the slot. Again she left the box and for about a minute occupied herself with a root in the ground nearby. Returning to the open end of the box she lay down in front of it and felt around beneath the box, as though searching for approach to the bottle. Shortly she returned to slot 1 and began moving the bottle with her right hand. Presently she happened to move it toward the open end of the box. Instantly she perceived her advantage, gave a growl of surprised interest, ran to the open end and looked in. Then she ran to slot 2 and reaching in was able to touch the bottle and to push it still farther toward the opening of the box. Once more returning to the opening she reached in and obtained the bottle. Six and one-half minutes were required for this solution of the problem.

Congo's change of attitude when she discovered that she could push the bottle toward the opening was impressive and significant. The sound which she made was unusual and her eagerness as she ran to the open end of the box, and thence to slot 2 to push the bottle still farther, were clearly enough indicative of her awareness of approaching success.

Having removed the bottle from the box, it took her some ten seconds to get out the paper cap which I had placed in the mouth to prevent pieces of banana from falling out. Then she pounded the bottle, shook it, turned it upside down, and thus promptly obtained her reward.

Although it was intended that all three of the slots should be used for the solution of the problem, I do not think that Congo used slot 3 in her final success. Because of the quickness of action I did not observe perfectly, but my impression was that she pushed the bottle far enough beyond slot 2 to reach it directly from the opening of the box, instead of going to slot 3.

This initial observation has been described at length because it indicates all of the essential features in Congo's adaptation. Subsequent trials exhibited her ability to obtain the bottle promptly. Indeed, in her second trial she obtained the food in forty-seven seconds, and in the third, in five seconds. In the latter she ran promptly to slot 1, pushed the bottle along toward the opening of the box with both hands until it reached the upper limit of the slot, then going to the opposite side of the box, with one hand she vigorously pushed the bottle the entire length of slot 2, so that when she ran to the opening of the box and looked in she was able to reach it easily. Pulling it out, she promptly turned it upside down and shook out the banana.

In variations of this experiment an orange was used in the box as lure, and at another time a baseball. The former had the disadvantage of being too fragile to withstand the rough usage which Congo gave it in her attempts to remove it from the box, and the latter could so easily be rolled up the inclined floor of the box that slots 2 and 3 were not necessarily used.

For the stick variation of the experiment, the width of the slots was narrowed to five-eighths inch by nailing a strip of board along the upper edge of each, so that Congo could not use her hand or even her fingers to reach the bait. A soft wood stick 18 inches long by 2 inches by $\frac{3}{8}$ inches was placed on the ground about three feet west of the box. With this Congo could, if she so desired, reach through any one of the slots to move the food-containing bottle toward the open end of the box.

When at 9:42 on February 18 Congo was introduced to this variation of the slot box experiment, she came to the situation eagerly and with evident expectation of success. Interest, optimism, enthusiasm were manifest, undoubtedly because of her previous agreeable experiences with the slot box. Naturally her initial attempt was to reach the bottle with her fingers, but after about a half minute of such futile effort she stopped, patted her chest with impatience, and also pounded the box. Then looking about she picked up the stick and taking it directly to slot 1 tried to push it through the slot. She was clumsy in this, just as in the use of the stick in the platform and stick and similar experiments. Repeatedly she pushed it lengthwise against the side of the box instead of so orienting it that the end would enter the slot. After several seconds of such activity she placed the stick in her mouth and with teeth and hands broke it into small bits. Subsequently these bits were used as the whole had been. Then followed sporadic attempts to work with the bits of stick, with occasional periods of concentrated effort.

Her intent was clear, but she obviously lacked ability to carry it directly into effect. Although it might be inferred that she broke the stick in order that she might use it more readily, and that she thereby exhibited adaptive behavior in the shaping of an implement, I doubt the correctness of this interpretation. Instead, I suspect that she was discouraged, impatient, and in destructive mood, without considering the usefulness of the stick, broke it.

During the thirty-minute interval of the trial she several times worked for minutes at slot 1. The following is descriptive of one such interval. Leaving the opening of the box, where she had been looking at the bait, she went to slot 1; thence to a root which she pulled from the ground and broke off. This piece of root about two feet long she carried to slot 1 and, breaking it into pieces, tried to push bits into the slot. Both her teeth and fingers were used in breaking up the root and in trying to insert it into the slot. The process of destruction continued until it was practically useless as an implement. She then took up the bits either singly or by the handful and tried to apply them to the slot. Apparently during this time her interest was almost continuously on the problem, and her persistence and expectation of success seemed to match her concentration of attention.

This variation of the slot box experiment would appear to be of extraordinary interest as indicating Congo's endeavor to use the stick as implement in a novel and quite unusual type of situation. She did not, it is true, succeed, but she nevertheless exhibited the essential idea or intent. Ultimately, with practice, she undoubtedly would have succeeded in using a stick promptly and efficiently in the slot box. Chiefly for the sake of obtaining motion picture records, two additional trials were given. In the last of these, discouragement, coupled with pronounced impatience, appeared. She gave relatively little attention to the problem and spent much of her time in beating her chest or endeavoring to escape from the situation.

Problem 22. Round-about course, with stick. To test Congo's ability to vary the use of stick as implement in accordance with circumstances, the following modification of the platform and stick situation was made toward the close of my period of work.

On the platform described on page 405 was nailed a wooden block, 24 inches long by 2 inches in each of its other dimensions. One end of this block was placed against the left side-rail of the platform (from Congo's point of view) at a distance of thirty inches from the grill, and the other end was thirty-six inches from the grill. My purpose was to discover whether, if a desired object were placed in the angle between the side-rail and the block of wood, she would use a stick to push it free from the barrier and to draw it around to her right toward the grill. It would seem a very simple problem, and by certain chimpanzees Köhler actually found it to be readily soluble. For the gorilla, however, the case was quite different. She was given three trials with the following results.

One-half orange was placed as prospective reward and Congo was given a 24-inch stick. With this she immediately attempted to reach, but as it proved too short for convenient use she was given instead a 42-inch stick. After she had tried for a few seconds to obtain the orange, she deliberately broke it in half, thus rendering it useless. Then she left the grill and walked about the cage, possibly in search of a stick. When she again appeared at the grill she was given a stick thirty inches long, with which she persistently swept the platform. Always she reached in the direction of the orange, but usually the end of the stick moved above it and toward the left, for she held her hand near the platform instead of raising it so that the stick would approach the orange. For several minutes she worked without even touching the orange. Mostly the stick was held in her right hand, but sometimes in her left, and occasionally with both hands.

The trial was continued for thirty minutes, and although during this interval she worked hard, much of the time she made no evident progress toward the solution of her problem. Two or three times she just touched the orange. Once as she did so she pushed it a few inches away from her. Almost always she moved the stick so that had it come into contact with the orange it would have swept it toward the left into the angle between the side-rail and the wooden barrier between her and the reward. When the trial was discontinued she, despite discouragements, was still at work.

The first trial was made on March 9 at 8:32; at 11:10 a second trial was given. Again one-half orange was placed as prospective reward and Congo was given the 30-inch stick. Eagerly she went to work. Handling the stick inexpertly as previously, she shortly pushed the food directly away from her a distance of several inches. This undoubtedly was unintentional. It discouraged her and she promptly quit work and left the grill for about a minute. Then returning she pushed the orange against the side-rail of the platform where it was practically inaccessible. Thereupon I restored it to its original position and she continued her efforts to obtain it. This trial also continued for thirty minutes, but she worked little during the last fifteen minutes.

The next day a third trial was given, with failure as result. Congo directed the stick more accurately than before, but she tended always to work the orange toward her left where it became inaccessible. It will be recalled that early in the platform and stick experiment she acquired the tendency to sweep objects toward her left. In arranging the present experiment I naturally took this habit into account and decided to set a problem which would demand adaptation by use of the stick to move the reward toward the right, instead of the left, side of the platform.

There is no reason to doubt the ability of Congo to solve this problem with a sufficient number of trials. Actually she was given one and one-half hours to work at it. From her performance in other experiments which demanded the use of an implement, it is not unreasonable to suppose that a score or more of thirty-minute trials might be necessary for adaptation and the acquisition of a fair degree of skill. Whether or not Congo had any measure of understanding of this problematic situation is difficult to decide. My impression is that she did not, and that she exhibited definite inferiority to the chimpanzee of like age and experience in experimentally arranged situations.

Summary of Section V

During the winter of 1926 Congo's ability to use sticks was tested in four situations, in no one of which did she succeed promptly and without assistance. I have therefore stated that she seemingly lacked natural or acquired ability to use the stick as implement, and further that she entirely failed to use it on her own initiative as an implement to reach, pull, or strike with, although she did spontaneously use it as an aid in climbing.

During the winter of 1927, in addition to repeating the previous experiments which involved the use of sticks, I devised new situations, so that the total number described in this section is nine. The list with the outstanding result in each follows.

(1) Shelf and stick experiment. In this Congo, having failed utterly of adjustment in 1926, promptly succeeded, either by reason of transfer of ability or of maturation, in 1927.

(2) Platform and stick—a problem which was beyond the gorilla's unaided adaptive ability in 1926, and which she solved only after long tuitional assistance from the experimenter. In 1927 she promptly succeeded in this experiment without assistance.

(3) Suspended food and stick experiment. This originally elicited tendency to use the stick to climb upon and push off from. Neither in 1926 nor in 1927 did it call forth ability to use sticks to strike with. In both seasons success was achieved in this experiment.

(4) Suspended food and auxiliary stick experiment, presented first in 1927, and yielding success. The notion of using a short stick to obtain a longer one, which in turn could be used to climb upon, appeared early, but skill in putting the idea into effect developed slowly.

(5) Pipe and stick or rod experiment yielded failure in the first period of work, despite persistent tuitional efforts of the experimenter. In 1927 repetition indicated that maturation had not prepared the way for ready solution of the problem.

(6) Box and pole experiments, presented first in 1927, yielded no evidences of adaptation until the experimenter had assisted by presentation of imitative copy and tuition. Perfect adaptation to the situation was finally achieved as the result of a large number of trials. In this connection it is of interest to note that the box and pole experiment, in practically the same form as presented to Congo, has been solved by the orangoutan and chimpanzee quickly and apparently with ease.

(7) Box and pole to pipe and rod transfer experiment, presented in 1927, yielded immediate adaptation to the pipe and rod situation, although in all previous trials Congo had failed to use the rod as an implement. The experiment seemingly demonstrates transfer of ability from the box and pole situation to that of the pipe and rod.

(8) Slot box experiment. First presented in 1927, this immediately yielded success by the use of the hand as means of manipulating the food container. When the experiment was so modified that a stick must be used, the idea of employing the stick was promptly exhibited, but ability to manipulate the implement properly was lacking. Presumably as in the case of the box and pole experiment, it would have been acquired had sufficient opportunity been afforded.

(9) Round-about course with stick experiment. This variation of the platform and stick situation, presented first in 1927, yielded negative results. The stick was used as in the shelf and stick and platform and stick situations, but unadaptively.

Critical review of the results of this particular assemblage of experiments would seem to justify the statement that Congo at the beginning of my observations possessed very little if any ability to use sticks as implements, and that such ability was acquired slowly and with extreme effort by suggestion, setting of imitative copy, and tuitional aid from the experimenter. For stick problems the following comparisons among anthropoids are indicated. In (1) initial equipment, (2) initiative and versatility in attempting to solve problems, (3) response to opportunity for imitation, (4) response to tuitional assistance, and (5) speed, adequacy of adaptation and degree of manual skill achieved, Congo is markedly inferior to the orang-outan and chimpanzee of comparable age and experience.

Comparison of the account of the stick as instrument in my first report, pages 40-69, with the present description of repetitional and supplementary experiments, indicates that in the second period of observation Congo began with the advantage not only of her previous experience in like problems, but also of certain progress toward maturation. She possessed interest in sticks and other objects as possible implements, greater initiative, versatility, and inventiveness than in the winter of 1926, and also, it appears to me, somewhat improved insight, or approach to insight, into the nature and essential features of the problematic situations. There can, I think, be no doubt that she profited markedly by her experience in the experiments of 1926, and on this account, and also because of her normal maturation and splendid adaptation to conditions of life in captivity, succeeded much better in the stick-as-implement problems of 1927 than in those of 1926.

SIMPLE MECHANISMS, AND OTHER UNFAMILIAR OBJECTS, AS EXHIBITORS OF ADAPTIVE ABILITY

Congo's ability, as previously observed by me, to adapt to unfamiliar objects, and more particularly to what are usually designated as mechanical devices, was so meager that it seemed highly desirable to repeat the experiments of this category and to supplement them by variation of conditions and the presentation of other types of problem. In this section I shall describe six forms of experiment. The apparatus used in each was simple, and such as the chimpanzee speedily learns to operate.

Problem 11. Diagonal rope. This is a repetition of problem 2 of the original list. The observations now to be described were made under conditions identical with those of the previous winter, except that the rope was twenty-six instead of twenty-four inches from the grill at its nearest point and thirty-eight instead of thirty-six inches at the farthest point of reach. The experimental setting was arranged with Congo absent from her cage and out of sight. The rope was baited by tying to it, at the point thirty-eight inches from the grill, a paper bag containing food.

In the first repetitional trial, Congo, as soon as admitted to her cage, noticed the rope with suspended bag, but instead of running to the south end of the grill to reach directly for the bag she went hurriedly to the north end, reached for the rope at its nearest point, and seizing it with her left hand held it until she had grasped it somewhat farther to the south with her right hand. She then proceeded hand over hand until she reached the opposite end of the grill. There with a determined effort she reached for the bag with her right hand and grasping it promptly broke it from its attachment to the rope. Thus with perfect technique she solved the problem without a moment's hesitation. The time required was minimal, probably about five seconds.

The only other repetition of this experiment was made on March 3, for motion picture record. In this case also Congo's response was perfectly adapted to the requirements of the situation.

From this description, by comparison with the gorilla's initial response to the diagonal rope situation, it appears that she remembered the situation and its requirements perfectly after an interval of one year and was able to respond even more quickly and skillfully than in her best performance of the previous season. Granted that the situation is easily adapted to, it still has obvious value as a method of exhibiting the retention of acquired forms of response, and it seems not improbable that if used in standardized form for the comparative study of certain aspects of adaptivity in children and anthropoid apes, it may prove serviceable beyond one's natural expectation.

Problem 2. Hooked rope. This also is repetitional. The conditions of experiment 3 of the original list were reproduced, except for the necessarily greater size and strength of apparatus. Thus, for example, the post which carried the rope was placed eighty-four instead of seventy-two inches from the grill, and the food carrier, to escape Congo's grasp, was located a few inches farther from the grill (38 inches) than previously. The experimental setting was prepared with Congo absent from her cage and out of sight.

On January 18, at 12:15, as indicated in the list of experiments on page 397 Congo was given opportunity to demonstrate memory of this situation and solution of the problem. She was brought into the cage and held on her leash until the observer had taken his position a few feet from the apparatus. On being released she immediately approached the grill and began to work at the mechanism. Because of the nature of mistakes in this and subsequent trials her behavior will be described briefly but in detail. In this, the first trial, she went directly to the ring arm of the rope and pulled on it, then to the carrier arm and pulled on it. Thereupon she returned to the ring arm and removed the ring from the stout nail which held it in position on the lower bar of the grill. Pushing the ring between the grill bars to fall on the platform outside, she again pulled on the ring arm. Next she shifted quickly to the carrier arm and pulling the carrier with its burden of sweet potato within reach, deftly extracted the food. Her speed of action and the brief interval required for each of these moves are indicated by the total time required for success, approximately thirty seconds. Although false moves stand out conspicuously in this performance, it is excellent, as compared with early trials in the hooked rope situation. Moreover, it supplies wholly convincing indications of memory.

On successive days, four additional trials were given, which exhibit speedy achievement of perfection in response.

In the second trial, she pulled first momentarily on the carrier arm, then hastened to the ring arm, skillfully removed the ring although the tension of the rope made it somewhat difficult, and instantly with clear intent shifted to the carrier arm and hauled in the food container. The total time of work approximated one minute. The third trial shows further elimination of unnecessary moves, for although she went first to the carrier arm and pulled slightly on it, she immediately shifted to the ring arm, removed the ring and without pulling on the ring arm proceeded to the carrier arm. After pushing for a moment on the rope, she pulled in the food container and obtained her reward. This performance also required nearly a minute.

Markedly contrasting with the preceding trials are those numbered 4 and 5. In 4, Congo attacked the ring directly and immediately removed it, then shifted to the carrier arm and drew the reward to her. This perfect performance required about ten seconds. Improvement seemed scarcely possible, yet in the next and last repetitional trial she reduced her time.

Brought to the open door of the cage and released, she rushed to the grill, instantly removed the ring, and by the simplest and most direct of movements drew the food container to her. The time required approximated five seconds.

It appears therefore that although her first response to this problematic situation, after an interval of one year during which she presumably had no experience with it or similar problems, was imperfect, she remembered the situation and was capable of prompt and perfect adaptation. It is important to note that in her tenth and final trial in this problem during the winter of 1926, she made several false moves and required approximately thirty seconds for success. Her achievements in trials 4 and 5 of the repetitional series are markedly superior to the best performance of the previous year. Hence it is fair to say that she not only remembered the solution of the hooked rope problem, but actually improved in adaptive ability during the year intervening between her opportunities for work.

Problem 15. Milk bottle. Already reference has been made to Congo's ability to obtain food from such containers as, for example, the milk bottle used in slot box, and the tin can of the hooked rope experiment. Partly because of these casual references (see also Yerkes, 1927, p. 72ff.), but chiefly on account of the unexpectedly illuminating character of the results, it seems worth while to describe briefly in the present category certain experimental observations which were made with the milk bottle as object demanding adaptation.

The milk bottle problem, simple in the extreme from our point of view because all that was required was the skillful extraction of solid food therefrom, was first presented in 1926. Although she succeeded in obtaining the desired food, Congo did so awkwardly and in a manner very inferior to the most efficient method. Therefore it seemed desirable to repeat the experiment, and also to present it in the new form which is designated as variation A.

When on February 4, the milk bottle experiment was first repeated, the usual type of one-quart glass bottle containing a whole banana, which fitted the mouth of the bottle rather closely, was placed on the ground before Congo. She took it up, almost instantly turned it upside down and shook it so that the banana projected beyond the mouth of the bottle. It then was grasped and pulled out by her hand. This success contrasted sharply in speed and directness with the best performance of a year earlier. She made no attempt to force her fingers into the bottle, nor did she attempt to bite it. A day later the experiment was repeated in a second trial, when again success was promptly and efficiently achieved.

This experiment also indicates actual increase in proficiency, as well as definite memory of the problematic object.

The variation in the milk bottle problem designated as A consisted in filling it partially with milk instead of with banana. Usually from one-half to one pint of milk was used. To obtain the liquid content of course required a wholly different sort of adaptation from that previously demanded.

When on February 20 the bottle containing milk was first presented to Congo, she promptly tipped it over and let the milk flow out on the ground. The whole of the contents was wasted, although once she put the mouth of the bottle to her lips and tasted the milk. As this result appeared to justify further observation, the simple experimental situation was presented on successive days, with the omission of February 24 and 27, until March 9, a total of sixteen trials. The results may be summarized.

In the first few trials she carelessly upset the bottle and spilled most of the milk, although as the work progressed she became increasingly interested in placing the mouth of the bottle to her lips or her eye to the mouth of the bottle so that she could examine the milk. Occasionally she succeeded in getting a few drops of milk into her mouth, but it was by licking them from the bottle instead of pouring them into her mouth.

In trial 5 a bottle about one-fourth filled with milk and sealed with a paper cap was handed to her. Taking it up she immediately removed the stopper with her fingers. Then she deliberately tilted the bottle over with mouth away from her and let most of the milk run out. It formed a pool on the ground before her from which she tried to drink, but promptly it disappeared in the sand. Then taking up the bottle she looked into the opening and touched the mouth with her lips. As she tilted it toward her face the remaining milk slowly poured out and a few drops fell into her mouth. Several times she applied her lips to the opening of the bottle as though attempting to drink from it. Following this description of behavior I wrote in my notebook: "She seems unconscionably slow in adapting to such practical situations as this, and she also is extraordinarily wasteful of food. Is this possibly a species peculiarity—destructiveness and wastefulness of food—due to the nature and abundance of the food supply in the gorilla's habitat? Or is it due to the adaptive limitations of the mountain gorilla?"

In trials 6 to 10 appeared gradual adaptation through the effort, on Congo's part, to approximate the mouth of the bottle to her own mouth and to pour out the milk so that she could drink it. In several trials very little milk was thus obtained, almost all of it falling to the ground because of her clumsiness and general inaptitude in managing bottle and lips. One of the conspicuous defects in her method was failure to raise her head sufficiently. Often she lay on the ground, and although she raised the bottle she held her head so low that the milk flowed out quickly and very little of it entered her mouth. Following the seventh trial I recorded that she was making appreciable but slow progress and that she seemed greatly interested in the problem and intent on getting the milk. Marked success characterized the eighth trial because the head was held higher and the milk was poured more slowly. At least a quarter of it was drunk.

It was not until the twelfth trial that notably adaptive behavior appeared. Sitting straight up, Congo took the milk bottle, removed the cap, and proceeded to drink skillfully, except that she poured so fast that much of the milk escaped at the corners of her mouth. Had she poured more slowly and deliberately the performance would have been perfect. In about a minute the bottle was emptied, and immediately cast aside. Since obviously there was opportunity for further improvement in adaptation the experiment was continued. The most efficient performance appeared in trial 14, when Congo, sitting upright with back against the trunk of a tree, took the bottle in hand and drank at least half of its contents with scarcely a drop spilled. Then she lazily stretched herself on her belly and continuing to drink, spilled only a little.

This may seem a futile and monotonous recital, but one discovers in attempting to gain adequate knowledge of an organism's behavior that the seemingly trivial may have unexpected significance when considered in relation to other observations. The contrast between Congo's response to the milk-containing bottle in her first and in her fourteenth trials may not greatly surprise the reader, but the slowness of adaptation certainly will. From all that is known of the mental characteristics of the manlike apes one might naturally expect the gorilla, orangoutan, and chimpanzee to learn in the course of a single trial so to handle the milk-containing bottle that its contents could be drunk instead of lost on the ground. I have said that the milk bottle experiment in its original form and its variation was peculiarly illuminating. It may here be added that even more markedly and convincingly than various more complicated experimental situations, it exhibits Congo's slowness of adaptation to practical problems. Perhaps she did not do her best. Had she been extremely hungry, possibly she would quickly have discovered how to handle the bottle successfully. I suspect that in this particular experiment the motivation sometimes was relatively low, for as a rule she had worked all the morning in experiments and had received, as result of success in some of them, the greater part of her breakfast and sometimes also a part of her luncheon. The milk, given usually between twelve-thirty and one-thirty p. m. in problem 15, was a portion of what she would have received regularly in the middle of the day if experiments had not been in progress. She was not, I think, overfed at the time, but certainly her appetite was not keen, and sometimes possibly she was almost as much interested in playing with the bottle as in drinking its contents.

I have suggested this ground of explanation or excuse for slow adaptation to what seems to us a very simple situation because the facts demand it, and also because many readers will wonder whether the motivation was optimal or even adequate. But having admitted the possibility of sub-optimal motivation in the milk bottle experiment, I must also in fairness say that, under practically identical conditions, the adaptation of the young chimpanzee is very rapid by comparison, and there is no tendency to waste the food. This would make it seem that the surprising behavior of Congo is characteristic of her, possibly also of her species, and even if alterable by changes in motivation, nevertheless is fairly indicative of her relative slowness in learning and wastefulness in the handling of food.[5]

Problem 14. Wound chain. The wound chain experiment, it will be recalled from the previous report, was presented in 1926 with full expectation that Congo would solve it promptly because of her extensive experience with like situations when moored to trees or stakes. That she failed utterly in two trials of fifty-five and sixty minute duration, respectively, was both surprising and inexplicable. It therefore was with unusual curiosity that I re-presented the situation in the winter of 1927. Essential data concerning the long series of repetitions

---

[5]Four chimpanzees, the youngest probably under the age of Congo and the oldest possibly two years beyond Congo's age, when given opportunity to take milk from milk bottle as was Congo, succeeded initially even better than did the gorilla after a fortnight of practice. Their success, furthermore, was achieved even though they had just taken a hearty meal and were not eager for the milk. In a second trial on the following day, given before breakfast, each chimpanzee emptied the milk bottle promptly and with skill. Like Congo, these animals had previous familiarity with cups and could drink from them, but so far as I know they had not had experience in trying to get either solids or liquids from a bottle. These unpublished observations will be reported elsewhere in greater detail, together with related data.

of this experiment, and also of the related variation A, appear in the list of experiments on page 399. Plate 9, figure 2, presents the wound chain situation.

In its first re-presentation, February 3 at 11:33, a stout wire chain was wound four times counter-clockwise about a section approximately one foot in diameter of the trunk of the oak tree which had served as the scene of the experiment in the previous winter (Tree 2). This portion of the multiple trunk was widely enough separated from the other sections to enable Congo readily to climb around it if she so desired. The chain extended from the tree a distance of about eight feet so that when attached to its free end she had approximately ten feet reach from the tree. Some six feet beyond the end of the chain a plate containing two sweet potatoes and a piece of turnip was placed on the ground. Congo when brought to this situation apparently sized it up promptly and almost immediately climbed the section of the tree which held the chain, and going around it clockwise descended to the ground with a full length of chain. Again she started to climb for another circuit, but for some reason stopped midway and, returning to the ground, walked toward the plate of food and succeeded in reaching it.

Particularly impressive in this performance were her appreciation of the relation of the chain to the tree and the indications of practical judgment. It seemed that these must spring from her long experience at the adjoining tree, to which for months she had been moored for a time almost daily. Thus in the very first repetitional trial she succeeded. Naturally the observer thought that her more ample experience had enabled her to do after a year what she was unable to do in 1926. But he was puzzled when in the next three trials, in conditions similar to those of the first, she failed to obtain her reward, and indeed made only incipient motions toward unwinding the chain. Was the easy initial success purely accidental; was motivation inadequate in subsequent trials, or were there inhibiting influences which would have obscured even optimal motivation? It was hoped to obtain an answer by continuance and variation of the experiment.

On February 7, the day following the fourth trial in the regular experiment, the wound chain situation was arranged as variation A at Congo's home tree (Tree 1), to which she was accustomed to be fastened for exercise and play, and with which presumably she was very familiar. The chain was wound twice counter-clockwise about one section of the tree and extended approximately five feet from the tree toward a plate containing her breakfast, the major part of which still remained despite previous work. The plate was fifteen to sixteen feet from the base of the tree and to the south of it. When brought from her cage to the experiment Congo looked up and about the tree as though appraising the situation, and then running directly to the trunk which carried the chain she climbed around it clockwise and promptly measured the length of the free chain by approaching the plate. It was insufficient to enable her to reach the food, so she hastily returned to the tree and with the slack of the chain held in one hand, as if to render more obvious its relation to the tree, she again climbed about the trunk clockwise. Then, descending to the ground, she pulled the chain to make sure that it was free and clear, and proceeded to the plate, which she easily reached with one foot and drew to her. The total time required for this successful performance was about thirty seconds. There was no hesitation whatever in initial attack on the problem or in carrying out the phases of its solution.

This response makes one still more curious as to why the gorilla should not act similarly when the same problem is set on an adjoining tree less than twenty feet away and with the chain wound similarly about a section of the trunk.

On the following day variation A of the experiment was repeated, except that the chain was wound clockwise instead of counter-clockwise. Success came so quickly that it was difficult for the experimenter to follow Congo's movements and to time the performance. Certainly it did not require more than ten seconds.

On February 9, trial 3 of variation A resulted in success, trial 5 of the regular experiment in failure, and trial 4 of variation A in success. When brought to the regular experiment for trial 5, Congo started about the trunk of the tree in the direction required to unwind the chain. Then she suddenly stopped and descended to the ground. It looked as though she knew how to solve the problem, but for some reason did not care to try. On the chance that motivation was inadequate I promptly added to the sweet potatoes already on the plate two ripe bananas, of which she was inordinately fond, and an apple. She looked intently at the offering, seemed interested and eager for it, but made no effort to get it. Instead, for the greater part of the thirty-minute interval, she either climbed about the tree gathering moss, leaves, and bark, or played on the ground near the trunk.

Again it should be emphasized that effort was made to present the same problem in each situation; namely, in variation A at Tree 1, to which Congo was accustomed to be moored, and in the regular experiment at Tree 2, a similar tree only a few yards from the familiar oak. Somewhat different types of chain were used initially, but it was subsequently proved by experiment that this did not influence the behavior.

Beginning on February 10, settings of the regular experiment and of variation A were presented daily in that order. At the home tree conditions were made increasingly difficult by complex windings of the chain, whereas at the other tree they were rendered as simple as possible. Various sections of the two trees were used, and in several of the trials two or three sections were employed simultaneously, the chain often being wound in opposite directions about adjacent portions of the trunk in order to render the task of unwinding more complex and to give me opportunity to note Congo's observational ability and the manner in which she followed the course of the chain.

On February 10, trial 6 of the regular experiment yielded failure, trial 5 of variation A success. In the latter case the problem was more complicated than previously and she made a number of false moves, spending nearly a minute in solving her problem. The outstanding features of her performance were pauses and obvious visual inspection of the relation of the chain to the tree, especially when she made a mistake. Usually she saw what should be done, but often her movements tended to get ahead of her visual observation and she was compelled to retrace her steps and by actually pulling on the chain with her hand test its freedom of motion and discover anew the direction which she should take.

Again, on February 11, trial 7 of the regular experiment exhibited only initial movement toward the unwinding of the chain, whereas trial 6 of variation A yielded prompt solution, *despite slight desire for the reward of food.*

On February 12 the results were similar in that the regular experiment, even with an extreme simplification of the problem, failed to command Congo's interested attention, whereas trial 7 of variation A, with a new and somewhat complicated setting involving three sections of the trunk of the tree, yielded solution, after a number of errors, in about one minute. The latter trial clearly exhibited Congo's method. At each critical point in the process of unwinding she stopped to observe the direction which the chain took, gathered it up in one hand and either pushed or threw it before her so that it should be clear of the tree trunk and she should not have to retrace her steps and run the risk of getting it tangled. This technique, doubtless the product of long experience, is excellent. Yet again on February 13 the two forms of experiment were presented successively, with complete failure as usual at the unfamiliar tree and success at the home tree.

On subsequent days between February 17 and March 5, four additional trials, 9 to 12, were given in variation A, the conditions being varied for the purpose of exhibiting observational ability, method, and the effect of exchanging the chains which had been used in the two forms of experiment. Thus, in trials 10 and 11 the other chain was substituted for the one regularly used at Congo's home tree. She nevertheless worked diligently at her problem and solved it. This proves that the relatively unfamiliar chain did not inhibit effort.

The attempt to discover reasons for Congo's failure in the regular form of the experiment was continued through a total of sixteen trials, of which numbers 10 to 16 were given between February 15 and March 5. Failure is recorded for trials 10 and 11. In trial 12, on February 18, the familiar chain from the home tree was used at Tree 2. It was wrapped about a section of the trunk three times clockwise, with six feet free. Although she made no attempt to unwind the chain, she two or three times fingered and looked at it as though interested, and twice I thought she was about to start to climb about the trunk. At this point it may be said that no variations, such for example as the exchange of chains in the two forms of experiment, essentially altered Congo's attitudes toward the problem in the diverse settings or her performance.

Finally, on February 19, I decided to concentrate the entire resources of the day on this particular experiment and to offer what would be relatively a magnificent reward for effort. To this end the experimental situation was set as usual; the familiar chain from the home tree was employed at the unfamiliar tree, and the food plate, sixteen feet northward of the tree, contained two large sweet potatoes, two baked bananas, and an orange. Prior to the experiment Congo had taken nothing except a cup of milk for approximately fifteen hours. Several times prior to the trial, which was made at 10:02, she had vocally begged for food while waiting in her cage. When brought to the experiment and attached to the chain she seemed quite ready to work. Within two minutes she began to fool with the chain. Then she moved toward the plate as far as the chain would permit. Returning she walked about the tree in various directions, now gazing toward the house or elsewhere, and again walking about restlessly. It may here be remarked that restlessness is ordinarily a good sign in a problematic situation. It seems to indicate that hope of success has not been abandoned and that things are happening inside.

At precisely 10:08 Congo started about the trunk of the tree counter-clockwise, but she retraced her steps without completing the turn. Fingering the chain as if to satisfy herself that she had started in the right direction, she again moved about the tree, holding the chain in front of her, and this time passing all the way around the trunk in the correct direction. She next descended to the ground and taking the chain in hand proceeded to go around the tree trunk again in the same fashion. Thus she completed the unwinding of the chain and with its full length available, walked deliberately to the plate and emptied it of its contents.

In addition to the unusually large reward offered and the fact that she had not previously had any portion of her breakfast except her cup of milk, an exceptional condition in this trial was an approaching shower. It is entirely possible that dislike of being away from the shelter of her cage during rainfall may have stirred her to attempt the early completion of her task. At any rate the trial demonstrated that under appropriate conditions she could as readily solve the wound chain problem at the unfamiliar tree as at the home tree. Whether the difference in attitude in the two locations is due to motivation or to specific inhibiting factors does not yet appear.

Naturally it appealed to the experimenter as of considerable interest to discover whether the barriers having once been passed, Congo would continue to work smoothly and successfully in the regular wound chain experiment. Therefore on the following day, in trial numbered 14, she again faced the problem which had been so long unsolved, but which in trial 1 and again in trial 13 she had shown herself capable of solving. In this case the setting of the experiment was as usual. Other experiments had preceded this particular one, Congo had had a portion of her breakfast, and on the plate appeared one baked banana and half of a sweet potato. With little hesitation she attacked the problem and in less than twenty seconds she had succeeded in unwinding the chain and in obtaining her reward. It would seem then that resistance to effort had been overcome and that she was as ready to work at the unfamiliar tree as at the familiar one.

The situation was re-presented as trial 15 on February 21, and the new chain as originally used at the unfamiliar tree was employed. It was twice wound about the middle trunk of the tree counter-clockwise, then it was wound twice about an adjacent trunk clockwise. These turns were alternated, one counter-clockwise about the first trunk, one clockwise about the second trunk, then another counter-clockwise about the first trunk, and finally another clockwise about the second trunk. Otherwise the conditions were as usual, the ordinary food reward being in position. Beginning promptly Congo worked at the problem for several minutes, but the windings of the chain were difficult to follow and after a time she became discouraged and gave up, so the final result was failure.

In the final trial of the regular wound chain experiment, no. 16 given on March 5, Congo evidently was very desirous of the food reward. Nevertheless she made no effort to unwind the chain. Following her utter failure in this situation, the same problem was immediately set at the home tree, as trial 12 of variation A. Success was achieved in about seven minutes.

It appears that the wound chain problem is readily soluble at the familiar mooring tree, whereas it is seldom solved at the adjacent and relatively unfamiliar tree. The experiments demonstrate Congo's ability to unwind the chain at either tree, and indeed during both winters, she was observed to unwind or untangle her mooring chain in diverse situations, as for example, when wound about stakes, boxes, rods, or other paraphernalia of experimentation. The conclusion is that some undiscovered inhibitory influence restrained her when in the regular setting of the wound chain experiment. This occasionally could be overcome by strong motivation. The experiment is described thus at length, although as a matter of fact only summarily since my notes are extensive, because it throws extraordinarily interesting if somewhat puzzling and inadequate light on certain traits or assemblages of traits exhibited by Congo. Undoubtedly persistent inquiry into the conditions of her behavior would be richly repaid. Unfortunately the circumstances of my work were such that I could not follow the inquiry further.

Problem 8. Hasp and padlock. In this experiment, as presented during the winter of 1926, Congo failed utterly. In the repetition described below she succeeded in solving the problem, but without indication of insight.

For purposes of repetition, a wooden box 18 by 5 by 5 inches, inside measurements, and therefore somewhat larger than the original, was used. The hinged lid of this box, as formerly, was held shut by a hasp into the staple of which a padlock could be slipped. Figure 1 of plate 7 presents the box as set for an experiment, except that for photography it was faced away from instead of toward the grill. Whereas in 1926 the experiment was presented in the cage, in the repetitions the box was fastened on the platform outside the grill within easy reach as she worked through the grill. Either sweet potato, banana, or both, were placed in this box, with Congo observing, and the lock was slipped into position. Thereupon the box was shoved into its standard position before the grill and, unless she earlier succeeded in removing the lock, she was given fifteen minutes for work.

The first five trials, given at the rate of one trial per day, yielded no evidence whatever of progress toward the solution of this simple problem. It seemed instead as though she had a subtle conviction that the lock could not be removed, for her attention was devoted chiefly to the box itself, and she strove in varied ways to loosen it or to open the lid. But since at the conclusion of a trial I usually removed the lock and permitted her to open the lid to obtain the food, her interest in the locking mechanism steadily increased. My procedure of course gave certain slight opportunity for imitation, but it will be recalled that during the winter of 1926 I exhausted my resources in trying to teach the gorilla to remove an open lock.

In the sixth trial. without previous indication of approaching success, Congo in thirty-eight seconds by what appeared to be mere fumbling with the lock, removed it from the staple. It seemed like sheer accident, so I promptly re-set the mechanism for trial 7, which was completed by success in fifty-five seconds. Thereafter in trials given at the rate of two a day, she regularly succeeded in from three seconds to four minutes.

Returning on February 3 to the initial procedure of one trial per day, I observed her performance closely in order if possible to discover her method. She worked steadily, using the knuckles of both hands to push the lock about on the face of the box. Evidently she noticed the relation of the lock stem to the staple, for her interest and activity obviously increased when the stem was nearly free from the staple. Thus by continuous manipulation of the lock she succeeded in removing it from the staple in forty-nine seconds. The minimum time was achieved in trial 17 on March 2, three seconds.

Thus finally, after prolonged opportunity during the winter of 1926 and several trials a year later, Congo learned to manipulate successfully the open lock in a kind of problematic situation which for the chimpanzee is very easy of mastery. But whereas this ape grasps the lock with its hand and removes it directly, deftly, and with apparent appreciation of its relation to the staple, the gorilla succeeded by means of random manipulation which is best described by the word fumbling. In less time than it required for Congo to learn to manipulate the open lock, an average specimen of chimpanzee would, I believe, learn to use a lock and key, so great is the difference between these anthropoids in mechanical aptitude and accompanying versatility and manual dexterity.

Problem 9. Spring snap. Although spring snaps had been familiar to Congo for many months prior to the observations now to be described, this experiment is new. The type of harness snap employed is represented by figure 2 of plate 7. It was used to fasten the lid of the box precisely as was the padlock of experiment no. 8. My first opportunity for systematic observation of Congo's attitude toward this mechanism was provided by the box and pole experiment, no. 7 in the list, for during the early trials of this experiment, from January 25 to February 2, a spring snap was used to fasten the lid of the box, and Congo therefore had opportunity to obtain the food within the box either by removing the snap and opening the lid or by pushing it out with the pole. As a matter of fact, during eight trials, the usual duration of which was thirty minutes, the gorilla, although she occasionally fooled with the snap for a few seconds, never made obvious progress toward the successful manipulation of the mechanism. Usually it appeared as though she examined it in order to assure herself that the lid was locked. So far then as initiative in the solution of this mechanical problem is concerned, the result of the first group of experiments was failure. But instead of abandoning the problem at this point I decided to present it in the same setting as the hasp and padlock experiment; that is, on the platform before the grill and with spring snap instead of padlock as fastening mechanism.

After the box and pole trial of February 2, the spring snap problem was presented as above indicated, before the grill. Congo, returned to her cage for the experiment, immediately attacked the snap and before I was able to get in position for observation, she had succeeded in removing it. How this happened I do not know. I suspect it must have been an accident, for never before had she succeeded, or indeed exhibited approach to discovery of method of operating the mechanism. Certainly in this instance not more than three seconds was required for the removal of the snap. Naturally I immediately re-set the apparatus in order to test her ability to repeat her success, but as I anticipated, she worked vainly and at random, and although given fifteen minutes for effort, finally failed. Similarly, on three succeeding days, a trial of fifteen minutes' duration daily yielded failure. Then it was decided to convert the experiment into a test of imitative learning and the following procedure was adopted.

With box on platform thirty inches from the grill, and there-fore beyond Congo's reach, I gave her opportunity to watch me place food within it, close the lid, fasten it with snap, remove and replace the snap slowly and with exaggerated movement of hand, and finally open the lid, close it, replace the snap, and push the mechanism into position for use. Some-times she watched intently throughout the demonstration, but more frequently after a few seconds she would turn away from the grill with indications of impatience. Following the demonstration, she was allowed a period of ten minutes to work at the snap.

Under these conditions of imitative learning the experiment was presented from February 7 daily, with two exceptions as indicated in the list on page 398, until the 19th, without solution of the problem, but with certain surprising observations rel-ative to motivation. For example, on February 10, a warm wet day which I supposed would be unfavorable for experimental work, Congo belied my judgment and expectation by working willingly, even eagerly, and instead of objecting to being out in the open and obliged to work for her breakfast, she actually begged for continuance after I had finished the day's work and returned her to her cage. It was quite obvious that she desired company and the entertainment of experimental work, which is certainly more than could be said of many human subjects who have served in psycho-biological experiments!

A typical observation for this period of the experiment is that of trial 8 on February 15. Imitative copy was set as usual and Congo when allowed to work fumbled with the snap for some fifteen seconds, then went away to amuse herself about the cage. Returning presently she worked with the snap for about six seconds, then mounted to the grill shelf, where she lay for several minutes. Returning once more to the snap she worked for only a moment. During the ten-minute interval there was absolutely no indication of progress and only a small amount of time was given to the problem.

By contrast with the above, her behavior in the spring-snap-imitation experiment on February 19, trial 11, is extremely interesting and important. Because of a sudden shower she was in her cage just prior to this trial. Apparently she was quite ready for something to do. I let her see me place a large orange in the box and then proceeded to demonstrate the removal of the snap as usual. When the mechanism was presented to her for work she began instantly and for four minutes labored almost continuously. She poked at the snap, turned, twisted, and pulled it; only once did she go away and then for but a moment. Once I heard the spring bolt of the snap click; a second later again, and in the next two minutes I heard it several times. She was working with extreme concentration, intense interest, and apparently with approaching localization of attack on the spring bolt. As I watched her fumble with the snap I wondered what she would do if the mechanism were two or three times as large, and therefore easier of manipulation with her short, thick fingers. In my notes on these observations I commented: "Why this great accession of interest in an experiment which at various times in the past fortnight she has virtually given up? Is it the cloudy day, with somewhat lower temperature, coupled with higher humidity and possibly a more stimulating atmosphere? Hunger certainly does not account for her unusual interest and activity." Previously she had succeeded, to my great surprise, in the wound chain experiment and had received her entire breakfast as reward. She had then spent an hour in her cage without attention from the experimenter. Possibly this, combined with her unwonted success in the wound chain experiment and the lure of the large orange, conditioned her favorably for the spring snap problem. Still I am puzzled, for I had no reason to expect other than the usual futile fumbling activity; and whereas previously I have felt reasonably certain that success in removing the snap was almost entirely accidental, I am now warned by the clicking of the spring bolt that the mechanism is being attacked in a manner which promises early success.

In the very next trial, no. 12 of February 20, she watched

the setting of the apparatus and my demonstration with evident impatience, meanwhile trying, even by reaching out with straws, to get hold of the box. This most unusual behavior undoubtedly resulted from her previous near success. She made it perfectly clear that she wished to work for herself instead of watching me operate the mechanism. With the box within reach she began to work feverishly, pulling, turning, and twisting the snap as in the preceding trial. In fifty-five seconds she removed the snap; precisely how I am unable to say, for her hands entirely obscured the mechanism from view.

From this time on the spring-snap-imitation experiment was repeated to enable me to discover her method of operating the mechanism and the rapidity of acquisition of skill. With reference to the first item, I discovered that she did not specifically attack the movable part of the spring snap but instead rubbed it vigorously with the knuckles of her fingers and thus sooner or later, forcing the bolt back, gave the snap an opportunity to spring out of the staple. This manipulation is little better than fumbling and it offers no evidence of insight. It is amazingly different from that of the chimpanzee, which in my experience either of its own initiative or quickly by aid of imitative copy, learns to operate this type of spring snap directly and efficiently by specific attack on the spring bolt, which is drawn back and the open hook of the snap thereupon skillfully removed from the staple of the hasp by a single movement of the animal's wrist. More striking contrast can scarcely be imagined than between Congo's method of removing the spring snap and that of a comparable specimen of the chimpanzee.

From the record of trial 17 given on February 26 are taken the following typical supporting observations. Congo began work instantly, eagerly, and with evident expectation of success. With the backs of her fingers and chiefly the knuckles of her right hand she pushed the snap about. Quickly she got it off (fifty-six seconds), but it seemingly was rather good luck than insight, for what happened was that she pressed hard against the snap again and again and finally got it into such a position that as her downward moving fingers forced the spring bolt back the snap either sprang or fell out of the staple. She worked without observation of the relation of bolt to remainder of snap or of the snap itself to the staple. There can be no doubt that her solution is an original one, and that my imitative copy instead of influencing her actions specifically merely stirred her to effort.

Yet another psychologically important result of this experiment is Congo's failure to carry over her interest in the spring snap or her ability to manipulate it to other situations than those of the experiment just described. For the purpose of motion picture photography the spring snap box was arranged on the platform outside the grill with the snap facing away from the grill instead of toward it. It was with extreme difficulty that I succeeded in holding Congo's attention on the mechanism in this position or in getting her to work at it, and not once in several trials was I able to induce her to remove the snap. In almost all of the experiments of this report in which she was moored to a stake during the progress of observation, a spring snap of the type described was used at one or both ends of the leash. Yet only once or twice, even after the series of experiments which I have described, did I observe her manipulating one of these snaps. Twice she succeeded by accident in freeing herself from a stake during an experiment, but it was by a sudden jerk on the chain and not by manipulation of the snap itself. It therefore appears that transfer of ability to operate a spring snap did not occur. This is contrary to the result of the box and pole and pipe and rod experiment, but in general it is consistent with Congo's behavior in other experiments. Indeed her behavior in the spring-snap-imitation experiment gave me the impression that her ability to solve the problem was very closely bound up with the particular situation in which she attained success. Obviously her success was the result of crude, ill-directed efforts, and lacked accompanying insight. Whether the mechanism was operated in a few seconds, a few minutes, or not at all, depended rather on good luck than good management.

From the observational results presented in the foregoing pages it would appear that my earlier tentative conclusions relative to the narrowly limited mechanical ability or aptitude of Congo are wholly confirmed. Although in the winter of 1927 she succeeded in solving simple mechanical problems in which she had previously failed, this indicates, I believe, rather the combined results of general adaptation to experimental situations and maturation than increased aptitude for dealing with mechanisms or greater insight into their essential characteristics and relations. Also supporting the conclusion that she is mechanically inapt in a truly remarkable degree is the repeatedly confirmed observation that she gave almost no attention to such mechanisms as the locks, hooks, snaps, and like devices which were used about her cage, in the construction of experimental apparatus, and for mooring her to trees. A notable illustrative instance is the following. On the inside of the door leading into her cage was a light hook such as is used on screen doors, which served to hold the door closed after one had entered the cage. It might naturally be supposed that Congo could, if she had so desired, either thrust the door open by force or lift the hook out of its eye, but during my months of observation of the animal and daily use of this device to hold the door shut, I never once saw her manipulate it. Were this not a typical observation, I should report others. It is a clear case of mechanical inaptitude. The chimpanzee is highly gifted in this respect, as compared with Congo. I think the same statement might be applied to the orang-outan, but as I have not had opportunity to make strictly comparable experiments and should have to depend upon intimate experimental acquaintance with only one specimen, I prefer to limit the comparison as indicated above.

SUMMARY OF SECTION VI

In this section, six experiments with their results have been summarily described. Of these, five were repetitions of experiments presented in essentially the same form in 1926, two were presented also in novel variations, and one experiment was first given in 1927.

The situations and Congo's response are as follows:

(1) Diagonal rope experiment, in which Congo promptly succeeded in 1926 and to which on repetition in 1927 she instantly reacted with perfect adaptation. Her response may cause the reader to suspect that this problem is too easy of solution to yield significant results. This inference, according to H. C. Bingham,[6] is not justified by the responses of young children.

(2) Hooked rope experiment. When it was initially presented, Congo reacted with gradual adaptation which afforded scant evidence of insight. Finally, she mastered the problem. On repetition the following winter she reacted successfully, although imperfectly, but after a few trials she exhibited a degree of adaptation or perfection of response not previously attained. It would thus seem that either the ripening of her specific experience or her general maturation during the interval between observations facilitated adaptation.

(3) Milk bottle experiment. In its original form, with the bottle containing solid food, this experiment yielded success initially and also in its repetitions after an interval of a year. The results of repetition were as usual superior to the original performances. Variation A of this experiment, which involved use of the bottle as milk container, was mastered very slowly and awkwardly by the gorilla. On first presentation, she was entirely incapable of adaptation, and it was only after daily practice for a fortnight that she achieved a fair amount of proficiency in drinking from the bottle. By contrast, the chimpanzee of comparable age and experience, as far as known adapts not only much more quickly than did Congo but also more perfectly.

(4) Wound chain experiment. To this situation Congo in 1926 responded negatively, although adaptation might reason-

---

[6] Unpublished observations.

ably have been expected. When the same situation was presented the following winter her response was at first positive, although subsequently she often refused to work in the experiment. When the problem was shifted from its original setting to the tree to which she was customarily moored for exercise, she immediately reacted positively and, indeed, exhibited quite unusual interest, eagerness, and skill. The reasons for her negativism in the one setting of the wound chain experiment and her positive response in the other are obscure. It would appear to be only in part a matter of motivation, and perhaps it is chiefly due to previous experience and to inhibiting factors or conditions appearing in connection with a specific situation. The detailed records of this experiment suggest many problems in motivation and indicate that the situation is worthy of intensive study with a view to careful analysis of attitude and of the relations of behavior to controllable internal and external conditions.

(5) Hasp and padlock experiment. Whereas Congo completely failed in this simple experiment during 1926, she succeeded a year later. Her success was due to what seemed more like random activity than action with insight. At no time did she exhibit skill in the manipulation of hasp and padlock comparable with that of the chimpanzee.

(6) Spring snap experiment. Presented first in experimental form in the winter of 1927, this situation for a long time baffled Congo. For months she had been familiar with spring snaps and similar mechanisms, but in no instance had she exhibited interest or the ability to operate them. Not only did she fail, in a long series of trials, to master the spring snap, but even the provision of imitative copy merely stirred her interest and eagerness to work at the snap. Finally she mastered it by random action which looked like fumbling, instead of by direct and definite attack on the movable bolt of the snap.

These several experiments very definitely indicate that Congo's behavioral adaptivity increased markedly during the year between observations. Her mechanical ability, initially meager, seemed only slightly greater after a year. The evidences of memory or persistence of effects of earlier experiences in the various experiments are abundant and wholly convincing. In almost every respect Congo's responses to mechanisms are inferior to those of the chimpanzee.

VII

BOXES AS IMPLEMENTS

During my first period of work with Congo she exhibited no natural ability to use a box as aid or implement in the solution of problems. Although in a few instances imitative copy was set, it is possible, and I suspect probable, that her ultimate success in using one box, and also in placing two boxes, the one upon the other, in order to obtain suspended food, was rather an expression of initiative and originality than of imitative tendency. Her slow and narrowly limited progress in the use of boxes during the winter of 1926, and my uncertainties as to the effects of imitative copy, made it especially desirable to re-present various forms of box problem the following winter.

Originally this type of problem had been presented in only two forms; namely, with either one or more boxes available for use on her initiative, or with similar situation in which the experimenter appeared as setter of imitative copy. The following winter four types of problem were used, but in no instance was a previously presented situation precisely duplicated. Repetition therefore is not an applicable term. The four experiments whose results will be presented in this section are: (1) greatest dimension of box; (2) box stacking with two boxes; (3) with three boxes, and (4) with four boxes.

Problem 10. Greatest dimension of box. This situation demanded merely the use of a single box so oriented with reference to the objective that its greatest dimension could be utilized. The experiment was set under Tree 3 from a limb of which at distance of eighty-eight inches from the ground there hung a paper bag containing food. A stake to which Congo could be moored during observations was driven into the ground a few feet off center, center being defined as the point on the ground directly beneath the suspended food. Five feet east of center and within easy reach was placed a wooden box 28 by 12 by 12 inches, and numbered for convenience of designation as O.

Congo a year earlier had demonstrated her ability to use successfully a box of unequal dimensions. This therefore is in principle a repeated experiment.

In her first trial, given January 26, Congo when brought to this problematic situation instantly ran to the box and rolled it over twice toward the center. She then ran to the stake and pulling the box toward her in that direction mounted it and looked first toward the limb of the tree and then toward the bag of food. The next few minutes she spent either gazing about or lying on the box. After a time she arose and grasping the box placed it almost on center with its greatest dimension vertical. She then tried to mount it, but its relatively small base and great height rendered this difficult for her. In four attempts it tipped toward her each time. Had she succeeded in mounting it she would have obtained her reward immediately. Actually she abandoned what must have seemed to her futile effort, and lay down to rest. Returning to her task after some minutes she first placed the box wrongly, but in her very next move she set it on end nearly under the food and again tried to mount it. Because of the obvious unfairness of the situation, I stepped up and holding the box firmly enabled her to climb upon it. Instantly she mounted and secured the bag of food. If in this case success were reckoned from the beginning of observation to the moment at which she first tried to mount the box in correct position, it would be nine minutes.

Following this trial the length of box O was reduced to twenty-four inches, on the assumption that Congo could use it readily in the dimensions 24 by 12 by 12 inches. The second trial was given with the reward eighty-four inches above the ground, and the modified box in position. When brought to the experiment she at once ran to the box, carried it almost to center, and tried to set it on end. It tipped over, and as it lay on one side she mounted it and reached for the bag with both hands, but missed it by two or three inches. Without stopping for a second attempt she scrambled to the ground, promptly set the box on end, mounted it with ease, and on the first attempt readily reached and secured her reward. The time required for success was about forty-five seconds.

Congo's eagerness for this experiment when she first saw the situation and was given opportunity to go to work was remarkable. Evidently she knew that she could succeed and was pleased.

A month later the experiment was tried in a different setting, under Tree 4, but with box O and the reward in the same relation as in the second trial. Again she exhibited ability properly to orient and place the box with reference to her objective and to obtain the latter. In this instance success required slightly less than one minute.

There can be no doubt about the gorilla's appreciation of the greatest as contrasted with the other dimensions of the box and her ability to utilize visual data in properly relating the box as implement to the food to be reached. Not only did this experiment in repetition yield success, but the performances described above are markedly better than those observed a year earlier. One may infer therefrom memory and mental development.

Problem 12. Box stacking with two boxes. It will be recalled that after prolonged opportunity for initiative, Congo finally in the 1926 period of observation succeeded in using two boxes successfully to obtain food. Whether in this she derived certain aid from her human environment I am not certain; at the time I was suspicious that she did. But however that may be, she finally acquired a fair measure of skill in solving this type of problem. Undoubtedly it is safer to assume that her response was partly imitation and partly the result of independent initiative.

In the interim between the box stacking performances of 1926 and the experiments now to be described, Congo had been used by Mr. Ben Burbridge as subject in motion picture studies, for certain of which box stacking was required. In all probability she obtained but little practice, as the sole interest of the photographer was to obtain as quickly as possible records of her performance in using boxes. Mr. Burbridge informed me that he had never seen her stack or pyramid more than two boxes. This of course has important bearing upon the subsequent experiments with three and four boxes.

The first trial of the experiment with two boxes was given under Tree 3. The stake to which the subject was moored was placed some two feet off center, and she was given about nine feet of chain for freedom of motion. The reward was suspended in a paper bag ninety-two inches above the ground. Two wooden boxes were placed within reach. The larger, an eighteen-inch cube, was five feet east of center, and the smaller, a twelve-inch cube, was five feet west of center.

When brought to the experiment for her first trial (whether or not it may properly be described as repetitional is in doubt) Congo ran directly to the larger box and rolled it over three times toward the center until it was in excellent position for use. Then she hastened directly to the smaller box, paused a moment to sit on it, and taking it in her arms carried it to the larger box, placed it squarely upon the latter, mounted the pyramid which she had thus constructed, and without difficulty reached the bag of food. The whole performance occupied somewhat less than one minute. Her technique was perfect and the only obvious possibility of improvement was the elimination of the delay at the smaller box when she stopped to sit on it as if interested in the feel of it.

This performance was so far superior to anything which I had observed in 1926 that I at once inferred that Congo must have had considerable experience in the handling and use of boxes during my absence, but, as already stated, Mr. Burbridge did not confirm my suspicion. Assuredly development, maturation, or however else one may choose to designate the changes in connection with growth and the ripening of experience, had splendidly prepared her for the solution of this problem.

The outcome of the first trial in the experiment with two boxes was so definite that it was not repeated immediately. After a month, on March 1, opportunity occurred for a second trial in a different setting. My reasons for trying experiments in different settings are suggested by the description of the wound chain experiments.

In this second re-presentational trial the situation was arranged under a different oak, Tree 4. To secure the food suspended eighty-eight inches above the ground a fifteen-inch cubical box was placed six feet east of center and the twelve-inch box six feet west of center.

Congo's performance demands detailed description. With the first opportunity she began to work. Going to 15[7] she took it in her arms and carried it toward center. Then she tried to place it on its edges or corners between the center and the stake. Several times she lifted it toward the reward, and once placing it before her she mounted and from it reached toward the food. Discouraged by this futile effort, she climbed down and carried it toward 12, where she dropped it and climbing upon it reached down and drew 12 up to her so that she could place it on 15. With the two boxes, she was about three feet west of center. Looking toward the food she evidently perceived that it was out of reach, but nevertheless she stood erect on 15, holding 12 in her arms toward the food as if testing her reach and momentarily uncertain. She now looked at the observer for a few seconds; then leaving the boxes ran away, and when she returned, devoted a few seconds to freeing her chain which had become wound about the stake. Evidently she was somewhat puzzled, and uncertain what to do. Having freed the chain she went to 15 and again placed it nearly on center. Then mounting it she reached down and drawing up 12 placed it upon 15. At first she tried to stand it on its corners or edges, but after a few seconds she put it squarely on 15 and mounting the pyramid

[7]The boxes are designated hereafter by their size: 15, for example, refers to the fifteen-inch cube.

reached for the reward. She was too far off center, and could barely touch the suspended food without risk of losing her balance. Unwilling to take this risk she descended to 15 and re-located 12 somewhat nearer the banana, so that it projected over the edge of 15. Again she mounted, but still too far away for safe reach she descended when the boxes began to tip, and once more shifted the position of 12. This time it extended precariously far beyond the edge of 15. With the boxes in this instable position she slowly mounted 12 and by careful reaching grasped the food just as the pyramid toppled under her. Thus success was achieved in a trifle less than five minutes of almost continuous work.

This performance has been described in detail because it is more characteristic, illuminating, and, I believe, fair to Congo's actual status in relation to this type of experiment than is that of the previous trial. Evidently she remembered how to use two boxes, but was neither swift nor expert in the task save as circumstances favored her. Why she happened to work so skillfully in the first trial and so much less so in the second is uncertain. I strongly suspect it was a matter of attitude. Trial 1 was given in a location where she had previously achieved success in several types of experiment. Her attitude naturally was one of eager, expectant hopefulness, and she therefore solved immediately the problem for which she carried over from the previous year the necessary experience. For trial 2, by contrast, the experiment was set in a new situation, farther from the cage and her usual grounds of experimentation, which lacked both familiarity and the value of associated successes. My surmise may be wrong, but I believe this suggested explanation is more probably correct than the assumption that in the one case she was more hungry, eager for food, or for similar reasons more strongly motivated than in the other.

Problem 13. Box stacking with three boxes. By Congo's success in the use of two boxes to obtain suspended food I was encouraged to present in order three and subsequently four boxes. For both of these experiments, except the preliminary trial of problem 13, Tree 4, the oak some twenty-five yards north of the cage, and of all the trees used most remote from it, was employed. To a limb of this tree the food was suspended as reward, and a standard set of boxes, two of which have already been mentioned in connection with the previous experiment, was used as indicated in the following paragraphs. The boxes were all constructed of light wood and were cubes measuring 9, 12, 15, and 18 inches. Their weights were respectively 6, 12, 25, and 30 pounds.

The first trial of this experiment may be considered preliminary. It was arranged under Tree 3 in the site of the 1926 box experiment, and Congo, by the proximity of the trunk of the tree and some low branches, was constantly tempted to try other methods of obtaining the food than the stacking of boxes. Food in a paper bag was suspended one hundred and six inches above the ground, and three boxes, each six feet off center, were available as follows: 18-inch cube, east; 15-inch cube, west; and 12-inch cube, north of center. The subject had ten feet of free chain.

Prevented from using tree trunk or branches as avenues of approach to her reward, she attempted to use the boxes. After some minutes of work with 18 and 12, she turned to 15 and tried to pull 18 upon it. Although she several times attempted to stack the three boxes, she never placed them in the relation 18, 15, 12 and never in stable equilibrium. Several times as she tried to mount the pile she either tipped the boxes over or fell off. Repeatedly, as she worked with the boxes, she paused to beat her chest or the boxes, in evident impatience or resentment of her task.

Because of the obvious unsatisfactoriness of this location for the three-box experiment, this preliminary trial was discontinued after an interval of ten minutes. In the meantime Congo had demonstrated her interest in the problem and her willingness to attempt to use three boxes to obtain the reward. Whereas previously she had usually taken up the second box and lifted it into position on the basal box, in this trial she more frequently mounted the first box, or the second if two were in position, and pulled the other box or boxes up into position. Possibly she would have succeeded in solving the problem had she placed the boxes in the order 18, 15, 12, thus constructing a stable pyramid.

For the regular trials of problem 13, beginning January 31, the situation was arranged under Tree 4. In this location all subsequent experiments with three and with four boxes were made. The setting was eminently satisfactory because there was no opportunity for her to use either limbs or the tree trunk. The mooring stake was located about eighteen inches southwest of center; the bait, unless otherwise specified consisting of a baked banana and a baked sweet potato, was suspended one hundred and six inches above the ground, and the boxes were placed as in the preliminary trial six feet off center, 12 to the north, 15 to the west, and 18 to the east. She was given ten feet of free chain. The time of each trial was thirty minutes.

Whereas in the preliminary trial definite effort to use the three boxes had been observed, this did not appear in the first regular trial. She worked with all of the boxes, but never did she give convincing evidence of desire to place them in pyramidal formation. Possibly the new setting of the experiment was responsible for this seeming inferiority of the performance in trial 1 to that in the preliminary trial.

Similarly in the second trial there was failure to use three boxes. Once it was recorded that Congo suddenly rushed to the boxes and began to use them as though she had just realized that by so doing she might obtain the food. She seized 18 and placed it about three feet off center; then she pulled 15 upon it. Mounting the pile she looked toward the bait, which however was too far away to be reached. The suddenness of her approach to the boxes may indicate a compelling impulse, possibly involving imagery or other form of ideational process. Shortly thereafter she purposely knocked

15 from 18 and ran about the stake the length of her chain
as if impatient with the boxes and her task. So the description
continues, without indication of progress toward the solution
of the problem. One additional incident is worthy of report.
She succeeded in piling 18 upon 15, but they were instably
placed and as she mounted the pile the boxes fell. Congo
falling with them struck the ground heavily on her back. It
was the first time I saw her fall in such a manner as to cause
discomfort. She came down with a dull thud, apparently
entirely unprepared for the mishap and unable to save herself from an uncomfortable jar. One discovers in this good
reason why she should not attempt to jump. No emotional
expression was observed, nor did she seem particularily disconcerted.

Obvious diminution of interest in the experiment appeared
in trial 3, and neither in it nor trial 4 did indication of progress
appear. In trial 5, contrary to the experimenter's intention,
she succeeded in obtaining her reward by placing 15 upon 18
on center and reaching from them. She was not able to grasp
the food, but by touching it with her finger tips dislodged it.

In order if possible to increase the motivation, in trial 6
a hand of ripe bananas, consisting of about a dozen, was placed
one hundred and seven inches from the ground. Just beneath
the hand there dangled in horizontal position a single banana.
It was one hundred and four inches from the ground. The bait
in this trial was unusually conspicuous because of the bright
yellow color and the large quantity.

Although at first Congo feigned indifference, it was obvious that the food was almost constantly in mind and that
she was searching for ways of getting at it. Two or three
times she used 15 and 18, but from them she was unable to
reach her objective. Then returning to her task from a brief
respite, she mounted 18, pulled 15 upon it, and standing on
15 reached down for 12. From that height it was a difficult
task, but grasping 12 firmly she lifted it and, standing erect
on 15, raised it toward the banana instead of placing it under

her feet. In this she persisted for several seconds, but without being able to touch the food. Discouraged, she descended to the ground, dropping 12 as she went, and thereupon removed 15 from 18.

This was an excellent attempt, and although Congo failed of success it is obvious tnat had she placed 12 on 15 she could have obtained her reward. Especially in this trial the observer was made to feel the difficulty for her of transition from the use of two to three boxes. Her behavior suggested the question: Is it more intelligent to strive for the seemingly impossible or to abandon effort? Quite evidently she gives up when effort seems fruitless.

Because the large prospective reward appeared to increase Congo's interest and effort, it was continued in trial 7. She came to the experiment eagerly, and after several minutes of varied activity directly, and with definite intent it seemed, pulled 18 to center, drew 15 upon it, and reaching from the pile almost touched the reward. Encouraged thereby she nevertheless descended to the ground and, knocking 15 from 18, attempted from 18 to pull both 15 and 12 to her. She was able to get both in her hands simultaneously, but she failed to raise them. Her next move was to pull 15 upon 18 and then reaching down from 15 to draw up 12 and place it upon 15. The pyramid thus constituted was perfect and, instantly mounting it, she easily reached the bananas and, grasping four of them, sat down on 12 to devour them. This initial success in the use of three boxes is shown in figure 2 of plate 10.

Chiefly to test the influence of diminished quantity of reward, two bananas, instead of a hand, were offered in trial 8. They were conspicuously located about one hundred and six inches from the ground. Brought to the experiment, Congo went to work immediately. Having assembled the boxes about her, she mounted 18 and tried to pull 12 upon it. Next she turned to 15 and attempted to place the boxes in the order 18, 12, 15. The pile was instable and toppled over. Sitting upon 18 she now pulled 15 to her and after some difficulty placed it squarely on 18. Then standing on 18 she reached down and grasping 12 pulled it up and placed it securely on 15. Once more, as in trial 7, she had achieved a perfect pyramid. With proper caution she mounted it and standing erect reached the bananas. She then sat down on 12, but finding it uncomfortably small she knocked it out of her way and sat on 15. Approximately two minutes were required for this excellent performance.

Subsequent repetitions of this experiment, trials 9 to 12, were made for purpose of photographic record (see plate 10), demonstration, or to indicate further the motivating value of large versus small quantities of food as prospective reward. The general outcome of the observations was that Congo's ability to use three boxes when she so desired, to obtain suspended food, was convincingly demonstrated. The motivation appeared to be extremely variable. In general, a large quantity of food seemed more likely to attract attention and stimulate effort, but as indicated by the description of trial 8, the customary quantity might yield as prompt and signal success as an extraordinarily large quantity. Although no considerable skill was attained by Congo in the manipulation of three boxes to construct a pyramid, she exhibited tendency to place the boxes appropriately near center and in such relation as to constitute a stable structure. To the experimenter her difficulty in making the transition from solution of the two-box to that of the three-box problem is puzzling. The preliminary trial with three boxes clearly enough indicated tendency to try to use all of the boxes, but in the regular trials it seemed at first as though she were restricted to the use of two boxes, and that the necessity for employment of three constituted a veritably new type of problem. This suspicion is further confirmed by the results of the experiment with four boxes, now to be described.

Problem 19. Box stacking with four boxes. In the situation described for the previous experiment, the box stacking observations were continued with placement of the reward which necessitated the use of four boxes. A hand of bananas one hundred and fifteen inches above the ground, unless otherwise specified, was offered as reward, and as means of obtaining it, the four cubical boxes previously described were placed six feet off center as follows: 9 to the south, 12 to the north, 15 to the west, and 18 to the east.

In the very first trial Congo eagerly began work, with every indication of expected success. Gathering the boxes about her she began to pile them and in the course of a few minutes she had constructed and proved the uselessness of 18, 9, 12; 18, 12, 9, and 15, 18, 12. In case of the last of these structures she had placed the basal box practically on center, but the pile was instable and promptly fell. Several times she succeeded in arranging the boxes in the order 15, 18, 12, but this construction of course did not suffice to bring her within reach of the reward. The really essential point in the record of this trial is that in the course of the regular thirty-minute interval of work Congo did not attempt to use the fourth box as part of the pyramid, nor indeed was there indication of attention to it.

The second trial exhibited marked diminution of interest and expectation of success. She amused herself by playing with the boxes, throwing them about in the air as though they were toys. Only a small part of her time was given to manipulation of the boxes in relation to the food. Again she showed entire willingness to work with two or three of the boxes in combination, but it seemed not to occur to her that the fourth might be added to the structure.

As my available time for the continuation of this experiment was limited, I decided at this point to attempt to facilitate solution of the four-box problem by eliminating certain of the initial steps in pyramid construction. To this end for trial 3 I pre-arranged the situation by placing 18 on center, 15 upon 18, 12 six feet west of center, and 9 six feet east of center. A hand of bananas was suspended one hundred and fifteen inches from the ground. When brought into this situation Congo paid little attention to boxes or food. Deliberately she knocked 15 from 18; then she proceeded to play with 12, throwing it into the air and moving it about rapidly with hands and feet. Apparently she had definitely given up the problem and was not to be tempted to undertake its solution. Again as I watched her, I wondered whether perhaps in the long run it is good judgment to refuse to attempt the seemingly impossible. Here Congo, as in certain other experiments, after sizing up the situation, definitely refused to work.

In the next trial, 4, she was extremely rambunctious, but only slightly interested in the problematic situation. It was her delight apparently to knock the boxes about as though irritated by them and impatient of their presence.

The fifth trial found her in optimistic mood. She had just succeeded easily in the slot box experiment and, it seemed, was greatly encouraged by the experience. In preparation for her I had arranged the boxes as follows: 18, 15, 12 were pyramided on center and 9 was six feet to the west of center. Instantly, when given opportunity, she mounted the pyramid, and then lifting 12 she moved it about and readjusted it to suit herself. Then again she climbed upon it and looked toward the food without reaching for it. Next she got down and removed 12 and 15 from 18. Presently she took up 9 and carried it toward the other boxes. Thus she approximated all four boxes to the stake. They were within easy reach and 18 was excellently placed as base of the pyramid. But instead of attempting to construct it she lay down beside the boxes and amused herself with them, her chain, and acorns in the sand about her. The concluding paragraph of my notes on this trial reads: "Evidently box stacking does not generalize in the sense that when the gorilla has learned to use two boxes together she can by virtue of this acquired ability use additional boxes as necessity requires. Apparently there is marked difference between the spread or transfer of training from box to box and from stick to straw, cloth, or any other functional substitute for a stick. It is clear that Congo is not likely to succeed in the four-box experiment unless somehow given a strong impetus toward effort."

The sixth trial was entirely without result. She came to the experiment unwillingly, and either refused to work or manipulated the boxes carelessly and with evident lack of interest.

The seventh trial, given on March 2, had as its background an unusual preparation. Prior to it Congo had been given opportunity to use, in order, for the achievement of reward one box, two boxes, and three boxes. This was done with the thought that success in the use of boxes in forms of experiment which she had already mastered might favor determined effort to use four boxes. The conditions of trial 7 differed somewhat from prior trials. A hand of bananas hung one hundred and fourteen inches above the ground with a single banana hanging horizontally just beneath the hand. Box 18 was placed on center and the others six feet off center, 15 to the east, 12 to the west, and 9 to the north.

Congo came to the experiment eagerly. Her attitude contrasted sharply with that in trial 6, when she evidently ignored the problem. This I believe clearly indicates the importance for motivation of her recent experiences in the other forms of box problem. Actually, in the half hour which she was given for work, she manipulated the boxes rather persistently in varied ways, and despite a temperature of 45° and a cold wind, she made a number of excellent attempts to pyramid them. Once, with 18, 15, 12 well placed, it seemed as though she might succeed, but descending from her excellent pyramid she intentionally knocked it over and going directly to box 9 touched it, without carrying it toward the other boxes. So the trial continued, with varied uses of three boxes, but no detectable approach to the use of the fourth.

Nothing new appeared in trial 8; but in trial 9 all four of the boxes were used in various combinations but never together, nor was there convincing evidence that she had the idea of constructing a pile or pyramid of four boxes. Impatience, as indicated by chest beating, was conspicuous throughout the trial.

In trial 10, on March 6, appeared what may tentatively be described as the imaginal solution of the four-box problem. Success was not actually achieved, but Congo's behavior would seem to indicate that she had at last hit upon the idea of using the fourth box. In this trial a hand of bananas hung approximately one hundred and seventeen inches from the ground. Boxes 18, 15, 12 were pyramided on center and 9 was six feet west of center. It was necessary only for her to carry 9 to the pyramid and properly place it. Although she had been eager for other experiments on this date, when brought to the box stacking stake she exhibited a negativistic attitude by turning her back on the boxes. Nevertheless, she soon mounted the pyramid and looked at the bait. Then she jumped from 15 to the ground, a very unusual thing for her to do, and ran away the length of her chain. Passing box 9 she noticed it and stopping drew it to her. Then while looking at it *she started* as if suddenly realizing that the box was potentially useful. Taking it up she hurried with it to the pyramid and tried to place it on top. The reach was too great for her and in her efforts she knocked box 12 off of the pile. Putting 9 in place of 12, she mounted the pyramid but of course without advantage. Next she dropped 9 to the ground and reaching for 12, while standing on 15, drew it up and placed it in position, thus reconstituting the pyramid 18, 15, 12. Once more she mounted the pile and standing up vainly reached toward the bananas. As she started to climb down she knocked 12 off and then clambering to the ground intentionally pulled 15 off of 18. It was clearly an expression of dissatisfaction.

As she had shown desire to use the fourth box, the placement of which on top of the pyramid was extremely difficult, I now stepped up and replaced 12 so that the pyramid, directly on center, was constituted by 18, 15, 12. Quickly Congo mounted this pyramid and from the top reached for 9, but in doing so she knocked 12 to the ground. Thereupon she dropped 9. Once more I replaced 12, and she, mounting the pile, looked about for 9. Failing to reach it, she knocked 12 out of her way. A third time I replaced it and as she mounted the pyramid I placed box 9 so that she could reach it and, if she so desired, raise it to her level. This she succeeded in doing. Then standing on 12 she held 9 toward the bait, raising it thus three times as if to reach the bananas with it (see plate 11, figure 1). She then turned it over several times in her hands, as if uncertain how to place it on the pyramid. After a few seconds she placed it squarely on 12 and mounting the pyramid of four boxes readily reached the bananas. As the pyramid, although perfectly formed, was instable, fearing that otherwise she might fall and injure herself, I steadied it with one hand as she reached. Actually she did fall despite my precaution, for having grasped several of the bananas she fell with them to the ground as the pyramid collapsed.

Barring the experimenter's assistance in this experiment, Congo's behavior was essentially the same as in the transition from the use of two to the use of three boxes.

Trial 11, like 10 in its setting, resulted in success, but only with the assistance of the experimenter, who again held 9 so that Congo standing on the pyramid could grasp and draw it to her. Of peculiar interest in this trial and the preceding one was her method of mounting the pyramid and reaching down from the topmost box for additional building materials. For an animal of her weight and degree of clumsiness this procedure is unsatisfactory, but so also and perhaps in equal degree is the method of placing the boxes from the ground. It was entirely possible for her to place three boxes by either method, but by neither could the fourth box of this particular series readily be put into position. Doubtless had the boxes been considerably larger so that Congo could stand on any one of them and from it reach to the topmost, a combination of methods might have been effectively used. Considering the difficulties of the situation, the aid offered by the experimenter would seem justifiable, and although it possibly modified Congo's natural solution of the problem, it nevertheless leaves in clear light her desire and intent to use four boxes simultaneously.

The twelfth trial yielded conspicuous and almost independent success. The conditions were as previously described, except that box 9 was only four feet from center. Having mounted the pyramid Congo promptly removed 12 and replaced it with 9. This is peculiarly significant as indicating association of 9 with the food. She then lifted 9 upwards in the air toward the bananas, whereupon she placed it on 15 and reached to the ground for 12. Standing as she did on top of the pile, this naturally was a difficult process, and although she made an excellent attempt to raise it toward her the pyramid was endangered, so stepping up I held 12 against the base of the pyramid so that she could grasp it firmly and lift it. Taking it up she stood on 15 and held both 9 and 12 in her arms. Promptly I stepped back to try to obtain a photograph of her manipulation of the boxes. Intent on the photographic record, I cannot say certainly whether she placed 12 or 9 on 15, but at any rate in a very few seconds she had completed the pyramid and was reaching for the bananas. She easily grasped several of them, and then as the pyramid toppled she fell lightly to the ground. The time required for this success was three minutes and twenty-one seconds. As indicating ability to use the fourth box it is excellent.

A subsequent trial, in which the boxes were distributed in their initial positions, resulted in failure on Congo's part to stack them successfully. In the course of the half hour allowed her she made several attempts to construct a usable pyramid, but in no case did she place the boxes in proper order or succeed in getting all four into a single structure.

Summary of Section VII

In reviewing the four box experiments of this section it is eminently worthy of note that Congo used boxes as implements much more readily and skillfully in the winter of 1927 than a year previously. Especially conspicuous was her memory for the use of the greatest dimension of a box and of two boxes simultaneously, and her very considerable imaginal and manual skill in properly placing and using either a box or boxes in problems 10 and 12 of the present series.

Whereas the experimenter had expected the use of additional boxes to be merely a matter of practice in stacking or pyramiding, it is made clear by the three-box and four-box experiments as described in this section that each additional box essentially alters the problematic situation, and to an extent which may be found to vary very greatly in accordance with the previous experience of the individual or with individuals of the species, constitutes a new problem. Whereas in the winter of 1926, the experimenter undertook to assist Congo in the solution of box experiments, in the present series of observations her solutions, as far as intent is concerned, were entirely spontaneous. It was only in the four-box experiment that she was given any aid, and in that case only after she had exhibited the idea of using the four boxes in relation.

The characteristics of Congo's adaptations to these problems, her peculiar difficulties and her modes of achieving success, suggest on the one hand the desirability of a carefully standardized series of box problems, and on the other its application under comparable conditions to children ranging in chronological age from two years on, and to the several types of manlike ape. In the circumstances of my study of Congo it was entirely impossible to standardize methods or to use ideally those already standardized. There were, as indicated by description of observations, a number of varying factors in each experimental situation which could be only partially controlled. There is no reason to apologize for this, but it is essential to recognize the circumstances and to safeguard against misleading inferences by taking them fully into account.

In the box experiments Congo, clearly enough, was complexly motivated. Irrespective of degree of hunger or desire for the reward which happened to be offered, she might come to either a familiar or an unfamiliar type of situation with eagerness or reluctance, hopefulness or discouragement, depending upon the result of a preceding experiment or possibly of other experiments which happen to have been set in the situation in which she finds herself. Whereas with certain of the mammalia, notably the much studied rodents, a few reasonably controllable external stimuli may appear chiefly to control or condition the nature and speed of adaptation or habit formation, such clearly is not the case with Congo, or indeed with any of the types of anthropoid ape. Instead, motivation involves numerous internal factors, knowledge of which must be sought in previous experience. Immediate stimuli may be of almost negligible value by comparison with these representational processes.

DELAYED RESPONSE AND OTHER METHODS OF EXHIBITING MNEMONIC PROCESS

In 1926 only a few problematic situations were arranged for the special study of memory in Congo, and those few as often yielded negative as positive results. The following winter, aside from the repetition of experiments to discover the status of previously acquired habits and the nature and extent of mental development, attention was directed to the study of mnemonic processes by such special methods as the delayed response experiment and the burial of food. The results are definitely positive and of unusual interest and importance, especially as suggesting supplementary lines of inquiry.

Problem 17. Delayed response. The suggestion which led to this experiment came from W. S. Hunter's (1913) description of the delayed reaction method as applied to animals and children. The method now to be described differs importantly from that of Hunter, not because I sought thus to improve on the original but because the characteristics of my subject and the general situation in which I worked suggested the desirability of a different apparatus and procedure.

The delayed response experiment was arranged under the large water-oak, Tree 3, some ten yards northerly of the cage. The situation had the advantage of the shade of the large tree and also of a clear level sandy area some thirty feet in each direction. Taking the mooring post as the center of the mechanism, there were placed at the ends of the north-south and east-west diameters and sixteen feet from the center, four similar wooden boxes, the inside measurements of which were: length 12 inches, depth 6 inches, width 4½ inches. Each box was made of ⅞-inch pine and carried a lid which although fitting tightly could readily be lifted. This lid was not hinged or in any other way fastened to the box. The boxes were coated with strong colored enamel paint, white, black, red, and green, respectively. In relation to the mooring post they were placed as follows: white to the north, green to the east, black to the south, red to the west.

Congo was moored to the post and her freedom of motion regulated by a rope and chain system. In the top of the post, which projected some ten inches above the ground, was a stout swivel spring snap to which was attached a two-inch steel pulley. A like pulley was fastened to a large limb of the oak tree approximately sixteen feet above and exactly over the mooring post. To another limb of the tree approximately fifteen feet northeast of the first and twelve feet from the ground another pulley was fastened, and some eighteen feet northeast of the post a stake, with cleat to which rope could easily be fastened, was driven into the ground. Beside this stake was placed a seat for the observer and a box on which his notebook and timing mechanisms could rest. A half-inch manila rope extended from the last mentioned stake through the three pulleys above described, and at its end carried a spring snap which was prevented from passing through the pulley on the mooring post by a knot in the rope. To this snap there was attached a piece of chain three feet long, which in turn terminated in a spring snap. The latter as desired could be hooked into the ring of Congo's collar.

With the rope drawn taut against the knot and securely fastened to the stake beside the observer's seat, Congo could be attached to the mooring post by the short chain. This gave her approximately four feet range and she could walk about the post in that radius without tangling the chain or rope, since the swivel snap and swivels also in the pulleys provided that the mechanism should turn with her. As the boxes were sixteen feet from the post they were eight to ten feet beyond Congo's reach.

The chain-rope system was so planned and arranged that she could be held at the post for any desired interval and at the appropriate moment released to seek food in one or other of the boxes. To effect release the experimenter merely loosened the rope from the stake beside him and allowed Congo as much leeway as necessary to reach a box. As soon as she had made definite choice, either obtaining her reward or failing to do so as the case might be, she was promptly drawn back to the post and there held. By this simple device it proved possible to regulate the movement of the animal with entire satisfactoriness. Only once in the course of the weeks of experimentation did the chain and rope become tangled so that it was necessary for the observer to straighten them out before the subject could be released for response.

Plate 12 presents the delayed response situation. In figure 1 Congo is shown moored to the central post with the Negro Bill standing close by, and by appropriate symbols the positions of the release mechanism, the observer, and of the several food boxes are indicated. Figure 2 is a close-up of the mooring post and its attached mechanism.

During experiments the observer sat between the white and the red boxes close to the trunk of the oak tree and with his right side toward Congo. She was familiarized with the apparatus and its operation by five preliminary trials, February 17 to 21 inclusive, in each of which she was permitted to obtain food from every box. The order was varied from day to day and the attention of the investigator was directed to acquainting her so far with the apparatus and accustoming her to it that having seen food placed in a given box she would attempt to obtain it as soon as released. By the end of the fifth preliminary trial she was working so freely and well that it seemed desirable to proceed with the regular course of experimentation. Thereupon it was decided to begin with a delay of five minutes.

It was on February 21 that the initial trials, each of five minutes, were given. With Congo waiting at the post and everything arranged for observation, I let her see me place in the black box a quart cup of milk. As soon as the box was covered I started my stop watch and promptly took my place beside the release mechanism, where I observed and recorded her behavior during the five-minute interval of delay. At first she struggled hard to get free, evidently with desire to get to the milk. At the proper moment, with Congo oriented away from the black box, I loosened the rope and, at once appreciating the measure of freedom thus given, she proceeded directly and rapidly to the black box and eagerly drank the milk.

A similar positive result was obtained in a second trial with the same interval of delay. Congo struggled hard to break from her mooring post, but she exhibited no irritation and the apparatus worked perfectly.

The conditions and results of a series of delayed response observations extending from February 21 to March 10 are presented in tabular form herewith. The information provided comprehends date, hour, and number of trial, correct or food-containing box, designated by appropriate capital letter, period of delay in minutes, location of the animal during major portion of period of delay, P indicating presence at mooring post and A indicating absence from mooring post. In the latter case Congo ordinarily was engaged in work on other experiments. And finally, the result of the experiment, + indicating a correct first choice and — an incorrect first choice. Letter or letters following the minus sign designate box or boxes chosen. Trials designated by a or b following the number of trial are repetitions. Thus, for example, in trial 3, involving use of the red box, Congo failed. Immediately she was returned to the mooring post, shown the food in the red box and held for a period of five minutes before being permitted to choose. In other words, trial 3 was immediately repeated as trial 3a under the same conditions as originally. In one instance, namely trial 31, also with the red box, two repetitions were necessary before she chose correctly. In this case she was absent from the delayed response situation in trial 31 and in its first repetition, whereas for the second repetition she was present throughout the interval of delay.

DELAYED RESPONSE EXPERIMENTS

Date and hour	Trial number	Designation of box	Period of delay	Location of animal	Response
Feb. 21, 12:50 p.m.	1	B	5'	P	+
" " 12:57 p.m.	2	G	5'	P	+
" 22, 9:32 a.m.	3	R	5'	P	— G
" " 9:38 a.m.	3a	R	5'	P	+
" " 9:45 a.m.	4	W	6'	P	+
" —" 12:12 p.m.	5	G	8'	P	+
" " 12:24 p.m.	6	B	10'	P	+
" 23, 9:11 a.m.	7	G	6'	P	+
" " 9:20 a.m.	8	R	8'	P	+
" " 12:13 p.m.	9	B	10'	P	+
" " 12:26 p.m.	10	W	12'	P	+
" 24, 4:40 p.m.	11	R	12'	P	+
" " 4:55 p.m.	12	G	15'	P	— W
" " 5:14 p.m.	12a	G	15'	P	+
" 25, 9:08 a.m.	13	W	12'	P	+
" " 9:23 a.m.	14	B	15'	P	+
" " 12:16 p.m.	15	G	15'	P	— W
" " 12:33 p.m.	15a	G	15'	P	+
" " 12:50 p.m.	16	R	18'	P	+
" 26, 9:37 a.m.	17	B	16'	P	+
" " 9:56 a.m.	18	W	20'	P	— R
" " 10:21 a.m.	18a	W	20'	P	+
" " 12:20 p.m.	19	R	25'	P	+
" " 12:48 p.m.	20	G	30'	P	— B R[a]
" " 4:05 p.m.	21	G	25'	P	+
" " 4:32 p.m.	22	B	30'	P	+
" 27, 9:26 a.m.	23	R	25'	P	+
" " 9:55 a.m.	24	W	35'	P	+
" " 12:21 p.m.	25	B	40'	P	+
" 28, 8:55 a.m.	26	G	45'	P	— W G
" " 11:00 a.m.	27	R	60'	P	— B R
" " 4:07 p.m.	28	W	60'	P	+
Mar. 1, 8:45 a.m.	29	B	30'	P	+
" " 9:20 a.m.	30	G	120'	A	— B G
" 2, 9:18 a.m.	31	R	60'	A	— G
" " 10:20 a.m.	31a	R	60'	A	— B
" " 11:25 a.m.	31b	R	60'	P	+
" 4, 9:50 a.m.	32	W	60'	A	+
" 5, 9:45 a.m.	33	B	90'	A	— W B
" 6, 10:00 a.m.	34	R	120'	P	+
" 7, 9:09 a.m.	35	G	150'	P	+
" " 4:00 p.m.	36	G	10'	P	+
" 8, 9:12 a.m.	37	B	180'	A	+
" 9, 9:15 a.m.	38	(Special experiment, described in text.)			
" 9-10, 9:30 a.m.	39	W	1440'	A	—

[a]Food not obtained.

The following points in technique and procedure are of importance. The interval of delay was determined, from the instant of covering the food-containing box to the instant of Congo's release, by the use of an additive stop watch. The observer, except during the trials when Congo was absent from the delayed response situation or in delays of more than an hour, with few exceptions, sat continually at his post facing east with his right side toward Congo and the mooring post. Most of the time he was engaged in writing. In the early experiments when the moment for release arrived, Congo's attention was attracted by light clapping of the experimenter' hands thrice; later she gave attention the instant the experimenter moved toward the release stake. In no instance was she released until she was facing in some other direction than toward the correct box, and in almost all of the trials she directly faced the experimenter when released, and at the same time usually held the rope with one hand ready to pull on it and to move toward one of the boxes. Throughout the series of experiments the food-reward offered was relatively large. Sometimes it consisted of an entire meal, but oftener a cup containing nearly a quart of milk, or the solid food of a meal (one or two sweet potatoes and one to three baked bananas) was used separately.

Congo's initial responses surprised me greatly, for she chose correctly with evident ease and assurance, although during the period of delay she made no attempt to hold her orientation and apparently attended to the varied happenings about her as though unaware of the near presence of food. The chances of a correct choice, aside from memory, would presumably be one in four. Actually, she chose incorrectly about once in four times, and even then she almost never failed to locate the correct box on first repetition.

From the first, effort was made to prevent her from using as basis for choice odor of food, peculiarities in the appearance of the correct box aside from location and color, and cues derived from the actions of the experimenter. At no time was attempt made to conceal the experimenter; instead he practiced rigorous uniformity of action, gazing always directly at the mooring post and observing Congo indirectly as she was released and oriented toward a box. Possible choice by odor was checked in two ways, and it was proved that she was not depending on this cue. One check was the direction of wind, for since the observations were conducted in the open it frequently happened that the wind was so steady and strong that unless it carried from the correct box toward the mooring post Congo could not possibly obtain stimulus. The second check was obtained by surreptitiously placing food with strong odor in each of the three boxes designated as incorrect. In no instance was Congo misled by this condition. Further check on the possible derivation of cues from the observer is supplied by the results of trial 38, which at this point may appropriately be described in detail.

This trial was arranged for the express purpose of discovering whether the observer could determine the choice in the absence of food. The conditions, following a trial with three-hour delay on the previous day, in which Congo chose correctly, were as follows. At 9:15 Congo was brought to the delayed response situation. Food was not placed in any box, but the experimenter selected red as the box to be chosen. After being held at the post for five minutes she was released in accordance with the usual procedure. At the moment she was facing the observer. Instantly she turned to the post, pulled on the rope, wheeled sharply to her left, and facing the white box went directly to it and opened it as though expecting food. Promptly she was returned to the post in preparation for repetition of the experiment as trial 38a. In this case the experimenter selected black as the correct box. In due course Congo was again released facing the observer, but instead of holding her orientation she wheeled to her right, grasped the rope, pulled on it, then turned sharply to her left and went directly to the green box. Once more she was returned to the post, this time in preparation for repetition designated as trial 38b. The experimenter selected white as the correct box. Congo, however, by procedure similar to that in the previous trials, chose the black box. Again she was returned to the stake and this time, in trial 38c, for which the observer selected the green box as correct, she definitely, and evidently on the basis of choice made in advance of release, went directly to the red box.

In no case, despite the selection of a given box by the experimenter, was it chosen by Congo. It is noteworthy that in this series of four trials she chose in order white, green, black, red, proceeding clockwise about the circle. Whether this was accidental or evidence of method cannot be stated.

In view of the evidence from the detailed records of delayed response experiments, and especially the results of various check experiments, I state with assurance that Congo did not depend upon secondary cues for correct response. Instead, the food-box situation, as originally experienced, in some psycho-physiological manner persisted until the moment of response. Reaction may have been to the total situation, to visual configuration, or to position. In all probability the factor of position was of primary importance, and although there was no opportunity to analyze the situation in order to determine the value of different factors, it is not unlikely that the visual qualities of the several food containers were entirely neglected in favor of the positional situation.

Congo's prompt adaptation to the conditions of this experiment and her well-nigh perfect performance throughout the course of the work, doubtless will surprise the reader no less than they did the experimenter. Where discontent and impatience had been expected, she exhibited placidity and willingness to await her opportunity; and whereas attempts to destroy the mechanism and constant interference with its operation had been anticipated, these failed to appear. From the start the task seemed to appeal to her as interesting and worth while, and despite the rapidly lengthening periods of delay she worked quite as well at the end of the series of trials as at the beginning. Usually the motivation was adequate; I think I might safely say optimal. In this experiment, on many of the days of its continuance, Congo obtained at least half of her daily ration and at times almost the whole.

Two trials, separated widely in extent of delay and date, as well as other conditions, will be described somewhat in detail to supplement the general statements which have been made. The first is trial 15. It extended from 12:16 to 12:32 on February 25. The green box was baited with a quart of milk and Congo was held for a fifteen-minute interval. The trial followed a shower, and although the sky had cleared, water dripped from the tree above us. She came to the mooring post from her cage with a rush, evidently keen for the experiment. At five minutes after the beginning of the trial she was noticed to look toward the green box, but most of the time she sat quietly beside the stake amusing herself as usual by playing with the mechanism, with the sand about her, or with objects which she happened to find on the ground. Apparently she was perfectly contented. Most of the time she faced toward the west away from the sun, doubtless because of the direct sunlight. When released she was facing me; a moment previously she had faced the green. As the rope was loosened she started toward the white box and continuing to it lifted the lid and looked in. Then she instantly made for the green box, but she was drawn back to the stake and held there. I thereupon re-baited the green box by taking out the cup of milk, showing it to her, and replacing it in the box. Thus preparation was made for the immediate repetition of this trial which had resulted in incorrect choice. Throughout the second period of delay Congo was quiet, apparently little if any disturbed, or at least giving no evidence of disturbance over her failure to locate the milk in her previous choice. When she was released in trial 15a she was facing the experimenter. Instantly she started toward the north but soon sharply swung around to the green box and opening it took the cup of milk. There could be no doubt about the definiteness and decisiveness of her choice.

At this point a word may be said in justification of immediate repetition of a trial in which the subject failed. The chief reason for this procedure was disciplinary. By means of it Congo, it was thought, might be held to careful choice. Furthermore, it was considered poor technique to remove the animal from the delayed response situation without reward, and equally poor to give her the reward except following a correct choice. Beginning with trial 20, certain variations in procedure appear. Thus in this particular trial, which resulted in incorrect choice, a second opportunity for choice was immediately given, but it also was incorrect, and as it was impossible to repeat the trial with its thirty-minute interval of delay, the experiment was terminated without reward. In trials 26, 27, 30, and 33, initial incorrect choice was immediately followed by opportunity for a second choice, which in every instance was correct. These facts are indicated in the final column of the table of delayed response experiments on page 485, in which, following the minus symbols, appear the letters indicative of the box or boxes chosen.

By contrast with trial 15, trial 37 is of peculiar significance. It extended from 9:12 to 12:12 on March 8. The black box was baited with Congo's entire breakfast, which consisted of a cup of milk, two baked bananas, one large sweet potato, and one half orange. The interval of delay was three hours. For this experiment she was taken to the situation, held at the post while the box was baited, and a few minutes later removed from the delayed response situation to work for about an hour in various other experiments. She was taken first to the box and stick and pipe and rod combination experiment of March 8; then to the four-box experiment; thence to the mirror experiment, and finally, shortly after 10:00 o'clock, she was returned to the delayed response situation and there waited quietly for the remainder of the three-hour interval. During the four experiments enumerated, she had obtained food rewards as follows: one banana from the pipe, one-half orange from the box in box and pole, and three bananas in the four-box experiment. Presumably her hunger must have been considerably reduced and consequently her eagerness for the food which she had previously seen placed in the black box.

During the interval of nearly two hours while she waited at the mooring post she was normally quiet, contented, and seemingly entirely satisfied to bide her time. As I stepped up to release her she directly faced me for a moment, then as she felt the rope give, she swung abruptly to her right and pulling on the rope made for the black box. Reaching it she immediately lifted the cover and at her leisure, but apparently with keen relish, took her belated breakfast.

The experiments prove conclusively that maintenance of orientation is not necessary for correct response and that varied distractions during the interval of delay are not necessarily disturbing. The tabulated results indicate that when removed from the delayed response situation for purposes of diversion during a considerable part of the interval of delay, Congo was more often wrong than right in her choice. For example, in trials 30 and 31 she chose wrongly; also in 31a; whereas in 31b, when she had been returned to the situation and held there, she chose correctly. Likewise in trial 33 her first choice was incorrect. On the other hand, in trials 32 and again in 37, she succeeded in spite of prolonged absence from the situation and varied distractions. The numerical results I consider somewhat misleading. They are few, and in my opinion the significant thing is that successes appear at the end of the series and under conditions which practically preclude the probability of chance. It cannot be doubted, however, that removal from the situation and occupation with other experiments increases the probability of incorrect choices.

Following demonstration that Congo could react correctly after delay of three hours, it was decided to test her with an overnight delay. This was done in the following manner in trial 39.

At 9:30 a.m. on March 9, she was taken to the delayed

response situation and watched me place in the white box two oranges and three raw bananas. Thereupon she was promptly transferred to other experiments and the day's work proceeded as usual and without further reference to delayed response. On the morning of March 10, shortly after 9:00 a.m., she was removed from her cage to the front of the house so that she should certainly be out of sensory contact with the delayed response situation. I then substituted for the food which had on the previous day been placed in the white box her entire breakfast, which consisted of a cup of milk, one large sweet potato, and one baked banana. At 9:15 she was brought to the mooring post and for fifteen minutes awaited opportunity for reaction. She exhibited ordinary patience, although obviously eager for her breakfast.

The following observations were recorded. When I arose to loosen the rope at 9:30 she directly faced me with evident eager anticipation; then grasping the rope she made directly for the north end of her cage, passing midway between the red and the black boxes without attention to either. Promptly I drew her back to the mooring post and recorded in my notes that lacking definite memory of the baited box she had attempted to get to a store of surplus food which I had carelessly left on a packing box at the end of her cage and which she knew was there, because when brought to the delayed response situation she had seized the box with one foot, upsetting it and throwing the food upon the ground. It had been replaced instead of being removed to a greater distance and it evidently now competed with the delayed response situation.

With Congo waiting at the post, I removed the food from the end of the garage to a bench directly back of the tree under which we were working. I had been accustomed to keep the surplus supply of food during delayed response experiments on this bench, which since it was directly back of the large trunk of the tree could not be seen by Congo.

With everything quiet and apparently in readiness, at 9:33 I again approached the release stake. Congo faced me and when released ran directly toward the tree trunk behind which I had concealed the food. Since it was clear that she was not choosing a box I again drew her back to the mooring post. Thereupon I again removed the food, this time to the distant garage, hoping that I might thus eliminate it as a distraction.

Once more at 9:35 she was released, and again she moved directly to the tree, possibly with intent to climb. As I drew her back to the post she caught the lid of the white box with one foot and pulled it off. Her position was such that she probably could not see the food within the box, and although after reaching the post she looked back toward it, her subsequent behavior definitely suggests that she had not seen the food.

Waiting again until everything was quiet I released her at 9:37 for a fourth choice. For a third time she went directly toward the tree trunk and was drawn back to the mooring post. Again a short wait, and at 9:39 she was released for the fifth time. After moving directly toward the tree she attempted to pass between the black and the red boxes, but I succeeded in drawing her back to the post without permitting her to touch either box.

At 9:41 I released her for the sixth time, whereupon she faced the white box directly and going to it uncovered it and took her breakfast. She ate carelessly, spilling much of her milk, perhaps because of emotional disturbance.

This completes the record of trial 39 with its twenty-four hour period of delay. One may, I suspect, fairly infer from Congo's behavior that she had forgotten the location of the food and that in her choices more remote, but also more nearly visible, food dominated. It is, however, noteworthy that when she first chose a box it should have been the one which contained her breakfast. This may or may not mean that there was some vestige of mnemonic process.

The results of the delayed response experiment contrast arrestingly with those obtained in other forms of the same experiment and with other animals by Hunter. Ordinarily the period of delay preceding correct choice in mammals which are able to react correctly independently of orientation does not exceed five minutes. It would appear then from these initial delayed response results that Congo belongs by virtue of her mnemonic processes in the class with man. Whether under the conditions of experimentation used for her, certain other mammals may react as successfully remains to be discovered. In any event her reactions are of extraordinary interest and importance. Naturally they will be followed up in supplementary experiments at the earliest opportunity.

Problem 20. Buried food. A second type of experimental situation used to give rough measurement of the span of memory is no. 20 of the list. Suggestion of this mode of inquiry was first taken from Köhler (1925, p. 290 ff.), who by the simple procedure of permitting chimpanzees to observe the burial of desired food demonstrated that they could remember its presence and location for at least sixteen and one-half hours. As a means of supplementing my delayed response experiments, and also of checking up the negative results on memory yielded by the buried food-jar experiment of 1926 (Yerkes, 1927, pp. 90-94), I made the following observations.

Prior to the simple experiments now to be described, Congo had been given no buried food tests by me subsequent to those described in my previous report, nor had she been observed to dig in the sand while at work in other experiments or while in her cage. Occasionally she scratched on the surface of the sand, but digging as if in search of some object I had not observed since the previous winter. Thus it would appear that conditions were favorable for use of the buried food test of memory.

The first of four trials now to be described was made on March 1. Following the two-box experiment, and while Congo was still moored to the stake of that situation some fifteen feet from the box of the box-and-pole situation, I permitted her to see me dig a hole in line with the box and about twelve inches from its northerly end. I made the hole about twelve inches in diameter and five inches deep, placed paper in the bottom of it, and on the paper one large orange, three raw bananas, and one baked banana. Over the food I then placed, partly for cleanliness and partly to reduce the risk of guidance by odor, a tin baking pan, ten inches in diameter and two inches deep. This pan was then covered by two to three inches of sand and the surface smoothed over carefully so that when the sand had dried, the spot should be indistinguishable from its surroundings. As she watched this performance Congo evidently was intensely interested. When she saw me cover the food she growled and turning her back ran away. On the completion of the food burying I removed her from the box stacking situation to her home tree with definite intent to return her to the buried food situation, weather permitting, after a delay of twenty-four hours.

The conclusion of the observation occurred on March 2 at 9:20 a.m. Congo was brought to the buried food situation after seeing the delayed response experiment prepared for trial 31. She was moored to the stake between the pipe and rod and the box and stick apparatus instead of to the box stacking stake. This was done purposely in order to make the test somewhat more difficult. She had observed the burying of the food from a different position, namely from the east, whereas when returned she was placed to the west of the box, at the north end of which the food was concealed.

At the moment of release the delay lacked twenty minutes of twenty-four hours. When released for action Congo was diverted for a few minutes by a ladder which she succeeded in grasping and dragging to her. As soon as this was removed she started to walk about the box and almost immediately she went to its north end and began to dig in the sand. The digging was vigorous and she promptly uncovered the tin pan. This seemed to surprise and puzzle her; for a minute or so she scraped at the top of the tin pan, then she pulled it off the food and quickly devoured what was beneath. Her response was convincingly positive. Clearly enough she remembered something, possibly the presence and location of the food.

A second buried-food experiment may be described more briefly. With similar precautions, an orange and three bananas at 9:40 a.m. on March 2 were buried at the south end of the box previously referred to. Congo watched the process from the box stacking stake at a distance of some fifteen feet. Returning to the situation on March 4 after a delay of forty-eight hours, she was placed as in the case of the previous experiment, on the opposite side of the buried food box from that in which she had observed the concealment of the reward. Almost immediately when released she went to the south end of the box and began to scratch in the sand about two feet west of the food. After a few minutes of scratching she went to the north end and there dug almost exactly where the food had been located for the previous experiment. Shortly returning to the south end she scratched about eighteen inches south of the right spot, then momentarily at two other spots. Returning again to the north end of the box she dug vigorously. Then to the south end, where she dug in very nearly the right spot, but failed to reach the tin pan. After she had been permitted to work for five minutes and had amply demonstrated her memory of the buried food, although she had not located it with precision and had failed to uncover it, the observation was discontinued in favor of other experiments in which it was deemed desirable that she should obtain her daily ration.

Congo's behavior in this experiment indicated initial memory of the more recently buried food, together with memory of her previous experience in obtaining food at the opposite end of the box. Undoubtedly had she been given a few additional minutes to work she would have obtained the supply at the south end of the box. It thus appears that for at least forty-eight hours effects of such an experience as that described may persist.

In yet a third experiment of this kind Congo was permitted to see a supply of food buried at the northeasterly corner of the platform outside the cage grill and almost in precisely the spot where during the winter of 1926 the food jar had repeatedly been buried in a similar form of experiment which initially yielded no evidence of memory.

The food was buried on March 4, and on March 5, after a delay of approximately twenty-six hours, Congo when returned to the situation and given opportunity to work, rather promptly went to the proper spot and began to dig about eight inches too near the grill. After a few seconds she stopped and went away to attend to other things, but shortly returning she dug at yet another point slightly nearer the food. Again she went away, and suffering distractions her return was delayed for some minutes. Subsequently she dug several times nearly over the food, and once in exactly the right spot (see plate 13), but as the dirt had been packed rather tightly, she failed to dig deeply enough and consequently did not discover what she was seeking. The evidence of memory nevertheless was positive.

In a final, and fourth, buried food experiment the food was concealed in the customary way near the south end of the slot box and in line with it. Congo from a stake twenty-five feet to the east intently watched the process. This was 10:00 a.m. on March 8. At 9:45 on March 10 she was moored to the stake of the slot box and given opportunity to exhibit memory for the concealed food. Evidence of memory did not appear so long as the observer was at hand; but when after some minutes he left the situation in order to discover whether his presence was possibly inhibiting Congo, she rather promptly began to dig in the right spot and almost immediately secured her reward. It was impossible to say with certainty whether her successful response was delayed by the presence of the experimenter, nor can one be certain that she did not in this or any or all of the similar experiments obtain odor cues from the concealed food.

Although the buried food tests apparently confirm the results of the delayed response experiment, this form of test is in a variety of respects unsatisfactory and in my opinion it is of slight value by comparison with more readily controllable types of situation. There is evidence that memory of locations in which food has been concealed persists not merely for forty-eight hours, but for several days. Thus, for example, when returned to some of the spots described in the above experiments after approximately a week, Congo exhibited definite memory of her previous experiences in those locations. Probably like responses would be exhibited by various other mammals. Consequently it is doubtful whether in this type of experiment the gorilla exhibits anything distinctive, peculiar to her species, or indeed strikingly different from that of organisms of much simpler neural organization and mental constitution. It is not intended to belittle this procedure as a crude test or method of sounding for memory, but merely to indicate that by comparison with other evidences herein presented the results of the buried food experiments of Köhler and the writer are of relatively little importance.

Summary of Section VIII

Evidence of mnemonic processes is supplied by all of the experiments with Congo; and in most instances repetition in 1927 of the experiments of 1926 definitely proved that effects of experience had persisted and that she resumed her work either where she had left it the previous winter or with indications that adaptation had continued during the interval.

It is needless at this point to review the varied evidences from the score or more of experiments. The only one which yielded either negative or uncertain results was the pipe and stick or rod experiment, and even in that it may be argued that Congo remembered her failure and therefore was in a measure prejudiced against the situation. Memory of various objects and events was noted from day to day, and often anticipatory responses indicated that the gorilla, on the basis of her previous experience in problematic situations, expected certain happenings. For example, one morning when she was called to the cage door to be taken out for observation, instead of responding she went to the corner of the nest-room, from which she could see the trees under which several of the experiments were at that time being set, and very obviously looked over the situations. Perhaps she was looking for the rewards of effort which might be expected, or possibly instead she was interested in discovering which of the several problems were to be presented to her. In any event, marked interest in what was coming was evident in her attitude. This was observed on several days, as were also similar indications of anticipation of experiences.

Presumably several sorts of mnemonic process and imaginal experience existed in connection with the behavior which has been described. It is not possible to describe them in terms either of sense mode or of neurological process. There is risk possibly of over-estimating the importance of the relatively long periods of delay during which the gorilla could retain the psycho-biological condition necessary for correct reaction to a situation. It is rather the behavior of the animal during the period of delay and at the moment of decision and choice than the duration of the delay that impress me as of peculiar significance.

In memory, as far as exhibited, Congo seemingly compares more favorably with the chimpanzee and orang-outan than in speed, versatility, and efficiency of adaptation to problematic situations. I have already demonstrated in a series of observations which will shortly be published, that the chimpanzee not only endures as long delays as did Congo in the delayed response experiment, but that it also reacts as readily and decisively. It may well be suspected that the delayed response of the gorilla, as of any other organism which can successfully withstand long intervals, has as neurological basis a physiological condition or process which is lacking in the rodents, and possibly in all of the mammals except the primates. One may naturally enough suppose that the capacity for correct response after hours, days, weeks, or years of delay may be due to the physiological equivalent of imaginal or other representational processes and that such processes occur only in organisms of highly complex nervous system. If this proves to be true, it will doubtless also appear that such types of mnemonic process as are necessary to imaginal response, condition alike ideational adaptation and the forms of memory response which I have demonstrated in the gorilla and the chimpanzee by means of the delayed response experiment. Speculation at this stage of the inquiry, although helpful to the investigator, seems scarcely worthy of publication.

MISCELLANEOUS OBSERVATIONS, BEARING ON BEHAVIORAL ADAPTATION

Miscellaneous observations, too numerous and varied to describe in detail, throw additional light on the features of adaptation which have been considered in the foregoing sections. They indicate, even more clearly than the results of formal experiments, certain changes or developments in behavior and are therefore worthy of consideration.

In general, my daily records of Congo's activities within and without experiments confirm the conclusion that her adaptations are relatively slow and less convincingly indicative of insight than are those of comparable chimpanzees and orang-outans. They generally confirm the descriptive statements of my initial report, but in certain directions, as I shall now attempt to indicate, they reveal remarkable and thought-provoking changes.

During my first period of observation Congo was only slightly destructive. Unfamiliar objects falling into her hands were hastily examined with fingers, nose, and mouth, but proving inedible they rarely were damaged and ordinarily they were thrown aside and utterly ignored after initial inspection. A year later I was much surprised to find destructiveness as pronounced in her as in the chimpanzee of like age. She was more interested in unfamiliar things, and instead of contenting herself with discovering whether or not they were edible, she proceeded in either case to try to dismember them. In 1926, experimental work with her was relatively simple and easy because she seldom tried to destroy the apparatus; but in 1927 nothing was safe from her aggression, and having been seized, from her strength of jaws and limbs. Whether this is a normal, predictable change in behavior, accompanying physical growth and psycho-physical development, is not indicated by the literature or by my observations. It is conceivable that increased familiarity with her new environment and general adaptation to conditions of life in captivity released her from certain inhibitions, and that whereas during the first winter she was reluctant to take liberties with the objects about her, she subsequently came to act more freely, spontaneously, and naturally. My suspicion, however, is that the change is due rather to normal psycho-physical development than to adaptation.

Curiosity similarly was strangely lacking or disguised in 1926, while in 1927 it was considerably more obvious and played a rather important rôle in the animal's adaptation to new situations. It remained, nevertheless, far below the normal level for the chimpanzee, and whereas Congo, when in the presence of an unusual object or as observer of strange happenings, might inspect, examine, test, or observe in a few ways, the chimpanzee would do so far more persistently and with greater versatility of response. Here, as also in the case of general adaptation, Congo's repertoire of response seemed meager in comparison with our own and also with that of the chimpanzee. Often where one would expect the keenest curiosity she appeared indifferent. But once more emphasis must be laid on temperamental characteristics, for in the second winter she was as introverted, aloof, independent, inclined to indirection, given to simple forms of craft, cunning, and attempts to mislead the observer, as during the initial period of study. Possibly these characteristics and the response pictures which they suggest are incompatible with lively expressions of curiosity. It may even be suspected that were she entirely free from the suspicion of being observed, she might act differently and supply much more varied evidences of curiosity.

Imitativeness was described in the first report as little in evidence. Reiteration of this statement is justified by the observations of 1927. It may not be said that Congo is unimitative of members of her species, but throughout our work she was but slightly imitative of me. During 1926 she seemed oftener to be negativistic than otherwise when I set imitative copy. The following winter she clearly was more interested in what I did and more inclined to obtain the objective toward which my actions tended, even though she failed to observe or was unable or unwilling to imitate my actions. Almost never did I notice evidence that my setting of copy for her in experiments which she had failed to solve did more than encourage her to renewed or more vigorous efforts of her own particular kind. Even my tuitional attempts slightly, if at all, modified her modes of response. Often they stirred her to redoubled effort to secure the prospective reward, and occasionally they seemed somewhat to modify her method of attack on the problem. This is strikingly different from common experience with the chimpanzee, which readily and eagerly imitates man as well as members of its species. It seemingly watches for opportunity to imitate, with respect alike to mode of response and objective attained (means and end), whereas Congo seemed oblivious of the features of imitative copy and intent only on the objective which both imitator and imitatee had in view.

Once more the question inevitably suggests itself: Is this astounding difference in imitative tendency and in the nature of imitative response to be attributed to type of organism or to stage of psycho-physical development? Possibly Congo, although of the same age chronologically as some of the chimpanzees which I have studied, is less advanced in development because of markedly slower growth and maturation of the nervous system. When I first reported to Mr. Ben Burbridge experimental results with her which contrasted unfavorably with those obtained with chimpanzees of comparable age, he immediately said that he believed the gorilla developed more slowly than the chimpanzee and possibly even than man. The suggestion must be taken seriously in the face of important problems, like those suggested above, whose solution is contingent on definite information. The indications are fairly convincing that in general the physical development of Congo is slightly if at all slower than that of the chimpanzee, but it is entirely possible that in temporal relations the psychoneurological development of the several anthropoids differs markedly. Possibly, then, a year or two hence Congo may exhibit changes in curiosity and imitativeness comparable with the change in destructiveness which I have noted as occurring between the winter of 1926 and that of 1927. If this suspicion should prove to be correct, it may invalidate all of the comparative statements which I have made. For although chronological age, as estimated by anthropometric data, is our only present basis of comparison, it is admittedly unsatisfactory and should as promptly as possible be either supplemented or replaced by physiological age.

In the previous report, a section was devoted to the discussion of fooling, aping, and imitating. Therein it was asserted that Congo exhibits in far less degree than do the other great apes random investigative activity, copying or seemingly purposeless and almost automatic repetition of the acts of others, and intelligent imitation. At once less of an investigator and less imitative than the chimpanzee, she is also, it would appear from my varied observations, less willing or eager to work persistently in the face of discouraging conditions. Eager and optimistic in the first stages of work on a problem, she tends after a time to abandon it as insoluble, unless in the meantime she achieves an encouraging measure of success. Otherwise expressed, the gorilla, like not a few men, roughly measures or estimates the probability of success, and if the chances seem to be against her, gives up the task. What at the start appears to her impossible she will not even attempt.

Herein appears what may be one of the most important differences between this anthropoid and mankind, for whereas Congo either refused to work, or shortly abandoned effort, in problematic situations which must have seemed to her impossible of solution, some men commonly stigmatized as foolish, eagerly and insistently strive for what is unpredictable. This may be not only the most important difference between man and other organisms, but also the secret of human progress and the key to the development of human types of civilization and culture. Certainly if no representatives of our genus were willing to attempt the impossible, and even to devote their lives to a goal which may be many generations distant, progress would be relatively slow. The chimpanzee is more nearly an investigator, although of primitive type, than any other of the great apes, and therein it is comparable with man. That it likewise most closely resembles man in its attitude toward the seemingly unattainable goal is not yet evident. In future observation of the anthropoids and other primates it will be of very considerable interest and significance to trace origins, developments, and relationships of the attitudes, reactive tendencies, and modes of adaptation which are comprehended in the concepts research and gambling. For although some may object to the latter term to designate willingness to strive for the unpredictable, it nevertheless suggests many of the essential points to be observed, and until replaced by a better term may well enough serve our need.

Although Congo in varied situations in which I have observed her during months of almost continuous work, adapted slowly, she nevertheless exhibited, the more clearly perhaps because of the slowness of her mastery of the problems, several different types of learning process. The following are more or less clearly and frequently manifested, sometimes in isolation, again in combination:

(1) Adaptation based upon reflex or automatized simple or complex acts, the elicitation and repetition of which in a given situation yielded satisfaction in the form of freedom, food, or other desired objects or opportunities for activity.

(2) Adaptation resulting from what to all appearances is random trial of different activities and the ultimate discovery and, finally, regular repetition of the particular act or succession of acts which yields satisfaction.

Both of these modes of response have repeatedly been exhibited and analyzed in lowly organized creatures, and are well described in numerous general works on animal behavior. They are exhibited by Congo, but because of other modes of learning, habit-formation, or adaptation, they tend to be overlooked.

(3) Differing from (2) in directness and possibly also in the nature of the neurological processes is a form of adaptation which involves inspection of the situation, with resulting exclusion of certain obviously possible acts and the limitation of trial to certain modes of response which more or less closely approximate adequacy. Finally, from among these acts, one which is not necessarily the most nearly adequate of all, but as a rule is highly adapted, becomes the preferred and regular mode of response. This variety of adaptation involves not only observation but discrimination and selection on the basis of previous experience.

(4) Adaptation with insight appears as a step in advance of method (3), for in it the organism, following observation of the problematic situation, exhibits immediately an appropriate act whose occurrence or use in the absence of previous familiarity with the situation indicates at least observational appreciation of some of the essential relations of the problem. In the previous mode of learning there is a measure of insight or an approach to it, but in the present mode insight is the conspicuous and all-important feature. In only a few of the problematic situations presented to Congo did she respond immediately and adequately. Perhaps the slot box experiment, problem no. 16, is as good an illustration of adaptation on the basis of insight as can be cited. But certainly the diagonal rope experiment, problem no. 11, and the auxiliary stick experiment, problem no. 6, supply excellent evidence of insight.

(5) So often do combinations of these modes of adaptation appear that it would be inexcusable to omit the category of mixed response. The use of automatisms, process of trial, inspectional analysis with a measure of insight, all may appear in the solution of any given problem.

All things considered, I must conclude that Congo has decidedly less insight in the types of problematic situation in which I have had opportunity to observe all of the great apes than has the chimpanzee or orang-outan, and although possibly this may be due to slower psycho-physical development, I should be surprised if that proved to be the fact. As I review the score or more of experiments conducted during each of my two periods of observation, I am impressed first of all by the frequency of initial failure to master problems; next, by the slowness with which the gorilla profited by imitative and tuitional assistance, and finally, by the very limited, partial or slowly appearing appreciation of the essential features or relations of the problematic situations. Of her insight I have no doubt. Many times she gave impressive evidence of memory and anticipation of experiences, and although my primary interest is in the facts of behavior and their structural conditions, I still deem it altogether desirable, and from certain points of view of the utmost importance, to couple these facts with the phenomena of consciousness.

AFFECTIVE EXPRESSIONS AND MOTIVATION

The observations of 1927, with few and minor exceptions, confirm my earlier description of the affective traits and behavior of Congo (Yerkes, 1927, pp. 169-177), but additional and more varied evidences of affective as well as of cognitive processes were obtained. It seemed to the observer that she was at once more expressive, more keenly interested in her environment, and better able to adapt herself to novel situations, but in the first instance it may well be that emotional expressions were more frequently noted because of the observer's increasing familiarity with his subject and ability to understand her behavior. Vocal expressions were slightly if at all more frequent than in the winter of 1926, and it was only in bodily attitude and facial conditions that there appeared to be greater expressivity.

Playfulness was much in evidence, and some of the most favorable opportunities to observe emotional expressions appeared in connection with it. Congo frequently sought opportunity to play with human companions or with the dogs about Shady Nook. From day to day extreme variations appeared, for now she would be active, energetic, frolicsome, eager for play or work as circumstances suggested, and again lethargic, negativistic, and only slightly responsive to playful approaches. These daily variations of course vitally affected work in experiments. Unfortunately no method was available to identify and measure her mood or degree of interest and optimism. Had this been possible, the data would have very considerable significance for the interpretation of experimental results.

Few opportunities appeared for sustained observation of emotional expression during play. The following is one of the rare and exceptionally valuable records. Mr. R. L. Boyd, a neighbor of the Burbridges, who was fond of Congo and had been in the habit of playing with her at intervals ever since her arrival at Shady Nook, kindly volunteered one day to engage her in playful activity while I secured pictorial records. The gorilla's initial approach and early behavior were clearly indicative of extreme satisfaction or joy. With characteristic roughness and abandon she patted, pounded, and mauled her playfellow, biting at his clothing, rolling over or upon him, and romping excitedly and good-naturedly as might a child. Occasionally in the rough and tumble she nipped with her teeth rather too sharply and Mr. Boyd had to defend himself by slapping her. After some minutes of such play near the cage Mr. Boyd took Congo to the river bank in front of the house where, with greater freedom, the sport was continued. Although there was not much vocalization on Congo's part, one could not mistake her pleasure in the social activity. Presently it occurred to Mr. Boyd to try to test her response to water by taking her to a nearby pier which ran into the river. This was attempted, but before she had gone fifty yards from the Burbridge house, her familiar environment, she began to hold back on the leash and to exhibit unwillingness to go farther. As she was dragged or coaxed forward, indications of timidity and fear appeared. Evidently she was increasingly disturbed and correspondingly reluctant to proceed. No sound was uttered, but with evident determination she set herself against forward progress. Arrived at a fence which must be passed on the way to the pier she made a determined effort to get away, and in doing so she bit Mr. Boyd's hand so sharply that she succeeded in partially freeing herself and gaining temporary advantage. Recovering his grip on the leash Mr. Boyd again coaxed her forward and she proceeded, but clearly against her will and alert for opportunity to escape and return home. Arrived on the pier she took the first opportunity to jump off into the water, careless apparently of that element as well as of the height of some six or eight feet from which she jumped. No sooner had she struck the water, which was only about a foot deep, than she headed for the shore and home. There was no vocalization whatever, and the bodily attitude and general behavior alone were indicative of fear and resentment. Clearly she was deeply stirred.

Arriving at her home tree, to which her leash was thereupon attached, she threw herself on her back on the ground and there, completely relaxed, lay with arms and legs outstretched. For several minutes she rested thus, evidently greatly fatigued by her adventure.

This initially playful incident has been described in detail because almost any other primate with which I am familiar would have vocalized vigorously in such a situation. Congo, no less stirred in all probability and certainly no less determined to have her own way, nevertheless maintained silence. Fortunately I was able to get excellent still and motion picture records of Congo romping with Mr. Boyd.

Often between experiments, on off days, or at the beginning or end of our day's work, I too engaged in frolics with my subject. Her behavior exhibited little versatility, her stock procedure being to run either toward or from her playfellow and attempt either to grasp or avoid him. She was inordinately fond of being pommeled and retaliated in kind and with considerable interest. Although ticklish in the arm pits, groins, back of the neck, and on the ribs, she seemed greatly to enjoy the experience of slight irritation, and when in cheerful mood would actively respond with varied involuntary as well as voluntary movements of head, facial muscles, and limbs, and also with persistent chuckling and occasionally low throaty growls which may be likened to human laughter. Indeed, these sounds often reminded the observer of the involuntary laughter of a person who is tickled. At such times smiles often appeared, and in addition to the sounds mentioned, grunting and something resembling purring.

Brief mention has been made of timidity and fear, but Congo is not by nature a timid creature. She exhibited no pronounced fear of any person or of other animate or inanimate objects about Shady Nook. Of a stick which was used by the Negro caretaker to defend himself she was appropriately apprehensive, but never so far disturbed that she expressed herself in other than the protective manner that a child would naturally exhibit. During both of my periods of work I was surprised by the infrequent and relatively mild expressions of fear and anger. Not once did I observe anything remotely approaching terror or rage. Timidity and resentment manifested themselves occasionally in connection with the day's work or play; resentment was the more common, and yet even in connection with it I usually felt that she was much more patient and considerate of the desires of the observer than most human subjects of comparable age would have been. All of my efforts to induce anger or rage failed to elicit any pronounced emotional expression. Naturally I supposed that sufficiently disappointing or exasperating situations would induce in so young an animal the temper tantrum or violent expression of displeasure which is natural to child and chimpanzee alike. But such was not the case.

In the day's work, as already suggested, appeared different and also varying moods. There were good and bad days primarily because of Congo's condition of depression or exultation, hopefulness or the opposite. Moods were even more in evidence than transient emotions. If I were to attempt a brief characterization of Congo's affective life I should say that it is one of moods rather than of feelings and emotions in the human sense. In the previous report attention was given to evidences of good and bad working days, and their relation to the affective condition of Congo. During my recent period of work evidence of dependence of experimental results upon moods continued to accumulate. Thus, for example, there appeared not only pronounced variations in days but also in experiments. Brought to a given situation, Congo might go to work eagerly or refuse to attend to it. An illustration may be taken from the box stacking experiment. A large reward had been offered for effort, but Congo, although undoubtedly hungry, behaved as though indifferent to the food. She acted as though she were not interested, but in so doing I suspect that she misrepresented or disguised her true feeling, purpose, and intent. Possibly this is what is meant by "Harvard indifference"!

From records for February 18 the following affective data bearing on motivation are taken. The day was an extraordinarily eventful one. Congo led off with a pronounced and unexpected success in the pipe and rod and box and pole experiment, and not only did she use the same type of tool in different situations, but she also sought, as opportunity offered, to use different objects—sticks, straws, chains, papers, cloths—for the same purpose. Success seemed characteristic of the day. Brought to a new problematic situation, the slot box and stick experiment, she worked with eagerness and definite indications of insight, and although she failed to obtain the reward she exhibited prolonged and diligent effort. Now, it happens that the slot-box experiment in its original form was one in which the gorilla succeeded initially, to her very obvious satisfaction. Thus the slot box itself had acquired certain affective value and Congo came to the new situation optimistically because of her previous easy success. She was misled in that she failed to appreciate that the problem presented by the box had been modified by the narrowing of the slots and that now a stick or other implement must be used instead of her fingers. This behavioral situation is mentioned because of its extraordinarily important bearing on the problem of motivation. The matter deserves further consideration.

Commonly we students of animal behavior assume that some particular factor or condition which we have selected as incentive to effort or achievement is actually the essential factor in motivation. Hunger, for example, escape from close confinement, achievement of opportunity to play, are assumed to be the controlling elements. Yet day after day and in varied types of experiment and under differing conditions in the same experiment, I have observed that my chosen incentive, deriving from food offered as reward, became subordinated to other factors which I had not anticipated and should little have suspected of being capable of swamping hunger. I could

indeed exhibit instance after instance of complicated motivation in which the factors are both immediate and remote, deriving often from previous experiences either in the same problematic situation or in other related situations. There were
many times in which my chosen incentive obviously determined the direction of Congo's effort, but I suspect that there
were quite as many in which it was of coördinate importance
with others or even of minor significance. Without careful
analysis and attempts properly to control motivation our ostensibly quantitative studies in habit-formation are almost certain to yield misleading results. From my observations with
Congo and other anthropoid apes, I suspect that a large part
of the work on habit-formation in the mammalia is incapable
of evaluation or interpretation because of inadequate descriptions of motivation. If there were any semblance of quantitative description in my accounts of the adaptive behavior of
Congo, I should be extremely doubtful of their value and correspondingly apologetic. But as a fact I have been aware,
almost from the first, of the complicated nature of motivation
in my subject and have attempted to discover factors and relations. I am now wholly convinced that the intensive study of
motivation is an essential preparation for reliable measurement
of rapidity, duration, and other aspects of adaptation.

By reflection on motivation in Congo I am reminded of my
varying suspicion that, on the one hand, she was naïve, stupid,
or on the other, unexpectedly deep, far-sighted, and given to
the practice of craft and cunning. The longer I observe her
and the more intimate I become with the nature and conditions
of her behavior, the more I suspect that her apparent super-
ficiality or stupidity is grossly misleading. It is her nature
apparently to act as though somewhat indifferent to situations
which would arouse the interest and hopeful expectancy of
various other types of primate. Not only is she silent where
one might expect vocal expressions of feeling, emotion, or
mood; she also is seemingly stupid or inapt in situations which
the other anthropoids promptly master. Is it because she

cannot adapt to them or instead because she is motivated by a greater number and variety of factors, and especially by more internal or psycho-physiological factors than, for example, the chimpanzee or orang-outan? This question may not be answered other than tentatively from my data. Like the questions concerning the origin and nature of "research" and "gambling"-attitudes toward the seemingly impossible (p.505) this problem opens to one's imagination vistas of genetic inquiry and description which when once definitely mastered and set forth in proper proportions and relations will surely have extraordinary scientific and practical significance.

Inasmuch as in the primates we commonly expect to find vocal expressions among the more important aspects of affective response, it is appropriate to conclude this section with brief description of Congo's vocal repertoire. In the winter of 1926 she produced only a few varieties of sound, and those infrequently. During the following winter she vocalized only slightly, if at all, more frequently, nor did she exhibit new sounds. The following list of vocal responses is chiefly confirmatory of previous description. It comprehends the chuckle, low throaty growl, and purr-like sounds associated with tickling or occurring in excitement during play; the shrill tremulous and also tenuous cry similar to the distant neighing of a horse or call of the screech owl; the very low throaty purr, sometimes changing into a succession of grunts and suggestive of the cat or the pig, according as the rhythmic purr or the less rapid grunt dominated, and the sharp rhythmic cry made with protruded lips by quick inspiration. Both Mrs. Burbridge and Bill described to me a scream indicative of resentment or disappointment, which appeared in connection with delayed feeding or like disappointing situations. Congo never made this cry in my hearing. As suitable occasions must frequently have appeared, I am forced to infer that in some manner of which I am unconscious, I inhibited this emotional expression.

A single additional incident and the discussion of affectivity is concluded. I was giving Congo a cup of milk through her grill. She had drained the cup and was attempting to grasp it with one hand when I commanded her to keep hands off. She wished to put her fingers into the cup in order to scrape from its sides some thick milk which adhered to them. Irritated by my prohibition, she turned from the grill, made a circuit of the cage and came back to face me. Her attitude and every motion as she walked stiffly about the cage betokened petulance. It was an amusing emotional pantomime, executed in utter silence.

SOCIAL RELATIONS

Opportunities to observe Congo's responses to social stimuli and to obtain general knowledge of her social traits were limited by circumstances beyond my control. No other mountain gorillas, or indeed any infrahuman primates, were available, and the only objects which contributed substantially to the social values of Congo's environment were a mirror which was used in an experiment, two dogs, the Burbridges, Bill, the experimenter, and occasional visitors. My observations are meager and unrelated and doubtless they are also wholly inadequate by comparison with what might be obtained in the natural habitat of the species. I do not set great store by the materials of this section, but they seem to me worthy of presentation as indicating social attitude, psycho-physical development, and bases for motivation.

As during my first period of observation, so likewise in the winter of 1927, the only experiment definitely planned to exhibit social responses was that with the mirror, problem no. 21. When originally presented, the mirror commanded Congo's intense interest and elicited varied investigative behavior. Both attitude and responsiveness persisted throughout the series of trials, and when at the end of his period of work the observer reluctantly discontinued the experiment, it appeared that Congo was as eager as ever for the companionship of her mirror image. It was natural then that on first opportunity I should re-present the situation as a means of discovering developmental or other changes in her behavior:

Problem 21. Mirror. This time the preparations for the experiment were more carefully and intelligently made than originally. I wished not only to observe the gorilla's responses when she was in the presence of the mirror image and free to manipulate it as she liked, but also to make still and motion picture records. Experience indicated that construction must necessarily be very substantial. I therefore obtained a heavy plate glass mirror 18 by 30 inches and mounted it in a correspondingly heavy wooden frame, of which the outside measurements were 24 by 32 inches. This in turn was mounted in another substantial wooden frame which was held vertically by posts driven into the sand in a clear space somewhat easterly of the oak trees under which most of the experiments were set (see plate 14). The mirror faced southwest. It was backed by seven-eighth inch boards, between which and the glass newspapers were placed to lessen risk of breakage. About three feet west of the mirror frame a mooring stake was driven into the ground. So far as I know, Congo had not seen her mirror image since my previous observations in this type of experiment.

On March 4, and thereafter on four days, of which the last was March 8, she was brought to the mirror experiment and for approximately ten minutes given opportunity to investigate the mirror, her image, or other aspects of the situation as she might desire. Her total time in the situation during the five trials above mentioned certainly did not exceed one hour. The essential features of her behavior may be described very briefly, chiefly for the sake of contrast with those of the previous winter.

In the first trial she evidently was somewhat distracted and disconcerted by the new situation. Her interest was by no means so-keen as the previous year. Nevertheless, she exhibited during the interval almost all of the features of response which I have previously recorded. These included examination of the image visually and tactually from directly in front, attempts to kiss it, reaching behind the mirror with hand or hands, actually going around back of the frame and examining it, pounding on the mirror itself and also on the back of the frame, and varied antics which related especially to the examination of her own body. Some of her attitudes in this or subsequent trials are represented in plates 14 and 15.

In the second trial there was increase of interest and repetition of her characteristic investigative acts. In addition she vigorously kicked the surface of the mirror and pulled at the frame as though trying to dislodge the image. This did not appear in 1926, possibly because the mirror frame was held in the hands of the experimenter instead of being securely mounted in a self-supporting frame.

So remarkable do the variety and persistence of her responses to the mirror image seem to me that I deem it desirable to present my detailed original record of her behavior in trial 3.

"Congo looked at the image closely, then began to pound on the surface of the mirror; then away for two or three seconds; behind the mirror frame; then again in front looking at the image and pounding the face. Away, sitting behind the mirror with her back to the frame. I am not sure whether this was merely to escape a cool southerly wind, or whether she was actually seeking contact with the other animal. Next she pressed her face to the image and touched it with her lips. Then she patted or pounded the image and also rubbed it with the backs of her hands, her arms, and her lips. Repeatedly she attempted to climb the mirror frame, but this I prevented for fear she would try to reach a telephone wire which was not far above the frame. Pounding the mirror, especially from its front, that is, the image side, was the most frequent of all of her antics. This she did vigorously. Again looked at the image, as though curious about it. In fact, her whole attitude expressed curiosity rather than emotional disturbance. She did not seem to be as much stirred by the image as last year, but just to be inquisitive about it. Now sitting back to back with the mirror frame; next pounding the image; examining it face to face, with lip against lip; again pounding the image and rubbing it with her hands; then away; returning she again pounded the image. Next she went to the stake and fooled with the chain for a few seconds. It may be that the cool breeze influenced her behavior a good deal throughout the period of observation. Lying before the image she put up one foot and looked at it with apparent curiosity. There is, more than previously, a tendency to examine herself in detail, and it seems to be a more mature sort of behavior than that of last year. Going behind the mirror she pounded it, and apparently tried to get inside of it, not only in the back but from the edge toward the west. Then she sat against it back to back. Returning to the front she pounded the image and looked at it intently, touched it with her face; then beat her chest and again peered at the image. Observation discontinued.

"How long Congo would keep up this behavior I do not know. I have never yet kept her in the proximity of the mirror long enough to let her get tired of it and go away. Always it has been a ten-minute or approximately ten-minute period. That she can stand perfectly."

To the end of the series of observations her interest in the mirror image continued unabated. In comparison with that of the previous winter it seemed more mature and intellectual as contrasted with emotional, thus suggesting psycho-physical development. Once more I venture to express my surprise that despite other reward than the satisfaction of activity itself, she was as markedly interested in her mirror image at the end as at the beginning of this experiment.

The relations of this young anthropoid with the two dogs resident at Shady Nook, as described in my initial report, were those of companion and playmate. There was evidence of mutual interest and delight, especially on the part of the Airedale Betty and the gorilla. The bulldog Bobby was distinctly less friendly to Congo and as often as not resented her playful advances. When, in the winter of 1927, I returned to Jacksonville, Betty was still at hand, but Bobby had disappeared and in his place there was a mongrel male, perhaps collie and setter. As previously Congo was interested in the dogs as playmates, and especially when moored to Tree 1 for her daily outing, often romped with them as she might with a member of her species. Usually however the dogs were reluctant to come close to her and held aloof, thus limiting forms of play to chasing, leaping about, and playful seizing with jaws or extremities. The only thing to be especially remarked about the playful relations is that Congo had become so large, strong, and rough that the dogs were somewhat afraid of her when I began to observe their relations in January 1927. Their timidity steadily increased and by March it was rare to see her in direct contact with either of her former playmates. They would race about near her, tempting her to grab for them, but were cautious to keep beyond reach.

The really notable thing, and the primary excuse for this account of Congo's social relations with the dogs, is the evidence of developmental change afforded by what presumably should be designated as sex play. In 1926 almost nothing suggestive of sex interest in other animals in her environment and no form of sex play was observed; therefore the peculiar and very considerable genetic interest of the following data.

On January 19, 1927, while Congo was chained to her oak tree, both Betty and the mongrel male, which we shall for convenience designate as collie, were at hand, and although the latter was timid and stand-offish, Congo succeeded in getting hold of him and drawing him to her. I happened to be watching closely and I noticed that she appeared to be unusually gentle and considerate of his feelings. This I at first inferred to be caution on her part lest he bite her. Having drawn him within reach she in a calm leisurely way proceeded to examine him, smelling his face, legs, body, the while also using her eyes. Then, the dog remaining passive, she raised one hind leg and turning him on his side exposed the genitalia. There followed manual, olfactory, and visual examination. Her attitude and expression were indicative of interest and perplexity. She acted slowly, as if puzzled by the new sense data. Again she explored his head, legs, and body, and then returned to the genitalia. Once the dog attempted to draw away from her, but she held him firmly and gently. Now pulling the animal toward her she turned him on his back and stepping astride assumed a male copulatory position and executed appropriate movements. This persisted for a few seconds, when stepping from above the dog she threw herself on her back and drew him, belly down, upon her. Thus she held him for a few seconds in what had every appearance of sex embrace. The dog however, instead of coöperating or remaining passive, made vigorous efforts to escape.

This behavior is similar to what is definitely recognized as sex play in young chimpanzees. Whether it is legitimate to designate Congo's reaction to the collie as sex behavior is uncertain. But in any event, nothing like it was observed during the winter of 1926 and it presumably indicates developmental change.

Similar observations were made on January 20 when I purposely arranged an experimental setting by coaxing the collie within Congo's reach. She was very eager to play with him, but he resisted her and escaped. Somewhat later she was observed to play with Betty in a manner suggesting her previous response to the collie, for she repeatedly drew Betty upon her belly and held her thus. It was on this date that I discovered a possible clue to Congo's extraordinary response to the sensory data which she obtained from the genitalia of the collie on January 19. I observed that one side of his scrotum had been badly cut or torn and that one of the testicles was seriously injured and suppurating. Consequently the condition was such as to provide unusually strong olfactory stimulus and perhaps in consequence to stir Congo unwontedly. Treatment of the collie was necessary and for about two weeks he was absent from Shady Nook.

A number of times Congo was observed to use Betty as a sex object. Always Betty remained passive, or if too roughly handled, attempted to escape. Congo's usual performance was to throw herself on her back and draw Betty upon her with evident desire to bring the genital parts into contact. Thereupon she manipulated the dog's body with her hands, feet, or both, producing movements simultaneously of her own body and that of the dog and inducing friction. The intent seemed clear and the behavior unquestionably yielded satisfaction to the gorilla.

Why, one is impelled to ask, the appearance of sex play in such pronounced form and so conspicuously at this time, whereas heretofore and indeed during the whole period of work in the winter of 1926, no sign of it was observed? Daily variations in sex interest and desire appeared to be marked, for at times, and indeed usually, Congo either paid little attention to the dogs or merely romped with them as already described, while again she seemed interested exclusively in the one or other animal as a possible sex object. Marked preference for the male as contrasted with the female was noticed from the first. She used Betty as a sex object only if the collie was unavailable. There was some indication also during 1927 that she was more interested in men than in women. This was remarked by the Burbridges, and although I had slight opportunity to confirm their suspicion I am inclined to think it is correct.

From February 4, when the collie was returned to Shady Nook, observation of his relations with Congo was resumed and I verified and supplemented my initial record of behavior. Thus, for example, on the day of his return Congo, on getting hold of him, kept him within her grasp for about fifteen minutes with obvious efforts to use him as a sex object. Her gentleness was marked. She examined his genitalia olfactorily, and on completion of her investigation assumed the male copulatory position. Thereafter she attempted to pull the collie upon her, but at first wholly passive he presently effected his escape. Betty was then used in the position of the male, while Congo lay on her back.

It can scarcely be doubted in the light of knowledge of the development of sex behavior in the various primates that this is adolescent sex play, and that its appearance indicates development of Congo during my period of acquaintance with her and approach to adolescence. I suspect that at the time of these observations (February 1927) she was in her sixth year.

A few times it was observed that Congo made attempts to bring the external genitalia into contact with inanimate objects, such for example as timbers or boxes. I at first assumed that this was an effort to relieve irritation, but in the light of her social responses to dogs I doubt the correctness of this interpretation.

When first observed by me in December, 1925, Congo gave little evidence of interest in people or of desire to interest them in her. She seemed aloof and eager to escape rather than to court observation. There was no evidence whatever of acting or of desire for applause. Gradually during her sojourn at Shady Nook this social attitude gave place to more friendly and perhaps also more selfish behavior. In March, 1927 she welcomed visitors and often quite evidently sought to hold their attention by acting. There can be little doubt that this change resulted from the practical experience that satisfactions of one sort or another may be derived from persons, even though they be only casual visitors. Both early and late she was more interested in children than in adults, in Negroes than in Caucasians, and perhaps I may safely add, for the winter of 1927, in males than in females. Whereas initially she displayed only moderate interest in me, this grew with our acquaintance and her discovery that I had control of the food supply. Finally she came to regard me, it appeared, as a friend as well as a benefactor and to associate me with problematic situations of the experimental sort which almost invariably included as a conspicuous factor something edible. From day to day I noted extreme differences in her attitude toward me. They were usually readily enough correlated with her physical condition or mood. One day she might be quiescent, only mildly interested in anything that I could do or demand of her, easy to handle, unusually gentle, and if not docile at least largely controllable; and the very next day she might be rambunctious, energetic, determined to have her own way, rough, and even if eager for food and interested in problematic situations, too impatient of restraints or disappointments to get on well with me or with her problems.

One of the many things which first surprised and then puzzled me was her limited obedience. Of the many anthropoid apes with which I have worked as psycho-biologist, there are few which did not sooner or later and in most situations reasonably well obey commands. Congo never did so unless it happened to suit her convenience and whim. My only way of making certain that she would do what I desired or commanded her to was physical restraint. I depended upon her stout leather collar with an equally stout chain attached. An illustration, which is significant for a variety of reasons, I take from my method of handling her in connection with experiments. Each morning it was necessary for me to attach a chain to her collar, and having done so to remove her from the cage to the site of an experiment. Throughout my weeks of work with her, I first of all called to or commanded her to come to the door of the cage so that I might conveniently attach the leash. Occasionally she would start toward me, but almost always she would, instead, retreat to the farthest corner of the cage, usually climbing to the roof of the nest-room where she was so far out of reach that I had to climb for her, and when I entered the cage and followed her she would do her best to keep out of reach. For a time I inferred that she did not wish to leave the cage and was merely delaying the experiments as long as possible; but subsequently, when I knew to a certainty that she was interested in the experiments and eager for their rewards, she displayed the same behavior. My present interpretation is that she converted my necessity and my appearance in the cage into an occasion for play. Compelling me to climb about and chase her into a corner, she experienced some of the satisfactions which she doubtless craved and which normally she would have obtained abundantly from her juvenile companions. But even if my interpretation be correct, it is none the less remarkable that she should persist in negative reaction to my commands. A chimpanzee or an orang-outan of like age and average docility certainly would have come to me on command, either initially or after a few days of training. Congo I never succeeded in training, and in March, 1927, on the completion of my period of work, she was just as difficult for me to capture as she had been in January. I cite this not as an exception, but as typical of her temperament and behavior toward me.

That the gorilla ordinarily was much influenced by my presence or actions in the experimental situations I very much doubt. Usually she ignored me in favor of the problematic situation itself. There were a few situations in which she came to recognize me as a disturbing agent. For example, in the buried food experiments I seemingly acquired an inhibiting value because I sometimes removed her from the situation before she had opportunity to get her reward. This I admit would have been inexcusably bad technique had I intended to continue the form of experiment. It was bad in any event if I wished to avoid prejudicing the animal against me in ways which might affect all of my observations.

As I contrast gorilla behavior, as represented in Congo, with that of the chimpanzee, I am forced to the tentative conclusion that the social stimulus is much less important in the former than in the latter. Possibly gorilla and orang-outan are nearly on a par in this respect, while the chimpanzee is above all a social organism.

XII

SUMMARY AND CONCLUSIONS

Whereas my first report on the mind of a gorilla presents results of a general survey of the behavioral characteristics of a female specimen of *Gorilla beringei,* this, a second part of the same study, deals more specifically with evidences of developmental and other forms of modification or change appearing in mnemonic processes, adaptivity, and expressivity. In reading this summary statement of results and conclusions the reader is requested to bear in mind important reservations and limitations which appear in the previous report (Yerkes, 1927, p. 178).

When first observed by me in the winter of 1926, the gorilla Congo weighed approximately sixty-five pounds. A year later when I resumed my investigation, her weight had doubled. From her arrival in America from Africa in October, 1925, until the conclusion of my observations in March, 1927, her health was perfect, her growth rapid, and her general condition eminently favorable for psycho-biological studies.

Between January, 1926 and January, 1927, many of Congo's behavioral characteristics changed markedly. Destructiveness, almost lacking in 1926, constantly appeared the following winter. Curiosity, interest in the experimenter and in other familiar or unfamiliar persons, also increased. Imitativeness and emotional expressiveness increased slightly. In all respects the subject was noticeably more mature during the second period of observation. She was increasingly self-reliant and correspondingly more at home in her captive environment, better adapted to the general conditions of experimentation, and if anything slightly more coöperative than in 1926.

In the first report, twenty-four problematic situations, with Congo's responses to them, are described; in the present report, twenty-two. Of the latter, thirteen are repetitions of experiments of the previous winter and the remainder are new problems. The purpose of repetition was to observe evidences of memory, of improved adaptation prior to additional practice, and of increase in adaptivity. Almost all of the new forms of experiment were arranged to supplement the earlier problems or to throw light on mnemonic processes.

For convenience of presentation, experimental and other observations have been grouped in seven categories: (1) the stick, or functional substitutes, as implement; (2) simple mechanisms and other familiar objects as exhibitors of adaptive ability; (3) boxes as implements; (4) delayed response and other methods of exhibiting mnemonic processes; (5) miscellaneous general observations; (6) affective expressions and motivation, and (7) social relations. Significant results for each of these observational categories will be presented in order in the following paragraphs.

When initially studied, Congo lacked ability to use sticks or functionally equivalent objects as implements. Slowly by imitational and tuitional effort she was enabled to adapt to certain situations which demanded the use of simple implements. When various stick experiments were repeated in 1927 she exhibited keen interest and immediate adaptation superior in many instances to that achieved the previous winter. This is important as indicating improvement between experiences. Whereas in 1926 the stick experiments yielded almost no indications of insight, in 1927 there were varied evidences. For a summary statement concerning the results of each of the nine stick experiments the reader is referred to page 432.

Evidence of transfer of ability from one problematic situation to a differing one appeared in two experiments: the shelf and stick and the pipe and rod. During the winter of 1926 Congo failed to solve the shelf and stick problem, although she mastered certain similar problems, but when the shelf and stick situation was re-presented after an interval of one year, she adapted to it almost immediately and perfectly, presumably on the basis of her previous experience in similar problematic situations and by reason of transfer. An explicit test of transfer was made with the pipe and rod experiment after Congo had mastered the essentially similar box and pole experiment. The result was positive. In general, however, evidences of spread or transfer of acquired interests and adaptations were meager.

Mechanisms, even of the simplest sort, baffled Congo in the first period of observation, and the results of such experiments were almost uniformly negative. Repetitions, a year later, yielded certain evidences of memory, but more especially indications of ability to solve types of problem which she had previously failed to master. In most instances, adaptation was slow and lacked conspicuous characteristics of insight. Such mechanisms, for example, as the padlock and spring snap, were operated by fumbling instead of by appropriate localized attack. The results of the second period of observation confirm my initial conclusion that Congo has little mechanical ability or aptitude. The reader will find on pages 458-60 a summary of the results of the six experiments which belong in this category.

Boxes were not promptly used as implements by Congo in 1926, but encouraged by imitative copy and tuitional effort on the part of the experimenter, she finally achieved solution of the greatest-dimension and the two-box problems. The experiments revealed little initiative, originality, or insight. Similar experiments in 1927, some of them virtually repetitions of earlier ones, and others new to the subject, yielded more abundant positive results. The problems which had been solved the previous winter were met with surprisingly adequate response on re-presentation. Indeed, it was clear that she had continued to improve during the rest interval. New problems, involving the use of three and four boxes, demonstrated an increase of adaptivity over that of 1926, while also proving that each additional box essentially alters the situation and tends to render it problematic. One might naturally suppose that having learned to pile one box upon another in order to reach a desired reward, an animal physically capable of the task would use additional boxes as necessary and available. Such was not the case for Congo. A more nearly adequate summary of the box stacking experiments appears on pages 478-80. Certain memory tests in 1926 yielded negative results, whereas similar tests in 1927 gave positive results. A form of delayed response experiment which involved opportunity for choice of any one of four objects, one of which prior to delay had been associated with food, demonstrated that Congo could respond correctly after a delay of three hours, and either with or without distractions. The situation was not analyzed because of lack of opportunity, but it is assumed that the factor of position or location was of primary importance for the response of the gorilla and that the visual configuration was of subordinate value. Heretofore, no organism except man has been proved capable of correct response in the delayed reaction type of situation after an interval of more than five minutes.[9] It is possible that the experiment demonstrates in Congo the existence of a neural process which appears only in the most complexly organized of creatures, and perhaps differentiates man and the anthropoid apes from all other animals.

Additional proof of mnemonic processes was supplied by buried food experiments, in which ability to respond appropriately after delays of one and two days was observed. These statements relative to mnemonic processes are supplemented by summary of the delayed response and buried food experiments on pages 498-500.

The following modes of adaptation by Congo to problematic situations are based upon the results of general observation and experimentation: (1) adaptation based on reflex or automatized acts, the repetition of which happened to yield satisfaction; (2) trial and the elimination of useless activities; (3) inspectional elimination and selection, by virtue of which the process of trial is abbreviated; (4) adaptation with insight,

---

[9]It is not improbable that the various forms of delayed response experiment differ so importantly as to yield incomparable results. The fact remains to be determined.

as a result of which appropriate response is direct, immediate, and reasonably adequate, and finally (5) various combinations of these several methods.

Initially characterized by me as aloof, shut-in, independent, unexpressive, Congo confirmed this description by her behavior in the winter of 1927. Although playful, she was remarkably self-controlled, and although facial, attitudinal, and vocal emotional expressions were observed, they were rare, seldom pronounced, and they often failed to appear in provocative situations.

Motivation, seemingly a relatively simple matter in many of the mammalia, is obviously complex and highly variable in Congo. Although in the experiments chief reliance was placed on food as a lure or incentive, it often happened that she worked well when not eager for her reward and as often poorly when obviously hungry. Immediate affective conditions and varied effects of previous experience played their important parts in motivation. Good and bad work-days depended often on Congo's mood, and that in turn was sometimes traceable to physical condition, and again to successes or failures in experiments. Likewise, situations acquired affective values from Congo's experience in experiments. Evidently one may not work with the gorilla as with rats, mice, guinea pigs, and other relatively unintelligent mammals, on the assumption that some one chosen motivating factor will commonly dominate and in effect determine the nature of response. Results with the gorilla indicate that analysis of motivation and careful control of factors are absolutely essential to profitable quantitative studies of behavioral adaptation. They suggest the possibility that much of the ostensibly quantitative work on habit-formation in animals is of uncertain value because of the investigator's neglect of motivation or ignorance of its varying constituents.

Congo's social environment was so simple that little could be learned about the value of social stimuli and the nature of her social behavior. She was obviously more interested in persons, both familiar and unfamiliar, the second winter than the first, and whereas in 1926 she seemingly preferred to be ignored, in 1927 she enjoyed visitors and acted to a limited extent for their entertainment. A mirror experiment, which in 1926 exhibited the gorilla's marked and sustained interest in her mirror image, while at the same time demonstrating varied investigative response, furnished strikingly similar evidence when re-presented in 1927. The second series of observations indicated a somewhat more intellectual, as contrasted with emotional, attitude.

No evidence of sex interest or anything resembling sex play was observed in the winter of 1926, but in 1927, in certain of her relations with her dog companions and also occasionally in reaction to inanimate objects, sex behavior appeared. There was decided preference for the male over the female dog, and, as opportunity offered, occasional use of either male or female as sex object. Congo assumed, at various times, the sex-play attitude of either male or female mammal.

Compared with chimpanzees and orang-outans of like age, Congo is remarkably slow in adaptation, and limited in initiative, originality, and insight. Many of the types of problem described in this and the preceding report have been presented by the writer to all three types of anthropoid ape. With the exception of a few types of problem, the chimpanzee leads in rapidity of solution, variety of response, and evidence of insight. The orang-outan takes second place, and Congo third. In the previous report, comparisons of her behavior with that of the chimpanzee and orang-outan were made with extreme caution and conservatism. Since then, results have abundantly justified the general conclusion stated above.

The common belief that the gorilla is mentally the most highly developed of the anthropoid apes receives no support from my observations. This, however, far from proves its inferiority to the chimpanzee and orang-outan, for a single specimen of a single species of gorilla is a minimum of observational material! Several possible reasons for the seeming inferiority of Congo to comparable specimens of chimpanzee and orang-outan suggest themselves. A few seem worthy of mention. (1) This particular specimen of gorilla may be of less than average ability, or she may be retarded in her psycho-physical development. (2) *Gorilla beringei* may regularly and normally develop psycho-physically more slowly than do other anthropoid apes. This might be true even though general physical development occurs at approximately the same rate in the several anthropoid types. (3) The temperamental characteristics of Congo, and perhaps also of her species, may be relatively unfavorable to adaptation to life in captivity and to the ready solution of such problematic situations as I presented.

So numerous are the experimental leads revealed by observation of Congo, so suggestive of important psycho-biological questions the results already obtained, and so problematic the relation of my results to the characteristics of the species *Gorilla beringei,* that it is manifestly important to study additional individuals and also to obtain comparable data for the two species, *Gorilla gorilla* and *Gorilla beringei*. Now that Congo has successfully adapted to conditions of life in the United States, it is hoped that her psycho-physical development may be systematically followed to maturity.

LIST OF REFERENCES

Burbridge, Ben. The gorilla hunt. *Forest and Stream,* 1926, 96; 1927, 97.

Hobhouse, L. T. Mind in evolution. 2nd ed. 1915, London.

Hunter, Walter S. The delayed reaction in animals and children. *Behav. Monog.,* 1913, 2, no. 1, Pp. v +86.

Köhler, Wolfgang. The mentality of apes. 1925, New York.

Yerkes, Robert M. The mind of a gorilla. *Genetic Psychol. Monog.,* 1927, 2, nos. 1 and 2, Pp. 193.

LIST OF ILLUSTRATIONS

Plate 1. Portraits of Congo, March, 1927
Fig. 1, upper. Interested stare. Fig. 2, lower. Beating chest in impatience.

Plate 2. Portraits of Congo, March, 1927
Fig. 1, upper. Calm observation. Fig. 2, lower. Eating
sweet potato.

Plate 3. Playmates
Fig. 1, upper. Congo and Betty at play. Fig. 2, lower. After a romp.

Plate 4. Scene of observations

Fig. 1, upper. Congo's cage, with grill and experiment boxes in foreground. Fig. 2, lower. Congo ready for work inside the grill.

Plate 5. Box and pole, pipe and rod experiments

Fig. 1, upper. Congo standing on head to look through box. Fig. 2, middle. Pushing the pole along outside of box. Fig. 3, lower. About to thrust rod into pipe.

Plate 6. Slot-box experiment

Fig. 1, upper. Slot-box, showing slot no. 3 and milk bottle
ready to be put into box. Fig. 2, lower. Congo at work at
slot no. 1; slots nos. 2 and 3 are visible.

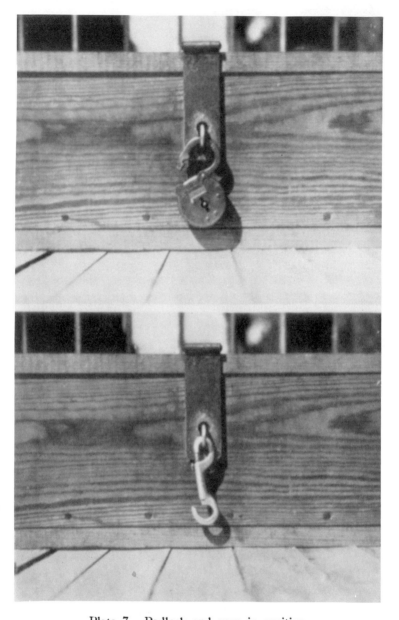

Plate 7. Padlock and snap in position

Fig. 1, upper. Open lock in staple of hasp as used in experiment. Fig. 2, lower. Spring snap in staple of hasp, ready for presentation to Congo.

Plate 8.   Congo working through the grill

Fig. 1, upper.   Hands occupied with lock on box, left foot ready to assist.   Fig. 2, lower.   Hands and feet coöperating in manipulation of straws.

Plate 9. Characteristic attitudes
Fig. 1, upper. An interval of rest in the difficult box and
pole experiment. Fig. 2, lower. Congo sitting as though
baffled in the wound chain situation.

Plate 10. The use of three boxes

Fig. 1, upper. A precarious stage in the process of stacking. Fig. 2, lower. A stable structure successfully used.

Plate 11.   The use of four boxes
Fig. 1, upper. Last stage in the process of stacking. Fig 2,
lower. Four boxes successfully used.

Plate 12. The delayed response experiment

Fig. 1, upper. Congo moored to central stake; Bill standing
by; o, release mechanism and position of observer; w, g, b, r,
white, green, black, and red food-boxes respectively. Fig. 2,
lower. Close-up of mooring stake and mechanism in use.

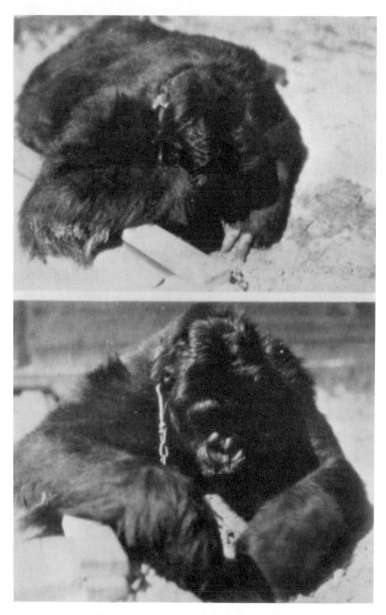

Plate 13. Digging for buried food

Plate 14. The mirror situation
Fig. 1, upper. The mirror ready for use. Fig. 2, lower.
Congo reaching behind mirror for visual object.

Plate 15.   Responses to the mirror image
Fig. 1, upper. Kissing the image.   Fig. 2, lower. Cheek to cheek.

INDEX

Adaptation, increase of, 460;
in experiments, 488;
speed of, 419, 443, 501;
to milk bottle, 439;
types of, 505.
Adolescence, approach to, 522.
Affective traits, 508.
Akeley, Carl, 377.
Anger, 511.
Anthropometry, 385, 386.
Apparatus, construction of, 389.
Attention and interest, 430.
Attitude, change of, 427;
in experiments, 391, 429, 449,
455, 464, 474, 489;
toward experimenter, 384, 393,
523;
toward people, 523;
toward the seemingly impossible, 471, 474, 504.

Bingham, Harold C., 425, 459.
Box and pole, 398, 415, 433.
to pipe and rod transfer, 400,
421, 433.
Box problems, standardization of,
479.
Box, greatest dimension of, 399,
462.
Box stacking, with two boxes,
399, 464;
with three boxes, 399, 467;
with four boxes, 400, 472.
Boxes, as implements, 462;
method of designating, 466;
method of placing, 472;
summary, use of, 478, 528.
Boyd, R. L., 508ff.
Burbridge, Ben, 377, 381, 384, 388,
395, 503;
"The Gorilla Hunt," 383;
and box stacking. 464, 465.
Burbridge, James, 377, 383, 388.
Buried food, 400, 494;
method, 498.

Categories, problem, 527.
Chest-beating, 429.
Chimpanzee compared with gorilla, 411, 434, 443, 452, 456,
458, 494, 499, 507, 525, 531.

Climatic conditions 388.
Clumsiness of gorilla, 470.
Companionship, 516.
Comparison of gorilla with other
apes, 411, 434, 443, 452, 456,
458, 494, 499, 501, 503, 504, 507,
511, 525, 531.
Complication of experiments, 423.
Concrete versus abstract, 404.
Confusion of instruments, 425.
Congo, method of handling in
experiments, 389, 482;
traits of, 530.
Construction of pyramids, 471,
473, 477.
Cues in delayed response experi-
ment, 487.
Curiosity, 502.

Delayed response, 481,
table of, 485.
Destructiveness, 501, 526.
Diagonal rope, 399, 436, 459.
Diet, 386.
Discouragement, 431.
Distraction and delayed reponse,
491.
Dogs as playmates, 519.

Emotional expressions, 429, 508.
Experiments, conditions of, 389;
essential data on, 397;
list of, 397;
location of, 397;
program of, 396;
time of, 391.
Experimenter, influence of, 525.

Fatigue, 510.
Fear, 510.
Feeding and motivation, 392.
Food, 386;
as incentive, 391, 486;
contact with, 426;
container, 427, 440;
waste of, 443.
Foresight and plan, 412.
Fumbling versus insight, 456.

Gambling, 505, 514.
Gorilla sanctuary, 378.

550

GENETIC PSYCHOLOGY MONOGRAPHS

Greatest dimension of box. 399,
462.
Growth, rate of, 386, 503.

Handedness, 406, 431.
Harvard indifference, 512.
Hasp and padlock, 398, 451, 460.
Hooked rope, 397, 437, 459.
Hunter, W. S., 481, 493.

Ideation and mnemonic process,
500.
Ideation or insight, 403, 421, 429,
432, 434, 456, 469, 476, 499,
506, 507.
Illustrations, list of, 533.
Image, 404.
Imitation, 396, 415, 416, 418, 454,
457, 462, 502.
Impatience, 456.
Impulses, conflict of, 416.
Indifference feigned, 470.
Indirectness of method, 412.
Inhibition and motivation, 448,
449.
Inhibition of effort, 444, 446, 497.
Initiative, 396, 417.
Insight, see ideation.

Jumping, 476;
absence of, 411.

Köhler, W., 494, 498.

Learning, methods of, 505, 529.
List of problems, 397.
Literature on gorilla, 382.
Location of experiments, 397.

Mechanical ability, 436, 451 ff.,
457, 528;
summary discussion, 458.
Memory, evidences of, 498.
for experiments, 384, 437;
for buried food, 494;
in delayed response, 486;
of experimenter, 383;
summary of results, 529.
Memory experiments, 481;
summary of, 498.
Mental development, 386, 395.
Mental traits of Congo, 513.
Method, delayed response, 482;
of operating snap, 455;
of placing boxes, 472, 473.

Methods, nature of, 396.
Milk bottle, 400, 439, 459.
Mind versus behavior, 381.
Mirror image, response to, 516.
Miscellaneous observations, 501.
Mnemonic processes, 481, 529.
Moods, 511.
Motivation, and moods, 511;
and quantity of food, 448, 471;
factors in, 393, 475, 512;
in experiments, 391, 455, 512;
in rodents, 480;
satisfactoriness of, 392, 393;
summary discussion of, 530;
variability, 472, 479;
versus hunger, 447.

Negativism, 460, 476, 502.
Nutrition, 386.

Obedience, limitation of, 523.
Observational ability, 409, 423,
447, 452, 464.
Obstruction to use of stick, 430.
Odor as cue, 487.
Orang-outan compared with go-
rilla, 434, 458, 499, 507, 531.
Orientation and delayed response,
491.
Originality, 457.

Photographic recording, 426.
Physical measurements, 384, 386,
526.
Pipe and stick or rod, 398, 414,
433.
Platform and stick, 398, 405,
433.
Playfulness, 508.
Problems and tasks, 395.

Reach, standing, 410.
References, list of, 532.
Representative process, 404.
Research activity, 505, 514.
Restlessness, 448.
Reward, quantity of, 448, 471.
Ringling, John, 377.
Round-about course, with stick,
400, 430, 434.

Sexual development, 386, 531.
Sexual play, 520.

CLASSICS IN PSYCHOLOGY

An Arno Press Collection

Angell, James Rowland. **Psychology:** On Introductory Study of the Structure and Function of Human Consciousness. 4th edition. 1908

Bain, Alexander. **Mental Science.** 1868

Baldwin, James Mark. **Social and Ethical Interpretations in Mental Development.** 2nd edition. 1899

Bechterev, Vladimir Michailovitch. **General Principles of Human Reflexology.** [1932]

Binet, Alfred and Th[éodore] Simon. **The Development of Intelligence in Children.** 1916

Bogardus, Emory S. **Fundamentals of Social Psychology.** 1924

Buytendijk, F. J. J. **The Mind of the Dog.** 1936

Ebbinghaus, Hermann. **Psychology: An Elementary Text-Book.** 1908

Goddard, Henry Herbert. **The Kallikak Family.** 1931

Hobhouse, L[eonard] T. **Mind in Evolution.** 1915

Holt, Edwin B. **The Concept of Consciousness.** 1914

Külpe, Oswald. **Outlines of Psychology.** 1895

Ladd-Franklin, Christine. **Colour and Colour Theories.** 1929

Lectures Delivered at the 20th Anniversary Celebration of Clark University. (Reprinted from *The American Journal of Psychology*, Vol. 21, Nos. 2 and 3). 1910

Lipps, Theodor. **Psychological Studies.** 2nd edition. 1926

Loeb, Jacques. **Comparative Physiology of the Brain and Comparative Psychology.** 1900

Lotze, Hermann. **Outlines of Psychology.** [1885]

McDougall, William. **The Group Mind.** 2nd edition. 1920

Meier, Norman C., editor. **Studies in the Psychology of Art: Volume III.** 1939

Morgan, C. Lloyd. **Habit and Instinct.** 1896

Münsterberg, Hugo. **Psychology and Industrial Efficiency.** 1913

Murchison, Carl, editor. **Psychologies of 1930.** 1930

Piéron, Henri. **Thought and the Brain.** 1927

Pillsbury, W[alter] B[owers]. **Attention.** 1908

[Poffenberger, A. T., editor]. **James McKeen Cattell: Man of Science.** 1947

Preyer, W[illiam] **The Mind of the Child: Parts I and II.** 1890/1889

The Psychology of Skill: Three Studies. 1973

Reymert, Martin L., editor. **Feelings and Emotions:** The Wittenberg Symposium. 1928

Ribot, Th[éodule Armand]. **Essay on the Creative Imagination.** 1906

Roback, A[braham] A[aron]. **The Psychology of Character.** 1927

I. M. Sechenov: Biographical Sketch and Essays. (Reprinted from *Selected Works* by I. Sechenov). 1935

Sherrington, Charles. **The Integrative Action of the Nervous System.** 2nd edition. 1947

Spearman, C[harles]. **The Nature of 'Intelligence' and the Principles of Cognition.** 1923

Thorndike, Edward L. **Education:** A First Book. 1912

Thorndike, Edward L., E. O. Bregman, M. V. Cobb, et al. **The Measurement of Intelligence.** [1927]

Titchener, Edward Bradford. **Lectures on the Elementary Psychology of Feeling and Attention.** 1908

Titchener, Edward Bradford. **Lectures on the Experimental Psychology of the Thought-Processes.** 1909

Washburn, Margaret Floy. **Movement and Mental Imagery.** 1916

Whipple, Guy Montrose. **Manual of Mental and Physical Tests:** Parts I and II. 2nd edition. 1914/1915

Woodworth, Robert Sessions. **Dynamic Psychology.** 1918

Wundt, Wilhelm. **An Introduction to Psychology.** 1912

Yerkes, Robert M. **The Dancing Mouse** and **The Mind of a Gorilla.** 1907/1926

DATE DUE

OCT 1			